Honda CBR600F2 & F3

Service and Repair Manual

by Mark Coombs & Matthew Coombs

Models covered:

(2070 - 248 - 10Y3)

Honda CBR600F2 (F-M, F-N, F-P, F-R). 599cc. 1991 to 1994
Honda CBR600F3 (F-S, F-T, F-V, F-W). 599cc. 1995 to 1998

Note: *The 598cc CBR600F (F-H, F-J, F-K and F-L) models, 1987 to 1990, are covered in Manual No. 1730*

ABCDE
FGHIJ

A book in the **Haynes Service and Repair Manual Series**

ISBN 1 85960 538 9

British Library Cataloguing in Publication Data
A catalogue record for this book is available from the British Library

Library of Congress Catalog Card Number 98-72826

Printed in the USA

Haynes Publishing
Sparkford, Yeovil, Somerset BA22 7JJ, England

Haynes North America, Inc
861 Lawrence Drive, Newbury Park, California 91320, USA

Editions Haynes
4, Rue de l'Abreuvoir
92415 COURBEVOIE CEDEX, France

Haynes Publishing Nordiska AB
Box 1504, 751 45 UPPSALA, Sweden

Contents

Contents

REPAIRS AND OVERHAUL

REFERENCE

The Birth of a Dream

by Julian Ryder

There is no better example of the Japanese post-War industrial miracle than Honda. Like other companies which have become household names, it started with one man's vision. In this case the man was the 40-year old Soichiro Honda who had sold his piston-ring manufacturing business to Toyota in 1945 and was happily spending the proceeds on prolonged parties for his friends. However, the difficulties of getting around in the chaos of post-War Japan irked Honda, so when he came across a job lot of generator engines he realised that here was a way of getting people mobile again at low cost.

A 12 by 18-foot shack in Hamamatsu became his first bike factory, fitting the generator motors into pushbikes. Before long he'd used up all 500 generator motors and started manufacturing his own engine, known as the 'chimney', either because of the elongated cylinder head or the smoky exhaust or perhaps both. The chimney made all of half a horsepower from its 50 cc engine but it was a major success and became the Honda A-type. Less than two years after he'd set up in Hamamatsu, Soichiro Honda founded the Honda Motor Company in September 1948. By then, the A-type had been developed into the 90 cc B-type engine, which Mr Honda decided deserved its own chassis not a bicycle frame. Honda was about to become Japan's first post-War manufacturer of complete motorcycles. In August 1949 the first prototype was ready. With an output of three horsepower, the 98 cc D-type was still a

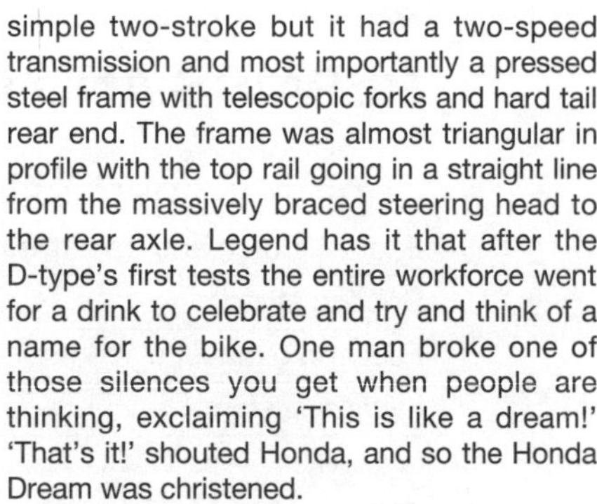

simple two-stroke but it had a two-speed transmission and most importantly a pressed steel frame with telescopic forks and hard tail rear end. The frame was almost triangular in profile with the top rail going in a straight line from the massively braced steering head to the rear axle. Legend has it that after the D-type's first tests the entire workforce went for a drink to celebrate and try and think of a name for the bike. One man broke one of those silences you get when people are thinking, exclaiming 'This is like a dream!' 'That's it!' shouted Honda, and so the Honda Dream was christened.

> 'This is like a dream!'
> 'That's it'
> shouted Honda

Mr Honda was a brilliant, intuitive engineer and designer but he did not bother himself with the marketing side of his business. With hindsight, it is possible to see that employing Takeo Fujisawa who would both sort out the home market and plan the eventual expansion into overseas markets was a masterstroke. He arrived in October 1949 and in 1950 was made Sales Director. Another vital new name was Kiyoshi Kawashima, who along with Honda himself, designed the company's first four-stroke after Kawashima had told them that the four-stroke opposition to Honda's two-strokes sounded nicer and therefore sold better. The result of that statement was the overhead-valve 148 cc E-type which first ran in July 1951 just two months after the first drawings were made. Kawashima was made a director of the Honda Company at 34 years old.

The E-type was a massive success, over 32,000 were made in 1953 alone, but Honda's lifelong pursuit of technical innovation sometimes distracted him from commercial reality. Fujisawa pointed out that they were in danger of ignoring their core business, the motorised bicycles that still formed Japan's main means of transport. In May 1952 the F-type Cub appeared, another two-stroke despite the top men's reservations. You could buy a complete machine or just the motor to attach to your own bicycle. The result was certainly distinctive, a white fuel tank with a circular profile went just below and behind the saddle on the left of the bike, and the motor with its horizontal cylinder and bright red cover just below the rear axle on the same side of the bike. This was the machine that turned Honda into the biggest bike maker in Japan

The CB250N Super Dream became a favorite with UK learner riders of the late seventies and early eighties

with 70% of the market for bolt-on bicycle motors, the F-type was also the first Honda to be exported. Next came the machine that would turn Honda into the biggest motorcycle manufacturer in the world.

The C100 Super Cub was a typically audacious piece of Honda engineering and marketing. For the first time, but not the last, Honda invented a completely new type of motorcycle, although the term 'scooterette' was coined to describe the new bike which had many of the characteristics of a scooter but the large wheels, and therefore stability, of a motorcycle. The first one was sold in August 1958, fifteen years later over nine-million of them were on the roads of the world. If ever a machine can be said to have brought mobility to the masses it is the Super Cub. If you add in the electric starter that was added for the C102 model of 1961, the design of the Super Cub has remained substantially unchanged ever since, testament to how right Honda got it first time. The Super Cub made Honda the world's biggest manufacturer after just two years of production.

Honda's export drive started in earnest in 1957 when Britain and Holland got their first bikes, America got just two bikes the next year. By 1962 Honda had half the American market with 65,000 sales. But Soichiro Honda had already travelled abroad to Europe and the USA, making a special point of going to the Isle of Man TT, then the most important race in the GP calendar. He realised that no matter how advanced his products were, only racing success would convince overseas markets for whom 'Made in Japan' still meant cheap and nasty. It took five years from Soichiro Honda's first visit to the Island before his bikes were ready for the TT. In 1959 the factory entered five riders in the 125. They did not have a massive impact on the event being benevolently regarded as a curiosity, but sixth, seventh and eighth were good enough for the team prize. The bikes were off the pace but they were well engineered and very reliable.

The TT was the only time the West saw the Hondas in '59, but they came back for more the following year with the first of a generation of bikes which shaped the future of motorcycling - the double-overhead-cam four-cylinder 250. It was fast and reliable - it revved to 14,000 rpm - but didn't handle anywhere near as well as the opposition. However, Honda had now signed up non-Japanese riders to lead their challenge. The first win didn't come until 1962 (Aussie Tom Phillis in the Spanish 125 GP) and was followed up with

The GL1000 introduced in 1975, was the first in Honda's line of Goldwings

a world-shaking performance at the TT. Twenty-one year old Mike Hailwood won both 125 and 250 cc TTs and Hondas filled the top five positions in both races. Soichiro Honda's master plan was starting to come to fruition, Hailwood and Honda won the 1961 250 cc World Championship. Next year Honda won three titles. The other Japanese factories fought back and inspired Honda to produce some of the most fascinating racers ever seen: the awesome six-cylinder 250, the five-cylinder 125, and the 500 four with which the immortal Hailwood battled Agostini and the MV Agusta.

Photo courtesy of Kel Edge

Carl Fogarty in action at the Suzuka 8 Hour on the RC45

When Honda pulled out of racing in '67 they had won sixteen rider's titles, eighteen manufacturer's titles, and 137 GPs, including 18 TTs, and introduced the concept of the modern works team to motorcycle racing. Sales success followed racing victory as Soichiro Honda had predicted, but only because the products advanced as rapidly as the racing machinery. The Hondas that came to Britain in the early '60s were incredibly sophisticated. They had overhead cams where the British bikes had pushrods, they had electric starters when the Brits relied on the kickstart, they had 12V electrics when even the biggest British bike used a 6V system. There seemed no end to the technical wizardry and when in 1968 the first four-cylinder CB750 road bike arrived the world changed for ever. They even had to invent a new word for it: superbike. Honda raced again with the CB750 at Daytona and won the World Endurance title with a prototype DOHC version that became the CB900 roadster. There was the six-cylinder CBX, the first turbocharged production bike, they invented the full-dress tourer with the Goldwing and came back to GPs with the revolutionary oval-pistoned NR500 four-stroke, a much-misunderstood bike that was more rolling experiment than racer. It was true, though, that Mr Honda was not keen on two-strokes - early motocross engines had to be explained away to him as lawnmower motors! However, in 1982 Honda raced the NS500, an agile three-cylinder lightweight against the big four-cylinder opposition in 500 GPs. The bike won in the first year and in '83 took the world title for Freddie Spencer. In four-stroke racing the V4 layout took over from the straight four, dominating TT, F1 and Endurance championships and when Superbike arrived Honda were ready with the RC30. On the roads the VFR V4 became an instant classic while the CBR600 invented another new class of bike on its way to becoming a best-seller.

An early CB750 Four

And then there was the NR750. This limited-edition technological tour-de-force embodied many of Soichiro Honda's ideals. It used the latest techniques and materials in every component, from the oval-piston, 32-valve V4 motor to the titanium coating on the windscreen, it was - as Mr Honda would have wanted - the best it could possibly be. A fitting memorial to the man who has shaped the motorcycle industry and motorcycles as we know them today.

The CBR600F2 and F3 models

Since its introduction in 1987, the Honda CBR600 has undergone two comprehensive redesigns which while following the same basic layout as the original F1 machine of 1987 to 1990 changed the bike comprehensively. This manual deals with the bike's last two incarnations, the so-called F2 and F3 models. The original CBR600F1 is covered in manual No. 1730.

The really big change came between F1 and F2, with a completely revised powerplant in a diamond rather than cradle frame - although it was still made of steel. The motor got the short-stroke treatment, going from 63 x 48 mm to 65 x 45.2 mm for the 1991 F-M model, the first of the F2s. The cylinder head layout was also completely revised in order to keep up with the 100 hp middleweights now emanating from the other Japanese factories in this most competitive of market sectors worldwide.

The F3 arrived in 1995 as the F-S model and while nowhere near as radical a jump as the F2 it had some significant differences. Typically, Honda improved every area of the bike incrementally to give an overall power, acceleration and top speed gain but they managed to maintain the CBR600's character and all-round abilities compared to the much more race-track orientated 600s from the opposition. Customers voted with their wallets and kept the CBR at the top of the sales tree on both sides of the Atlantic for its entire model life. It also boasts the dubious distinction of being the most-stolen bike in the US!

Internally, the F3 motor got new pistons, lighter con-rods, a more compact combustion chamber, shorter inlet tracts and a degree of downdraft for the bigger 36 mm carburetors. The exhaust system was revised as well. The front forks were updated with new 12-position rebound damping adjustment and held in strengthened triple clamps. At the back a less-linear rising rate linkage operated the same rear shock as fitted to the F2. Rear rim size went up half an inch to a full five inches, mainly for the benefit of racers.

The 1997 CBR600F3 model

The result of all the detail changes kept the CBR competitive in Supersport class racing all over the world, even in the new World Series which has run alongside the World Superbike Championship since 1997 where the Honda has to compete with the 748 Ducati as well as the racier Japanese machinery. This is all the more remarkable as Supersport regulations mean that standard road suspension and wheels have to be retained. The CBR doesn't boast such cutting-edge technology as upside-down forks, but it still wins races. And uniquely in the Supersport 600 class you can carry a passenger on the roads in some comfort. That's what I call an all-rounder.

And that's the secret of the CBR600's immense commercial success. The buying public knows that it will have staying power, that it will not go out of fashion in a year as race replicas have a habit of doing, and that its residual value will therefore be good. In the real world on real roads a four-cylinder 600 is the sort of bike that'll do all you want at a price you can afford and it has all the performance you need (as opposed to want!) - just look at the lap times in the Supersport class at the Isle of Man TT. If the Supersport 600 class is the all-rounders' sector then the CBR is the all-rounder's all-rounder, the one constant factor in that area of the market.

The first F2, the CBR600F-M, was a considerable leap forward, a sharpening up which gave the bike the sportiness the F1 was short on. The final set of modifications that produced the F3 continued the job yet maintained the CBR's unmatched versatility. That seems to be a trick that only Honda can pull off.

Acknowledgements

Our thanks are due to Paul Branson Motorcycles of Yeovil who supplied the machines featured in the illustrations throughout this manual. We would also like to thank NGK Spark Plugs (UK) Ltd for supplying the color spark plug condition photos and the Avon Rubber Company for supplying information on tire fitting.

Thanks are also due to Honda (UK) Ltd and Kel Edge for supplying color transparencies.

The introduction 'The Birth of a Dream' was written by Julian Ryder.

About this manual

The aim of this manual is to help you get the best value from your motorcycle. It can do so in several ways. It can help you decide what work must be done, even if you choose to have it done by a dealer; it provides information and procedures for routine maintenance and servicing; and it offers diagnostic and repair procedures to follow when trouble occurs.

We hope you use the manual to tackle the work yourself. For many simpler jobs, doing it yourself may be quicker than arranging an appointment to get the motorcycle into a dealer and making the trips to leave it and pick it up. More importantly, a lot of money can be saved by avoiding the expense the shop must pass on to you to cover its labor and overhead costs. An added benefit is the sense of satisfaction and accomplishment that you feel after doing the job yourself.

References to the left or right side of the motorcycle assume you are sitting on the seat, facing forward.

We take great pride in the accuracy of information given in this manual, but motorcycle manufacturers make alterations and design changes during the production run of a particular motorcycle of which they do not inform us. No liability can be accepted by the authors or publishers for loss, damage or injury caused by any errors in, or omissions from, the information given.

Safety first!

Professional mechanics are trained in safe working procedures. However enthusiastic you may be about getting on with the job at hand, take the time to ensure that your safety is not put at risk. A moment's lack of attention can result in an accident, as can failure to observe simple precautions.

There will always be new ways of having accidents, and the following is not a comprehensive list of all dangers; it is intended rather to make you aware of the risks and to encourage a safe approach to all work you carry out on your bike.

Asbestos

● Certain friction, insulating, sealing and other products - such as brake pads, clutch linings, gaskets, etc. - contain asbestos. Extreme care must be taken to avoid inhalation of dust from such products since it is hazardous to health. If in doubt, assume that they do contain asbestos.

Fire

● Remember at all times that petrol is highly flammable. Never smoke or have any kind of naked flame around, when working on the vehicle. But the risk does not end there - a spark caused by an electrical short-circuit, by two metal surfaces contacting each other, by careless use of tools, or even by static electricity built up in your body under certain conditions, can ignite petrol vapour, which in a confined space is highly explosive. Never use petrol as a cleaning solvent. Use an approved safety solvent.

● Always disconnect the battery earth terminal before working on any part of the fuel or electrical system, and never risk spilling fuel on to a hot engine or exhaust.

● It is recommended that a fire extinguisher of a type suitable for fuel and electrical fires is kept handy in the garage or workplace at all times. Never try to extinguish a fuel or electrical fire with water.

Fumes

● Certain fumes are highly toxic and can quickly cause unconsciousness and even death if inhaled to any extent. Petrol vapour comes into this category, as do the vapours from certain solvents such as trichloro-ethylene. Any draining or pouring of such volatile fluids should be done in a well ventilated area.

● When using cleaning fluids and solvents, read the instructions carefully. Never use materials from unmarked containers - they may give off poisonous vapours.

● Never run the engine of a motor vehicle in an enclosed space such as a garage. Exhaust fumes contain carbon monoxide which is extremely poisonous; if you need to run the engine, always do so in the open air or at least have the rear of the vehicle outside the workplace.

The battery

● Never cause a spark, or allow a naked light near the vehicle's battery. It will normally be giving off a certain amount of hydrogen gas, which is highly explosive.

● Always disconnect the battery ground (earth) terminal before working on the fuel or electrical systems (except where noted).

● If possible, loosen the filler plugs or cover when charging the battery from an external source. Do not charge at an excessive rate or the battery may burst.

● Take care when topping up, cleaning or carrying the battery. The acid electrolyte, evenwhen diluted, is very corrosive and should not be allowed to contact the eyes or skin. Always wear rubber gloves and goggles or a face shield. If you ever need to prepare electrolyte yourself, always add the acid slowly to the water; never add the water to the acid.

Electricity

● When using an electric power tool, inspection light etc., always ensure that the appliance is correctly connected to its plug and that, where necessary, it is properly grounded (earthed). Do not use such appliances in damp conditions and, again, beware of creating a spark or applying excessive heat in the vicinity of fuel or fuel vapour. Also ensure that the appliances meet national safety standards.

● A severe electric shock can result from touching certain parts of the electrical system, such as the spark plug wires (HT leads), when the engine is running or being cranked, particularly if components are damp or the insulation is defective. Where an electronic ignition system is used, the secondary (HT) voltage is much higher and could prove fatal.

Remember...

✘ **Don't** start the engine without first ascertaining that the transmission is in neutral.

✘ **Don't** suddenly remove the pressure cap from a hot cooling system - cover it with a cloth and release the pressure gradually first, or you may get scalded by escaping coolant.

✘ **Don't** attempt to drain oil until you are sure it has cooled sufficiently to avoid scalding you.

✘ **Don't** grasp any part of the engine or exhaust system without first ascertaining that it is cool enough not to burn you.

✘ **Don't** allow brake fluid or antifreeze to contact the machine's paintwork or plastic components.

✘ **Don't** siphon toxic liquids such as fuel, hydraulic fluid or antifreeze by mouth, or allow them to remain on your skin.

✘ **Don't** inhale dust - it may be injurious to health (see Asbestos heading).

✘ **Don't** allow any spilled oil or grease to remain on the floor - wipe it up right away, before someone slips on it.

✘ **Don't** use ill-fitting spanners or other tools which may slip and cause injury.

✘ **Don't** lift a heavy component which may be beyond your capability - get assistance.

✘ **Don't** rush to finish a job or take unverified short cuts.

✘ **Don't** allow children or animals in or around an unattended vehicle.

✘ **Don't** inflate a tyre above the recommended pressure. Apart from overstressing the carcass, in extreme cases the tyre may blow off forcibly.

✔ **Do** ensure that the machine is supported securely at all times. This is especially important when the machine is blocked up to aid wheel or fork removal.

✔ **Do** take care when attempting to loosen a stubborn nut or bolt. It is generally better to pull on a spanner, rather than push, so that if you slip, you fall away from the machine rather than onto it.

✔ **Do** wear eye protection when using power tools such as drill, sander, bench grinder etc.

✔ **Do** use a barrier cream on your hands prior to undertaking dirty jobs - it will protect your skin from infection as well as making the dirt easier to remove afterwards; but make sure your hands aren't left slippery. Note that long-term contact with used engine oil can be a health hazard.

✔ **Do** keep loose clothing (cuffs, ties etc. and long hair) well out of the way of moving mechanical parts.

✔ **Do** remove rings, wristwatch etc., before working on the vehicle - especially the electrical system.

✔ **Do** keep your work area tidy - it is only too easy to fall over articles left lying around.

✔ **Do** exercise caution when compressing springs for removal or installation. Ensure that the tension is applied and released in a controlled manner, using suitable tools which preclude the possibility of the spring escaping violently.

✔ **Do** ensure that any lifting tackle used has a safe working load rating adequate for the job.

✔ **Do** get someone to check periodically that all is well, when working alone on the vehicle.

✔ **Do** carry out work in a logical sequence and check that everything is correctly assembled and tightened afterwards.

✔ **Do** remember that your vehicle's safety affects that of yourself and others. If in doubt on any point, get professional advice.

● If in spite of following these precautions, you are unfortunate enough to injure yourself, seek medical attention as soon as possible.

Model code is printed on the color code label located behind the right side cover

Frame number is stamped on the right side of the steering head

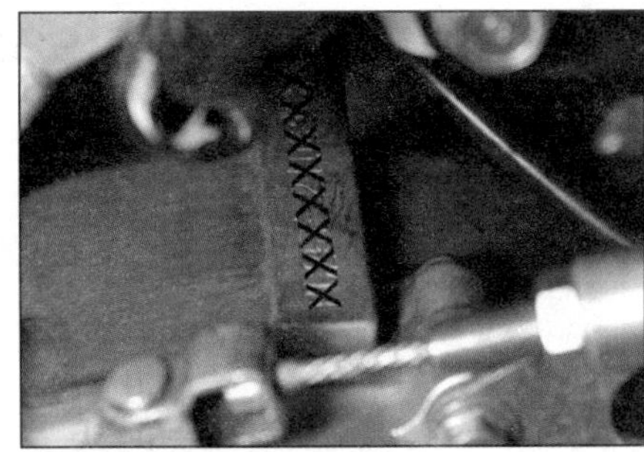

Engine number is stamped on the right side of the crankcase

Frame and engine numbers

The frame serial number is stamped into the right side of the steering head. The engine number is stamped into the right upper side of the crankcase, directly above the clutch unit. Both of these numbers should be recorded and kept in a safe place so they can be furnished to law enforcement officials in the event of a theft.

The frame serial number, engine serial number and carburetor identification number should also be kept in a handy place (such as with your driver's license) so they are always available when purchasing or ordering parts for your machine.

Identifying model years

The procedures in this manual identify the bikes by model code. The model code (eg CBR600F-**M**) is printed on the color code label, which is stuck on the right side of the frame, behind the right side cover. The model code and production year can also be determined from the engine and frame serial numbers as follows:

	Engine number	Frame number
UK models		
CBR600F-M (1991)	PC25E-2000105 to 2020536	PC25-2000059 to 2011020
CBR600F-N (1992)	PC25E-2103197 to 2127440	PC25-2100030 to 2115605
CBR600F-P (1993)	PC25E-2206510 to 2223238	PC25-2201237 to 2212108
CBR600F-R (1994)	PC25E-2305716 to 2324608	PC25-2300751 to 2312384
CBR600F-S (1995)	PC25E-2400095 on	PC31-2000062 on
CBR600F-T (1996)	PC25E-2500001 on	PC31A-TM000001 on
CBR600F-V (1997)	PC25E-2600001 on	PC31A-VM100001 on
CBR600F-W (1998)	PC25E-2700001 on	PC31A-WM200001 on
California models		
CBR600F-M (1991)	PC25E-2000088 to 2018016	PC251-MM000007 to MM001169
CBR600F-N (1992)	PC25E-2100796 to 2126855	PC251-NM100004 to NM101462
CBR600F-P (1993)	PC25E-2200011 to 2219170	PC251-PM200001 to PM201540
CBR600F-R (1994)	PC25E-2300001 to 2324323	PC251-RM300001 to RM301734
CBR600F-S (1995)	PC25E-2400102 on	PC251-SM400009 on
CBR600F-T (1996)	PC25E-2500001 on	PC251-TM500001 on
CBR600F-V (1997)	PC25E-2600001 on	PC251-VM600001 on
CBR600F-W (1998)	PC25E-2700001 on	PC251-WM700001 on
US models (except California)		
CBR600F-M (1991)	PC25E-2000086 to 2018015	PC250-MM000008 to MM005872
CBR600F-N (1992)	PC25E-2100001 to 2126787	PC250-NM100001 to NM107517
CBR600F-P (1993)	PC25E-2200006 to 2219565	PC250-PM200003 to PM207591
CBR600F-R (1994)	PC25E-2300001 to 2324269	PC250-RM300001 to RM308445
CBR600F-S (1995)	PC25E-2400100 on	PC250-SM400009 on
CBR600F-T (1996)	PC25E-2500001 on	PC250-TM500001 on
CBR600F-V (1997)	PC25E-2600001 on	PC250-VM600001 on
CBR600F-W (1998)	PC25E-2700001 on	PC250-WM700001 on

Buying spare parts

Once you have found all the identification numbers, record them for reference when buying parts. Since the manufacturers change specifications, parts and vendors (companies that manufacture various components on the machine), providing the ID numbers is the only way to be reasonably sure that you are buying the correct parts.

Whenever possible, take the worn part to the dealer so direct comparison with the new component can be made. Along the trail from the manufacturer to the parts shelf, there are numerous places that the part can end up with the wrong number or be listed incorrectly.

The two places to purchase new parts for your motorcycle - the accessory store and the franchised dealer - differ in the type of parts they carry. While dealers can obtain virtually every part for your motorcycle, the accessory dealer is usually limited to normal high wear items such as shock absorbers, tune-up parts, various engine gaskets, cables, chains, brake parts, etc. Rarely will an accessory outlet have major suspension components, cylinders, transmission gears, or cases.

Used parts can be obtained for roughly half the price of new ones, but you can't always be sure of what you're getting. Once again, take your worn part to the wrecking yard (breaker) for direct comparison.

Whether buying new, used or rebuilt parts, the best course is to deal directly with someone who specializes in parts for your particular make.

1 Engine/transmission oil level

Before you start:

✔ Make sure you always have an adequate supply of the correct oil (see below).
✔ Place the motorcycle on its centerstand, making sure it is on level ground.
✔ Start the engine and allow it to reach normal operating temperature.
Caution: Do not run the engine in an enclosed space such as a garage or workshop.
✔ Stop the engine and let it stand undisturbed for a few minutes to allow the oil level to stabilize.

The correct oil

● Modern, high-revving engines place great demands on their oil. It is very important that the correct oil for your bike is used.
● Always top up with a good quality oil of the specified type and viscosity and do not overfill the engine.

Oil type	API grade SE, SF or SG
Oil viscosity	SAE 10W40

Bike care:

● If you have to add oil frequently, you should check whether you have any oil leaks. If there is no sign of oil leakage from the joints and gaskets the engine could be burning oil (see Fault Finding).

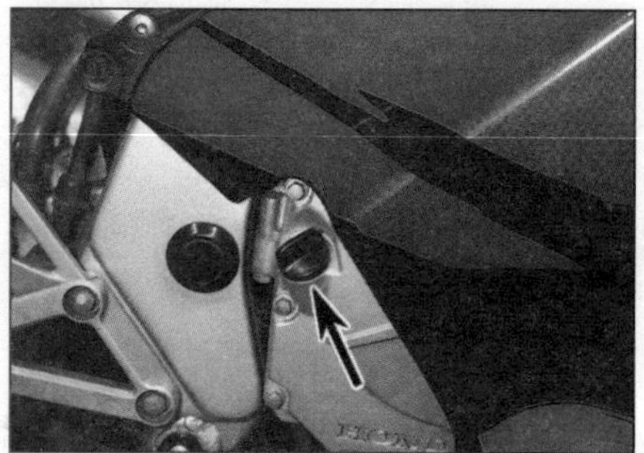

1 Unscrew the oil filler cap (arrow) from the right side crankcase cover. The dipstick is integral with the oil filler cap, and is used to check the engine oil level. Using a clean rag or paper towel, wipe off all the oil from the dipstick.

2 Insert the clean dipstick back into the engine, but do not screw it in. Remove the dipstick and observe the level of the oil, which should be somewhere in between the upper and lower level marks (arrows).

3 If the level is below the lower mark, top the engine up with the recommended grade and type of oil, to bring the level up to the upper mark on the dipstick. Do not overfill.

2 Coolant level

> ***Warning: DO NOT remove the radiator pressure cap to add coolant. Topping up is done via the coolant reservoir tank filler. DO NOT leave open containers of coolant about, as it is poisonous.***

Before you start:

✔ Make sure you have a supply of coolant available (a mixture of 50% distilled water and 50% corrosion inhibited ethylene glycol anti-freeze is needed).
✔ Place the motorcycle on its centerstand, making sure it is on level ground.
✔ Start the engine and allow it to reach normal operating temperature, then stop it.
Caution: Do not run the engine in an enclosed space such as a garage or workshop.

Bike care:

● Use only the specified coolant mixture. It is important that anti-freeze is used in the system all year round, and not just in the winter. Do not top the system up using only water, as the system will become too diluted.
● Do not overfill the reservoir tank. If the coolant is significantly above the UPPER level line at any time, the surplus should be siphoned or drained off to prevent the possibility of it being expelled out of the overflow hose.
● If the coolant level falls steadily, check the system for leaks (see Chapter 1). If no leaks are found and the level continues to fall, it is recommended that the machine is taken to a Honda dealer for a pressure test.

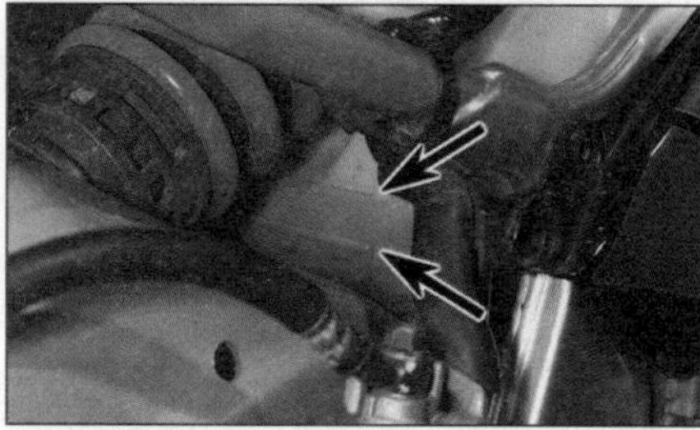

1 The coolant reservoir is located behind the right side cover. Remove the cover (see Chapter 8). The coolant level is visible through the translucent plastic body of the reservoir, and should be between the UPPER and LOWER level lines (arrows).

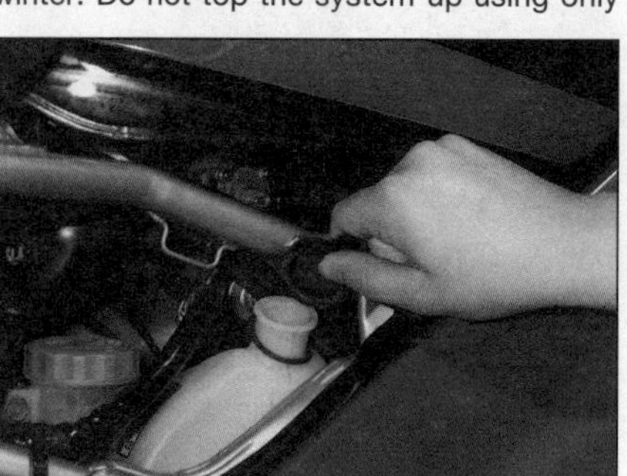

2 If the coolant level is not in between the UPPER and LOWER markings, remove the reservoir filler cap.

3 Top the coolant level up with the recommended coolant mixture. Fit the cap securely, then install the side cover (see Chapter 8).

3 Brake fluid levels

Before you start:

✔ Support the motorcycle in an upright position on its centerstand, and turn the handlebars until the top of the front master cylinder is as level as possible. The rear master cylinder reservoir is located below the seat on the right side of the machine.

✔ Make sure you have the correct hydraulic fluid. DOT 4 is recommended.

✔ Wrap a rag around the reservoir to ensure that any spillage does not come into contact with painted surfaces.

✔ Access to the front reservoir cap screws is restricted by the windshield. If a short or angled screwdriver is not available, remove the fairing to access the screws (see Chapter 8).

Bike care:

● The fluid in the front and rear brake master cylinder reservoirs will drop slightly as the brake pads wear down.

● If any fluid reservoir requires repeated topping-up this is an indication of a hydraulic leak somewhere in the system, which should be investigated immediately.

● Check for signs of fluid leakage from the hydraulic hoses and components - if found, rectify immediately.

● Check the operation of both brakes before taking the machine on the road; if there is evidence of air in the system (spongy feel to lever or pedal), it must be bled (see Chapter 7).

1 Look closely at the inspection window in the front brake master cylinder reservoir. Make sure that the fluid level, visible in the sightglass, is above the LOWER mark on the reservoir.

2 To top up, unscrew the retaining screws and lift off the cover, diaphragm plate and diaphragm.

3 Using a good quality brake fluid of the recommended type, from a freshly opened container, top up the reservoir to the upper level mark; this mark is in the form of a line, cast on the inside of the front face of the reservoir.

4 When the fluid level is correct, clean and dry the diaphragm, fold it into its compressed state and install it in the reservoir, making sure it is properly seated.

5 Install the diaphragm plate and the reservoir cover and tighten its screws securely.

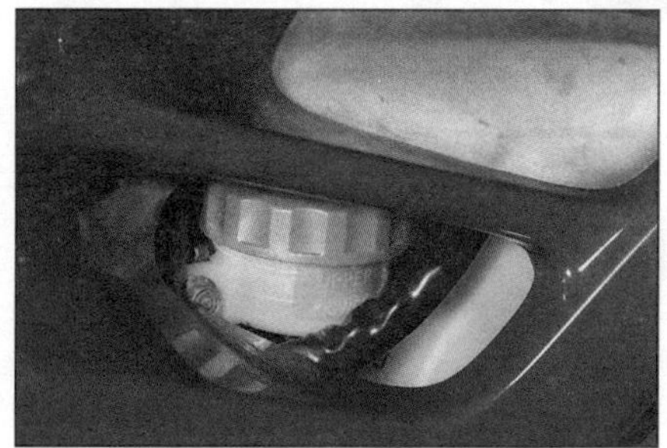

6 Check the level in the rear brake reservoir, visible through the holes in the right side cover. Make sure that the fluid level, visible through the translucent material of the reservoir, is between the UPPER and LOWER marks on the reservoir.

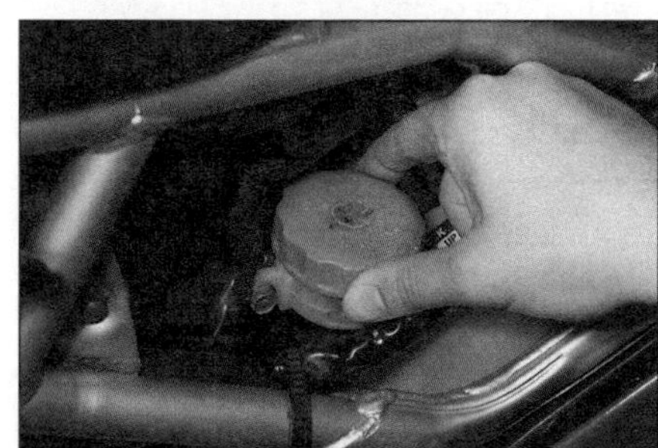

7 If the level is low, the fluid must be replenished. Remove the right side cover (see Chapter 8) and remove all dust and dirt from the area around the cap. Unscrew the reservoir cap and remove the diaphragm plate and diaphragm.

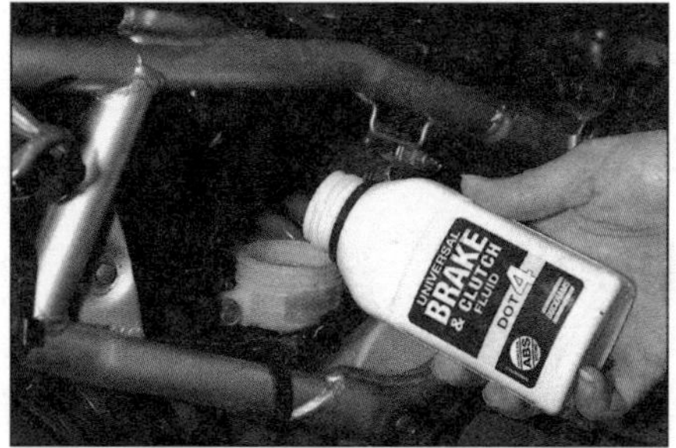

8 Using DOT 4 brake fluid, from a freshly opened container, top up the reservoir to the UPPER level mark.

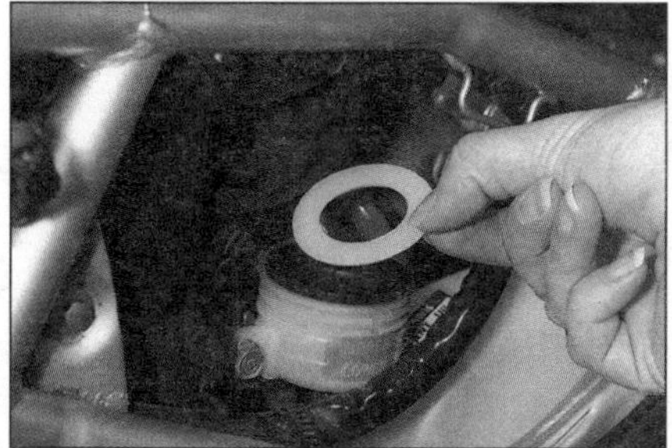

9 When the fluid level is correct, clean and dry the diaphragm, fold it into its compressed state and install it in the reservoir followed by the diaphragm plate. Install the reservoir cap and the right side cover.

4 Suspension, steering and final drive

Suspension and Steering:

- Check that the front and rear suspension operate smoothly and without binding.
- Check that the suspension is adjusted as required.
- Check that the steering moves smoothly from lock-to-lock.

Final drive:

- Check that the drive chain slack isn't excessive, and adjust if necessary (see Chapter 1).
- If the chain looks dry, lubricate it (see Chapter 1).

5 Tires

The correct pressures:

- The tire pressures must be checked when **cold**, not immediately after riding. Note that low tire pressures may cause the tire to slip on the rim or come off. High tire pressures will cause abnormal tread wear and unsafe handling.
- Use an accurate tire pressure gauge.
- Proper air pressure will increase tire life and provide maximum stability and ride comfort.

Tire pressures (cold)	
Front	36 psi (2.5 Bar)
Rear	42 psi (2.9 Bar)

Tire care:

- Check the tires carefully for cuts, tears, embedded nails or other sharp objects and excessive wear. Operation of the motorcycle with excessively worn tires is extremely hazardous, as traction and handling are directly affected.
- Check the condition of the tire valve and ensure the dust cap is in place.
- Pick out any stones or nails which may have become embedded in the tire tread. If left, they will eventually penetrate through the casing and cause a puncture.
- If tire damage is apparent, or unexplained loss of pressure is experienced, seek the advice of a tire fitting specialist without delay.

Tire tread depth:

- At the time of writing UK law requires that tread depth must be at least 1 mm over ¾ of the tread breadth all the way around the tire, with no bald patches. Many riders, however, consider 2 mm tread depth minimum to be a safer limit. Honda recommend the following limits:

Tire tread minimum depth	
Front	1.5 mm
Rear	2.0 mm

- Many tires now incorporate wear indicators in the tread. Identify the triangular pointer on the tire sidewall to locate the indicator bar and replace the tire if the tread has worn down to the bar.

1 Check the tire pressures when the tires are **cold** and keep them properly inflated.

2 Measure tread depth at the center of the tire using a tread depth gauge.

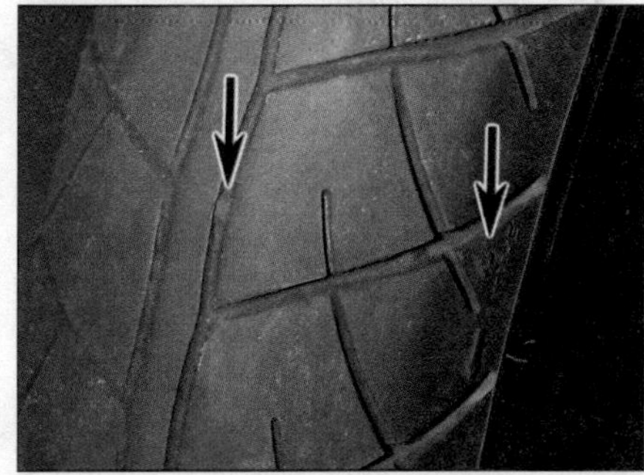

3 Tire tread wear indicator bar and its location marking (usually either an arrow, a triangle, the letters TWI, or the manufacturer's own mark) on or near the sidewall (arrow).

6 Legal and safety checks

Lighting and signaling:

- Take a minute to check that the headlight, taillight, brake light, instrument lights and turn signals all work correctly.
- Check that the horn sounds when the switch is operated.
- A working speedometer graduated in mph is a statutory requirement in the UK.

Safety:

- Check that the throttle grip rotates smoothly and snaps shut when released, in all steering positions. Also check for the correct amount of freeplay (see Chapter 1).
- Check that the engine shuts off when the kill switch is operated.
- Check that sidestand return spring holds the stand securely up when retracted.

Fuel:

- This may seem obvious, but check that you have enough fuel to complete your journey. If you notice signs of fuel leakage - rectify the cause immediately.
- Ensure you use the correct grade unleaded (recommended) or low-lead fuel - see Chapter 4 Specifications.

Chapter 1
Routine maintenance and servicing

Contents

Degrees of difficulty

Easy, suitable for novice with little experience 

Fairly easy, suitable for beginner with some experience 

Fairly difficult, suitable for competent DIY mechanic 

Difficult, suitable for experienced DIY mechanic 

Very difficult, suitable for expert DIY or professional

Specifications

Engine

Spark plugs	
Type	NGK CR9EH9 or ND U27FER9
Electrode gap	0.8 to 0.9 mm (0.031 to 0.035 in)
Valve clearances (COLD engine)	
Intake	0.13 to 0.19 mm (0.005 to 0.007 in)
Exhaust	0.19 to 0.25 mm (0.007 to 0.010 in)
Engine idle speed	
California models	1400 ± 100 rpm
All other US and UK models	1200 ± 100 rpm
Cylinder compression pressures	
M, N, P and R (1991 to 1994) models	12.6 to 12.9 bars (179 to 183 psi)
S, T, V and W (1995 to 1998) models	13.0 to 13.4 bars (185 to 191 psi)
Carburetor synchronization	
Maximum vacuum difference between any two cylinders	30 mm (1.2 in) Hg
Cylinder numbering (from left side to right side of the bike)	1-2-3-4

Miscellaneous

Brake pad minimum thickness	see text
Freeplay adjustments	
Throttle grip	2 to 6 mm (0.08 to 0.24 in)
Choke lever	2 to 3 mm (0.08 to 0.12 in)
Clutch lever	10 to 20 mm (0.4 to 0.8 in)
Drive chain	15 to 25 mm (0.6 to 1.0 in)
Minimum tire tread depth	See *'Daily (pre-ride) checks'*
Tire pressures (cold)	See *'Daily (pre-ride) checks'*

Torque settings

	Nm	ft-lbs
Engine oil pan drain plug	38	27
Oil filter	10	7
Spark plugs	12	9
Engine mounting bracket 10 mm bolt - S, T, V and W (1995 to 1998) models	45	33
Timing inspection cap	18	13

Recommended lubricants and fluids

Engine/transmission oil	
Type	API grade SE, SF or SG
Viscosity	SAE 10W40
Capacity - M, N, P and R (1991 to 1994) models	
With filter change	3.5 liters (3.7 US qt, 6.2 Imp pts)
Oil change only	3.2 liters (3.4 US qt, 5.6 Imp pts)
After engine rebuild	4.0 liters (4.3 US qt, 7.0 Imp pts)
Capacity - S, T, V and W (1995 to 1998) models	
With filter change	3.7 liters (3.9 US qt, 6.5 Imp pts)
Oil change only	3.4 liters (3.6 US qt, 6.0 Imp pts)
After engine rebuild	4.2 liters (4.4 US qt, 7.4 Imp pts)
Coolant	
Mixture type	50% distilled water, 50% corrosion inhibited ethylene glycol antifreeze
Capacity	
Radiator and engine	2.4 liters (2.53 US qt, 4.2 Imp pt)
Coolant reservoir	0.35 liters (0.38 US qt, 0.7 Imp pt)
Brake fluid	DOT 4

Miscellaneous

Drive chain	SAE 80 to 90W gear oil
Wheel bearings	Medium weight, lithium-based multi-purpose grease
Swingarm pivot bearings	Molybdenum disulfide grease
Suspension linkage bearings	Molybdenum disulfide grease
Shock absorber mounting bearings	Molybdenum disulfide grease
Cables and lever pivots	Chain and cable lubricant or 10W40 motor oil
Sidestand/centerstand pivots	Medium-weight, lithium-based multi-purpose grease
Brake pedal/shift lever pivots	Chain and cable lubricant or 10W40 motor oil
Throttle grip	Multi-purpose grease or dry film lubricant

Note: *The pre-ride inspection outlined at the front of this manual covers checks and maintenance that should be carried out on a daily basis. Always perform the pre-ride inspection at every maintenance interval (in addition to the procedures listed). The intervals listed below are the shortest intervals recommended by the manufacturer for each particular operation during the model years covered in this manual. Your owner's manual may have different intervals for your model.*

Daily (pre-ride)

- ☐ See *'Daily (pre-ride) checks'* at the beginning of this manual.

After the initial 600 miles (1000 km)

Note: *This check is usually performed by a Honda dealer after the first 600 miles (1000 km) from new. Thereafter, maintenance is carried out according to the following intervals of the schedule.*

Every 600 miles (1000 km)

- ☐ Check, adjust and lubricate the drive chain (Section 1)

Every 4000 miles (6000 km) or 6 months (whichever comes sooner)

- ☐ Check and adjust the idle speed (Section 2)
- ☐ Check the brake pads (Section 3)
- ☐ Check and adjust the clutch (Section 4)
- ☐ Clean and gap the spark plugs - US models (Section 5)
- ☐ Lubricate the clutch and brake lever pivots, the shift/brake lever pivots and the sidestand/centerstand pivots (Section 6)

Every 8000 miles (12,000 km) or 12 months (whichever comes sooner)

Carry out all the items under the 4000 mile (6000 km) check, plus the following

- ☐ Replace the engine oil and filter (Section 7)
- ☐ Check the fuel system hoses and filter (Section 8)
- ☐ Check the battery (Section 9)
- ☐ Check and adjust the throttle and choke cables (Section 10)
- ☐ Clean and gap the spark plugs - UK models (Section 11)
- ☐ Replace the spark plugs - US models (Section 12)
- ☐ Check/adjust the carburetor synchronization (Section 13)
- ☐ Check the condition of the EVAP and PAIR system hoses - California models only (Section 14)
- ☐ Check the cooling system (Section 15)

Every 8000 miles (12,000 km) or 12 months (whichever comes sooner) (continued)

- ☐ Check the condition of the exhaust system (Section 16)
- ☐ Check the brake system (Section 17)
- ☐ Check the condition of the wheels and tires (Section 18)
- ☐ Check and adjust the headlight aim (Section 19)
- ☐ Check the sidestand (Section 20)
- ☐ Check the operation of the front and rear suspension (Section 21)
- ☐ Check and adjust the steering head bearings (Section 22)
- ☐ Check the tightness of all nuts, bolts and fasteners (Section 23)

Every 12,000 miles (18,000 km) or 18 months (whichever comes first)

Carry out all the items under the 4000 mile (6000 km) check, plus the following

- ☐ Replace the air cleaner element (Section 24)
- ☐ Change the brake fluid (Section 25)

Every 16,000 miles (24,000 km) or two years (whichever comes sooner)

Carry out all the items under the 8000 mile (12,000 km) check, plus the following

- ☐ Replace the spark plugs - UK models (Section 26)
- ☐ Check and adjust the valve clearances (Section 27)

Every 24,000 miles (36,000 km) or three years (whichever comes sooner)

Carry out all the items under the 12,000 mile (18,000 km) and 8000 mile (12,000 km) checks, plus the following

- ☐ Replace the coolant (Section 28)

Non-scheduled maintenance

- ☐ Check the cylinder compression (Section 29).

Component locations on right side

1 *Rear brake fluid reservoir*
2 *Coolant reservoir*
3 *Throttle cable upper adjuster*
4 *Front brake fluid reservoir*
5 *Cooling system pressure cap*
6 *Oil filter*
7 *Clutch cable lower adjuster*
8 *Engine oil dipstick*
9 *Rear brake light switch*

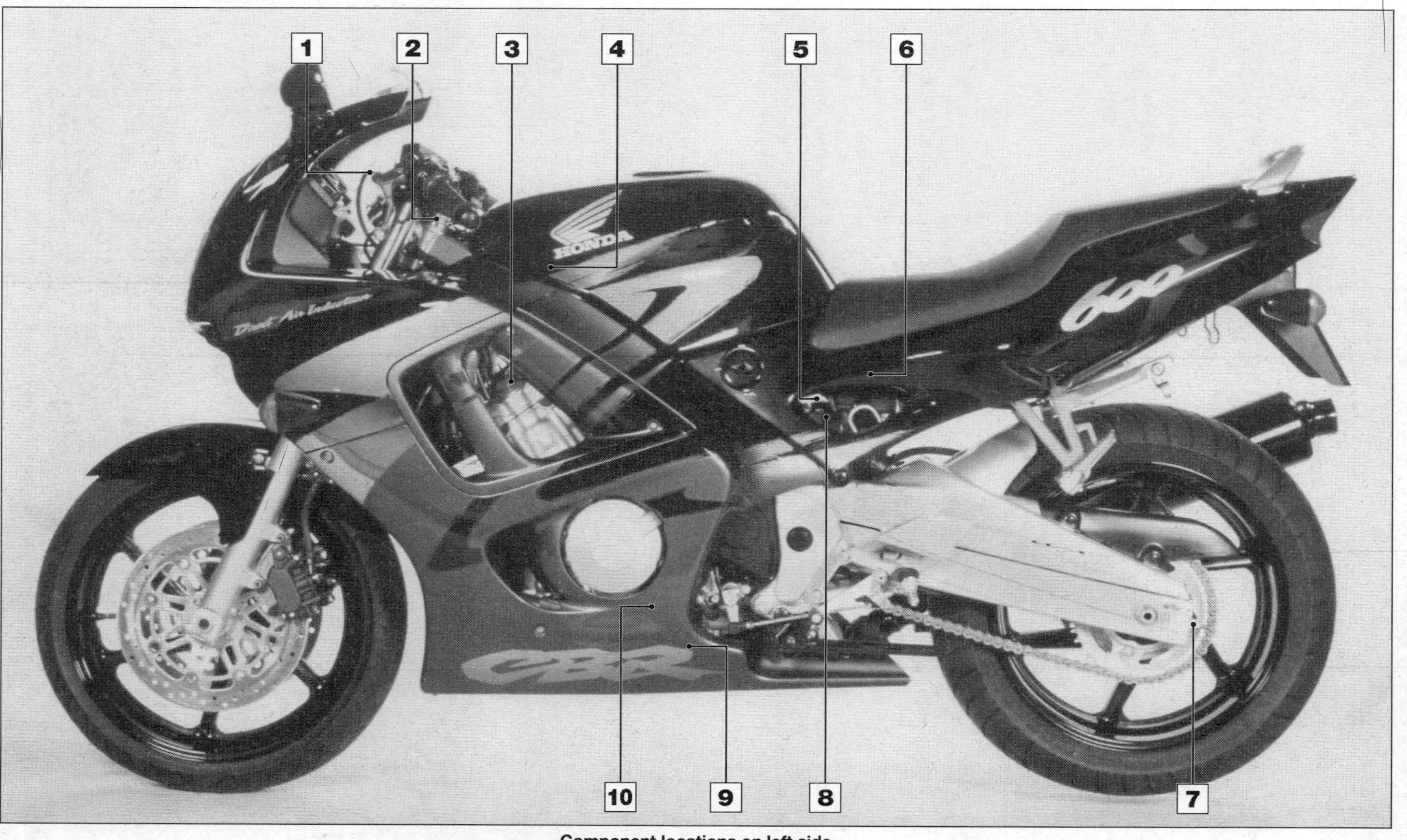

Component locations on left side

1 Clutch cable upper adjuster
2 Steering head bearings
3 Spark plugs
4 Air filter
5 Idle speed adjuster
6 Battery
7 Drive chain adjuster
8 Fuel filter and pump (S, T, V and W models)
9 Engine oil drain plug
10 Coolant drain plug on water pump

Introduction

1 This Chapter is designed to help the home mechanic maintain his/her motorcycle for safety, economy, long life and peak performance.

2 Deciding where to start or plug into the routine maintenance schedule depends on several factors. If the warranty period on your motorcycle has just expired, and if it has been maintained according to the warranty standards, you may want to pick up routine maintenance as it coincides with the next mileage or calendar interval. If you have owned the machine for some time but have never performed any maintenance on it, then you may want to start at the nearest interval and include some additional procedures to ensure that nothing important is overlooked. If you have just had a major engine overhaul, then you may want to start the maintenance routine from the beginning. If you have a used machine and have no knowledge of its history or maintenance record, you may desire to combine all the checks into one large service initially and then settle into the maintenance schedule prescribed.

3 Before beginning any maintenance or repair, the machine should be cleaned thoroughly, especially around the oil filter, spark plugs, valve cover, side panels, carburetors, etc. Cleaning will help ensure that dirt does not contaminate the engine and will allow you to detect wear and damage that could otherwise easily go unnoticed.

4 Certain maintenance information is sometimes printed on decals attached to the motorcycle. If the information on the decals differs from that included here, use the information on the decal.

Every 600 miles (1000 km)

1 Drive chain and sprockets - check, adjustment and lubrication

Check

1 A neglected drive chain won't last long and can quickly damage the sprockets. Routine chain adjustment and lubrication isn't difficult and will ensure maximum chain and sprocket life.

2 To check the chain, place the bike on its centerstand and shift the transmission into Neutral. Make sure the ignition switch is off.

3 Push up on the bottom run of the chain and measure the slack midway between the two sprockets, then compare your measurements to the value listed in this Chapter's Specifications **(see illustration)**.

1.3 Checking drive chain slack

Caution: If the machine is ridden with more than 50 mm (2.0 in) (M, N, P and R models) or 40 mm (1.6 in) (S, T, V and W models) of slack in the drive chain, the chain will contact the frame and swingarm, causing severe damage.

As wear occurs, the chain will actually stretch, necessitating adjustment to take up some slack from the chain. In some cases where lubrication has been neglected, corrosion and galling may cause the links to bind and kink, which effectively shortens the chain's length. If the chain is tight between the sprockets, rusty or kinked, it's time to replace it with a new one.

Caution: Repeat the chain slack measurement along the length of the chain - ideally, every inch or so. If you find a tight area, mark it with felt pen or paint, and repeat the measurement after the bike has been ridden. If the chain's still tight in the same area, it may be damaged or worn. Because a tight or kinked chain can damage the transmission countershaft bearing, it's a good idea to replace it.

4 Check the entire length of the chain for damaged rollers, loose links and pins and replace if damage is found. **Note:** *Never install a new chain on old sprockets, and never use the old chain if you install new sprockets - replace the chain and sprockets as a set.*

5 Remove the engine sprocket cover (see Chapter 6). Check the teeth on the engine sprocket and the rear wheel sprocket for wear **(see illustration)**.

6 Also inspect the drive chain slider on the swingarm for excessive wear. If it has worn to the wear limit line, or is damaged or deteriorated, remove the swingarm (see Chapter 6) and replace it. It is secured to the swingarm by two screws.

Adjustment

7 Rotate the rear wheel until the chain is positioned with the tightest point at the center of its bottom run.

8 Slacken the rear axle nut and the locknut on each chain adjuster **(see illustrations)**.

9 Turn the axle adjusting nuts on both sides of the swingarm until the proper chain tension is obtained (get the adjuster on the chain side close, then set the adjuster on the opposite side) **(see illustration)**. Be sure to turn the adjusting nuts evenly to keep the rear wheel in alignment. If the adjusting nuts reach the end of their travel, the chain is excessively worn and should be replaced with a new one (see Chapter 6). The chain wear decals will also indicate the need for chain replacement when the pointer on the chain adjuster aligns with the 'replace chain' zone of the decal **(see illustration)**.

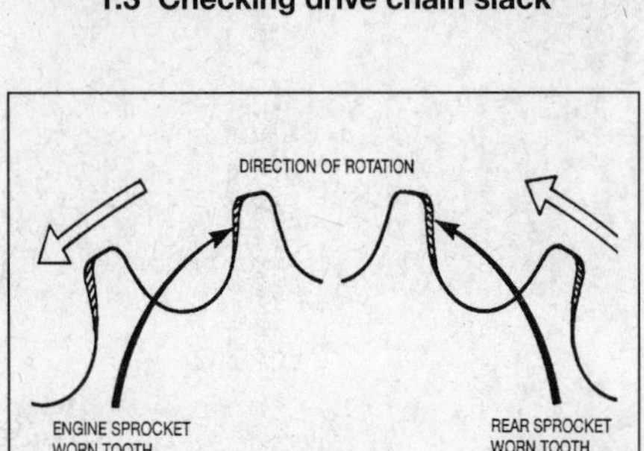

1.5 Check the sprockets in the areas indicated to see if they are worn excessively

1.8a Slacken the axle nut (arrow) . . .

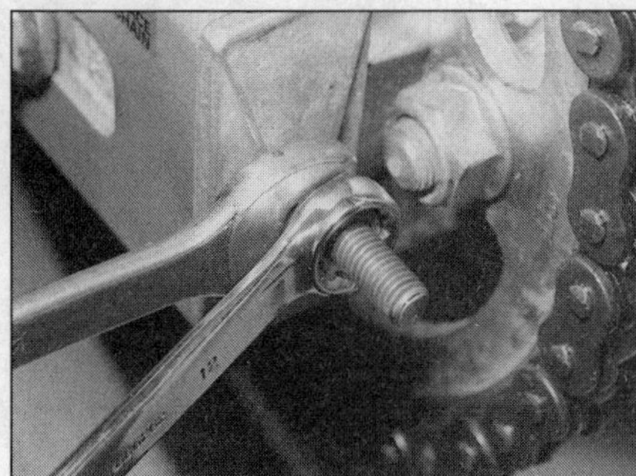

1.8b . . . and each chain adjuster locknut . . .

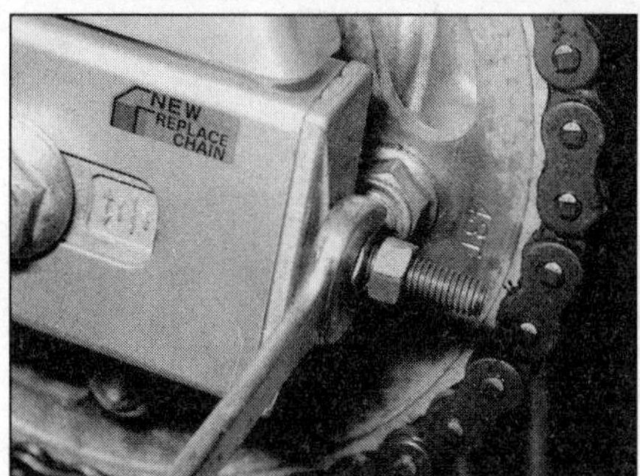

1.9a . . . then rotate the adjuster nut as required to obtain the correct chain tension

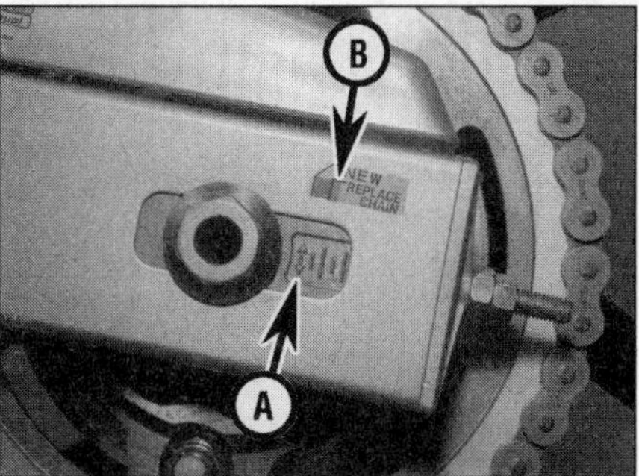

1.9b When the arrow (A) aligns with the red 'REPLACE CHAIN' indicator (B), the chain must be replaced

1.10a Make sure the adjuster alignment marks are equal on each side

10 When the chain has the correct amount of slack, check that the wheel is correctly aligned by making sure the alignment marks on each adjuster are in the same position relative to the back of the adjustment cutout in the swingarm **(see illustration)**. Tighten the axle nut to the torque listed in Chapter 7 Specifications **(see illustration)**.

11 With the axle nut tightened, tighten the chain adjuster locknuts to the specified torque setting listed in Chapter 7 Specifications.

Lubrication

12 If required, wash the chain in paraffin (kerosene), then wipe it off and allow it to dry, using compressed air if available. If the chain is excessively dirty it should be removed from the machine and allowed to soak in the paraffin (see Chapter 6).

Caution: Don't use petrol, solvent or other cleaning fluids which might damage the internal sealing properties of the chain. Don't use high-pressure water. The entire process shouldn't take longer than ten minutes - if it does, the O-rings in the chain rollers could be damaged.

13 For routine lubrication, the best time to lubricate the chain is after the motorcycle has been ridden. When the chain is warm, the lubricant will penetrate the joints between the side plates better than when cold. **Note:** *Honda specifies SAE 80 to SAE 90 gear oil only; do not use chain lube unless it is marked as suitable for O-ring chains.* Apply the oil to the area where the side plates overlap - not the middle of the rollers.

Apply the oil to the top of the lower chain run, so centrifugal force will work the oil into the chain when the bike is moving. After applying the lubricant, let it soak in a few minutes before wiping off any excess.

1.10b Once the chain is correctly tensioned, tighten the rear axle nut to the specified torque

Every 4000 miles (6000 km) or 6 months

2 Idle speed - check and adjustment

1 The idle speed should be checked and adjusted before and after the carburetors are synchronized and when it is obviously too high or too low. Before adjusting the idle speed, make sure the valve clearances and spark plug gaps are correct. Also, turn the handlebars back-and-forth and see if the idle speed changes as this is done. If it does, the throttle cables may not be adjusted correctly, or may be worn out. This is a dangerous condition that can cause loss of control of the bike. Be sure to correct this problem before proceeding.

2 The engine should be at normal operating temperature, which is usually reached after 10 to 15 minutes of stop and go riding. Place the motorcycle on the centerstand and make sure the transmission is in Neutral.

3 The idle speed adjuster screw is accessed via the cutout in the left side cover **(see illustrations)**. Turn the adjuster screw until the idle speed listed in this Chapter's Specifications is obtained.

4 Snap the throttle open and shut a few times, then recheck the idle speed. If necessary, repeat the adjustment procedure.

5 If a smooth, steady idle can't be achieved, the fuel/air mixture may be incorrect. Refer to Chapter 4 for additional carburetor information.

2.3a Idle speed screw (arrow) - M, N, P and R (1991 to 1994) models

2.3b Idle speed screw (arrow) - S, T, V and W (1995 to 1998) models

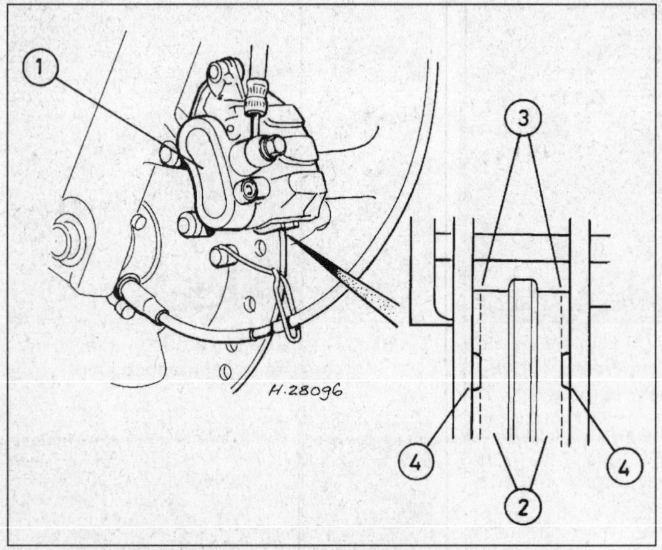

3.1a Front brake pad wear indicator groove details

1 *Front brake caliper*
2 *Pads*
3 *Wear limit*
4 *Minimum thickness cutout*

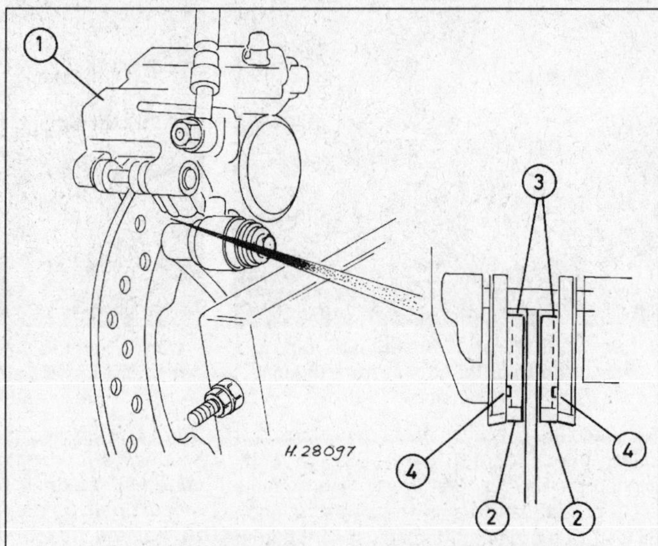

3.1b Rear brake pad wear indicator groove details

1 *Rear brake caliper*
2 *Pads*
3 *Wear limit*
4 *Minimum thickness cutout*

3 Brake pads - wear check

1 A quick check of the brake pads can be made without removing them from the caliper. The pad wear can be judged by looking at the thickness of the pad from the rear of the caliper (both front and rear) **(see illustrations)**.

2 If either pad has worn down to, or beyond the cutout in the friction material, both pads must be replaced as a set. However, it is recommended that the pads be removed and a more detailed inspection be carried out as described in Sections 2 and 6 of Chapter 7.

4 Clutch - check and adjustment

1 Check that the clutch cable operates smoothly and easily.

2 If clutch lever operation is heavy or stiff, remove the cable as described in Chapter 2 and lubricate it as described in Section 6. Install the lubricated cable, making sure it takes the smoothest possible route.

3 With the cable operating smoothly, check that the clutch cable freeplay is correctly adjusted. Freeplay is measured in terms of free travel at the ball end of the lever before the clutch is activated, and should be as given in this Chapter's Specifications. If adjustment is required, slacken the cable adjuster locknut on the clutch lever mounting bracket, then screw the adjuster in or out as required until the freeplay is correct **(see illustration)**. Tighten the locknut securely.

4 If there is insufficient range in the handlebar adjuster it will be necessary to remove the right lower fairing panel (see Chapter 8) and adjust the freeplay at the lower adjuster on the crankcase **(see illustration)**. Screw the upper adjuster fully inwards and slacken the locknut on the lower adjuster. Rotate the lower adjuster nut until the required freeplay is obtained at the handlebar lever, then securely tighten the lower adjuster locknut and install the fairing lower panel. If necessary, fine adjustments can then be made using the handlebar adjuster.

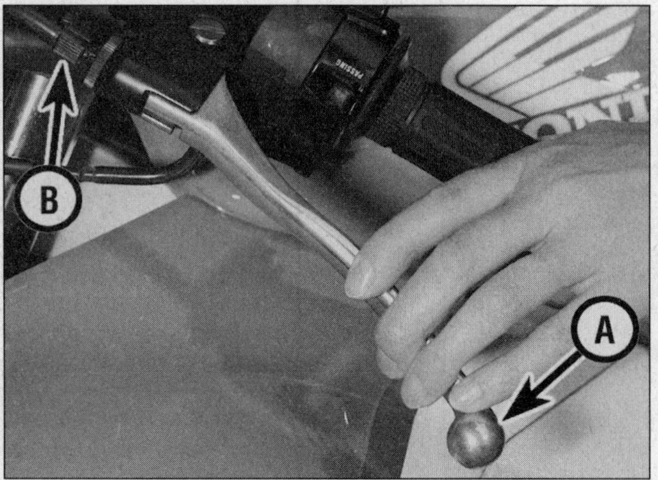

4.3 Clutch cable freeplay measured in terms of travel at the lever ball end (A); adjust using upper adjuster (B)

4.4 Adjusting the clutch cable lower adjuster

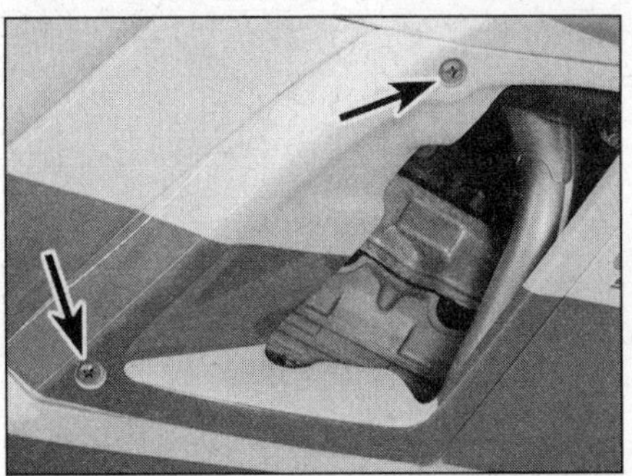
5.2 Release the screws (arrows) and remove both access covers to reach the spark plugs

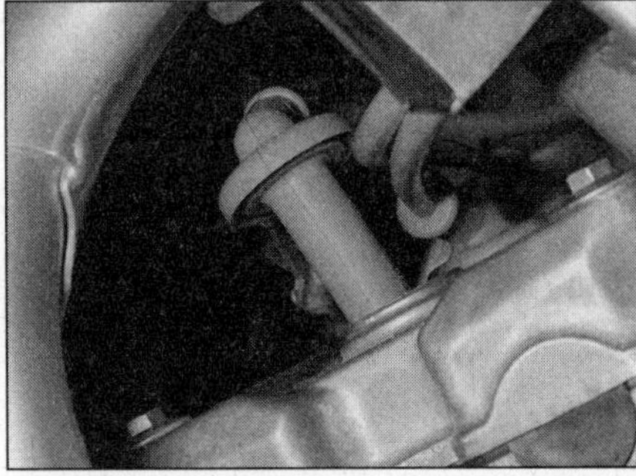
5.3a Disconnect the spark plug caps . . .

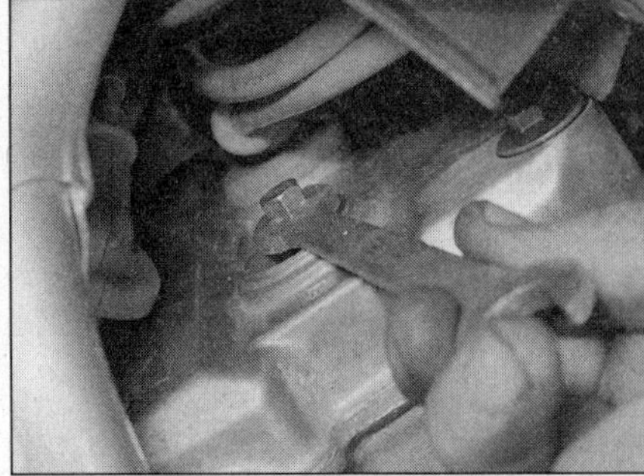
5.3b . . . then unscrew the spark plugs . . .

5 Spark plug gaps - check and adjustment (US models)

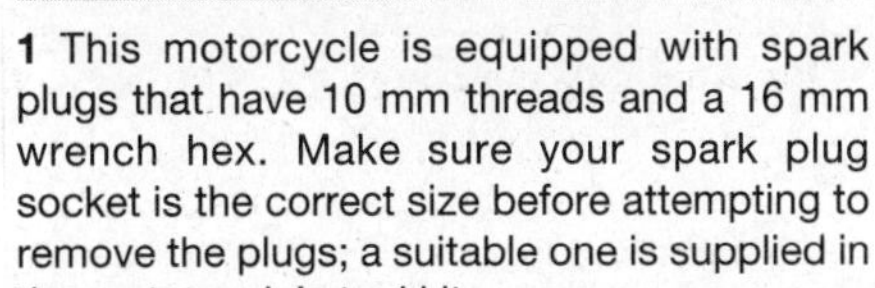

1 This motorcycle is equipped with spark plugs that have 10 mm threads and a 16 mm wrench hex. Make sure your spark plug socket is the correct size before attempting to remove the plugs; a suitable one is supplied in the motorcycle's tool kit.

2 Release the fasteners and remove the access covers from the left and right lower fairing panels (see Chapter 8, if necessary) **(see illustration)**.

3 Disconnect the spark plug caps from the spark plugs. If available, use compressed air to blow any accumulated debris from around the spark plugs. Remove the plugs and lay them out in relation to their cylinder number; if any plug shows up a problem it will then be easy to identify the troublesome cylinder **(see illustrations)**.

4 Inspect the electrodes for wear. Both the center and side electrodes should have square edges and the side electrode should be of uniform thickness. Look for excessive deposits and evidence of a cracked or chipped insulator around the center electrode. Compare your spark plugs to the color spark plug reading chart. Check the threads, the washer and the ceramic insulator body for cracks and other damage.

5 If the electrodes are not excessively worn, and if the deposits can be easily removed with a wire brush, the plugs can be regapped and re-used (if no cracks or chips are visible in the insulator). If in doubt concerning the condition of the plugs, replace them with new ones, as the expense is minimal.

6 Cleaning spark plugs by sandblasting is permitted, provided you clean the plugs with a high flash-point solvent afterwards.

7 Before installing new plugs, make sure they are the correct type and heat range. Check the gap between the electrodes, as they are not preset. For best results, use a wire-type gauge rather than a flat (feeler) gauge to check the gap. If the gap must be adjusted, bend the side electrode only and be very careful not to chip or crack the insulator nose **(see illustrations)**. Make sure the washer is in place before installing each plug.

8 Since the cylinder head is made of aluminum, which is soft and easily damaged, thread the plugs into the head by hand.

Since the plugs are recessed, slip a short length of hose over the end of the plug to use as a tool to thread it into place. The hose will grip the plug well enough to turn it, but will start to slip if the plug begins to cross-thread in the hole - this will prevent damaged threads and the resultant repair costs.

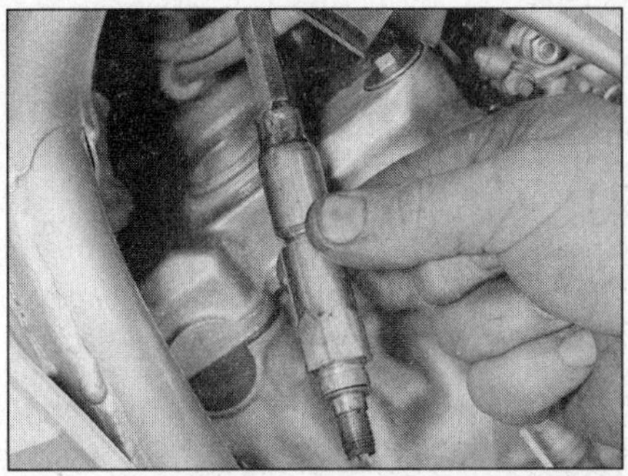
5.3c . . . and remove them from the engine

9 Once the plugs are finger-tight, the job can be finished with a socket. If a torque wrench is available, tighten the spark plugs to the specified torque listed in this Chapter's Specifications. If you do not have a torque wrench, tighten the plugs finger-tight (until the washers bottom on the cylinder head) then use a wrench to tighten them an additional 1/4 turn. Regardless of the method used, do not over-tighten them.

10 Reconnect the spark plug caps and reinstall the access covers.

Stripped plug threads in the cylinder head can be repaired with a thread insert - see 'Tools and Workshop Tips' in the Reference section.

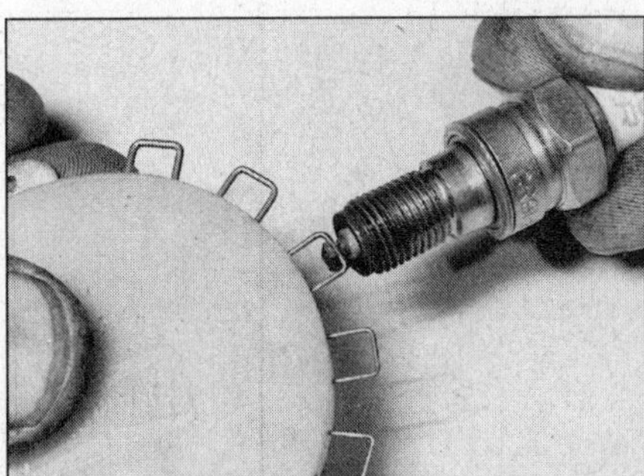
5.7a A wire type gauge is recommended to measure spark plug electrode gap

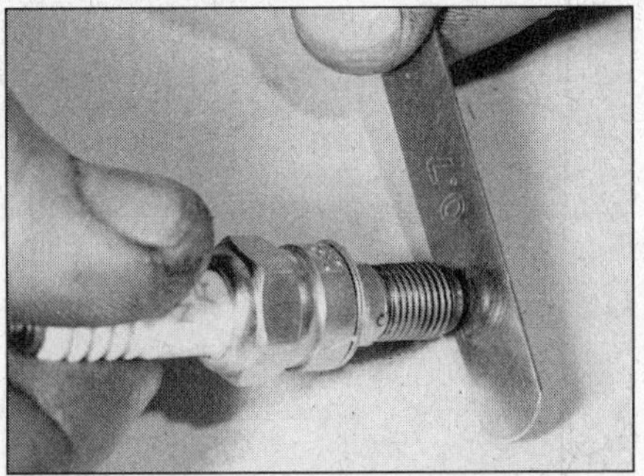
5.7b Using a feeler gauge to measure spark plug electrode gap

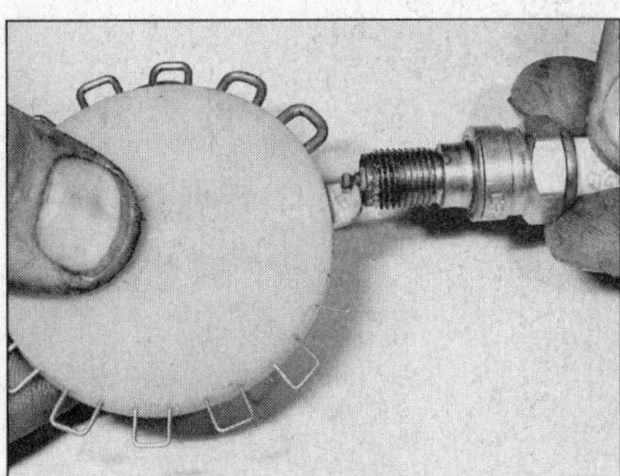
5.7c Electrode gap is adjusted by bending the side electrode

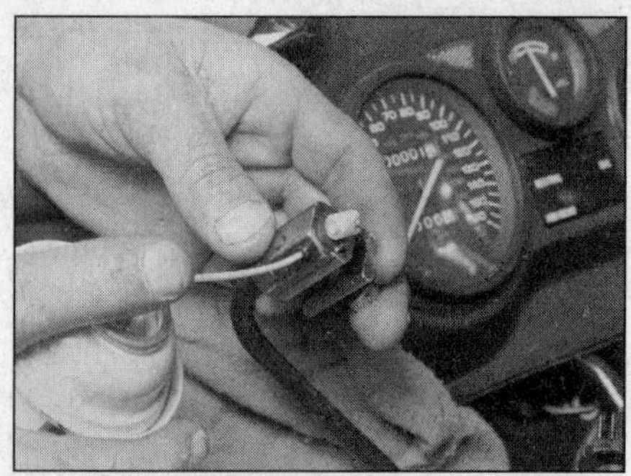

6.3a Lubricating a cable with a pressure lubricator. Make sure the tool seals around the inner cable

6 Lubrication - general

1 Since the controls, cables and various other components of a motorcycle are exposed to the elements, they should be lubricated periodically to ensure safe and trouble-free operation.

2 The footpegs, clutch and brake lever, brake pedal, shift lever and side and centerstand pivots should be lubricated frequently. In order for the lubricant to be applied where it will do the most good, the component should be disassembled. However, if chain and cable lubricant is being used, it can be applied to the pivot joint gaps and will usually work its way into the areas where friction occurs. If motor oil or light grease is being used, apply it sparingly as it may attract dirt (which could cause the controls to bind or wear at an accelerated rate). **Note:** *One of the best lubricants for the control lever pivots is a dry-film lubricant (available from many sources by different names).*

3 To lubricate the cables, disconnect the relevant cable at its upper end, then lubricate the cable with a pressure adapter, or if one is not available, using the set-up shown **(see illustrations)**. See Chapter 4 for the choke and throttle cable removal procedures, and Chapter 2 for clutch cable removal details.

4 The speedometer cable (M, N, P and R, 1991 to 1994 models only) should be removed from its housing and lubricated with motor oil or cable lubricant. Do not lubricate the upper few inches of the cable as the lubricant may travel up into the speedometer head.

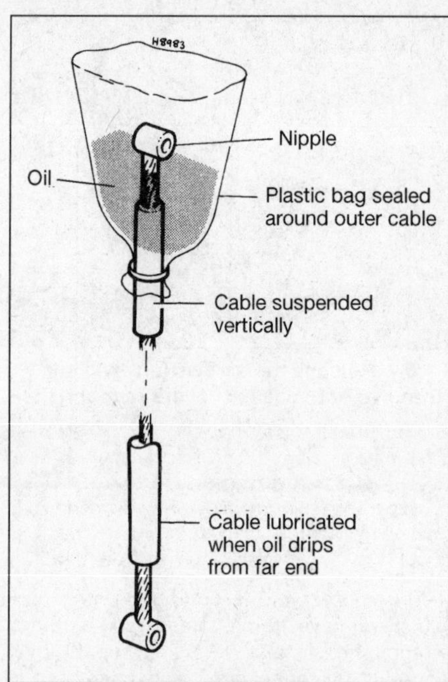

6.3b Lubricating a cable with a makeshift funnel and motor oil

Every 8000 miles (12,000 km) or 12 months (whichever comes sooner)

Carry out all the items under the 4000 mile (6000 km) check, plus the following

7 Engine oil/filter - change

1 Consistent routine oil and filter changes are the single most important maintenance procedure you can perform on a motorcycle. The oil not only lubricates the internal parts of the engine, transmission and clutch, but it also acts as a coolant, a cleaner, a sealant and a protectant. Because of these demands, the oil takes a terrific amount of abuse and should be replaced often with new oil of the recommended grade and type. Saving a little money on the difference in cost between a good oil and a cheap oil won't pay off if the engine is damaged.

2 Before changing the oil and filter, warm up the engine so the oil will drain easily.

Warning: Be careful when draining the oil, as the exhaust pipes, the engine and the oil itself can cause severe burns.

3 Put the motorcycle on the centerstand and position a clean drain pan below the engine. Unscrew the oil filler cap to vent the crankcase and act as a reminder that there is no oil in the engine **(see illustration)**. Refer to Chapter 8 and remove the lower fairing panels.

4 Next, remove the drain plug from the oil pan and allow the oil to drain into the pan **(see illustration)**. Discard the sealing washer on the drain plug; it should be replaced whenever the plug is removed.

5 Make sure the drain pan is under the filter, then slacken the oil filter using a chain wrench or strap wrench **(see illustration)**. Unscrew the filter from the engine and empty its contents into the drain pan. If additional maintenance is planned for this time period, check or service another component while the oil is allowed to drain completely.

6 Clean the filter threads and housing on the crankcase with solvent or clean shop towels. Wipe any remaining oil off the filter sealing area of the crankcase.

7.3 Remove the oil filler cap (arrow)

7.4 Unscrew the oil drain plug and allow the oil to drain

7.5 If the oil filter is tight, use a strap wrench or chain wrench to loosen it

7.8a Apply a smear of engine oil to the filter sealing ring . . .

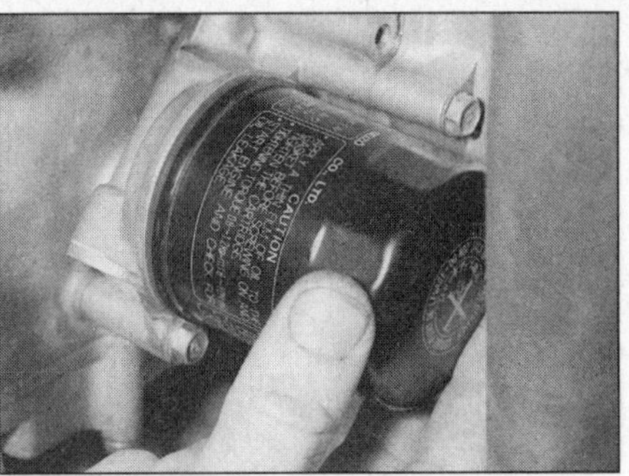

7.8b . . . and screw the filter onto the engine

7.9 Select a filter wrench to fit the molded hex of the filter

7 Slip a new sealing washer over the drain plug. Fit the plug to the oil pan and tighten it to the specified torque setting. Avoid over-tightening, as damage to the oil pan will result.
8 Apply a smear of clean oil to the sealing ring of the new filter and screw it into position on the engine. Tighten the filter firmly by hand **(see illustrations)**.
9 If you have a filter wrench, the filter should be tightened to the specified torque setting **(see illustration)**.

Before refilling the engine, check the old oil carefully. If it is very metallic colored, then the engine is experiencing wear from break-in (new engine) or from insufficient lubrication. If there are flakes or chips of metal in the oil, then something is drastically wrong internally and the engine will have to be disassembled for inspection and repair. If there are pieces of fiber-like material in the oil, the clutch is experiencing excessive wear and should be checked.

10 If inspection of the oil turns up nothing unusual, refill the crankcase to the proper level with the recommended type and amount of oil and install the filler cap (see *Daily (pre-ride) checks* if necessary) **(see illustration)**. Start the engine and let it run for two or three minutes. Shut it off, wait a few minutes, then check the oil level. If necessary, add more oil to bring the level up to the upper mark. Check around the drain plug and filter for leaks.
11 The old oil drained from the engine cannot be re-used and should be disposed of properly. Check with your local refuse disposal company, disposal facility or environmental agency to see whether they will accept the used oil for recycling. Don't pour used oil into drains or onto the ground.

OIL BANK LINE
0800 66 33 66

To find the location of your local oil recycling bank, call this UK number free. In the US note that any oil supplier must accept used oil for recycling.

8 Fuel system - check and filter cleaning

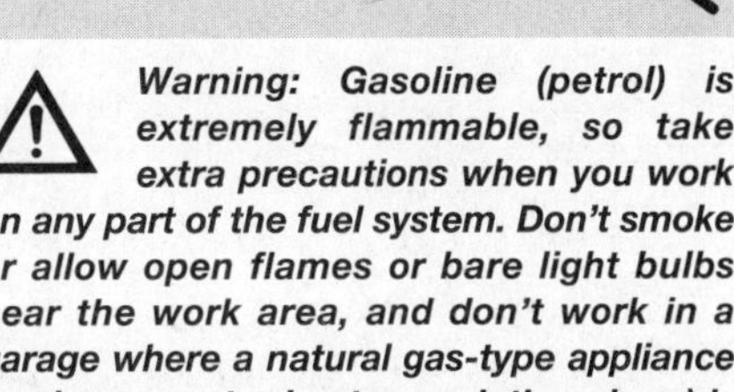

Warning: Gasoline (petrol) is extremely flammable, so take extra precautions when you work on any part of the fuel system. Don't smoke or allow open flames or bare light bulbs near the work area, and don't work in a garage where a natural gas-type appliance (such as a water heater or clothes dryer) is present. If you spill any fuel on your skin, rinse it off immediately with soap and water. When you perform any kind of work on the fuel system, wear safety glasses and have a fire extinguisher suitable for a Class B type fire (flammable liquids) on hand.

1 Check the fuel tank, the tank breather hose (not California models), the fuel tap, the lines and the carburetors, and on S, T, V and W (1995 to 1998) models check the fuel pump for leaks and evidence of damage.
2 If the carburetor gaskets are leaking, the carburetors should be disassembled and rebuilt by referring to Chapter 4.
3 If the fuel tap is leaking, tightening the retaining nut may help but if leakage persists, the tap should be disassembled and repaired or replaced with a new one.
4 If the fuel lines are cracked or otherwise deteriorated, replace them with new ones.
5 On M, N, P and R (1991 to 1994) models, check the vacuum hose connecting the fuel tap to No. 1 cylinder intake port. If it is cracked or otherwise damaged, replace it with a new one.
6 The fuel filter which is attached to the fuel tap may become clogged and should be removed and cleaned periodically. In order to clean the filter, the fuel tank must be drained and the fuel tap removed.
7 Remove the fuel tank (see Chapter 4). Drain the fuel into an approved fuel container.
8 Once the tank is emptied, unscrew the nut and remove the tap and filter. Recover the O-ring from the retaining nut.
9 Clean the filter with solvent and blow it dry with compressed air. If the filter is torn or otherwise damaged, replace it. Check the O-ring and replace it if it is damaged or worn.

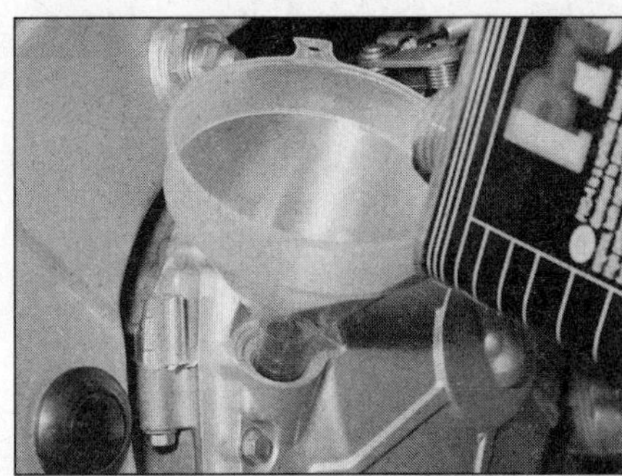

7.10 Fill the engine with the correct amount of the specified type and grade of oil

10 Install the O-ring, filter and fuel tap to the tank and securely tighten the retaining nut. Install the tank (see Chapter 4) and refill. Check carefully for leaks around the retaining nut.
11 On S, T, V and W (1995 to 1998) models, an in-line fuel filter is fitted in the fuel pipe from the fuel pump **(see illustration)**. If the filter is dirty or clogged or otherwise needs replacing, remove the fuel tank (see Chapter 4). Have a rag handy to soak up any residual fuel and disconnect the pipes from the filter. Slip the filter out of its bracket and install the new filter so that its arrow points in the direction of fuel flow (ie towards the pump). Secure the pipes to the filter with the retaining clips. Install the fuel tank (see Chapter 4), turn the tap ON and check that there are no fuel leaks.

8.11 In-line fuel filter (arrow) - S, T, V and W (1995 to 1998) models

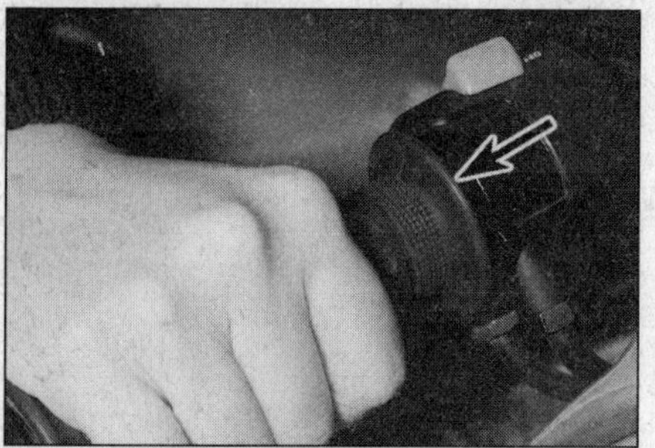
10.3 Throttle cable freeplay is measured in terms of twistgrip rotation at the grip flange (arrow) . . .

10.4 . . . and adjusted using the upper cable adjuster (arrow)

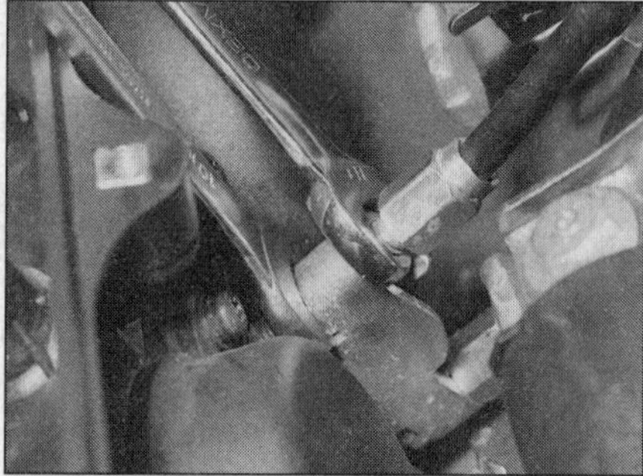
10.5 Adjusting the throttle cable lower adjuster

9 Battery - check

1 All models covered in this manual are fitted with a sealed battery, which requires no maintenance.

Caution: Do not attempt to remove the battery caps to check the electrolyte level or battery specific gravity. Removal will damage the caps, resulting in electrolyte leakage and battery damage.

2 All that should be done is to check that its terminals are clean and tight and that the casing is not damaged or leaking. See Chapter 9 for further details.

3 If the machine is not in regular use, disconnect the battery and give it a refresher charge every month to six weeks, as described in Chapter 9.

10 Throttle and choke operation/grip freeplay - check and adjustment

Throttle cables

1 Make sure the throttle grip rotates easily from fully closed to fully open with the front wheel turned at various angles. The grip should return automatically from fully open to fully closed when released.

2 If the throttle sticks, this is probably due to a cable fault. Remove the cables as described in Chapter 4 and lubricate them as described in Section 6. Install each cable, routing them so they take the smoothest route possible. If this fails to improve the operation of the throttle, the cables must be replaced. Note that in very rare cases the fault could lie in the carburetors rather than the cables, necessitating the removal of the carburetors and inspection of the throttle linkage (see Chapter 4).

3 With the throttle operating smoothly, check for a small amount of freeplay at the grip. The amount of freeplay in the throttle cables, measured in terms of twistgrip rotation, should be as given in this Chapter's Specifications **(see illustration)**. If adjustment is necessary, adjust the idle speed first (see Section 2).

4 Slacken the locknut on the cable upper adjuster and rotate the adjuster until the correct amount of freeplay is obtained, then tighten the locknut **(see illustration)**. If it is not possible to obtain the correct freeplay with the upper adjuster, it will also be necessary to make adjustment at the lower adjuster, situated on the carburetors.

5 To gain access to the lower adjuster remove the fuel tank and air filter housing as described in Chapter 4 **(see illustration)**. Screw the cable upper adjuster in to obtain the maximum possible freeplay, then slacken the lower adjuster locknut and set the cable freeplay using first the lower adjuster and then, if necessary, the upper adjuster. Once the freeplay is correct tighten the locknuts securely.

6 Check that the throttle twistgrip operates smoothly and snaps shut quickly when released.

Warning: Turn the handlebars all the way through their travel with the engine idling. Idle speed should not change. If it does, the cables may be routed incorrectly. Correct this condition before riding the bike (see Chapter 4).

Choke cable

7 Remove the fuel tank and air filter housing as described in Chapter 4. Operate the handlebar-mounted lever while observing the movement of the carburetor choke mechanism **(see illustration)**. The mechanism should extend smoothly when the lever is pulled, and return home fully when the lever is returned.

8 If the choke mechanism does not operate smoothly this is probably due to a cable fault. Remove the cable as described in Chapter 4 and lubricate it as described in Section 6. Install the cable, routing it so it takes the smoothest route possible. If this fails to improve the operation of the choke, the cable must be replaced. Note that in very rare cases the fault could lie in the carburetors rather than the cable, necessitating the removal of the carburetors and inspection of the choke plungers as described in Chapter 4.

9 With the choke mechanism operating smoothly, check for a small amount of freeplay at the base of the choke lever. The amount of freeplay is measured in terms of lever travel, before the mechanism starts to operate. This should be as given in this Chapter's Specifications. To adjust the cable, slacken the choke cable clamping screw, situated on the carburetors, then move the lower end of the outer cable until the required amount of freeplay is obtained **(see illustration)**. Tighten the clamping screw securely.

10 Once the choke mechanism is correctly adjusted, install the air filter housing and fuel tank as described in Chapter 4.

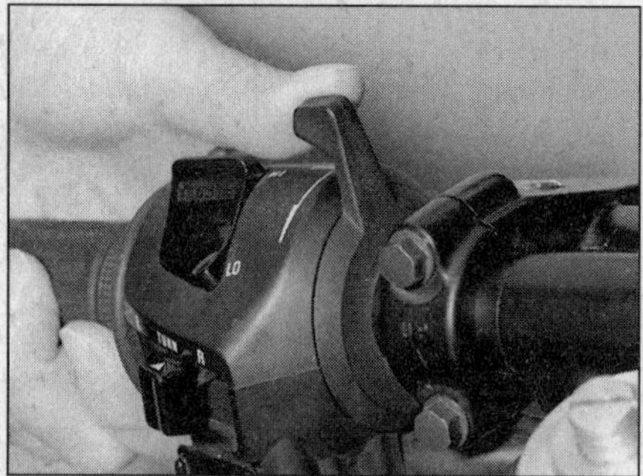
10.7 Check that the choke lever operates smoothly and easily

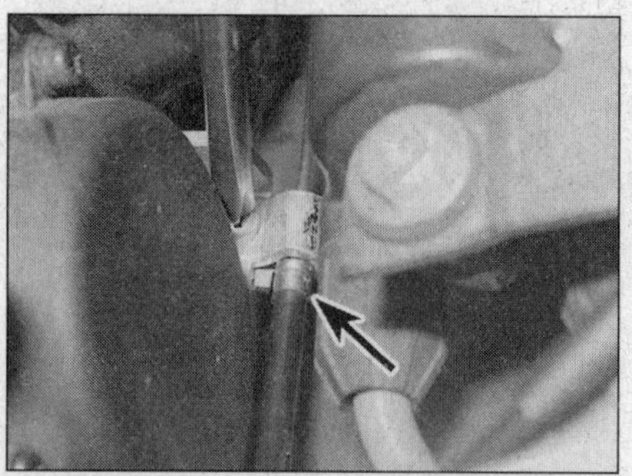
10.9 Slacken the screw and reposition the outer cable (arrow) in the clamp

11 Spark plug gaps - check and adjustment (UK models)

See Section 5 'Spark plug gaps - check and adjustment (US models)' under the 4000 mile (6000 km) or 6 months heading for details.

12 Spark plugs - replacement (US models)

See Section 5 'Spark plug gaps - check and adjustment (US models)' under the 4000 mile (6000 km) or 6 months heading for details.

13 Carburetor synchronization - check and adjustment

Warning: Gasoline (petrol) is extremely flammable, so take extra precautions when you work on any part of the fuel system. Don't smoke or allow open flames or bare light bulbs near the work area, and don't work in a garage where a natural gas-type appliance (such as a water heater or clothes dryer) is present. If you spill any fuel on your skin, rinse it off immediately with soap and water. When you perform any kind of work on the fuel system, wear safety glasses and have a fire extinguisher suitable for a Class B type fire (flammable liquids) on hand.

1 Carburetor synchronization is simply the process of adjusting the carburetors so they pass the same amount of fuel/air mixture to each cylinder. This is done by measuring the vacuum produced in each cylinder. Carburetors that are out of synchronization will result in decreased fuel mileage, increased engine temperature, less than ideal throttle response and higher vibration levels.

2 To properly synchronize the carburetors, you will need some sort of vacuum gauge setup, preferably with a gauge for each cylinder, or a manometer, which is a calibrated tube arrangement to indicate engine vacuum. The equipment used should be suitable for a four cylinder engine. On M, N, P and R (1991 to 1994) models, two adapters are required to screw into the holes in No. 3 and 4 cylinder intake ports. On S, T, V and W (1995 to 1998) models, one adapter is required to screw into the hole in No. 1 cylinder intake port.

3 Because of the nature of the synchronization procedure and the need for special instruments, most owners leave the task to a Honda dealer service department or a reputable motorcycle repair shop.

4 Start the engine and let it run until it reaches normal operating temperature, then shut it off.

5 Remove the fuel tank as described in Chapter 4, and the lower fairing panels as described in Chapter 8. On S, T, V and W (1995 to 1998) models, also remove the engine mounting bracket on each side, noting the positions of the spacers **(see illustration)**.

6 On M, N, P and R (1991 to 1994) models, undo the screw from the underside of No. 3 and 4 intake ports and screw in the adapters. On S, T, V and W (1995 to 1998) models, undo the screw from the side of No. 1 intake port and screw in the adapter.

Warning: Take great care not to burn your hands on the hot engine unit.

On M, N, P and R (1991 to 1994) models, detach the hose and cap from the unions on Nos. 1 and 2 cylinder intakes respectively. On S, T, V and W (1995 to 1998) models, detach the caps from the unions on Nos. 2, 3 and 4 cylinder intakes. Hook up the vacuum gauge set or the manometer according to the manufacturer's instructions **(see illustrations)**.

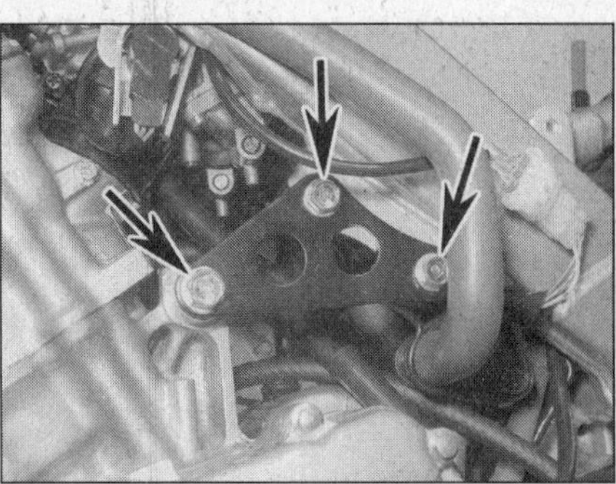

13.5 Unscrew the three bolts (arrows) securing each bracket and remove the brackets

Make sure there are no leaks in the setup, as false readings will result.

7 Arrange a temporary fuel supply, either by using a small temporary tank or by using extra long fuel pipes to the now remote fuel tank on a nearby bench (the fuel tap should be positioned in the RES position, and on M, N, P and R (1991 to 1994) models the vacuum hose should be attached to its union on the tap and a vacuum applied to it, then it should be sealed so the vacuum remains).

8 Start the engine and make sure the idle speed is correct. If it isn't, adjust it (see Section 2). If the gauges are fitted with damping adjustment, set this so that the needle flutter is just eliminated but so that they can still respond to small changes in pressure.

9 The vacuum readings for all of the cylinders should be the same, or at least within the tolerance listed in this Chapter's Specifications. If the vacuum readings vary, adjust as necessary.

10 The carburetors are adjusted by the three screws situated between each carburetor, in the throttle linkage. The screws are accessible from the rear of the air filter housing. **Note:** *Do not press down on the screws while adjusting them, otherwise a false reading will be*

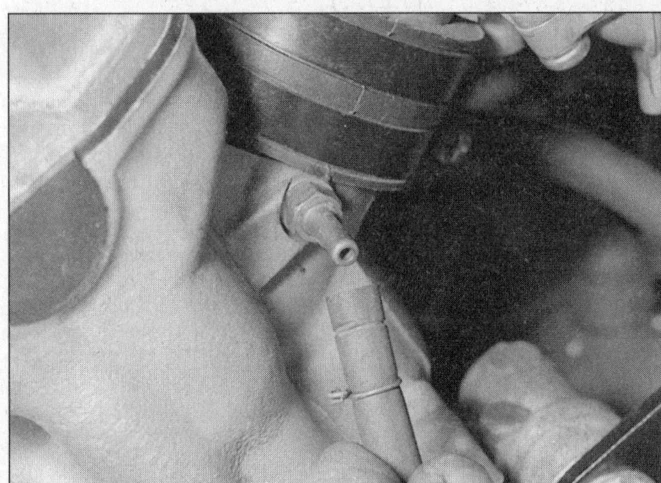

13.6a On M, N, P and R (1991 to 1994) models, disconnect the fuel tap vacuum hose from the No. 1 intake port and connect the gauge to the adapter

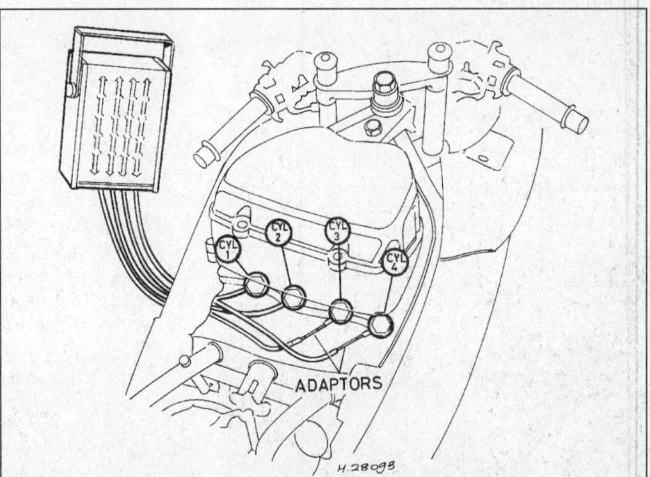

13.6b Screw the adapters into No. 3 and 4 (M, N, P and R models) or No. 1 (S, T, V and W models) intake ports and connect the vacuum gauge/manometer as shown

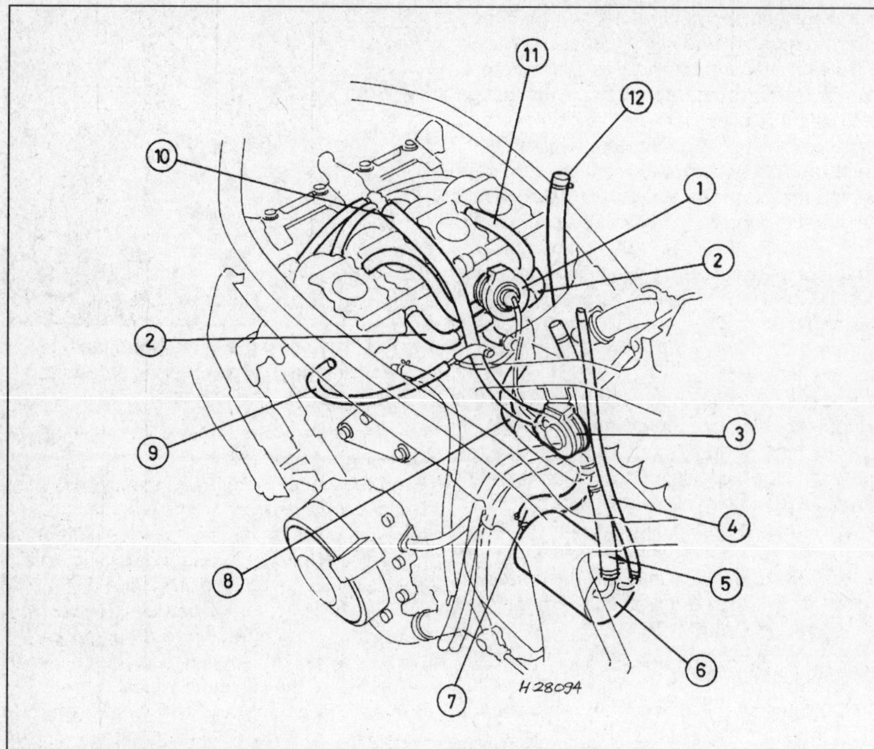

14.2 Evaporative emission control (EVAP) system hoses - California models

1 *Evaporative emission carburetor air vent control valve*
2 *Fuel tubes*
3 *Evaporative emission purge control valve*
4 *No. 1 tube (to fuel tank)*
5 *No. 4 tube*
6 *Canister*
7 *Air vent tube*
8 *No. 4 tube*
9 *Fuel tap vacuum tube*
10 *No. 5 tube*
11 *No. 6 tubes*
12 *Pulse secondary air injection (PAIR) control valve air intake hose*

obtained. When all the carburetors are synchronized, open and close the throttle quickly to settle the linkage, then recheck the gauge readings, readjusting if necessary.

11 When the adjustment is complete, recheck the vacuum readings and idle speed, then stop the engine. Remove the vacuum gauge or manometer. Unscrew the adapters, where fitted, and fit the screws, tightening them securely. On M, N, P and R (1991 to 1994) models, attach the vacuum hose to No. 1 cylinder. Otherwise, fit the cap(s) onto the union(s). On S, T, V and W (1995 to 1998) models, if removed, install the engine mounting brackets with their spacers and tighten the 10 mm bolt to the torque setting specified at the beginning of the Chapter.

12 Detach the temporary fuel supply and install the fuel tank and fairing section as described in Chapters 4 and 8.

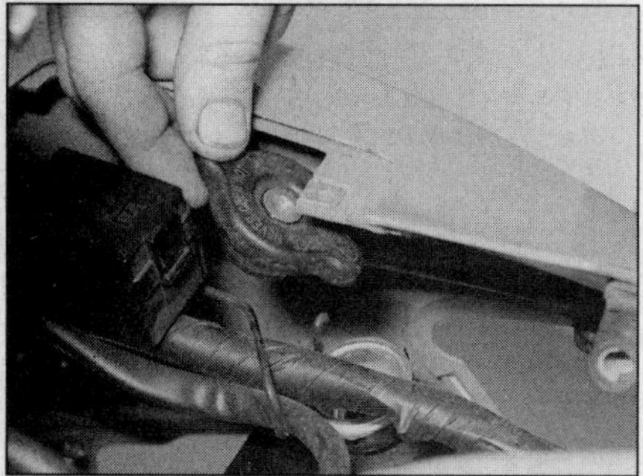

15.8 Remove the radiator pressure cap as described in text

14 Emission control systems (California models only) - check

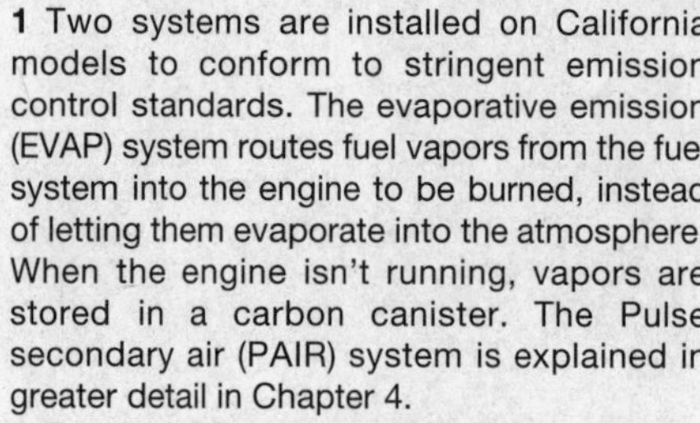

1 Two systems are installed on California models to conform to stringent emission control standards. The evaporative emission (EVAP) system routes fuel vapors from the fuel system into the engine to be burned, instead of letting them evaporate into the atmosphere. When the engine isn't running, vapors are stored in a carbon canister. The Pulse secondary air (PAIR) system is explained in greater detail in Chapter 4.

2 To begin the inspection of the system, remove the side covers, seat and fuel tank (see Chapters 4 and 8 if necessary). Inspect the hoses from the fuel tank and carburetors to the canister, which is mounted underneath the bike, for cracking, kinks or other signs of deterioration **(see illustration)**. Details of the correct routing of all hoses is given on a label attached to the air filter housing.

3 Label and disconnect the hoses, then remove the canister from the machine.

4 Inspect the canister for cracks or other signs of damage. Tip each canister so the nozzle points down. If fuel runs out of the canister, it is probably damaged internally, so it would be a good idea to replace it.

15 Cooling system - check

Warning: The engine must be cool before beginning this procedure.

1 Check the coolant level as described in *'Daily (pre-ride) checks'*.

2 Remove the left and right lower fairing panels as described in Chapter 8.

3 The entire cooling system should be checked for evidence of leakage. Examine each rubber coolant hose along its entire length. Look for cracks, abrasions and other damage. Squeeze each hose at various points. They should feel firm, yet pliable, and return to their original shape when released. If they are dried out or hard, replace them with new ones.

4 Check for evidence of leaks at each cooling system joint. Tighten the hose clips carefully to prevent future leaks.

5 Check the radiator for leaks and other damage. Leaks in the radiator leave telltale scale deposits or coolant stains on the outside of the core below the leak. If leaks are noted, remove the radiator (see Chapter 3) and have it repaired by a professional or replace it with a new one.

Caution: Do not use a liquid leak stopping compound to try to repair leaks.

6 Check the radiator fins for mud, dirt and insects, which may impede the flow of air through the radiator. If the fins are dirty, force water or low pressure compressed air through the fins from the rear face. If the fins are bent or distorted, straighten them carefully with a screwdriver.

7 On M, N, P and R (1991 to 1994) models, remove the fusebox access cover from the upper fairing and undo the right upper fairing retaining screw. Pull the fairing gently away from the machine to gain access to the radiator pressure cap. On S, T, V and W (1995 to 1998) models, it is advisable to remove the upper fairing to access the cap.

8 Remove the pressure cap by turning it counterclockwise (anti-clockwise) until it reaches a stop **(see illustration)**. If you hear a hissing sound (indicating there is still pressure in the system), wait until it stops. Now press down on the cap and continue turning the cap until it can be removed. Check the condition of the coolant in the system. If it is rust-colored or if accumulations of scale are visible, drain, flush and refill the system with new coolant (See Section 28). Check the cap seal for cracks and other damage. If in doubt about the pressure cap's condition, have it tested by a dealer service department or replace it with a new one. Install the cap by turning it clockwise until it reaches the first stop then push down on the cap and continue turning until it can turn further.

9 Check the antifreeze content of the coolant with an antifreeze hydrometer. Sometimes coolant looks like it's in good condition, but might be too weak to offer adequate protection. If the hydrometer indicates a weak mixture, drain, flush and refill the system (see Section 28).

10 Start the engine and let it reach normal operating temperature, then check for leaks again. As the coolant temperature increases, the fan should come on automatically and the temperature should begin to drop. If it does not, refer to Chapter 3 and check the fan and fan circuit carefully.

11 If the coolant level is consistently low, and no evidence of leaks can be found, have the entire system pressure checked by a Honda dealer service department, motorcycle repair shop or service station.

16 Exhaust system - check

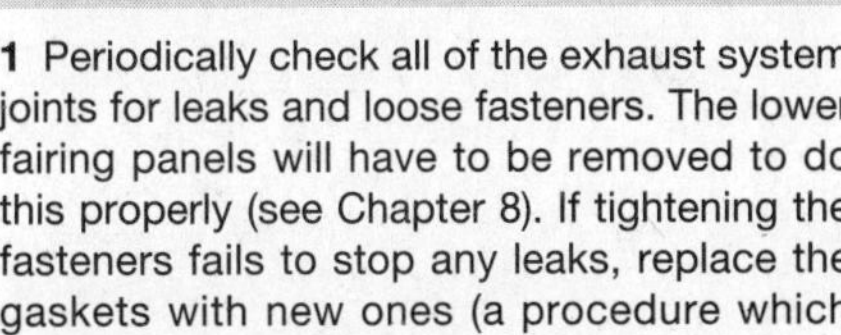

1 Periodically check all of the exhaust system joints for leaks and loose fasteners. The lower fairing panels will have to be removed to do this properly (see Chapter 8). If tightening the fasteners fails to stop any leaks, replace the gaskets with new ones (a procedure which requires disassembly of the system). Refer to Chapter 4 for further information.

2 The exhaust pipe flange nuts at the cylinder heads are especially prone to loosening, which could cause damage to the head. Check them frequently and keep them tight.

17 Brake system - general check

1 A routine general check of the brakes will ensure that any problems are discovered and remedied before the rider's safety is jeopardized.

2 Check the brake lever and pedal for loose connections, excessive play, bends, and other damage. Replace any damaged parts with new ones (see Chapter 7).

3 Make sure all brake fasteners are tight. Check the brake pads for wear (see Section 3) and make sure the fluid level in the reservoirs is correct (see *'Daily (pre-ride) checks*'). Look for leaks at the hose connections and check for cracks in the hoses. If the lever or pedal is spongy, bleed the brakes as described in Chapter 7.

4 Make sure the brake light operates when the front brake lever is depressed. The front brake light switch is not adjustable. If it fails to operate properly, replace it with a new one (see Chapter 9).

5 Make sure the brake light is activated just before the rear brake pedal takes effect. If adjustment is necessary, hold the switch and turn the adjusting ring on the switch body until the brake light is activated when required **(see illustration)**. If the switch doesn't operate the brake lights, check it as described in Chapter 9.

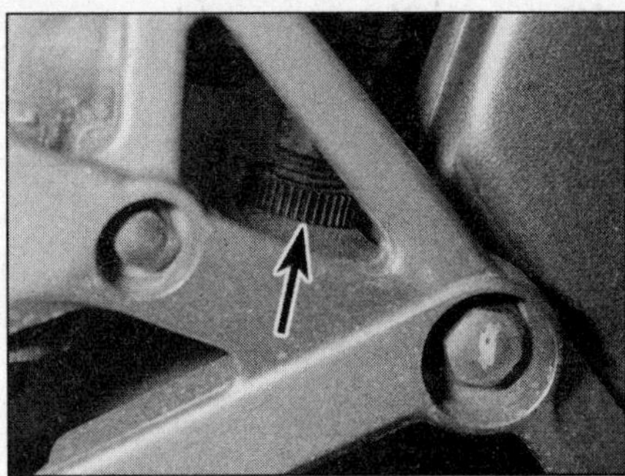

17.5 Adjust rear brake light switch by turning the adjusting ring (arrow)

18 Tires/wheels - general check

Tires

1 Check the tire condition and tread depth thoroughly - see *Daily (pre-ride) checks*.

Wheels

2 Cast wheels are virtually maintenance free, but they should be kept clean and checked periodically for cracks and other damage. Also check the wheel runout and alignment (see Chapter 7). Never attempt to repair damaged cast wheels; they must be replaced with new ones. Check the valve rubber for signs of damage or deterioration and have it replaced if necessary. Also, make sure the valve stem cap is in place and tight.

19 Headlight aim - check and adjustment

Note: *An improperly adjusted headlight may cause problems for oncoming traffic or provide poor, unsafe illumination of the road ahead. Before adjusting the headlight aim, be sure to consult with local traffic laws and regulations - for UK models refer to 'MOT Test Checks' in the Reference section.*

1 The headlight beam can adjusted both horizontally and vertically. Before making any adjustment, check that the tire pressures are correct and the suspension is adjusted as required. Make any adjustments to the headlight aim with the machine on level ground, with the fuel tank half full and with an assistant sitting on the seat. If the bike is usually ridden with a passenger on the back, have a second assistant to do this.

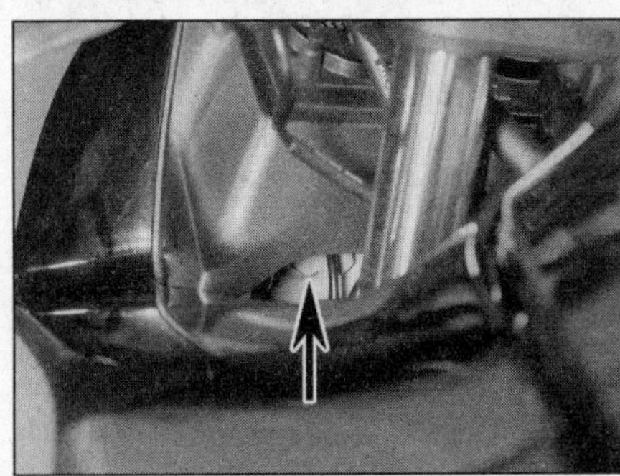

19.3a Horizontal beam adjuster (arrow)

2 Undo the two screws or release the two trim clips and remove the headlight access cover from the base of the upper fairing assembly. Take care not to break the cover tabs when releasing it.

3 The headlight aim is altered using the adjusters on the rear of the headlight unit **(see illustrations)**. The knob on the top left corner of the assembly adjusts the horizontal position of the beam and the knob on bottom right corner of the assembly alters the vertical position of the beam.

4 Rotate the adjusters as required until the headlight beam is correctly aimed, then install the access cover.

20 Sidestand - check

1 The sidestand return spring must be capable of retracting the stand fully and holding the stand retracted when the motorcycle is in use. If the spring is sagged or broken it must be replaced.

2 Lubricate the sidestand pivot regularly (see Section 6).

4 The sidestand switch prevents the motorcycle being started if the stand is extended. Check its operation by shifting the transmission into neutral, retracting the stand and starting the engine. Pull in the clutch lever and select a gear. With the clutch lever held in, extend the sidestand. The engine should stop as the sidestand is extended. If the sidestand switch does not operate as described, check its circuit (see Chapter 9).

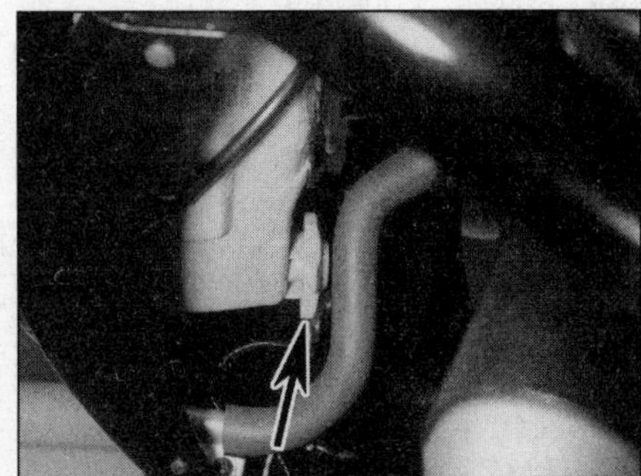

19.3b Vertical beam adjuster (arrow)

21.3 Check above and below the fork seals (arrow) for signs of oil leakage

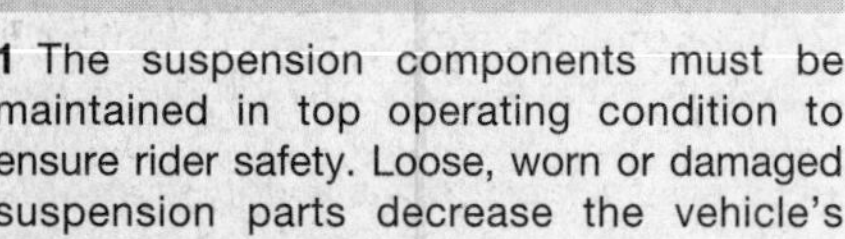

21 Suspension - check

1 The suspension components must be maintained in top operating condition to ensure rider safety. Loose, worn or damaged suspension parts decrease the vehicle's stability and control.
2 While standing alongside the motorcycle, apply the front brake and push on the handlebars to compress the forks several times. See if they move up-and-down smoothly without binding. If binding is felt, the forks should be disassembled and inspected as described in Chapter 6.
3 Carefully inspect the area around the fork seals for any signs of fork oil leakage **(see illustration)**. If leakage is evident, the seals must be replaced as described in Chapter 6.
4 Check the tightness of all suspension nuts and bolts to be sure none have worked loose.
5 Inspect the rear shock for fluid leakage and tightness of the mounting nuts. If leakage is found, the shock should be replaced.
6 Set the bike on its centerstand. Grab the swingarm on each side, just ahead of the axle. Rock the swingarm from side to side - there should be no discernible movement at the rear. If there's a little movement or a slight clicking can be heard, make sure the pivot shaft nut is tight. If the pivot nut is tight but movement is still noticeable, the swingarm will have to be removed and the bearings replaced as described in Chapter 6.
7 Inspect the tightness of the rear suspension nuts and bolts.

22 Steering head bearings - check and adjustment

1 This motorcycle is equipped with caged ball type steering head bearings which can become dented, rough or loose during normal use of the machine. In extreme cases, worn or loose steering head bearings can cause steering wobble - a condition that is potentially dangerous.

Check

2 To check the bearings, place the motorcycle on its centerstand and block the machine so the front wheel is in the air.
3 Point the wheel straight-ahead and slowly move the handlebars from side-to-side. Any dents or roughness in the bearing races will be felt and the handlebars will not move smoothly.
4 Next, grasp the wheel and try to move it forward and backward **(see illustration)**. Any looseness in the steering head bearings will be felt as front-to-rear movement of the fork legs. If play is felt in the bearings, adjust the steering head as follows.

Freeplay in the fork due to worn fork bushes can be misinterpreted for steering head bearing play - do not confuse the two.

Adjustment

5 Referring to Chapter 6 for further information, carefully pry off the snap-ring from the top of each fork tube.
6 Slacken the right handlebar clamp bolt. Slide the handlebar off of the fork tube and support it to prevent straining the hydraulic hose or the possible leakage of brake fluid from the master cylinder.
7 Slacken the left handlebar clamp bolt. Slide the handlebar off of the fork tube and position it clear of the triple clamp.
8 Slacken the top triple clamp bolts then pry off the cap from the steering stem top nut. Slacken and remove the nut and lift off the top triple clamp.
9 Using a suitable C-wrench, slacken and remove the adjuster nut locknut.
10 Remove the lock washer and discard it; a new one must be fitted on reassembly.
11 Slacken the adjuster nut slightly until pressure is just released, then turn it slowly clockwise until resistance is just evident. The object is to set the adjuster nut so that the bearings are under a very light loading, just enough to remove any freeplay.
Caution: Take great care not to apply excessive pressure because this will cause premature failure of the bearings.
12 With the bearings correctly adjusted, fit a new lock washer to the adjuster nut. Bend down two opposite lock washer tabs into the grooves of the adjuster nut.
13 Install the locknut and tighten it finger-tight only.
14 Hold the adjuster nut, to prevent it from moving, and tighten the locknut approximately 90° more until its slots align with the remaining lock washer tabs. Secure the locknut in position by bending up the lock washer tabs into its slots.

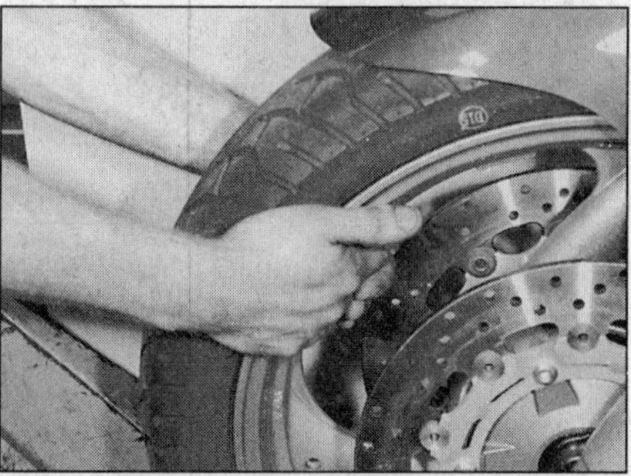
22.4 Grasp the front wheel and try to pull it back and forth to check for play in the steering head bearings

15 Fit the top triple clamp to the steering stem then install the stem top nut and tighten it and both the clamp bolts to their specified torque settings (see Chapter 6). Fit the cap.
16 Check the bearing adjustment as described above and re-adjust if necessary.
17 With the bearing adjustment correctly set, install the handlebars to the top of the fork tubes, ensuring that the lug on the bottom of each casting is correctly located with the cutout on the top triple clamp.
18 Fit the snap-ring to each fork tube making sure they are correctly located in their grooves. Then tighten the handlebar clamp bolts to the specified torque while pushing each handlebar fully forwards (see Chapter 6).

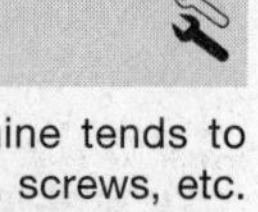

23 Fasteners - check

1 Since vibration of the machine tends to loosen fasteners, all nuts, bolts, screws, etc. should be periodically checked for proper tightness.
2 Pay particular attention to the following:

Spark plugs
Engine oil drain plug
Gearshift lever
Footpegs, sidestand and centerstand
Engine mounting bolts
Shock absorber mounting bolts
Handlebar and triple clamp bolts
Rear suspension linkage bolts
Front axle and clamp bolts
Rear axle nut
Exhaust system bolts/nuts

3 If a torque wrench is available, use it along with the torque specifications at the beginning of this and other Chapters.

Every 12,000 miles (18,000 km) or 18 months (whichever comes first)

Carry out all the items under the 4000 mile (6000 km) check:

24 Air filter element - change

Caution: If the machine is continually ridden in wet or dusty conditions, the filter should be replaced more frequently.

1 Remove the fuel tank (see Chapter 4).

2 On S, T, V and W (1995 to 1998) models, slacken the clamp screws securing the DAI (Direct Air Injection) system ducts to the front of the air filter cover **(see illustration)**. On all models, undo the seven retaining screws and remove the cover from the air filter housing **(see illustration)**.

3 Lift out the air filter element noting which way around it is fitted and which side is up and discard it **(see illustration)**.

4 Wipe out the housing with a clean rag.

5 Fit the new element to the housing, making sure it is the correct way round and up. Install the cover and securely tighten its retaining screws. On S, T, V and W (1995 to 1998) models, reconnect the DAI ducts.

6 Install the fuel tank as described in Chapter 4.

7 To clean the filter in between replacement service intervals, tap the element on a hard surface to shake out dirt. If compressed air is available, use it to clean the element by blowing from the bottom of the element upwards. If the element is extremely dirty or torn, replace it with a new one.

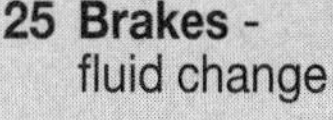

25 Brakes - fluid change

The brake fluid should be replaced at the prescribed interval or whenever a master cylinder or caliper overhaul is carried out. Refer to the brake bleeding section in Chapter 7, noting that all old fluid must be pumped from the fluid reservoir and hydraulic line before filling with new fluid.

Old brake fluid is invariably much darker in color than new fluid, making it easy to see when all old fluid has been expelled from the system.

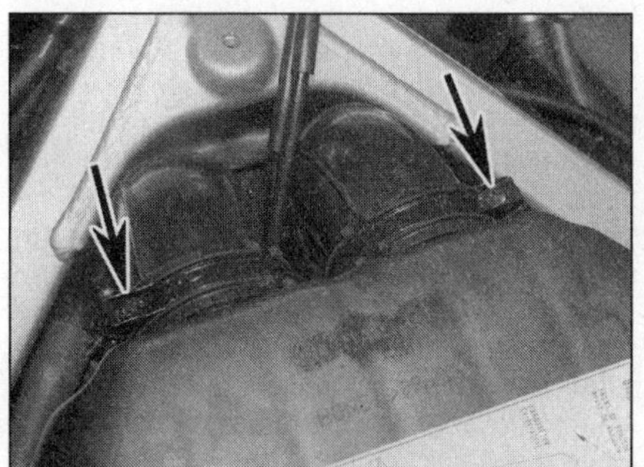

24.2a On S, T, V and W (1995 to 1998) models slacken the air duct clamp screws (arrows)

24.2b Remove the air filter housing cover . . .

24.3 . . . then lift out the filter element

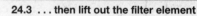

Every 16,000 miles (24,000 km) or two years

Carry out all the items under the 8000 mile (12,000 km) check, plus the following:

26 Spark plugs - replacement (UK models)

See Section 5 'Spark plug gaps - check and adjustment (US models)' under the 4000 mile (6000 km) or 6 months heading for details.

27 Valve clearances - check and adjustment

1 The engine must be completely cool for this maintenance procedure, so let the machine sit overnight before beginning.

2 Remove the valve cover as described in Chapter 2. To further improve access, remove the ignition HT coils as described in Chapter 5 then unclip and remove the rubber insulating cover, situated directly above the valve cover, from the frame.

3 Draw the valve positions on a piece of paper, numbering both the intake and exhaust valves from 1 to 8, from the left end of the engine.

4 Unscrew the timing inspection cap from the crankshaft right end cover. On S, T, V and W models (1995 to 1998), refer to Chapter 2 *'Cam chain tensioner - removal and installation'* and retract the tensioner plunger using the special tool; there is no need to remove the tensioner body.

5 Turn the crankshaft, with a socket placed on the crankshaft bolt, until the line next to the 'T' mark on the rotor is aligned with the index mark, in the form of a cutout on the crankshaft cover. Now, check the position of the camshaft sprockets - the 'IN' mark on the intake camshaft sprocket and the 'EX' mark on the exhaust camshaft sprocket should be aligned with the cylinder head surface with each mark the correct way up and on the outside of its respective sprocket **(see illustrations)**. If the marks are not correctly

27.5a Remove the center cap from the crankshaft right cover and rotate the crankshaft using a socket and extension bar

27.5b Position the crankshaft so the line next to the 'T' mark is aligned with the cutout (arrow) . . .

27.5c . . . and the IN and EX marks (arrows) on the camshaft sprockets are level with the cylinder head surface

positioned, turn the crankshaft through 360° (one complete turn). **Note:** *Turn the engine in the normal direction of rotation (clockwise), viewed from the right end of the engine.*

6 With the engine in this position, on M, N, P and R models (1991 to 1994), all four valves for cylinder No. 1 can be checked. On S, T, V and W models (1995 to 1998), the intake valves for No. 1 and 3 cylinders can be checked.

7 Insert a feeler gauge of the correct thickness (see Specifications) between each cam lobe and follower and check that it is a firm sliding fit **(see illustration)**. If it is not, use the feeler gauges to obtain the exact clearance. **Note:** *The intake and exhaust valve clearances are different.*

27.7 Measuring a valve clearance

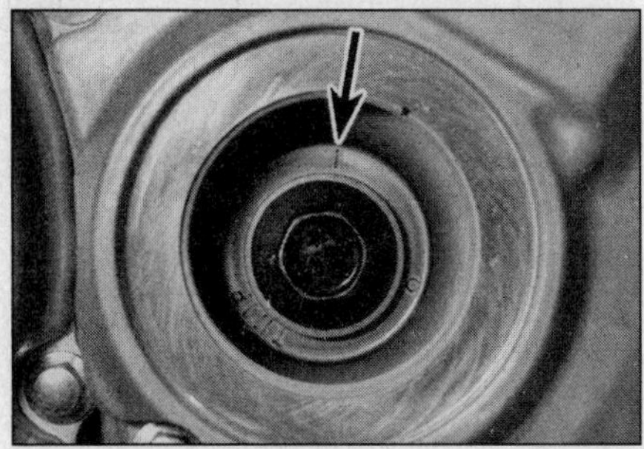

27.9 Rotate the crankshaft through 180° so that the index line (arrow) on the rotor is vertical

8 Record the clearance of each valve next to its relevant location on the piece of paper.

9 With the specified valves measured, rotate the crankshaft through 180° (half a turn) until the index line on the rotor is vertical **(see illustration)**. On M, N, P and R models (1991 to 1994), all four valves for cylinder No. 2 cylinder can be checked. On S, T, V and W models (1995 to 1998), the exhaust valves for No. 2 and 4 cylinders can be checked.

10 Rotate the crankshaft through another 180° (half a turn) until the 'T' mark on the rotor is again aligned with the crankcase cover cutout **(see illustration 27.5b)**. On M, N, P and R models (1991 to 1994), all four valves for cylinder No. 4 cylinder can be checked. On S, T, V and W models (1995 to 1998), the intake valves for No. 2 and 4 cylinders can be checked.

11 Rotate the crankshaft through 180° (half a turn) until the index line on the rotor is vertical again **(see illustration 27.9)**. On M, N, P and R models (1991 to 1994), all four valves for cylinder No. 3 cylinder can be checked. On S, T, V and W models (1995 to 1998), the exhaust valves for No. 1 and 3 cylinders can be checked.

12 If any of the clearances need to be adjusted the relevant camshaft(s) must be removed as described in Chapter 2.

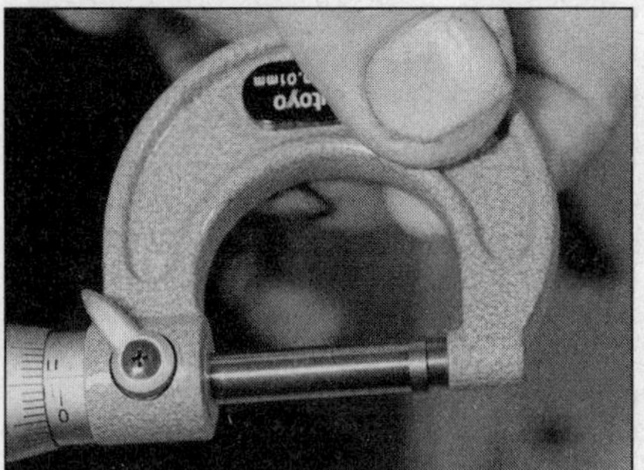

27.14a Measuring shim thickness

13 With the camshaft removed, using a magnet, lift the follower on the valve to be adjusted out of the cylinder head and remove the shim. Note that the shim is likely to stick to the inside of the follower so take great care not to lose it as the follower is removed. If more than one follower and shim is to be removed, make sure they are not interchanged.

14 The shim size should be stamped on its face, however, it is recommended that the shim is measured to check that it has not worn. The size marking is in the form of a three figure number, eg 180 indicating that the shim is 1.800 mm thick **(see illustrations)**. Where the number does not equal a shim thickness, it should be rounded up or down, eg 182 or 183 both indicate that the shim is 1.825 mm thick. Shims are available in 0.025 mm increments from 1.200 to 2.800 mm. The new shim thickness required can then be calculated as follows. **Note:** *Always aim to get the clearance at the mid-point of the specified range.*

15 If the valve clearance was less than specified, subtract the measured clearance from the specified clearance then deduct the result from the original shim thickness. For example:

27.14b Shim thickness is indicated by three numbers stamped on its surface

Sample calculation - intake valve clearance too small

Clearance measured (A) - 0.08 mm
Specified clearance (B) - 0.16 mm (0.13 to 0.19 mm)
Difference (B - A) - 0.08 mm
Shim thickness fitted - 2.475 mm
Correct shim thickness required is 2.475 - 0.08 = 2.395 mm

16 If the valve clearance was greater then specified, subtract the specified clearance from the measured clearance, and add the result to the thickness of the original shim. For example:

Sample calculation - exhaust valve clearance too large

Clearance measured (A) - 0.35 mm
Specified clearance (B) - 0.22 mm (0.19 to 0.25 mm)
Difference (A - B) - 0.13 mm
Shim thickness fitted - 1.975 mm
Correct shim thickness required is 1.975 + 0.13 = 2.105 mm

17 Obtain the correct thickness shims from your Honda dealer. Where the required thickness is not equal to the available shim thickness, round off the measurement to the nearest available size.

18 Install the shim in position on top of the relevant valve, making sure it is correctly seated in the valve spring retainer.

19 Install the followers in their respective positions in the cylinder head, making sure each one squarely enters its bore.

20 Install the camshaft(s) as described in Chapter 2.

21 Rotate the crankshaft a few times, to settle all disturbed components, and recheck all valve clearances as described above. If necessary, repeat the adjustment procedure.

22 On S, T, V and W models (1995 to 1998), release the stopper key from the cam chain tensioner. Install a new sealing washer on the tensioner bolt and tighten the bolt securely.

23 When all the valve clearances are correctly set, install the ignition coils and rubber installing cover (if removed). Install the valve cover as described in Chapter 2.

24 Apply a smear of oil to the timing inspection cap O-ring and tighten the cap to the specified torque setting.

Every 24,000 miles (36,000 km) or three years (whichever comes sooner)

Carry out all the items under the 12,000 mile (18,000 km) and 8000 mile (12,000 km) checks, plus the following

28 Cooling system - draining, flushing and refilling

***Warning:** Allow the engine to cool completely before performing this maintenance operation. Also, don't allow antifreeze to come into contact with your skin or the painted surfaces of the motorcycle. Rinse off spills immediately with plenty of water. Antifreeze is highly toxic if ingested. Never leave antifreeze lying around in an open container or in puddles on the floor; children and pets are attracted by its sweet smell and may drink it. Check with local authorities (councils) about disposing of antifreeze. Many communities have collection centers which will see that antifreeze is disposed of safely. Antifreeze is also combustible, so don't store it near open flames.*

Draining

1 Remove the left and right lower fairing panels as described in Chapter 8.

2 On M, N, P and R (1991 to 1994) models, remove the fusebox access cover from the upper fairing and undo the right upper fairing retaining screw. Pull the fairing gently away from the machine to gain access to the radiator pressure cap **(see illustration 15.8)**. On S, T, V and W (1995 to 1998) models, it is advisable to remove the upper fairing to access the cap.

3 Position a suitable container beneath the water pump, then remove the drain bolt and sealing washer from the pump cover **(see illustration)**.

4 Remove the pressure cap by turning it counterclockwise (anti-clockwise) until it reaches a stop. If you hear a hissing sound (indicating there is still pressure in the system), wait until it stops. Now press down on the cap and continue turning the cap until it can be removed. As the cap is removed the flow of coolant will increase, be prepared for this.

5 Once the flow of coolant has stopped from the pump, position the container beneath the front of the engine and remove the drain bolt from the bottom of the oil cooler casing.

6 Drain the coolant reservoir. Refer to Chapter 3 for reservoir removal procedure. Wash out the reservoir with water.

Flushing

7 Flush the system with clean tap water by inserting a garden hose in the radiator filler neck. Allow the water to run through the system until it is clear and flows cleanly out of both drain holes. If the radiator is extremely corroded, remove it by referring to Chapter 3 and have it cleaned professionally.

8 Clean the holes then install the drain bolts and sealing washers, tightening them securely.

28.3 Coolant drain bolt (arrow) on water pump cover

9 Fill the cooling system with clean water mixed with a flushing compound. Make sure the flushing compound is compatible with aluminum components, and follow the manufacturer's instructions carefully.

10 Start the engine and allow it reach normal operating temperature. Let it run for about ten minutes.

11 Stop the engine. Let it cool for a while, then cover the pressure cap with a heavy shop towel and turn it counterclockwise (anti-clockwise) to the first stop, releasing any pressure that may be present in the system. Once the hissing stops, push down on the cap and remove it completely.

12 Drain the system once again.

13 Fill the system with clean water and repeat the procedure in Steps 10 to 12.

Refilling

14 Fit new sealing washers to the drain bolts and install them in the oil cooler and pump cover, tightening each one securely.

15 Fill the system with the proper coolant mixture (see this Chapter's Specifications) **(see illustration)**.

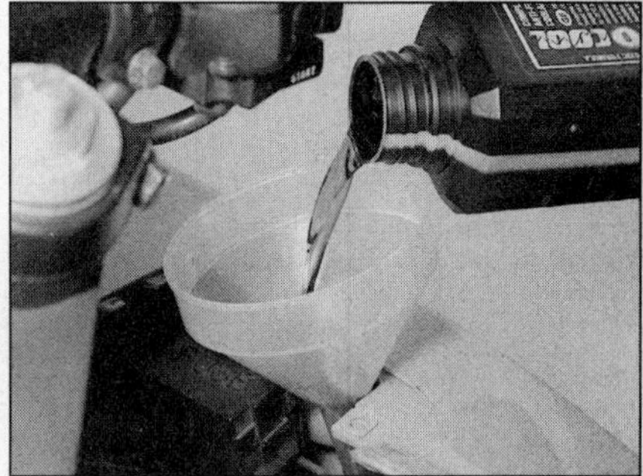

28.15 Fill the cooling system using a funnel to avoid spilling coolant over the bodywork

16 When the system is full (all the way up to the top of the radiator filler neck), start the engine and allow it to idle for 2 to 3 minutes. Flick the throttle twistgrip part open 3 or 4 times, so that the engine speed rises to approximately 4000 - 5000 rpm, then stop the engine. This process will bleed any trapped air bubbles from the system.

17 Top up the coolant level to the base of the filler neck and install the pressure cap. Top up the coolant reservoir to the UPPER level mark.

18 Start the engine and allow it to reach normal operating temperature, then shut it off.

19 Let the engine cool then remove the pressure cap as described in Step 11. Check that the coolant level is still up to the radiator filler neck. If it's low, add the specified mixture until it reaches the top of the filler neck. Reinstall the cap.

20 Check the coolant level in the reservoir and top up if necessary (see *'Daily (pre-ride) checks'*).

21 Check the system for leaks. If all is well, install the fairing panels (Chapter 8).

22 Do not dispose of the old coolant by pouring it down the drain. Instead pour it into a heavy plastic container, cap it tightly and take it into an authorized disposal site or service station - see Warning at the beginning of this Section.

Non-scheduled maintenance

29 Cylinder compression - check

1 Among other things, poor engine performance may be caused by leaking valves, incorrect valve clearances, a leaking head gasket, or worn pistons, rings and/or cylinder walls. A cylinder compression check will help pinpoint these conditions and can also indicate the presence of excessive carbon deposits in the combustion chambers.

2 The only tools required are a compression gauge and a spark plug wrench. Depending on the outcome of the initial test, a squirt-type oil can may also be needed.

3 Refer to the procedure under the *'Fault Finding Equipment'* heading in the Reference Section. The cylinder compression figure is given in the Specifications at the beginning of this Chapter.

Chapter 2
Engine, clutch and transmission

Contents

Degrees of difficulty

Easy, suitable for novice with little experience 	**Fairly easy,** suitable for beginner with some experience 	**Fairly difficult,** suitable for competent DIY mechanic 	**Difficult,** suitable for experienced DIY mechanic 	**Very difficult,** suitable for expert DIY or professional

Specifications

General

Capacity	599 cc
Bore	65.0 mm (2.56 in)
Stroke	45.2 mm (1.78 in)
Compression ratio	
M, N, P and R (1991 to 1994) models	11.6 to 1
S, T, V and W (1995 to 1998) models	12.0 to 1

Camshafts

Intake cam lobe height	
California models	
Standard	34.540 to 34.780 mm (1.3598 to 1.3693 in)
Service limit	34.51 mm (1.359 in)
All other models	
Standard	36.140 to 36.380 mm (1.4228 to 1.4323 in)
Service limit	36.11 mm (1.422 in)
Exhaust cam lobe height	
California models	
Standard	33.580 to 33.820 mm (1.3220 to 1.3315 in)
Service limit	33.55 mm (1.321 in)
All other models	
Standard	35.300 to 35.540 mm (1.3898 to 1.3992 in)
Service limit	35.27 mm (1.389 in)

Camshafts (continued)

Camshaft journal OD	
Standard	23.959 to 23.980 mm (0.9433 to 0.9441 in)
Service limit	23.955 mm (0.9430 in)
Camshaft bearing cap ID	
Standard	24.000 to 24.021 mm (0.9449 to 0.9457 in)
Service limit	Not available
Camshaft bearing oil clearance	
Standard	0.020 to 0.062 mm (0.0008 to 0.0024 in)
Service limit	0.1 mm (0.004 in)
Camshaft runout	Less than 0.05 mm (0.002 in)
Camshaft follower OD	
Standard	25.978 to 25.993 mm (1.0228 to 1.0233 in)
Service limit	25.968 mm (1.0224 in)

Cylinder head

Maximum warpage	0.10 mm (0.004 in)
Cylinder head follower bore ID	
Standard	26.010 to 26.026 mm (1.0240 to 1.0246 in)
Service limit	26.040 mm (1.0252 in)

Valves, guides and springs

Intake valve stem OD	
Standard	3.975 to 3.990 mm (0.1565 to 0.1571 in)
Service limit	3.965 mm (0.1561 in)
Exhaust valve stem OD	
Standard	3.965 to 3.980 mm (0.1561 to 0.1567 in)
Service limit	3.955 mm (0.1557 in)
Valve guide ID - intake and exhaust	
Standard	4.000 to 4.012 mm (0.1575 to 0.1580 in)
Service limit	4.040 mm (0.1590 in)
Intake valve stem-to-guide clearance	
Standard	0.010 to 0.037 mm (0.0004 to 0.0015 in)
Service limit	0.075 mm (0.0029 in)
Exhaust valve stem-to-guide clearance	
Standard	0.020 to 0.047 mm (0.0008 to 0.0019 in)
Service limit	0.085 mm (0.0033 in)
Intake valve guide projection above cylinder head	13.1 to 13.3 mm (0.516 to 0.524 in)
Exhaust valve guide projection above cylinder head	11.3 to 11.5 mm (0.445 to 0.453 in)
Valve seat width	
Standard	0.9 to 1.1 mm (0.035 to 0.043 in)
Service limit	1.5 mm (0.06 in)
Valve spring free length - M, N, P, R, S and T (1991 to 1996) models	
Inner springs	
Standard	31.92 mm (1.257 in)
Service limit	30.62 mm (1.206 in)
Outer springs	
Standard	35.36 mm (1.392 in)
Service limit	33.86 mm (1.333 in)
Valve spring free length - V and W (1997 and 1998) models	
Standard	38.25 mm (1.506 in)
Service limit	37.05 mm (1.460 in)

Clutch

Friction plate thickness	
Standard	2.92 to 3.08 mm (0.115 to 0.121 in)
Service limit	2.60 mm (0.102 in)
Plain plate maximum warpage	0.3 mm (0.012 in)
Clutch spring free length - M, N, P and R (1991 to 1994) models	
Standard	48.9 mm (1.93 in)
Service limit	47.5 mm (1.87 in)
Clutch spring free length - S, T, V and W (1995 to 1998) models	
Standard	49.7 mm (1.96 in)
Service limit	48.3 mm (1.90 in)
Clutch drum center collar OD	
Standard	34.975 to 34.991 mm (1.3770 to 1.3776 in)
Service limit	34.965 mm (1.3766 in)

Clutch (continued)

Clutch drum center collar ID	
Standard	21.994 to 22.007 mm (0.8659 to 0.8664 in)
Service limit	22.017 mm (0.8668 in)
Mainshaft OD at clutch center collar contact point	
Standard	21.980 to 21.993 mm (0.8654 to 0.8659 in)
Service limit	21.95 mm (0.864 in)

Lubrication system

Oil pressure	4.9 bars (71 psi) at 6000 rpm, 80°C (176°F)
Oil pump rotor tip-to-outer rotor clearance	
Standard	0.15 to 0.20 mm (0.006 to 0.008 in)
Service limit	0.20 mm (0.008 in)
Oil pump outer rotor-to-body clearance	
Standard	0.15 to 0.22 mm (0.006 to 0.009 in)
Service limit	0.35 mm (0.014 in)
Oil pump rotor endfloat	
Standard	0.02 to 0.07 mm (0.001 to 0.003 in)
Service limit	0.10 mm (0.004 in)
Oil pump drive sprocket ID - S and T (1995 and 1996) models	
Standard	35.025 to 35.075 mm (1.3789 to 1.3836 in)
Service limit	35.17 mm (1.38 in)
Oil pump drive sprocket ID - V and W (1997 and 1998) models	
Standard	35.025 to 35.145 mm (1.3789 to 1.3809 in)
Service limit	35.17 mm (1.38 in)
Oil pump drive sprocket collar OD	
Standard	34.050 to 34.075 mm (1.3405 to 1.3415 in)
Service limit	34.03 mm (1.34 in)

Starter clutch

Driven gear OD	
Standard	51.699 to 51.718 mm (2.0354 to 2.0361 in)
Service limit	51.684 mm (2.0348 in)

Shift drum and forks

Shift fork end thickness	
Standard	5.93 to 6.00 mm (0.233 to 0.236 in)
Service limit	5.90 mm (0.232 in)
Shift fork bore ID	
Standard	12.000 to 12.021 mm (0.4724 to 0.4733 in)
Service limit	12.030 mm (0.4736 in)
Shift fork shaft OD	
Standard	11.957 to 11.968 mm (0.4707 to 0.4712 in)
Service limit	11.95 mm (0.470 in)

Cylinder block

Cylinder bore ID	
Standard	65.000 to 65.015 mm (2.5591 to 2.5596 in)
Service limit	65.10 mm (2.563 in)
Maximum ovality (out-of-round)	0.10 mm (0.004 in)
Maximum taper	0.10 mm (0.004 in)
Cylinder-to-piston clearance	
Standard	0.010 to 0.045 mm (0.0004 to 0.0018 in)
Service limit	0.10 mm (0.004 in)
Maximum gasket face warpage	0.10 mm (0.004 in)

Pistons

Piston OD (measured 11 mm (0.433 in) up from base of skirt)	
Standard	64.970 to 64.990 mm (2.5579 to 2.5587 in)
Service limit	64.90 mm (2.555 in)
Piston pin bore ID	
Standard	17.002 to 17.008 mm (0.6694 to 0.6696 in)
Service limit	17.02 mm (0.670 in)
Piston pin OD	
Standard	16.993 to 17.000 mm (0.6690 to 0.6693 in)
Service limit	16.98 mm (0.669 in)
Piston-to-piston pin clearance	
Standard	0.002 to 0.015 mm (0.0001 to 0.0006 in)
Service limit	0.04 mm (0.0016 in)

Piston rings

Top ring-to-groove clearance	
Standard	0.025 to 0.060 mm (0.0010 to 0.0024 in)
Service limit	0.08 mm (0.003 in)
Second ring-to-groove clearance	
Standard	0.015 to 0.050 mm (0.0006 to 0.0016 in)
Service limit	0.08 mm (0.003 in)
Top ring end gap	
Standard	0.20 to 0.35 mm (0.008 to 0.014 in)
Service limit	0.5 mm (0.02 in)
Second ring end gap	
Standard	0.35 to 0.50 mm (0.014 to 0.020 in)
Service limit	0.7 mm (0.03 in)
Oil control ring side rail end gap	
Standard	0.2 to 0.7 mm (0.01 to 0.03 in)
Service limit	1.0 mm (0.04 in)

Connecting rods and bearings

Connecting rod side clearance - M, N, P and R (1991 to 1994) models	
Standard	0.05 to 0.20 mm (0.002 to 0.008 in)
Service limit	0.3 mm (0.012 in)
Connecting rod side clearance - S, T, V and W (1995 to 1998) models	
Standard	0.10 to 0.25 mm (0.004 to 0.01 in)
Service limit	0.3 mm (0.012 in)
Connecting rod piston pin bore ID	
Standard	17.016 to 17.034 mm (0.6699 to 0.6706 in)
Service limit	17.04 mm (0.671 in)
Connecting rod crankpin bore ID - M, N, P and R (1991 to 1994) models	
Size group 1	36.000 to 36.008 mm (1.4173 to 1.4176 in)
Size group 2	36.008 to 36.016 mm (1.4176 to 1.4180 in)
Connecting rod crankpin bore ID - S, T, V and W (1995 to 1998) models	
Size group 1	34.000 to 34.008 mm (1.3386 to 1.3389 in)
Size group 2	34.008 to 34.016 mm (1.3389 to 1.3392 in)
Crankshaft crankpin OD - M, N, P and R (1991 to 1994) models	
Size group A	32.992 to 33.000 mm (1.2989 to 1.2992 in)
Size group B	32.984 to 32.992 mm (1.2986 to 1.2989 in)
Crankshaft crankpin OD - S, T, V and W (1995 to 1998) models	
Size group A	31.492 to 31.500 mm (1.2408 to 1.2411 in)
Size group B	31.484 to 31.492 mm (1.2404 to 1.2408 in)
Connecting rod bearing oil clearance	
Standard	0.028 to 0.052 mm (0.0011 to 0.0020 in)
Service limit	0.06 mm (0.002 in)
Bearing insert thicknesses - M, N, P and R (1991 to 1994) models	
Brown	1.494 to 1.498 mm (0.0588 to 0.0590 in)
Green	1.490 to 1.494 mm (0.0587 to 0.0588 in)
Yellow	1.486 to 1.490 mm (0.0585 to 0.0587 in)
Bearing insert thicknesses - S, T, V and W (1995 to 1998) models	
Brown	1.244 to 1.248 mm (0.0489 to 0.0491 in)
Green	1.240 to 1.244 mm (0.0488 to 0.0489 in)
Yellow	1.236 to 1.240 mm (0.0486 to 0.0488 in)

Crankshaft and main bearings

Maximum crankshaft runout	0.05 mm (0.002 in)
Crankcase main bearing bore ID - M, N, P and R (1991 to 1994) models	
Size group A	36.000 to 36.008 mm (1.4173 to 1.4176 in)
Size group B	36.008 to 36.016 mm (1.4176 to 1.4180 in)
Size group C	36.016 to 36.024 mm (1.4180 to 1.4183 in)
Crankcase main bearing bore ID - S, T, V and W (1995 to 1998) models	
Size group A	36.000 to 36.007 mm (1.4173 to 1.4176 in)
Size group B	36.007 to 36.014 mm (1.4176 to 1.4179 in)
Size group C	36.014 to 36.021 mm (1.4179 to 1.4181 in)
Crankshaft journal OD - M, N, P and R (1991 to 1994) models	
Size group 1	32.992 to 33.000 mm (1.2989 to 1.2992 in)
Size group 2	32.984 to 32.992 mm (1.2986 to 1.2989 in)
Crankshaft journal OD - S, T, V and W (1995 to 1998) models	
Size group 1	32.993 to 33.000 mm (1.2989 to 1.2992 in)
Size group 2	32.986 to 32.993 mm (1.2986 to 1.2989 in)
Main bearing oil clearance	
Standard	
1991 models	0.023 to 0.047 mm (0.0009 to 0.0019 in)
1992-on models	0.020 to 0.045 mm (0.0008 to 0.0018 in)
Service limit (all models)	0.05 mm (0.002 in)

Crankshaft and main bearings (continued)

Bearing insert thicknesses - M, N, P and R (1991 to 1994) models	
Brown	1.492 to 1.496 mm (0.0587 to 0.0589 in)
Green	1.488 to 1.492 mm (0.0586 to 0.0587 in)
Yellow	1.484 to 1.488 mm (0.0584 to 0.0586 in)
Pink	1.480 to 1.484 mm (0.0583 to 0.0584 in)
Bearing insert thicknesses - S, T, V and W (1995 to 1998) models	
Brown	1.507 to 1.511 mm (0.0593 to 0.0595 in)
Green	1.503 to 1.507 mm (0.0592 to 0.0593 in)
Yellow	1.499 to 1.503 mm (0.0590 to 0.0592 in)
Pink	1.495 to 1.499 mm (0.0589 to 0.0590 in)

Transmission shafts

Ratios - M, N, P and R (1991 to 1994) models	
1st	2.9285 to 1 (41/14T)
2nd	2.0625 to 1 (33/16T)
3rd	1.5882 to 1 (27/17T)
4th	1.3684 to 1 (26/19T)
5th	1.2000 to 1 (24/20T)
6th	1.0861 to 1 (25/23T)
Ratios - S, T, V and W (1995 to 1998) models	
1st	2.9285 to 1 (41/14T)
2nd	2.0625 to 1 (33/16T)
3rd	1.6470 to 1 (28/17T)
4th	1.3684 to 1 (26/19T)
5th	1.2000 to 1 (24/20T)
6th	1.0861 to 1 (25/23T)
Gear ID	
Mainshaft 5th and 6th gears	
Standard	28.000 to 28.021 mm (1.1024 to 1.1032 in)
Service limit	28.04 mm (1.104 in)
Countershaft 2nd, 3rd and 4th gears	
Standard	31.000 to 31.025 mm (1.2205 to 1.2215 in)
Service limit	31.04 mm (1.222 in)
Gear bushing OD	
Mainshaft 5th and 6th gears	
Standard	27.959 to 27.980 mm (1.1007 to 1.1016 in)
Service limit	27.94 mm (1.100 in)
Countershaft 3rd and 4th gears	
Standard	30.950 to 30.975 mm (1.2185 to 1.2195 in)
Service limit	30.93 mm (1.218 in)
Countershaft 2nd gear	
Standard	30.959 to 30.980 mm (1.2189 to 1.2197 in)
Service limit	30.94 mm (1.218 in)
Gear bushing ID	
Mainshaft 5th gear	
Standard	24.985 to 25.006 mm (0.9837 to 0.9845 in)
Service limit	25.016 mm (0.9849 in)
Countershaft 2nd gear	
Standard	27.985 to 28.006 mm (1.1018 to 1.1026 in)
Service limit	28.021 mm (1.1032 in)
Gear-to-bushing clearance	
Mainshaft 5th and 6th gear	0.020 to 0.062 mm (0.0008 to 0.0024 in)
Countershaft 2nd, 3rd and 4th gears	0.020 to 0.070 mm (0.0008 to 0.0028 in)
Mainshaft OD at 5th gear bushing point	
Standard	24.967 to 24.980 mm (0.9830 to 0.9835 in)
Service limit	24.960 mm (0.9827 in)
Mainshaft OD at clutch outer guide	
Standard	21.980 to 21.993 mm (0.8654 to 0.8659 in)
Service limit	21.95 mm (0.8694 in)
Countershaft OD at 2nd gear bushing point	
Standard	27.967 to 27.980 mm (1.0904 to 1.1016 in)
Service limit	27.96 mm (1.101 in)
Shaft-to-bushing clearance	
Mainshaft 5th gear	0.005 to 0.039 mm (0.0002 to 0.0015 in)
Countershaft 2nd gear	0.005 to 0.039 mm (0.0002 to 0.0015 in)

Torque settings

	Nm	ft-lbs
Engine upper rear mounting		
Adjusting bolt	15	11
Locknut	65	47
Engine rear mounting bolt nuts	45	33
Engine front mounting bolt nuts	65	47
Engine mounting bracket 10 mm bolt - S, T, V and W (1995 to 1998) models	45	33
Engine sprocket bolt	55	40
Valve cover bolts	10	7
Camchain tensioner bolts	10	7
Camshaft bearing cap bolts	12	9
Camshaft sprocket bolts	20	14
Camchain upper guide bolts	12	9
Timing inspection cap	18	13
Cylinder head bolts (see text)	48	35
Clutch center nut		
M, N, P and R (1991 to 1994) models	85	61
S, T, V and W (1995 to 1998) models	110	80
Clutch cover bolts	12	9
Oil pump sprocket bolt	15	11
Gearshift drum cam bolt	23	17
Gearshift pedal clamp bolt		
M, N, P and R (1991 to 1994) models	16	12
S, T, V and W (1995 to 1998) models	20	14
Starter clutch roller assembly bolts	16	12
Alternator rotor bolt	105	76
Crankshaft end cover bolts	12	9
Pulse generator rotor bolt	60	43
Crankcase bolts		
6 mm bolts	12	9
8 mm bolts	24	18
10 mm bolt	40	29
Connecting rod bearing cap nuts	26	19

1 General information

The engine/transmission unit is of water-cooled four-cylinder in-line design, fitted transversely across the frame. The sixteen valves are operated by double overhead camshafts, chain driven off the right end of the crankshaft. The engine/transmission unit is constructed in aluminum alloy with the crankcase being divided horizontally. The crankcase incorporates a wet sump, pressure fed lubrication system, and houses a chain driven dual rotor oil pump.

The alternator and flywheel are situated on the left end of the crankshaft with the starter clutch being built into the rear of the flywheel. The water pump is mounted on the left side of the crankcase and is driven off the oil pump shaft.

The clutch is of the wet multi-plate type and is gear driven off the crankshaft. The transmission is of the six-speed constant mesh type. Final drive to the rear wheel is by chain and sprockets. The drive sprocket is mounted on the end of the countershaft (output shaft).

2 Operations possible with the engine in the frame

The components and assemblies listed below can be removed without having to remove the engine/transmission assembly from the frame. If however, a number of areas require attention at the same time, removal of the engine is recommended.

Gearshift selector mechanism components
Shift drum and forks
Starter motor
Starter motor clutch
Alternator
Clutch assembly
Oil pan, oil pump and relief valves
Valve cover
Camchain tensioner
Camshafts
Camchain, sprockets and guides
Cylinder head

3 Operations requiring engine removal

It is necessary to remove the engine/transmission assembly from the frame and separate the crankcase halves to gain access to the following components.

Transmission shafts
Crankshaft and bearings
Piston/connecting rod assemblies and bearings

4 Major engine repair - general note

1 It is not always easy to determine when or if an engine should be completely overhauled, as a number of factors must be considered.

2 High mileage is not necessarily an indication that an overhaul is needed, while low mileage, on the other hand, does not preclude the need for an overhaul. Frequency of servicing is probably the single most important consideration. An engine that has regular and frequent oil and filter changes, as well as other required maintenance, will most likely give many miles of reliable service. Conversely, a neglected engine, or one which has not been broken in properly, may require an overhaul very early in its life.

3 Exhaust smoke and excessive oil consumption are both indications that piston rings and/or valve guides are in need of attention, although make sure that the fault is not due to oil leakage. Refer to *Fault Finding Equipment* in the Reference section and perform a cylinder compression check to determine for certain the nature and extent of the work required.

4 If the engine is making obvious knocking or rumbling noises, the connecting rod and/or main bearings are probably at fault.

5 Loss of power, rough running, excessive valve train noise and high fuel consumption rates may also point to the need for an overhaul, especially if they are all present at the same time. If a complete tune-up does not remedy the situation, major mechanical work is the only solution.

6 An engine overhaul generally involves restoring the internal parts to the specifications of a new engine. During an overhaul the piston rings are replaced and the cylinder walls are bored and/or honed. If a rebore is done, then new pistons will also be required. The main and connecting rod bearings are usually replaced during a major overhaul. Generally the valve seats are serviced as well, since they are usually in less than perfect condition at this point. While the engine is being overhauled, other components such as the carburetors and the starter motor can also be rebuilt. The end result should be a like new engine that will give as many trouble-free miles as the original.

7 Before beginning the engine overhaul, read through the related procedures to familiarize yourself with the scope and requirements of the job. Overhauling an engine is not all that difficult, but it is time consuming. Plan on the motorcycle being tied up for a minimum of two weeks. Check on the availability of parts and make sure that any necessary special tools, equipment and supplies are obtained in advance.

8 Most work can be done with typical shop hand tools, although a number of precision measuring tools are required for inspecting parts to determine if they must be replaced. Often a dealer service department or motorcycle repair shop will handle the inspection of parts and offer advice concerning reconditioning and replacement. As a general rule, time is the primary cost of an overhaul so it does not pay to install worn or substandard parts.

9 As a final note, to ensure maximum life and minimum trouble from a rebuilt engine, everything must be assembled with care in a spotlessly clean environment.

5 Engine - removal and installation

Warning: Engine removal and installation should be carried out with the aid of an assistant; personal injury or damage could occur if the engine falls or is dropped. An hydraulic floor-type jack should be used to support and lower the engine to the floor if possible (they can be rented at low cost).

Removal

1 Set the bike on its centerstand. If the machine is dirty, wash it thoroughly before starting any major dismantling work. This will make work much easier and rule out the possibility of caked on lumps of dirt falling into some vital component. Work can also be made easier by raising the machine to a suitable working height on a hydraulic ramp or a suitable platform.

2 Remove the fuel tank (see Chapter 4).

3 Remove the lower fairing panels as described in Chapter 8.

4 Drain the engine oil and remove the oil filter as described in Chapter 1.

5 Drain the coolant as described in Chapter 1.

6 Undo the three bolts and remove the cover from the battery box. Disconnect both battery cables from the battery.

Warning: Always disconnect the battery negative lead first and reconnect it last.

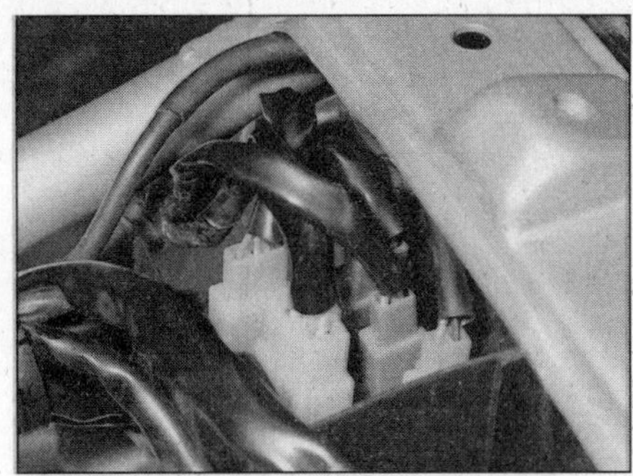

5.12a Trace the wiring back to the connectors in the junction box and disconnect them from the main harness

7 Remove the exhaust system as described in Chapter 4.

8 Remove the carburetors as described in Chapter 4 and plug the cylinder head intake openings with clean shop towels.

9 Disconnect the spark plug caps from the plugs.

10 Undo the two bolts securing the clutch cable bracket to the clutch cover and disconnect the inner cable from the operating lever. Screw the bracket retaining bolts back into the crankcase cover for safe-keeping.

11 Peel back the rubber cover then undo the nut and disconnect the lead from the starter motor. Screw the nut back onto the starter motor terminal for safe-keeping.

12 Trace the wiring back from the alternator, pulse generator and engine switches (the neutral switch, coolant temperature sender and oil pressure switch are all connected to the same wiring connector) in the junction box. Disconnect the three wiring connectors then release the wiring from underneath the junction box. Work back along the wiring, releasing it from any relevant retaining clips so that it is free to be removed with the engine unit **(see illustrations)**.

13 Disconnect the sidestand switch wiring connector in the junction box, then work back along the wire, freeing it from any relevant retaining clips. Completely free the wiring from the crankcase so that it will not interfere with engine/transmission unit removal.

14 On S, T, V and W (1995 to 1998) models, disconnect the speed sensor wiring connector above the clutch housing **(see illustration)**,

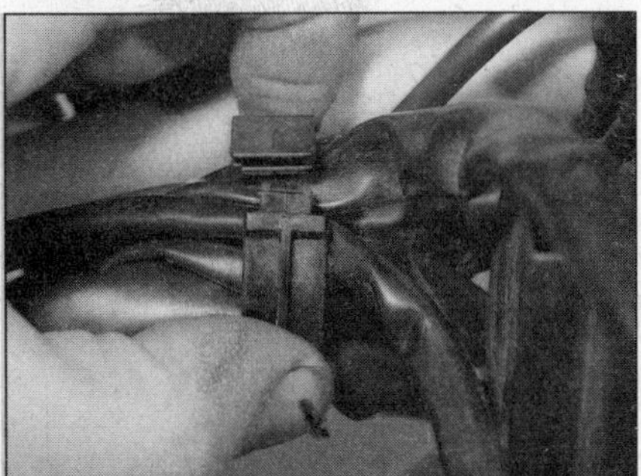

5.12b Work back along the wiring, freeing it from all the relevant retaining clips . . .

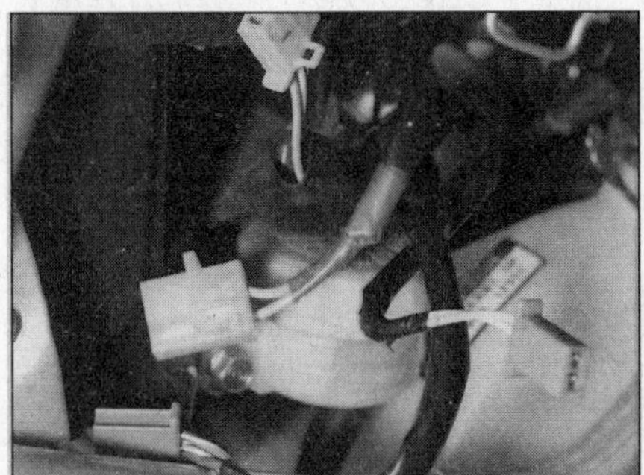

5.12c . . . so that the wiring is free to be removed with the engine

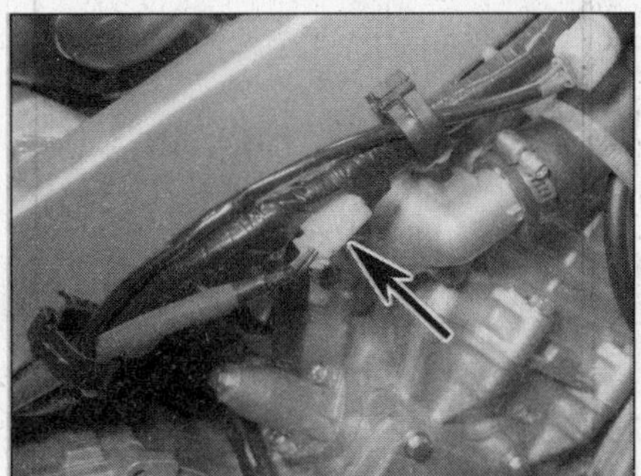

5.14 Disconnect the speed sensor wiring connector (arrow)

5.19 Slacken the clips and disconnect the coolant hoses from the water pump

5.21 Position a jack and block of wood underneath the engine and support the weight of the unit

5.22a Remove the left front engine mounting nut, bolt and spacer (arrow) . . .

then work back along the wire, freeing it from any relevant retaining clips so that it will not interfere with engine/transmission unit removal.

15 Undo the clamp bolt and disconnect the gearshift lever linkage from the engine, noting its alignment on the shaft (there should be a punch mark on the end of the shaft which aligns either with a punch mark on the linkage arm, or with the slot in the arm.

16 Unscrew the two screws securing the sprocket cover to the engine unit, noting the position of the wiring clamp.

17 Remove the engine sprocket cover and the drive chain guide plate.

18 Have an assistant apply the rear brake, then slacken and remove the engine sprocket retaining bolt and washer. Slide the sprocket off the countershaft then separate the sprocket from the chain. Note that if the drive chain is tight it may be necessary to slacken the drive chain adjustment to allow the sprocket to be slid off the shaft.

19 Slacken the retaining clips and disconnect the cooling system hoses from the thermostat housing and water pump **(see illustration)**.

20 Undo the radiator two lower mounting bolts and swing the radiator away from the frame to prevent it being damaged during engine removal.

21 Position a jack and block of wood beneath the engine and raise the jack so that it is supporting the weight of the engine/transmission unit **(see illustration)**.

22 Undo the engine left and right front mounting nuts and bolts and recover the spacers from between the frame downtubes and engine unit. Note that the left spacer is thicker than the right spacer **(see illustrations)**.

23 Unscrew the retaining bolts then remove both the left and right upper mounting brackets and recover the spacer fitted between each bracket and the engine **(see illustrations)**.

24 Slacken and remove the engine lower rear mounting nut and bolt.

25 Slacken and remove the engine upper rear mounting nut and bolt. With the bolt removed, loosen the large locknut situated on the right side of the frame then, using a suitable Allen wrench, slacken the adjuster bolt and recover the spacer which is fitted between the bolt and engine unit **(see illustrations)**.

26 Make a final check to make sure that all wires and hoses are disconnected.

27 Slowly and carefully lower the engine unit out of the frame.

Warning: The engine unit is heavy and may cause injury if it falls. Be sure it is securely supported. Have an assistant help you steady the engine as it is lowered out of position.

5.22b . . . and the right front mounting nut, bolt and spacer

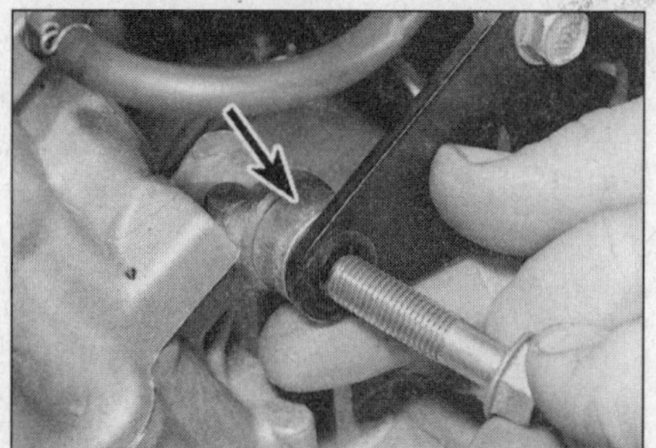
5.23a Unscrew the upper mounting bracket bolt and recover the spacer (arrow) . . .

5.23b . . . then undo the two bolts and remove the mounting bracket from the frame

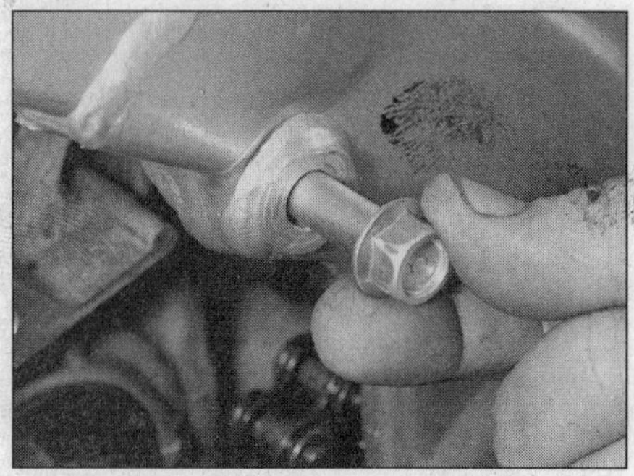
5.25a Slide out the upper rear mounting bolt . . .

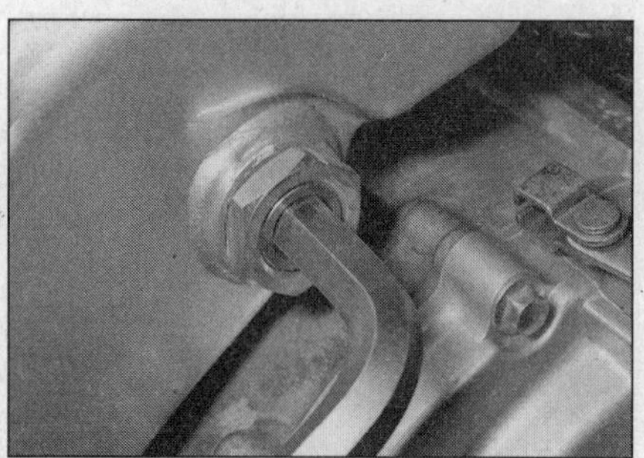
5.25b . . . then slacken the locknut and unscrew the adjuster bolt with an Allen wrench . . .

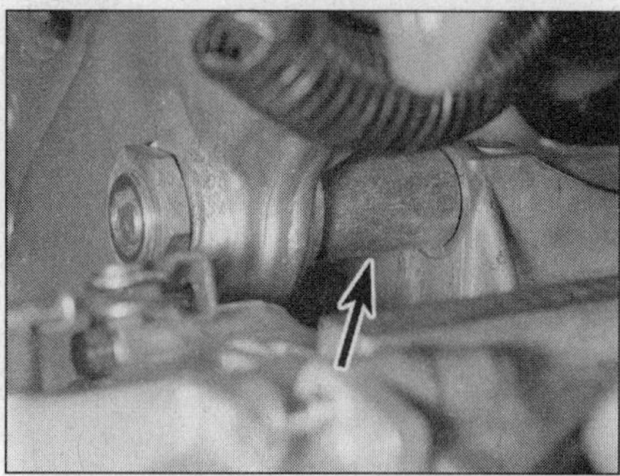
5.25c . . . and recover the spacer (arrow)

28 With the aid of an assistant lift the engine unit off the jack and lower it carefully onto the work surface, taking care not to break the long fins cast onto the bottom of the oil pan. These fins are there specifically for the engine to stand on and keep it in an upright position **(see illustration)**.

5.28 Lowering the engine to the floor

Installation

29 With the aid of an assistant place the engine unit on top of the jack and block of wood and carefully raise the engine unit into position in the frame.

30 Slide the engine lower rear bolt into position from the left of the bike and fit the nut, tightening it by hand only.

31 Locate the upper mounting spacers in position and install the mounting brackets, tightening the bolts by hand only.

32 Insert the front mounting spacers between the frame and engine, noting the thicker spacer is fitted on the left, and insert the bolts. Tighten the nuts by hand only.

33 Position the spacer on the right side of the engine unit and insert the upper, rear mounting bolt from the left side. Do not fit the nut yet.

34 With all the other engine mountings tightened by hand only, tighten the upper rear mounting adjusting bolt to the specified torque setting. Hold the adjuster bolt stationary then tighten its locknut to the specified torque setting **(see illustration)**. Fully insert the bolt and fit its nut.

5.34 Adjust the upper rear mounting (see text) then tighten the locknut to the specified torque

35 With the upper rear mounting bolts correctly adjusted, tighten all other mounting bolts securely (to the torque listed in this Chapter's Specifications where given) **(see illustrations)**.

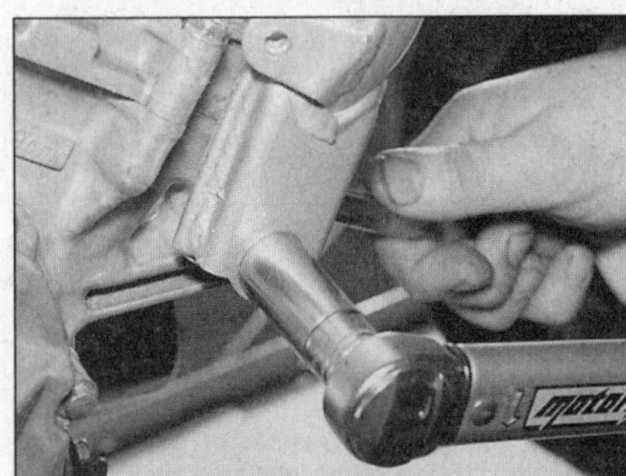

5.35a Tighten the front mounting bolts to the specified torque . . .

5.35b . . . and tighten all others securely

36 The remainder of the installation procedure is a direct reversal of the removal sequence, noting the following points.

a) Tighten all nuts and bolts to the specified torque settings (where given).
b) Align the punch marks on the gearshift pedal and shaft when locating the pedal on the shaft splines.
c) Make sure all wiring is correctly routed and retained by all the relevant clips and ties.
d) Adjust the drive chain as described in Chapter 1.
e) Fill the engine oil and cooling systems as described in Chapter 1.
f) Prior to installing the lower fairing panels start the engine and check for signs of coolant/oil leakage.

6 Engine disassembly and reassembly - general information

Note: *Refer to 'Tools and Workshop Tips' in the Reference section of this manual for further information.*

Disassembly

1 Before disassembling the engine, the external surfaces of the unit should be thoroughly cleaned and degreased. This will prevent contamination of the engine internals, and will also make working a lot easier and cleaner. A high flash-point solvent, such as kerosene (paraffin) can be used, or better still, a proprietary engine degreaser. Use old paintbrushes and toothbrushes to work the solvent into the various recesses of the engine casings. Take care to exclude solvent or water from the electrical components and intake and exhaust ports.

Warning: The use of gasoline (petrol) as a cleaning agent should be avoided because of the risk of fire.

2 When clean and dry, arrange the unit on the workbench, leaving suitable clear area for working. Gather a selection of small containers and plastic bags so that parts can be grouped together in an easily identifiable manner. Some paper and a pen should be on hand to permit notes to be made and labels attached where necessary. A supply of clean shop towels is also required.

3 Before commencing work, read through the appropriate section so that some idea of the necessary procedure can be gained. When removing various engine components it should be noted that great force is seldom required, unless specified. In many cases, a component's reluctance to be removed is indicative of an incorrect approach or removal method. If in any doubt, re-check with the text.

4 When disassembling the engine, keep 'mated' parts together (including gears, pistons, valves, etc). These 'mated' parts must be reused or replaced as an assembly.

5 Engine/transmission disassembly should be done in the following general order with reference to the appropriate Sections.

Remove the camshafts
Remove the cylinder head
Remove camchain, sprockets and guides
Remove the clutch
Remove the oil pump
Remove the external shift mechanism
Remove the alternator rotor
Remove the starter motor (see Chapter 9)
Remove the water pump (See Chapter 3)
Remove the oil pan
Separate the crankcase halves
Remove the connecting rod/piston assemblies
Remove the crankshaft
Remove the transmission shafts/gears
Remove the shift cam/forks

Reassembly

6 Reassembly is accomplished by reversing the general disassembly sequence.

7 Valve cover - removal and installation

Note: *The valve cover can be removed with the engine in the frame. If the engine has been removed, ignore the steps which do not apply.*

Removal

1 Remove the left and right lower fairing sections (see Chapter 8). On S, T, V and W (1995 to 1998) models, also remove the upper fairing assembly (see Chapter 8).

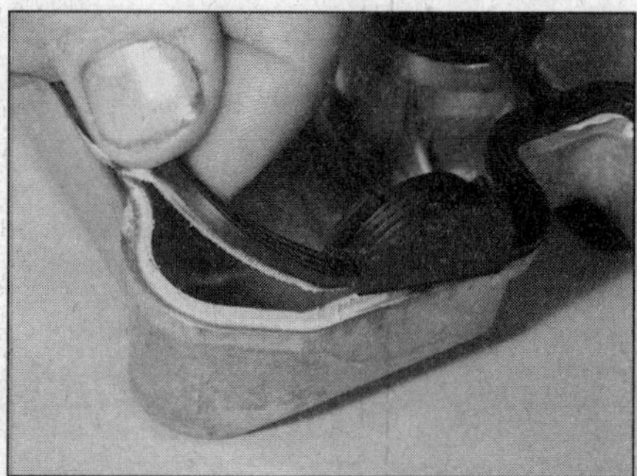
7.9 Apply a smear of sealant to the valve cover groove and fit the seal to the cover

7.10 Fit the cover to the cylinder head making sure the seal remains correctly seated

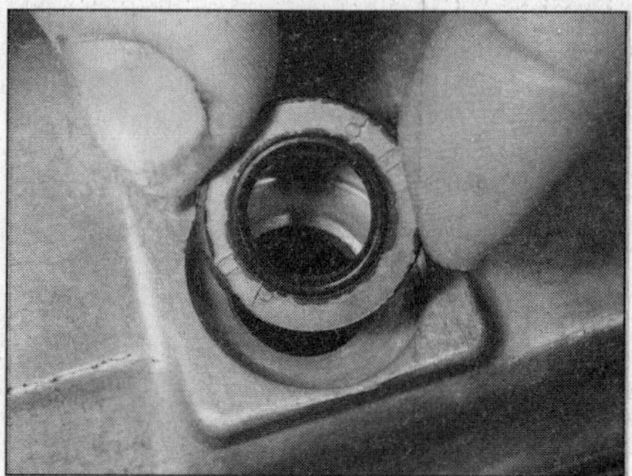
7.11 Fit the valve cover bolt seals so that their UP marks are facing upwards . . .

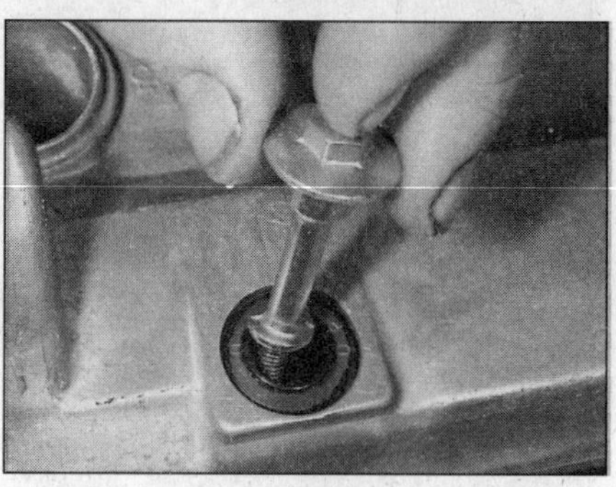
7.12 . . . then install the cover bolts

2 Remove the air filter housing as described in Chapter 4.

3 Disconnect the radiator fan wiring connector. Slacken and remove the radiator mounting bolts and recover the spacers from the mounting dampers. On M, N, P and R (1991 to 1994) models, unbolt the horn mounting bracket from the left side of the frame. On S, T, V and W (1995 to 1998) models, unhook the radiator filler neck. Move the radiator to disengage it from its upper locating peg and move it forward to improve access to the valve cover. Tie the radiator to the fork legs.

4 Release the retaining clip and disconnect the breather hose from the center of the valve cover. Disconnect the spark plug caps from the plugs and position them clear of the cover.

5 Slacken and remove the six cover bolts along with their sealing washers.

6 Lift the valve cover away from the head and maneuver it out from between the frame tubes. Recover the valve cover rubber seal.

7 Examine the rubber seal for signs of damage or deterioration and replace if it is cracked or brittle. Also check the cover bolt seals for signs of damage and replace if necessary.

Installation

8 Remove all traces of sealant from the cover groove and rubber seal.

9 Ensure the cover is clean and dry, then apply a small bead of sealant to the cover grooves. Fit the seal to the cover, making sure it is correctly located. The sealant will help to hold the seal in position as the cover is fitted **(see illustration)**.

10 Carefully install the cover on the cylinder head taking great care not to dislodge the seal **(see illustration)**. With the cover in position, lift it slightly and check that the seal is correctly located in the cover outer and spark plug hole grooves.

11 Fit the sealing washers to the cylinder head cover making sure the 'UP' mark on each one is facing upwards **(see illustration)**.

12 Install the six cover bolts and tighten them to the torque setting listed in this Chapter's Specifications **(see illustration)**. On S, T, V and W (1995 to 1998) models, tighten the front outer bolts first.

13 The remainder of installation is the reverse of removal.

8 Camchain tensioner - removal and installation

M, N, P and R (1991 to 1994) models

Removal

1 Set the bike on its centerstand.

2 Remove the right lower fairing panel as described in Chapter 8.

3 Unscrew the two bolts securing the camchain tensioner to the rear of the cylinder block/crankcase and remove them along with their sealing washers.

4 Remove the camchain tensioner and gasket **(see illustration)**. Discard the gasket and bolt sealing washers; new ones must be used on installation.

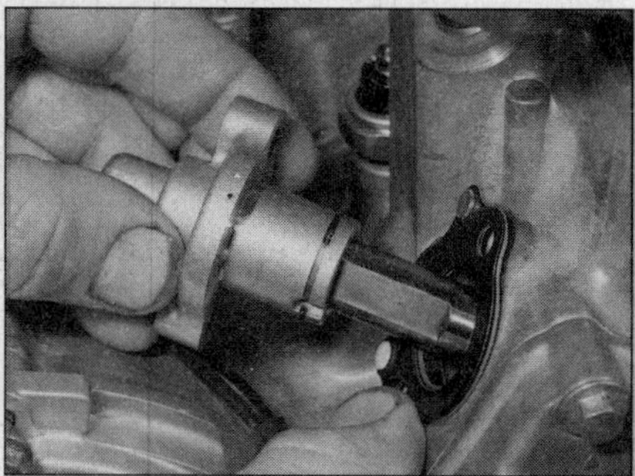
8.4 Remove the camchain tensioner and gasket noting which way around the gasket is fitted

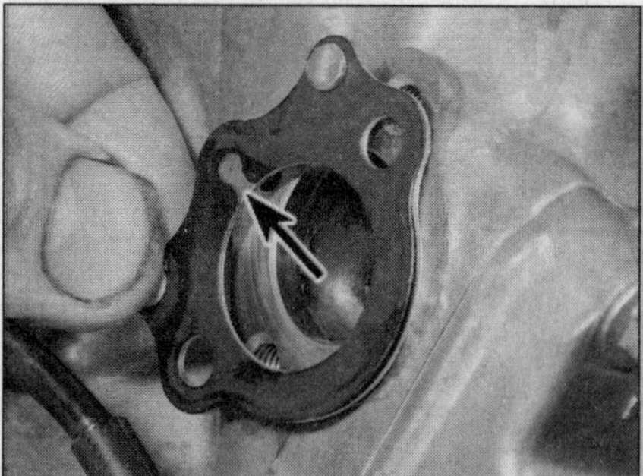
8.6 The gasket must be fitted with its oilway (arrow) facing towards the tensioner

Installation

5 Prior to installation, it is necessary to prime the camchain tensioner with oil. To do this, fill a suitable container with clean engine oil. Submerge the camchain tensioner in the oil and remove all air from the tensioner by slowly pushing the plunger in and out. Continue doing this until air bubbles stop being expelled from the plunger, then allow the plunger to extend fully. Remove the tensioner from the oil bath and wipe clean.

6 Ensure the tensioner and cylinder block/crankcase surfaces are clean and dry and fit the new gasket to the tensioner, making sure the gasket is fitted with its oilway facing towards the camchain tensioner **(see illustration)**. ***Caution: If the gasket is installed the wrong way around excess oil pressure will be exerted on the tensioner resulting in premature wear of the camchain.***

7 Fit a new sealing washer to each bolt and fit the camchain tensioner to the engine. Tighten the tensioner retaining bolts to the torque setting listed in this Chapter's Specifications.

8 Install the lower fairing panel as described in Chapter 8.

S, T, V and W (1995 to 1998) models

Removal

9 Remove the right lower fairing panel as described in Chapter 8. Unscrew the three bolts securing the right side engine mounting

8.9 Unscrew the three bolts (arrows) and remove the bracket

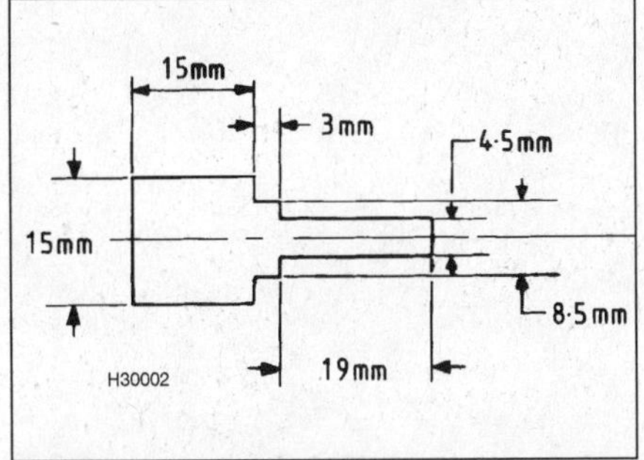

8.10a A copy of Honda's tensioner locking key can be made from a piece of 1 mm mild steel

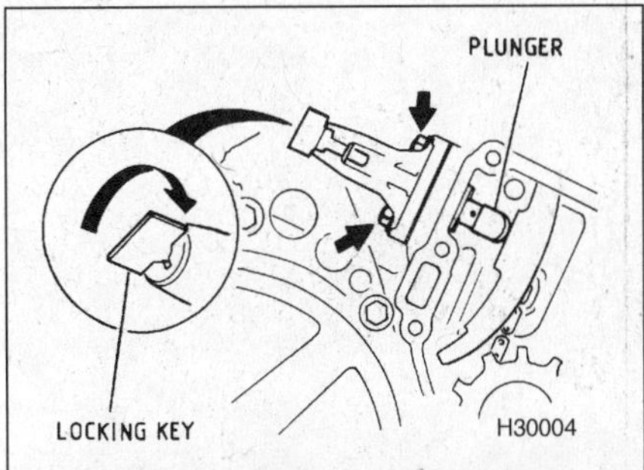

8.10b Locking key in position and tensioner plunger shown retracted. Tensioner mounting bolts arrowed

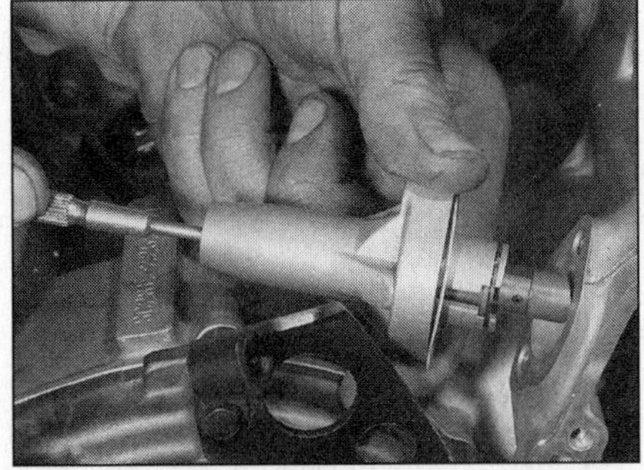
8.11 Tensioner plunger can be retracted using a small flat-bladed screwdriver as shown

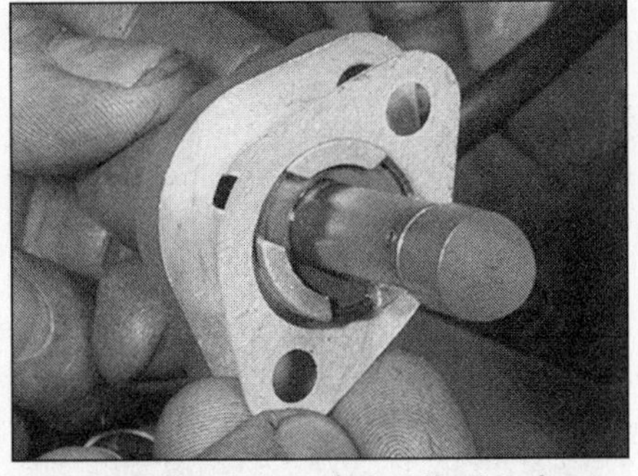
8.13 Install a new gasket at the tensioner-to-cylinder block joint

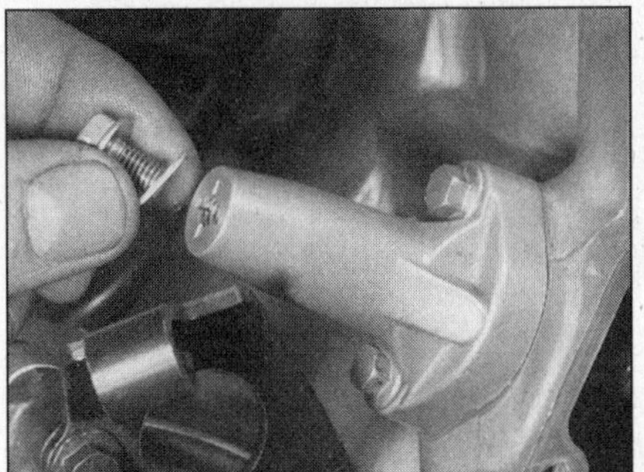
8.15 Use a new sealing washer on the tensioner end bolt

bracket and remove the bracket, noting its spacer **(see illustration)**.

10 Unscrew the bolt and sealing washer from the end of the camchain tensioner **(see illustration 8.15)**. If the Honda locking key or a home-made equivalent is available, insert it in the end of the tensioner so that it engages the slotted plunger and rotate the plunger fully clockwise, then push the key into the end of the tensioner body to hold it in this position **(see illustrations)**. Remove the two bolts to free the tensioner from the engine.

11 If the locking key is not available, use a small flat-bladed screwdriver to rotate the plunger fully clockwise and hold it in this position whilst the tensioner body bolts are removed **(see illustration)**. The plunger will spring back out once the screwdriver is removed, but can be easily reset on installation.

12 Discard the gasket; a new one must be used on installation. Do not dismantle the tensioner.

Installation

13 Ensure the tensioner and cylinder block surfaces are clean and dry and fit a new gasket to the tensioner **(see illustration)**.

14 If the locking key described above is available, insert it in the tensioner body and rotate the plunger fully clockwise to retract it into the body, then push the key shoulders into the end of the body to lock it **(see illustrations 8.10a and b)**. Install the tensioner on the engine and tighten its bolts to the specified torque setting. Remove the key and install the tensioner end bolt with a new sealing washer **(see illustration 8.15)**.

15 If the key is not available, rotate the plunger fully clockwise with a flat-bladed screwdriver and hold it in this position whilst the tensioner bolts are installed and fully tightened to the specified torque setting **(see illustration 8.11)**. Install the tensioner end bolt with a new sealing washer **(see illustration)**.

16 Install the fairing support bracket and fairing panel as described in Chapter 8.

9 Camshafts and followers - removal, inspection and installation

Note: *This procedure can be carried out with the engine in the frame.*

Removal

1 Remove the valve cover as described in Section 7. To further improve access to the camshafts remove the ignition HT coils as described in Chapter 5, then unclip and remove the rubber insulating cover (situated directly above the valve cover) from the frame.

2 On M, N, P and R (1991 to 1994) models, remove the camchain tensioner (see Section 8). On S, T, V and W (1995 to 1998) models, retract the tensioner plunger using the special tool; there is no need to remove the tensioner body (see Section 8).

3 Undo the three bolts and remove the upper camchain guide from the top of the cylinder head **(see illustrations)**.

4 Unscrew the two visible camshaft sprocket retaining bolts **(see illustration)**.

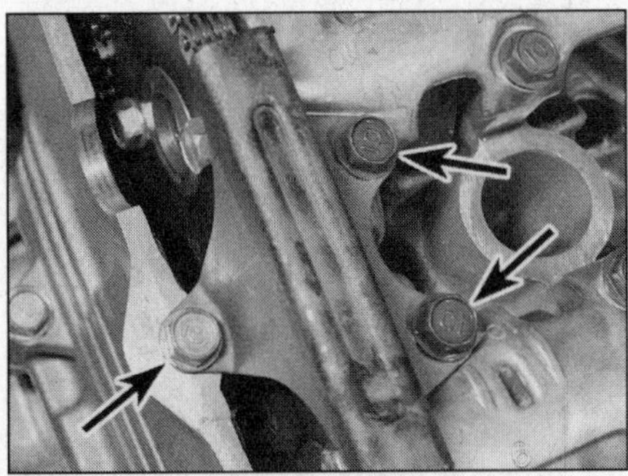
9.3a Undo the three bolts (arrows) . . .

9.3b . . . and remove the upper chain guide

9.4 Do not to drop the bolts down into the engine unit when unscrewing the camshaft sprocket bolts

9.8 Disengage each camshaft sprocket from the chain and remove them from the engine

9.9 Slacken the bearing cap bolts (see text), working in the reverse of the numerical sequence on each cap

9.10a Lift off the bearing cap and recover the locating dowels (arrows)

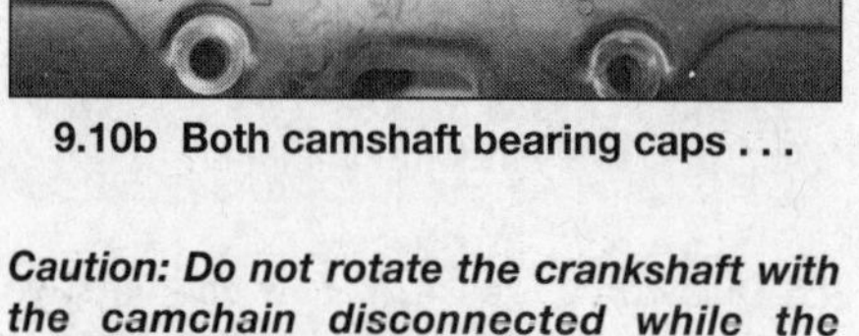

9.10b Both camshaft bearing caps . . .

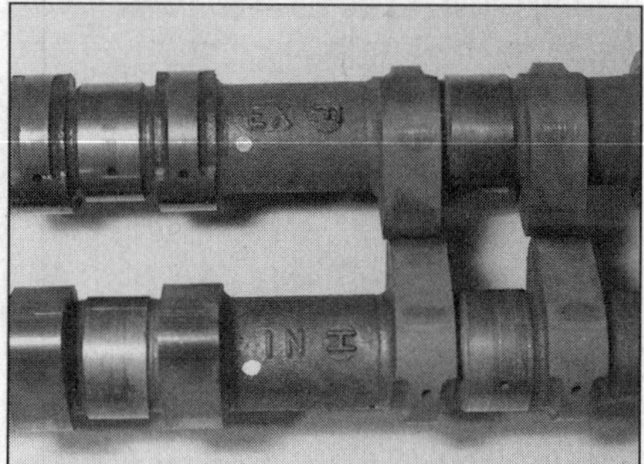
9.10c . . . and camshafts are marked IN and EX for identification purposes

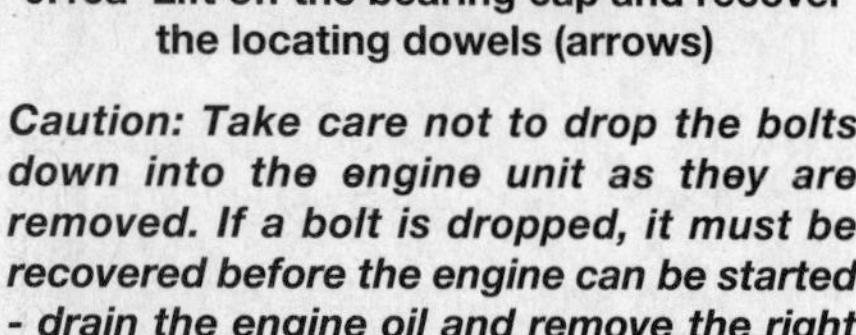

Caution: Take care not to drop the bolts down into the engine unit as they are removed. If a bolt is dropped, it must be recovered before the engine can be started - drain the engine oil and remove the right crankshaft end cover to recover the bolt.

5 Unscrew the timing inspection cap from the right crankshaft end cover.

6 Using a suitable socket, rotate the crankshaft clockwise until the remaining two camshaft sprocket retaining bolts are accessible.

7 Unscrew the two remaining camshaft sprocket bolts.

8 Disengage each sprocket from its camshaft and the camchain and remove it from the engine unit **(see illustration)**. Pass a piece of wire or screwdriver through the center of the camchain to prevent it dropping down inside the engine unit.

9.14 Check the lobes for wear - damage like this will require replacement (or repair) of the camshaft

Caution: Do not rotate the crankshaft with the camchain disconnected while the camshafts are in position.

9 Starting with the exhaust camshaft, working in the numerical sequence marked on the top of the bearing cap, loosen the bearing cap bolts by half a turn at a time to gently relieve the valve spring pressure on the cap **(see illustration)**. While slackening the bolts make sure that the bearing cap is lifting squarely away from the cylinder head and is not sticking on the cap locating dowels.

Caution: If the bolts are carelessly loosened and the cap does not come squarely away from the head, the cap is likely to break. If this happens the complete cylinder head assembly must be replaced; the bearing caps are matched to the cylinder head and cannot be replaced separately.

10 Once spring pressure is released from the cap, remove all the bolts then lift off the bearing cap and remove the camshaft. **Note:** *The camshafts and bearing caps are not interchangeable. The intake camshaft and bearing cap are marked 'IN' and the exhaust camshaft and bearing cap are marked 'EX'* **(see illustrations)**.

11 Repeat the operations in Steps 9 and 10 and remove the intake camshaft.

12 Obtain a container which is divided into sixteen compartments, and label each compartment with the number of its corresponding valve in the cylinder head.

13 Using a magnet, lift each follower out of the cylinder head and store it in its corresponding compartment in the container. Note that the shim is likely to stick to the inside of the follower so take great care not to lose it as the follower is removed. Remove the shims and store each one with its respective follower.

Inspection

Note: *Before replacing the camshafts or the cylinder head and bearing caps because of damage, check with local machine shops specializing in motorcycle engineering work. In the case of the camshafts, it may be possible for cam lobes to be welded, reground and hardened, at a cost far lower than that of a new camshaft. If the bearing surfaces in the cylinder head are damaged, it may be possible for them to be bored out to accept bearing inserts. Due to the cost of a new cylinder head it is recommended that all options be explored before condemning it as trash!*

14 Inspect the cam bearing surfaces of the head and the bearing caps. Look for score marks, deep scratches and evidence of spalling (a pitted appearance). Check the camshaft lobes for heat discoloration (blue appearance), score marks, chipped areas, flat spots and spalling **(see illustration)**.

15 Camshaft runout can be checked by supporting each end of the camshaft on V-blocks, and measuring any runout using a dial gauge. If the runout exceeds the specified limit the camshaft must be replaced.

9.16 Measure the height of the camshaft lobes with a micrometer

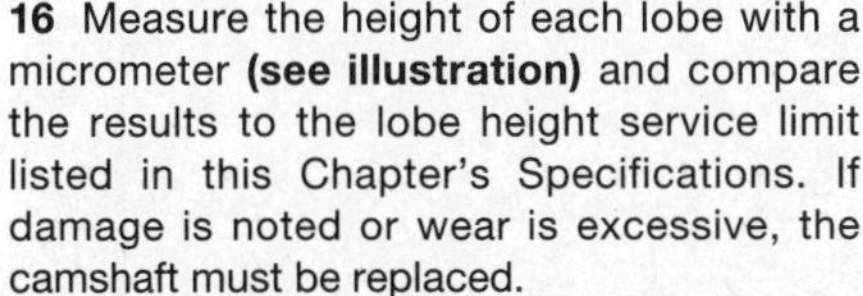

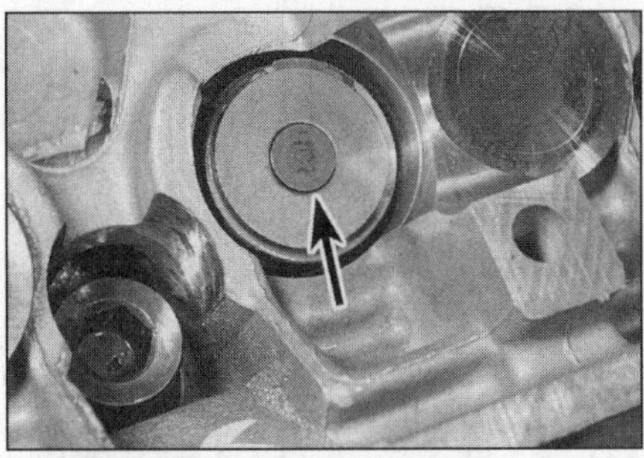

9.27 Make sure the shim (arrow) is correctly seated in the valve spring retainer . . .

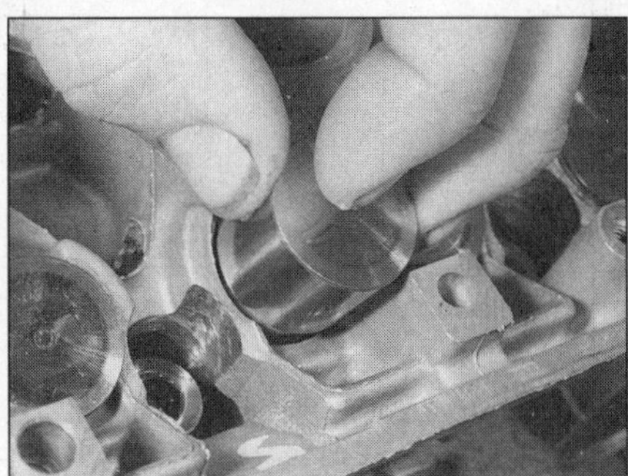

9.28 . . . and slide in the follower

16 Measure the height of each lobe with a micrometer **(see illustration)** and compare the results to the lobe height service limit listed in this Chapter's Specifications. If damage is noted or wear is excessive, the camshaft must be replaced.

17 The camshaft bearing oil clearance should then be checked. There are two possible ways of checking this, the first method is by direct measurement (see Steps 18 and 23) and the second by the use of a product known as Plastigage (see Steps 19 to 23).

18 If the first method is to be used, make sure the locating dowels are in position then fit the bearing caps to the head. Make sure the caps are correctly positioned (see note in Step 10). Tighten the retaining bolts to the specified torque in the numerical sequence marked on the top of each cap. Measure the diameter of each bearing cap journal and compare the measurements obtained with the service limit given in the Specifications at the start of this Chapter. If any journal is worn beyond the service limit, the cylinder head must be repaired/replaced. The camshaft bearing oil clearance can then be calculated by subtracting the camshaft bearing journal diameter from the bearing cap journal diameter.

19 If the second method is to be used, clean the camshafts, the bearing surfaces in the cylinder head and the bearing caps with a clean, lint-free cloth, then lay the camshafts in place in the cylinder head (see note in Step 10).

20 Cut strips of Plastigage and lay one piece on each bearing journal, parallel with the camshaft centerline. Make sure the bearing cap dowels are installed and fit the bearing caps in their proper positions (see note in Step 10). Ensuring the camshafts are not rotated at all, tighten the cap retaining bolts to the specified torque working as described in Steps 35 to 38.

21 Now unscrew the bolts as described in Steps 9 and 10 and carefully lift off the bearing caps, again making sure the camshafts are not rotated.

22 To determine the oil clearance, compare the crushed Plastigage (at its widest point) on each journal to the scale printed on the Plastigage container.

23 Compare the results to this Chapter's Specifications. If the oil clearance is greater than specified, measure the diameter of the cam bearing journal with a micrometer. If the journal diameter is less than the specified limit, replace the camshaft with a new one and recheck the clearance. If the clearance is still too great, replace the cylinder head and bearing caps with new parts (see the Note at the start of this sub-section).

24 Except in cases of oil starvation, the camchain wears very little. If the camchain has stretched excessively, which makes it difficult to maintain proper tension, replace it with a new one (see Section 23).

25 Check the sprockets for wear, cracks and other damage, replacing them if necessary. If the sprockets are worn, the camchain is also worn, and also the sprocket on the crankshaft. If wear this severe is apparent the camchain and all sprockets should be replaced.

26 Check the upper camchain guide for wear or damage. If it is worn or damaged, the camchain may be worn out. Refer to Section 23 for camchain replacement information.

Installation

27 Fit each shim to the top of its correct valve making sure it is correctly seated in the valve spring retainer **(see illustration)**. **Note:** *It is most important that the shims are returned to their original valves otherwise the valve clearances will be inaccurate.*

28 Install the followers in their respective positions in the cylinder head, making sure each one squarely enters its bore **(see illustration)**.

29 Unscrew the timing inspection cap from the right crankshaft end cover (if not already removed).

30 Using a suitable socket on the crankshaft bolt, rotate the crankshaft in a clockwise direction until the line situated next to the 'T' mark on rotor aligns with the index mark, in the form of a cutout, on the crankshaft cover **(see illustration)**.

31 Apply a smear of clean engine oil to the cylinder head camshaft bearings and followers **(see illustration)**.

32 Hook the camchain over the end of each camshaft and lay both camshafts in position on the cylinder head. **Note:** *Ensure the camshafts are fitted correctly; the intake camshaft is marked 'IN' and the exhaust camshaft 'EX'.* Position the camshafts so that the lobes of number 1 cylinder are pointing outwards (away from each other) **(see illustrations)**.

9.30 Align the line next to the T on the rotor with the index mark (arrow) on the right crankshaft end cover

9.31 Lubricate the camshaft bearings and followers with clean engine oil prior to installing the camshafts

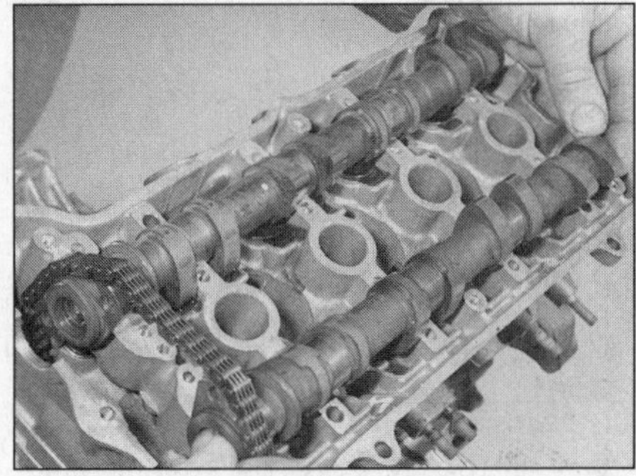

9.32a Engage both camshafts with the chain . . .

9.32b . . . and position them so the lobes of number 1 cylinder are pointing away from each other

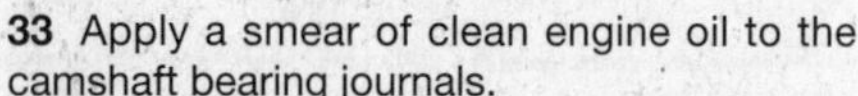

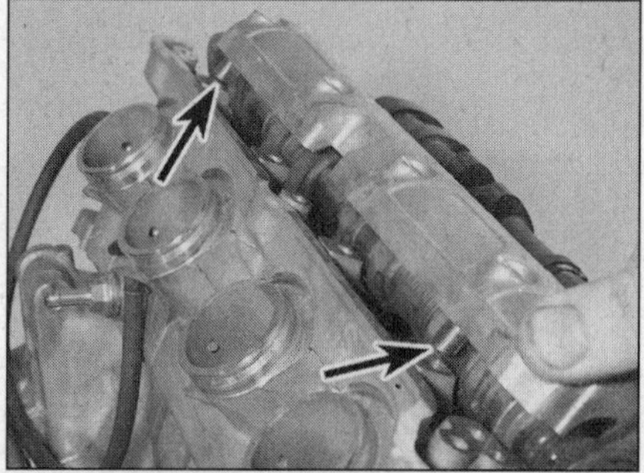

9.34 Install the bearing caps making sure the locating dowels (arrows) are in position

9.37 Tighten the bearing cap bolts to the specified torque as described in text

33 Apply a smear of clean engine oil to the camshaft bearing journals.

34 Make sure the locating dowels are in position and install the bearing caps on the head **(see illustration)**. **Note:** *Ensure the bearing caps are fitted correctly, the intake bearing cap is marked 'IN' and the exhaust bearing cap 'EX'.*

35 On S, T, V and W (1995 to 1998) models, apply some oil to the threads of the bearing cap bolts. On all models, screw in the bolts (noting that the longer bolts fit into the outer holes) by hand only until all bolts are contacting the caps. Do not install the number 10 bolts in the tightening sequence yet.

36 Starting with the intake bearing cap, working in the numerical sequence marked on the top of the bearing cap, tighten the bearing cap bolts by half a turn at a time to gradually draw the cap into position. While tightening the bolts make sure that the bearing cap is being pulled squarely down onto the cylinder head and is not sticking on the cap locating dowels.

Caution: If the bolts are carelessly tightened and the bearing cap is not drawn squarely onto the head, it is likely to break. If this happens the complete cylinder head assembly must be replaced; the bearing caps are matched to the cylinder head and cannot be replaced separately.

9.41 Engage the camshaft sprockets with the chain so that the IN and EX marks (arrows) are level with the cylinder head surface

37 Once the cap is in contact with the head, go around in the specified sequence and tighten the bolts to the torque setting listed in this Chapter's Specifications **(see illustration)**.

38 Repeat the procedure in Steps 36 and 37 and tighten the exhaust camshaft bearing cap bolts.

39 Make sure the crankshaft is still positioned as described in Step 30.

40 Keeping the front run of the camchain tight, locate the first sprocket with the camchain so that its EX mark is level with the upper surface of the cylinder head. Locate the sprocket on the end of the exhaust camshaft.

41 Engage the second sprocket with the camchain so that its IN mark is level with the upper surface of the cylinder head. Locate the sprocket on the end of the intake camshaft **(see illustration)**.

42 Remove all traces of old locking compound from the camshaft sprocket bolts using a wire brush.

43 Apply a drop of fresh locking compound to each bolt. Fit one bolt to each visible camshaft sprocket hole, tightening them lightly only at this stage **(see illustration)**.

44 On M, N, P and R (1991 to 1994) models, insert a finger or wooden dowel through the tensioner aperture and apply light pressure to the camchain tensioner guide. This will prevent the chain 'jumping' on the sprockets as the crankshaft is rotated.

45 Using a suitable socket, rotate the crankshaft clockwise until it is possible to insert the two remaining sprocket bolts.

46 Screw the bolts into position and tighten them to the torque setting listed in this Chapter's Specifications **(see illustrations)**.

47 Rotate the crankshaft clockwise until the other sprocket bolts are accessible then tighten them to the specified torque setting.

48 Align the 'T' mark on the crankshaft rotor with the index mark on the cover (see Step 30) and check that both the sprocket timing marks are correctly aligned with the cylinder head upper surface **(see illustration 9.41)**. If the marks aren't lined up, disengage the sprocket(s) from the chain and adjust their position.

49 Once all timing marks are correctly aligned, fit the upper camchain guide and tighten its bolts to the specified torque.

50 On M, N, P and R (1991 to 1994) models, install the camchain tensioner (see Section 8). On S, T, V and W (1995 to 1998) models, release the stopper key from the cam chain tensioner. Install a new sealing washer on the tensioner bolt and tighten the bolt securely.

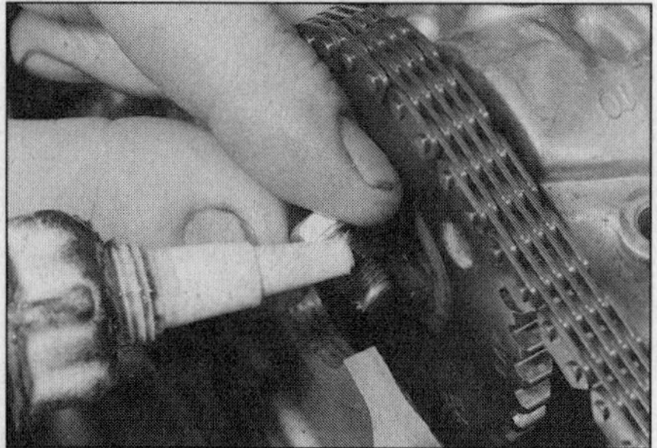

9.43 Apply thread locking compound to the camshaft sprocket bolts and screw two bolts into the visible holes

9.46a Rotate the crankshaft then install the two remaining bolts . . .

9.46b . . . and tighten all the sprocket bolts to the specified torque setting

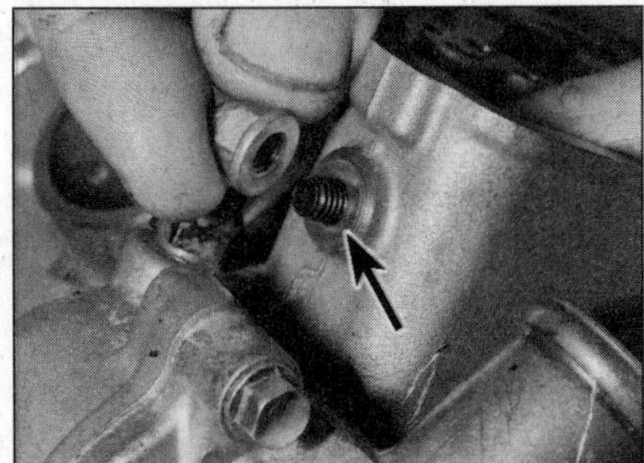

10.5a Slacken and remove the nut and sealing washer (arrow) . . .

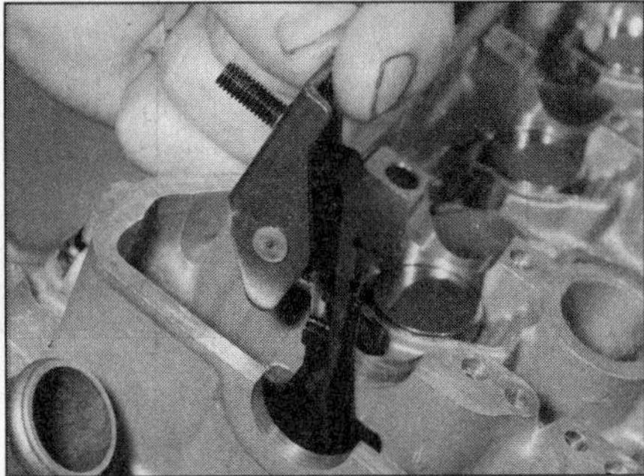

10.5b . . . and lift the rear camchain guide out from the head

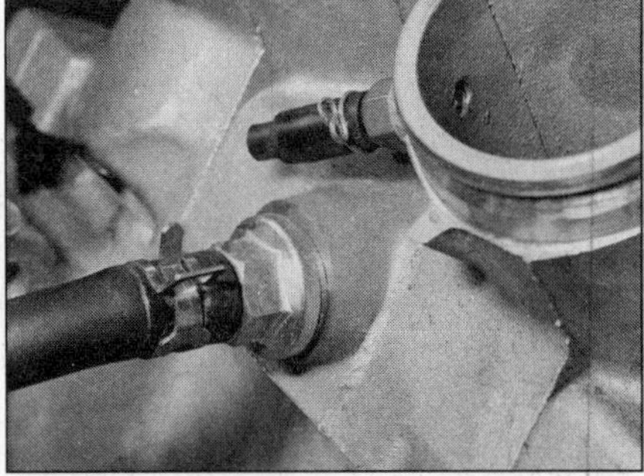

10.6 Release the retaining clip and detach the small coolant hose from the rear of the head

51 Rotate the crankshaft a few times, to settle all disturbed components, and check all valve clearances as described in Chapter 1, making adjustments as necessary.
52 Lubricate all bearing surfaces with clean engine oil and fit the valve cover as described in Section 7.
53 Apply a smear of oil to the timing inspection cap O-ring and tighten the cap to the specified torque setting.
54 Install any components removed to improve access.

10 Cylinder head - removal and installation

Caution: The engine must be completely cool before beginning this procedure or the cylinder head may become warped.
Note: *This procedure can be performed with the engine in the frame. If the engine has already been removed, ignore the preliminary steps which don't apply.*

Removal

1 Remove the exhaust system as described in Chapter 4.
2 Remove the carburetors as described in Chapter 4. On California models also remove the Pulse secondary air injection (PAIR) control valve as described in Chapter 4.
3 Drain the cooling system as described in Chapter 1.
4 Remove the camshafts and followers as described in Section 9.
5 Slacken and remove the nut and sealing washer securing the camchain rear guide to the cylinder head and lift out the guide **(see illustrations)**.
6 On M, N, P and R (1991 to 1994) models, release the clip and disconnect the single small coolant hose from the rear of the cylinder head (between cylinders 1 and 2) **(see illustration)**. On S and T (1995 and 1996) models, release the clips and disconnect the two small coolant hoses from the rear of the cylinder head (one between cylinders 1 and 2, one on the thermostat housing). On V and W (1997 and 1998) models, release the clips and disconnect the three small coolant hoses from the rear of the cylinder head (one between cylinders 1 and 2, one between cylinders 3 and 4 and one on the thermostat housing). Note which hose fits where before detaching them.
7 Slacken the clip and disconnect the main coolant hose from the thermostat housing.
8 Unscrew the two small cylinder head bolts from the right end of the head **(see illustration)**.
9 Disconnect the wiring connector from the coolant temperature sender unit which is screwed into the right end of the head.
10 Working from the outside to the inside in a criss-cross pattern, slacken the cylinder head bolts by half a turn at a time. Once all pressure is released from the bolts, fully unscrew them and remove along with their washers.
11 Tap around the joint faces of the cylinder head with a soft-faced mallet to free the head. Don't attempt to free the head by inserting a screwdriver between the head and cylinder block - you'll damage the sealing surfaces.
12 Lift the head off the block, and remove it from the engine. Pass a piece of wire or a screwdriver through the camchain to prevent it falling down into the engine.
13 Remove the old head gasket and discard it. If loose, remove the cylinder head locating dowels from the cylinder block and store them with the head for safe-keeping.
14 Check the cylinder head gasket and the mating surfaces on the cylinder head and block for signs of leakage, which could indicate warpage. Check the flatness of the head as described in Section 12.

Installation

15 Ensure both cylinder head and block mating surfaces are clean and fit the locating dowels to the block (if removed). Apply a smear of engine oil to the surface of each cylinder bore **(see illustration)**.
16 Fit the new head gasket over the locating dowels **(see illustration)**.
17 Carefully lower the cylinder head onto the block while feeding the camchain up through the head. Pass a screwdriver or piece of wire through the chain to prevent it falling back into the engine **(see illustrations)**.
18 Apply a smear of clean engine oil to the threads and undersides of the cylinder head bolts **(see illustration)**.

10.8 Unscrew the two small cylinder head bolts from the right end of the head

10.15 Prior to installing the head, lubricate the bores with clean engine oil

10.16 Ensure the locating dowels (arrows) are in position and fit the new head gasket

10.17a Lower the head into position, passing the camchain up through the head . . .

10.17b . . . and pass a suitable tool through the chain to prevent it falling back into the engine

19 Fit the cylinder head bolts and washers and tighten them all by hand.

20 Working from the inside to the outside in a criss-cross pattern, tighten the cylinder head bolts to approximately half the specified torque setting given in the Specifications **(see illustration)**. Then go around in the same sequence and tighten the bolts to the full specified torque setting.

21 Install the two bolts to the right end of the cylinder head and tighten them securely.

22 Connect the small coolant hose(s) to the rear of the head and secure it/them with the clip(s). On S and T (1995 and 1996) models, the hose from the top union on the water pump cover fits onto the left side of the cylinder head and the hose from the carburetor heater system fits onto the thermostat housing. On V and W (1997 and 1998) models, the hose from the top union on the water pump cover fits onto the left side of the cylinder head, the hose from the bottom union on the water pump cover fits onto the right side of the cylinder head, and the hose from the carburetor heater system fits onto the thermostat housing.

23 Connect the main coolant hose to the thermostat housing and securely tighten its clip.

24 Connect the wiring connector to the temperature sender.

25 Lower the camchain rear guide into position, fit a new sealing washer and securely tighten its retaining nut.

26 Install the camshafts and followers as described in Section 9.

27 Fit the exhaust system, carburetors and, where necessary, the pulse secondary air injection (PAIR) control valve as described in Chapter 4.

28 Fill the cooling system (see Chapter 1).

11 Valves/valve seats/valve guides - servicing

1 Because of the complex nature of this job and the special tools and equipment required, servicing of the valves, the valve seats and the valve guides (commonly known as a valve job) is best left to a professional.

2 The home mechanic can, however, remove and disassemble the head, do the initial cleaning and inspection, then reassemble and deliver the head to a dealer service department or properly equipped motorcycle repair shop for the actual valve servicing. Refer to Section 12 for those procedures.

3 The dealer service department will remove the valves and springs, recondition or replace the valves and valve seats, replace the valve guides, check and replace the valve springs, spring retainers and keepers (collets) (as necessary), replace the valve seals with new ones and reassemble the valve components.

4 After the valve job has been performed, the head will be in like-new condition. When the head is returned, be sure to clean it again very thoroughly before installation on the engine to remove any metal particles or abrasive grit that may still be present from the valve service operations. Use compressed air, if available, to blow out all the holes and passages.

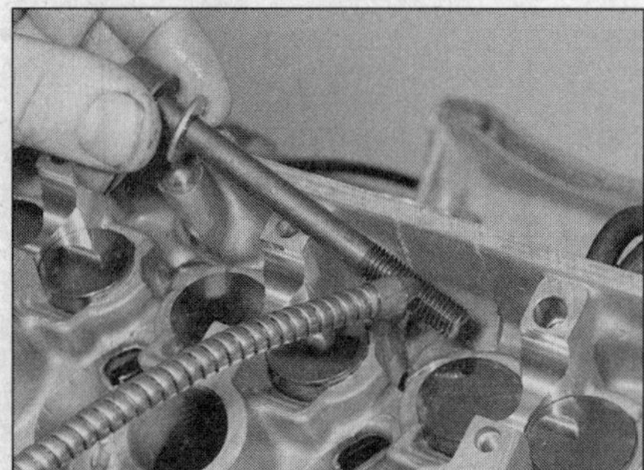

10.18 Apply a smear of oil to the threads and underside of the heads of the cylinder head bolts

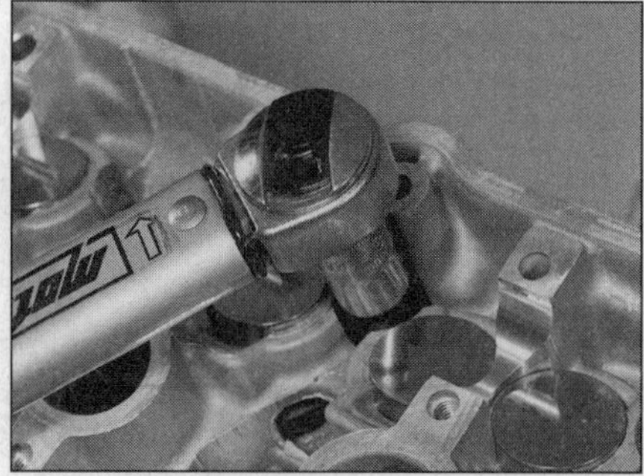

10.20 Tighten the head bolts to the specified torque as described in the text

12 Cylinder head and valves - disassembly, inspection and reassembly

1 As mentioned in the previous Section, valve servicing and valve guide replacement should be left to a dealer service department or motorcycle repair shop. However, disassembly, cleaning and inspection of the valves and related components can be done (if the necessary special tools are available) by the home mechanic. This way no expense is incurred if the inspection reveals that service work is not required at this time.

2 To properly disassemble the valve components without the risk of damaging them, a valve spring compressor is absolutely necessary.

Disassembly

3 Remove the followers and their shims if you haven't already done so (see Section 9). Store the components in such a way that they can be returned to their original locations without getting mixed up **(see illustrations)**.

4 Before the valves are removed, scrape away any traces of gasket material from the head gasket sealing surface. Work slowly and do not nick or gouge the soft aluminum of the head. Gasket removing solvents, which work very well, are available at most motorcycle shops and auto parts stores.

5 Carefully scrape all carbon deposits out of the combustion chamber area. A hand held wire brush or a piece of fine emery cloth can be used once the majority of deposits have been scraped away. Do not use a wire brush mounted in a drill motor, or one with extremely stiff bristles, as the head material is soft and may be eroded away or scratched by the wire brush.

6 Before proceeding, arrange to label and store the valves along with their related components so they can be kept separate and reinstalled in the same valve guides they are removed from (labeled plastic bags work well for this).

7 Compress the valve spring on the first valve with a spring compressor, then remove the keepers (collets) and the retainer from the valve assembly.

Caution: Take great care not to mark the cylinder head follower bore with the spring compressor.

Do not compress the springs any more than is absolutely necessary. Carefully release the valve spring compressor and remove the spring(s) and the valve from the head. If the valve binds in the guide (won't pull through), push it back into the head and deburr the area around the keeper (collet) groove with a very fine file or whetstone **(see Tool tip and illustrations)**.

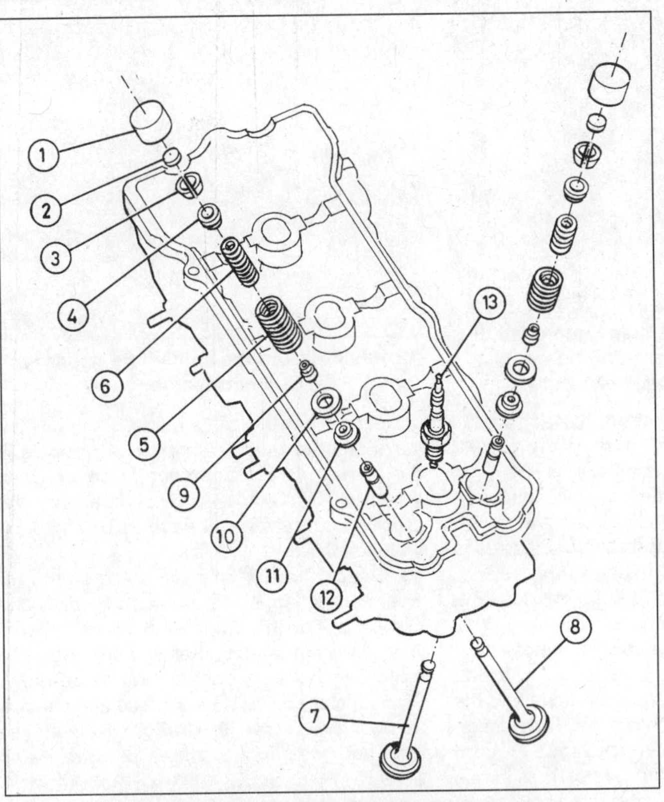

12.3a Cylinder head and valve components - M, N, P, R, S and T (1991 to 1996) models

1 Follower
2 Shim
3 Keepers (collets)
4 Spring retainer
5 Outer valve spring
6 Inner valve spring
7 Intake valve
8 Exhaust valve
9 Valve stem seal
10 Outer spring seat
11 Inner spring seat
12 Valve guide
13 Spark plug

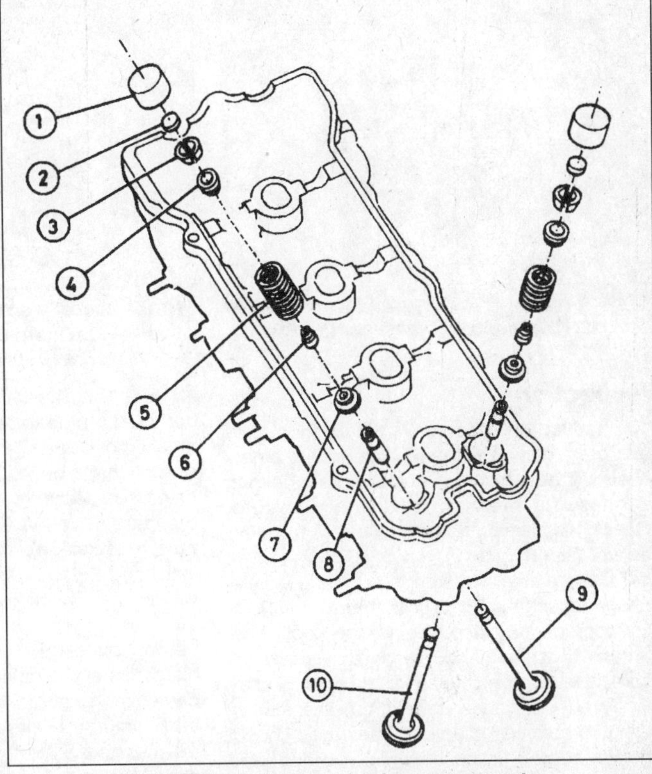

12.3b Cylinder head and valve components - V and W (1997 and 1998) models

1 Follower
2 Shim
3 Keepers (collets)
4 Spring retainer
5 Valve spring
6 Valve stem seal
7 Spring seat
8 Valve guide
9 Exhaust valve
10 Intake valve

8 Repeat the procedure for the remaining valves. Remember to keep the parts for each valve together so they can be reinstalled in the same location.

9 Once the valves have been removed and labeled, pull off the valve stem seals with pliers and discard them (the old seals should never be re-used), then remove the spring seats.

TOOL TiP

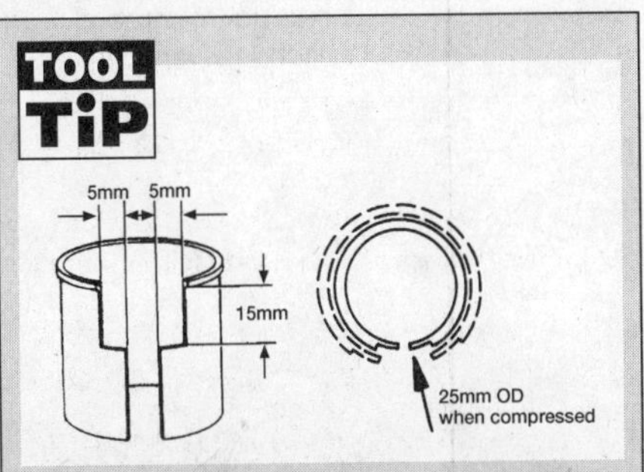

A protection sleeve for the follower bore can be made by cutting up a plastic container for a 35 mm film roll as shown.

10 Next, clean the cylinder head with solvent and dry it thoroughly. Compressed air will speed the drying process and ensure that all holes and recessed areas are clean.

11 Clean all of the valve springs, keepers (collets), retainers and spring seats with solvent and dry them thoroughly. Do the parts from one valve at a time so that no mixing of parts between valves occurs.

12 Scrape off any deposits that may have formed on the valve, then use a motorized wire brush to remove deposits from the valve heads and stems. Again, make sure the valves do not get mixed up.

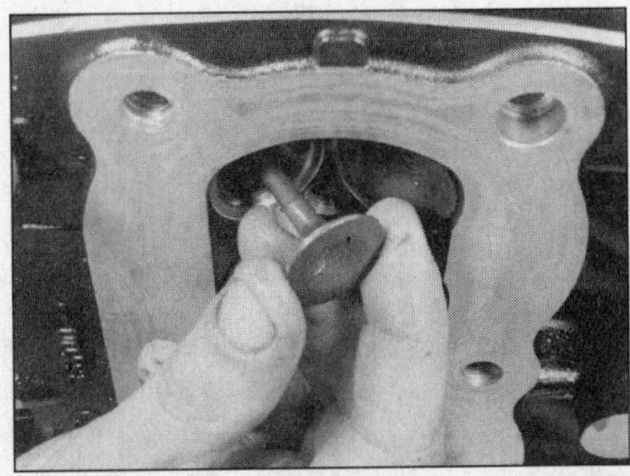

12.7a Take the valve out of the combustion chamber, but don't force it if it's stuck . . .

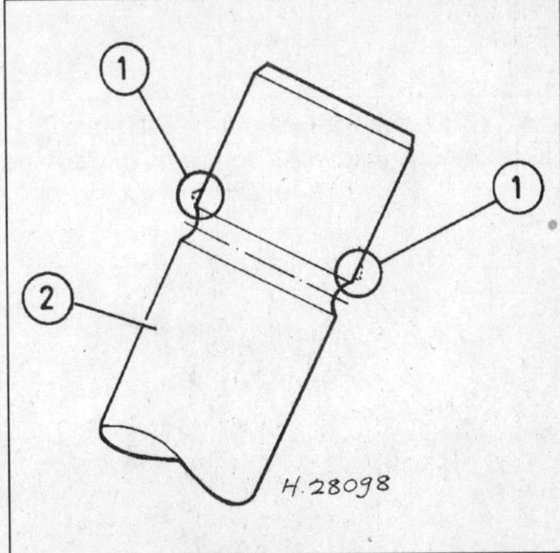

12.7b . . . check the area around the keeper (collet) groove for burrs and remove any that you find

1 Burrs (remove)
2 Valve stem

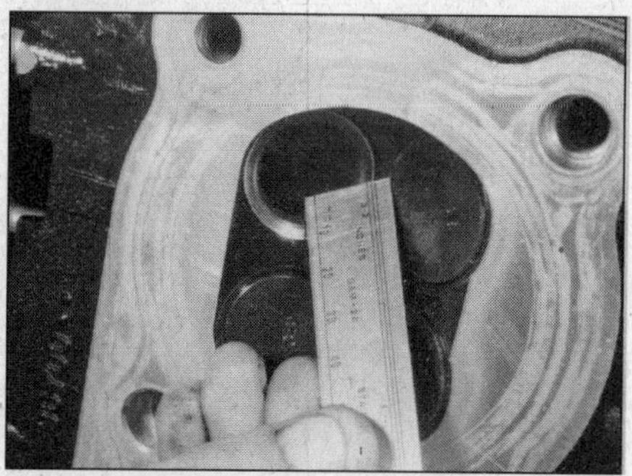
12.15 Measuring valve seat width

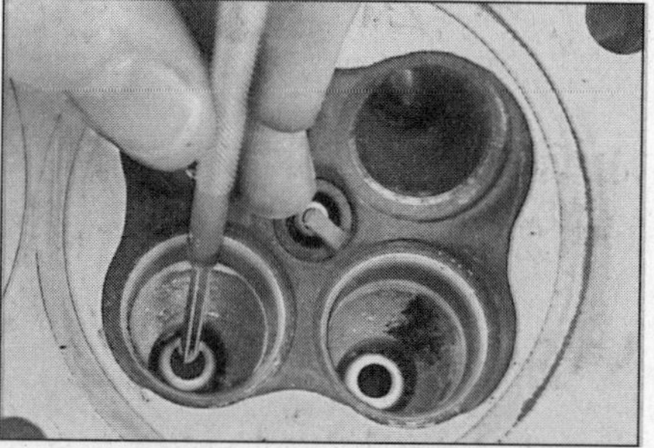
12.16a Insert a small-hole gauge into the valve guide and expand it so there's a slight drag when pulled out

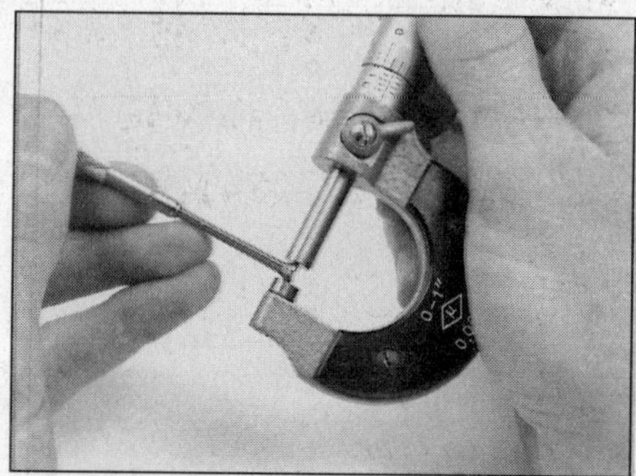
12.16b Measure the small-hole gauge with a micrometer

Inspection

13 Inspect the head very carefully for cracks and other damage. If cracks are found, a new head will be required. Check the cam bearing surfaces for wear and evidence of seizure. Check the camshafts and followers for wear as well (see Section 9).

14 Using a precision straight-edge and a feeler gauge, check the head gasket mating surface for warpage. Lay the straight-edge lengthwise, across the head and diagonally (corner-to-corner), intersecting the head stud holes, and try to slip a feeler gauge under it, on either side of each combustion chamber. The gauge should be the same thickness as the cylinder head warp limit listed in this Chapter's Specifications. If the feeler gauge can be inserted between the head and the straight-edge, the head is warped and must either be machined or, if warpage is excessive, replaced with a new one.

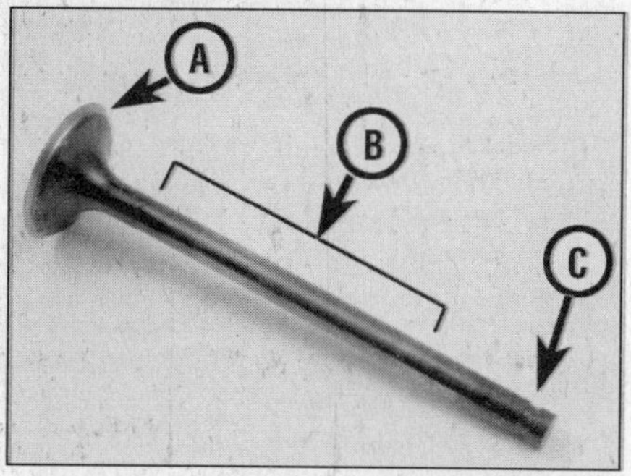

12.17 Check the valve face (A), stem (B) and keeper groove (C) for signs of damage or wear

15 Examine the valve seats in each of the combustion chambers. If they are pitted, cracked or burned, the head will require valve service that's beyond the scope of the home mechanic. Measure the valve seat width and compare it to this Chapter's Specifications **(see illustration)**. If it exceeds the service limit, or if it varies around its circumference, valve service work is required.

16 Clean the valve guides to remove any carbon build-up, then measure the inside diameters of the guides (at both ends and the center of the guide) with a small-hole gauge and micrometer **(see illustrations)**. Record the measurements for future reference. These measurements, along with the valve stem diameter measurements, will enable you to compute the valve stem-to-guide clearance. This clearance, when compared to the Specifications, will be one factor that will determine the extent of the valve service work required. The guides are measured at the ends and at the center to determine if they are worn in a bell-mouth pattern (more wear at the ends). If they are, guide replacement is an absolute must.

17 Carefully inspect each valve face for cracks, pits and burned spots **(see illustration)**. Check the valve stem and the keeper (collet) groove area for cracks. Rotate the valve and check for any obvious indication that it is bent. Check the end of the stem for pitting and excessive wear. The presence of any of the above conditions indicates the need for valve servicing.

18 Measure the valve stem diameter **(see illustration)**. By subtracting the stem diameter from the valve guide diameter, the valve stem-to-guide clearance is obtained. If the stem-to-guide clearance is greater than listed in this Chapter's Specifications, the guides and valves will have to be replaced with new ones.

19 Check the end of each valve spring for wear and pitting. Measure the free length and compare it to this Chapter's Specifications. Any springs that are shorter than specified have sagged and should not be re-used. Stand the spring on a flat surface and check it for squareness **(see illustration)**. Note that an inner and outer spring is fitted to the valves on M, N, P, R, S and T (1991 to 1996) models, whereas on V and W (1997 and 1998) models only one spring is fitted.

20 Check the spring retainers and keepers (collets) for obvious wear and cracks. Any questionable parts should not be re-used, as extensive damage will occur in the event of failure during engine operation.

21 If the inspection indicates that no service work is required, the valve components can be reinstalled in the head.

Reassembly

22 Before installing the valves in the head, they should be lapped to ensure a positive seal between the valves and seats. This procedure requires coarse and fine valve lapping compound (available at auto parts stores) and a valve lapping tool. If a lapping tool is not available, a piece of rubber or plastic hose can be slipped over the valve stem (after the valve has been installed in the guide) and used to turn the valve.

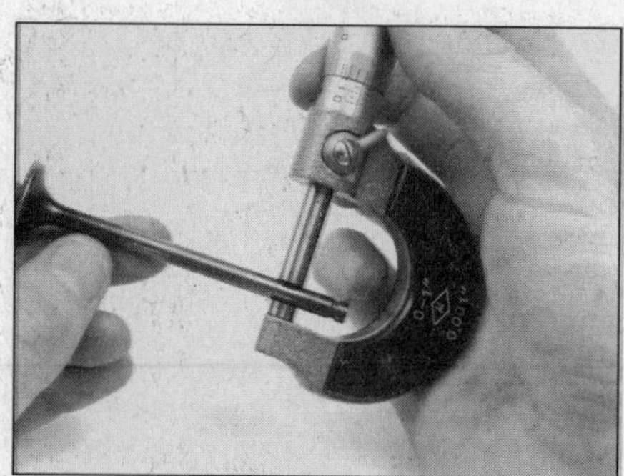
12.18 Measure the valve stem diameter with a micrometer

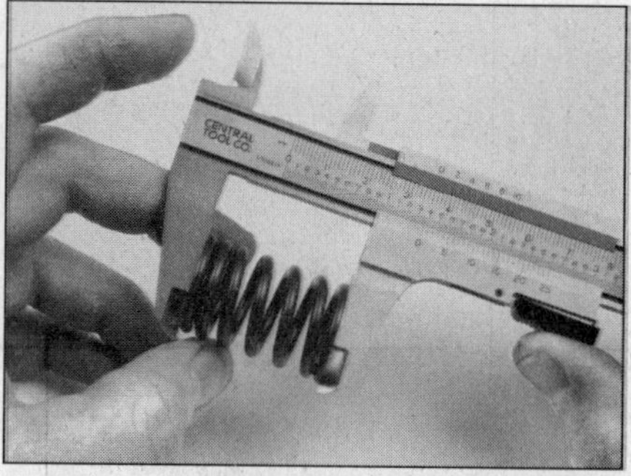

12.19a Measure the free length of the valve springs

12.19b Check the valve springs for squareness

12.23 Apply lapping compound very sparingly, in small dabs, to the valve face only

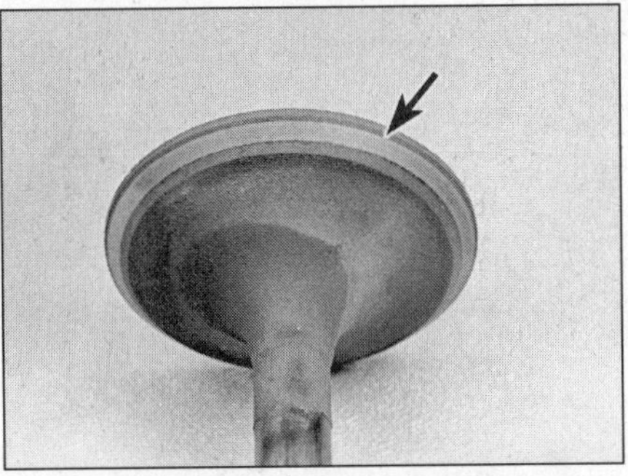
12.24a After lapping, the valve face should exhibit a uniform, unbroken contact pattern (arrow) . . .

12.24b . . . and the seat should be the specified width (arrow) with a smooth, unbroken appearance

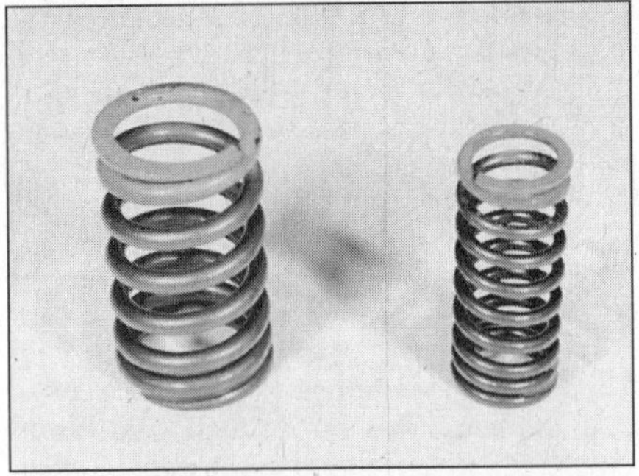
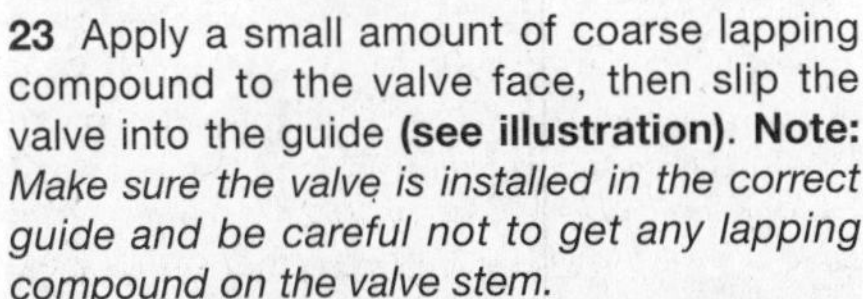
12.28a Install the valve springs with their tightly-wound coils downward (against the cylinder head)

12.28b A small dab of grease will help hold the keepers (collets) in place on the valve while the spring is released

23 Apply a small amount of coarse lapping compound to the valve face, then slip the valve into the guide **(see illustration)**. **Note:** *Make sure the valve is installed in the correct guide and be careful not to get any lapping compound on the valve stem.*

24 Attach the lapping tool (or hose) to the valve and rotate the tool between the palms of your hands. Use a back-and-forth motion rather than a circular motion. Lift the valve off the seat and turn it at regular intervals to distribute the lapping compound properly. Continue the lapping procedure until the valve face and seat contact area is of uniform width and unbroken around the entire circumference of the valve face and seat **(see illustrations)**.

25 Carefully remove the valve from the guide and wipe off all traces of lapping compound. Use solvent to clean the valve and wipe the seat area thoroughly with a solvent soaked cloth.

26 Repeat the procedure with fine valve lapping compound, then repeat the entire procedure for the remaining valves.

27 Lay the spring seats in place in the cylinder head, then install new valve stem seals on each of the guides. Use an appropriate size deep socket to push the seals into place until they are properly seated. Don't twist or cock them, or they will not seal properly against the valve stems. Also, don't remove them again or they will be damaged.

28 Coat the valve stems with clean engine oil, then install one of them into its guide. Next, install the springs and retainer, compress the springs and install the keepers (collets). **Note:** *Install the springs with the tightly-wound coils at the bottom (next to the spring seat).* When compressing the springs with the valve spring compressor, depress them only as far as is absolutely necessary to slip the keepers (collets) into place. **Note:** *Take great care not to mark the cylinder head follower bore with the spring compressor.* Apply a small amount of grease to the keepers (collets) to help hold them in place as the pressure is released from the springs **(see illustrations)**. Make certain that the keepers (collets) are securely locked in their retaining grooves.

29 Support the cylinder head on blocks so the valves can't contact the workbench top, then very gently tap each of the valve stems with a soft-faced hammer. This will help seat the keepers (collets) in their grooves.

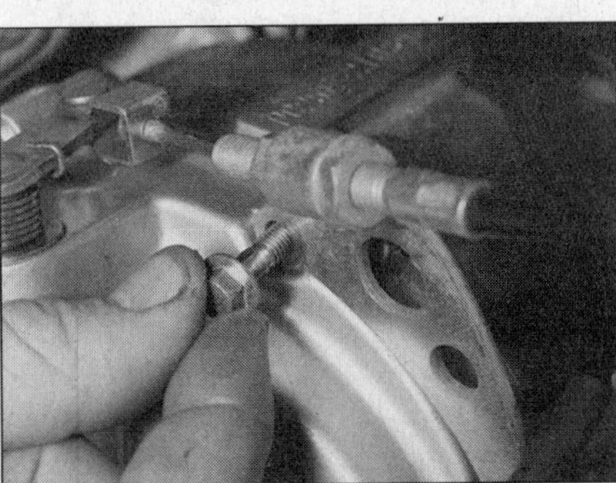
13.4a Undo the cable bracket bolts . . .

Check for proper valve sealing by pouring a small amount of solvent into each of the valve ports. If the solvent leaks past the valve(s) into the combustion chamber area, disassemble the valve(s) and repeat the lapping procedure, then reinstall the valve(s) and repeat the check. Repeat the procedure until a satisfactory seal is obtained.

13 Clutch - removal, inspection and installation

Note: *This procedure can be performed with the engine in the frame. If the engine has already been removed, ignore the preliminary steps which don't apply.*

Removal

1 Set the bike on its centerstand.

2 Remove the right lower fairing panel as described in Chapter 8.

3 Drain the engine oil as described in Chapter 1.

4 Undo the two bolts securing the clutch cable bracket to the clutch cover, then free the cable from the clutch lifting arm. Position the cable clear of the engine unit **(see illustrations)**.

5 Working in a criss-cross pattern, evenly slacken the clutch cover retaining bolts.

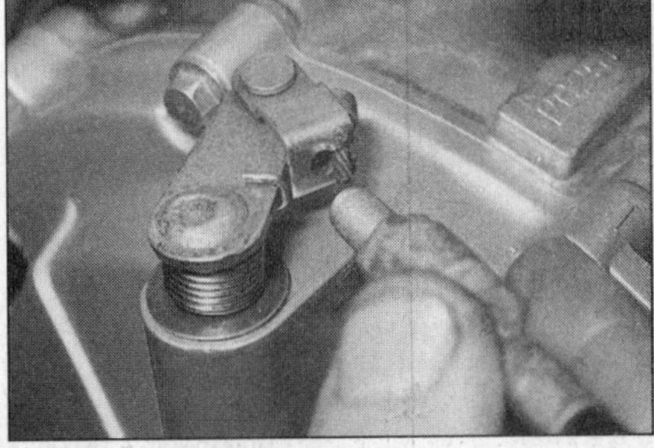
13.4b . . . then detach the cable from the lifting arm and position it clear of the engine unit

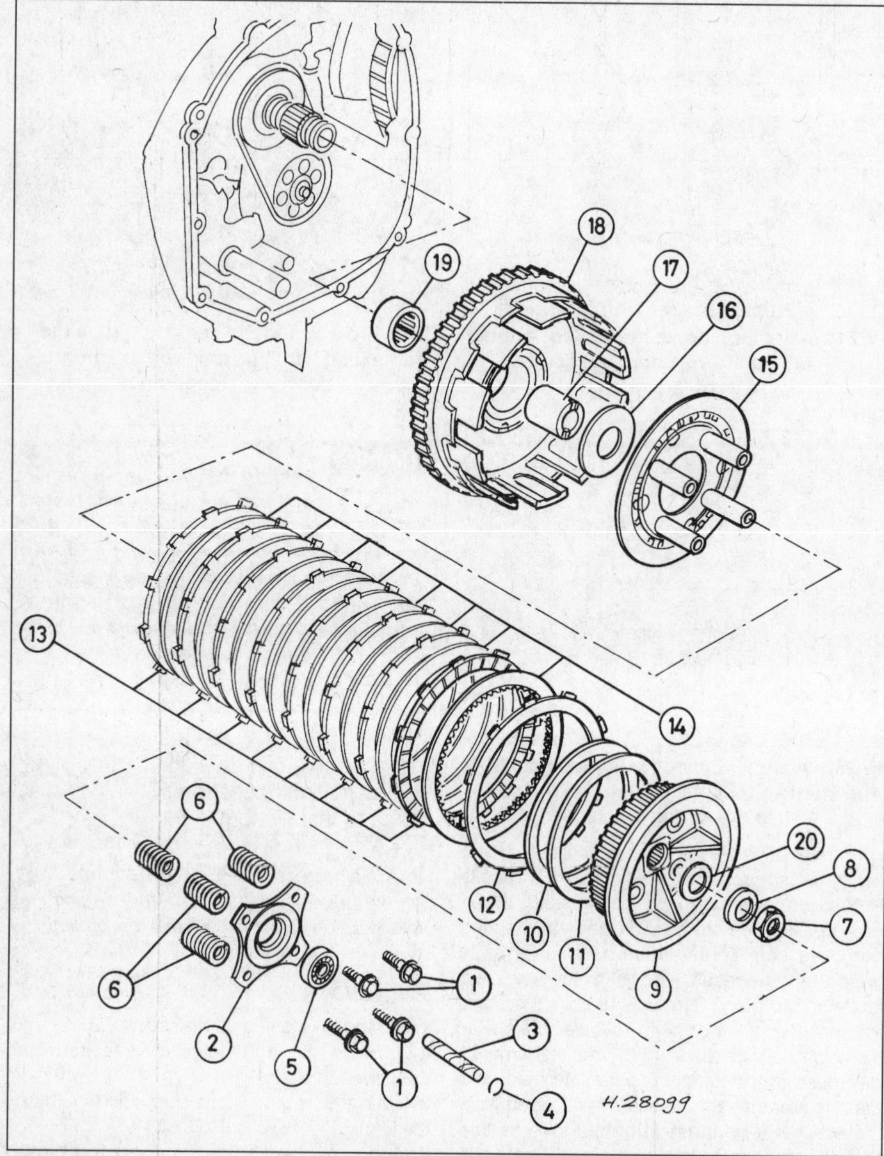

13.8a Exploded view of clutch

1 Lifting plate bolts
2 Lifting plate
3 Lifting rod
4 Snap-ring (M, N, P and R only)
5 Bearing
6 Springs
7 Center nut
8 Lock Washer
9 Center
10 Anti-judder spring
11 Spring seat
12 Outer friction plate
13 Inner friction plates
14 Plain plates
15 Pressure plate
16 Thrust washer
17 Bushing
18 Drum
19 Needle roller bearing
20 Thrust washer (S, T, V and W only)

13.8b Gradually unscrew the retaining bolts . . .

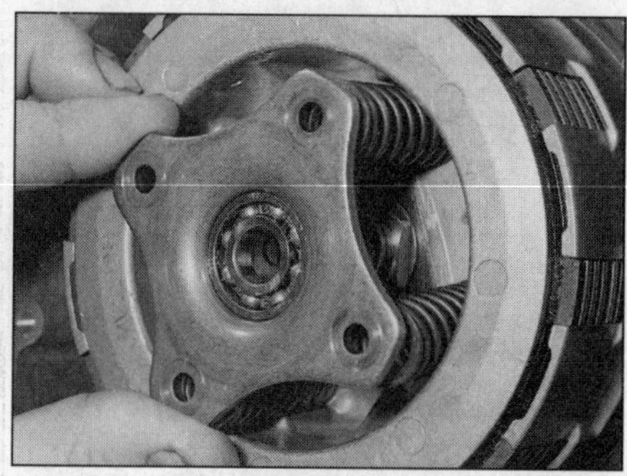

13.8c . . . then remove the lifting plate . . .

13.8d . . . and clutch springs

13.9 Unstake the clutch center nut using a suitable chisel

6 Lift the cover away from the engine, being prepared to catch any residual oil which may be released as the cover is removed. Take care not to lose the clutch pushrod from the cover.

7 Remove the gasket and discard it. Note the two locating dowels fitted to the crankcase and remove these for safe-keeping if they are loose.

8 Working in a criss-cross pattern, gradually slacken the clutch spring retaining bolts until spring pressure is released. Unscrew the bolts, then remove the clutch lifting plate and rod and recover the four springs **(see illustrations)**.

9 Unstake the clutch center nut using a hammer and suitable pointed-nose chisel, taking care not to damage the mainshaft end **(see illustration)**.

10 In the absence of the Honda service tool, Part Number 07JMB-MN50300, it will be necessary to devise some method of preventing the clutch center rotating as the center nut is slackened. If the engine is in the frame, lock the clutch through the transmission, by selecting top gear and applying the rear brake hard while the nut is slackened. If the engine is out of the frame, pass a close-fitting box wrench (ring spanner) over the countershaft (output shaft) splines, select top gear and hold the wrench while the nut is slackened.

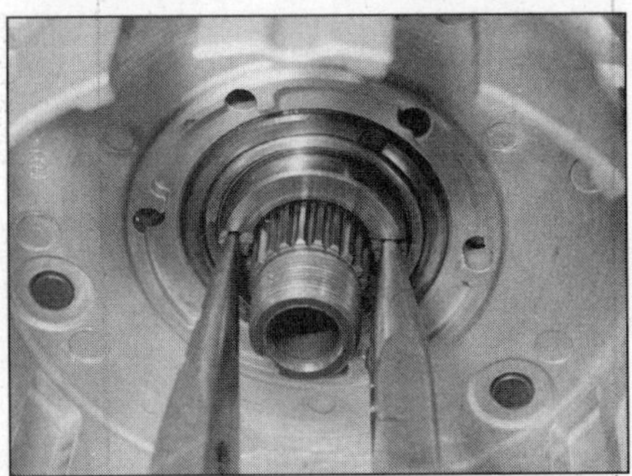
13.16 Withdraw the drum center bushing using two pairs of pliers

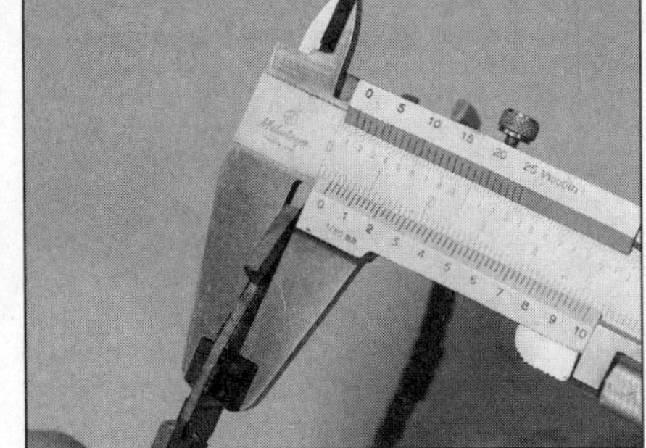
13.17 Measuring friction plate thickness

13.23 Check lifting plate bearing for roughness and replace if necessary

11 Remove the nut and discard it; a new one must be used on installation.

12 Remove the washer(s), noting the direction of fitting. Note that S, T, V and W (1995 to 1998) models have a thrust washer behind the lockwasher. **Note:** *The lock washer is marked 'OUTSIDE'.*

13 Withdraw the clutch center followed by the outer friction plate. **Note:** *The outer friction plate is different to the others. Mark the plate in some way to ensure that it is fitted in its original position.*

14 Remove the spring seat and anti-judder spring, noting which way around the spring is fitted, followed by the remaining plain and friction plates.

15 Remove the clutch pressure plate followed by the large thrust washer.

16 In order to withdraw the clutch drum it is first necessary to slide out the drum center bushing. Grip the lugs on the bushing with two pairs of suitable pliers and slide out the bushing while supporting the drum **(see illustration)**. With the bushing removed, carefully maneuver the clutch drum out from the crankcase.

Inspection

17 After an extended period of service the clutch friction plates will wear and promote clutch slip. Measure the thickness of each friction plate using a vernier caliper **(see illustration)**. If any plate has worn to or beyond the service limit given in the Specifications, the friction plates must be replaced as a set.

18 The plain plates should not show any signs of excess heating (bluing). Check for warpage using a flat surface and feeler gauges. If any plate exceeds the maximum permissible amount of warpage, or shows signs of bluing, all plain plates must be replaced as a set.

19 Inspect the clutch assembly for burrs and indentations on the edges of the protruding tangs of the friction plates and/or slots in the edge of the clutch drum with which they engage. Similarly check for wear between the inner tongues of the plain plates and the slots in the clutch center. Wear of this nature will cause clutch drag and slow disengagement during gear changes, since the plates will snag when the pressure plate is lifted. With care a small amount of wear can be corrected by dressing with a fine file, but if this is excessive the worn components must be replaced.

20 Also inspect the anti-judder spring and seat for signs of wear or distortion and replace if necessary.

21 Inspect the mainshaft, clutch drum center collar and clutch drum bearing surfaces for signs of wear and damage, along with the needle bearing. If access to the necessary measuring equipment can be gained, the condition of the above components can be judged by direct measurement. If any component shows signs of wear or damage, or has worn beyond its service limit given in the Specifications, it must be replaced.

22 Inspect the clutch drum needle roller bearing for signs of wear or damage. If replacement is necessary, the task should be entrusted to a Honda dealer. The bearing is a press fit in the drum and a hydraulic press and suitable spacers will be required to remove the original bearing and install the new one.

23 Check the clutch lifting plate bearing for wear **(see illustration)**. Ensure that the inner race of the bearing spins freely without any sign of notchiness and that there is no freeplay between the inner and outer races or the outer race and plate. If necessary, replace the bearing by driving the old bearing out of the plate and tapping the new bearing into position using a hammer and suitable tubular drift which bears only on the bearing's outer race.

24 Measure the free length of each clutch spring **(see illustration)**. If any one has settled to less than the service limit, the clutch springs must be replaced as a set.

25 On M, N, P and R (1991 to 1994) models, remove the snap-ring from the clutch lifting rod and discard it; the snap-ring must be replaced whenever it is disturbed.

26 Check that the clutch lifting arm and pushrod operate smoothly in the cover. Withdraw the pushrod from the cover and slide out the lifting arm and return spring. Inspect the needle bearings and seal fitted to the clutch cover for signs of wear or damage, along with the lifting arm and return spring **(see illustrations)**. **Note:** *The seal can be replaced but it is not possible to replace the bearings. If they are worn the complete cover must be replaced.*

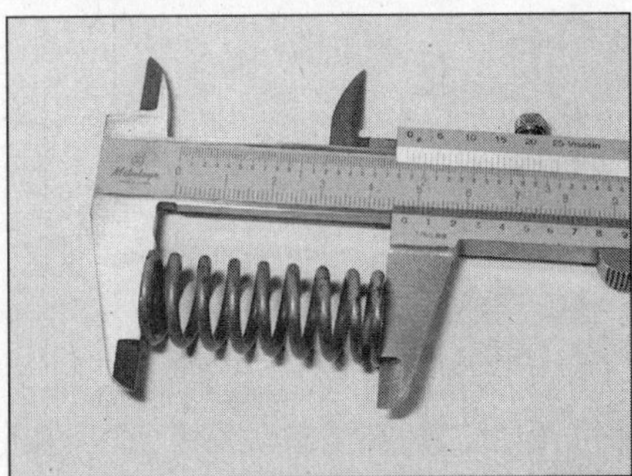
13.24 Measuring clutch spring free length

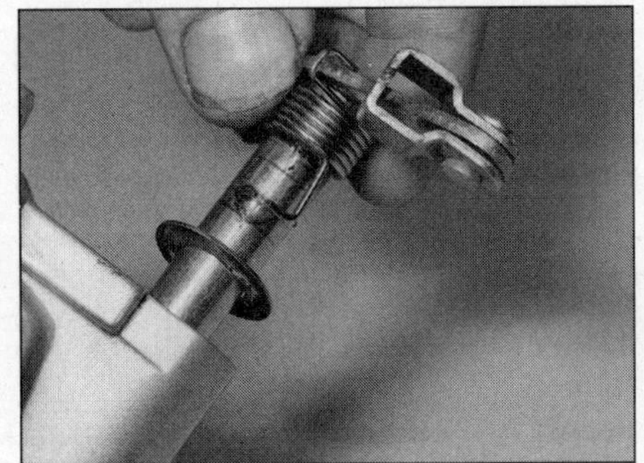
13.26a Withdraw the lifting arm, spring and washer from the clutch cover

13.26b Inspect the cover seal and bearings for wear or damage

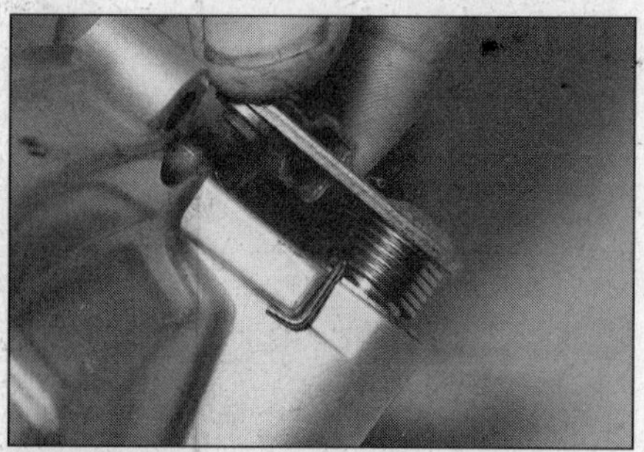
13.27a Make sure the lifting arm spring is correctly engaged with the cover cutout as shown . . .

13.27b . . . and install the pushrod with its rounded end facing away from the cover

13.29a Align the clutch drum holes with the oil pump sprocket dogs (arrows) . . .

13.29b . . . then engage the drum with the crankshaft gear

13.31a Install the center bushing making sure its removal lugs are facing outwards . . .

13.31b . . . and fit the thrust washer

27 Apply grease to the oil seal lip, needle bearings and pushrod and carefully insert the lifting arm and return spring. Make sure the spring is correctly seated, then fit the pushrod to the cover, making sure its rounded end is facing away from the cover (towards the clutch) **(see illustrations)**. Check the operation of the clutch lifting arm.

13.32a Fit the spring seat to the clutch center . . .

Installation

28 Remove all traces of gasket from the crankcase and clutch cover surfaces.

29 Maneuver the clutch drum into position. Engage the drum with the teeth of the crankshaft gear, noting it is also necessary to align it with the dogs on the oil pump drive gear sprocket. Rotate the oil pump sprocket to check the dogs are correctly engaged **(see illustrations)**. **Note:** *Make sure the drum is correctly engaged with the oil pump drive sprocket before proceeding.*

30 Apply a smear of clean engine oil to the clutch drum needle roller bearing and center bushing.

31 Slide the center bushing into position, making sure its removal lugs are facing outwards, and slide on the large thrust washer **(see illustrations)**.

32 Fit the spring seat to the clutch center followed by the anti-judder spring **(see illustrations)**. **Note:** *The anti-judder spring must be fitted with its convex side facing the spring seat.*

33 Using the mark made on dismantling, fit the outer friction plate to the clutch center **(see illustration)**. **Note:** *The outer friction plate has a slightly larger internal diameter than the other plates.*

34 Install a plain plate followed by one of the ordinary friction plates then alternately install all the remaining plain and friction plates **(see illustration)**. **Note:** *If new clutch plates are being fitted, apply a coating of oil to their surfaces to prevent seizure.*

35 Fit the pressure plate to the rear of the clutch center, making sure the raised dot on the rear of the pressure plate is aligned with

13.32b . . . then fit the anti-judder spring with its convex side facing the spring seat

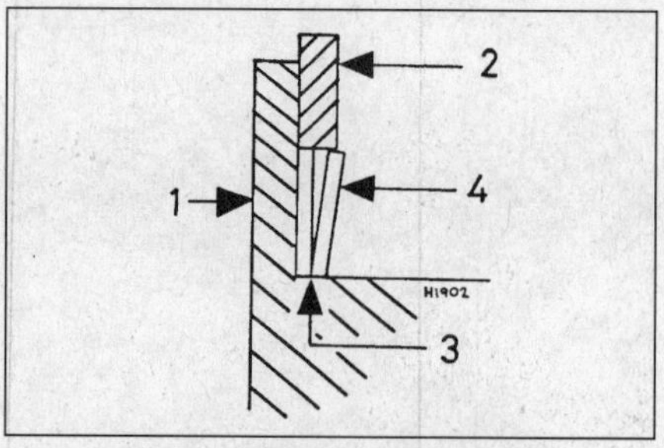

13.32c Correct fitting of anti-judder spring

1 Clutch center
2 Outer friction plate
3 Spring seat
4 Anti-judder spring

13.33 Fit the outer friction plate to the clutch center . . .

13.34 . . . followed by a plain plate

13.35a Make sure the pressure plate raised dot (arrow) . . .

13.35b . . . is aligned with the center raised dot (arrow) . . .

13.35c . . . when fitting the plate to the center

13.36 Install the assembly in the clutch drum aligning the friction plate tangs with the drum slots (arrows)

13.37 Fit the lock washer with the OUTSIDE mark facing outwards

13.38a Fit the new center nut . . .

13.38b . . . then tighten it to the specified torque setting . . .

13.38c . . . and stake it in position with a suitable punch

the raised dot on the front of the center **(see illustrations)**.

36 Install the assembly into the clutch drum while aligning the friction plate tangs with the slots in the drum, and the clutch center with the mainshaft splines **(see illustration)**.

37 On S, T, V and W (1995 to 1998) models, fit the thrust washer. On all models, fit the lock washer, ensuring that the OUTSIDE mark is facing outwards (away from crankcase) **(see illustration)**.

38 Fit a new clutch nut and tighten it to the specified torque setting while holding the clutch center using the method employed on removal. Secure it in position by staking it into the groove in the mainshaft using a suitable hammer and punch **(see illustrations)**.

39 Install the clutch springs, lifting plate and the clutch spring retaining bolts. Gradually tighten the four bolts evenly in a criss-cross pattern until they are all securely tightened.

40 On M, N, P and R (1991 to 1994) models, fit a **new** snap-ring to the clutch lifting rod making sure it is securely located in the rod groove, then slide the rod into position in the lifting plate bearing **(see illustrations)**. On S, T, V and W models, slide the headed lifting rod into the lifting plate bearing.

41 Make sure the locating dowels are in position and fit a new gasket to the crankcase **(see illustration)**.

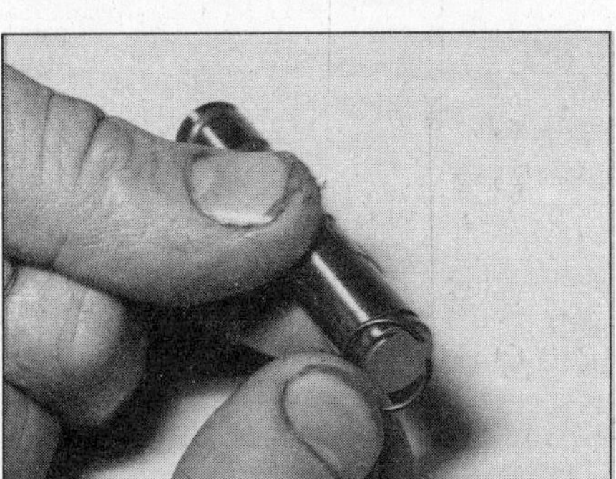
13.40a Fit a new snap-ring to the lifting rod (M, N, P and R models) . . .

13.40b . . . and slide the rod into the lifting plate

13.41 Fit the locating dowels (arrows) then position a new gasket on the crankcase . . .

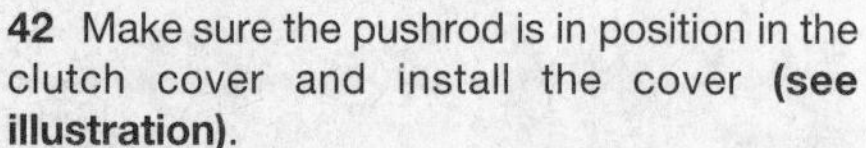

42 Make sure the pushrod is in position in the clutch cover and install the cover **(see illustration)**.

43 Fit all the cover retaining bolts, except the two which retain the clutch cable bracket, and tighten them by hand only.

44 Engage the clutch cable with the lifting arm then align the bracket with clutch cover and fit its retaining bolts.

45 Working in a criss-cross pattern tighten the clutch cover bolts to the torque listed in this Chapter's Specifications.

46 Fill the engine with the correct type and amount of oil as described in Chapter 1.

47 Adjust the clutch cable as described in Chapter 1.

48 Install the lower fairing panel as described in Chapter 8.

14 Clutch cable - replacement

1 Remove the right lower fairing panel as described in Chapter 8.

2 Slacken the lower cable adjuster locknut and detach the inner cable from the clutch lifting arm. Free the outer cable from its mounting bracket.

3 Work back along the cable, freeing it from any relevant retaining clips while noting the correct routing of the cable.

4 Detach the cable from the lever and remove it from the bike.

5 Install the new cable making sure it is correctly routed and retained by all necessary clips.

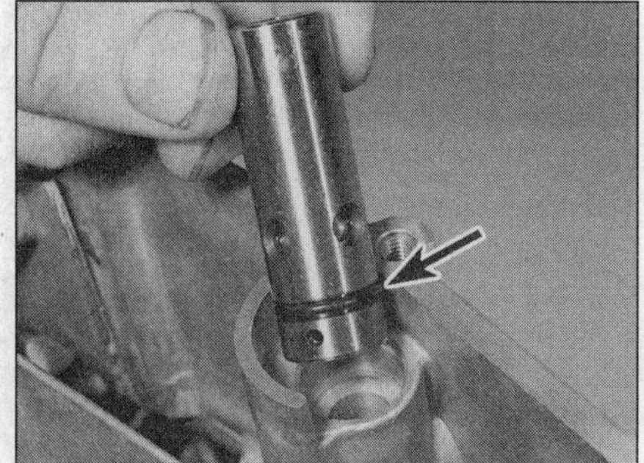

15.11 Fit a new O-ring (arrow) to the oil pressure relief valve prior to installation

13.42 . . . and install the cover

6 Adjust the cable (see Chapter 1), then install the lower fairing panel (see Chapter 8).

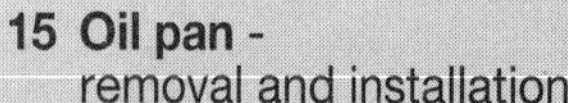

15 Oil pan - removal and installation

Note: *The oil pan can be removed with the engine in the frame. If work is being carried out with the engine removed ignore the preliminary steps.*

Removal

1 Remove the right and left lower fairing panels as described in Chapter 8.

2 Remove the complete exhaust system as described in Chapter 4.

3 Drain the engine oil as described in Chapter 1.

4 Working in a criss-cross pattern, gradually loosen the oil pan retaining bolts.

5 Remove all the bolts and lower the oil pan away from the crankcase. If the engine is in the frame, note that as the oil pan is removed, the oil pump pick-up strainer and oil pressure relief valve may fall out of the bottom of the crankcase.

6 On M, N, P, R, S and T (1991 to 1996) models, recover the gasket and discard it.

7 If they were not released when the oil pan was removed, remove the oil pump pick-up strainer and the oil pressure relief valve from the base of the crankcase. Remove the seal from the pick-up and the O-ring from the pressure relief valve and discard them.

8 Clean the pick-up strainer mesh in solvent. Check it for clogging or splitting and replace if necessary.

15.12a On M, N, P, R, S and T models, fit a gasket to the crankcase. Note the correct fitted positions of strainer and relief valve . . .

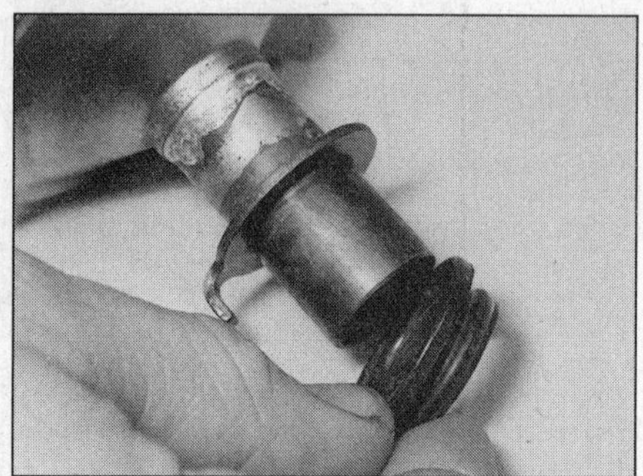

15.10a Fit the seal to the oil pump pick-up strainer making sure the seal flange is facing the strainer

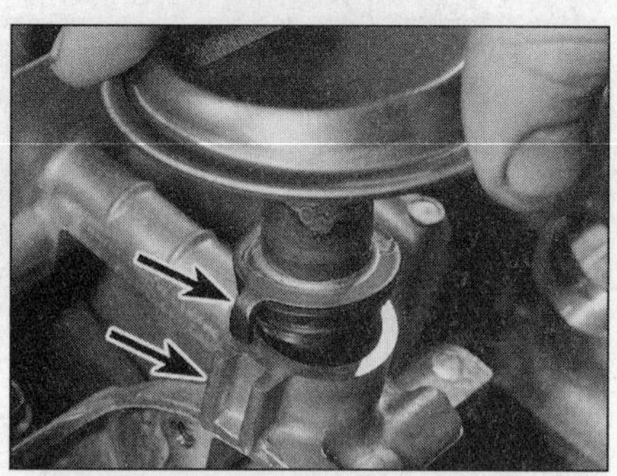

15.10b Install the strainer aligning its tab with the crankcase slot (arrow)

Installation

9 Remove all traces of gasket or sealant from the oil pan and crankcase mating surfaces.

10 Fit a new seal to the oil pump pick-up strainer making sure its flange is facing the strainer. Fit the strainer to the base of the crankcase aligning its tab with the slot in the crankcase **(see illustrations)**.

11 Fit a new O-ring to the oil pressure relief valve groove. Apply a smear of oil to the O-ring and ease the relief valve into position in the base of the crankcase **(see illustration)**.

12 On M, N, P, R, S and T (1991 to 1996) models, position a new gasket on the oil pan and fit the pan to the engine **(see illustrations)**. If the engine is in the frame, use a smear of grease on the gasket to hold it in place as the oil pan is installed. Make sure the gasket is correctly positioned then insert the retaining bolts and tighten them by hand.

15.12b . . . and install the oil pan

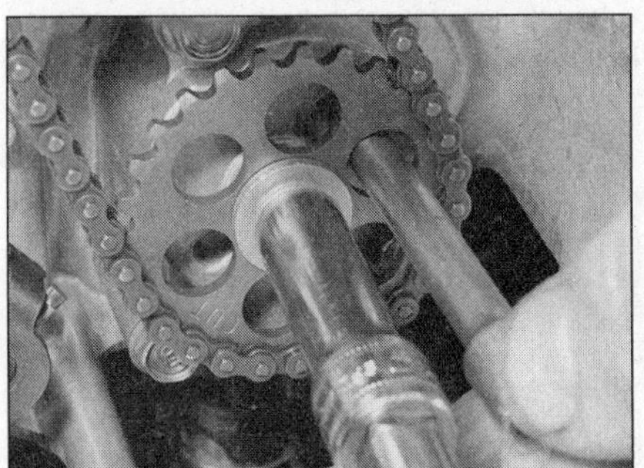

16.11 Insert a screwdriver through the oil pump sprocket hole to prevent rotation as the bolt is slackened

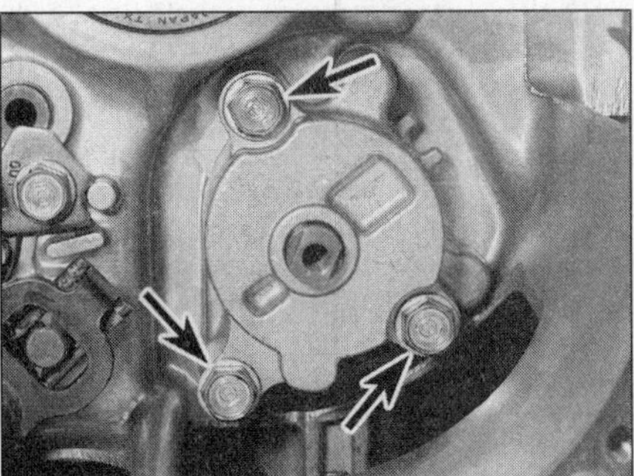

16.13a Undo the three bolts (arrows) . . .

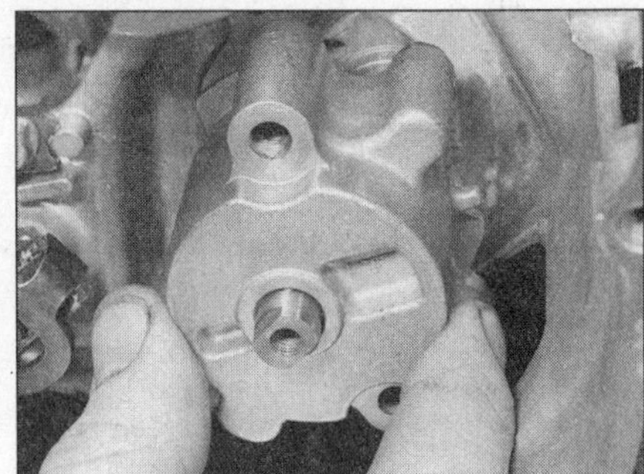

16.13b . . . and remove the oil pump

13 On V and W (1997 and 1998) models, apply a coating of a suitable sealant to the oil pan mating surface, then fit the pan to the engine and insert the retaining bolts and tighten them by hand.
14 Working in a criss-cross pattern, securely tighten all the oil pan retaining bolts.
15 Install the exhaust system as described in Chapter 4.
16 Fill the engine with the correct type and quantity of oil as described in Chapter 1. Start the engine and check for leaks.
17 If all is well, fit the fairing panels as described in Chapter 8.

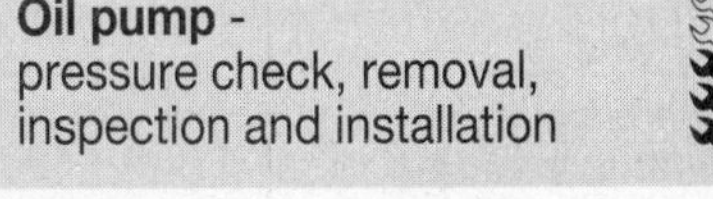

16 Oil pump - pressure check, removal, inspection and installation

Note: *The oil pump can be removed with the engine in the frame.*

Pressure check

1 To check the oil pressure, a suitable gauge and adapter piece (which screws into the oil pressure switch thread) will be needed.
2 Warm the engine up to normal operating temperature then stop it.
3 Remove the oil pressure switch as described in Chapter 9.
4 Screw the adapter into the oil pressure switch threads in the top of the crankcase and connect the gauge to the adapter.
5 Start the engine and increase the engine speed to 6000 rpm while watching the gauge reading. The oil pressure should be similar to that given in the Specifications at the start of this Chapter.
6 If the pressure is significantly lower than the standard, either the relief valve is stuck open, the oil pump is faulty, the oil pump pick-up strainer is blocked or there is other engine damage. Begin diagnosis by checking the oil pump pick-up strainer and relief valve (see Sections 15 and 17), then the oil pump. If those items check out okay, chances are the bearing oil clearances are excessive and the engine needs to be overhauled.
7 If the pressure is too high, the relief valve is stuck closed. To check it, see Section 17.
8 Stop the engine and unscrew the gauge and adapter from the crankcase.
9 Install the oil pressure switch as described in Chapter 9.

Removal

10 Remove the clutch as described in Section 13.
11 Slacken and remove the oil pump sprocket retaining bolt while preventing the sprocket turning by inserting a screwdriver through one of the sprocket holes **(see illustration)**.
12 Slide the drive sprocket off the mainshaft and remove the drive sprocket, chain and pump sprocket as an assembly. Remove the guide bushing from the center of the drive sprocket.
13 Undo the three bolts and remove the oil pump from the crankcase **(see illustrations)**.

Inspection

14 Wash the oil pump in solvent, then dry it off **(see illustration)**.
15 Remove the pump cover screw **(see illustration)**.
16 Lift off the cover and recover the locating dowel **(see illustration)**.
17 Remove the thrust washer from the pump driveshaft.
18 Slide out the driveshaft, noting which way around it is fitted, and remove the drive pin.
19 Remove the inner and outer rotors from the pump body.
20 Check the pump body and rotors for scoring and wear. If any damage or uneven or excessive wear is evident, replace the pump (individual parts aren't available). If you are rebuilding the engine, it's a good idea to install a new oil pump.

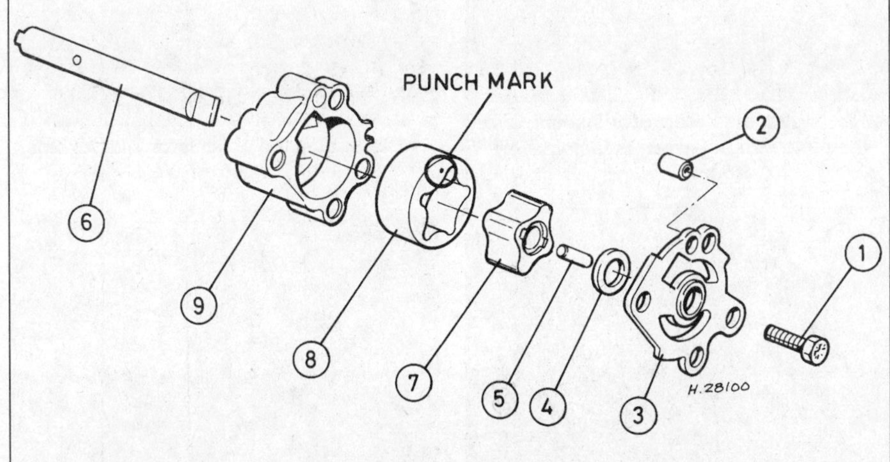

16.14 Exploded view of the oil pump

1 *Cover screw*
2 *Dowel*
3 *Cover*
4 *Thrust washer*
5 *Drive pin*
6 *Driveshaft*
7 *Inner rotor*
8 *Outer rotor*
9 *Body*

16.15 Undo the screw . . .

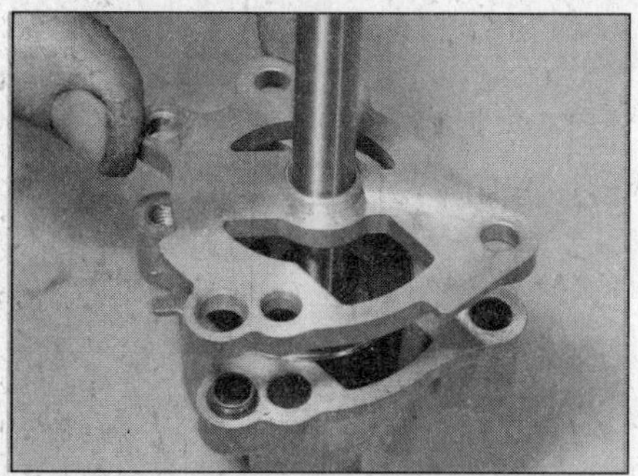

16.16 . . . and slide off the pump cover

16.21 Measuring outer rotor-to-body clearance

16.22 Measuring rotor tip clearance

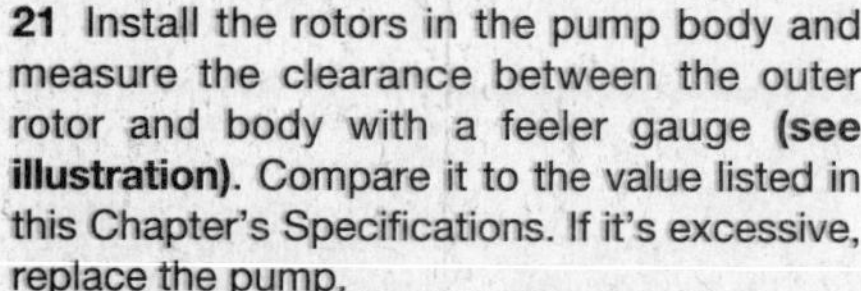

21 Install the rotors in the pump body and measure the clearance between the outer rotor and body with a feeler gauge **(see illustration)**. Compare it to the value listed in this Chapter's Specifications. If it's excessive, replace the pump.

22 Measure the clearance between the inner rotor tip and the outer rotor **(see illustration)**. Again, replace the pump if the clearance is excessive.

23 Lay a straight-edge across the rotors and pump body and measure the rotor endfloat (gap between the rotors and pump body) with a feeler gauge **(see illustration)**. If it's outside the limits listed in this Chapter's Specifications, replace the pump.

24 Inspect the pump drive chain and sprockets for wear and damage and replace if necessary. If replacement is necessary note that both sprockets and the chain should be replaced as a set.

25 If the pump is good make sure all components are clean and lubricate them with clean engine oil. Reassemble the pump as follows.

26 Fit the outer rotor making sure its punch mark is facing away from the pump body **(see illustration)**.

27 Install the inner rotor making sure its drive pin slot is facing away from the pump body **(see illustration)**.

28 Insert the driveshaft, making sure it is fitted the correct way around and insert the drive pin. Slide the driveshaft into position so that the drive pin is engaged in its slot in the inner rotor **(see illustrations)**.

29 Fit the thrust washer to the driveshaft **(see illustration)**.

30 Fit the locating dowel then install the pump cover and securely tighten the retaining screw.

Installation

31 Lubricate the pump rotors with clean engine oil and check that the pump driveshaft rotates freely.

32 Install the pump in the crankcase making sure its driveshaft end is correctly aligned with the slot in the end of the water pump shaft.

33 Fit the pump bolts and tighten them securely.

34 Engage both the drive sprocket and pump sprocket with the chain noting that the 'OUT' mark on the pump sprocket must be positioned so that it will be facing away from the pump when the chain is installed.

35 Fit the guide bushing to the center of the drive sprocket and slide the sprocket and chain assembly on the mainshaft. Engage the pump sprocket with the driveshaft and check the sprocket is fitted the correct way around **(see illustrations)**.

16.23 Measuring rotor endfloat

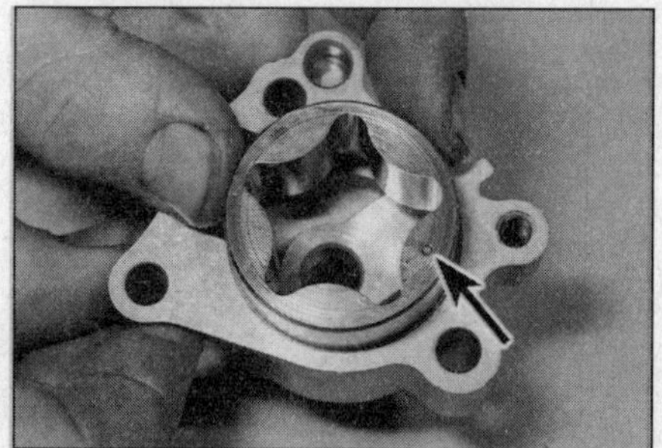

16.26 Install the outer rotor, making sure the punch mark (arrow) is facing away from the body

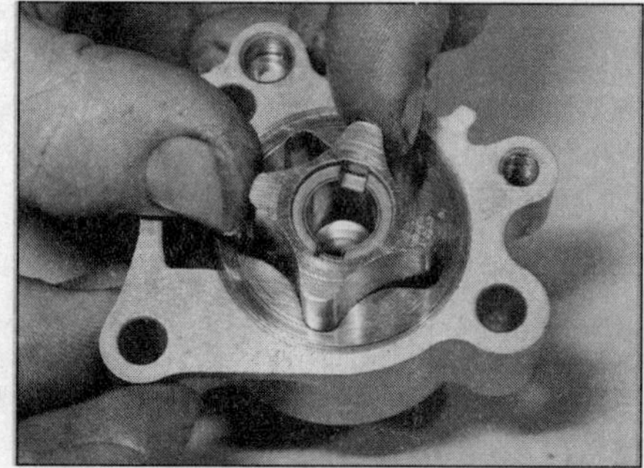

16.27 Install the inner rotor with its slot facing away from the body

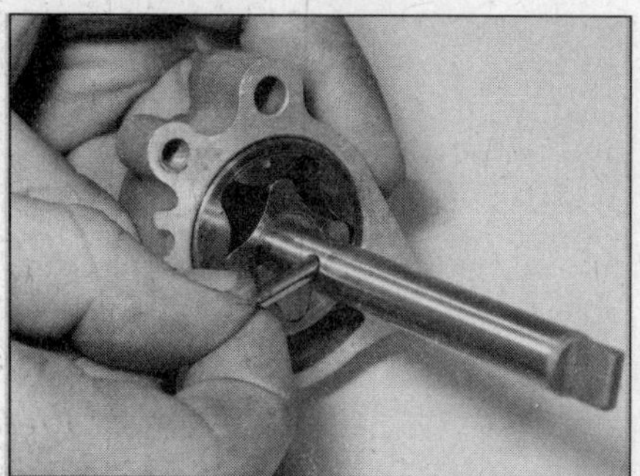

16.28a Insert the driveshaft and drive pin . . .

16.28b . . . making sure the pin is correctly located in the inner rotor slot (arrow)

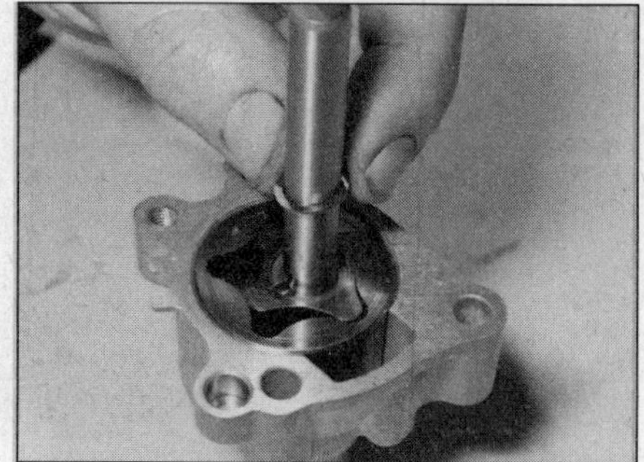

16.29 Do not omit the thrust washer from between the rotor and cover

16.35a Slide the guide bushing on the mainshaft . . .

36 Clean the sprocket bolt and apply a few drops of a suitable locking compound to its threads **(see illustration)**.

37 Fit the sprocket bolt and tighten it to the torque listed in this Chapter's Specifications. Prevent the sprocket from rotating by inserting a screwdriver through one of the sprocket holes.

38 Install the clutch as described in Section 13.

17 Oil pressure relief valve - removal, inspection and installation

Note: *The pressure relief valve can be removed with the engine in the frame.*

Removal

1 Remove the oil pan and pressure relief valve as described in Section 15.

Inspection

2 Push the plunger into the relief valve body and check for free movement. If the valve operation is sticky, remove the snap-ring, noting that it is under spring pressure, and withdraw the washer, spring and piston. Clean all the parts and inspect the piston and bore for wear and damage. Apply oil to all parts and reassemble the valve. Check its operation again as above - if it is still sticky it must be replaced (individual parts are not available).

Installation

3 Install the pressure relief valve and oil pan as described in Section 15.

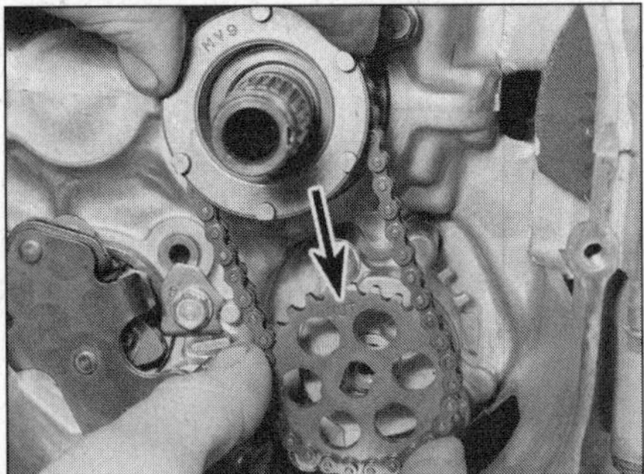

16.35b . . . and install the oil pump chain and sprocket assembly. The pump sprocket OUT mark (arrow) must face outwards

18 Oil cooler - removal and installation

Note: *The oil cooler can be removed with the engine in the frame. If work is being carried out with the engine removed ignore the preliminary steps.*

Removal

1 Remove the left and right lower fairing panels as described in Chapter 8. If required for improved access, remove the exhaust system (see Chapter 4).

2 Drain the engine oil as described in Chapter 1 and remove the oil filter. **Note:** *If the filter is damaged or disfigured on removal it must be replaced.*

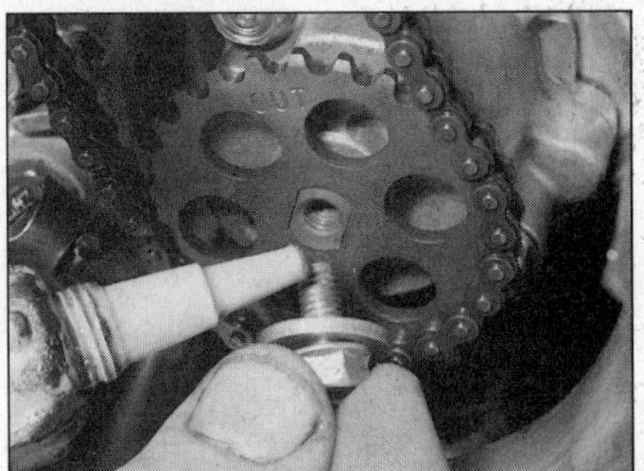

16.36 Apply thread locking compound to the threads of the oil pump sprocket retaining bolt prior to installation

3 Drain the coolant as described in Chapter 1.

4 Slacken the clip and disconnect the coolant hose from the left side of the cooler.

5 Undo the retaining bolts and remove the oil cooler assembly from the front of the crankcase **(see illustrations)**. Recover the sealing ring from the top of the cooler and discard it.

6 Remove the oil cooler collars from the crankcase/oil cooler (as applicable) noting which way around they are fitted. Recover the O-rings, there are four in total, and discard them.

Installation

7 Fit a new O-ring to the recess in each collar and fit the second new O-ring to the thinner end of each collar. Apply a smear of engine oil to each O-ring to ease installation.

8 Fit both collars to the crankcase making sure their thicker ends are facing the crankcase **(see illustrations)**.

18.5a Unscrew the oil cooler retaining bolts (arrows) . . .

18.5b . . . and remove the cooler assembly from the front of the engine

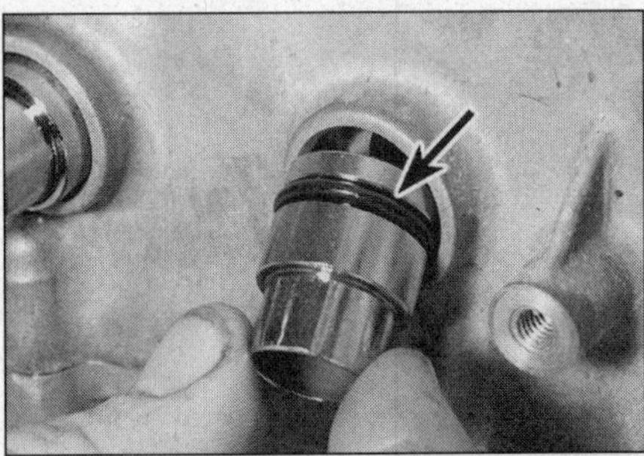

18.8a Fit a new O-ring (arrow) to each collar groove then install both collars with their thicker ends facing the crankcase

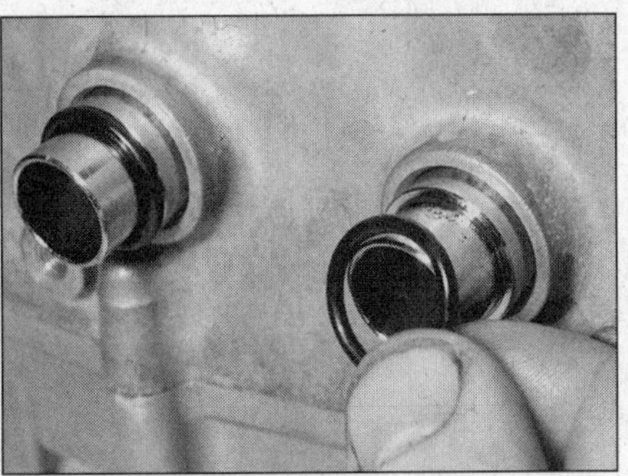

18.8b Fit a second new O-ring to each collar

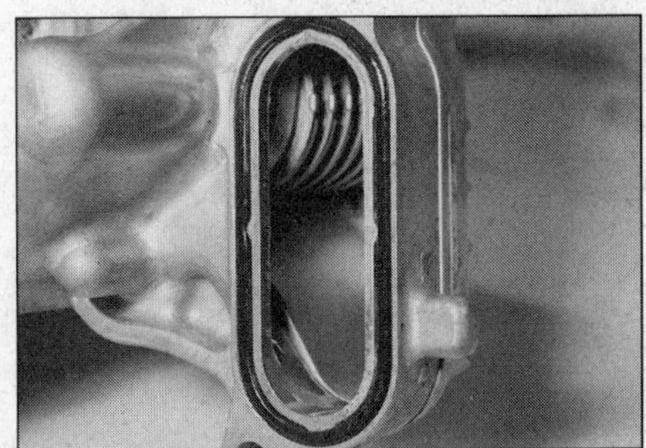

18.9 Make sure the sealing ring is correctly seated in the oil cooler groove prior to installation

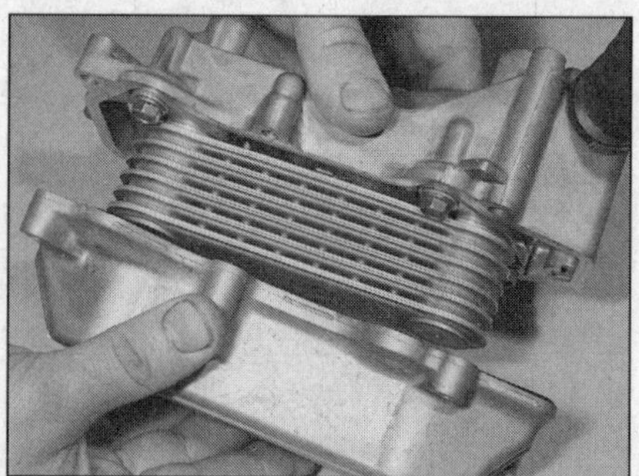
19.3 Remove the retaining bolt and remove the oil cooler housing cover

19.4 Oil cooler is retained by four bolts (arrows)

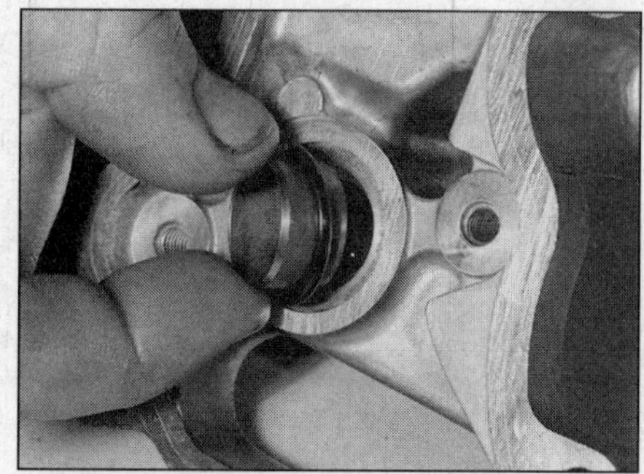
19.7 Fit a new O-ring to each collar and fit both collars to the housing

9 Fit a new sealing ring to the recess in the oil cooler **(see illustration)**.

10 Install the oil cooler on the front of the crankcase, making sure the sealing ring remains correctly seated in its groove. Align the cooler with the collars and push it firmly into position.

11 Fit the oil cooler mounting bolts and tighten them securely.

12 Connect the coolant hose and securely tighten its retaining clip.

13 Fit the oil filter (a new oil filter is recommended) and, if removed, install the exhaust system (see Chapter 4). Fill the cooling system as described in Chapter 1.

14 Fill the engine with the correct amount and type of oil as described in Chapter 1.

15 Start the engine and check for leaks.

16 Install the fairing panels as described in Chapter 8.

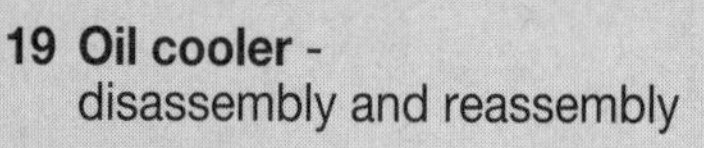

19 Oil cooler - disassembly and reassembly

Disassembly

1 Remove the oil cooler as described in Section 18.

2 Remove the coolant drain screw (if not already having done so) and unscrew the cover retaining bolt.

3 Lift off the oil cooler housing cover **(see illustration)**. Recover the cover seal and discard it.

4 Slacken and remove the four bolts and washers and remove the oil cooler **(see illustration)**. Recover the O-rings and discard them.

5 Remove the two collars from the housing.

Reassembly

6 Fit the collars to the oil cooler housing.

7 Fit a new O-ring to each collar and apply a smear of clean engine oil to each one **(see illustration)**.

8 Locate the oil cooler on the locating dowels making sure the arrow on the cooler is pointing in the same direction as the arrow on the housing **(see illustration)**. Fit the cooler mounting bolts and tighten them securely.

9 Fit a new seal to the recess in the oil cooler cover **(see illustration)**.

10 Fit the cover to the housing making sure the seal remains correctly seated. Fit the cover bolt and tighten it securely.

11 Fit the oil cooler assembly as described in Section 18.

20 Gearshift mechanism - removal, inspection and installation

Note: *The gearshift mechanism components can be removed with the engine in the frame. If work is being carried out with the engine removed ignore the preliminary steps.*

Removal

1 Remove the clutch as described in Section 13.

2 Undo the clamp bolt and disconnect the gearshift lever pedal from the engine.

3 Withdraw the gearshift shaft from the right side of the crankcase and recover the thrust washer from the shaft **(see illustration)**.

4 Unscrew the stopper arm bolt and remove the stopper arm, washer and spring, noting their correct fitted positions.

5 Unscrew the shift drum cam bolt and remove the cam. Remove the locating pin from the shift drum and store it with the cam for safe-keeping **(see illustrations)**.

Inspection

6 Inspect the gearshift shaft return spring post. If it's worn or damaged, replace it. If it's loose, unscrew it, apply a few drops of thread locking compound to the threads, reinstall the post and tighten it securely.

19.8 Fit the oil cooler making sure the arrows on the cooler and housing are pointing in the same direction

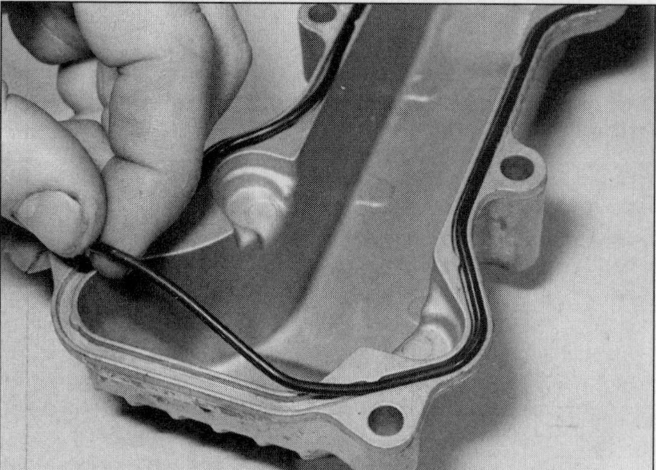
19.9 Make sure the seal is correctly seated in the housing cover groove

7 Check the gearshift shaft for straightness and damage to the splines. If the shaft is bent, you can attempt to straighten it, but if the splines are damaged it will have to be replaced.

8 Inspect the gearshift shaft return spring, and selector pawl and spring for damage. The return spring can be replaced individually but if the selector pawl or spring are damaged the complete shaft must be replaced. To replace the return spring, remove the snap-ring, and on S, T, V and W (1995 to 1998) models the inner thrust washer, and slide off the spring. Fit the new spring, making sure it is the correct way around and thus correctly engaged with the shaft, then on S, T, V and W (1995 to 1998) models fit the inner thrust washer, and secure it in position with the snap-ring. Note that the snap-ring should be fitted with its chamfered edge facing the return spring and must be correctly located in the shaft groove **(see illustrations)**.

9 Check the condition of the stopper lever and spring. Replace the stopper lever if it's worn where it contacts the shift drum cam. Replace the spring if it's distorted.

10 Inspect the pins on the end of the shift drum cam. If they're worn or damaged, replace the cam.

11 On S, T, V and W (1995 to 1998) models, unscrew the gearshift shaft oil seal retaining plate bolt and remove the plate. Check the condition of the gearshift shaft seal. If it has been leaking, lever it out **(see illustration)**. It's a good idea to replace it in any case, since

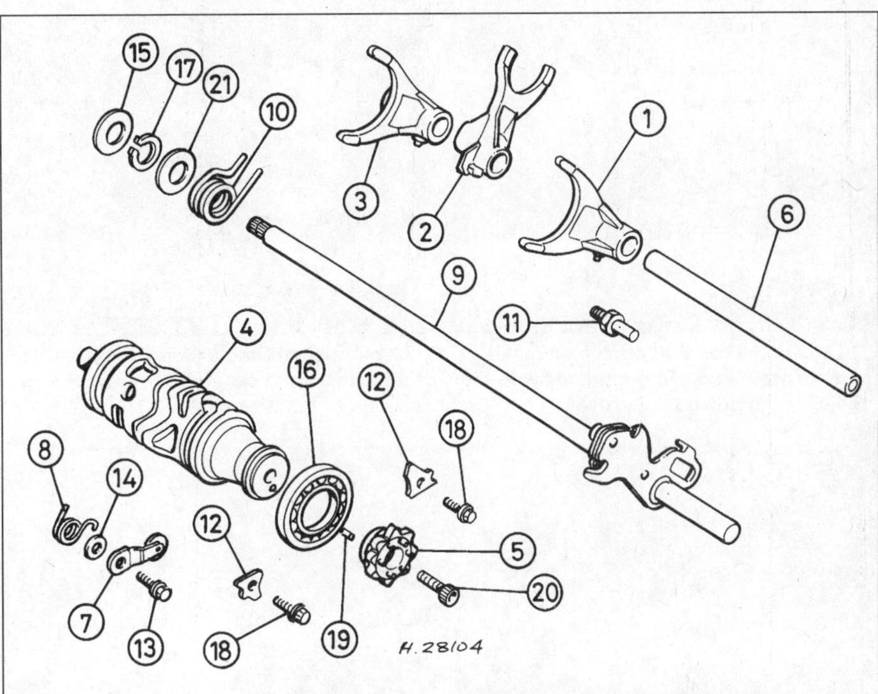

20.3 Gearshift mechanism components

1 Right shift fork
2 Center shift fork
3 Left shift fork
4 Shift drum
5 Shift drum cam
6 Shift fork shaft
7 Stopper arm
8 Spring
9 Gearshift shaft
10 Spring
11 Spring post
12 Retaining plate
13 Bolt
14 Washer
15 Thrust washer
16 Bearing
17 Snap-ring
18 Bolt
19 Locating pin
20 Bolt
21 Washer (S, T, V and W only)

20.5a Unscrew the bolt then remove the shift drum cam . . .

20.5b . . . and withdraw the locating pin

20.8a Slide the spring along the gearshift shaft . . .

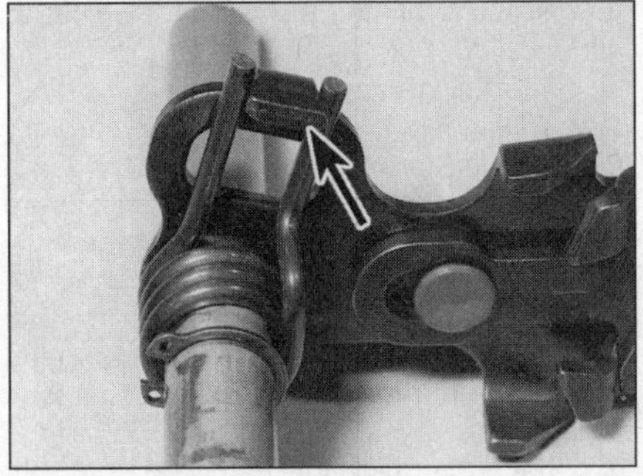

20.8b . . . and engage it with the tab (arrow); secure it in position with the snap-ring

20.11a Pry out the gearshift shaft oil seal with a screwdriver . . .

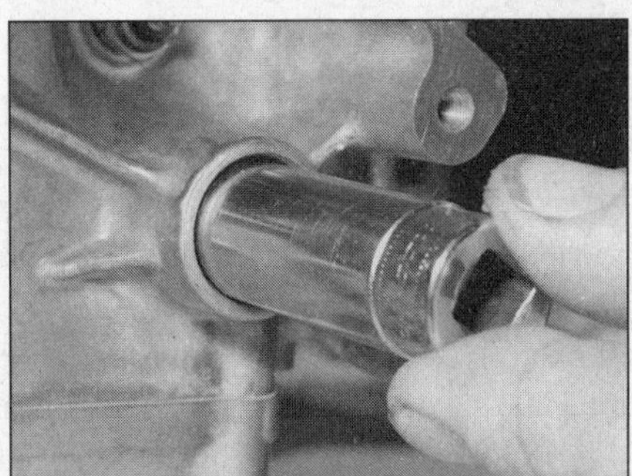

20.11b . . . and press the new seal into position with a suitable socket

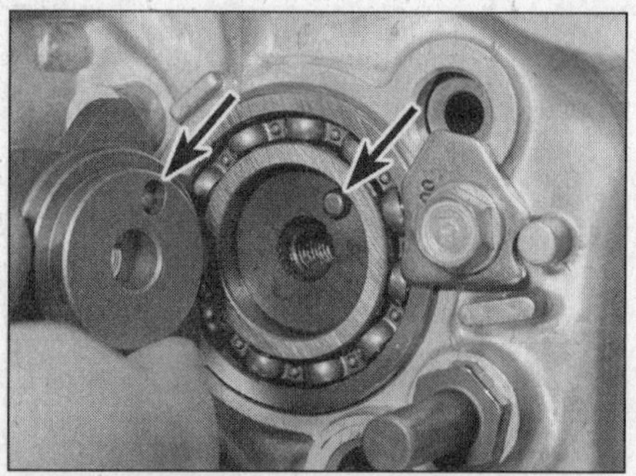

20.13 Install the shift drum cam making sure its hole is correctly engaged with the locating pin (arrows)

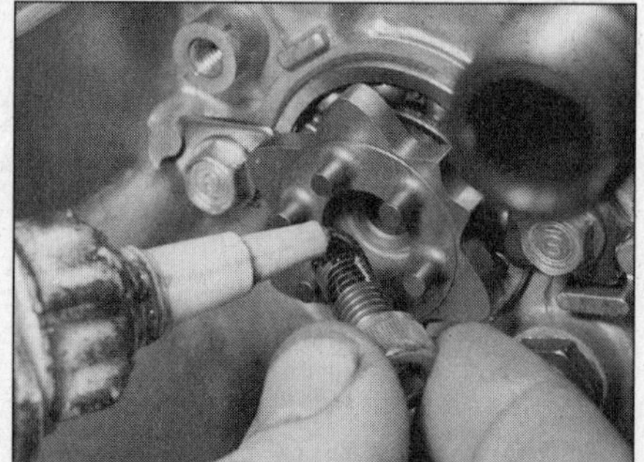

20.14 Apply thread locking compound to the shift drum cam bolt threads before installing it

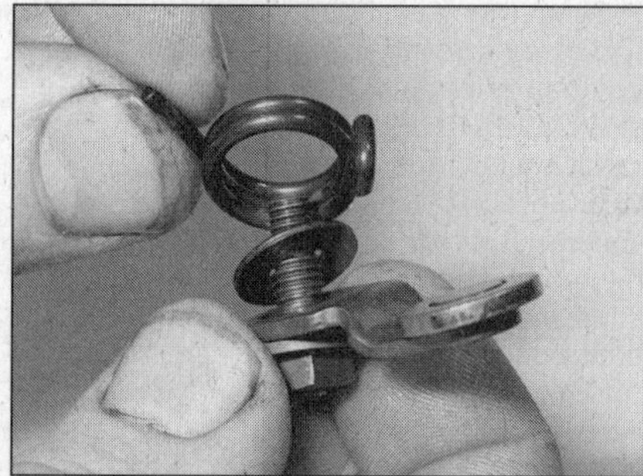

20.15a Fit the stopper arm, washer and spring to the bolt . . .

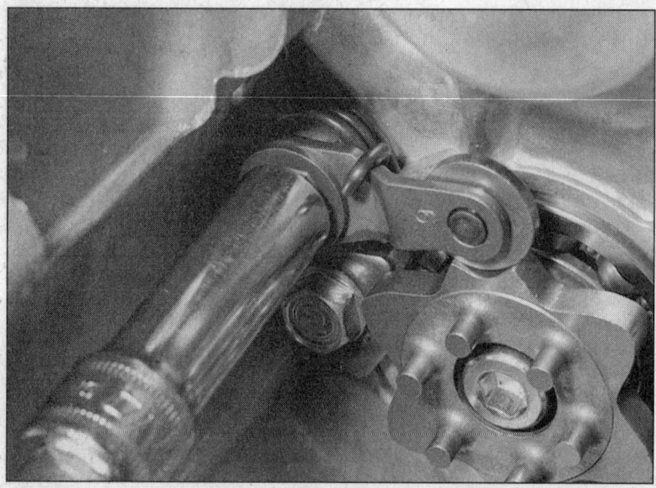

20.15b . . . and screw the assembly into position in the crankcase - the stopper arm must be correctly engaged with the cam's neutral detent

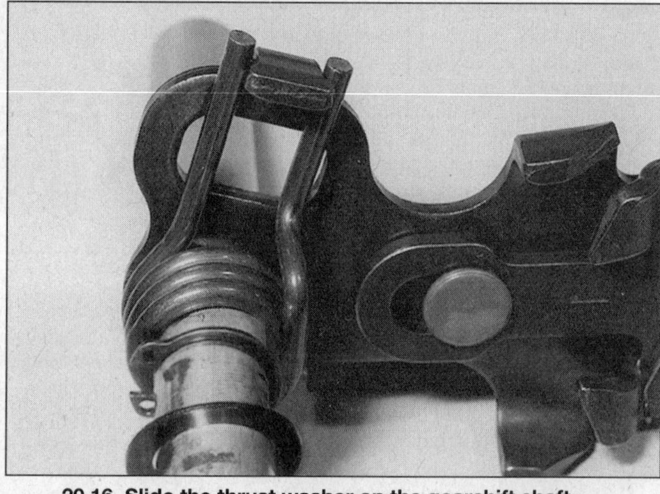

20.16 Slide the thrust washer on the gearshift shaft . . .

gaining access to it requires a fair amount of work. On S, T, V and W (1995 to 1998) models, check the condition of the gearshift shaft needle roller bearing behind the seal, and replace it if it is worn or damaged (refer to *Tools and Workshop Tips* in the Reference Section). Install a new seal with its sealing lip facing inwards. It should be possible to install the seal with thumb pressure, but if necessary, drive it in with a socket the same diameter as the seal's outer edge **(see illustration)**.

Installation

12 Fit the locating pin to the shift drum.

13 Fit the shift drum cam to the drum, aligning its hole with the locating pin **(see illustration)**.

14 Clean the shift drum cam bolt and apply a drop of locking compound to its threads **(see illustration)**. Install the bolt and tighten it to the torque setting listed in this Chapter's Specifications.

15 Fit the stopper arm, washer and spring to the retaining bolt, noting that the spring should be positioned to hold the stopper arm against the cam. Screw the stopper arm bolt into the crankcase. Using a screwdriver, lift the arm and position it on the shift drum cam. With the arm correctly positioned, securely tighten the bolt **(see illustrations)**.

16 Slide the thrust washer on the gearshift shaft **(see illustration)**.

17 Apply a smear of grease to the lip of the gearshift shaft oil seal and wrap the splines of the gearshift shaft with electrical tape, so the splines don't damage the seal as the shaft is installed.

18 Slide the gearshift shaft into the crankcase. Make sure the return spring is correctly located over its post and the selector pawls are aligned with the pins on the shift drum cam **(see illustration)**. Remove the tape.

19 Align the punch marks on the gearshift pedal and shaft and locate the gearshift pedal on the shaft splines. Fit the clamp bolt and tighten it to the specified torque setting **(see illustration)**.

20 Check the operation of the external shift mechanism then install the clutch as described in Section 13.

20.18 . . . and install the shaft in the crankcase making sure the spring engages correctly with the post (arrow) - components are shown in neutral position

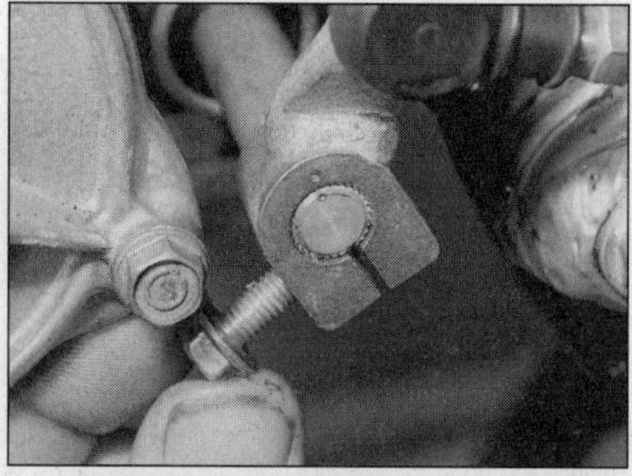

20.19 Align the punch marks when locating the gearshift pedal on the shaft splines

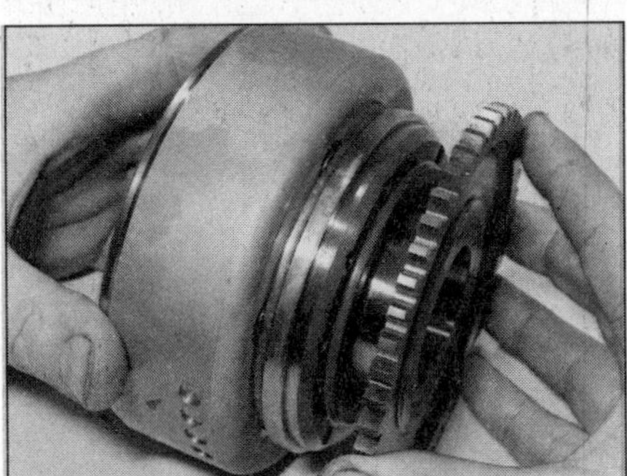

21.2 Remove the starter driven gear from the rear of the alternator rotor

21.3 Withdraw the shaft and remove the starter idler gear from the engine

21.5a Inspect the starter clutch rollers . . .

21 Starter motor clutch - removal, inspection and installation

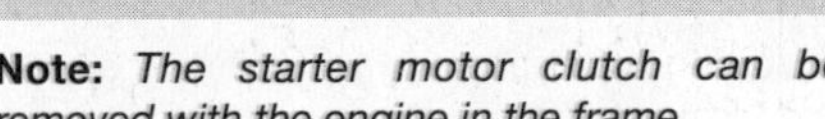

Note: *The starter motor clutch can be removed with the engine in the frame.*

Removal

1 Remove the alternator rotor as described in Section 22.

2 Remove the starter driven gear from the rear of the rotor **(see illustration)**.

3 Slide the idle gear off its shaft and remove the shaft from the crankcase **(see illustration)**.

Inspection

4 Inspect the starter idler gear and driven gear teeth and replace them as a pair if any teeth are chipped or missing. Check the idler shaft and gear bearing surfaces for signs of wear or damage, and replace if necessary.

5 Inspect the starter clutch rollers and driven gear contact surfaces for signs of wear and scoring **(see illustrations)**. The starter clutch rollers should be unmarked with no signs of wear such as pitting or flat spots. The degree of wear on the driven gear can be assessed by measuring the outside diameter of its boss and comparing it to the service limit given in the Specifications.

6 Inspect the crankshaft needle roller bearing and driven gear contact surfaces for wear or scoring and replace it if necessary. The bearing can be drawn off the crankshaft using a suitable puller. Install the new bearing, using a suitable tubular drift which contacts only the bearing inner race.

7 To replace the starter clutch roller assembly, clamp the rotor in a vise equipped with soft jaws then undo the six bolts and remove the clutch from the back of the rotor **(see illustration)**.

8 Clean the starter clutch bolts and apply a drop of locking compound to their threads **(see illustration)**.

9 Fit the new roller assembly to the rear of the rotor, install the bolts and tighten them to the specified torque setting **(see illustration)**.

Installation

10 Insert the idler gear shaft into the crankcase.

11 Apply a smear of clean engine oil to the shaft and slide on the idler gear.

12 Fit the driven gear to the rear of the alternator rotor, turning it counterclockwise (anti-clockwise) to help it engage with the starter clutch rollers.

13 Fit the alternator rotor as described in Section 22.

22 Alternator rotor - removal and installation

Note: *To remove the alternator rotor the special Honda rotor puller, Part Number 07733-0020001, or a pattern equivalent will be required. Do not attempt to remove the rotor using any other method. The alternator rotor can be removed with the engine in the frame. If work is being carried out with the engine removed, ignore the preliminary steps.*

21.5b . . . and the driven gear surface for signs of wear or damage - replace damaged components

Removal

1 Remove the fuel tank as described in Chapter 4.

2 Remove the left lower fairing panel as described in Chapter 8.

3 Drain the engine oil as described in Chapter 1.

4 Trace the wiring back from the left crankshaft end cover to the front of the junction box. Disconnect the alternator wiring connector and free the wiring from underneath the junction box. Work back along the wiring, noting its routing while releasing it from any relevant ties or clips.

5 Unscrew the cover retaining bolts and withdraw the cover squarely from the engine unit. **Note:** *Due to the magnetic pull of the*

21.7 Starter clutch is retained by six bolts (arrows)

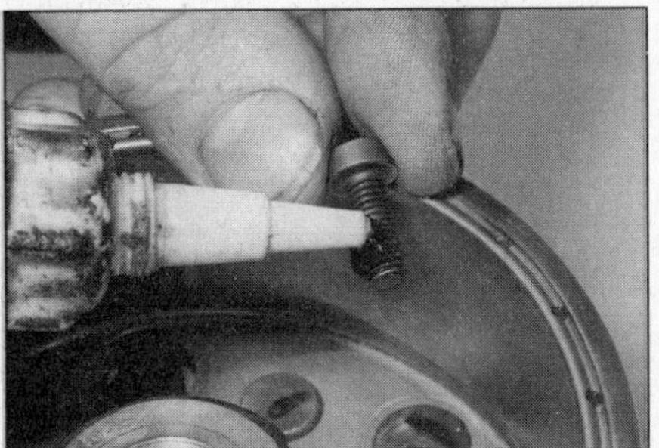

21.8 Apply thread locking compound to the starter clutch retaining bolts prior to installation . . .

21.9 . . . and tighten them to the specified torque setting

22.7a Retain the rotor with a large open-ended wrench and loosen the retaining bolt

22.7b Unscrew the retaining bolt and washer . . .

22.8 . . . and release the alternator rotor using the special Honda service tool

rotor, the cover may prove difficult to remove. Do not pry the cover away with a screwdriver as the mating surfaces will be damaged.

6 Remove the cover locating dowel from the crankcase and discard the gasket.

7 Slacken and remove the rotor retaining bolt and washer while holding the rotor to prevent it turning. The rotor can be retained using a large open-ended wrench on the rotor flats **(see illustrations)**. Alternatively, if the engine is still in the frame, the engine can be locked through the transmission by selecting top gear and applying the rear brake hard.

8 Screw the rotor puller tool into the center of the rotor and tighten it securely **(see illustration)**. Sharply tap on the end of puller tool to release the rotor's grip on the tapered shaft. Remove the rotor.

9 Recover the Woodruff key from the crankshaft and store it safely inside the flywheel rotor **(see illustration)**.

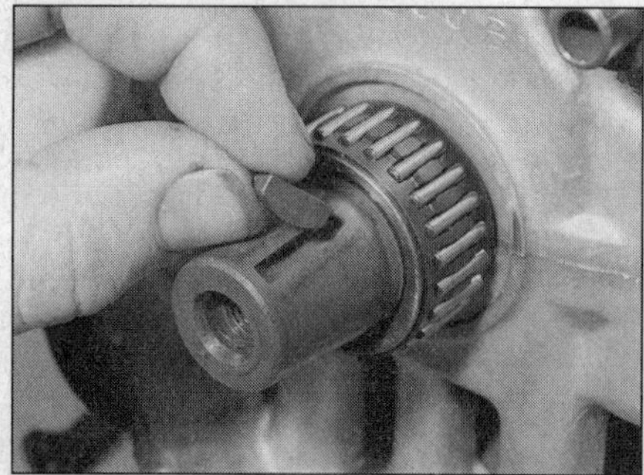
22.9 Remove the Woodruff key and store it with the rotor for safe-keeping

Installation

10 Degrease the rotor and crankshaft tapers and remove any metal particles of swarf from the rotor magnet. Remove all traces of gasket from the cover and crankcase mating surfaces.

11 Install the Woodruff key in the crankshaft taper.

12 Align the slot in the rotor taper with the Woodruff key and gently push the rotor on the crankshaft making sure the starter gear teeth are correctly meshed **(see illustration)**. Gently tap the rotor center with a soft-faced hammer to seat it on the crankshaft taper.

13 Fit the rotor bolt and washer and tighten it to the specified torque setting while holding the rotor using the method employed on removal.

14 Install the locating dowel and fit a new gasket to the crankcase **(see illustration)**.

15 Apply a smear of suitable sealing compound to the crankshaft left end cover wiring grommet and fit the cover to the engine **(see illustration)**.

16 Install the cover bolts and tighten them securely.

17 Make sure the wiring is correctly routed up to the junction box and reconnect the wiring connector. Secure the wiring in position with all the necessary clips and ties.

18 Fill the engine with the correct type and amount of oil as described in Chapter 1.

19 Install the fuel tank as described in Chapter 4.

20 Fit the fairing panel as described in Chapter 8.

23 Camchain and guides - removal, inspection and installation

Note: *The camchain and guides can be removed with the engine in the frame.*

Removal

Rear camchain guide

1 Remove the intake camshaft as described in Section 9.

2 Slacken and remove the nut and sealing washer securing the guide to the cylinder head and lift the guide out of position.

Front camchain guide

3 Remove the exhaust camshaft as described in Section 9.

4 Drain the engine oil as described in Chapter 1.

5 Trace the wiring back from the right crankshaft end cover to the front of the junction box. Disconnect the pulse generator wiring connector and free the wiring from underneath the junction box. Work back along the wiring, noting its routing while releasing it from any relevant ties or clips.

6 Unscrew the cover retaining bolts and withdraw the cover squarely from the engine unit **(see illustration)**. Note the position of the oil jet fitted behind the cover and make sure it stays in position.

7 Remove the cover locating dowels from the crankcase and discard the gasket.

22.12 The rotor slot must be correctly aligned with the key and the starter gear teeth correctly meshed (arrows)

22.14 Ensure the locating dowel (arrow) is in position then fit a new gasket . . .

22.15 . . . and install the cover

23.6 Unscrew the retaining bolts (arrows) and remove the right crankshaft end cover

23.8a Unscrew the bolt . . .

23.8b . . . and lift the front camchain guide out from the cylinder head

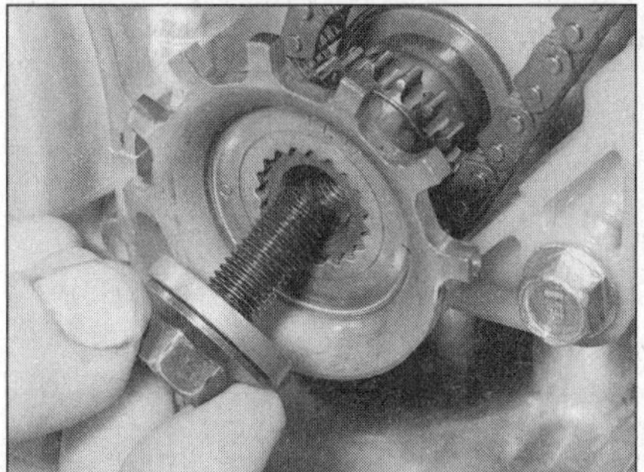
23.10a Unscrew the retaining bolt and washer . . .

23.10b . . . while retaining the alternator rotor with an open-ended wrench . . .

23.11 . . . and remove the pulse generator rotor

8 Unscrew the front camchain guide bolt and lift the guide upwards and out of the engine **(see illustrations)**. Remove the pivot bushing from the guide mounting bolt hole.

Camchain

9 Remove the front camchain guide as described in above in Steps 3 to 8 noting that both camshafts must be removed.

10 Slacken and remove the pulse generator rotor retaining bolt and washer. To prevent the crankshaft rotating, remove the left crankshaft end cover and hold the alternator rotor using a large open-ended wrench on the rotor flats (see Section 22) **(see illustrations)**. Alternatively, if the engine is still in the frame, the engine can be locked through the transmission by selecting top gear and applying the rear brake hard.

11 Slide off the pulse generator rotor **(see illustration)**.

12 Prior to removal, use paint or a suitable marker pen to mark the outside edge of the crankshaft camchain sprocket **(see illustration)**. This mark can then be used to make sure the sprocket is installed the correct way around.

13 Drop the chain down and remove it from the end of the crankshaft **(see illustration)**.

14 Slide the sprocket off of the crankshaft.

Inspection

15 Check the guides for deep grooves, cracking and other obvious damage, replacing them if necessary.

16 Check the camchain for binding and obvious damage and inspect the sprocket for damage such as chipped or missing teeth. If either of these conditions are visible, or if the chain appears to be stretched, both the camchain and sprockets (crankshaft and both camshaft sprockets) should be replaced as a set.

Installation

Rear camchain guide

17 Installation is the reverse of removal using a new sealing washer.

Front camchain guide

18 Remove all traces of gasket from the crankcase and cover mating surfaces. Make sure the oil jet is in position in the crankcase.

19 Lubricate the pivot bushing with engine oil and insert it into the guide, making sure the bushing shoulder is on the inside of the guide (between the guide and crankcase) **(see illustration)**.

20 Lower the guide into position through the top of the cylinder head.

21 Ensure the camchain is correctly engaged with the crankshaft sprocket then fit the guide bolt and tighten it securely.

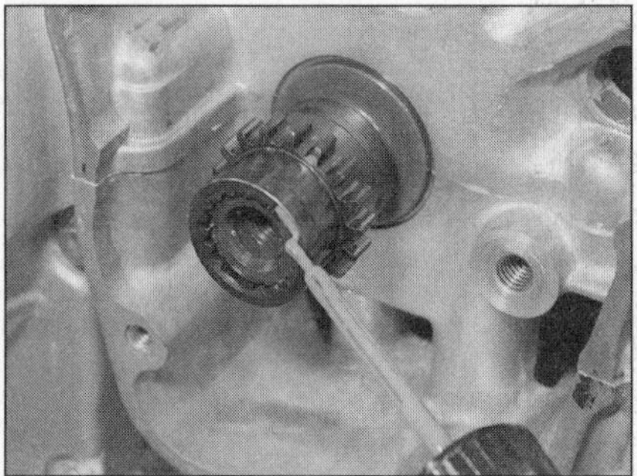
23.12 Make an identification mark on the crankshaft sprocket prior to removal

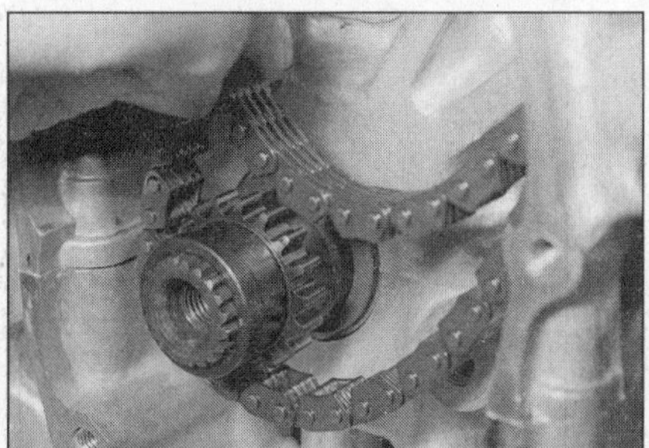
23.13 Drop the camchain down through the engine and remove it from the crankshaft

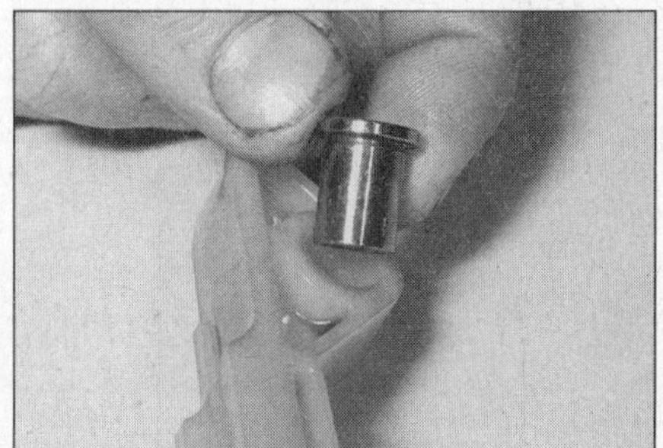
23.19 Fit the pivot bushing to the front camchain guide so that its collar will be positioned between the guide and crankcase

23.24 Apply sealant to the threads of the two right end cover bolts installed in the holes next to the triangular marks

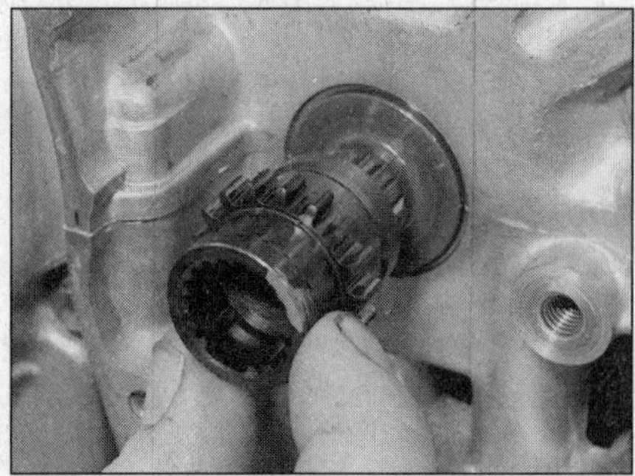
23.29 Slide the sprocket on the crankshaft using the mark made on removal to ensure correct fitting

22 Install the locating dowels and fit a new gasket to the crankcase.

23 Apply a smear of suitable sealing compound to the crankshaft right end cover wiring grommet and to the threads of two of the cover retaining bolts.

24 Fit the cover to the engine noting that the bolts smeared with sealant should be installed in the two holes next to the camchain tensioner. These holes are indicated by triangular marks cast on the cover **(see illustration)**. Tighten the cover bolts to the specified torque setting.

25 Make sure the wiring is correctly routed up to the junction box and reconnect the wiring connector. Secure the wiring in position with all the necessary clips and ties.

26 Fill the engine with the correct type and amount of oil as described in Chapter 1.

27 Install the camshaft as described in Section 9.

Camchain

28 Locate the chain over the crankshaft and lift it up through the engine unit. Pass a screwdriver through the chain to prevent it dropping back down into the engine unit.

29 Slide the sprocket on the crankshaft using the mark made on removal to ensure it is installed the correct way around **(see illustration)**.

30 Align the pulse generator rotor splines with those of the crankshaft and slide on the rotor. **Note:** *Make sure the rotor timing marks are facing outwards.*

31 Tighten the rotor bolt to the specified torque setting while preventing crankshaft rotation using the method employed on removal.

32 Install the front camchain guide as described in Steps 18 to 27.

24 Shift drum and forks - removal, inspection and installation

Note: *The shift drum and forks can be removed with the engine in the frame, though it is quite a tricky procedure. It is easier to remove the engine from the frame (see Section 5) and turn it upside down. It is easier still to access the components by separating the crankcase halves (the top end components can be left in situ). If a complete overhaul is being carried out the shift drum and forks may be left in position until after the crankcase halves have been separated.*

Removal

1 Remove the oil pan as described in Section 15.

2 Remove the gearshift mechanism components as described in Section 20.

3 Unscrew the bolts securing the shift drum bearing retaining plates to the crankcase and remove both plates, noting which way around they are fitted.

4 Withdraw the shift fork shaft slowly and remove the shift forks from the crankcase as they are released from the end of the shaft. When all three shift forks have been removed, fully withdraw the shaft from the crankcase.

5 Remove the bearing and withdraw the shift drum from the crankcase.

Inspection

6 The shift forks and shaft should be closely inspected to ensure that they are not badly damaged or worn.

7 Measure the width of both fork ends and the internal diameter of the shaft bore. If either fork end or the shaft bore has worn beyond its service limit the shift fork(s) must be replaced.

8 The shift fork shaft can be checked for trueness by rolling it along a flat surface. A bent shaft will cause difficulty in selecting gears and make the gearshift action heavy. Measure the diameter of the shaft at the points where it is in contact with the shift forks. If the shaft is bent or has worn beyond its service limit at any point it must be replaced.

9 Inspect the shift drum grooves and selector fork guide pins for signs of wear or damage. If either component shows signs of wear or damage the shift fork(s) and drum must be replaced.

10 Check that the shift drum bearing rotates freely and has no sign of freeplay between its inner and outer race. Replace the bearing if necessary.

Installation

11 Fit the bearing to the shift drum **(see illustration)**.

12 Lubricate the bearing and shift drum grooves with clean engine oil and insert the shift drum and bearing into position in the crankcase **(see illustration)**.

13 Apply a smear of engine oil to the shift fork shaft and slide the shaft partially into the crankcase **(see illustration)**.

14 The shift forks can be identified by the letter cast on each one; L denotes the left fork, C the center, and R the right **(see illustration)**. **Note:** *All shift forks must be installed in the crankcase so that the letter on each one faces towards the right side of the casing (clutch).*

15 Locate the right fork with its grooves in the gear and shift drum and slide in the shift fork shaft until it engages with the fork.

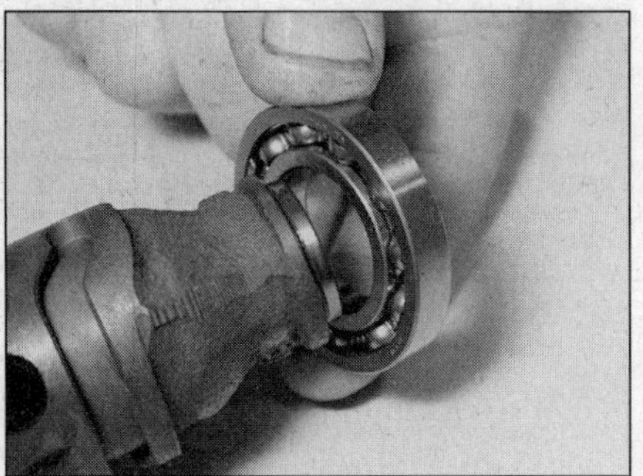
24.11 Fit the bearing to the shift drum . . .

24.12 . . . and insert the drum and bearing into the crankcase

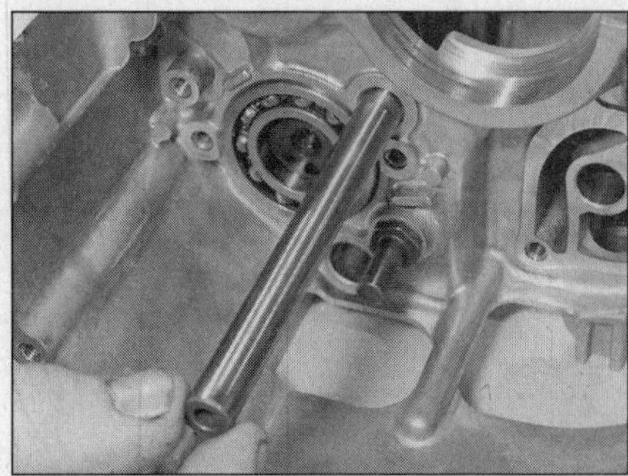
24.13 Locate the shift fork shaft in the crankcase

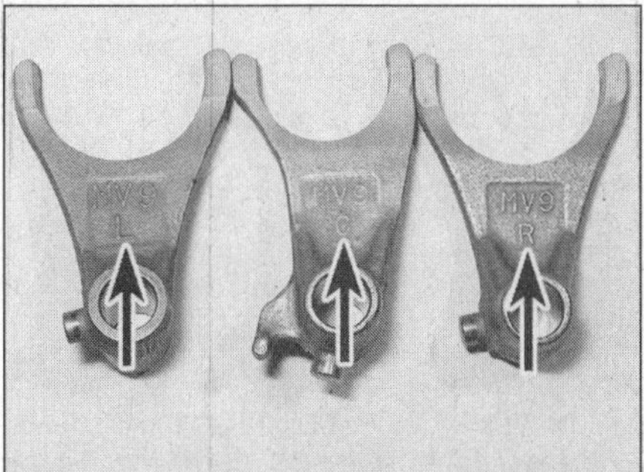

24.14 Each shift fork is marked with a letter to identify its correct fitted position (arrows)

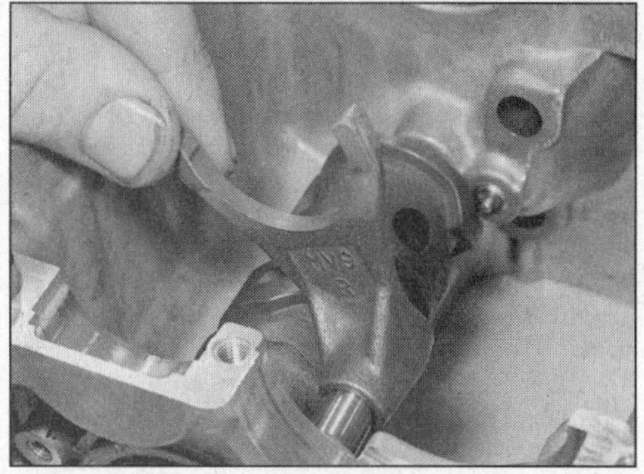

24.15a Making sure all shift forks are fitted with their markings facing the right, install the right fork . . .

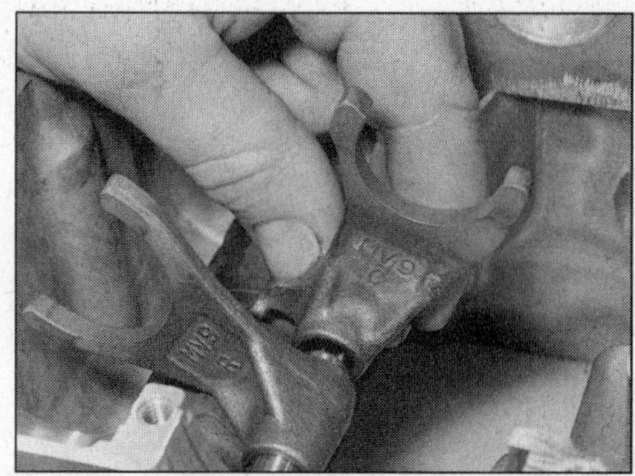

24.15b . . . followed by the center fork . . .

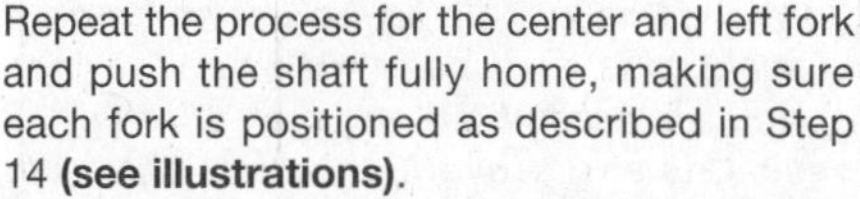

Repeat the process for the center and left fork and push the shaft fully home, making sure each fork is positioned as described in Step 14 **(see illustrations)**.

16 Clean the shift drum bearing plate bolts and apply a suitable locking compound to their threads.

17 Fit the bearing retaining plates making sure the 'OUT' marks are facing outwards (away from the crankcase). Fit the retaining bolts and tighten them securely **(see illustration)**.

18 Fit the gearshift mechanism components as described in Section 20.

19 Fit the oil pan as described in Section 15.

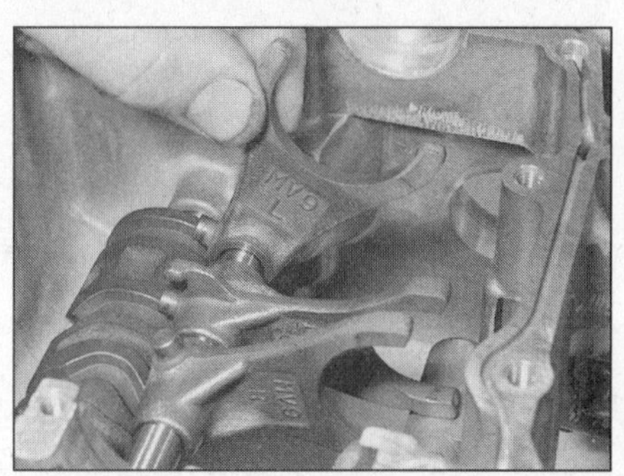

24.15c . . . and finally the left fork

24.17 Fit the bearing retaining plates with the OUT mark facing outwards making sure each is correctly engaged with the crankcase peg (arrow)

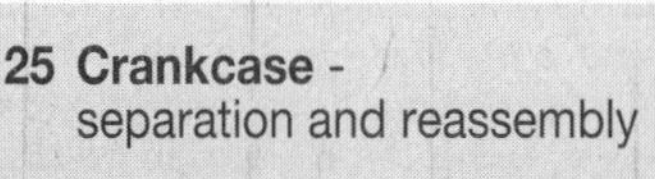

25 Crankcase - separation and reassembly

Separation

1 To examine and repair or replace the crankshaft, pistons and connecting rods, bearings and transmission components, the crankcase must be split into two parts.

2 To enable the crankcases to be split the engine must be removed from the frame and the following components first removed with reference to the relevant Sections.

a) Camshafts and followers
b) Cylinder head
c) Clutch
d) Oil pan
e) Oil pump
f) Oil cooler
g) Gearshift mechanism components
h) Alternator rotor
i) Camchain and guides
j) Speed sensor (S, T, V and W (1995 to 1998) models) (see Chapter 9)

Note: *If the crankcase halves are being separated purely to examine the transmission shafts or crankshaft then there is no need to remove the cylinder head.*

3 With all the relevant components removed proceed as follows.

4 Unbolt the two fairing mounting brackets from the front of the crankcase **(see illustrations)**.

5 Remove the oil jet which is located behind the crankcase right end cover. Remove the O-ring from the jet and discard it; a new one must be fitted on reassembly.

6 With the crankcase the right way up, slacken and remove the seven upper crankcase bolts from the top of the crankcase **(see illustration)**. **Note:** *As each bolt is removed, store it in its relative position in a cardboard template of the crankcase halves. This will ensure all bolts are installed in the correct location on reassembly.* Discard the sealing washers fitted to two of the bolts; new ones must be used on reassembly.

7 Turn the crankcase upside down, and unscrew the single 10 mm bolt and washer from the left rear corner of the crankcase **(see illustration)**.

25.4a Undo the bolts and remove the left . . .

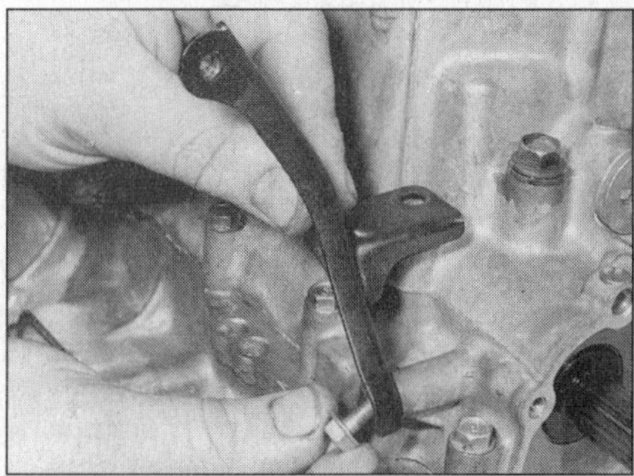

25.4b . . . and right fairing mounting brackets from the front of the crankcase

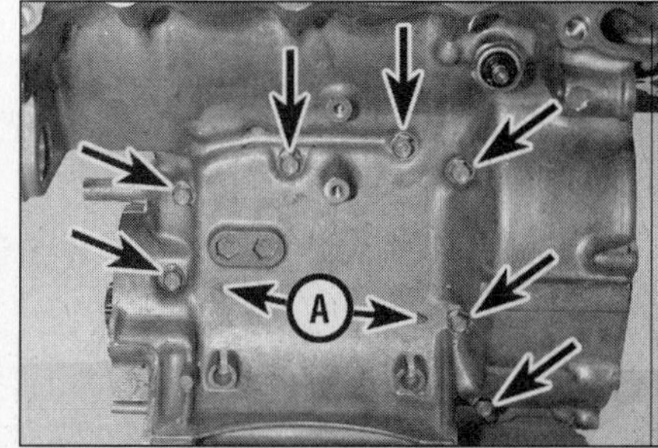

25.6 Upper crankcase bolts (arrows); note the triangular marks (A) next to the two bolts which are fitted with sealing washers

25.7 Large 10 mm bolt is situated at the left rear corner of the crankcase

25.9 Lower crankcase 8 mm bolts (arrows)

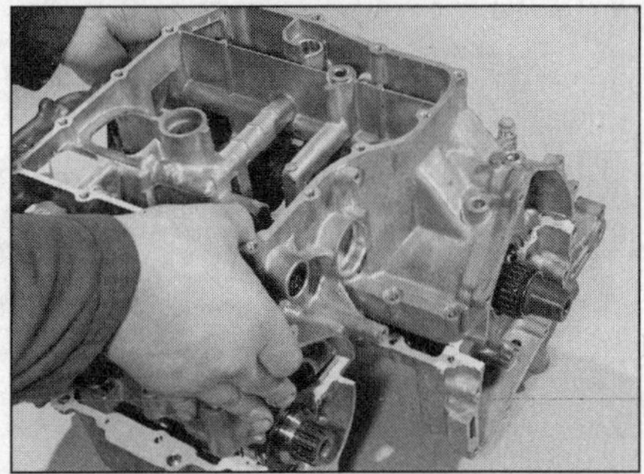
25.10 Lift the lower crankcase half off leaving the transmission and crankshaft in the upper half

8 Work around the crankcase and unscrew the 6 mm lower crankcase bolts (see note in Step 6).

9 Working in a criss-cross pattern, starting from the outside and working inwards, gradually slacken the ten 8 mm lower crankcase bolts **(see illustration)**. Once all the bolts are loose, unscrew and remove them along with their sealing washers (see note in Step 6).

10 Carefully lift the lower crankcase half, leaving the crankshaft and transmission shafts in the upper half of the crankcase **(see illustration)**. As the upper half is lifted away take care not to dislodge or lose any main bearing inserts. **Note:** *If it won't come easily away, make sure all fasteners have been removed. Don't pry against the crankcase mating surfaces or they will leak; initial separation can be achieved by tapping gently with a soft-faced mallet.*

25.11 Remove the locating dowels noting their correct fitted positions

11 Remove the three locating dowels from the upper crankcase half **(see illustration)**.

12 Remove the two oil jets from the upper crankcase half noting which way around they are fitted.

Reassembly

13 With the upper crankcase half turned over check the transmission shafts and crankshaft are correctly installed as described in Sections 30 and 31.

14 Remove all traces of sealant from the crankcase mating surfaces, being careful not to let any fall into the case as this is done.

15 Check that all components are installed and that they can rotate smoothly and easily.

16 Lubricate the transmission shafts and crankshaft with clean engine oil then use a rag soaked in high flash-point solvent to wipe over the gasket surfaces of both halves to remove all traces of oil.

17 Make sure the oil jet holes are clear. Fit both jets to the upper crankcase half making sure that the smaller diameter orifice of each jet is facing the lower crankcase half **(see illustration)**.

18 Install the three locating dowels in the upper crankcase half **(see illustration)**.

19 Apply a small amount of suitable sealant to the mating surface of the upper crankcase half **(see illustration)**.

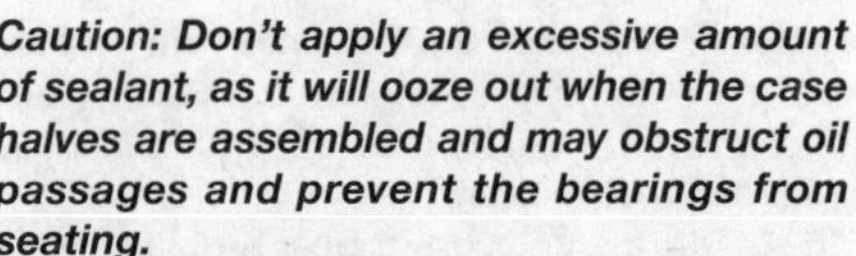
Caution: Don't apply an excessive amount of sealant, as it will ooze out when the case halves are assembled and may obstruct oil passages and prevent the bearings from seating.

20 Check the position of the shift cam, shift forks and transmission shafts - make sure they're in the neutral position.

21 Make sure that the main bearing inserts are in position and carefully lower the lower crankcase half onto the upper half. The shift forks must engage with their respective slots in the transmission gears as the halves are joined.

22 Check that the lower crankcase half is correctly seated and that all shafts are free to rotate. **Note:** *If the casings are not correctly seated, remove the lower crankcase half and investigate the problem. Do not attempt to pull them together using the crankcase bolts as the casing will crack and be ruined.*

23 Apply a smear of engine oil to the threads and undersides of the heads of the ten 8 mm lower crankcase bolts and install the bolts in their original locations **(see illustration)**.

24 Starting from the center and working outwards in a criss-cross pattern, tighten all the 8 mm bolts to approximately half the specified torque. Go around a second time in the same sequence and tighten them to the full torque setting given in the Specifications at the start of this Chapter.

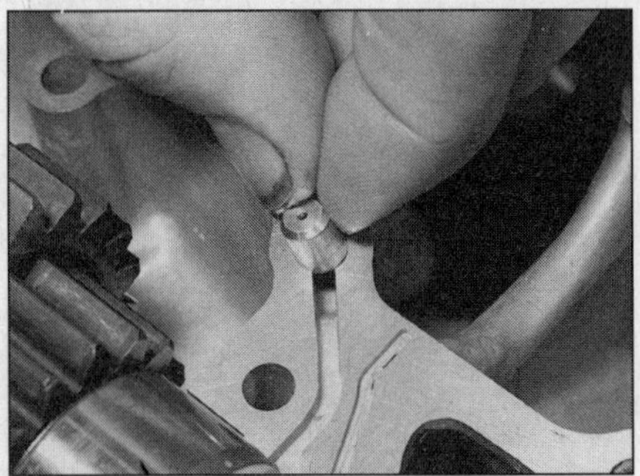
25.17 Fit the oil jets to the upper crankcase half - their smaller diameter orifices must face the lower half

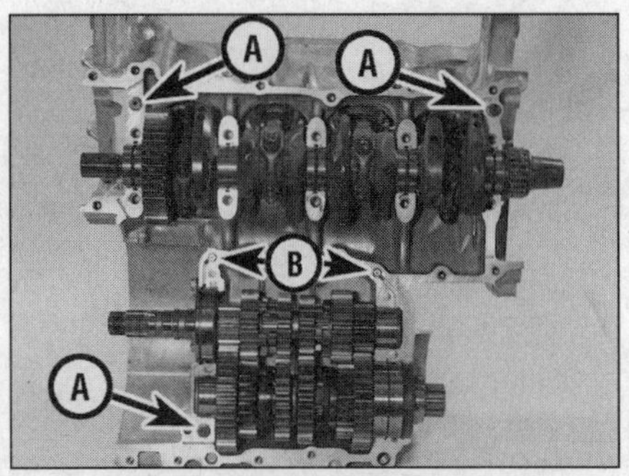

25.18 Correct fitted locations of locating dowels (A) and oil jets (B) in upper crankcase half

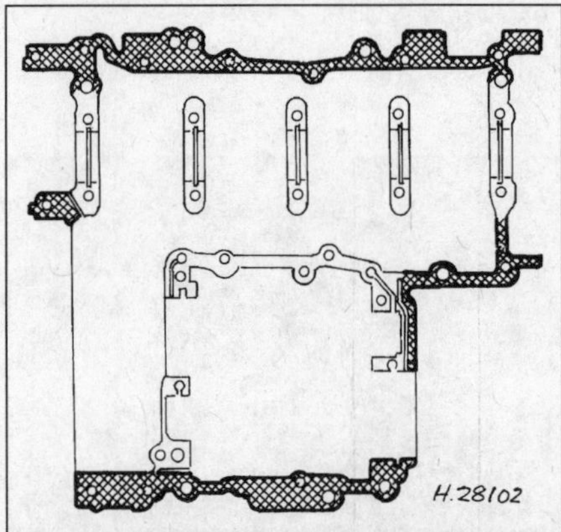

25.19 Apply a thin coat of sealant only to the shaded areas of the upper crankcase half

25 Fit the single 10 mm crankcase bolt and tighten it to the specified torque setting.

26 Fit the fourteen 6 mm bolts in their original locations and tighten them to the specified torque setting.

27 Turn the crankcase over so that it is upright and install the seven upper crankcase bolts and tighten them to the specified torque, noting that on S, T, V and W (1995 to 1998) models one of the bolts is 8 mm. Note that a new sealing washer must be fitted to both bolts fitted in the holes next to the triangular marks cast on the crankcase surface **(see illustration 25.6)**.

28 With all crankcase fasteners tightened, check that the crankshaft and transmission shafts rotate smoothly and easily. If there are any signs of undue stiffness or of any other problem, the fault must be rectified before proceeding further.

29 Fit the two fairing mounting brackets to the front of the crankcase and securely tighten their mounting bolts.

30 Fit a new O-ring to the oil jet. Apply a smear of oil to the O-ring to ease installation and insert the jet into position in the crankcase **(see illustration)**.

31 Install all other removed assemblies in the reverse of the sequence given in Step 2.

25.23 Lubricate the threads and underside of the heads of the 8 mm lower crankcase bolts prior to installation

25.30 Fit a new O-ring (arrow) to the oil jet and install it in the right end of the crankcase

26 Crankcase - inspection and servicing

1 After the crankcases have been separated, remove the crankshaft and transmission components, and the oil pressure switch and neutral switch (see Chapter 9). Clean the crankcases thoroughly with new solvent and dry them with compressed air.

Cylinder bores

Note: *Don't attempt to separate the liners from the cylinder block.*

2 Check the cylinder walls carefully for scratches and score marks.

3 Using the appropriate precision measuring tools, check each cylinder's diameter. Measure near the top, center and bottom of the cylinder bore, parallel to the crankshaft axis. Next, measure each cylinder's diameter at the same three locations across the crankshaft axis. Compare the results to this Chapter's Specifications. If the cylinder bores are tapered, out-of-round, worn beyond the specified limits, or badly scuffed or scored, have them rebored and honed by a dealer service department or a motorcycle repair shop. If a rebore is done, oversize pistons and rings will be required as well. Honda produce four sizes of oversize pistons (see Section 28).

4 As an alternative, if the precision measuring tools are not available, a dealer service department or motorcycle repair shop will make the measurements and offer advice concerning servicing of the cylinders.

5 If they are in reasonably good condition and not worn to the outside of the limits, and if the piston-to-cylinder clearances can be maintained properly (see Section 28), then the cylinders do not have to be rebored; honing is all that is necessary.

6 To perform the honing operation you will need the proper size flexible hone with fine stones, or a 'bottle brush' type hone, plenty of light oil or honing oil, some shop towels and an electric drill motor. Hold the upper crankcase half in a vise (cushioned with soft jaws or wood blocks) when performing the honing operation. Mount the hone in the drill motor, compress the stones and slip the hone into the top of the cylinder. Lubricate the cylinder thoroughly, turn on the drill and move the hone up and down in the cylinder at a pace which will produce a fine crosshatch pattern on the cylinder wall with the crosshatch lines intersecting at approximately a 60° angle. Be sure to use plenty of lubricant and do not take off any more material than is absolutely necessary to produce the desired effect. Do not withdraw the hone from the cylinder while it is running. Instead, shut off the drill and continue moving the hone up and down in the cylinder until it comes to a complete stop, then compress the stones and withdraw the hone. Wipe the oil out of the cylinder and repeat the procedure on the other cylinders. Remember, do not remove too much material from the cylinder wall. If you do not have the tools, or do not desire to perform the honing operation, a dealer service department or motorcycle repair shop will generally do it for a reasonable fee.

7 Next, the cylinders must be thoroughly washed with warm soapy water to remove all traces of the abrasive grit produced during the honing operation. Be sure to run a brush through the bolt holes and flush them with running water. After rinsing, dry the cylinders thoroughly and apply a coat of light, rust-preventative oil to all machined surfaces.

Crankcase castings

8 Remove any oil passage plugs that haven't already been removed. All oil passages should be blown out with compressed air.

9 All traces of old gasket sealant should be removed from the mating surfaces. Minor damage to the surfaces can be cleaned up with a fine sharpening stone or grindstone.

Caution: Be very careful not to nick or gouge the crankcase mating surfaces or leaks will result. Check both crankcase halves very carefully for cracks and other damage.

10 Small cracks or holes in aluminum castings may be repaired with an epoxy resin adhesive as a temporary measure. Permanent repairs can only be effected by argon-arc welding, and only a specialist in this process is in a position to advise on the economy or practical aspect of such a repair. If any damage is found that can't be repaired, replace the crankcase halves as a set.

11 Damaged threads can be economically reclaimed by using a diamond section wire thread insert, which is easily fitted after drilling and re-tapping the affected thread. Most motorcycle dealers and small engineering firms offer a service of this kind.

Refer to Tools and Workshop Tips in the Reference section for details of how to fit a thread insert and use screw extractors.

12 Sheared studs or screws can usually be removed with screw extractors, which are tapered, left thread screws of very hard steel. These are inserted into a pre-drilled hole in the stud, and usually succeed in dislodging the most stubborn stud or screw. If a problem arises which seems beyond your scope, it is worth consulting a professional engineering firm before condemning an otherwise sound casing. Many of these firms advertise regularly in the motorcycle press.

27 Main and connecting rod bearings - general note

1 Even though main and connecting rod bearings are generally replaced with new ones during the engine overhaul, the old bearings should be retained for close examination as they may reveal valuable information about the condition of the engine.

2 Bearing failure occurs mainly because of lack of lubrication, the presence of dirt or other foreign particles, overloading the engine and/or corrosion. Regardless of the cause of bearing failure, it must be corrected before the engine is reassembled to prevent it from happening again.

3 When examining the bearings, remove the main bearings from the case halves and the rod bearings from the connecting rods and caps and lay them out on a clean surface in the same general position as their location on the crankshaft journals. This will enable you to match any noted bearing problems with the corresponding crankshaft journal.

4 Dirt and other foreign particles get into the engine in a variety of ways. It may be left in the engine during assembly or it may pass through filters or breathers. It may get into the oil and from there into the bearings. Metal chips from machining operations and normal engine wear are often present. Abrasives are sometimes left in engine components after reconditioning operations such as cylinder honing, especially when parts are not thoroughly cleaned using the proper cleaning methods. Whatever the source, these foreign objects often end up imbedded in the soft bearing material and are easily recognized. Large particles will not imbed in the bearing and will score or gouge the bearing and journal. The best prevention for this cause of bearing failure is to clean all parts thoroughly and keep everything spotlessly clean during engine reassembly. Frequent and regular oil and filter changes are also recommended.

5 Lack of lubrication or lubrication breakdown has a number of interrelated causes. Excessive heat (which thins the oil), overloading (which squeezes the oil from the bearing face) and oil leakage or throw off from excessive bearing clearances, worn oil pump or high engine speeds all contribute to lubrication breakdown. Blocked oil passages will also starve a bearing and destroy it. When lack of lubrication is the cause of bearing failure, the bearing material is wiped or extruded from the steel backing of the bearing. Temperatures may increase to the point where the steel backing and the journal turn blue from overheating.

6 Riding habits can have a definite effect on bearing life. Full throttle low speed operation, or lugging (laboring) the engine, puts very high loads on bearings, which tend to squeeze out the oil film. These loads cause the bearings to flex, which produces fine cracks in the bearing face (fatigue failure). Eventually the bearing material will loosen in pieces and tear away from the steel backing. Short trip riding leads to corrosion of bearings, as insufficient engine heat is produced to drive off the condensed water and corrosive gases produced. These products collect in the engine oil, forming acid and sludge. As the oil is carried to the engine bearings, the acid attacks and corrodes the bearing material.

7 Incorrect bearing installation during engine assembly will lead to bearing failure as well. Tight fitting bearings which leave insufficient bearing oil clearances result in oil starvation. Dirt or foreign particles trapped behind a bearing insert result in high spots on the bearing which lead to failure.

8 To avoid bearing problems, clean all parts thoroughly before reassembly, double check all bearing clearance measurements and lubricate the new bearings with clean engine oil during installation.

28 Piston/connecting rod assemblies - removal, inspection and installation

Removal

1 Separate the crankcase halves as described in Section 25. Before removing the piston/connecting rods from the crankshaft measure the side clearance of each rod with a feeler gauge **(see illustration)**. If the clearance on any rod is greater than the service limit listed in this Chapter's Specifications, that rod will have to be replaced with a new one.

2 Using a center punch or paint, mark the relevant cylinder number on each connecting rod and bearing cap (number 1 cylinder on left end).

3 Unscrew the bearing cap nuts and withdraw the cap, complete with the lower bearing insert, from each of the four connecting rods **(see illustration)**. Push the connecting rods up and off their crankpins, then remove the upper bearing insert. Keep the cap, nuts and (if they are to be re-used) the bearing inserts together in their correct sequence.

4 Remove the ridge of carbon from the top of each cylinder bore. If there is a pronounced wear ridge on the top of each bore, remove with a ridge reamer.

5 Push each piston/connecting rod assembly up and remove it from the top of the bore making sure the connecting rod does not mark the cylinder bore walls.

Caution: Do not try to remove the piston/connecting rod from the bottom of the cylinder bore. The piston will not pass the crankcase main bearing webs. If the piston is pulled right to the bottom of the bore the oil control ring will expand and lock the piston in position. If this happens it is likely the ring will be broken.

6 Immediately install the relevant bearing cap, inserts and nuts on each piston/connecting rod assembly so that they are all kept together as a matched set.

7 Using a sharp scriber, scratch the number of each piston into its crown (or use a suitable marker pen if the piston is clean enough).

8 Support the first piston and, using a small screwdriver or scriber, carefully pry out a snap-ring from the piston groove **(see illustration)**.

9 Push the piston pin out from the opposite end to free the piston from the rod. You may have to deburr the area around the groove to enable the pin to slide out (use a triangular file for this procedure). If the pin is tight, tap it out using a suitable hammer and punch, taking care not to damage the piston. Repeat the procedure for the other pistons.

HAYNES HiNT ***If a piston pin is a tight fit in the bosses, soak a rag in boiling water then wring it out and wrap it around the piston - this will expand the alloy piston sufficiently to release its grip on the pin.***

Inspection

Pistons

10 Before the inspection process can be carried out, the pistons must be cleaned and the old piston rings removed.

28.1 Measuring connecting rod side clearance

28.3 On removal make sure the bearing shell stays in the cap

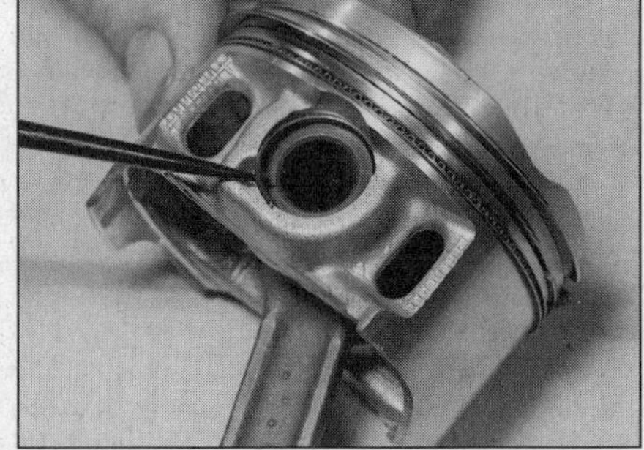

28.8 Using a scriber to pry out a piston pin snap-ring

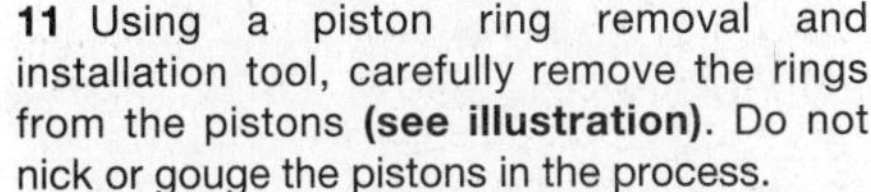

28.11 Remove the piston rings with a ring removal and installation tool

28.18 Measuring piston ring-to-groove clearance

28.19 Measuring piston diameter

11 Using a piston ring removal and installation tool, carefully remove the rings from the pistons **(see illustration)**. Do not nick or gouge the pistons in the process.

12 Scrape all traces of carbon from the tops of the pistons. A hand-held wire brush or a piece of fine emery cloth can be used once most of the deposits have been scraped away. Do not, under any circumstances, use a wire brush mounted in a drill motor to remove deposits from the pistons; the piston material is soft and will be eroded away by the wire brush.

13 Use a piston ring groove cleaning tool to remove any carbon deposits from the ring grooves. If a tool is not available, a piece broken off an old ring will do the job. Be very careful to remove only the carbon deposits. Do not remove any metal and do not nick or gouge the sides of the ring grooves.

14 Once the deposits have been removed, clean the pistons with solvent and dry them thoroughly. Make sure the oil return holes below the oil ring grooves are clear.

15 If the pistons are not damaged or worn excessively and if the cylinders are not to be rebored, new pistons will not be necessary. Normal piston wear appears as even, vertical wear on the thrust surfaces of the piston and slight looseness of the top ring in its groove. New piston rings, on the other hand, should always be used when an engine is rebuilt.

16 Carefully inspect each piston for cracks around the skirt, at the pin bosses and at the ring lands.

17 Look for scoring and scuffing on the thrust faces of the skirt, holes in the piston crown and burned areas at the edge of the crown. If the skirt is scored or scuffed, the engine may have been suffering from overheating and/or abnormal combustion, which caused excessively high operating temperatures. The oil pump and oil cooler should be checked thoroughly. A hole in the piston crown, an extreme to be sure, is an indication that abnormal combustion (pre-ignition) was occurring. Burned areas at the edge of the piston crown are usually evidence of spark knock (detonation). If any of the above problems exist, the causes must be corrected or the damage will occur again.

18 Measure the piston ring-to-groove clearance by laying a new piston ring in the ring groove and slipping a feeler gauge in beside it **(see illustration)**. Check the clearance at three or four locations around the groove. Be sure to use the correct ring for each groove; they are different. If the clearance is greater than the service limit, new pistons will have to be used when the engine is reassembled.

19 Calculate the piston-to-bore clearance by measuring the bore (see Section 26) and the piston diameter. Make sure that the pistons and cylinders are correctly matched. Measure the piston across the skirt on the thrust faces at a 90° angle to the piston pin, 11 mm up from the bottom of the skirt **(see illustration)**. Subtract the piston diameter from the bore diameter to obtain the clearance. If it is greater than specified, the cylinders will have to be rebored and new oversized pistons and rings installed.

20 Apply clean engine oil to the pin, insert it into the piston and check for freeplay by rocking the pin back-and-forth **(see illustration)**. If the pin is loose, new pistons and pins must be installed. If the necessary measuring equipment is available measure the pin diameter and piston pin bore and check the readings obtained do not exceed the limits given in this Chapter's Specifications. Replace components that are worn beyond the specified limit.

21 If the pistons are to be replaced, ensure the correct size of piston is ordered. Honda produces four oversizes of piston as well as standard pistons. The piston oversizes available are: +0.25 mm, +0.50 mm, +0.75 mm and +1.0 mm. **Note:** *Oversize pistons have their relevant size stamped on top of the piston crown, eg a 0.25 mm oversize piston will be marked 0.25.*

22 Install the rings on the pistons as described in Section 29.

Connecting rods

23 Check the connecting rods for cracks and other obvious damage. Lubricate the piston pin for each rod, install it in its original rod and check for play **(see illustration)**. If it wobbles, replace the connecting rod and/or the pin. If the necessary measuring equipment is available measure the pin diameter and connecting rod bore and check the readings obtained do not exceed the limits given in this Chapter's Specifications. Replace components that are worn beyond the specified limit.

24 Refer to Section 27 and examine the connecting rod bearing inserts If they are scored, badly scuffed or appear to have been seized, new bearings must be installed. Always replace the bearings in the connecting rods as a set. If they are badly damaged, check the corresponding crankpin. Evidence of extreme heat, such as discoloration, indicates that lubrication failure has occurred. Be sure to thoroughly check the oil pump and pressure relief valve as well as all oil holes and passages before reassembling the engine.

25 Have the rods checked for twist and bending at a dealer service department or other motorcycle repair shop.

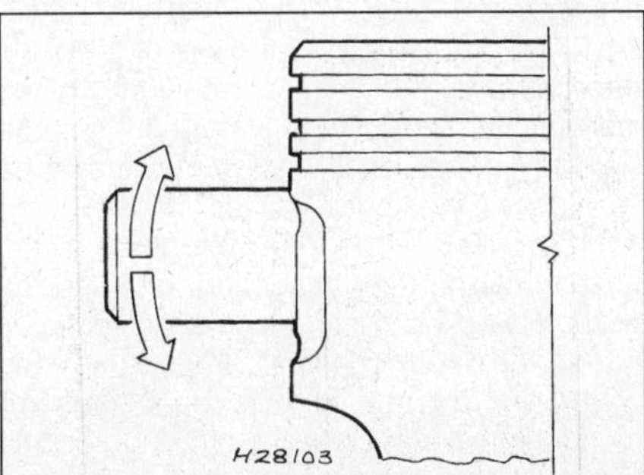

28.20 Slip the pin into the piston and try to wiggle it back-and-forth to check for freeplay

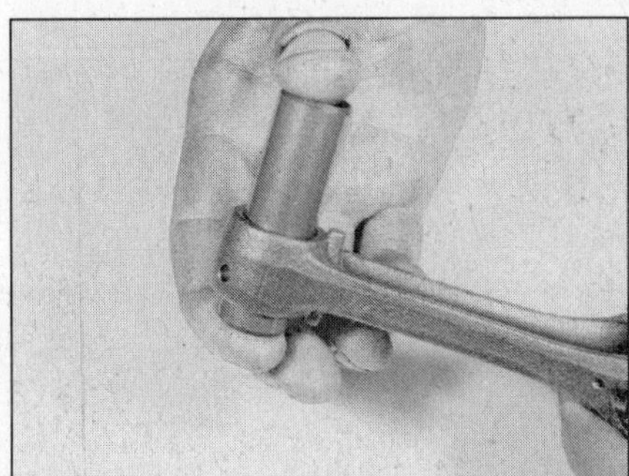

28.23 Slip the piston pin into the rod and rock it back-and-forth to check for looseness

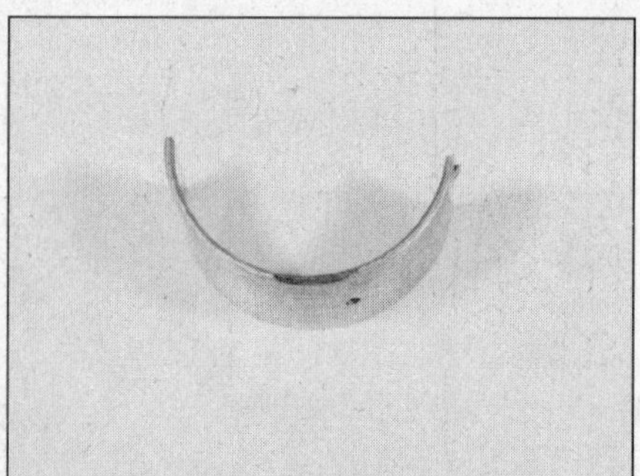

28.27 The color code is painted on the side of the bearing

26 If a connecting rod is to replaced, it is essential that the new rod is of the correct weight group to minimize vibration. The weight is indicated by a letter stamped on the big-end cap of each rod. This letter together with the connecting rod size mark (see Step 29) should be quoted when purchasing new connecting rod(s). **Note:** *Honda states that the maximum difference between any two connecting rods in the engine must be only one weight group.*

Bearing selection

27 The connecting rod bearing running clearance is controlled in production by selecting one of three grades of bearing insert. The grades are indicated by a color-coding marked on the edge of each insert **(see illustration)**. In order, from the thickest to the thinnest, the insert grades are: Brown, Green and Yellow. New bearing inserts are selected as follows using the crankpin and connecting rod size markings.

28 The standard crankpin journal diameter is divided into two size groups to allow for manufacturing tolerances. The size group of each crankpin can be determined by the letters which are stamped on the left end crank web **(see illustration)**.
Note: *Ignore the numbers as these refer to the main bearing journals.* On the web will be an L followed by four letters, made up of the letters A and B, for example LABAB. The letters indicate the diameter of each crankpin, starting with the left crankpin (number 1 cylinder) and finishing with the right crankpin

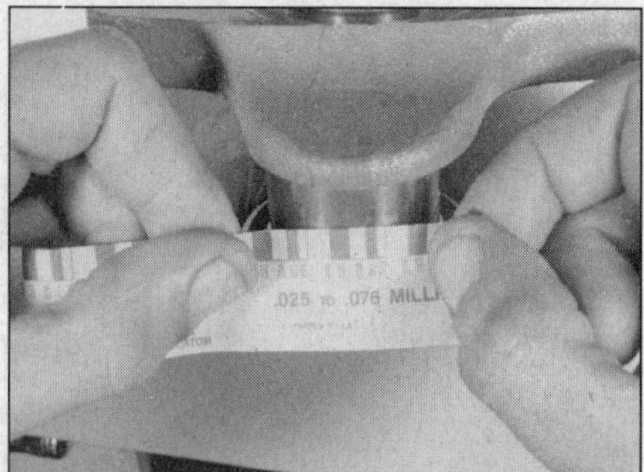

28.37 Place the Plastigage scale next to the flattened Plastigage to measure the bearing clearance

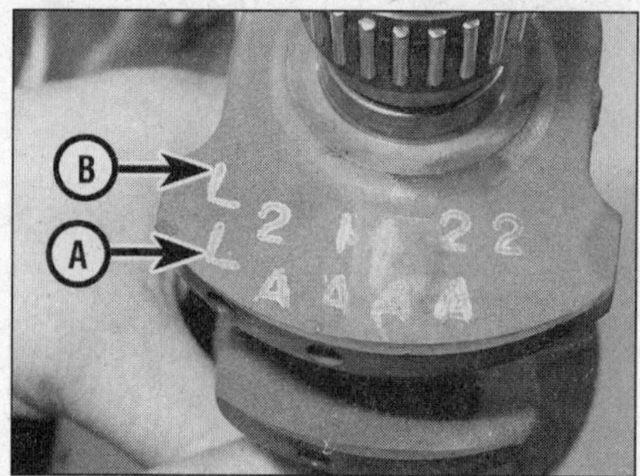

28.28 Crankshaft crankpin journal identification marks (A) and main bearing journal identification marks (B)

(number 4 cylinder). If the equipment is available, these marks can be checked by direct measurement.

29 The connecting rods are also divided into two size groups to allow for manufacturing tolerances. The size group is in the form of numbers (either 1 or 2) **(see illustration)**. **Note:** *Ignore the letter as this indicates the weight group of the connecting rod.* If the equipment is available, these marks can be checked by direct measurement.

30 Match the relevant connecting rod code with its crankshaft code and select a new set of bearing inserts using the following table.

Connecting rod mark	Crankshaft mark	Insert color
1	A	Yellow
1	B	Green
2	A	Green
2	B	Brown

Oil clearance check

31 Whether new bearing inserts are being fitted or the original ones are being re-used, the connecting rod bearing oil clearance should be checked prior to reassembly.

32 Clean the backs of the bearing inserts and the bearing locations in both the connecting rod and bearing cap.

33 Press the bearing inserts into their locations, ensuring that the tab on each insert engages in the notch in the connecting rod/bearing cap. Make sure the bearings are fitted in the correct locations and take care not to touch any insert's bearing surface with your fingers.

34 There are two possible ways of checking the oil clearance; the first method is by direct measurement (see Steps 35 and 38) and the second by the use of a product known as Plastigage (see Steps 36 to 38).

35 If the first method is to be used, fit the bearing cap to the connecting rod, with the bearing inserts in place. Make sure the cap is fitted the correct way around so the connecting rod and bearing cap weight/size markings are correctly aligned. Tighten the cap retaining nuts to the specified torque and measure the internal diameter of each assembled pair of bearing inserts. If the diameter of each corresponding crankpin journal is measured and then subtracted from the bearing internal diameter, the result will be the connecting rod bearing oil clearance.

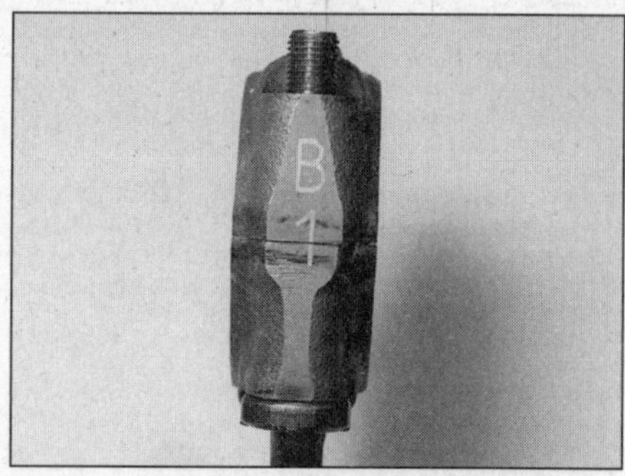

28.29 Connecting rod bearing diameter number and weight group letter

36 If the second method is to be used, cut several lengths of the appropriate size Plastigage (they should be slightly shorter than the width of the crankpin). Place a strand of Plastigage on each (cleaned) crankpin journal and fit the (clean) piston/connecting rod assemblies, inserts and bearing caps. Make sure the cap is fitted the correct way around so the connecting rod and bearing cap weight/size markings are correctly aligned and tighten the bearing cap nuts to the specified torque wrench setting while ensuring that the connecting rod does not rotate. Take care not to disturb the Plastigage. Slacken the bearing cap nuts and remove the connecting rod assemblies, again taking great care not to rotate the crankshaft.

37 Compare the width of the crushed Plastigage on each crankpin to the scale printed on the Plastigage envelope to obtain the connecting rod bearing oil clearance **(see illustration)**.

38 If the clearance is not within the specified limits, the bearing inserts may be the wrong grade (or excessively worn if the original inserts are being re-used). Before deciding that different grade inserts are needed, make sure that no dirt or oil was trapped between the bearing inserts and the connecting rod or bearing cap when the clearance was measured. If the clearance is excessive, even with new inserts (of the correct size), the crankpin is worn and the crankshaft should be replaced.

39 On completion carefully scrape away all traces of the Plastigage material from the crankpin and bearing inserts using a fingernail or other object which is unlikely to score the inserts.

Installation

40 Check that each piston has one new snap-ring fitted to it and insert the piston pin from the opposite side. If it is a tight fit, the piston should be warmed first. If the original pistons/connecting rods are being installed, use the marks made on disassembly to ensure each piston is fitted to its correct connecting rod.

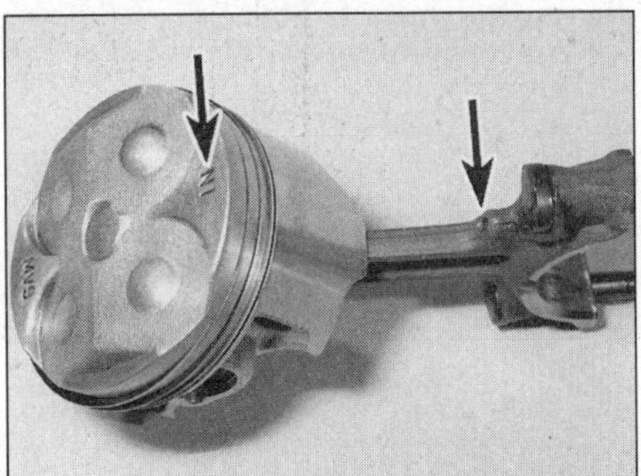

28.41 Make sure the piston IN mark is on the same side as the rod oilway (arrows)

28.42 Make sure both piston pin snap-rings are securely seated in the piston grooves

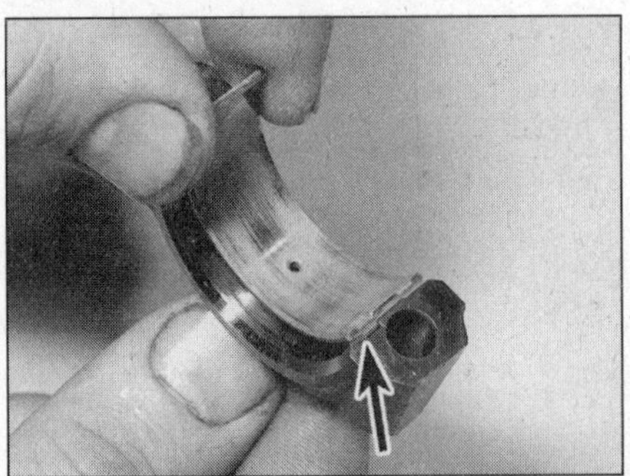

28.44 Install the bearings making sure each insert tab (arrow) is correctly engaged in its slot

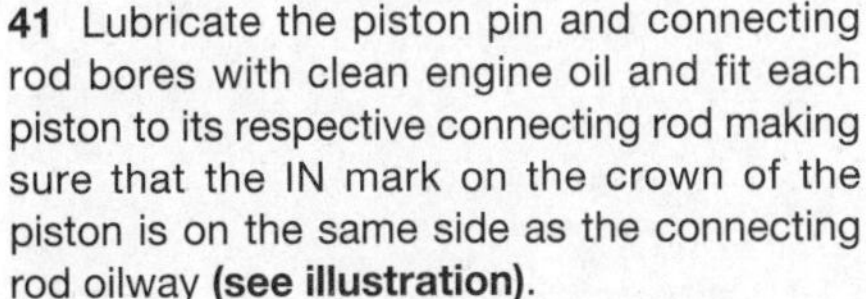

41 Lubricate the piston pin and connecting rod bores with clean engine oil and fit each piston to its respective connecting rod making sure that the IN mark on the crown of the piston is on the same side as the connecting rod oilway **(see illustration)**.

42 Push the piston pin through both piston bosses and the connecting rod bore. If necessary the pin can be tapped carefully into position, using a hammer and suitable drift, while supporting the connecting rod and piston. Secure each piston pin in position with a second new snap-ring, making sure it is correctly seated in the piston groove **(see illustration)**.

43 Clean the backs of the bearing inserts and the bearing recesses in both the connecting rod and bearing cap. If new inserts are being fitted, ensure that all traces of the protective grease are cleaned off using kerosene (paraffin). Wipe dry the inserts and connecting rods with a lint-free cloth.

44 Press the bearing inserts into their locations. Make sure the tab on each insert engages in the notch in the connecting rod or bearing cap **(see illustration)**. Make sure the bearings are fitted in the correct locations and take care not to touch any insert's bearing surface with your fingers.

45 Lubricate the cylinder bores, the pistons and piston rings then lay out each piston/connecting rod assembly in its respective position.

46 Starting with assembly number 1, position the top and second ring end gaps so they are 180 degrees apart then position the oil control ring side rails so that their end gaps are 180 degrees apart.

47 With the piston rings correctly positioned, clamp them in position with a piston ring compressor **(see illustration)**.

48 Insert the piston/connecting rod assembly into the top of its bore, taking care not to allow the connecting rod to mark the bore **(see illustration)**. Make sure the IN mark on the piston crown is on the intake side of the bore and push the piston into the position until the piston crown is flush with the top of the bore.

49 Ensure that the connecting rod bearing insert is still correctly installed. Taking care not to mark the cylinder bores, liberally lubricate the crankpin and both bearing inserts, then pull the piston/connecting rod assembly down its bore and onto the crankpin.

50 Fit the bearing cap and insert to the connecting rod. Make sure the cap is fitted the correct way around so the connecting rod and bearing cap weight/size markings are correctly aligned **(see illustration 28.29)**.

51 Apply a smear of clean engine oil the threads and underside of the bearing cap nuts. Fit the nuts to the connecting rod and tighten them evenly, in two or three stages, to the torque setting listed in this Chapter's Specifications **(see illustrations)**.

52 Check that the crankshaft is free to rotate easily, then install the three remaining assemblies in the same way.

28.47 Clamp the piston rings in position with a ring compressor . . .

29 Piston rings - installation

1 Before installing the new piston rings, the ring end gaps must be checked.

2 Lay out the pistons and the new ring sets so the rings will be matched with the same piston and cylinder during the end gap measurement procedure and engine assembly.

3 Insert the top ring into the top of the first cylinder and square it up with the cylinder walls by pushing it in with the top of the piston. The ring should be about 25 mm below the top edge of the cylinder. To measure the end gap, slip a feeler gauge between the ends of the ring and compare the measurement to the Specifications **(see illustration)**.

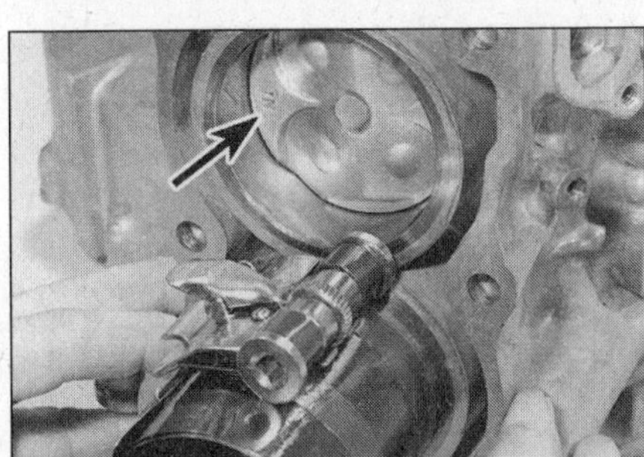

28.48 . . . and insert the piston/connecting rod assembly, making sure each piston IN mark (arrow) is on the intake side of the bore

28.51a Lubricate the threads and heads of the connecting rod bearing cap nuts . . .

28.51b . . . and tighten the nuts to the specified torque as described in text

29.3 Measuring piston ring end gap

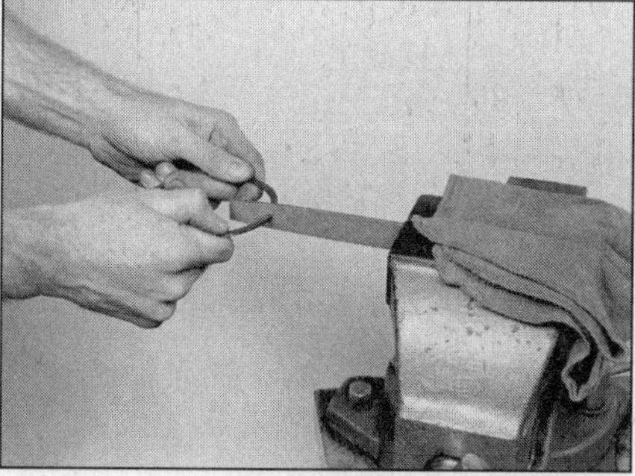
29.5 If the end gap is too small, clamp a file in a vise and file the ring ends to enlarge the gap slightly

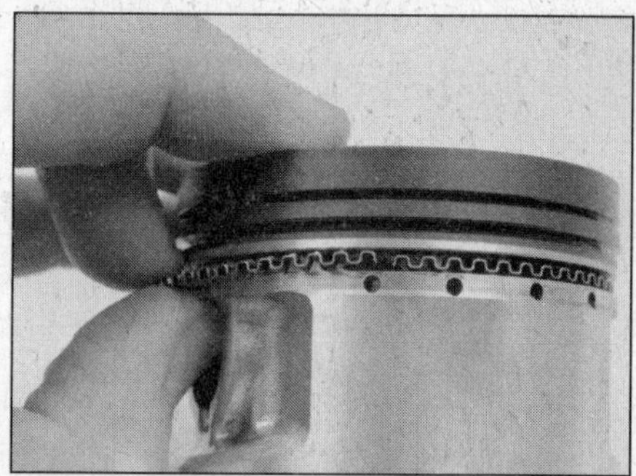
29.9a Installing the oil expander ring - make sure the ends don't overlap

4 If the gap is larger or smaller than specified, double check to make sure that you have the correct rings before proceeding.

5 If the gap is too small, it must be enlarged or the ring ends may come in contact with each other during engine operation, which can cause serious damage. The end gap can be increased by filing the ring ends very carefully with a fine file. When performing this operation, file only from the outside in **(see illustration)**.

6 Excess end gap is not critical unless it is greater than 1 mm. Again, double check to make sure you have the correct rings for your engine.

7 Repeat the procedure for each ring that will be installed in the first cylinder and for each ring in the remaining cylinders. Remember to keep the rings, pistons and cylinders matched up.

8 Once the ring end gaps have been checked/corrected, the rings can be installed on the pistons.

9 The oil control ring (lowest on the piston) is installed first. It is composed of three separate components. Slip the expander into the groove, then install the upper side rail. Do not use a piston ring installation tool on the oil ring side rails as they may be damaged. Instead, place one end of the side rail into the groove between the expander and the ring land. Hold it firmly in place and slide a finger around the piston while pushing the rail into the groove. Next, install the lower side rail in the same manner **(see illustrations)**.

10 After the three oil ring components have been installed, check to make sure that both the upper and lower side rails can be turned smoothly in the ring groove.

11 Install the second (middle) ring next. **Note:** *The second ring and top ring are identical in profile.* To avoid breaking the ring, use a piston ring installation tool and make sure that the identification mark (either a T or RN) is facing up **(see illustration)**. Fit the ring into the middle groove on the piston. Do not expand the ring any more than is necessary to slide it into place.

12 Finally, install the top ring in the same manner. Make sure the identifying mark (either a T or R) is facing up.

13 Repeat the procedure for the remaining pistons and rings.

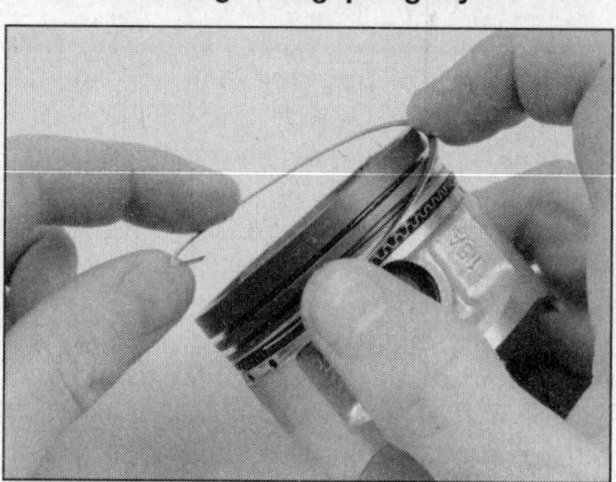
29.9b Installing an oil ring side rail - don't use a ring installation tool to do this

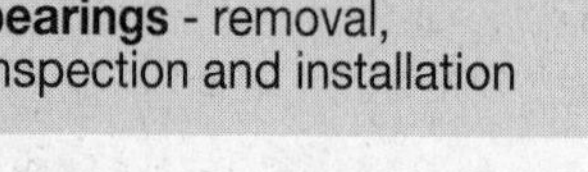

30 Crankshaft and main bearings - removal, inspection and installation

Removal

1 Separate the crankcase halves as described in Section 25.

2 Remove the piston/connecting rod assemblies as described in Section 28. **Note:** *If no work is to be carried out on the piston/connecting rod assemblies there is no need to remove them from the bores. The cylinder head can be left in position although the connecting rod bearing caps should be removed (see Section 28, Steps 1 to 3) and the pistons pushed up to the top of the bores so that the connecting rod ends are positioned clear of the crankshaft.*

30.3 Lifting the crankshaft out of position

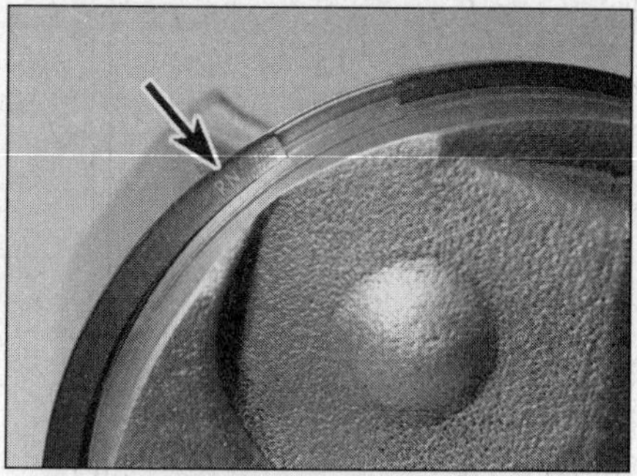
29.11 Make sure the second and top rings are installed with their identification mark (arrow) facing up

3 Lift the crankshaft out of the upper crankcase half, taking care not to dislodge the bearing inserts **(see illustration)**.

4 The main bearing inserts can be removed from the crankcase halves by pushing their centers to the side, then lifting them out. Keep the bearing inserts in order.

Inspection

5 Clean the crankshaft with solvent, using a rifle-cleaning brush to scrub out the oil passages. If available, blow the crank dry with compressed air. Inspect the starter clutch needle roller bearing as described in Section 21 **(see illustration)**.

6 Refer to Section 27 and examine the main bearing inserts. If they are scored, badly scuffed or appear to have been seized, new bearings must be installed. Always replace the main

30.5 Inspect the starter clutch needle roller bearing for signs of wear or damage

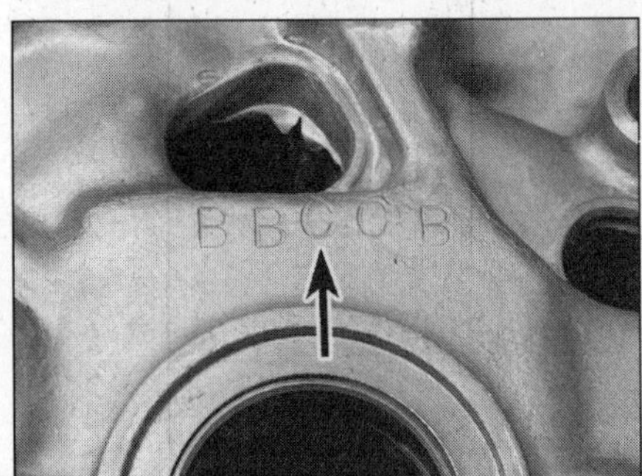

30.11 Crankcase main bearing bore diameter marks stamped on the left end of the upper crankcase half

bearings as a set. If they are badly damaged, check the corresponding crankshaft journal. Evidence of extreme heat, such as discoloration, indicates that lubrication failure has occurred. Be sure to thoroughly check the oil pump and pressure relief valve as well as all oil holes and passages before reassembling the engine.

7 The crankshaft journals should be given a close visual examination, paying particular attention where damaged bearing inserts have been discovered. If the journals are scored or pitted in any way a new crankshaft will be required. Note that undersizes are not available, precluding the option of re-grinding the crankshaft.

8 Set the crankshaft on V-blocks and check the runout with a dial indicator touching the center main bearing journal, comparing your findings with this Chapter's Specifications. If the runout exceeds the limit, replace the crank.

Bearing selection

9 The main bearing running clearance is controlled in production by selecting one of four grades of bearing insert. The grades are indicated by a color-coding marked on the edge of each insert **(see illustration 28.27)**. In order, from the thickest to the thinnest, the insert grades are: Brown, Green, Yellow and Pink. New bearing inserts are selected as follows using the crankshaft journal and crankcase main bearing bore size markings.

10 The standard crankshaft journal diameter is divided into two size groups to allow for manufacturing tolerances. The size group of each journal can be determined by the numbers which are stamped on the left end crank web **(see illustration 28.28)**. **Note:** *Ignore the letters as these refer to the crankpin journals.* On the web will be an L followed by five numbers, made up of the numbers 1 and 2, for example L12121. The numbers indicate the diameter of each crankshaft journal, starting with the left journal and finishing with the right journal. If the equipment is available, these marks can be checked by direct measurement.

11 The crankcase main bearing bore diameters are divided into three size groups to allow for manufacturing tolerances. The size group of each main bearing bore can be determined using the five letters stamped on the left end of the upper crankcase half **(see illustration)**. These wili be made up of the letters A, B or C. The first letter indicates the diameter of the left journal, and the last the diameter of the right journal. If the equipment is available, these marks can be checked by direct measurement.

12 Match the relevant crankcase code with its crankshaft code and select a new set of bearing inserts using the following table.

Crankshaft mark	Crankcase mark	Insert color
1	A	Pink
1	B	Yellow
1	C	Green
2	A	Yellow
2	B	Green
2	C	Brown

Oil clearance check

13 Whether new bearing inserts are being fitted or the original ones are being re-used, the main bearing oil clearance should be checked prior to reassembly.

14 Clean the backs of the bearing inserts and the bearing locations in both crankcase halves.

15 Press the bearing inserts into their locations, ensuring that the tab on each insert engages in the notch in the crankcase. Make sure the bearings are fitted in the correct locations and take care not to touch any insert's bearing surface with your fingers.

16 There are two possible ways of checking the oil clearance; the first method is by direct measurement (see Step 17 and 23) and the second by the use of a product known as Plastigage (see Steps 18 to 23).

17 If the first method is to be used, with the main bearing inserts in position, carefully lower the lower crankcase half onto the upper half. Make sure that the shift forks (if fitted) engage with their respective slots in the transmission gears as the halves are joined. Check that the lower crankcase half is correctly seated. **Note:** *Do not tighten the crankcase bolts if the casing is not correctly seated.* Install the ten 8 mm lower crankcase bolts in their original locations and, starting from the center and working outwards in a criss-cross pattern, tighten them to the specified torque setting. Measure the internal diameter of each assembled pair of bearing inserts. If the diameter of each corresponding crankshaft journal is measured and then subtracted from the bearing internal diameter, the result will be the connecting rod bearing oil clearance.

18 If the second method is to be used, ensure the main bearing inserts are correctly fitted and that the inserts and crankshaft are clean and dry. Lay the crankshaft in position in the upper crankcase.

19 Cut several lengths of the appropriate size Plastigage (they should be slightly shorter than the width of the crankshaft journal). Place a strand of Plastigage on each (cleaned) crankshaft journal.

20 Carefully lower the lower crankcase half onto the upper half. Make sure that the shift forks (if fitted) engage with their respective slots in the transmission gears as the halves are joined. Check that the lower crankcase half is correctly seated. **Note:** *Do not tighten the crankcase bolts if the casing is not correctly seated.* Install the ten 8 mm lower crankcase bolts in their original locations and, starting from the center and working outwards in a criss-cross pattern, tighten them to the specified torque setting. Make sure that the crankshaft is not rotated as the bolts are tightened.

21 Slacken and remove the crankcase bolts, working in a criss-cross pattern from the outside in, then carefully lift off the lower crankcase half, making sure the Plastigage is not disturbed.

22 Compare the width of the crushed Plastigage on each crankshaft journal to the scale printed on the Plastigage envelope to obtain the main bearing oil clearance **(see illustration 28.37)**.

23 If the clearance is not within the specified limits, the bearing inserts may be the wrong grade (or excessively worn if the original inserts are being re-used). Before deciding that different grade inserts are needed, make sure that no dirt or oil was trapped between the bearing inserts and the crankcase halves when the clearance was measured. If the clearance is excessive, even with new inserts (of the correct size), the crankshaft journal is worn and the crankshaft should be replaced.

24 On completion carefully scrape away all traces of the Plastigage material from the crankshaft journal and bearing inserts; use a fingernail or other object which is unlikely to score the inserts.

Installation

25 Clean the backs of the bearing inserts and the bearing recesses in both crankcase halves. If new inserts are being fitted, ensure that all traces of the protective grease are cleaned off using kerosene (paraffin). Wipe dry the inserts and crankcase halves with a lint-free cloth.

26 Press the bearing inserts into their locations. Make sure the tab on each insert engages in the notch in the casing **(see illustration)**. Make sure the bearings are fitted

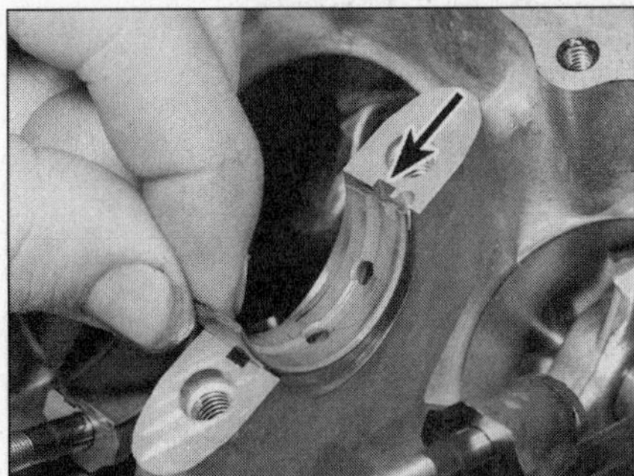

30.26 Install the main bearing inserts making sure each insert tab (arrow) is correctly engaged in the crankcase slot

30.27 Lubricate all bearing inserts with clean engine oil prior to installing the crankshaft

in the correct locations and take care not to touch any insert's bearing surface with your fingers.

27 Lubricate the bearing inserts in the upper crankcase with clean engine oil **(see illustration)**.

31.3a . . . then lift the countershaft . . .

28 Lower the crankshaft into position in the upper crankcase.

29 Fit the piston/connecting rod assemblies to the crankshaft as described in Section 28 if they were disconnected.

30 Reassemble the crankcase halves as described in Section 25.

31 Transmission shafts - removal and installation

Removal

1 Separate the crankcase halves as described in Section 25.

2 Unscrew the mainshaft bearing retaining plate bolts and remove the plate from the right side of the upper crankcase half, noting which way around it is fitted **(see illustration)**.

3 Lift the mainshaft and countershaft out of the crankcase. Do not lose the end plate from the right end of the countershaft **(see illustrations)**.

4 Recover the countershaft bearing half ring and dowel pin from the upper crankcase half and store them with the transmission shafts for safe-keeping **(see illustrations)**.

5 Remove the oil seal from the end of the countershaft and discard it; a new one must be used on installation.

6 If necessary, the transmission shafts can be disassembled and inspected for wear or damage as described in Section 32.

31.2 Undo the two bolts and remove the bearing retaining plate . . .

Installation

7 Install the countershaft bearing half ring and dowel pin in the upper crankcase.

8 Slide a new oil seal on the end of the countershaft making sure it is fitted with its sealing lip facing inwards **(see illustration)**.

9 Lower the mainshaft into position in the upper crankcase. Make sure the locating pin in the mainshaft bearing outer race is correctly locate in the groove in the crankcase.

10 Lower the countershaft into position in the crankcase half. Make sure the half ring groove, bearing pin and oil seal lip on the left end of the shaft are correctly engaged with the bearing half ring, crankcase notch and crankcase slot, and the hole in the needle bearing race on the right end of the shaft is correctly engaged with the dowel pin **(see illustrations)**.

11 Make sure both transmission shafts are correctly seated.

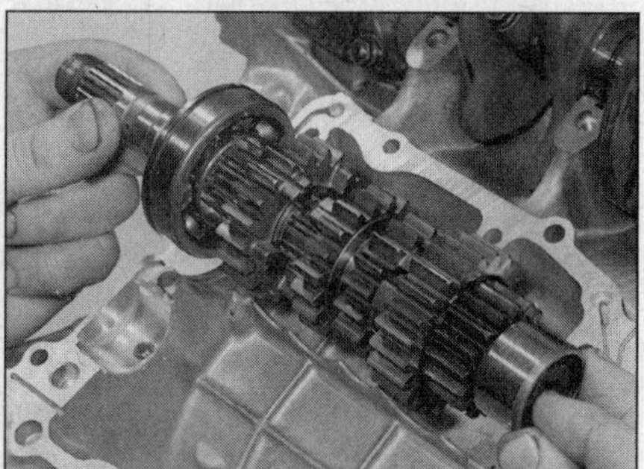

31.3b . . . and mainshaft out of the crankcase

31.4a Recover the countershaft bearing half ring . . .

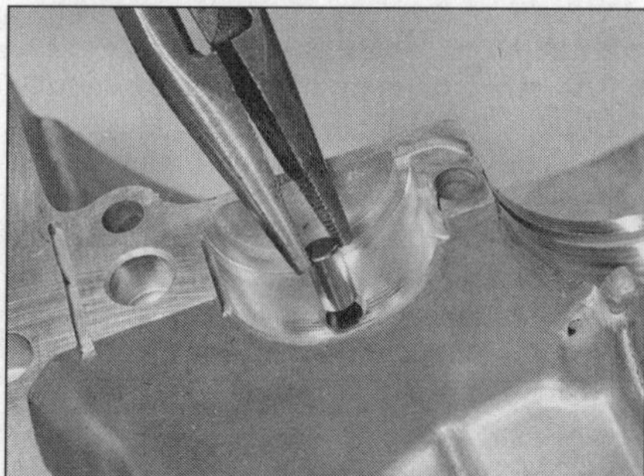

31.4b . . . and dowel pin from the upper crankcase half

31.8 Fit a new oil seal to the countershaft making sure its sealing lip is facing inwards

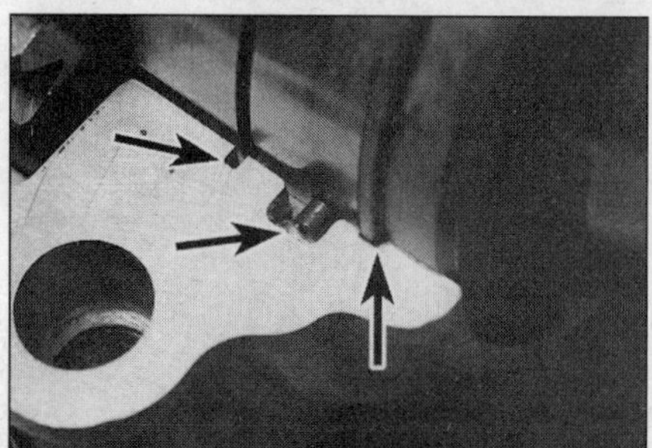

31.10a Lower the countershaft into position making sure the half ring, bearing pin and oil seal lip (arrows) . . .

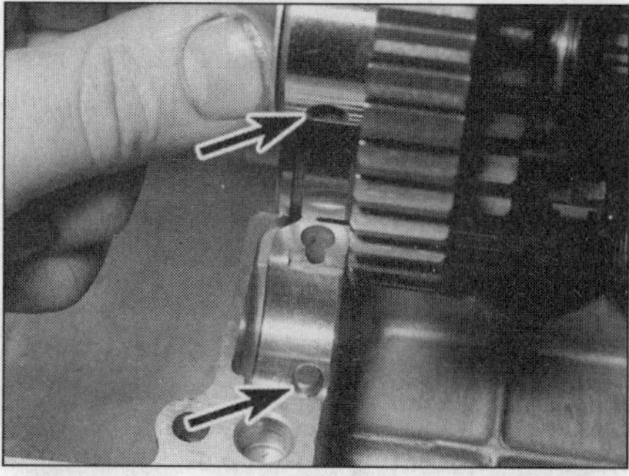

31.10b . . . and the bearing race hole and dowel pin (arrows) are correctly aligned

Caution: If the mainshaft bearing locating pin and/or countershaft half ring or dowel pin are not correctly engaged, the crankcase halves will not seat correctly.

12 Clean the mainshaft bearing plate bolts and apply a few drops of thread-locking compound to their threads.

13 Fit the bearing retaining plate to the crankcase making sure its OUT SIDE mark is facing outwards (away from the crankcase). Install the retaining bolts and tighten them securely **(see illustration)**.

14 Position the gears in the neutral position and check the shafts are free to rotate easily before proceeding further.

32 Transmission shafts - disassembly, inspection and reassembly

1 Remove the shafts from the casing as described in Section 31.

When disassembling the transmission shafts, place the parts on a long rod or thread a wire through them to keep them in order and facing the proper direction.

Mainshaft

Disassembly

2 Slide off the needle roller bearing and thrust washer from the left end of the shaft **(see illustration)**.

3 Slide off the 2nd gear.

4 Disengage the lock washer from the special splined washer and slide both off the mainshaft.

5 Remove the 6th gear followed by its splined bushing and thrust washer.

6 Remove the snap-ring using a suitable pair of snap-ring pliers.

7 Remove the 3rd/4th gear, noting which way around it is fitted.

8 Remove the second snap-ring.

9 Slide off the splined thrust washer followed by the 5th gear, 5th gear bushing and thrust washer.

Inspection

10 Wash all of the components in clean solvent and dry them off.

11 Check the gear teeth for cracking and other obvious damage. Check the gear bushings and the surface in the inner diameter of each gear for scoring or heat discoloration. If the gear or bushing is damaged, replace it.

12 Inspect the dogs and the dog holes in the gears for excessive wear. Replace the paired gears as a set if necessary.

13 The shaft is unlikely to sustain damage unless the engine has seized, placing an unusually high loading on the transmission, or the machine has covered a very high mileage. Check the surface of the shaft, especially where a pinion turns on it, and replace the shaft if it has scored or picked up. Inspect the threads of the shafts and check them for trueness by setting them up in V-blocks and measuring any runout with a dial gauge. Damage of any kind can only be cured by replacement.

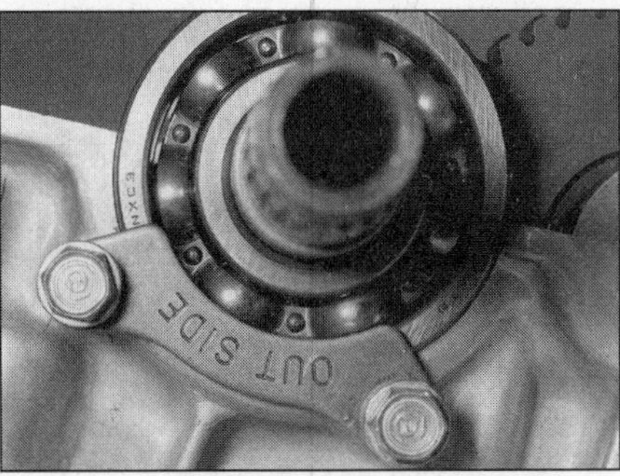

31.13 Ensure the mainshaft bearing retaining plate is fitted with its OUT SIDE mark facing outwards

14 Measure the internal diameter of all gears which run on bushings and the external diameter of the bushings which they run on. If either component has worn to or beyond its service limit it must be replaced. Using the above measurements calculate the gear to bushing clearance; if this exceeds the specified limit replace the relevant gear and bushing as a pair.

15 Check that the outer race of the bearing fitted to the end of the shaft rotates freely and has no sign of freeplay between its inner and outer races. If the bearing requires replacement, a bearing puller will be required to extract the bearing from its shaft. Note the position of the locating groove in the outer race of the bearing prior to removing it and ensure that the new bearing is fitted with the groove in the same position. Pull the bearing off of the shaft and fit the new bearing using a hammer and tubular drift which bears only on the inner race of the bearing.

Reassembly

16 During reassembly, always use new snap-rings. Lubricate the components with engine oil before assembling them.

Note: *If the thrust washers and snap-rings are examined closely it will be seen that they are chamfered on one side. During reassembly it is crucial that each thrust washer and snap-ring is fitted so its chamfer is on the correct side* **(see illustration)**.

17 Slide on the thrust washer making sure its chamfered edge is facing away from the integral 1st gear **(see illustration)**.

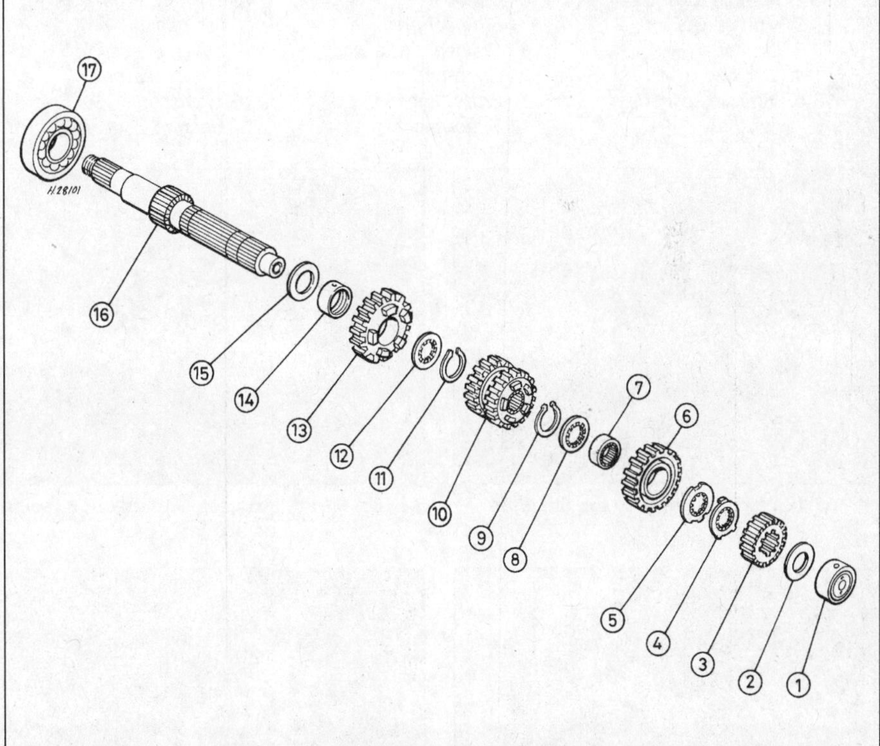

32.2 Mainshaft components

1 *Needle roller bearing*
2 *Thrust washer*
3 *2nd gear*
4 *Lock washer*
5 *Special splined washer*
6 *6th gear*
7 *6th gear bushing*
8 *Splined thrust washer*
9 *Snap-ring*
10 *3rd/4th gear*
11 *Snap-ring*
12 *Splined thrust washer*
13 *5th gear*
14 *5th gear bushing*
15 *Thrust washer*
16 *Mainshaft*
17 *Bearing*

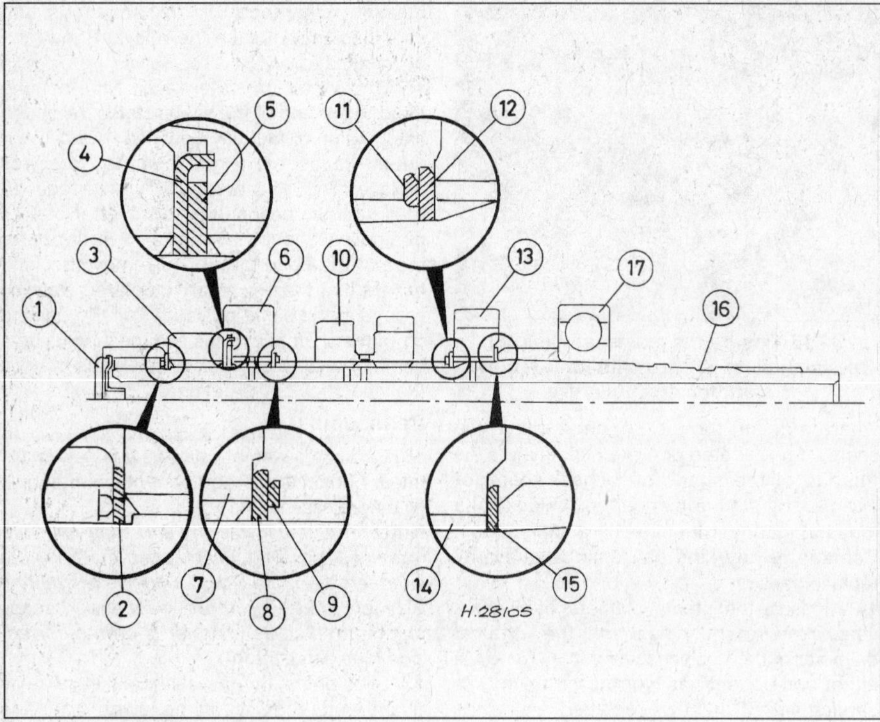

32.16 Correct fitted orientation of mainshaft snap-rings and thrust washers

1 *Needle roller bearing*
2 *Thrust washer*
3 *2nd gear*
4 *Lock washer*
5 *Special splined washer*
6 *6th gear*
7 *6th gear bushing*
8 *Splined thrust washer*
9 *Snap-ring*
10 *3rd/4th gear*
11 *Snap-ring*
12 *Splined thrust washer*
13 *5th gear*
14 *5th gear bushing*
15 *Thrust washer*
16 *Mainshaft*
17 *Bearing*

32.17 Slide on the thrust washer . . .

18 Slide on the 5th gear bushing then fit the 5th gear with its dogs facing towards the left end of the shaft. Fit the splined thrust washer with its chamfered edge facing the 5th gear **(see illustrations)**.

19 Secure the 5th gear components in position with a new snap-ring making sure its chamfered edge is facing the thrust washer **(see illustration)**. Check the snap-ring is correctly located in the mainshaft groove.

20 Install the 3rd/4th gear with its larger 4th gear facing the 5th gear. Engage the gear on the shaft splines ensuring that its oil holes are correctly aligned with the shaft oilways **(see illustration)**.

21 Fit a second new snap-ring to the shaft with its chamfered edge facing away from the 3rd/4th gear pinion. Make sure the snap-ring is correctly located in the shaft groove **(see illustration)**.

32.18a . . . followed by the 5th gear bushing

32.18b Fit the 5th gear with its dogs facing as shown . . .

32.18c . . . then fit the splined thrust washer

32.19 Secure 5th gear components in position with a snap-ring

32.20 Align the gear oil hole with the mainshaft oilway (arrows) when installing the 3rd/4th gear

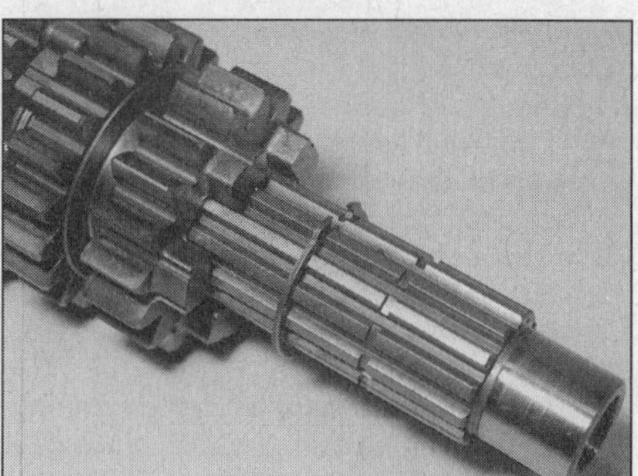

32.21 Fit a second snap-ring to the next groove . . .

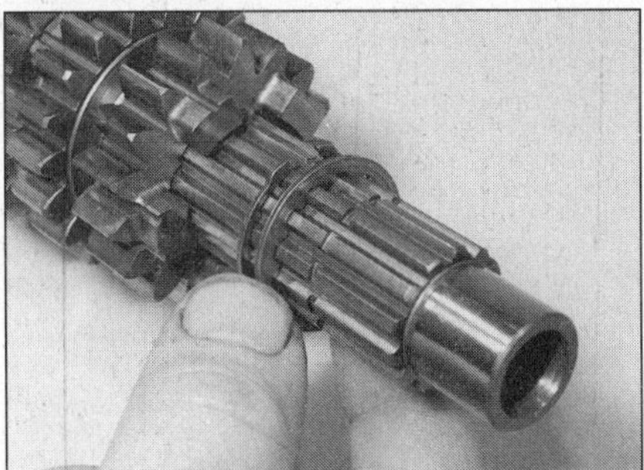

32.22 . . . then slide on a splined thrust washer

32.23a Fit the 6th gear splined bushing, aligning its oil holes with the shaft oilways . . .

32.23b . . . and fit the 6th gear with its dogs facing the 3rd/4th gear

32.24a Slide on the special splined washer . . .

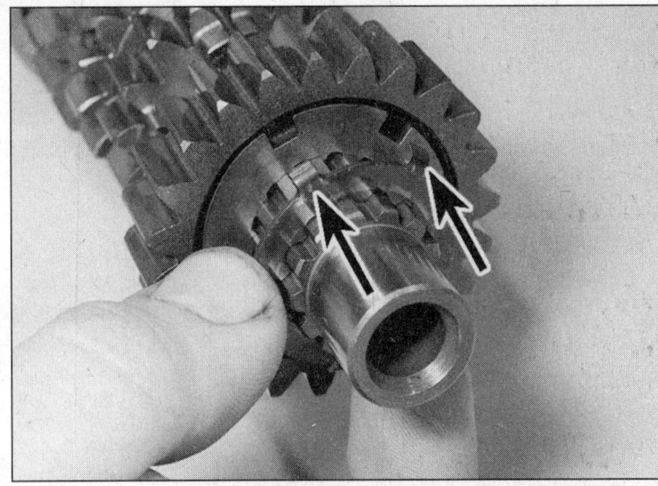

32.24b . . . then fit the lock washer engaging its tabs with the splined washer slots (arrows)

22 Slide on the splined thrust washer with its chamfered edge facing away from the snap-ring **(see illustration)**.

23 Align the 6th gear splined bushing oil holes with the shaft oilways and slide it along the shaft. Fit the 6th gear so that its dogs are facing the 3rd/4th gear **(see illustrations)**.

24 Slide the special splined washer along until it abuts the 6th gear, followed by the lock washer. Rotate the splined washer until its cutouts align with the lock washer tabs, then engage the lock washer with the splined washer to lock it in position **(see illustrations)**.

25 Fit the 2nd gear followed by the thrust washer, making sure the thrust washer chamfered edge faces the gear **(see illustrations)**.

26 Liberally oil the needle roller bearing and install it on the end of the shaft **(see illustration)**.

Countershaft

Disassembly

27 Remove the end plate from the right end of the countershaft and slide off the needle roller bearing **(see illustration overleaf)**.

28 Remove the thrust washer followed by the 1st gear, needle roller bearing and second thrust washer.

29 Remove the 5th gear noting which way around it is fitted.

30 Remove the snap-ring with a suitable pair of snap-ring pliers.

31 Slide off the splined washer followed by the 4th gear and splined bushing.

32 Disengage the lock washer from the special splined washer and slide both off the countershaft.

33 Remove the 3rd gear along with its splined bushing and thrust washer.

32.25a Fit the 2nd gear . . .

32.25b . . . followed by the thrust washer . . .

32.26 . . . then install the needle roller bearing

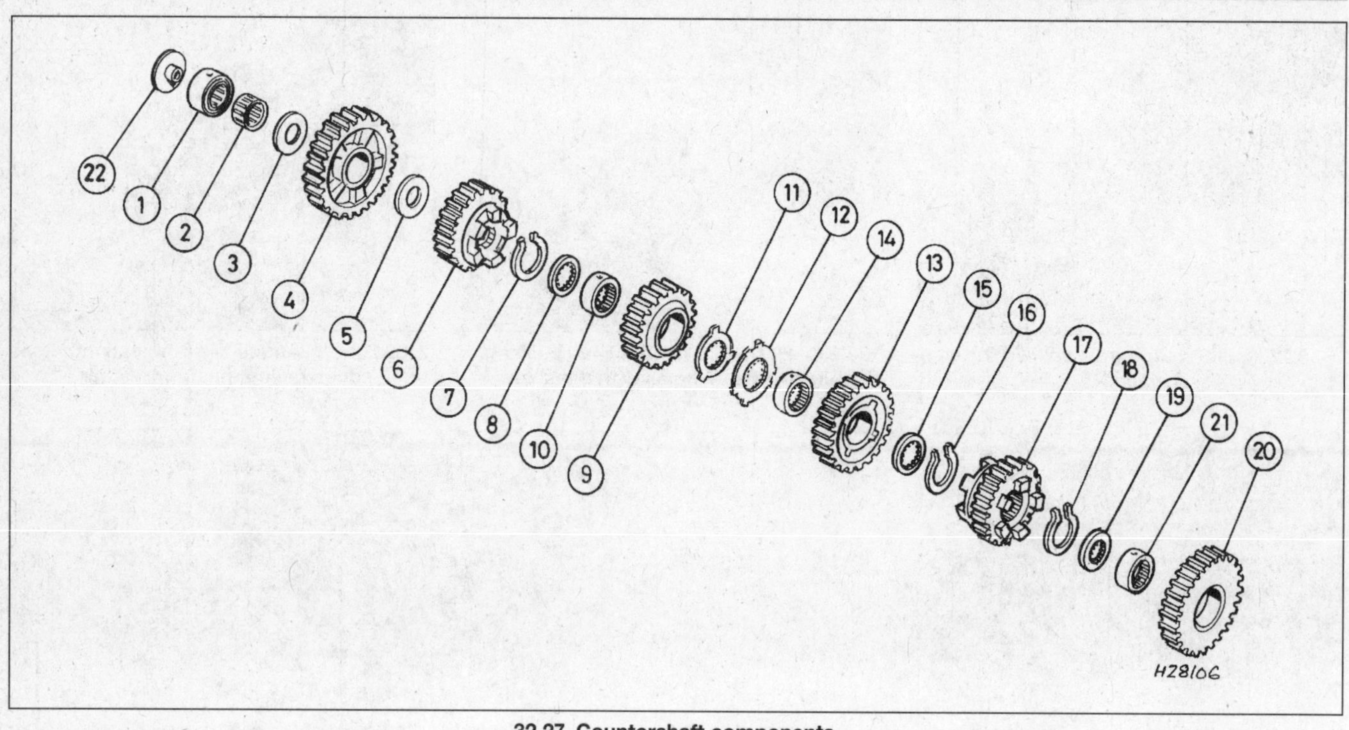

32.27 Countershaft components

1 Needle roller bearing
2 1st gear needle roller bearing
3 Thrust washer
4 1st gear
5 Thrust washer
6 5th gear
7 Snap-ring
8 Splined thrust washer
9 4th gear
10 4th gear bushing
11 Lock washer
12 Special splined washer
13 3rd gear
14 3rd gear bushing
15 Splined thrust washer
16 Snap-ring
17 6th gear
18 Snap-ring
19 Splined thrust washer
20 2nd gear
21 2nd gear bushing
22 End plate

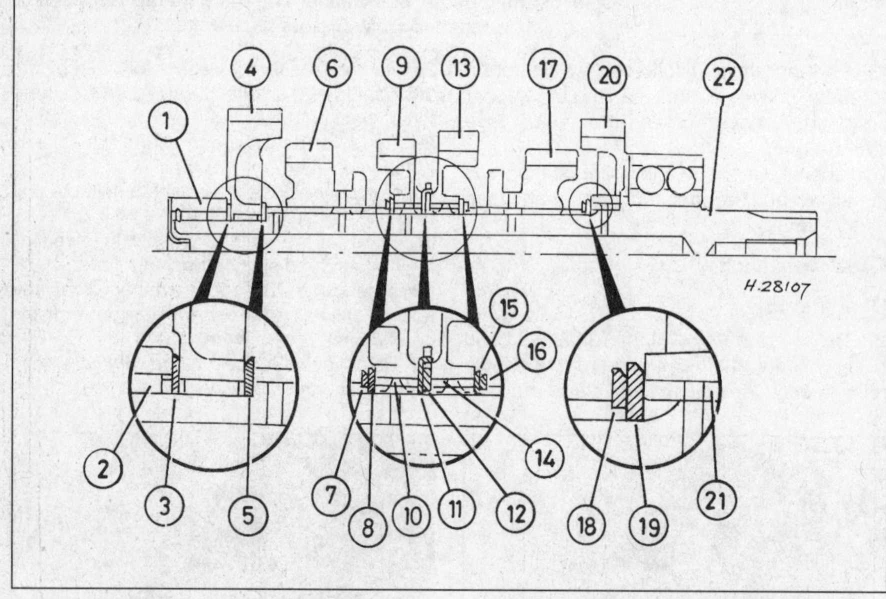

32.37 Correct fitted orientation of countershaft snap-rings and thrust washers

1 Needle roller bearing
2 1st gear needle roller bearing
3 Thrust washer
4 1st gear
5 Thrust washer
6 5th gear
7 Snap-ring
8 Splined thrust washer
9 4th gear
10 4th gear bushing
11 Lock washer
12 Special splined washer
13 3rd gear
14 3rd gear bushing
15 Splined thrust washer
16 Snap-ring
17 6th gear
18 Snap-ring
19 Splined thrust washer
20 2nd gear
21 2nd gear bushing
22 Countershaft

34 Remove the second snap-ring and slide off the 6th gear.

35 Remove the third snap-ring and slide off the splined thrust washer followed by the 2nd gear and 2nd gear bushing.

Inspection

36 Refer to Steps 10 to 15.

Reassembly

37 During reassembly, always use new snap-rings. Lubricate the components with engine oil before assembling them.

Note: *If the thrust washers and snap-rings are examined closely it will be seen that they are chamfered on one side. During reassembly it is crucial that each thrust washer and snap-ring is fitted so its chamfer is on the correct side* **(see illustration)**.

38 Slide on the 2nd gear bushing and install the 2nd gear so that its plain surface abuts the countershaft bearing. Fit the splined thrust washer with its chamfered edge facing the 2nd gear and secure the 2nd gear components in position with a new snap-ring. Fit the snap-ring with its chamfered edge facing the thrust washer and make sure it is correctly located in the countershaft groove **(see illustrations)**.

39 Fit the 6th gear to the shaft so that its shift fork groove is facing away from the 2nd gear. Align the gear oil holes with the shaft oilways and slide the gear on the shaft **(see illustration)**.

32.38a Fit the 2nd gear bushing . . .

32.38b . . . and install the 2nd gear with its plain surface facing the bearing

32.38c Slide on a splined thrust washer . . .

40 Fit a second new snap-ring with its chamfered edge facing away from the 6th gear. Ensure the snap-ring is correctly located in the shaft groove **(see illustration)**.

32.38d . . . and secure the 2nd gear components in position with a snap-ring

32.40 Fit a second snap-ring to the countershaft . . .

32.42b . . . and install the 3rd gear with its dog holes facing the 6th gear

41 Slide on the splined thrust washer with its chamfered edge facing away from the snap-ring **(see illustration)**.

42 Align the 3rd gear splined bushing oil holes with the shaft oilways and slide it along the shaft. Fit the 3rd gear so that its dog holes are facing the 6th gear **(see illustrations)**.

32.39 Slide on the 6th gear making sure its oil holes are correctly aligned with the shaft oilways (arrows)

32.41 . . . and slide on a splined thrust washer

32.43 Fit the special splined washer and lock washer engaging the lock washer tabs with the splined washer cutouts (arrows)

43 Slide the special splined washer along until it abuts the 3rd gear, followed by the lock washer. Rotate the splined washer until its cutouts align with the lock washer tabs then engage the lock washer with the splined washer to lock it in position **(see illustration)**.

44 Align the 4th gear splined bushing oil holes with the shaft oilways and slide it along the shaft. Fit the 4th gear so that its dog holes are facing away from the 3rd gear, then slide on the splined thrust washer with its chamfered edge facing the 4th gear **(see illustrations)**.

45 Secure the 4th gear components in position with a new snap-ring. Fit the snap-ring with its chamfered edge facing the thrust washer and make sure it is correctly located in the countershaft groove **(see illustration)**.

32.42a Fit the 3rd gear bushing, aligning its oil holes with the shaft oilways . . .

32.44a Slide on the 4th gear bushing, aligning its oil holes with the shaft oilways . . .

32.44b . . . and fit the 4th gear with its dog holes facing away from the 3rd gear

32.44c Slide on a splined thrust washer . . .

32.45 . . . and secure it in position with another snap-ring

32.46 Fit the 5th gear as shown

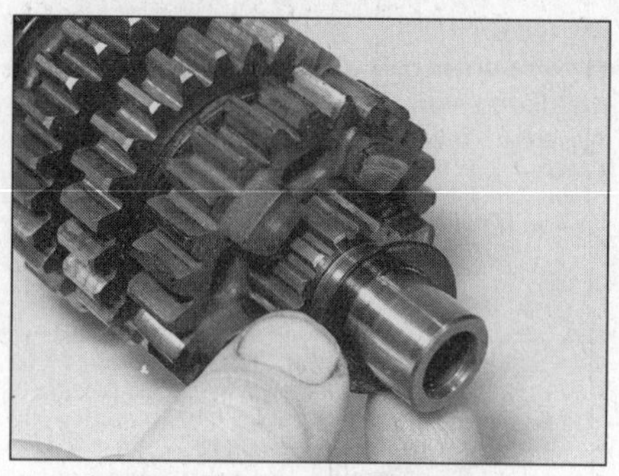
32.47a Install the thrust washer . . .

32.47b . . . followed by the 1st gear needle roller bearing . . .

46 Fit the 5th gear to the shaft so that its shift fork groove is facing the 4th gear **(see illustration)**. Align the gear oil holes with the shaft oilways and slide the gear on the shaft.

47 Fit the thrust washer to the countershaft with its chamfered edge facing away from the 5th gear then install the 1st gear needle roller bearing **(see illustrations)**.

48 Liberally lubricate the bearing, then fit the 1st gear so that its dog holes are facing the 5th gear and slide on the second thrust washer **(see illustrations)**. The chamfered edge of the thrust washer should face the 1st gear.

49 Lubricate the needle roller bearing assembly and fit it to the end of the countershaft. Fit the end plate to the bearing **(see illustration)**.

33 Initial start-up after overhaul

1 Make sure the engine oil and coolant levels are correct (see *'Daily (pre-ride) checks'*).

2 On M, N, P and R (1991 to 1994) models, turn the kill switch to the OFF position. Turn ON the ignition switch and crank the engine over with the starter until the oil pressure indicator light goes off (which indicates that oil pressure exists).

3 On S, T, V and W (1995 to 1998) models, pull off the spark plug caps and insert four spare spark plugs into the caps; lay the spark plug bodies against the cylinder head - make sure they make good ground (earth) contact with the head metal otherwise the ignition system may be damaged.

Warning: Do not remove the spark plugs from the engine to do this because atomized fuel from the spark plug holes could ignite.

Turn the kill switch to the RUN position and turn the ignition ON. Crank the engine over on the starter motor until the oil pressure indicator light goes off (which indicates that oil pressure exists). Turn the ignition OFF and remove the spare spark plugs. Install the spark plug caps.

4 On all models, make sure there is fuel in the tank, then turn the fuel tap to the ON position and operate the choke.

5 Start the engine and allow it to run at a moderately fast idle until it reaches operating temperature.

32.48a . . . then fit the 1st gear with its dog holes facing the 5th gear

32.48b Slide on another thrust washer . . .

32.49 . . . then fit the needle roller bearing and end plate

Warning: If the oil pressure indicator light doesn't go off, or it comes on while the engine is running, stop the engine immediately.

6 Check carefully for oil leaks and make sure the transmission and controls, especially the brakes, function properly before road testing the machine. Refer to Section 34 for the recommended break-in procedure.

7 Upon completion of the road test, and after the engine has cooled down completely, recheck the valve clearances (see Chapter 1) and check the engine oil and coolant levels (see *'Daily (pre-ride) checks'*).

34 Recommended break-in procedure

1 Any rebuilt engine needs time to break-in, even if parts have been installed in their original locations. For this reason, treat the machine gently for the first few miles to make sure oil has circulated throughout the engine and any new parts installed have started to seat.

2 Even greater care is necessary if the engine has been rebored or a new crankshaft has been installed. In the case of a rebore, the engine will have to be broken in as if the machine were new. This means greater use of the transmission and a restraining hand on the throttle until at least 500 miles (800 km) have been covered. There's no point in keeping to any set speed limit - the main idea is to keep from lugging (laboring) the engine and to gradually increase performance until the 500 mile (800 km) mark is reached. These recommendations can be lessened to an extent when only a new crankshaft is installed. Experience is the best guide, since it's easy to tell when an engine is running freely. The following recommendations, which Honda provides for new motorcycles, can be used as a guide.

a) 0 to 600 miles (0 to 1000 km): Keep engine speed below 5000 rpm. Vary the engine speed and don't use full throttle.

b) 600 to 1000 miles (1000 to 1600 km): Keep engine speed below 7000 rpm. Rev the engine freely through the gears, but don't use full throttle for prolonged periods.

c) After 1000 miles (1600 km): Full throttle can be used. Don't exceed maximum recommended engine speed (redline).

3 If a lubrication failure is suspected, stop the engine immediately and try to find the cause. If an engine is run without oil, even for a short period of time, severe damage will occur.

Notes

Chapter 3
Cooling system

Contents

Degrees of difficulty

Easy, suitable for novice with little experience 	**Fairly easy,** suitable for beginner with some experience 	**Fairly difficult,** suitable for competent DIY mechanic 	**Difficult,** suitable for experienced DIY mechanic 	**Very difficult,** suitable for expert DIY or professional

Specifications

Coolant

Mixture type	50% distilled water, 50% corrosion inhibited ethylene glycol antifreeze
Capacity	
Radiator and engine	2.4 lit (2.53 US qt, 4.2 Imp pt)
Coolant reservoir	0.35 lit (0.38 US qt, 0.7 Imp pt)

Radiator

Cap valve opening pressure	1.10 to 1.40 bars (16 to 20 psi)

Thermostat

Opening temperature	80 to 84°C (176 to 183°F)
Fully open	95°C (203°F)
Minimum valve lift	8 mm (0.32 in) @ 95°C (203°F)

Torque settings

	Nm	ft-lbs
Cooling fan thermostatic switch	10	7
Temperature gauge sender unit	10	7

1 General information

The cooling system uses a water/antifreeze coolant to carry away excess energy in the form of heat. The cylinders are surrounded by a water jacket from which the heated coolant is circulated by thermo-syphonic action in conjunction with a water pump, driven off the oil pump. The hot coolant passes upwards to the thermostat and through to the radiator (mounted on the frame's front downtubes to take maximum advantage of the passing airflow). The coolant then flows across the radiator core, where it is cooled by the passing air, down to the water pump and back up to the engine where the cycle is repeated. A thermostat is fitted in the system to prevent the coolant flowing through the radiator when the engine is cold, therefore accelerating the speed at which the engine reaches normal operating temperature. A thermostatically-controlled cooling fan is also fitted to aid cooling in extreme conditions.

The complete cooling system is partially sealed and pressurized, the pressure being controlled by a valve contained in the spring-loaded radiator cap. By pressurizing the coolant the boiling point is raised, preventing premature boiling in adverse conditions. The overflow pipe from the system is connected to a reservoir into which excess coolant is expelled under pressure. The discharged coolant automatically returns to the radiator when the engine cools.

Warning: Do not allow antifreeze to come in contact with your skin or painted surfaces of the motorcycle. Rinse off any spills immediately with plenty of water. Antifreeze is highly toxic if ingested. Never leave antifreeze lying around in an open container or in puddles on the floor; children and pets are attracted by its sweet smell and may drink it. Check with the local authorities about disposing of used antifreeze. Many communities will have collection centers which will see that antifreeze is disposed of safely.

Caution: Do not remove the pressure cap from the radiator when the engine is hot. Scalding hot coolant and steam may be blown out under pressure, which could cause serious injury. To gain access to the pressure cap, remove the right lower fairing panel (see Chapter 8), then remove the fuse access panel from the upper fairing and the upper fairing right mounting screw; ease the edge of the fairing away from the fuel tank so that the cap can be reached between the fairing and tank. When the engine has cooled, place a thick rag, like a towel over the radiator cap; slowly rotate the cap counterclockwise (anti-clockwise) to the first stop. This procedure allows any residual pressure to escape. When the steam has stopped escaping, press down on the cap while turning it counterclockwise (anti-clockwise) and remove it.

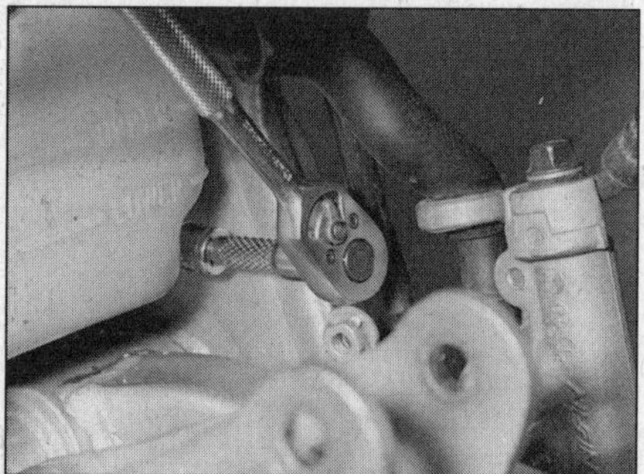

3.6a Unscrew the reservoir mounting bolt . . .

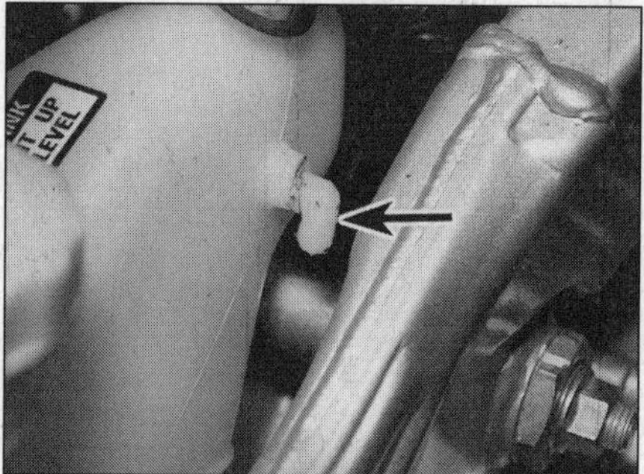

3.6b . . . then disengage the mounting hook (arrow) . . .

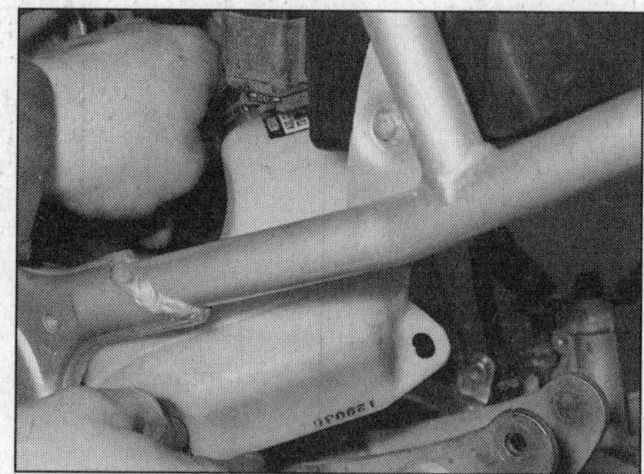

3.6c . . . and maneuver the coolant reservoir out from the frame

2 Radiator cap - check

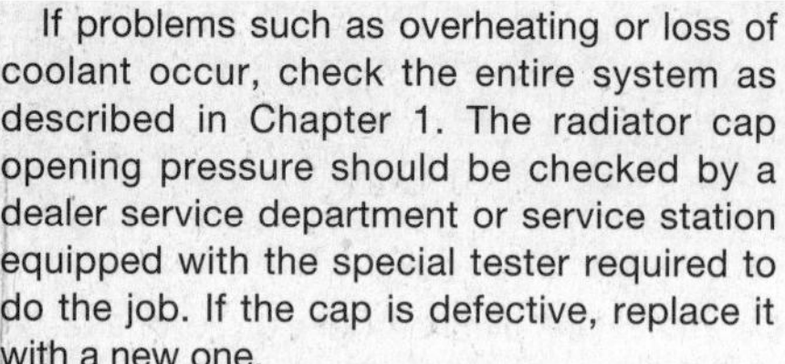

If problems such as overheating or loss of coolant occur, check the entire system as described in Chapter 1. The radiator cap opening pressure should be checked by a dealer service department or service station equipped with the special tester required to do the job. If the cap is defective, replace it with a new one.

3 Coolant reservoir - removal and installation

Removal

1 Drain the cooling system as described in Chapter 1.

2 Remove the right side cover (see Chapter 8, if necessary).

3 Remove the rear shock absorber as described in Chapter 6.

4 Disconnect the two hoses from the top and bottom of the reservoir and allow any residual coolant to drain from the reservoir.

5 Unscrew the rear brake master cylinder reservoir mounting bolt and reposition the brake reservoir clear of the coolant reservoir. Keep the brake reservoir upright to prevent fluid loss.

6 Undo the coolant reservoir mounting bolt and remove the reservoir from the machine. To release the reservoir upper locating hook from the frame, move the reservoir towards the rear of the bike **(see illustrations)**.

Installation

7 Installation is the reverse of the removal sequence noting the following.

a) *Apply a few drops of locking compound to the threads of the master cylinder reservoir bolt then fit the bolt and tighten it to the specified torque setting (see Chapter 7).*

b) *On completion refill the cooling system as described in Chapter 1.*

4 Cooling fan and thermostatic switch - check and replacement

Check

1 If the engine is overheating and the cooling fan isn't coming on, first check the cooling fan switch fuse. If the fuse is blown, check the fan circuit for a short to ground/earth (see the *wiring diagrams* at the end of this book).

2 If the fuse is sound, disconnect the wire from the fan switch which is fitted to the left side of the radiator. If necessary, remove the left side lower fairing to improve access to the switch as described in Chapter 8. Turn the ignition switch on and ground (earth) the fan switch wire. As the wire is grounded the fan should come on. If it does the fan switch is defective and must be replaced, although a more comprehensive test is described below in Steps 5 to 7.

3 If the fan does not come on the fault lies in either the cooling fan motor or relevant wiring. The wiring can be tested as described in Chapter 9.

4 To test the cooling fan motor, trace the wiring back from the motor and disconnect it at the connector. On M, N, P and R (1991 to 1994) models, remove the air filter housing as described in Chapter 4 to gain access to the fan motor wiring connector, mounted on the left side of the frame, in front of the ignition coils **(see illustration)**. On S, T, V and W (1995 to 1998) models, the connector is behind the left-hand end of the radiator **(see illustration)**. Using a 12 volt battery and two jumper wires, connect the battery across the terminals of the cooling fan block connector. Once connected

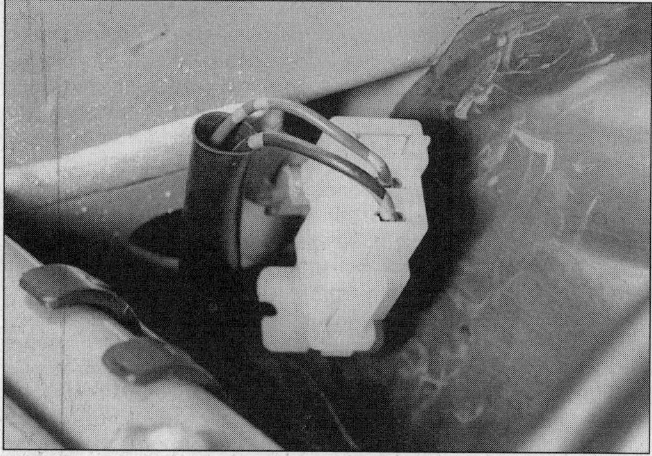

4.4a On M, N, P and R (1991 to 1994) models, the cooling fan wiring connector is clipped to the left side of the frame, in front of the ignition HT coils

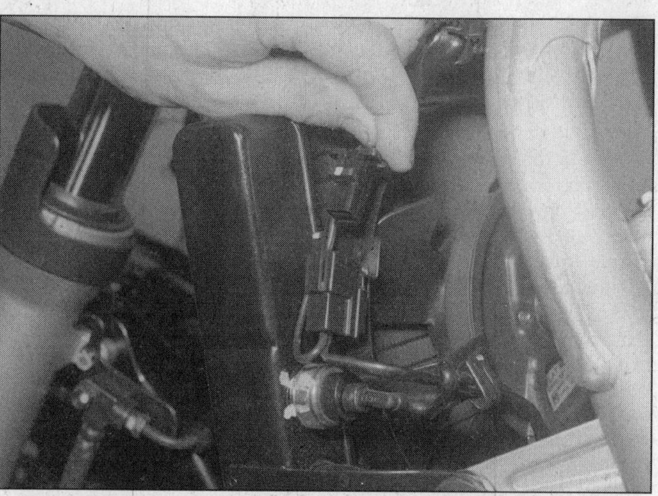

4.4b On S, T, V and W (1995 to 1998) models, the cooling fan wiring connector is behind the left end of the radiator

the fan should operate. If this is not the case the fan motor is faulty and must be replaced.

5 To fully test the fan switch, a heatproof container, a small gas-powered camping stove, a thermometer capable of reading up to 110°C (230°F) and an ohmmeter or multimeter will be required.

Warning: Antifreeze is poisonous. Don't use a cooking pan. Remove the switch as described in Steps 16 to 18.

6 Remove the switch (see below). Fill the container with coolant of the specified type and strength and suspend the switch on some wire so that just the sensing portion and threads are submerged. Connect one probe of the meter to the switch terminal and the other to the body of the switch. Suspend the thermometer so that its bulb is close to the switch **(see illustration)**. **Note:** *No components should be allowed to touch the container.*

7 Set the meter to the ohms x 1 scale and start to heat the coolant, stirring it gently, until the coolant is between 98 - 102°C (208 - 216°F).

Warning: This must be done very carefully to avoid the risk of personal injury.

With the coolant at this temperature the meter should show a reading of 0 ohms indicating that the switch has closed. Carry on heating the coolant until it reaches 102°C (216°F) then turn the stove off. Note the resistance reading of the switch as the temperature falls. When the coolant cools to 93°C (208°F) there should no longer be continuity between the meter probes. If this is not the case the fan switch is defective and must be replaced.

Replacement

Fan motor

8 Remove the radiator (see Section 7).

9 Disconnect the wiring connector from the thermostatic switch **(see illustration)**.

10 Unscrew the bolt from the bottom of the radiator and the two nuts (M, N, P and R (1991 to 1994) models) or bolts (S, T, V and W (1995 to 1998) models), from the top of the radiator. Separate the fan assembly from the radiator noting the correct position of the fan motor ground/earth lead **(see illustrations)**.

11 Unscrew the retaining nut and remove the fan blade from the motor **(see illustration)**.

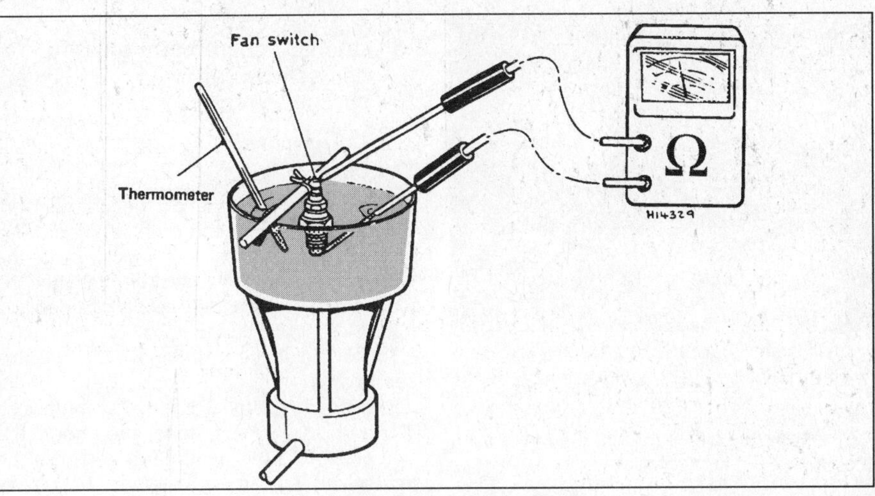

4.6 Fan switch testing set-up

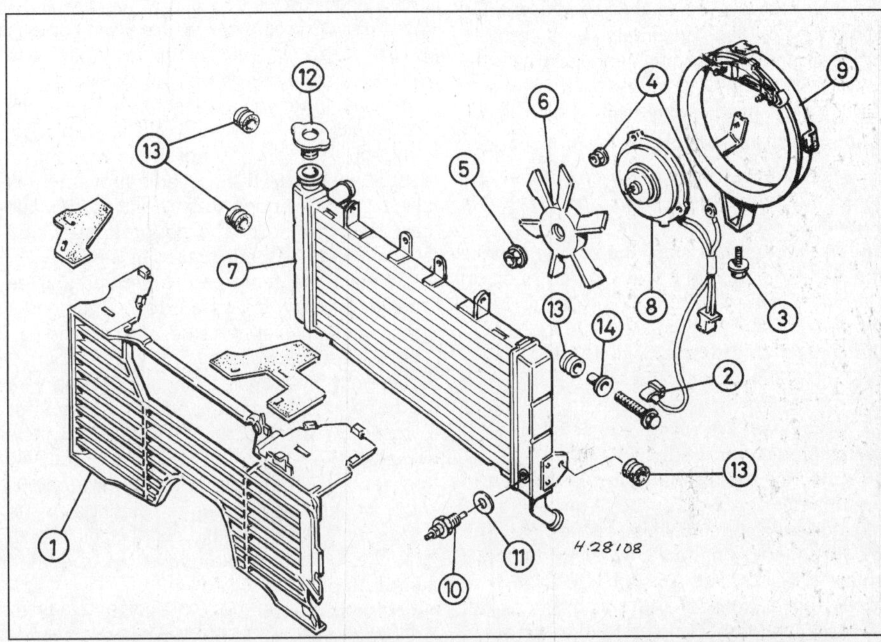

4.9 Radiator and associated components - M, N, P and R (1991 to 1994) models

1 Grille
2 Fan motor and switch wiring
3 Fan shroud bolt
4 Ground/earth lead and nut
5 Fan blade nut
6 Fan blade
7 Radiator
8 Fan motor
9 Fan shroud
10 Fan thermostatic switch
11 O-ring
12 Radiator cap
13 Mounting damper
14 Spacer

4.10a Unscrew the fan assembly retaining bolt . . .

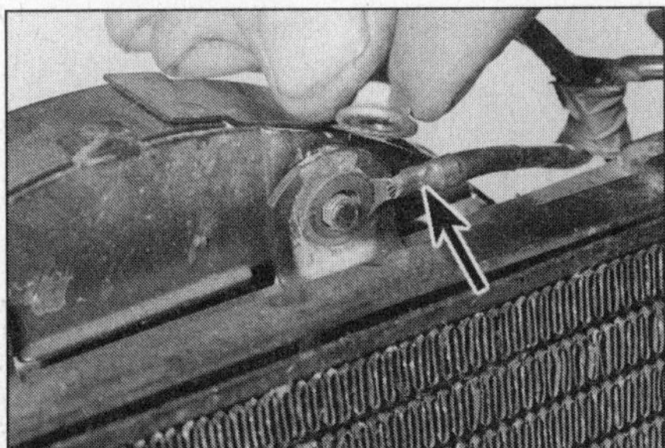

4.10b . . . and nuts or bolts, noting the correct fitted position of the ground/earth lead (arrow)

4.11 Fan blade is retained by a nut (arrow)

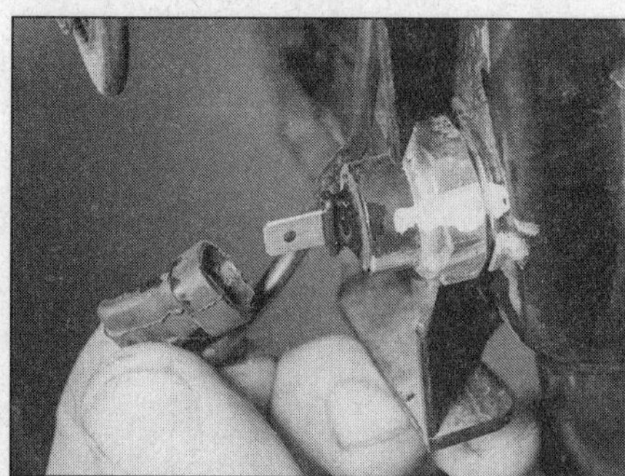

4.17 Disconnect the cooling fan switch wiring connector. The switch is a screw fit in the radiator

12 Release the clips and free the wiring from the back of the fan motor shroud.

13 Unscrew the nuts and separate the fan motor from the shroud.

14 Installation is the reverse of removal. On fitting the fan blade ensure its slot is correctly aligned with the motor shaft and make sure the motor ground/earth lead is correctly positioned.

15 Install the radiator as described in Section 7.

Thermostatic switch

Warning: The engine must be completely cool before this procedure.

16 To improve access to the switch, remove the left side fairing panel as described in Chapter 8. On M, N, P and R (1991 to 1994) models, the switch is threaded into the front of the radiator on the left side. On S, T, V and W (1995 to 1998) models, the switch is threaded into the back of the radiator, on the left side.

17 Disconnect the wiring connector from the switch **(see illustration)**.

18 Unscrew the switch from the left side of the radiator and recover the O-ring. Plug the radiator opening to minimize coolant loss.

19 Fit a new O-ring to the switch and apply a smear of sealant to the switch threads.

20 Remove the plug and quickly install the new switch, tightening it to the specified torque setting.

21 Connect the wiring connector to the switch and install the fairing panel.

22 Check the coolant level and if necessary, top up as described in *'Daily (pre-ride) checks'*.

5 Coolant temperature gauge and sender unit - check and replacement

Check

1 The circuit consists of the sender unit mounted in the right end of the cylinder head and the gauge assembly mounted in the instrument panel. If the system malfunctions check first that the battery is fully charged and that all fuses are in good condition.

2 To test the circuit, first remove the fuel tank (see Chapter 4) to gain access to the sender unit wiring connector. Turn the ignition switch ON and disconnect the wire from the temperature sender unit. Ground (earth) the sender unit wire to earth. When the wire is grounded the needle should swing immediately over to the H on the gauge.

Caution: Do not ground the wire for any longer than is necessary to take the reading, or the gauge may be damaged.

If the needle moves as described above, the sender unit is defective and must be replaced, although a more comprehensive test is described below. If the needle movement is still faulty, of if it does not move at all, the fault lies in the wiring or the gauge itself which should be tested as described in Step 4.

3 Remove the temperature sender unit as described below in Steps 5 to 7. The sender unit is tested in the same way as the fan switch, referring to Steps 5 to 7 of Section 4, noting that the container should be filled with oil rather than coolant and a thermometer capable of reading up to 120°C (248°F) will be required. Heat the oil gently, stirring it slowly to keep a uniform temperature throughout, while noting the resistance readings of the sender unit. A serviceable sender unit should give the following readings at the specified temperatures.

Temperature	80°C (176°F)	120°C (248°F)
Resistance	45 to 60 ohms	10 to 20 ohms

If the sender unit does not produce the specified resistances at the stated temperatures it must be replaced.

4 If the gauge appears to be faulty, remove the instrument cluster as described in Chapter 9, and check the relevant wiring connectors. If all appears to be well, the gauge is defective and must be replaced.

Replacement

Temperature sender unit

Warning: The engine must be completely cool before this procedure.

5 Remove the fuel tank, and on S, T, V and W (1995 to 1998) models the carburetors, as described in Chapter 4.

6 Disconnect the wiring connector from the switch.

7 Unscrew the sender unit from the cylinder head. Plug the head opening to minimize coolant loss.

8 Apply a smear of sealant to the switch threads.

9 Remove the plug and quickly install the new sender unit, tightening it to the specified torque setting.

10 Connect the wiring connector to the sender unit and install the fuel tank as described in Chapter 4.

11 Check the coolant level and, if necessary, top up as described in *'Daily (pre-ride) checks'*.

Temperature gauge

12 See Chapter 9.

6 Thermostat - removal, check and installation

Warning: The engine must be completely cool before carrying out this procedure.

Removal

1 The thermostat is automatic in operation and should give many years service without requiring attention. In the event of a failure, the valve will probably jam open, in which case the engine will take much longer than normal to warm up. Conversely, if the valve jams shut, the coolant will be unable to circulate and the engine will overheat. Neither condition is acceptable, and the fault must be investigated promptly.

2 Drain the cooling system (see Chapter 1).

3 Remove the right lower fairing panel as described in Chapter 8, if not already done.

4 Slacken the clip and disconnect the coolant hose from the thermostat housing **(see illustration)**.

5 Unscrew the three bolts and remove the thermostat housing **(see illustration)**. Recover the housing O-ring.

6 Remove the thermostat from the cylinder head.

Check

7 Examine the thermostat visually before carrying out the test. If it remains in the open position at room temperature, it should be replaced.

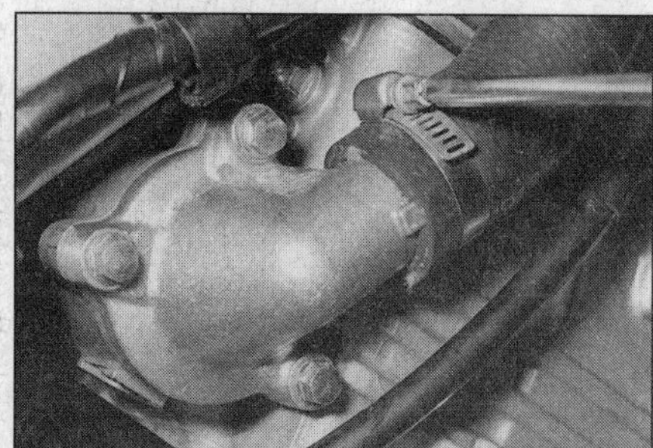

6.4 Slacken the retaining clip and disconnect the coolant hose from the thermostat housing

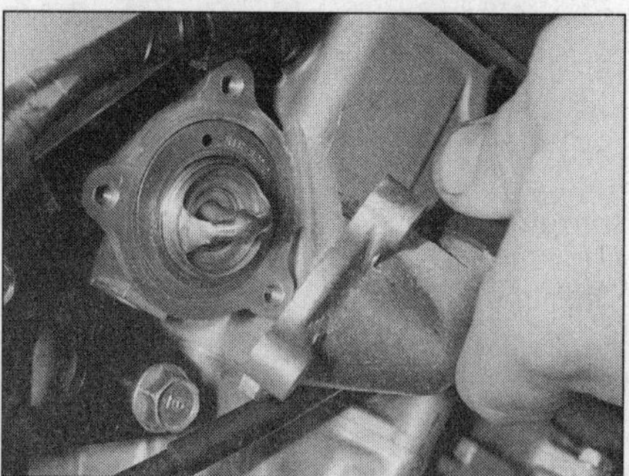

6.5 Remove the housing and lift out the thermostat

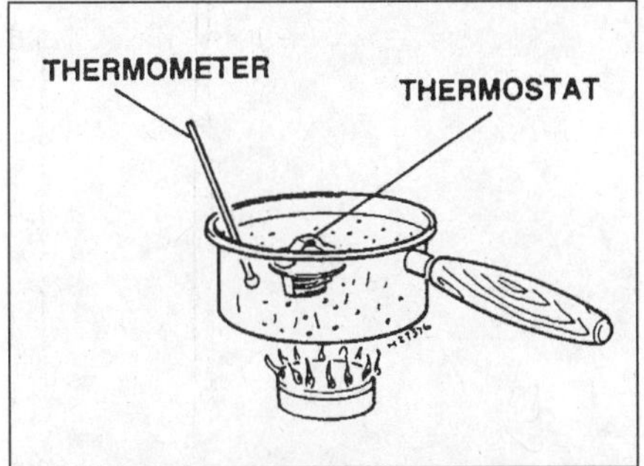

6.8 Thermostat opening check

8 Suspend the thermostat by a piece of wire in a container of cold water. Place a thermometer in the water so that the bulb is close to the thermostat **(see illustration)**. Heat the water, noting when the thermostat opens and how much valve lift it has when it is fully open, and compare the results with those given in the Specifications. If the readings obtained differ from those given, the thermostat is faulty and must be replaced.

9 In the event of thermostat failure, as an emergency measure only, it can be removed and the machine used without it. **Note:** *Take care when starting the engine from cold as it will take much longer than usual to warm up. Ensure that a new unit is installed as soon as possible.*

Installation

10 Set the motorcycle on its sidestand. This will ensure the thermostat will remain in position in the head.

11 Fit the thermostat to the cylinder head noting that its small bypass hole must be positioned at the top **(see illustration)**.

12 Fit a new O-ring to the housing cover and install the cover. Securely tighten the cover retaining bolts.

13 Reconnect the coolant hose and securely tighten its retaining clip.

14 Refill the cooling system as described in Chapter 1.

15 Fit all disturbed fairing sections as described in Chapter 8.

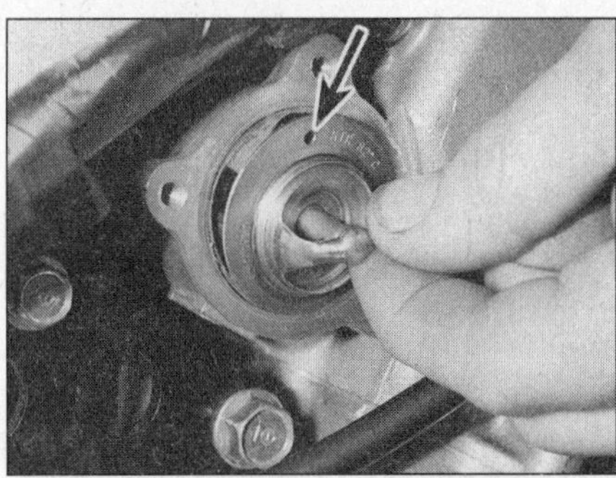
6.11 When installing the thermostat make sure that its bypass hole (arrow) is at the top

7 Radiator - removal and installation

Warning: The engine must be completely cool before carrying out this procedure.

Removal

1 Remove the left and right side lower fairing panels as described in Chapter 8.

2 On M, N, P and R (1991 to 1994) models, remove the air filter housing as described in Chapter 4.

3 Drain the cooling system as described in Chapter 1.

4 Slacken the retaining clips and disconnect the top and bottom hoses from the radiator **(see illustrations)**. On S, T, V and W (1995 to 1998) models, disconnect the top hose from the radiator itself rather than from the filler neck, and remove the radiator without the remote filler neck.

5 Release the retaining clip and disconnect the coolant reservoir hose from the radiator filler neck **(see illustration)**.

6 On M, N, P and R (1991 to 1994) models, free the fan motor wiring connector from the top of the frame and disconnect the connector **(see illustration)**. On S, T, V and W (1995 to 1998) models, disconnect the connector and free the wiring from the clamp **(see illustration 4.4b)**.

7 On M, N, P and R (1991 to 1994) models, undo the bolt and free the horn mounting bracket from the left side of the machine **(see illustration)**.

8 Unscrew the three radiator mounting bolts and recover the spacer from each radiator mounting damper **(see illustrations)**.

7.4a Slacken the retaining clips and disconnect the top . . .

7.4b . . . and bottom hoses from the radiator

7.5 Release the clip and disconnect the reservoir hose from the radiator neck

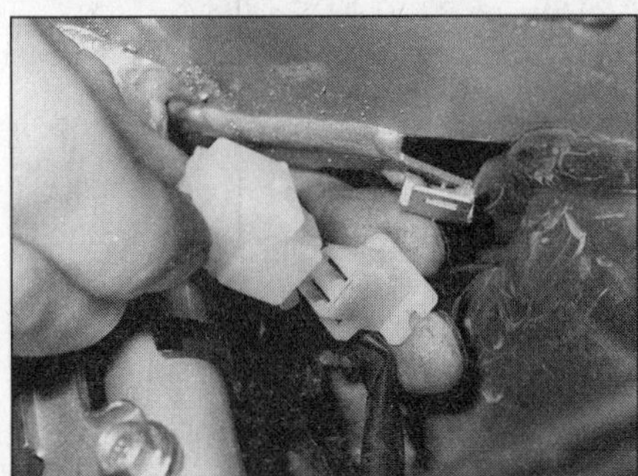
7.6 Disconnect the cooling fan wiring connector and release the connector from the frame

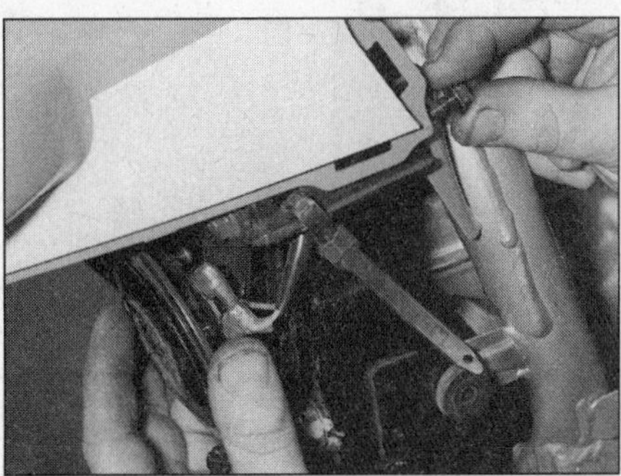
7.7 Unscrew the mounting bolt and remove the horn bracket assembly from the left side of the frame

7.8a Unscrew the three bolts . . .

7.8b . . . and recover the spacer from each radiator mounting

7.9 Removing the radiator assembly

7.10 Inspect the mounting dampers and replace them if they are damaged

9 Move the radiator to disengage it from its upper locating peg and carefully remove the radiator, taking great care not to damage the radiator fins **(see illustration)**.

10 Check the radiator mounting dampers for signs of damage or deterioration and replace if necessary **(see illustration)**.

Installation

11 Installation is the reverse of the removal sequence noting the following.

a) Locate the radiator on its mounting peg, fit the spacer to each mounting damper and securely tighten the mounting bolts.
b) Make sure that the fan wiring is correctly routed, in no danger of being caught by the fan and is retained by any relevant clips.
c) Ensure the coolant hoses are securely retained by their clips.
d) On completion refill the cooling system as described in Chapter 1.

8 Water pump - check, removal and installation

Check

1 Remove the left side lower fairing panel as described in Chapter 8 and visually check the area around the water pump for signs of leakage.

2 To prevent leakage of water or oil from the cooling system to the lubrication system and vice versa, two seals are fitted on the pump shaft. On the underside of the pump body there is also a drainage hole. If either seal fails this hole should allow the coolant or oil to escape and prevent the oil and coolant mixing.

3 The seal on the water pump side is of the mechanical type which bears on the rear face of the impeller. The second seal, which is mounted behind the mechanical seal is of the normal feathered lip type. However, neither seal is available as a separate item as the pump is a sealed unit. Therefore, if on inspection the drainage hole shows signs of leakage, the pump must be removed and replaced.

Removal

Warning: The engine must be completely cool before carrying out this procedure.

4 Remove the left side lower fairing panel (if not already done) as described in Chapter 8.

5 Drain the cooling system as described in Chapter 1.

6 Release the retaining clip(s) and disconnect the small hose(s) from the water pump cover - on M, N, P and R (1991 to 1994) models there is one hose, on S and T (1995 and 1996) models there are two, and on V and W (1997 and 1998) models there are three hoses **(see illustrations)**. Make a careful note of which fits where before detaching them.

7 Slacken the retaining clips and disconnect the main coolant hoses from the water pump body and cover **(see illustration)**.

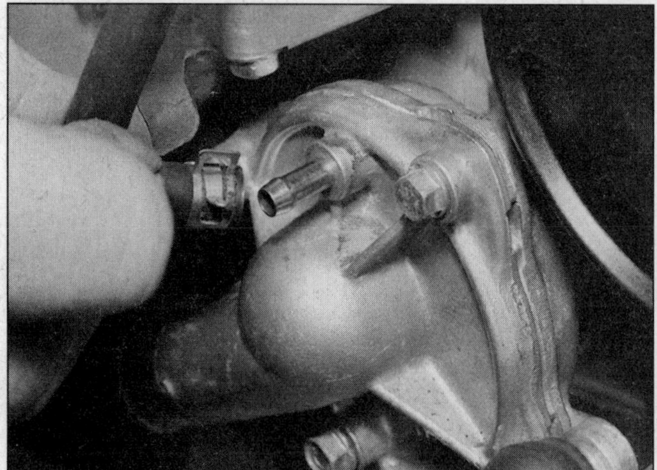
8.6a On M, N, P and R (1991 to 1994) models, disconnect the single small hose from the water pump cover

8.6b On V and W (1997 and 1998) models, disconnect the three small hoses (arrows) from the water pump cover

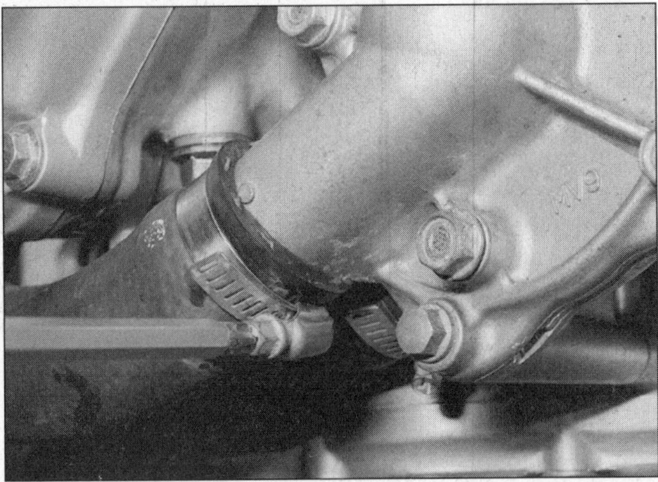

8.7 Slacken the retaining clips and disconnect the coolant hoses from the pump cover and body

8.8 Water pump mounting bolts (A) and cover retaining bolts (B)

8 Unscrew the mounting bolts and withdraw the water pump from the engine unit **(see illustration)**. Recover the O-ring from the water pump body.

9 Undo the remaining bolts and lift off the pump cover. Recover the sealing ring.

10 Wiggle the water pump impeller back-and-forth and in-and-out. If there is excessive movement the pump must be replaced.

Installation

11 Fit a new O-ring to the rear of the pump body and install the pump, aligning the slot in the impeller shaft with the projection on the oil pump shaft **(see illustrations)**.

12 Fit a new sealing ring to the pump body and fit the cover to the pump body **(see illustrations)**.

13 Install the cover retaining bolts and the pump mounting bolts and tighten them securely.

14 Reconnect the coolant hoses to the pump and cover, making sure each one is correctly positioned and securely retained by its clip. On S and T (1995 and 1996) models, the hose from the left side of the cylinder head fits onto the top union and the hose from the carburetor heater system fits onto the bottom union. On V and W (1997 and 1998) models, the hose from the left side of the cylinder head fits onto the top union, the hose from the carburetor heater system fits onto the middle rear-facing union, and the larger hose from the right-side of the cylinder head fits onto the bottom union.

15 Refill the cooling system (see Chapter 1).

8.11a Align the water pump impeller shaft slot with the oil pump shaft projection (arrows) . . .

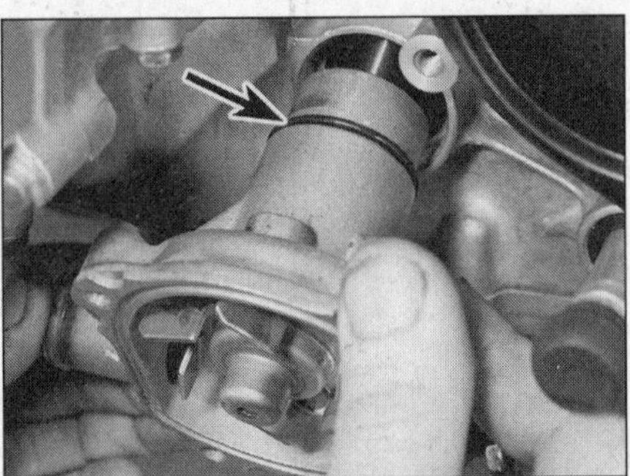

8.11b . . . and insert the pump in the crankcase. Do not forget the pump O-ring (arrow)

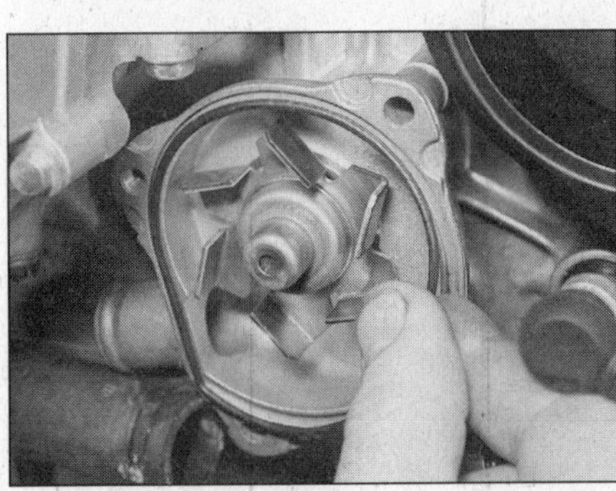

8.12a Fit a new sealing ring to the pump body . . .

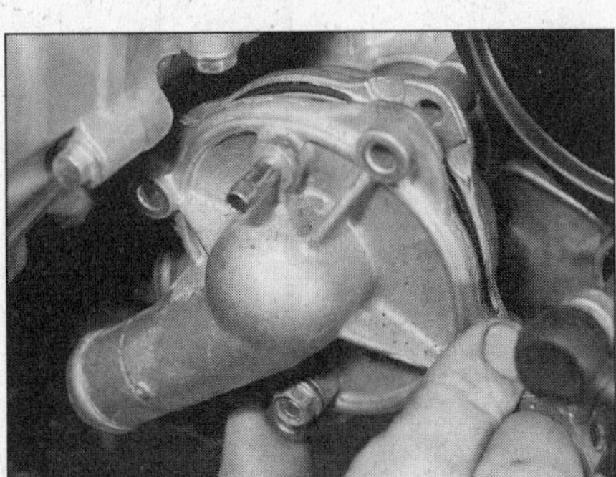

8.12b . . . and install the pump cover

9 Coolant hoses - removal and installation

Removal

1 Before removing a hose, drain the coolant as described in Chapter 1.

2 Use a screwdriver to slacken the hose clamps, then slide them back along the hose and clear of the union spigot.

Caution: The radiator unions are fragile. Do not use excessive force when attempting to remove the hoses.

Refer to Tools and Workshop Tips in the Reference section for radiator hose removal methods.

Installation

3 Slide the clips onto the hose and then work it on to its respective union.

If the hose is difficult to push on its union, it can be softened by soaking it in very hot water, or alternatively a little soapy water can be used as a lubricant.

4 Rotate the hose on its unions to settle it in position before sliding the clips into place and tightening them securely.

Notes

Chapter 4
Fuel and exhaust systems

Contents

Degrees of difficulty

Easy, suitable for novice with little experience 

Fairly easy, suitable for beginner with some experience 

Fairly difficult, suitable for competent DIY mechanic 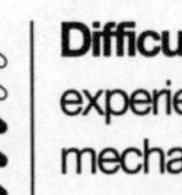

Difficult, suitable for experienced DIY mechanic 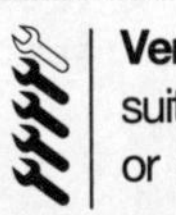

Very difficult, suitable for expert DIY or professional

Specifications

Fuel grade	Unleaded or leaded (according to local regulations), minimum 91 octane (research method)
Fuel tank capacity	
Main tank	
M, N, P and R models (1991 to 1994 models)	16 lit (4.23 US gal, 3.52 Imp gal)
S, T, V and W models (1995 to 1998 models)	17 lit (4.50 US gal, 3.70 Imp gal)
Reserve tank - all models	3.0 lit (0.8 US gal, 0.7 imp gal)
Carburetor	
M, N, P and R models (1991 to 1994 models)	
Type	Keihin CV 34 mm
Identification code	
California models	VP42A
US models (except California)	VP41A
UK models	VP40A
S and T models (1995 and 1996 models)	
Type	Keihin CV 36 mm
Identification code	
California models	VP62A
US models (except California)	VP61A
UK models	VP60A
V and W models (1997 and 1998 models)	
Type	Keihin CV 36 mm
Identification code	
California models	VP62A
US models (except California)	VP61A
UK models	VP60H

Jet sizes

M, N, P and R models (1991 to 1994 models)		
Main jet		
California models	132	
US models (except California) and UK models	135	
Pilot jet (all models)	38	
Pilot screw - initial setting (turns out)		
California models	2¾	
US models (except California)	2⅛	
UK models	2¼	
S and T models (1995 and 1996) models		
Main jet		
California models	135	
US models (except California) and UK models		
Nos. 1 and 4 carburetor	135	
Nos. 2 and 3 carburetor	138	
Pilot jet (all models)	40	
Pilot screw - initial setting (turns out)		
California models	1⅞	
US models (except California)	1½	
UK models	2	
V and W (1997 and 1998) models		
Main jet		
Nos. 1 and 4 carburetor	138	
Nos. 2 and 3 carburetor	140	
Pilot jet	40	
Pilot screw - initial setting (turns out)	2	

Carburetor adjustments

Float height (all models)	13.7 mm (0.54 in)
Idle speed	See Chapter 1

Torque settings

	Nm	ft-lbs
Engine mounting bracket 10 mm bolt - S, T, V and W (1995 to 1998) models	45	33
Exhaust system		
Muffler (silencer) clamp bolts	21	15
Front pipe nuts	20	14

1 General information and precautions

General information

The fuel system consists of the fuel tank, the fuel tap and filter, the carburetors and the connecting lines, hoses and control cables. On S, T, V and W (1995 to 1998) models, fuel is delivered to the carburetors by a fuel pump.

The carburetors used on these motorcycles are four Keihin CV carburetors. For cold starting, an enrichment circuit is actuated by a cable and the choke lever on the left handlebar.

Air is drawn to the carburetors from a molded plastic air filter housing containing a pleated paper type element. The S, T, V and W (1995 to 1998) models have a Direct Air Intake (DAI) system, which scoops air via a duct below the headlight. The system incorporates a solenoid valve which directs air via different routes according to engine speed.

The exhaust system is a four-into-one design.

Many of the fuel system service procedures are considered routine maintenance items and for that reason are included in Chapter 1.

Precautions

Warning: Gasoline (petrol) is extremely flammable, so take extra precautions when you work on any part of the fuel system. Don't smoke or allow open flames or bare light bulbs near the work area, and don't work in a garage where a natural gas-type appliance (such as a water heater or clothes dryer) is present. If you spill any fuel on your skin, rinse it off immediately with soap and water. When you perform any kind of work on the fuel system, wear safety glasses and have a fire extinguisher suitable for a class B type fire (flammable liquids) on hand.

Always perform service procedures in a well-ventilated area to prevent a build-up of fumes.

Never work in a building containing a gas appliance with a pilot light, or any other form of naked flame. Ensure that there are no naked light bulbs or any sources of flame or sparks nearby.

Do not smoke (or allow anyone else to smoke) while in the vicinity of gasoline (petrol) or of components containing it. Remember the possible presence of vapor from these sources and move well clear before smoking.

Check all electrical equipment belonging to the house, garage or workshop where work is being undertaken (see the Safety first! section of this manual). Remember that certain electrical appliances such as drill, cutters etc. create sparks in the normal course of operation and must not be used near gasoline (petrol) or any component containing it. Again, remember the possible presence of fumes before using electrical equipment.

Always mop up any spilt fuel and safely dispose of the shop towel or rag used.

Any stored fuel that is drained off during servicing work, must be kept in sealed containers that are suitable for holding gasoline (petrol), and clearly marked as such; the containers themselves should be kept in a safe place. Note that this last point applies equally to the fuel tank, if it is removed from the machine; also remember to keep its cap closed at all times.

Read the Safety first! section of this manual carefully before starting work.

Owners of machines used in the US, particularly California, should note that their machines must comply at all times with Federal or State legislation governing the permissible levels of noise and of pollutants such as unburnt hydrocarbons, carbon

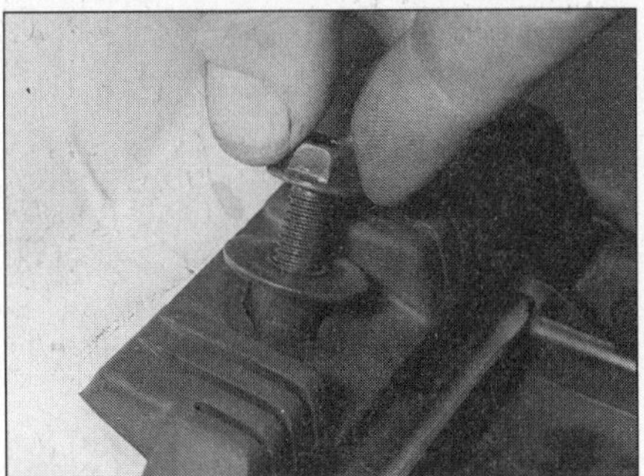
2.3a Unscrew the fuel tank rear mounting bolt and remove the spacer . . .

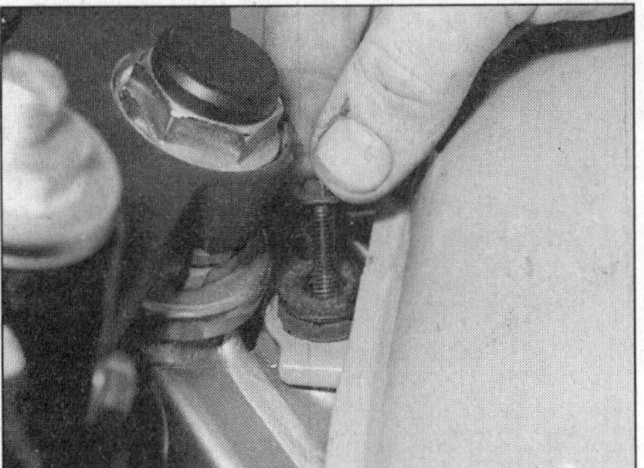
2.3b . . . then undo the front bolt . . .

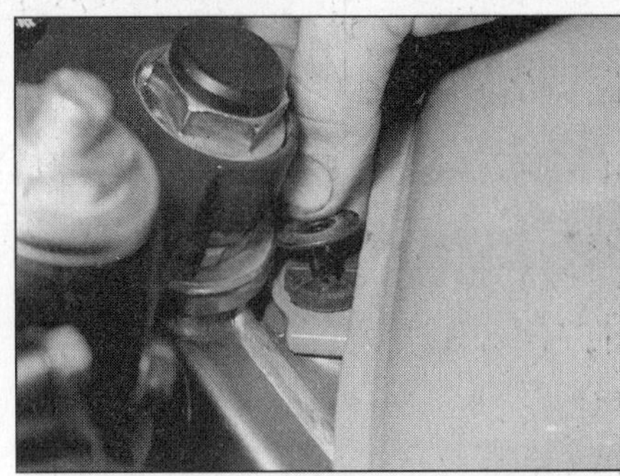
2.3c . . . and withdraw the spacer

monoxide etc. that can be emitted by those machines. All vehicles offered for sale must comply with legislation in force at the date of manufacture and must not subsequently be altered in any way which will affect their emission of noise or of pollutants.

In practice, this means that adjustments may not be made to any part of the fuel, ignition or exhaust systems by anyone who is not authorized or mechanically qualified to do so, or who does not have the tools, equipment and data necessary to properly carry out the task. Also if any part of these systems is to be replaced it must be replaced with only genuine Honda components or by components which are approved under the relevant legislation. The machine must never be used with any part of these systems removed, modified or damaged.

2.5a Release the retaining clip and disconnect the fuel hose (arrow) . . .

2 Fuel tank - removal and installation

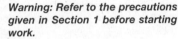

Warning: Refer to the precautions given in Section 1 before starting work.

Removal

1 Set the bike on its centerstand.
2 Remove the seat as described in Chapter 8.
3 Unscrew the fuel tank front and rear mounting bolts and remove the spacers from the center of each tank mounting damper **(see illustrations)**.
4 Ensure the fuel tap is turned OFF.
5 Disconnect the fuel hose, and on M, N, P and R (1991 to 1994) models, the vacuum hose, from the fuel tap **(see illustrations)**.
6 Lift up the rear of the fuel tank and disconnect the breather and drain hoses from the underside of the tank **(see illustration)**.
7 Lift the fuel tank away from the machine taking care not to lose the mounting damper from each side of the tank **(see illustration)**.
8 Inspect the tank mounting dampers for signs of damage or deterioration and replace if necessary.

Installation

9 Lower the fuel tank into position, making sure the mounting rubbers remain in position, and reconnect the breather and drain hoses to the rear of the tank**(see illustration 2.6)**.
10 Connect the fuel hose, and on M, N, P and R (1991 to 1994) models the vacuum hose, to the fuel tap, ensuring they are securely retained by their clips **(see illustrations 2.5a and b)**.
11 Fit the spacers to the mounting rubbers and install the mounting bolts, tightening them securely.
12 Fit the seat as described in Chapter 8.
13 Start the engine and check that there is no sign of fuel leakage.

3 Fuel tank - cleaning and repair

1 All repairs to the fuel tank should be carried out by a professional who has experience in this critical and potentially dangerous work. Even after cleaning and flushing of the fuel system, explosive fumes can remain and ignite during repair of the tank.
2 If the fuel tank is removed from the vehicle, it should not be placed in an area where sparks or open flames could ignite the fumes coming out of the tank. Be especially careful inside garages where a natural gas-type appliance is located, because the pilot light could cause an explosion.

4 Idle fuel/air mixture adjustment - general information

Due to the increased emphasis on controlling motorcycle exhaust emissions, certain governmental regulations have been formulated which directly affect the carburation

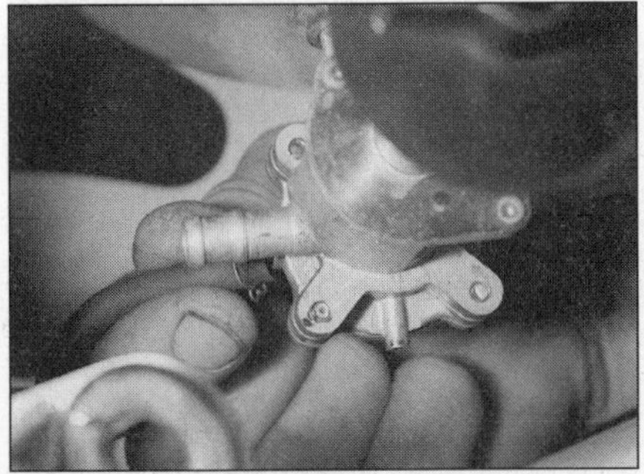
2.5b . . . and vacuum hose from the fuel tap

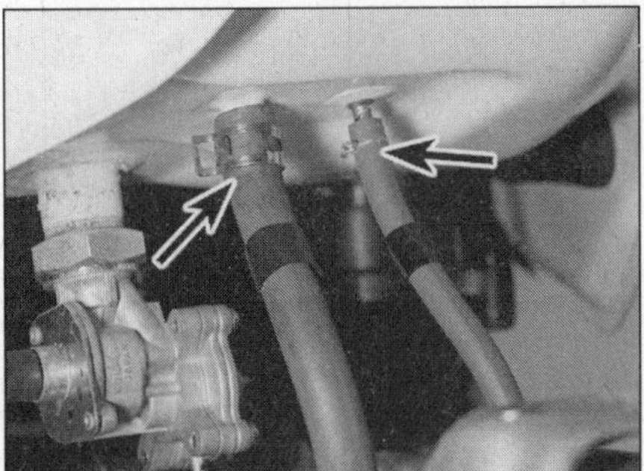
2.6 Lift the rear of tank and disconnect the breather and drain hoses (arrows)

2.7 Lift the fuel tank away from the machine and recover the mounting damper (arrow)

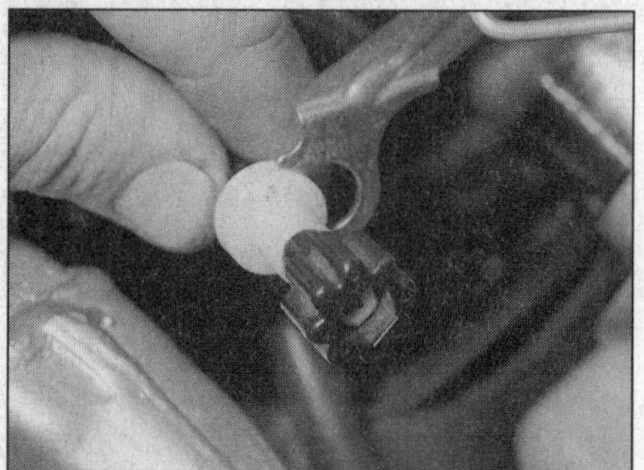
6.2 Free the idle speed adjusting screw from its frame bracket

6.4a Disconnect the sub-air cleaner hose (A) and the solenoid valve hose (B) . . .

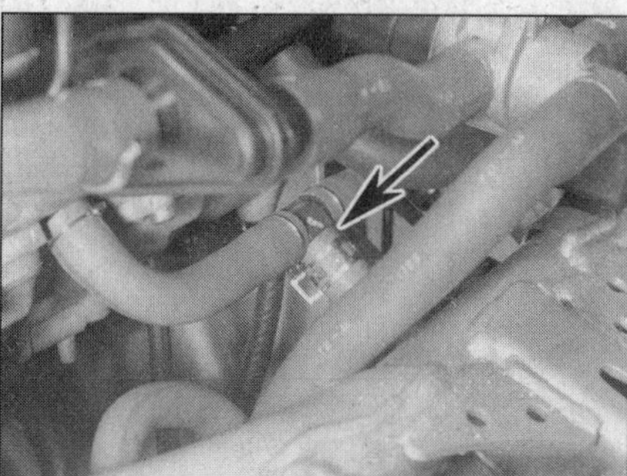
6.4b . . . then disconnect the fuel hose from the T-piece (arrow)

of this machine. In order to comply with the regulations, the carburetors on some models have a plastic limiter cap stuck onto the end of the pilot screw (which controls the idle fuel/air mixture) on each carburetor, so they can't be tampered with. These should only be removed in the event of a complete carburetor overhaul, and even then the screws should be returned to their original settings. The pilot screws on other models are accessible, but the use of an exhaust gas analyzer is the only accurate way to adjust the idle fuel/air mixture and be sure the machine doesn't exceed the emissions regulations.

If the engine runs extremely rough at idle or continually stalls, and if a carburetor overhaul does not cure the problem, take the motorcycle to a Honda dealer service department or other repair shop equipped with an exhaust gas analyzer. They will be able to properly adjust the idle fuel/air mixture to achieve a smooth idle and restore low speed performance.

5 Carburetor overhaul - general information

Poor engine performance, hesitation, hard starting, stalling, flooding and backfiring are all signs that major carburetor maintenance may be required.

Keep in mind that many so-called carburetor problems are really not carburetor problems at all, but mechanical problems within the engine or ignition system malfunctions. Try to establish for certain that the carburetors are in need of maintenance before beginning a major overhaul.

Check the fuel filter, the fuel lines, the tank cap vent (except California models), the intake manifold hose clamps, the vacuum hoses, the air filter element, the cylinder compression, the spark plugs and carburetor synchronization before assuming that a carburetor overhaul is required.

Most carburetor problems are caused by dirt particles, varnish and other deposits which build up in and block the fuel and air passages. Also, in time, gaskets and O-rings shrink or deteriorate and cause fuel and air leaks which lead to poor performance.

When the carburetor is overhauled, it is generally disassembled completely and the parts are cleaned thoroughly with a carburetor cleaning solvent and dried with filtered, unlubricated compressed air. The fuel and air passages are also blown through with compressed air to force out any dirt that may have been loosened but not removed by the solvent. Once the cleaning process is complete, the carburetor is reassembled using new gaskets and O-rings.

Before disassembling the carburetors, make sure you have a carburetor rebuild kit (which will include all necessary O-rings and other parts), some carburetor cleaner, a supply of rags, some means of blowing out the carburetor passages and a clean place to work. It is recommended that only one carburetor be overhauled at a time to avoid mixing up parts.

6 Carburetors - removal and installation

Warning: Refer to the precautions given in Section 1 before starting work.

Removal

1 Remove the air filter housing as described in Section 12.

2 Free the idle speed adjusting screw from its mounting bracket on the left side of the frame **(see illustration)**.

3 On California models, disconnect the relevant emission (EVAP) system hoses from the carburetors noting the correct fitted position of each hose.

4 On S, T, V and W models (1995 to 1998 models), disconnect the hose from the left side of the sub-air cleaner and the hose from the right side of the solenoid valve **(see illustrations)**. Position the valve aside and disconnect the fuel supply hose from the T-piece.

5 On S, T, V and W models (1995 to 1998 models), drain the coolant (see Chapter 1), then disconnect the carburetor heater system hoses from the thermostatic valve and from the water pump cover **(see illustration)**.

6 On S, T, V and W models (1995 to 1998 models), trace the wiring from the throttle position sensor on the outside of the left carburetor and disconnect it at the connector **(see illustration)**.

6.5 Disconnect the hose (arrow) from the thermostatic valve

6.6 Disconnect the throttle position sensor wiring connector (arrow)

6.7 Unscrew the three bolts (arrows) and remove the bracket

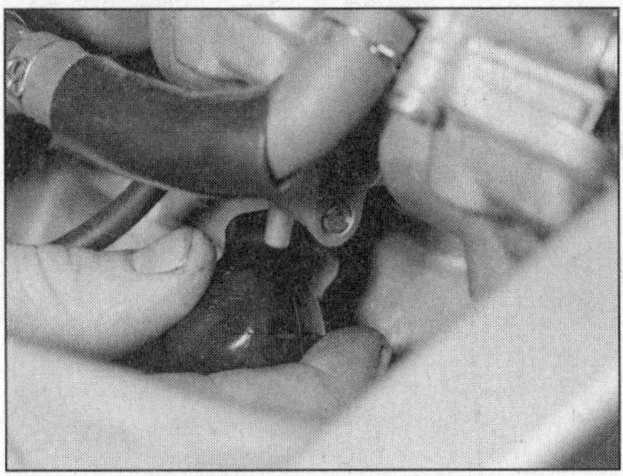

6.8 The retaining clip screws are accessed from underneath the carburetors

7 On S, T, V and W models (1995 to 1998 models), unscrew the three bolts securing the engine right mounting bracket and remove the bracket **(see illustration)**.

8 On all models, slacken the four retaining clips securing the carburetor intake manifolds to the cylinder head **(see illustration)**.

9 Slacken the choke outer cable clamp screw and detach the inner cable from the carburetor lever **(see illustration)**.

10 Slacken the throttle cable locknuts then free each outer cable from its mounting bracket.

11 Ease the carburetors away from the cylinder head then detach the inner cables from the throttle cam and remove the carburetors from the motorcycle **(see illustrations)**. **Note:** *Keep the carburetors the right way up to prevent fuel spillage from the float chambers and the possibility of the piston diaphragms being damaged.*

12 With the carburetors removed, place a container below the carburetor float chambers then slacken the drain screws and drain all the fuel from the carburetors. Once all the fuel has been drained, tighten all the drain screws securely.

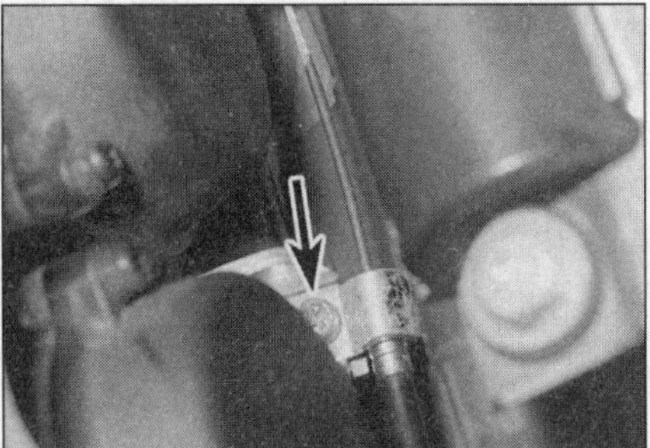

6.9 Slacken the screw (arrow) to release the outer cable and detach the inner cable from the linkage

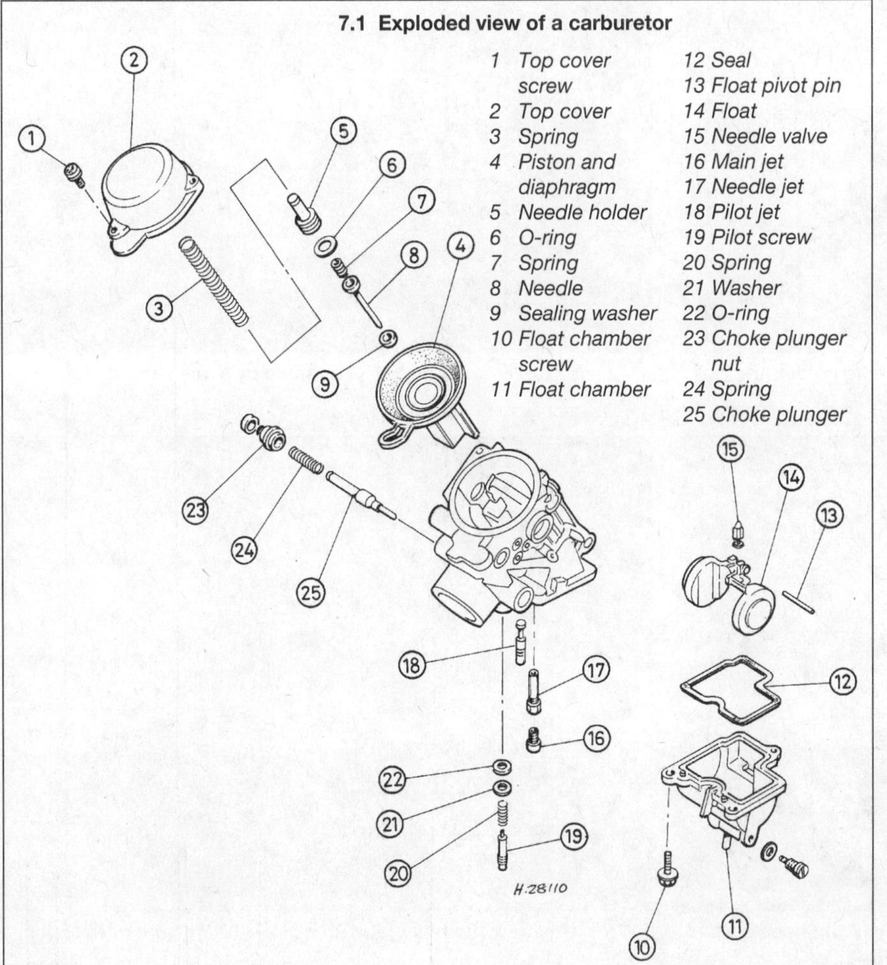

7.1 Exploded view of a carburetor

6.11a Free the carburetors from the cylinder head and the throttle cables from the mounting bracket . . .

6.11b . . . then detach both inner cables from the throttle cam (arrow)

Installation

13 Installation is the reverse of removal. Make sure the carburetor intake manifolds are fully engaged with the cylinder head and their retaining clips are securely tightened. Also make sure all disconnected hoses are fully engaged on their unions and secured by a clamp. Prior to installing the air filter housing, adjust the throttle and choke cables as described in Chapter 1. On S, T, V and W models (1995 to 1998 models), tighten the engine front (10 mm) mounting bracket bolt to the torque setting specified at the beginning of the Chapter.

7 Carburetors - disassembly, cleaning and inspection

Warning: Refer to the precautions given in Section 1 before proceeding.

Disassembly

1 Remove the carburetors from the machine as described in the previous Section. **Note:** *Do not separate the carburetors unless absolutely necessary; each carburetor can be dismantled sufficiently for all normal cleaning and adjustments while in place on the mounting brackets. Dismantle the carburetors separately to avoid interchanging parts.* Note that it is necessary to separate the carburetors to remove the choke plungers **(see illustration)**.

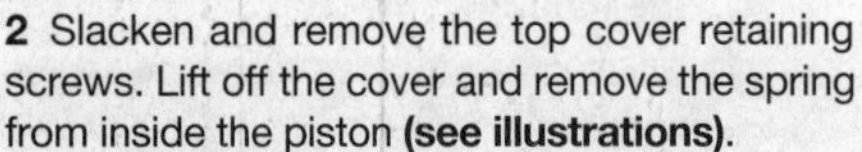

7.2a Undo the three screws and remove the top cover . . .

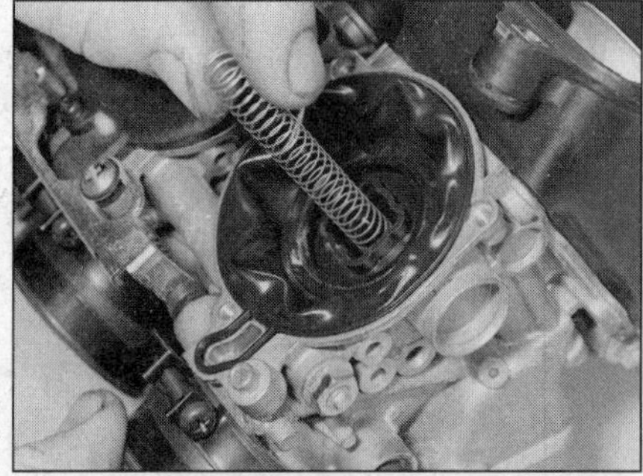

7.2b . . . then recover the spring from the piston

7.3 Withdrawing the diaphragm and piston assembly. Do not to damage the diaphragm

2 Slacken and remove the top cover retaining screws. Lift off the cover and remove the spring from inside the piston **(see illustrations)**.

3 Carefully peel the diaphragm away from its sealing groove in the carburetor and withdraw the diaphragm and piston assembly **(see illustration)**.

Caution: Do not use a sharp instrument to displace the diaphragm as it is easily damaged.

4 To remove the needle from the piston, screw a 4 mm bolt into the thread in the center of the needle holder (one of the top cover retaining screws will do), then use a pair of pliers to pull the needle holder out of the piston **(see illustration)**. Recover the O-ring and spring then tip the needle and sealing washer out of the piston.

5 Remove the retaining screws and remove the float chamber from the base of the carburetor **(see illustration)**. Recover the rubber seal.

6 Withdraw the float pivot pin, using a pair of pointed-nose pliers, and remove the float and needle valve assembly **(see illustration)**.

7.4 Screw one of the cover bolts into the needle holder and pull the holder out from the piston

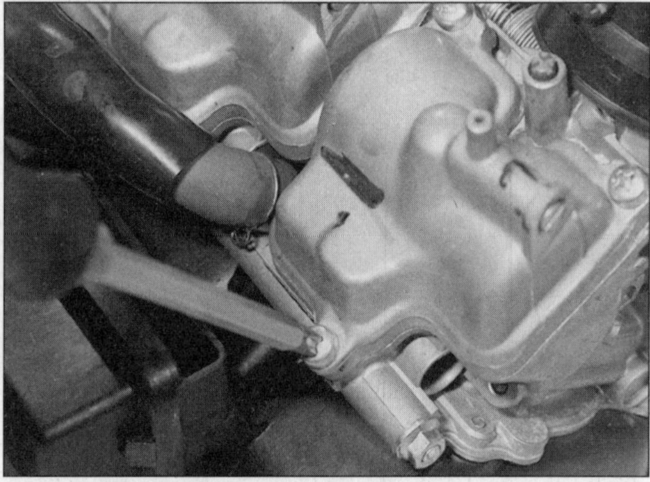

7.5 Float chamber is retained by three screws

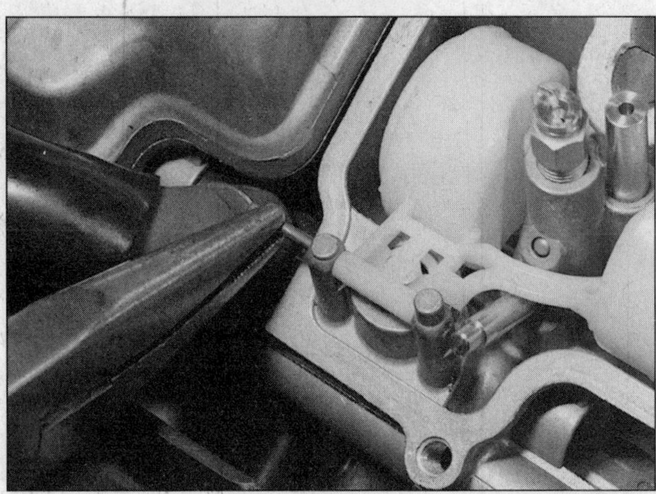

7.6 Withdraw the pivot pin and remove the float and needle valve from the carburetor

7.7a Unscrew the main jet with a close-fitting screwdriver . . .

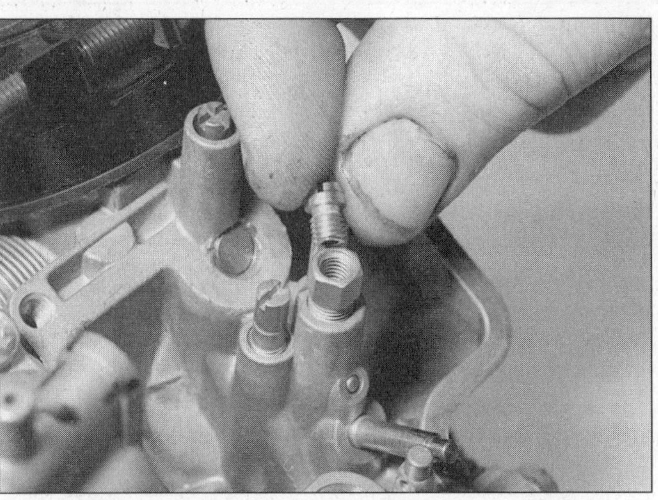

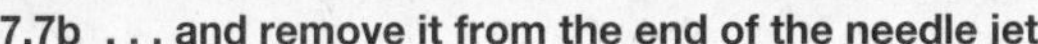
7.7b . . . and remove it from the end of the needle jet

7.8a Unscrew the needle jet . . .

7 Unscrew the main jet from the base of the needle jet **(see illustrations)**.

8 Unscrew the needle jet from the carburetor **(see illustrations)**.

9 Unscrew the pilot jet, situated next to the needle jet, from the carburetor **(see illustration)**.

10 Remove the plastic limiter cap (where fitted) from the pilot screw which is screwed into the base of the carburetor. The cap will be cemented in place and can be removed using a pair of pliers.

11 Screw the pilot screw in until it seats lightly, counting the number of turns necessary to achieve this, then remove the screw along with its spring, flat washer and O-ring. If the screw is bent or damaged in any way, all the pilot screws must be replaced as a set.

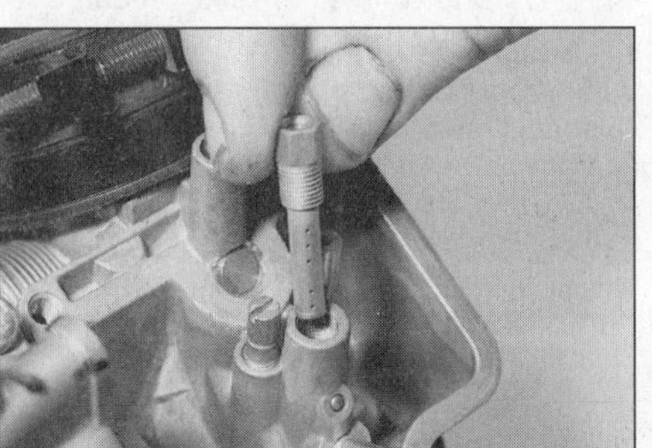
7.8b . . . and remove it from the carburetor

12 On S, T, V and W models (1995 to 1998 models), if required, remove the screws securing the throttle position sensor to the left (No.1) carburetor and draw the sensor off, noting how it fits.

13 If the carburetors have been separated, unscrew the valve nut and remove the choke plunger and spring from the carburetor. On S, T, V and W models (1995 to 1998 models), detach the hose from the union on each air cut-off valve, then remove the screw and draw the valve out of the carburetor. Remove the air jet. Discard the O-rings as new ones must be used.

Cleaning

Caution: Use only a petroleum based solvent for carburetor cleaning. Don't use caustic cleaners.

14 Submerge the metal components in the solvent for approximately thirty minutes (or longer, if the directions recommend it).

15 After the carburetor has soaked long enough for the cleaner to loosen and dissolve most of the varnish and other deposits, use a brush to remove the stubborn deposits. Rinse it again, then dry it with compressed air. Blow out all of the fuel and air passages in the main and upper body.

Caution: Never clean the jets or passages with a piece of wire or a drill bit, as they will be enlarged, causing the fuel and air metering rates to be upset.

Inspection

16 Check the operation of the choke plunger. If it doesn't move smoothly, replace it, along with the return spring. Inspect the needle on the end of the choke plunger and replace the plunger if it's worn or bent.

17 Check the tapered portion of the pilot screw for wear or damage. Replace the pilot screw if necessary **(see illustration)**.

18 Check the carburetor body, float chamber and top cover for cracks, distorted sealing surfaces and other damage. If any defects are found, replace the faulty component, although replacement of the entire carburetor will probably be necessary (check with your parts supplier for the availability of separate components).

19 Check the diaphragm for splits, holes and general deterioration. Holding it up to a light will help to reveal problems of this nature **(see illustration)**.

20 Insert the diaphragm piston in the carburetor body and check that it moves up-and-down smoothly. Check the surface of the piston for wear. If it's worn excessively or doesn't move smoothly in the bore, replace the carburetor.

7.9 Pilot jet is also a screw fit in the carburetor

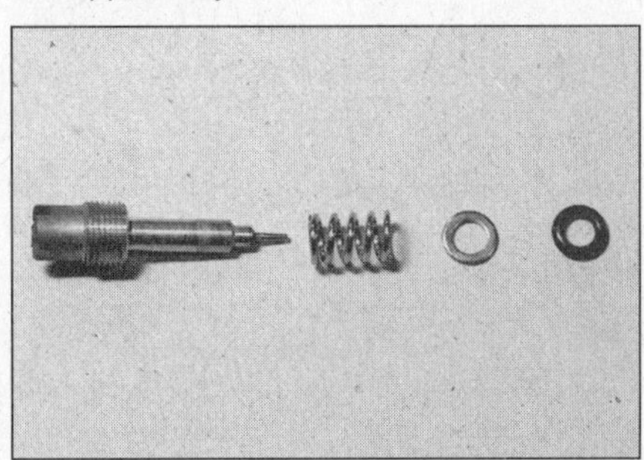
7.17 Pilot screw components - ensure the tapered portion of the screw is not bent or damaged

7.19 Check the piston diaphragm for signs of splitting and replace if necessary

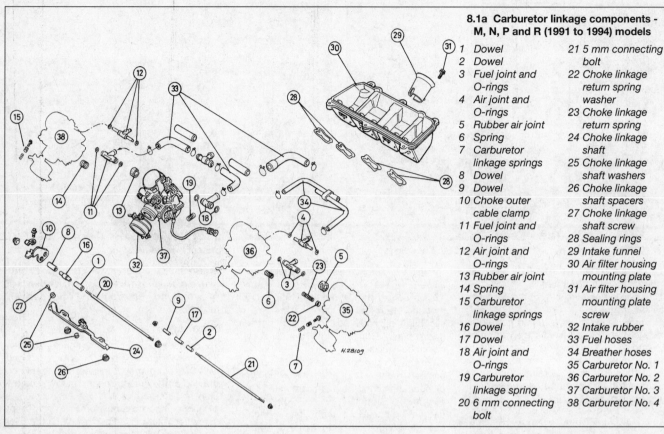

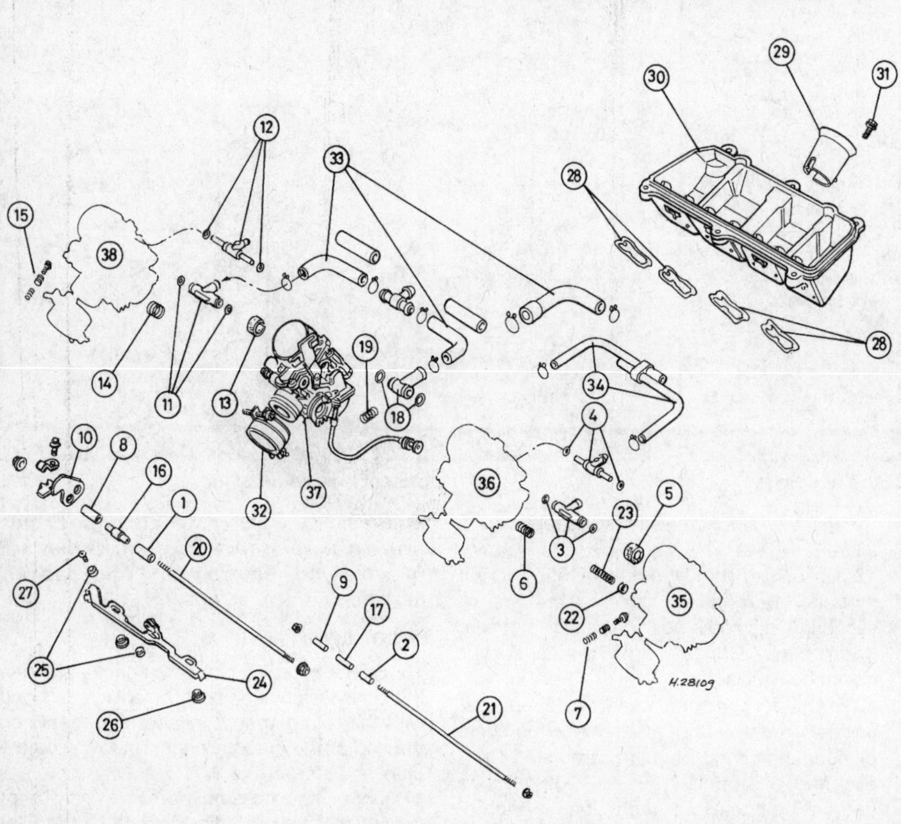

8.1a Carburetor linkage components - M, N, P and R (1991 to 1994) models

1 Dowel
2 Dowel
3 Fuel joint and O-rings
4 Air joint and O-rings
5 Rubber air joint
6 Spring
7 Carburetor linkage springs
8 Dowel
9 Dowel
10 Choke outer cable clamp
11 Fuel joint and O-rings
12 Air joint and O-rings
13 Rubber air joint
14 Spring
15 Carburetor linkage springs
16 Dowel
17 Dowel
18 Air joint and O-rings
19 Carburetor linkage spring
20 6 mm connecting bolt
21 5 mm connecting bolt
22 Choke linkage return spring washer
23 Choke linkage return spring
24 Choke linkage shaft
25 Choke linkage shaft washers
26 Choke linkage shaft spacers
27 Choke linkage shaft screw
28 Sealing rings
29 Intake funnel
30 Air filter housing mounting plate
31 Air filter housing mounting plate screw
32 Intake rubber
33 Fuel hoses
34 Breather hoses
35 Carburetor No. 1
36 Carburetor No. 2
37 Carburetor No. 3
38 Carburetor No. 4

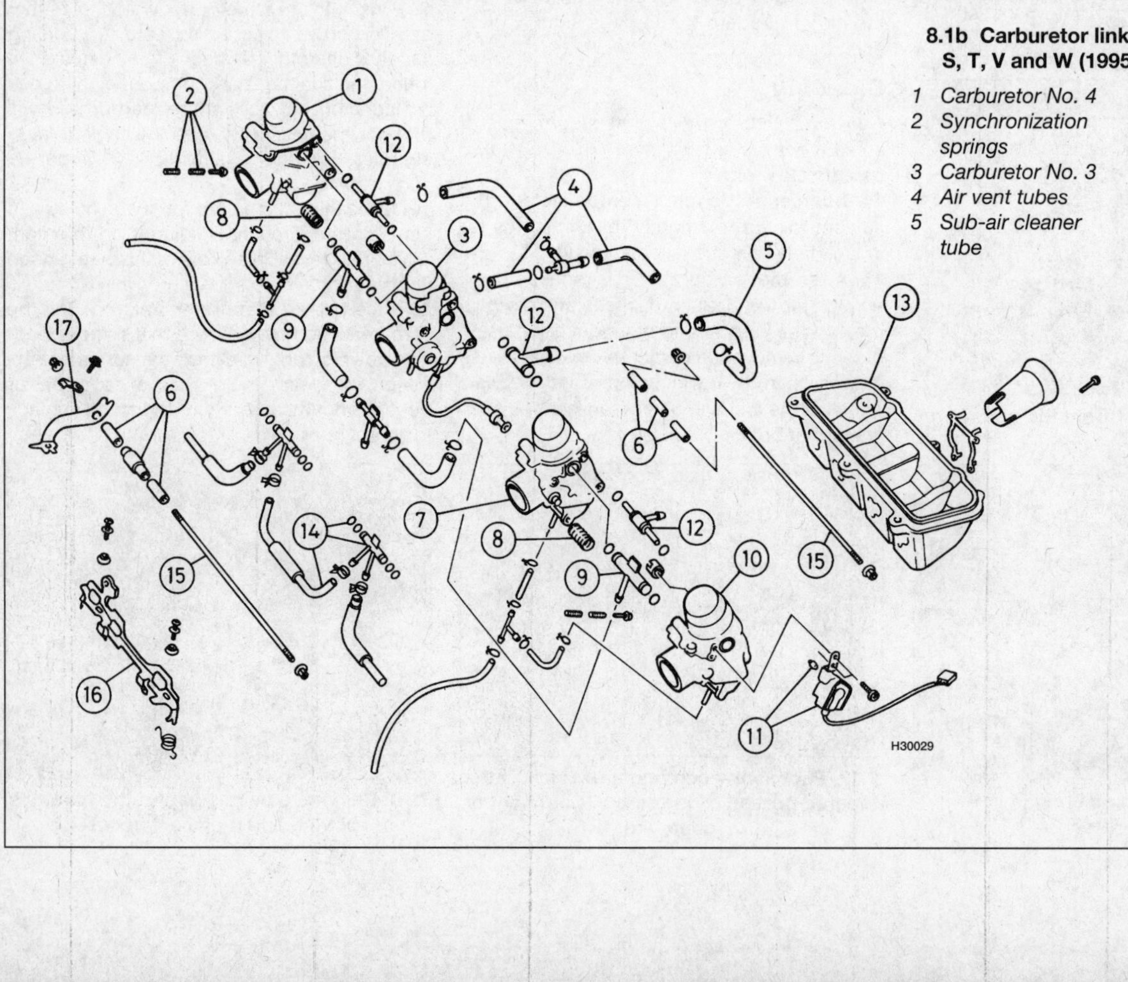

H.28109

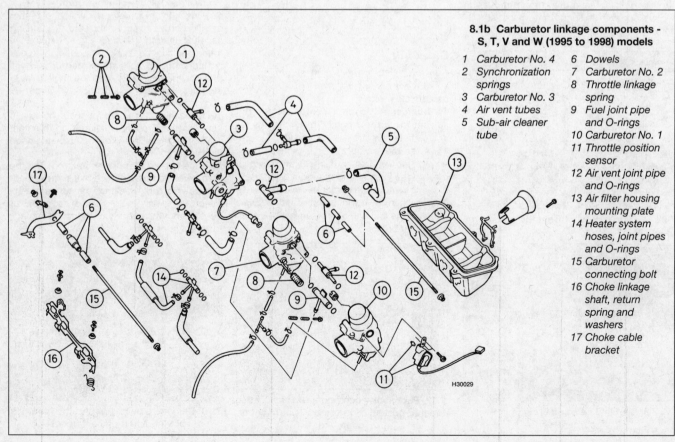

8.1b Carburetor linkage components - S, T, V and W (1995 to 1998) models

1 Carburetor No. 4
2 Synchronization springs
3 Carburetor No. 3
4 Air vent tubes
5 Sub-air cleaner tube
6 Dowels
7 Carburetor No. 2
8 Throttle linkage spring
9 Fuel joint pipe and O-rings
10 Carburetor No. 1
11 Throttle position sensor
12 Air vent joint pipe and O-rings
13 Air filter housing mounting plate
14 Heater system hoses, joint pipes and O-rings
15 Carburetor connecting bolt
16 Choke linkage shaft, return spring and washers
17 Choke cable bracket

H30029

8.3a On S, T, V and W (1995 to 1998) models bend up the lockplate tabs

8.3b Disconnect the breather hose . . .

8.3c . . . then undo the retaining screws and lift off the air filter mounting plate

8.4a Remove the choke linkage return spring and washer (arrow) . . .

8.4b . . . then undo the two retaining screws . . .

8.4c . . . and recover the washers

21 Check the jet needle for straightness by rolling it on a flat surface (such as a piece of glass). Replace it if it's bent or if the tip is worn.

22 Check the tip of the fuel inlet valve needle. If it has grooves or scratches in it, it must be replaced. Push in on the rod in the other end of the needle, then release it - if it doesn't spring back, replace the valve needle. If the needle valve seat is damaged the carburetor assembly must be replaced; it is not possible to replace the seat individually.

23 Check the float chamber gasket and replace it if it's damaged.

24 Operate the throttle shaft to make sure the throttle butterfly valve opens and closes smoothly. If it doesn't, replace the carburetor.

25 Check the floats for damage. This will usually be apparent by the presence of fuel inside one of the floats. If the floats are damaged, they must be replaced.

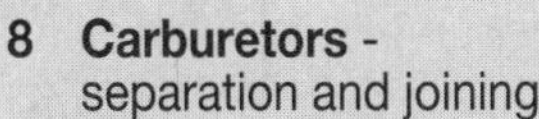

8 Carburetors - separation and joining

Warning: Refer to the precautions given in Section 1 before proceeding.

Separation

1 The carburetors do not need to be separated for normal overhaul. If you need to separate them (to replace a carburetor body, for example), refer to the following procedure **(see illustrations)**.

2 Remove the carburetors from the machine as described in Section 6. Mark the body of each carburetor with its cylinder number to ensure that it is positioned correctly on reassembly.

3 Undo the screws securing the air filter housing mounting plate to the rear of carburetors. On S, T, V and W models (1995 to 1998 models), first bend up the lockplate tabs **(see illustration)**. Disconnect the breather hose, then lift off the mounting plate, remove the intake funnels and recover the sealing rings from each carburetor **(see illustrations)**.

4 On M, N, P and R models (1991 to 1994 models) unhook the choke linkage return spring and washer from between number 1 and 2 carburetors **(see illustration)**. On S, T, V and W models (1995 to 1998 models), unhook the end of the return spring from the left end of the linkage bar between number 1 and 2 carburetors and remove the spring. Undo the two screws and washers securing the linkage shaft to the top of the carburetors then lift off the linkage shaft and recover the spacers from underneath the shaft **(see illustration)**.

5 Make a note of how the throttle linkage springs are arranged to ensure that they are fitted correctly on reassembly.

6 Evenly unscrew the two retaining nuts from the number 1 carburetor **(see illustration)**.

7 Carefully separate the carburetors while taking care not to damage the fuel and air vent joints, and on S, T, V and W models (1995 to 1998 models) the heater system joints, between each carburetor nor lose the screws from the throttle linkages. Keep a careful watch on all springs as the carburetors are separated; they should stay with the adjusting screws, but if they don't, find them and install them as shown in the illustration so they aren't lost **(see illustration)**.

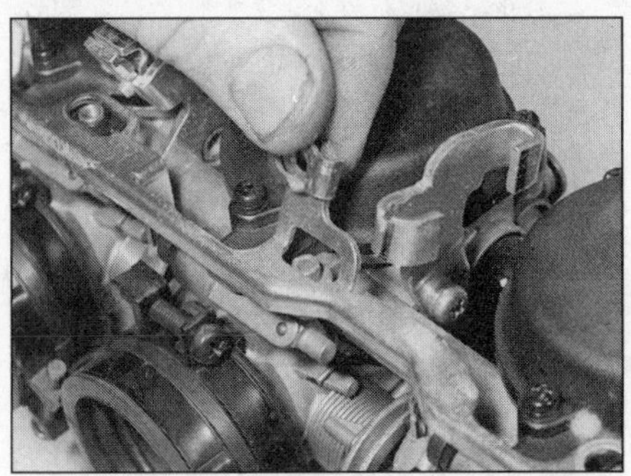

8.4d Lift off the choke linkage shaft . . .

8.4e . . . and recover the spacers from underneath it

8.6 Unscrew the carburetor retaining nuts (arrows) . . .

8.7 . . . then slide off the end carburetor and recover the spring

8.8a Recover the dowels from the carburetor (arrows) . . .

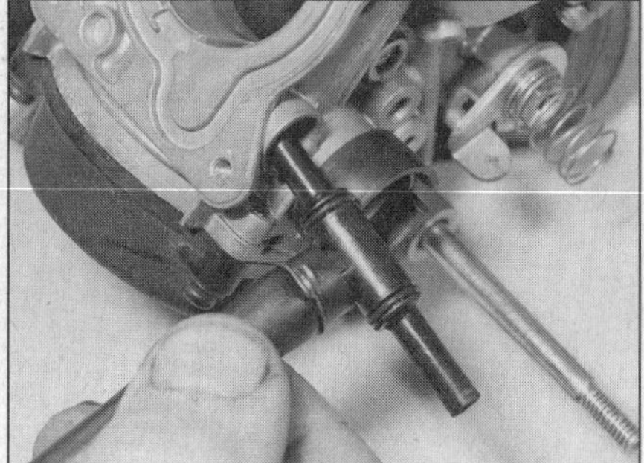
8.8b . . . and remove the fuel and air joint pieces

8.9a On reassembly renew all O-rings (arrows) . . .

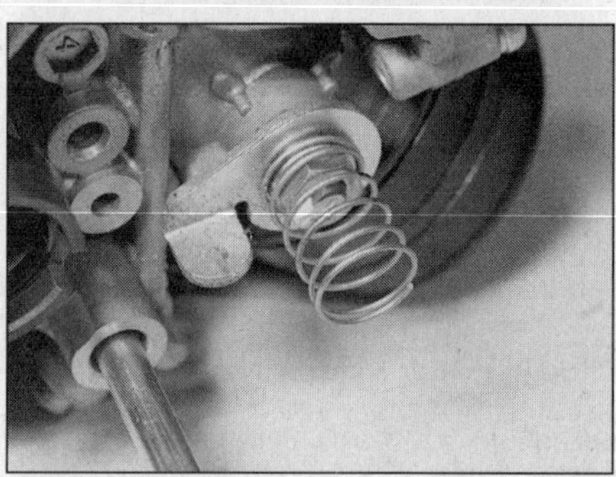
8.9b . . . and do not omit the springs from between each carburetor

8 Pull out the fuel fittings and vent line fittings, and on S, T, V and W models (1995 to 1998 models) the heater system fittings, and recover the dowels from the connecting bolt shafts **(see illustrations)**.

Joining

9 Assembly is the reverse of the disassembly procedure. Use new O-rings on the fuel and vent line fittings, and on S, T, V and W models (1995 to 1998 models) the heater system fittings, and smear them with oil. Check the operation of both the choke and throttle linkages ensuring that both operate smoothly and return quickly under spring pressure before installing the carburetors on the machine **(see illustrations)**. Check carburetor synchronization (see Chapter 1).

9 Carburetors - reassembly and float height check

Note: *When reassembling the carburetors, be sure to use the new O-rings, gaskets and other parts supplied in the rebuild kit. Do not overtighten the carburetor jets and screws as they are easily damaged.*

1 If the carburetors were separated, install the choke plunger in its bore, followed by its spring and nut. Tighten the nut securely and install the cap. On S, T, V and W models (1995 to 1998 models), install the air jet and air cut-off valve, using new O-rings, and secure the assembly with its screws. Connect the hose onto the union on the air cut-off valve.

2 Install the pilot screw (if removed) along with its spring, washer and O-ring, turning it in until it seats lightly **(see illustration)**. Now, turn the screw out the number of turns previously recorded. Where fitted, install a new limiter cap on the screw, applying a little bonding agent to hold it in position.

3 Screw the needle jet into position in the carburetor.

4 Screw the main jet into the end of the needle jet.

5 Screw the pilot jet into position.

6 Hook the needle valve over the float, then install the float and secure it with the pivot pin **(see illustration)**.

7 To check the float height, hold the carburetor so the float hangs down, then tilt it back until the valve needle is just seated, but

8.9c The carburetor throttle links must be correctly joined and the springs positioned as shown

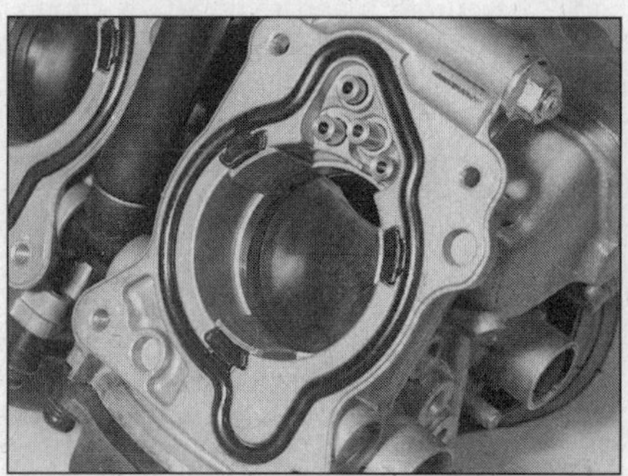
8.9d Do not omit the sealing rings fitted between the carburetors and air filter mounting plate

9.2 Assemble the pilot screw components on the screw and install the screw as described in text

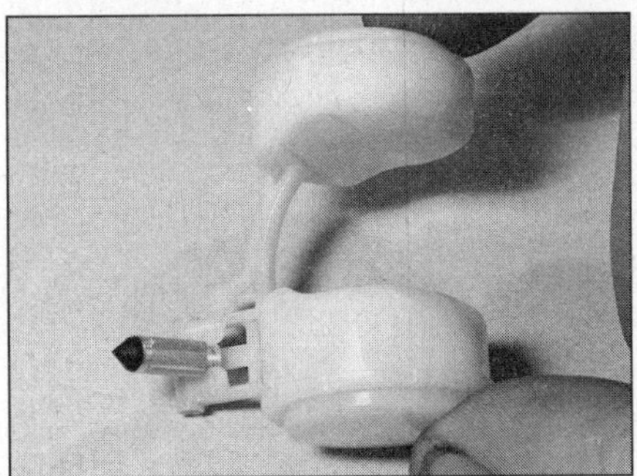

9.6 Make sure that the needle valve is correctly slotted into the float

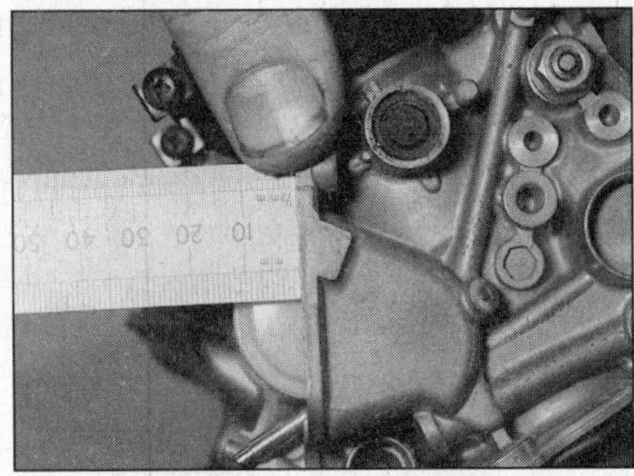

9.7 Measuring the float height

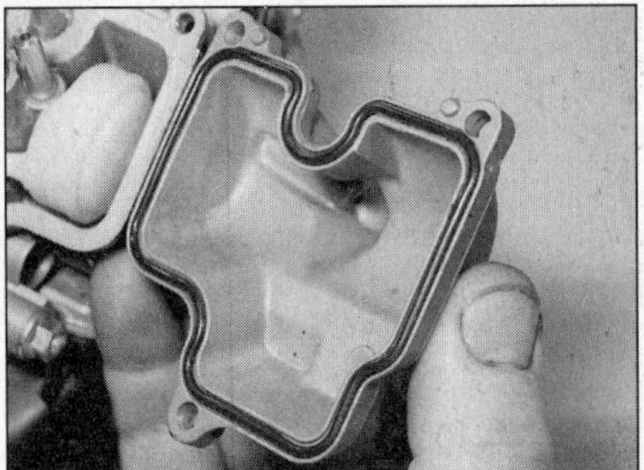

9.8 The rubber seal must be correctly located in its groove before installing the chamber on the carburetor

not so far that the needle's spring-loaded tip is compressed. Measure the distance between the gasket face and the bottom of the float with an accurate ruler **(see illustration)**. The correct setting should be as given in this Chapter's Specifications. The float height is not adjustable; if it is incorrect the float must be replaced. Repeat the procedure for all carburetors.

8 With the float height checked, fit the rubber seal to the float chamber and install the chamber on the carburetor **(see illustration)**.

9 Fit the washer to the needle and insert the needle into the piston. Position a new O-ring in the groove on the inside of the piston and fit the spring. Insert the needle holder into the center of the piston and press it into position until the O-ring is fully seated against the base of the piston **(see illustrations)**.

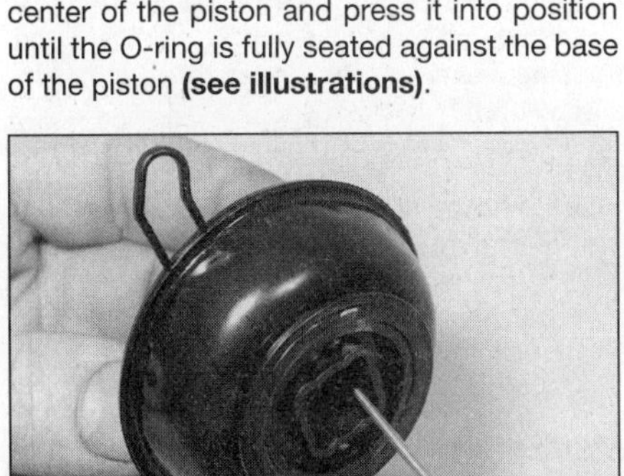

9.9a Insert the needle and sealing washer into the piston . . .

10 Insert the piston assembly into the carburetor body and lightly push it down, ensuring the needle is correctly aligned with the needle jet. Press the diaphragm outer edge into its groove, ensuring the diaphragm tongue is correctly seated in the cutout on the carburetor **(see illustration)**. Check the diaphragm is not creased, and that the piston moves smoothly up and down the bore.

11 Insert the spring and fit the top cover to the carburetor **(see illustration)**.

12 On S, T, V and W models (1995 to 1998 models), if removed, install the throttle position sensor, aligning the tab on the sensor with the groove in the end of the throttle shaft.

10 Throttle cables - removal and installation

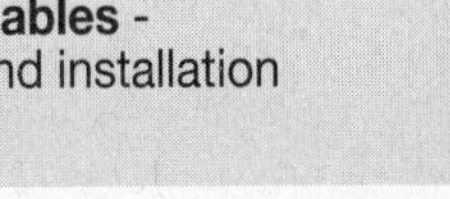

Warning: Refer to the precautions given in Section 1 before proceeding.

Removal

1 Remove the air filter housing (see Section 12).

2 Slacken the throttle cable locknuts then free each outer cable from its mounting bracket. Detach the inner cables from the throttle cam. If necessary to improve access to throttle cam, slacken the four retaining clips securing the carburetor intake manifolds to the cylinder head and disengage the carburetors from the cylinder head. Keep the carburetors upright to prevent fuel spillage.

3 Unscrew the two right handlebar switch screws and free the switch from the handlebar.

4 Disconnect the throttle cables from the throttle grip and unscrew each cable from the lower half of the handlebar switch. Mark each cable to ensure it is connected correctly on installation.

5 Remove the cables from the machine noting the correct routing of each cable.

Installation

6 Install the cables making sure they are correctly routed. The cables must not interfere with any other component and should not be kinked or bent sharply.

7 Screw the cables into the lower half of the handlebar switch, making sure they are correctly connected. Lubricate the end of each cable with multi-purpose grease and attach the cables to the throttle grip.

8 Fit the switch lower half to the handlebar, locating its peg in the handlebar hole. Fit the top half of the switch and securely tighten the screws.

9 Lubricate the end of each cable with multi-purpose grease and attach them to the carburetor throttle cam.

10 Make sure the cables are correctly connected and locate the outer cable adjusters in the mounting bracket.

11 Where necessary, fit the carburetors to the cylinder head and securely tighten the intake rubber clips.

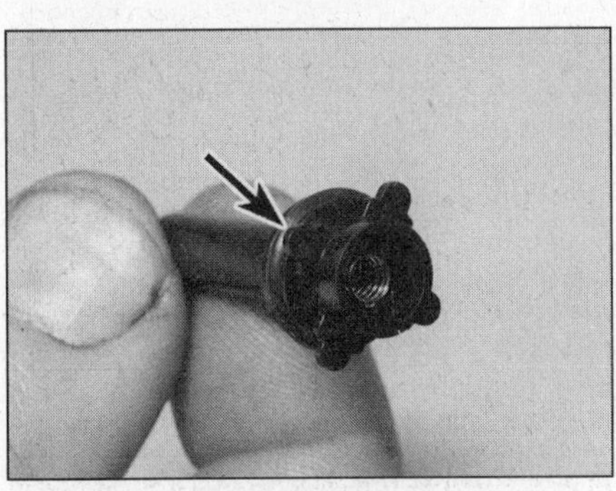

9.9b . . . and fit the needle holder and spring. Make sure the O-ring (arrow) is correctly positioned

9.10 Insert the piston and locate the diaphragm in the carburetor groove

9.11 Install the spring and cover while making sure the diaphragm remains correctly seated

11.2 Disconnecting the choke inner cable from the carburetor linkage

12 Adjust the cables as described in Chapter 1. Turn the handlebars back and forth to make sure the cables don't cause the steering to bind.

13 Install the air filter housing as described in Chapter 12. Prior to fitting the fuel tank, start the engine and turn the handlebars back and forth to make sure the idle speed doesn't rise as the bars are turned. If it does, the cables are incorrectly routed. Sort out the problem before riding the motorcycle.

14 Install the fuel tank.

11 Choke cable - removal and installation

Removal

1 Remove the air filter housing as described in Section 12.

2 Slacken the screw then free the choke outer cable from its retaining clamp and detach the inner cable from the carburetor choke linkage **(see illustration)**.

3 Unscrew the two left handlebar switch screws and free the switch from the handlebar.

4 Disconnect the choke cable from the choke lever and unscrew the cable from the lower half of the handlebar switch.

5 Remove the cable from the machine noting its correct routing.

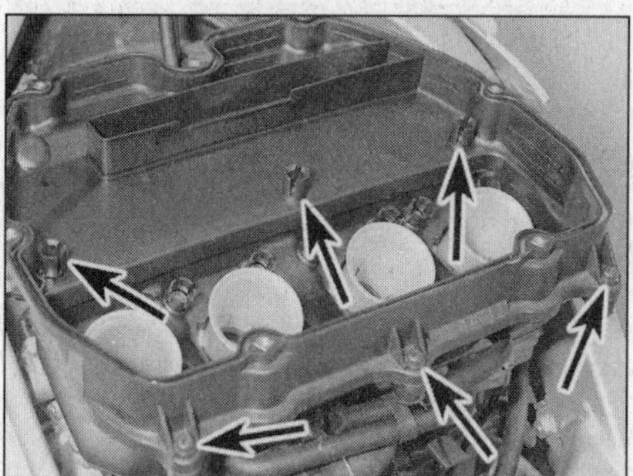

12.2a Air filter housing base screw locations (arrows)

Installation

6 Install the cable making sure it is correctly routed. The cable must not interfere with any other component and should not be kinked or bent sharply.

7 Screw the cable into the lower half of the handlebar switch. Lubricate cable end with multi-purpose grease and attach it to the choke lever.

8 Fit the switch lower half to the handlebar, locating its peg in the handlebar hole. Fit the top half of the switch and securely tighten the screws.

9 Lubricate the cable end with multi-purpose grease and attach it to the choke linkage.

10 Locate the outer cable in the retaining clamp and adjust the cable as described in Chapter 1.

11 Install the air filter housing as described in Section 12.

12 Air filter housing - removal and installation

Removal

1 Remove the air filter element as described in Chapter 1.

2 Undo the screws which secure the filter housing base in position **(see illustration)**. On S, T, V and W (1995 to 1998) models, note the positions of the DAI (Direct Air Induction) system solenoid valve and air hose holders **(see illustration)**.

12.2b On S, T, V and W (1995 to 1998) models, note the positions of the DAI system solenoid valve and air hose holders (arrows)

3 On M, N, P and R models (1991 to 1994 models), move the housing to the rear to disengage its front locating peg from the frame. Disconnect the breather hose from the right of the housing and remove the housing **(see illustration)**. On California models it will also be necessary to disconnect the pulse secondary air injection (PAIR) suction hose from the housing.

Installation

4 Installation is the reverse of removal ensuring that the throttle cables are both routed so that they pass on the left side of the housing base front locating peg **(see illustration)**.

13 Exhaust system - removal and installation

Removal

Muffler (silencer)

1 Set the bike on its centerstand.

2 Slacken and remove the muffler mounting nut and bolt and recover the washer and spacer from the rubber mounting **(see illustration)**.

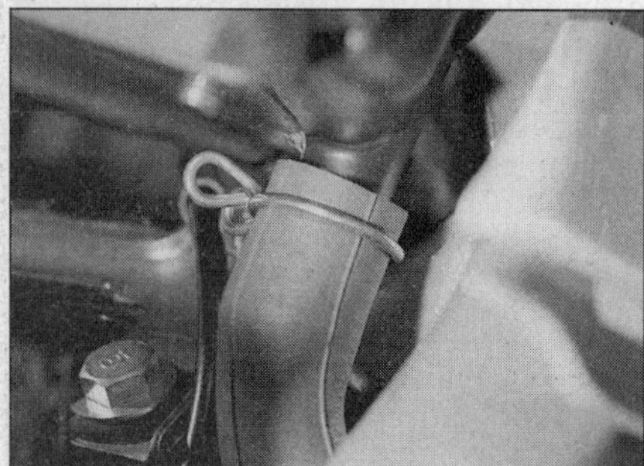

12.3 Lift up the housing base and disconnect the breather hose from its right end

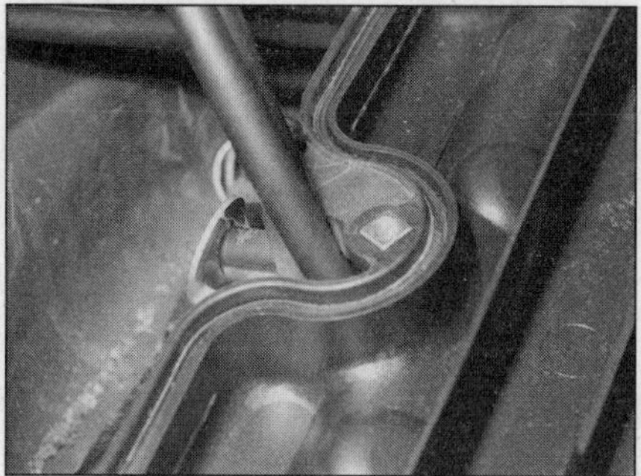

12.4 The throttle cables must pass on the left side of the air filter housing base front locating peg as shown

13.2 Remove the muffler (silencer) mounting nut and bolt

13.8 Remove the exhaust-to-frame mounting nut and bolt

13.12 On installation tighten the muffler (silencer) clamp bolts to the specified torque

13.13a Do not omit the spacer from the exhaust front pipe mounting . . .

3 Loosen the muffler clamp bolts then release the muffler from the exhaust front pipe using a twisting motion. Remove the muffler and recover the sealing ring.

Complete system

4 Set the bike on its centerstand.

5 Remove the lower fairing panels as described in Chapter 8.

6 Slacken and remove the muffler mounting nut and bolt and recover the washer and spacer from the rubber mounting.

7 Unscrew the six nuts securing the exhaust pipes to the front of the cylinder head and release the retaining plates from the cylinder head studs.

8 Slacken and remove the nut and bolt securing the exhaust system to the base of the frame then remove the exhaust assembly from the bike and recover the gaskets from the cylinder head ports **(see illustration)**.

Installation

9 Inspect the rubber mountings for signs of damage and replace if necessary.

Muffler (silencer)

10 Fit a new sealing ring to the front pipe and insert the spacer into the rear of the rubber mounting.

11 Install the muffler then fit the muffler mounting bolt, washer and nut and tighten it securely.

12 Tighten the muffler clamp bolts to the specified torque setting **(see illustration)**.

Complete system

13 Fit the spacer to the exhaust front pipe rubber mounting so that its flange is on the inside and insert the spacer into the rear of the muffler rubber mounting **(see illustrations)**.

14 Position a new gasket in each of the cylinder head ports. A dab of grease can be used to hold them in position **(see illustration)**.

15 Install the exhaust front pipe assembly, aligning the pipes with the cylinder head ports, and fit the mounting nut, washer and bolt.

16 Slide the retaining plates onto the studs and fit the nuts. Tighten the exhaust front pipe nuts to the specified torque setting, starting with the center nut of each retaining plate first, followed by the two outer nuts **(see illustration)**.

17 Securely tighten the front pipe mounting bolt.

18 Insert the spacer into the rear of the rubber mounting then fit the muffler mounting bolt, washer and nut and tighten securely.

13.13b . . . or the muffler (silencer) rubber mounting

19 Install the fairing panels as described in Chapter 8.

14 Pulse secondary air injection (PAIR) system - California models only

General information

1 On California models to reduce the amount of unburnt hydrocarbons released in the exhaust gases, a Pulse secondary air injection

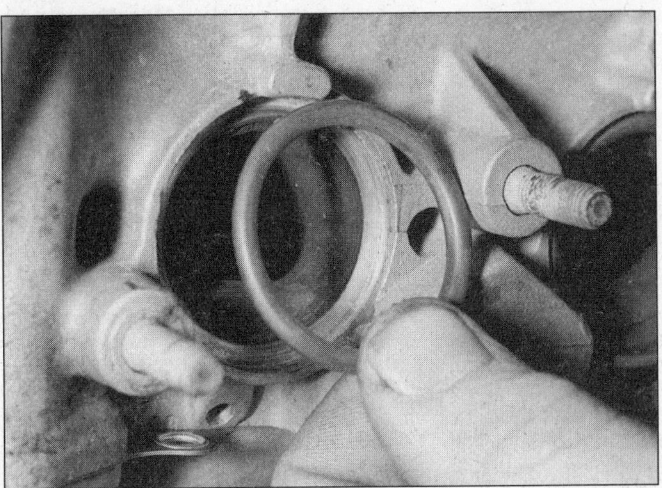
13.14 Fit a new gasket to each cylinder head port

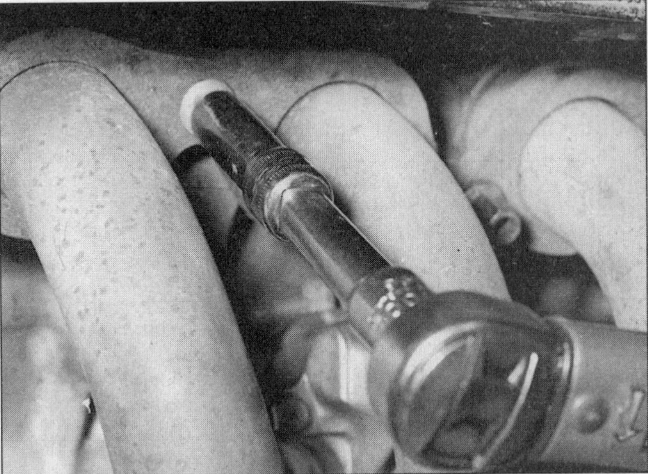
13.16 Tighten the front pipe nuts to the specified torque setting (see text)

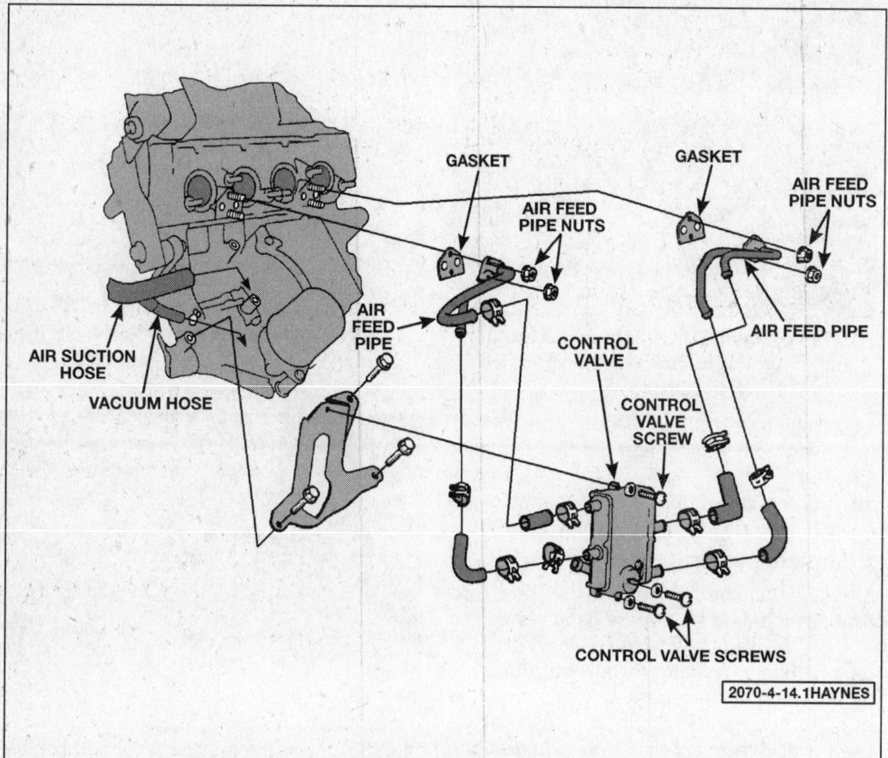

14.1 Pulse secondary air injection (PAIR) system components - California models

(PAIR) system is fitted **(see illustration)**. The system consists of the pulse air control valve assembly, which is mounted on the front of the engine unit, and the air feed pipe linking the control valve to the cylinder head. The control valve is linked to one of the intake ducts by a vacuum hose and to the air cleaner housing by a suction hose.

2 When the engine is running, the depression present in the intake duct acts on the vacuum diaphragm in the control valve and opens up the valve.

3 With the valve open, whenever there is a negative pulse in the exhaust system, filtered air is drawn from the air filter housing through the control valve and into the exhaust ports in the cylinder head. This fresh air promotes the burning of any excess fuel present in the exhaust gases, so reducing the amount of harmful hydrocarbons reduced into the atmosphere via the exhaust gases.

4 The control valve assembly is fitted with a pair of one-way check valves to prevent the exhaust gases passing through the control valve and into the air filter housing.

5 The system is not adjustable and can be tested only by a Honda dealer. Checks which can be performed by the owner are given in Chapter 1.

Removal

6 Remove the right and left lower fairing panels as described in Chapter 8.

7 Slacken the retaining clips and disconnect the vacuum hose and air hose from the right side of the control valve.

8 Undo the three screws and washers securing the control valve to the front of the crankcase.

9 Unscrew the four nuts and release the air feed pipes from the front of the cylinder head.

10 Remove the control valve assembly, complete with pipes and hoses, from the front of the engine unit.

11 Recover the gaskets from front of the cylinder head and discard them.

12 If necessary, unbolt the control valve mounting bracket from the front of the crankcase.

13 Inspect the pipes and hoses for signs of cracks and splits and replace damaged components.

Installation

14 Ensure the air feed pipe and cylinder head mating surfaces are clean and dry. Install the mounting bracket (where removed).

15 Fit a new gasket to each of the cylinder head unions, making sure each gasket is fitted the correct way around.

16 Install the control valve assembly locating the feed pipes on the cylinder head studs. Fit the feed pipe nuts and control valve retaining screws and tighten them securely.

17 Connect the vacuum hose and air suction hose to the control valve and secure in position with the retaining clips.

18 Fit the fairing panels as described in Chapter 8.

15 Direct Air Induction system (DAI) - check

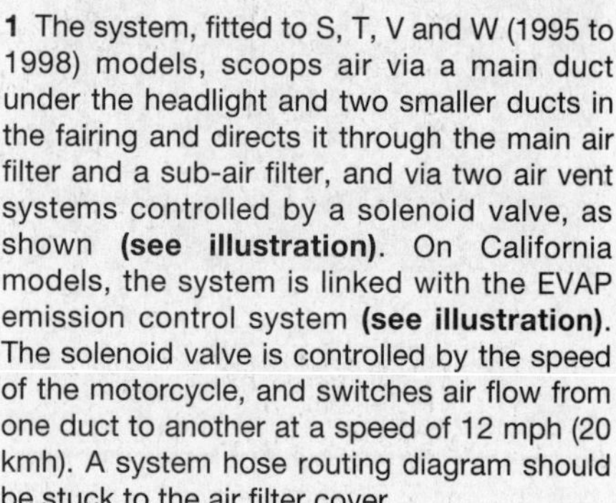

1 The system, fitted to S, T, V and W (1995 to 1998) models, scoops air via a main duct under the headlight and two smaller ducts in the fairing and directs it through the main air filter and a sub-air filter, and via two air vent systems controlled by a solenoid valve, as shown **(see illustration)**. On California models, the system is linked with the EVAP emission control system **(see illustration)**. The solenoid valve is controlled by the speed of the motorcycle, and switches air flow from one duct to another at a speed of 12 mph (20 kmh). A system hose routing diagram should be stuck to the air filter cover.

2 Remove the fuel tank (see Chapter 4). Check that all ducts and hoses are clear and clean any dirt or debris off the mesh in the front of the scoop below the headlight. Disconnect each tube in turn from its union and blow through it. Also check all hoses for kinks, damage or deterioration in the form of cracks, and replace them if necessary. Check that all ducts and hoses are secure on their unions.

3 Check the sub-air cleaner and the air vent filters for clogging and clean or replace them as required.

4 To check the solenoid valve on UK and US models (except California), detach the three hoses from the valve, noting which fits where (each hose and its union on the valve are numbered) **(see illustration)**. With the ignition switched OFF, the valve should allow air to enter the No. 4 hose union and exit the No. 6 union. With the ignition switched ON, the valve should allow air to enter the No. 7 hose union and exit the No. 6 union. Now remove the front sprocket (see Chapter 6) and position the sprocket and chain well clear of the countershaft end; refit the sprocket cover for safety. Start the engine and select a gear. With the speedometer indicating more than 12 mph (20 kmh) the valve should allow air to enter the No. 4 hose union and exit the No. 6 union.

Caution: Use a hand-operated pump only when checking the solenoid valve, high pressure air will damage the valve.

Caution: Do not allow the engine to overheat when carrying out this check.

5 To check the solenoid valves on California models, detach the three hoses from the EVAP valve, noting which fits where (each hose and its union on the valve are numbered). With the ignition switched OFF, the valve should allow air to enter the No. 4 hose union (adjacent the No. 8 union) and exit the No. 4 union on the other side. With the ignition switched ON, the valve should allow air to enter the No. 8 hose union and exit the No. 4 union on the other side. Now detach the hoses from the solenoid valve. Remove the front sprocket (see Chapter 6) and position the sprocket and chain well

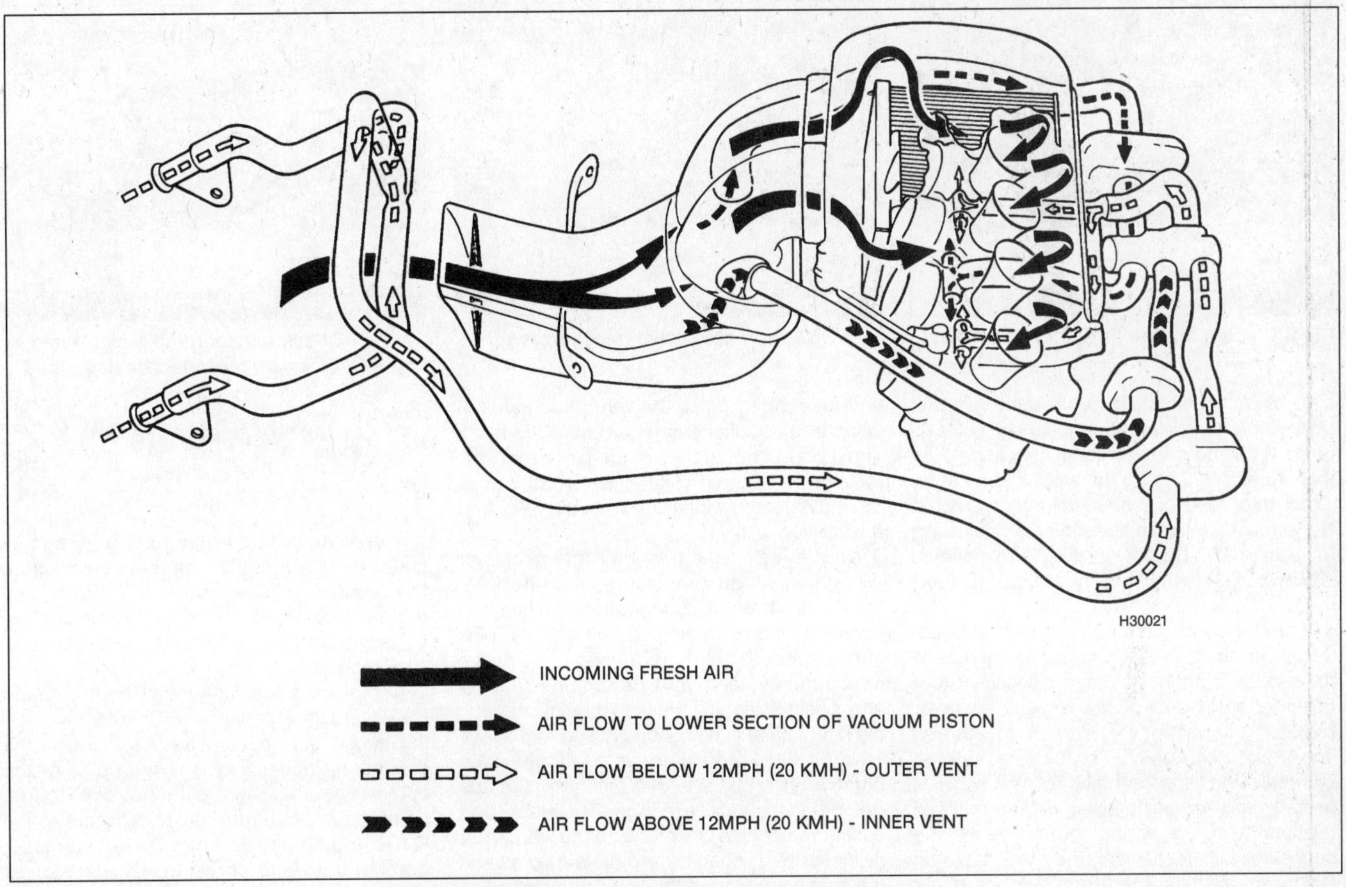

H30021

INCOMING FRESH AIR

AIR FLOW TO LOWER SECTION OF VACUUM PISTON

AIR FLOW BELOW 12MPH (20 KMH) - OUTER VENT

AIR FLOW ABOVE 12MPH (20 KMH) - INNER VENT

15.1a Direct Air Intake (DAI) system - except California

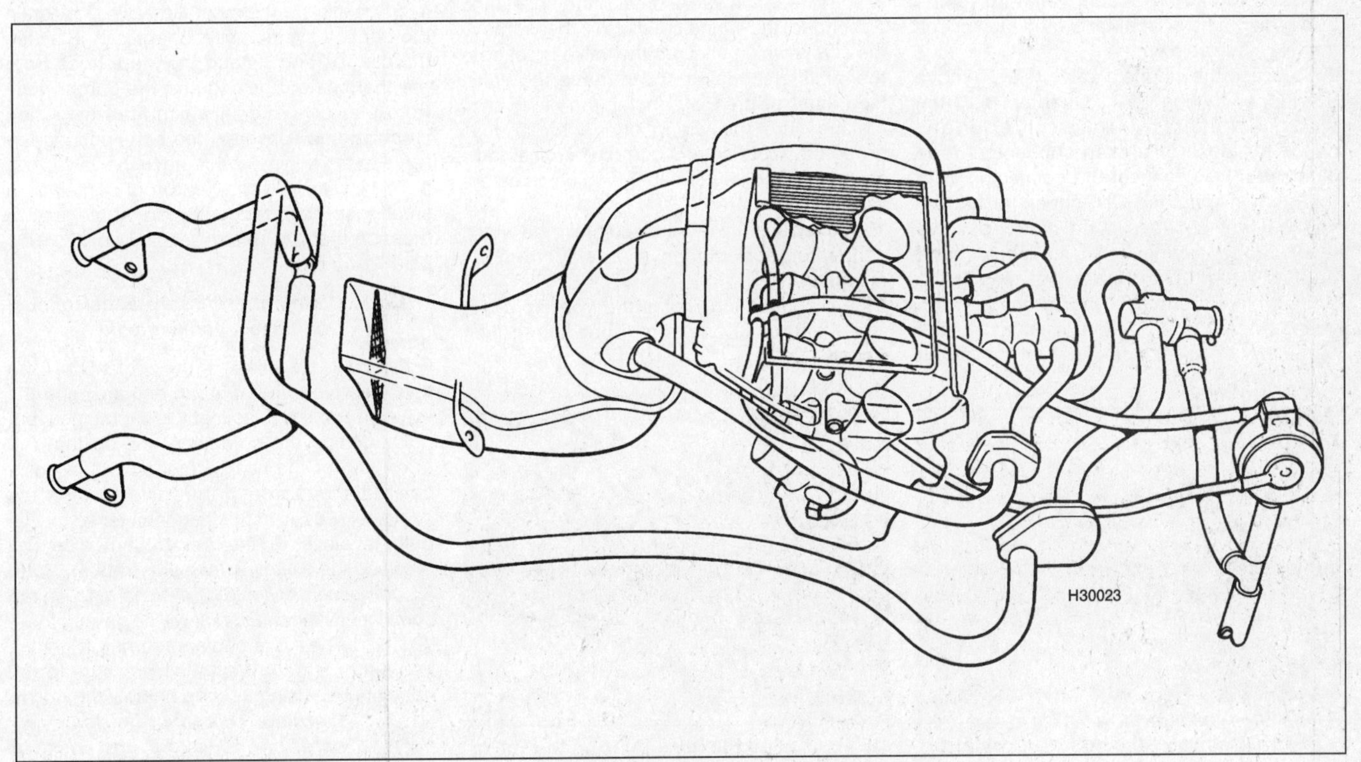

15.1b Direct Air Intake (DAI) system - California models

15.4 Disconnect the three hoses (arrows)

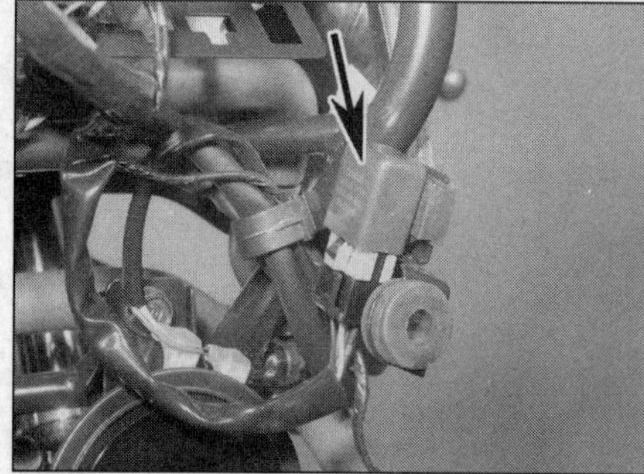
15.7 Solenoid valve relay (arrow)

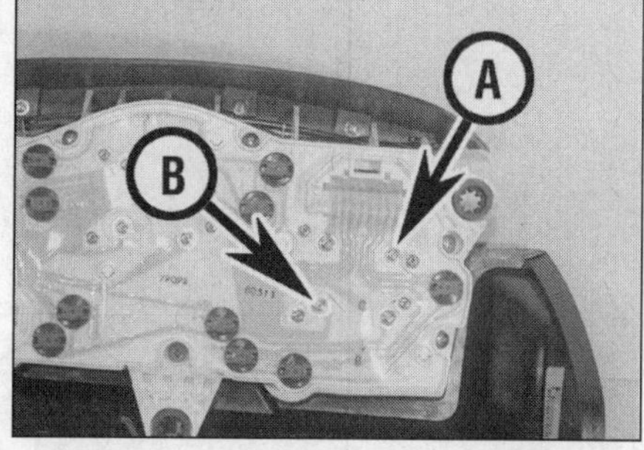

15.8 Check between the pink (A) and green/black (B) terminals as described

clear of the countershaft end; refit the sprocket cover for safety. Start the engine and select a gear. With the speedometer indicating less than 12 mph (20 km/h) the valve should allow air to enter the No. 4 hose union and exit the No. 6 union. With the speedometer indicating more than 12 mph (20 km/h) the valve should allow air to enter the No. 7 hose union and exit the No. 6 union.

6 If the valve does not perform as described, first check the fuse (see Chapter 9), then trace the wiring from the valve and disconnect it at the connector and check for any loose or broken connections. With the ignition switched ON, check for battery voltage between the orange/black (positive (+ve) probe) and green (negative (-ve) probe) terminals on the wiring loom side of the connector (when checking the EVAP valve on California models, then terminals are black and green). If no voltage is recorded, check the relevant wiring circuit, referring to the wiring diagrams in Chapter 9, and then check the relay (see below).

7 To check the solenoid valve relay, remove the upper fairing (see Chapter 8), then disconnect the relay wiring connector and check for loose or broken connectors **(see illustration)**. Reconnect the connector. With the ignition switched ON, check for battery voltage first between each black (positive (+ve) probe) terminal on connector and ground (earth), then between the orange/black terminal and ground. If no voltage is recorded on either or both black terminals, check the relevant wiring circuit and fuse, referring to the wiring diagrams in Chapter 9. If voltage is recorded at the black terminals but not at the orange/black terminal, replace the relay. If voltage is recorded at all three, check the wiring between the relay and the valve.

8 Now check that the instrument cluster wiring connectors are secure, and check for loose or broken connections. Using a continuity tester connected between the pink and green/black terminals on the speedometer, and with the engine running and a gear selected, check that below 12 mph (20 km/h) there is no continuity and that above 12 mph (20 km/h) there is continuity **(see illustration)**. If the results are not as described, check the speed sensor and speedometer (see Chapter 9). If the results are as described, check the pink wire between the speedometer and the solenoid valve relay. If the wiring is good, replace the valve.

9 To replace the valve, detach the hoses and disconnect the wiring connector, then remove the screw which secures the valve bracket to the air filter housing and remove the valve **(see illustration 15.4)**. Install the new valve, making sure the wiring connector and all hoses are securely and correctly connected - each hose and its corresponding union on the valve are numbered.

10 To replace the relay, disconnect the wiring connector and detach the relay from its mounting.

11 On completion, install the front sprocket (see Chapter 6) and the upper fairing (see Chapter 8).

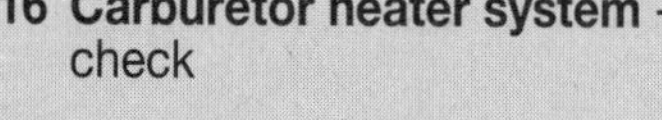

16 Carburetor heater system - check

1 The system, fitted only to S, T, V and W (1995 to 1998) models, directs coolant from the cooling system into a duct in the carburetors via a thermostatic valve. The valve shuts off the flow of coolant at a specific temperature.

2 Remove the fuel tank (see Chapter 4) and the lower fairing panels (see Chapter 8).

3 Check the coolant hoses from the thermostat housing on the right side of the engine via the thermostatic valve to the carburetors, and from the carburetors to the water pump cover for leaks, damage, deterioration and cracking. Check that all clamps are secure. If any of the hoses are damaged or deteriorated, replace them.

4 To check the thermostatic valve, first drain the cooling system (see Chapter 1). Slacken the clamps and detach the input hose from the thermostat housing and the output hose from the valve, noting which fits where **(see illustrations)**. Unscrew the bolt securing the valve to the engine and remove the valve.

5 To test the valve, a heatproof container, a small gas-powered camping stove and a thermometer capable of reading up to 110°C (230°F) are required.

Warning: Antifreeze is poisonous. Don't use a cooking pan.

6 Fill the container with coolant of the specified type and strength and suspend the valve on some wire so that it is submerged, but not touching the container, and so that the open end of the hose attached to the gold-colored (input) side of the valve is out of the container. Suspend the thermometer so that its bulb is close to the switch, but also not touching the container **(see illustration)**. **Note:** *No components should be allowed to touch the container as false readings will be given.*

7 Start to heat the coolant, stirring it gently, and either apply a gentle air pressure to the coolant hose using a pump or blow through it.

Warning: This must be done very carefully to avoid the risk of personal injury.

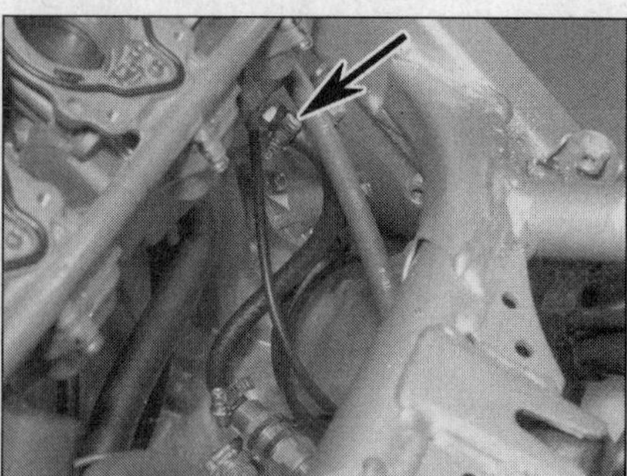
16.4a Disconnect the hose (arrow) from the thermostat housing . . .

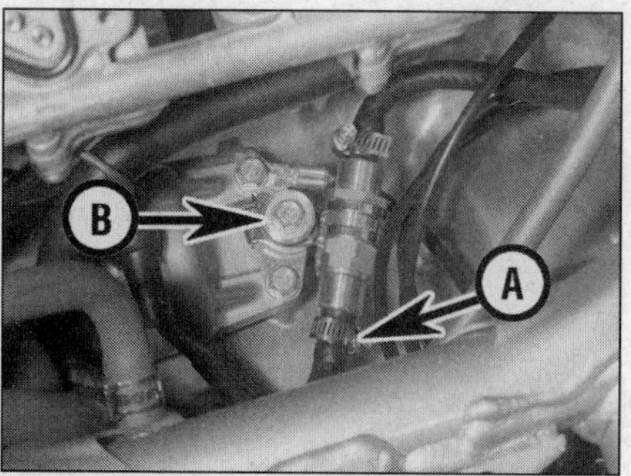

16.4b . . . and the hose (A) from the valve, then remove the valve mounting bolt (B)

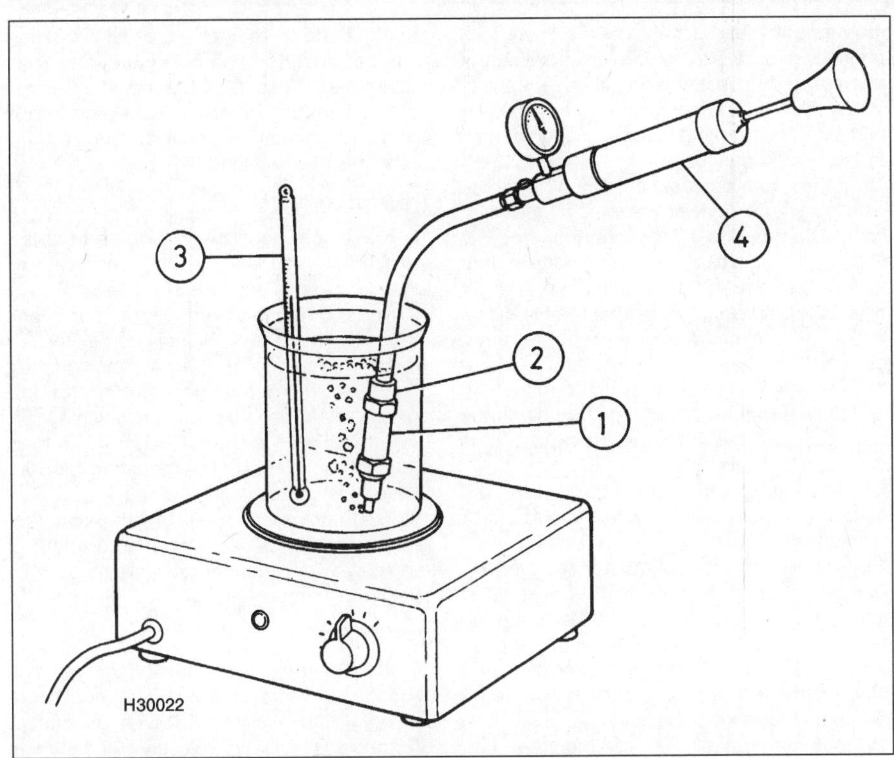

16.6 Thermostatic valve test set-up

1 Thermostatic valve 2 Gold-colored side 3 Thermometer 4 Pressure pump

The valve should be open and allow air to pass until the coolant reaches 73 to 77°C (163 to 171°F), whereupon it should start to close. If the valve is permanently closed, closes sooner than the specified temperature, or remains open, replace it as it is faulty.

8 Install the valve, making sure the hose from the thermostat housing attaches to the gold-colored (input) side of the valve. Make sure all hoses are correctly routed and securely connected, then fill the cooling system (see Chapter 1) and check it for leaks.

9 Install the fuel tank (see Chapter 4) and the lower fairing panels (see Chapter 8).

17 Fuel pump - check, removal and installation

Warning: Gasoline (petrol) is extremely flammable, so take extra precautions when you work on any part of the fuel system. Don't smoke or allow open flames or bare light bulbs near the work area, and don't work in a garage where a natural gas-type appliance (such as a water heater or clothes dryer) is present. If you spill any fuel on your skin, rinse it off immediately with soap and water. When you perform any kind of work on the fuel system, wear safety glasses and have a fire extinguisher suitable for a class B type fire (flammable liquids) on hand.

Check

1 The S, T, V and W (1995 to 1998) models are fitted with a fuel pump. The fuel pump is located behind the left side cover **(see illustration)**. The fuel cut-off relay is located on the frame above the passenger right footrest bracket **(see illustration)**. Remove the seat and both side covers to access all areas (see Chapter 8).

2 The fuel pump is controlled through the fuel cut-off relay so that it runs whenever the ignition is switched ON and the ignition is operative (ie, only when the engine is turning over). As soon as the ignition is killed, the relay will cut off the fuel pump's electrical supply (so that there is no risk of fuel being sprayed out under pressure in the event of an accident).

3 It should be possible to hear or feel the fuel pump running whenever the engine is turning over - either place your ear close beside the pump or feel it with your fingertips. If you can't hear or feel anything, check the circuit fuse (see Chapter 9). If the fuse is good, check the pump and relay for loose or corroded connections or physical damage and rectify as necessary.

4 If the circuit is fine so far, switch the ignition OFF. Unplug the relay's wiring connector and connect across the relay's black/white and black/blue terminals with a short length of insulated jumper wire. Switch the ignition ON; the pump should operate.

5 If the pump now works, either the relay or its wiring is at fault. Test the wiring as follows.

6 Check for full battery voltage at the relay's black/white terminal with the ignition switch ON. If there is no battery voltage, there is a fault in the circuit between the relay and the fuse - turn off the ignition, then trace and

17.1a Fuel pump location

17.1b Fuel cut-off relay (arrow)

rectify the fault as outlined in Chapter 9; refer to the wiring diagrams at the end of that Chapter.

7 If battery voltage was present, disconnect the wire connectors from the relay, fuel pump and ignition control module. Using an ohmmeter, check for continuity between the blue/yellow wire on the relay's wire connector and the blue/yellow wire on the control module's wire connector. Check for continuity between the black/blue wire on the relay's wire connector and the black/blue wire on the fuel pump's wire connector. Continuity should be indicated in all tests; if not, trace and rectify the fault as described in Chapter 9. Reconnect all wire connectors.

8 If the pump still does not work, trace the wiring from the pump and disconnect it at the black 2-pin wiring connector. Using a fully charged 12 volt battery and two insulated jumper wires, connect the positive (+ve) terminal of the battery to the pump's black/blue terminal, and the negative (-ve) terminal of the battery to the pump's green terminal. The pump should operate. If the pump does not operate it must be replaced.

9 If the pump works, check for battery voltage at the black/blue terminal on the supply side of the connector. If there is no voltage, check the wiring as above. If all the relevant wiring and connectors are good, then the relay is at fault. The only definitive test of the relay is to substitute one that is known to be good. If substitution does not cure the problem, bear in mind that the ignition control module could be faulty.

10 If the pump operates but is thought to be delivering an insufficient amount of fuel, first check that the fuel tank breather hose is unobstructed (except California models), that all fuel hoses are in good condition and not pinched or trapped. Check that the fuel filters in the fuel tank and fuel delivery hose are not blocked.

11 The fuel pump's output can be checked as follows: make sure the ignition switch is OFF. Remove the left lower fairing panel as described in Chapter 8.

12 Disconnect the fuel hose from the carburetor T-piece and place the end into a graduated beaker.

13 Disconnect the fuel cut-off relay wiring connector. Using a short length of insulated jumper wire, connect across the black and the black/blue wire terminals of the connector.

14 Turn the ignition switch ON and let fuel flow from the pump into the beaker for 5 seconds, then switch the ignition OFF.

15 Measure the amount of fuel that has flowed into the beaker, then multiply that amount by 12 to determine the fuel pump flow rate per minute. The minimum flow rate required is 700 cc (23.7 US fl oz, 24.6 Imp fl oz) per minute. If the flow rate recorded is below the minimum required, then the fuel pump must be replaced.

Removal

16 Make sure both the ignition and the fuel tap are switched OFF. Remove the seat and left side cover as described in Chapter 8.

17 Trace the wiring from the fuel pump and disconnect it at the black 2 pin connector.

18 Using a rag to mop up any spilled fuel, disconnect the two fuel hoses from the fuel pump, noting which pipe fits on which nozzle, then remove the pump with its rubber mounting sleeve from the mounting bracket, taking care not to snag the wiring.

19 To remove the fuel cut-off relay, first remove the right side cover, then disconnect the relay wiring connector and remove the relay from its mounting lug.

Installation

20 Installation is a reverse of the removal procedure. Make sure the fuel hoses are correctly and securely fitted to the pump. Start the engine and check carefully that there are no leaks at the pipe connections.

Chapter 5
Ignition system

Contents

Degrees of difficulty

Easy, suitable for novice with little experience 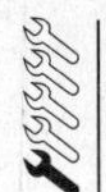

Fairly easy, suitable for beginner with some experience 

Fairly difficult, suitable for competent DIY mechanic

Difficult, suitable for experienced DIY mechanic

Very difficult, suitable for expert DIY or professional

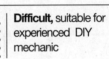

Specifications

General

Firing order	1-2-4-3
Cylinder identification	1-2-3-4 left to right

Ignition timing

Initial:	
M, N, P and R (1991 to 1994) models - except California	15° BTDC @ 1200 ± 100 rpm
S, T, V and W (1995 to 1998) models - except California	10° BTDC @ 1200 ± 100 rpm
All California models	5° BTDC @ 1400 ± 100 rpm
Full advance:	
US models (except California)	27° BTDC @ 8500 ± 100 rpm
California models	29° BTDC @ 8500 ± 100 rpm
UK models	42° BTDC @ 5500 ± 100 rpm

Pulse generator

Resistance	460 to 580 ohms @ 20°C (68°F)

Ignition HT coils

Primary winding resistance	2.5 to 3.1 ohms @ 20°C (68°F)
Secondary winding resistance	
With plug wires (HT leads) and plug caps	21 to 25 K ohms @ 20°C (68°F)
Without plug wires (HT leads)	11 to 15 K ohms @ 20°C (68°F)

Spark plugs

Type	See Chapter 1
Electrode gap	0.8 to 0.9 mm (0.031 to 0.035 in)

Torque settings

	Nm	ft-lbs
Crankshaft right end cover		
Retaining bolts	12	9
Center cap	18	13

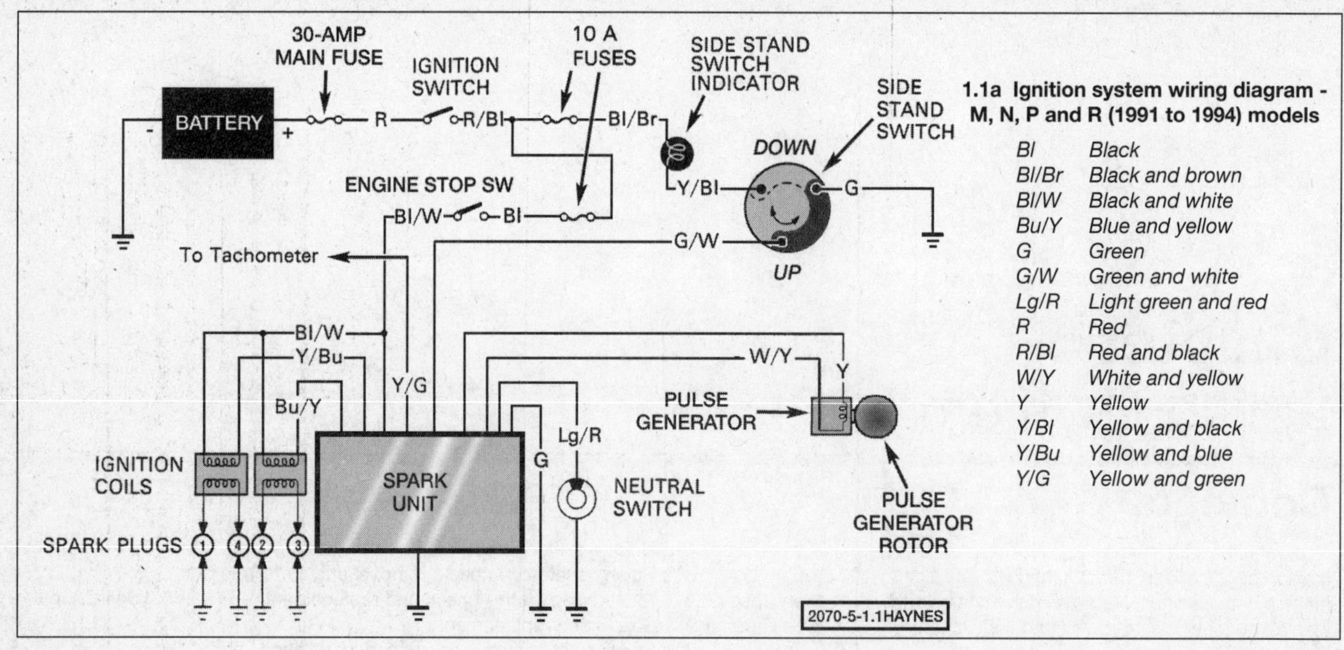

1.1a Ignition system wiring diagram - M, N, P and R (1991 to 1994) models

Bl	*Black*
Bl/Br	*Black and brown*
Bl/W	*Black and white*
Bu/Y	*Blue and yellow*
G	*Green*
G/W	*Green and white*
Lg/R	*Light green and red*
R	*Red*
R/Bl	*Red and black*
W/Y	*White and yellow*
Y	*Yellow*
Y/Bl	*Yellow and black*
Y/Bu	*Yellow and blue*
Y/G	*Yellow and green*

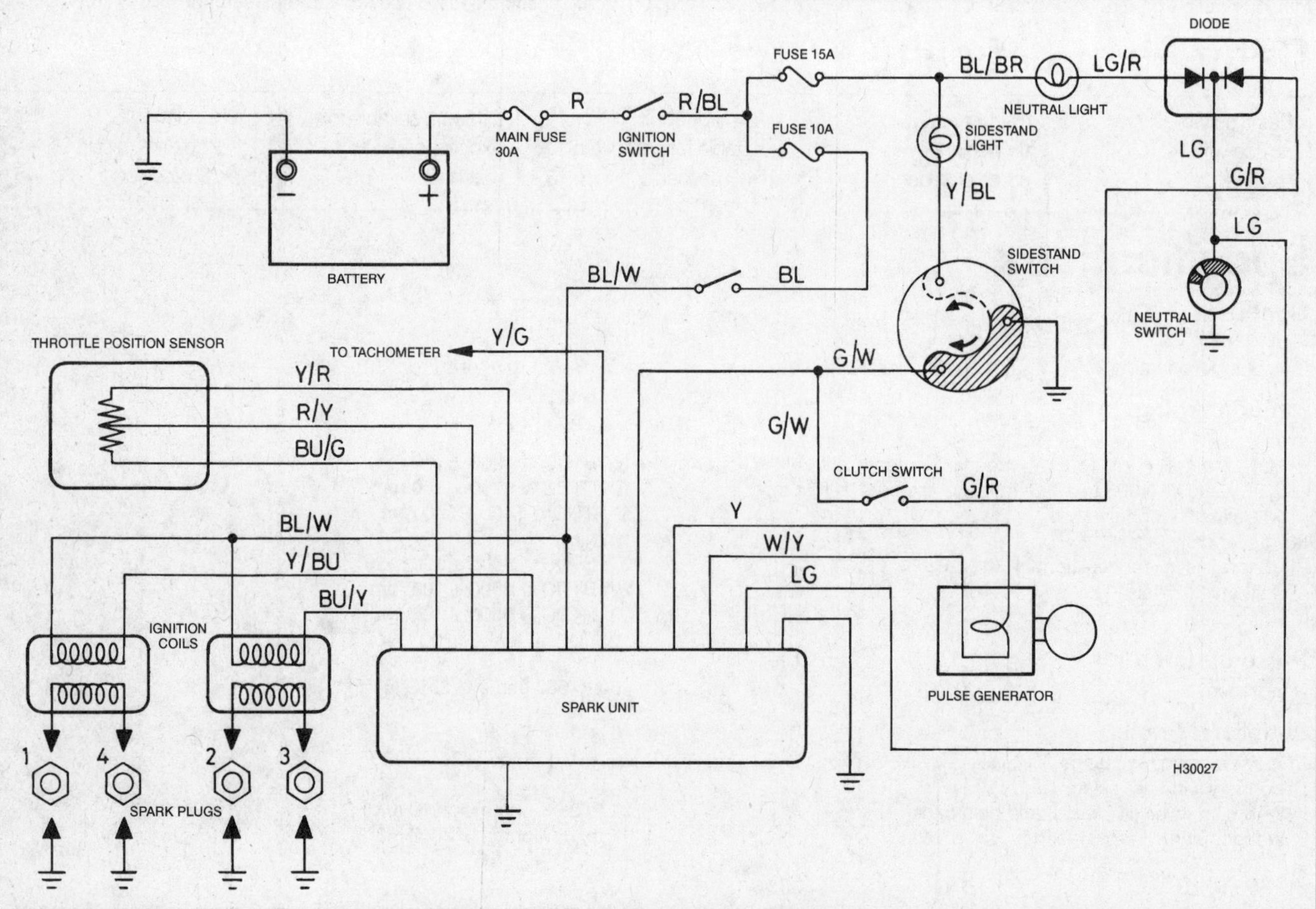

1.1b Ignition system wiring diagram - S (1995) model

BL	*Black*	*BU/Y*	*Blue and yellow*	*LG*	*Light green*	*Y/BL*	*Yellow and black*
BL/BR	*Black and brown*	*G*	*Green*	*LG/R*	*Light green and red*	*Y/BU*	*Yellow and blue*
BL/W	*Black and white*	*G/R*	*Green and red*	*R*	*Red*	*Y/G*	*Yellow and green*
BU/G	*Blue and green*	*G/W*	*Green and white*	*R/Y*	*Red and yellow*	*Y/R*	*Yellow and red*

1 General information

These models are fitted with a magnetically-triggered electronic ignition system, which due to its lack of mechanical parts is totally maintenance-free. The system comprises a rotor, pulse generator, spark unit and two ignition HT coils **(see illustrations)**.

The raised triggers on the rotor, which is fitted to the right end of the crankshaft, magnetically operate the pulse generator as the crankshaft rotates. The pulse generator sends a signal to the spark unit which then supplies the ignition coils with the power necessary to produce the spark at the plugs. Each coil supplies two spark plugs.

Cylinders 1 and 4 operate off one coil and cylinders 2 and 3 off the other. For any given cylinder, the plug is fired twice for every engine cycle, but one of the sparks occurs during the exhaust stroke and therefore performs no useful function. This arrangement is usually known as a 'spare spark' or 'wasted spark' system.

Because of their nature, the individual ignition system components can be checked but not repaired. If ignition system troubles occur, and the faulty component can be isolated, the only cure for the problem is to replace the part with a new one. Keep in mind that most electrical parts, once purchased, can't be returned. To avoid unnecessary expense, make very sure the faulty component has been positively identified before buying a replacement part.

2 Ignition system - check

Warning: The energy levels in electronic systems can be very high. On no account should the ignition be switched on while the plugs or plug caps are being held. Shocks from the HT circuit can be most unpleasant. Secondly, it is vital that the plugs are soundly grounded (earthed) when the system is checked for sparking. The ignition system components can be seriously damaged if the HT circuit becomes isolated.

1 As no means of adjustment is available, any failure of the system can be traced to failure of a system component or a simple wiring fault. Of the two possibilities, the latter is by far the most likely. In the event of failure, check the system in a logical fashion, as described below.

2 Disconnect the plug wires (HT leads) from No. 1 and No. 2 cylinder spark plugs and connect each lead to a spare spark plug. Lay each plug on the engine with the threads contacting the engine. If necessary, hold each spark plug with an insulated tool.

Warning: Don't remove one of the spark plugs from the engine to perform this check - atomized fuel being pumped out of the open spark plug hole could ignite, causing severe injury!

3 Having observed the above precautions, check that the kill switch is in the RUN position, turn the ignition switch to ON and turn the engine over on the starter motor. If the system is in good condition a regular, strong blue spark should be evident at each plug electrode.

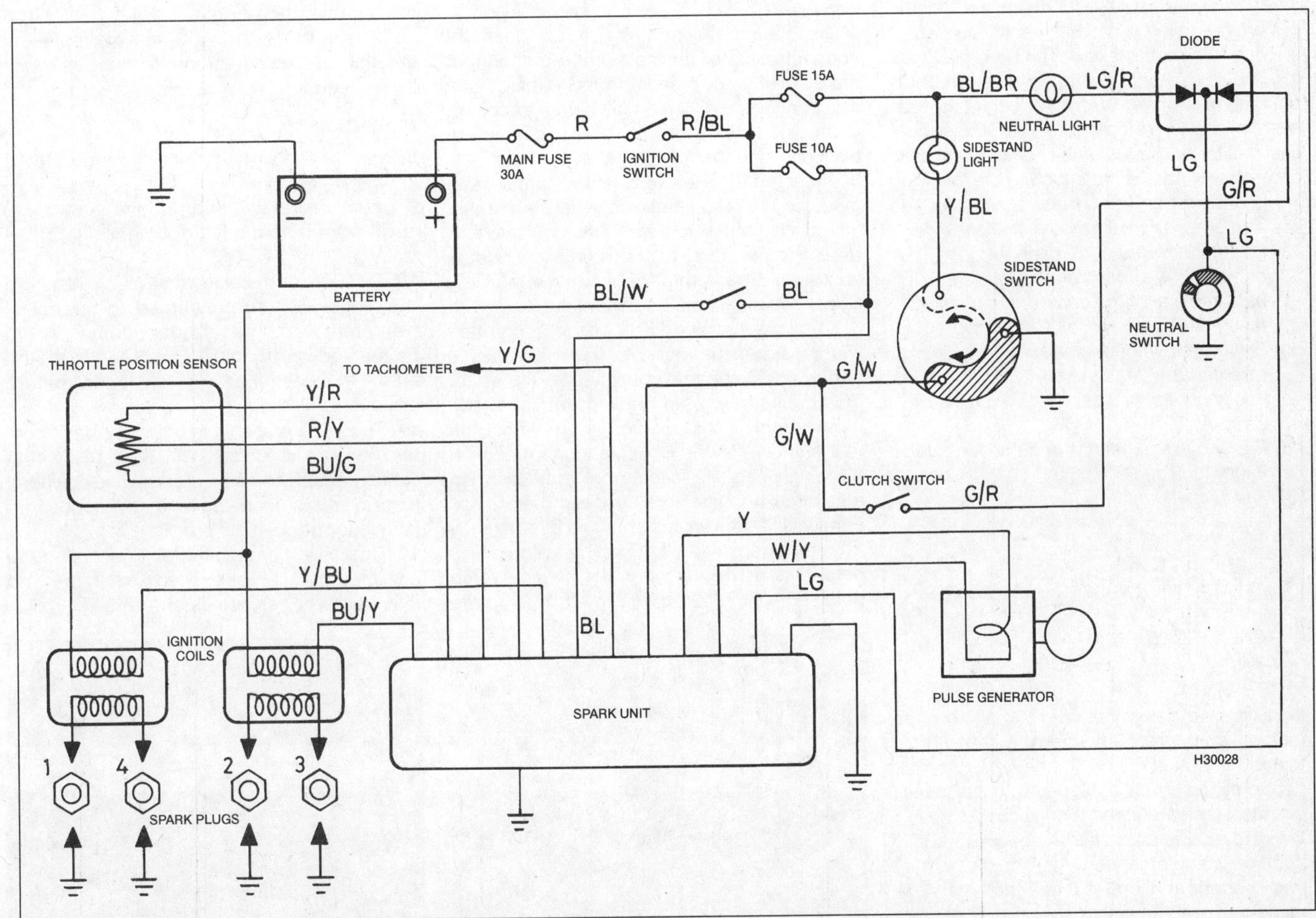

1.1c Ignition system wiring diagram - T, V and W (1996 to 1998) models

see illustration 1.1b for color key

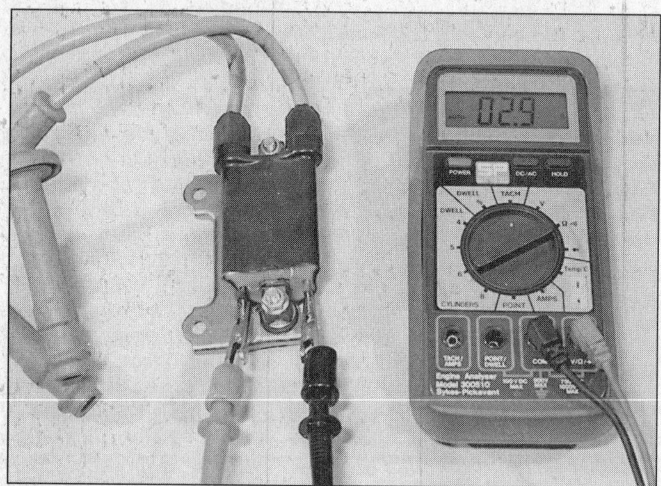
3.5 Measuring ignition HT coil primary winding resistance

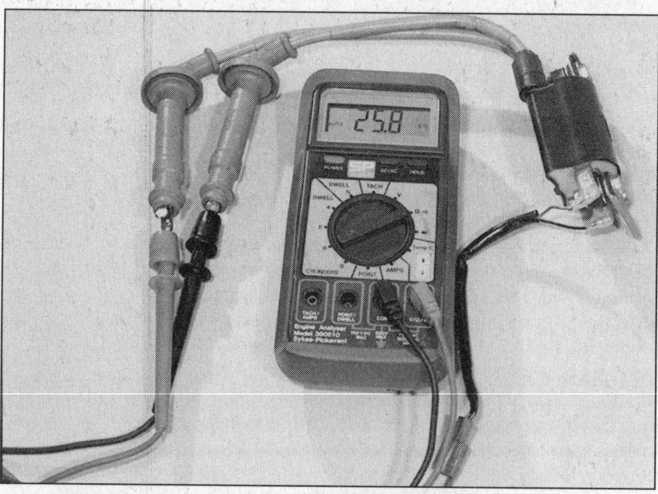
3.6 Measuring ignition HT coil secondary winding resistance (plug caps fitted)

If the spark appears thin or yellowish, or is non-existent, further investigation will be necessary. Before proceeding further, turn the ignition off and remove the key as a safety measure.

4 Ignition faults can be divided into two categories, namely those where the ignition system has failed completely, and those which are due to a partial failure. The likely faults are listed below, starting with the most probable source of failure. Work through the list systematically, referring to the subsequent sections for full details of the necessary checks and tests. **Note:** *Before checking the following items ensure that the battery is fully charged and that all fuses are in good condition.*

a) Loose, corroded or damaged wiring connections, broken or shorted wiring between any of the component parts of the ignition system (see Chapter 9).
b) Faulty ignition or engine kill switch (see Chapter 9).
c) Faulty neutral or sidestand switch (see Chapter 9).
d) Faulty pulse generator or damaged rotor.
e) Faulty ignition HT coil(s).
f) Faulty spark unit.

3 Ignition coils - check, removal and installation

Check

1 In order to determine conclusively that the ignition coils are defective, they should be tested by an authorized Honda dealer service department which is equipped with the special electrical tester required for this check.

2 However, the coils can be checked visually (for cracks and other damage) and the primary and secondary coil resistances can be measured with an ohmmeter. If the coils are undamaged, and if the resistances are as specified, they are probably capable of proper operation.

3 To gain access to the coils, remove the air filter housing as described in Chapter 4. Undo the retaining screws and remove the access covers from the left and right side of the fairing to gain access to the plug wires (HT leads).

4 Disconnect the primary circuit electrical connectors from the coil(s) and disconnect the plug wires (HT leads) from the plugs that are connected to the coil being checked. Mark the locations of all wires before disconnecting them.

5 Set the meter to the ohms x 1 scale and measure the resistance between the primary (low tension) terminals. This will give a resistance reading of the primary windings and should be within the limits given in the Specifications **(see illustration)**.

6 To check the condition of the secondary windings, set the meter to the K ohm scale and connect the meter probes to the spark plug caps, noting the reading obtained **(see illustration)**. If this reading is not within the range shown in the Specifications, unscrew the plug wires (HT leads) from the coils then measure the resistance between the HT coil terminals. If both values obtained differ greatly from those specified it is likely that the coil is defective. **Note:** *If only the first reading obtained is suspect, then the fault lies in the plug wire/HT lead/spark plug caps rather than the coil itself.*

7 Should any of the above checks not produce the expected result, the coil should be taken to a Honda dealer or auto-electrician for a more thorough check. If the coil is confirmed to be faulty, it must be replaced; the coil is a sealed unit and cannot therefore be repaired.

Removal

8 Remove the air filter housing as described in Chapter 4.

9 Undo the screws and remove the access cover from both the left and right side of the fairing.

10 Disconnect the plug wires (HT leads) from the plugs that are connected to the coil(s) being removed. The cylinder number should be marked on the plug wire/HT lead; if not, mark the locations of all leads before disconnecting them.

11 Trace the primary circuit wiring back from the coil(s) and disconnect it at the wiring connector(s). The connectors are color-coded to prevent them being wrongly connected **(see illustration)**.

12 Unscrew the retaining bolts securing the coil mounting bracket(s) to the frame and remove the coil(s) **(see illustration)**.

3.11 Ignition HT coil primary wiring connectors (arrows)

3.12 Ignition HT coil bracket retaining bolts (arrows)

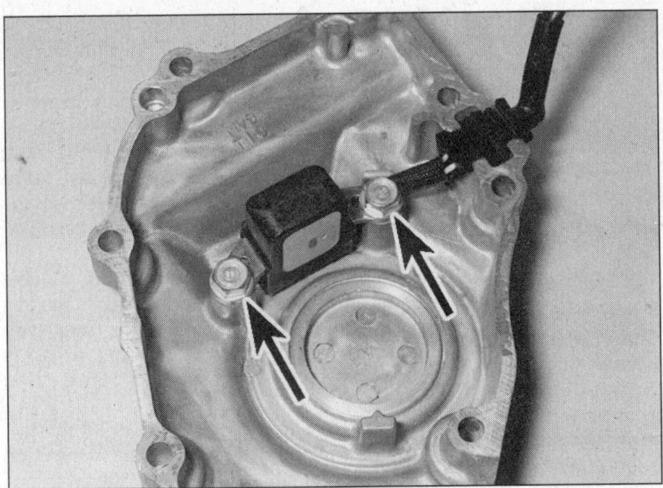
4.11 Pulse generator is secured to right cover by two bolts (arrows)

4.15a Install the locating dowels (arrows) . . .

Installation

13 Installation is the reverse of removal making sure the wiring connectors and HT leads are securely connected.

4 Pulse generator - check, removal and installation

Check

1 Remove the fuel tank as described in Chapter 4.

2 Disconnect the red two-pin block connector situated in the junction box. Using a multimeter set to the ohms x 100 scale measure the resistance between the White/yellow and Yellow wires on the generator side of the connector.

3 Compare the reading obtained with that given in the Specifications at the start of this Chapter. The pulse generator must be replaced if the reading obtained differs greatly from that given, particularly if the meter indicates a short circuit (no measurable resistance) or an open circuit (infinite, or very high resistance).

4 If the generator is thought to be faulty, first check that this is not due to a damaged or broken wire from the coil to the connector; pinched or broken wires can usually be repaired.

4.15b . . . and fit a new gasket to the crankcase. Ensure the oil jet (arrow) is in position

Removal

5 Remove the fuel tank as described in Chapter 4.

6 Remove the right lower fairing panel as described in Chapter 8.

7 Drain the engine oil as described in Chapter 1.

8 Trace the wiring back from the right crankshaft end cover to the junction box. Disconnect the pulse generator wiring connector and free the wiring from underneath the battery box. Work back along the wiring, noting its routing while releasing it from any relevant ties or clips.

9 Unscrew the cover retaining bolts and remove the cover squarely from the engine unit. Note the position of the oil jet fitted behind the cover and make sure it stays in position.

10 Remove the cover locating dowels from the crankcase and discard the gasket.

11 Remove the bolts which secure the pulse generator to the cover and remove the generator **(see illustration)**.

12 Examine the rotor triggers for signs of damage such as chipped or missing teeth and replace if necessary.

Installation

13 Fit the pulse generator to the cover and securely tighten its retaining bolts.

14 Remove all traces of old gasket from the crankcase and cover mating surfaces. Make sure the oil jet is in position in the crankcase.

15 Install the locating dowels and fit a new gasket to the crankcase **(see illustrations)**.

16 Apply a smear of suitable sealing compound to the right crankshaft end cover wiring grommet and to the threads of two of the cover retaining bolts.

17 Fit the cover to the engine noting that the bolts smeared with sealant should be installed in the two holes next to the cam chain tensioner. These holes are indicated by triangular marks cast in the cover **(see illustrations)**. Tighten the cover bolts to the torque setting listed in this Chapter's Specifications.

4.17a Fit the cover to the crankcase and install the bolts . . .

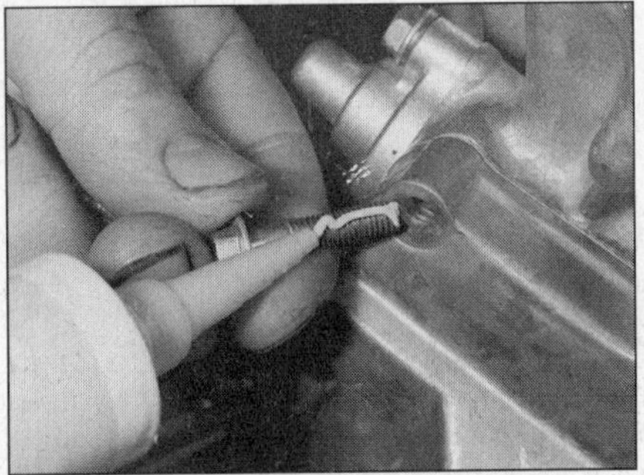
4.17b . . . making sure that sealant is applied to the threads of the two bolts . . .

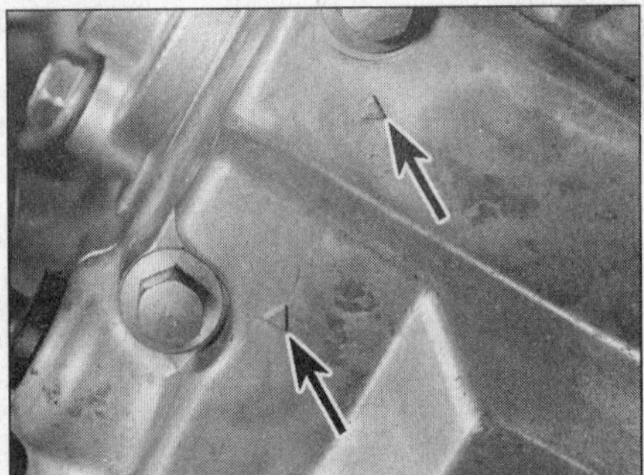
4.17c . . . that are fitted in the holes marked with the triangular marks (arrows)

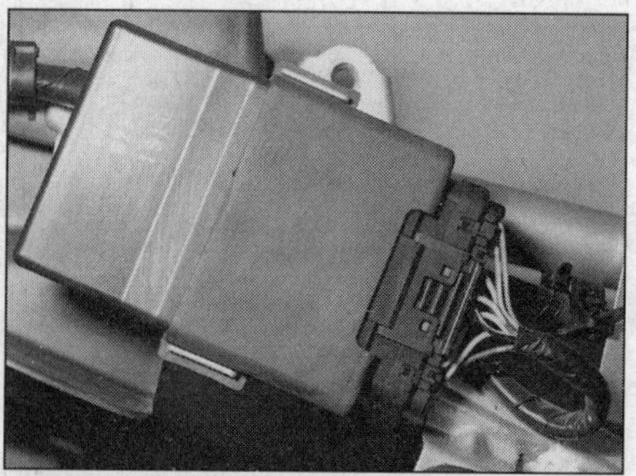

5.2 The spark unit is located behind the right side cover

18 Make sure the wiring is correctly routed up to the junction box and reconnect the wiring connector. Secure the wiring in position with all the necessary clips and ties.
19 Fill the engine with the correct type and amount of oil as described in Chapter 1.
20 Install the fuel tank and fairing panel as described in Chapters 4 and 8.

5 Spark unit - removal, check and installation

Removal

1 Remove the right side cover (see Chapter 8, if necessary).
2 Disconnect the wiring connector from the spark unit **(see illustration)**.
3 Slide the spark unit out of its rubber retainer and remove it from the motorcycle.

Check

4 If the tests shown in the preceding Sections have failed to isolate the cause of an ignition fault, it is likely that the spark unit itself is faulty. However, to assess the condition of the spark unit a special electronic test unit and adapter, only available to a Honda dealer, will be required.

6.5 Unscrew the center cap from the right crankshaft end cover to reveal the timing marks

Installation

5 Installation is the reverse of removal ensuring the wiring connector is securely connected.

6 Ignition timing - general information and check

General information

1 Since no provision exists for adjusting the ignition timing and since no component is subject to mechanical wear, there is no need for regular checks; only if investigating a fault such as a loss of power or a misfire, should the ignition timing be checked.
2 The ignition timing can only be checked while the engine is running using a stroboscopic (timing) lamp. The inexpensive neon lamps should be adequate in theory, but in practice may produce a pulse of such low intensity that the timing mark remains indistinct. If possible, one of the more precise xenon tube lamps should be used, powered by an external source of the appropriate voltage. **Note:** *Do not use the machine's own battery as an incorrect reading may result from stray impulses within the machine's electrical system.*

Check

3 Warm the engine up to normal operating temperature then stop it.
4 Remove the right lower fairing panel as described in Chapter 8.
5 Unscrew the center cap from the right crankshaft end cover to reveal the pulse generator rotor **(see illustration)**. Recover the cap sealing ring. The timing mark is stamped on the center of the rotor.
6 On M, N, P and R (1991 to 1994) models (except California) the timing mark is the line situated next to the 'F' on the rotor **(see illustration)**. On California models the mark is the two punch marks situated between the two lines.
7 On S, T, V and W (1995 to 1998) models (except California) the timing mark is the three punch marks situated between the two lines on the rotor **(see illustration)**. On California models the mark is the two punch marks situated between the two lines.
8 Connect the timing light to the No. 1 cylinder HT lead as described in the manufacturer's instructions. Start the engine and aim the light at the inspection hole.

Highlight the rotor timing mark with white paint to make it more visible under the stroboscopic light.

9 With the machine idling at the specified speed, the rotor timing mark should align with the index mark, in the form of a cut-out in the edge of the crankshaft end cover **(see illustration)**.
10 To check the ignition advance function, slowly increase the engine speed while observing the timing mark. Starting at approximately 1600 rpm on M, N, P and R (1991 to 1994) models (except California), 1900 rpm on M, N, P and R (1991 to 1994) California models, and 1500 rpm on all S, T, V and W (1995 to 1998) models, the 'F' mark

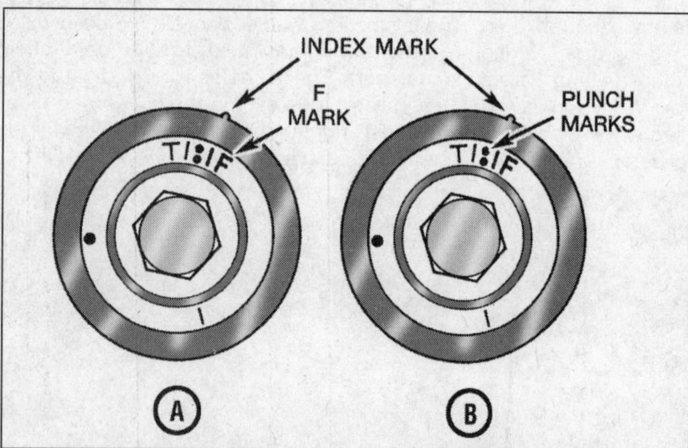

6.6 Ignition timing rotor markings and index mark - M, N, P and R (1991 to 1994) models

A UK models and US models except california
B California models

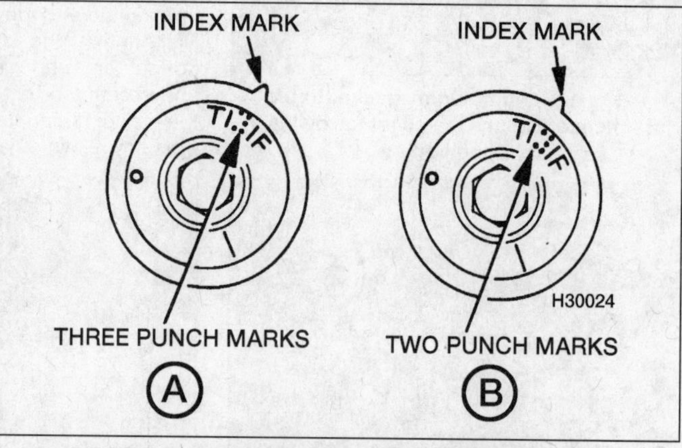

6.7 Ignition timing rotor markings and index mark - S, T, V and W (1995 to 1998) models

A UK models and US models except california
B California models

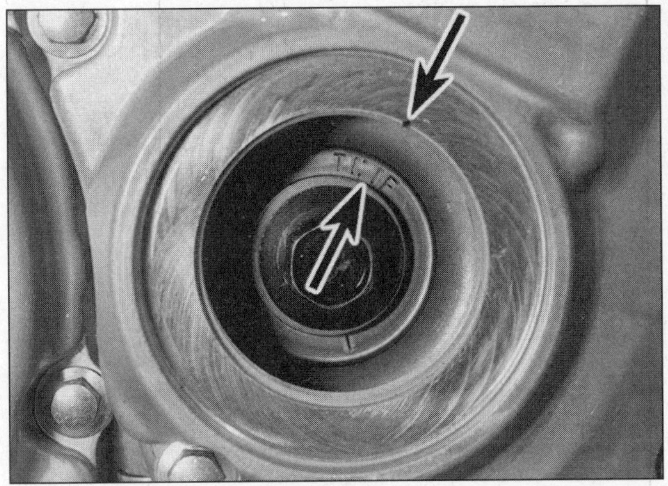
6.9 The correct rotor mark must align with the cut-out index mark in the crankcase cover (arrows)

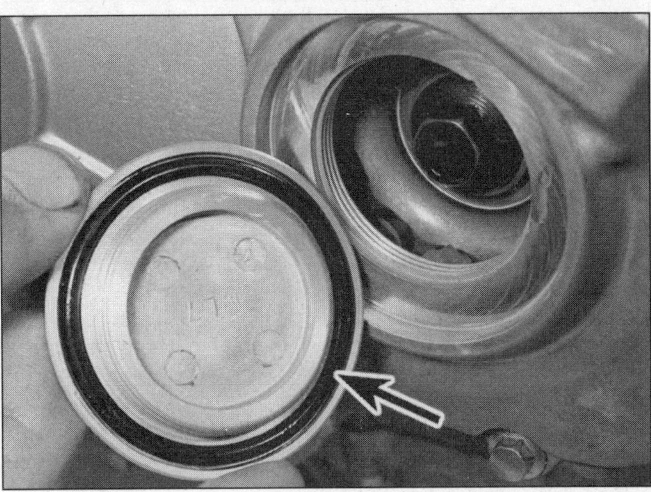
6.12 On installation fit a new O-ring (arrow) to the end cover center cap

should move counterclockwise (anti-clockwise), increasing in relation to the engine speed.

11 As already stated, there is no means of adjustment of the ignition timing on these machines. If the ignition timing is incorrect one of the ignition system components is at fault, and system must be tested as described in the preceding Sections of this Chapter.

12 When the check is complete, fit a new sealing ring to the center cap and lubricate it with a smear of clean engine oil **(see illustration)**. Install the cap and tighten it to the specified torque setting.

13 Install the fairing panel as described in Chapter 8.

7 Throttle position sensor - check and replacement

Check

1 The throttle position sensor is fitted to the carburetors on S, T, V and W (1995 to 1998) models only. Remove the air filter housing (see Chapter 4).

2 The throttle sensor is mounted on the outside of the left-hand carburetor. In order to determine conclusively that the throttle sensor is defective, it should be tested by a Honda dealer equipped with the special electrical adapter required for this check.

3 However, the sensor can be checked visually (for cracks and other damage) and the wiring between the sensor and the spark unit checked for continuity.

4 Trace the wiring to the 3-pin connector and disconnect it **(see illustration)**. Also disconnect the spark unit wiring connector. Check the connectors for loose or corroded terminals.

5 Using a multimeter set to resistance or a continuity tester, check the three wires which run from the throttle sensor connector to the spark unit connector for continuity. There should be continuity from one end of the wire to the other. If not, this is probably due to a damaged or broken wire between the connectors; pinched or broken wires can usually be repaired.

6 If the sensor is suspected of being faulty, take it to a Honda dealer for testing. If it is confirmed to be faulty, it must be replaced; the sensor is a sealed unit and cannot therefore be repaired.

Replacement

7 Remove the carburetors (see Chapter 4).

8 The throttle sensor is mounted on the outside of No. 1 carburetor. Unscrew the sensor mounting screws and remove the sensor, noting how it fits.

9 Install the sensor, aligning the slot with the boss on the end of the throttle shaft, and tighten its screws securely.

10 Install the carburetors (see Chapter 4).

7.4 Disconnect the throttle position sensor wiring connector

Chapter 6
Frame, suspension and final drive

Contents

Degrees of difficulty

Easy, suitable for novice with little experience 

Fairly easy, suitable for beginner with some experience 

Fairly difficult, suitable for competent DIY mechanic

Difficult, suitable for experienced DIY mechanic 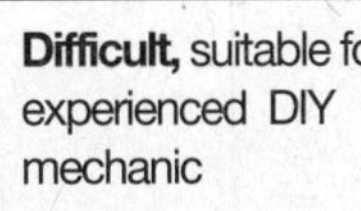

Very difficult, suitable for expert DIY or professional

Specifications

Front forks

Spring free length	
M and N (1991 and 1992) models	
New	443.2 mm (17.45 in)
Service limit	434.3 mm (17.10 in)
P and R (1993 and 1994) models	
New	429.3 mm (16.90 in)
Service limit	420.7 mm (16.60 in)
S, T, V and W (1995 to 1998) models	
New	317.9 mm (12.50 in)
Service limit	311.5 mm (12.30 in)
Oil capacity - per leg	
M and N (1991 and 1992) models	508 cc (17.1 US fl oz, 17.9 Imp fl oz)
P and R (1993 and 1994) models	460 cc (15.5 US fl oz, 16.2 Imp fl oz)
S and T (1995 and 1996) models	463 cc (15.7 US fl oz, 16.3 Imp fl oz
V and W (1997 and 1998) models	460 cc (15.5 US fl oz, 16.2 Imp fl oz)
Oil level*	
M and N (1991 and 1992) models	118 mm (4.65 in)
P and R (1993 and 1994) models	135 mm (5.31 in)
S and T (1995 and 1996) models	117 mm (4.61 in)
V and W (1997 and 1998) models	120 mm (4.72 in)
Fork oil type	SAE 10W fork oil

**Oil level is measured from the top of the tube with the fork spring removed and the leg fully compressed. On P, R, S T, V and W models (1993 to 1998) the damper rod should also be fully compressed.*

Rear shock absorber

Spring free length	
M and N (1991 and 1992) models	
New	139.2 mm (5.48 in)
Service limit	136.4 mm (5.37 in)
P and R (1993 and 1994) models	
New	134.9 mm (5.31 in)
Service limit	132.2 mm (5.20 in)

Final drive

Chain type (original equipment)	
M and N (1991 and 1992) models	RK50MFOX or DID50VA7 (108 links)
P and R (1993 and 1994) models	RK50MFO or DID50V4 (108 links)
S and T (1995 and 1996) models	RK50MFO or DID50V4 (108 links)
V and W (1997 and 1998) models	RK50ROZ1 or DID525HV (108 links)
Joining link pin projection from side plate (unstaked) - S, T, V and W (1995 to 1998) models	
RK type chain	1.2 to 1.4 mm (0.05 to 0.055 in)
DID type chain	1.15 to 1.55 mm (0.045 to 0.06 in)
Joining link staked ends diameter	
S and T (1995 and 1996) models	
RK type chain	5.55 to 5.85 mm (0.219 to 0.230 in)
DID type chain	5.50 to 5.80 mm (0.217 to 0.228 in)
V and W (1997 and 1998) models	
RK type chain	5.49 to 5.94 mm (0.216 to 0.233 in)
DID type chain	5.50 to 5.80 mm (0.217 to 0.228 in)

Torque settings

	Nm	ft-lbs
Handlebar clamp bolt	27	20
Triple clamp pinch bolts		
Top triple clamp	23	17
Bottom triple clamp	40	29
Front forks		
Top bolts	23	17
Damper rod Allen bolt		
M, N, P and R (1991 to 1994) models	23	17
S, T, V and W (1995 to 1998) models	20	14
Steering stem adjuster nut (see text)	25	18
Steering stem top nut	105	76
Shock absorber mounting bolt nuts	45	33
Rear suspension linkage pivot bolt nuts	45	33
Swingarm pivot shaft nut	110	80
Front sprocket bolt	55	40
Rear sprocket nuts	90	65

1 General information

All models covered in this manual employ a diamond type frame which uses the engine unit as a stressed member. The frame is constructed in box section steel.

Front suspension is by a pair of oil-damped, coil spring, telescopic fork legs.

Rear suspension is by Honda's 'Pro-Link' system in which the swingarm acts on a gas-charged, hydraulically-damped suspension unit via a two piece linkage.

Final drive is by sealed O-ring chain. A rubber damper (often called a 'cush drive') is installed between the rear wheel coupling and the wheel.

2 Frame - inspection and repair

1 The frame should not require attention unless accident damage has occurred. In most cases, frame replacement is the only satisfactory remedy for such damage. A few frame specialists have the jigs and other equipment necessary for straightening the frame to the required standard of accuracy, but even then there is no simple way of assessing to what extent the frame may have been over stressed.

2 After the machine has accumulated a lot of miles, the frame should be examined closely for signs of cracking or splitting at the welded joints. Corrosion can also cause weakness at these joints. Loose engine mount bolts can cause ovaling or fracturing of the mounting tabs. Minor damage can often be repaired by welding, depending on the extent and nature of the damage.

3 Remember that a frame which is out of alignment will cause handling problems. If misalignment is suspected as the result of an accident, it will be necessary to strip the machine completely so the frame can be thoroughly checked.

3 Footpegs and brackets - removal and installation

Removal

Rider's footpegs

1 Remove the cotter pin (split pin) and washer, then slide out the pivot pin and remove the footpeg from the bracket along with its return spring **(see illustration).**

2 If necessary, undo the retaining screws and separate the rubber pad from the footpeg.

Left rider's footpeg bracket

3 Set the bike on its centerstand.

4 Slacken and remove the pivot bolt securing the gearshift lever to the footpeg bracket. Free the linkage from the bracket and recover the washer from behind the lever.

5 Undo the two retaining bolts and remove the bracket assembly from the frame.

Right rider's footpeg bracket

6 Remove the fuel tank (see Chapter 4).

7 Trace the wiring back from the brake light switch and disconnect it at its wiring connector, situated in the junction box.

8 Unscrew the banjo union bolt from the top of the master cylinder. Discard the sealing washers on each side of the fitting. Wrap the end of the hose in a clean rag and suspend the hose in an upright position or bend it down carefully and place the open end in a clean container. The objective is to prevent excessive loss of brake fluid, fluid spills and system contamination.

9 Remove the bolt securing the master cylinder reservoir to the frame. Unscrew the reservoir cap and pour the contents into a container.

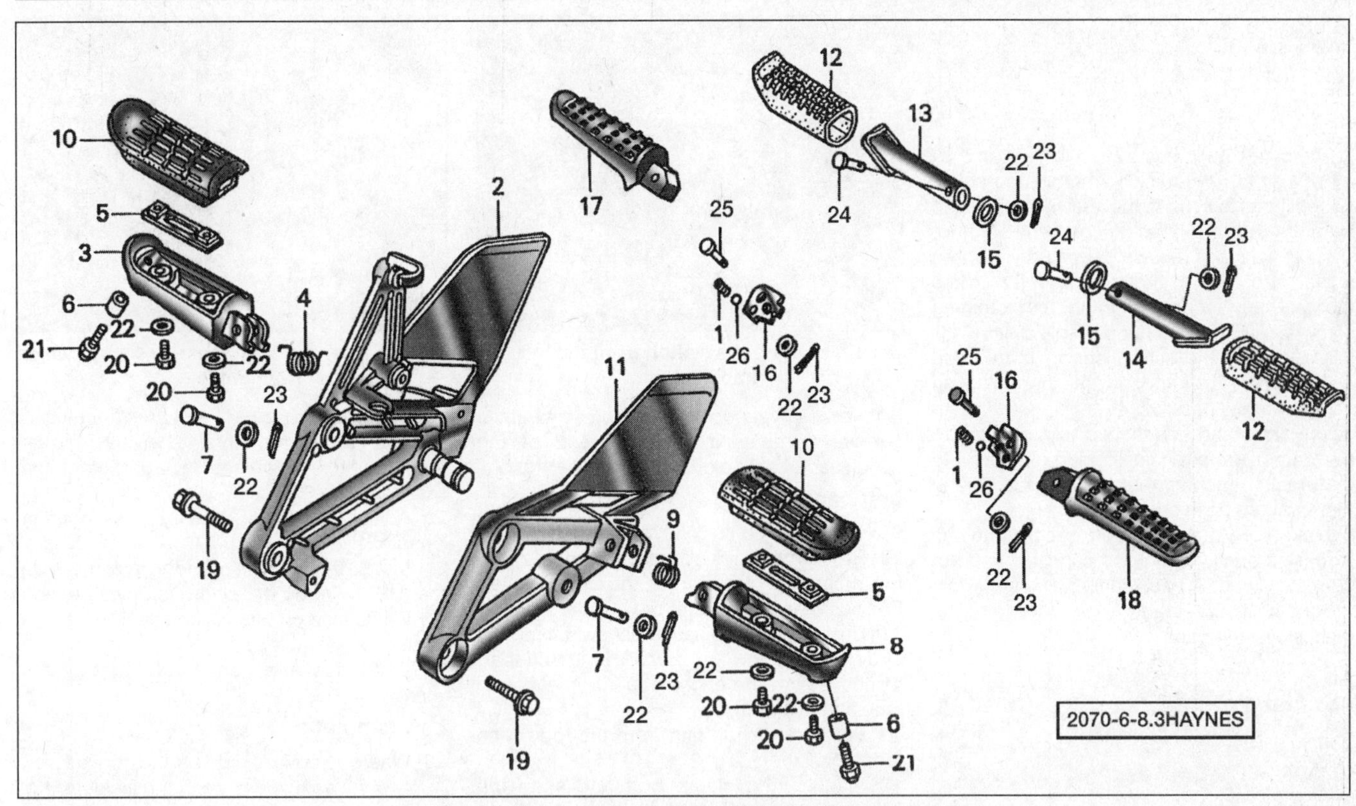

3.1 Exploded view of the footpeg and bracket components

1 Spring
2 Rider's right footpeg bracket
3 Rider's right footpeg
4 Return spring
5 Retaining plate
6 Spacer
7 Pivot pin
8 Rider's left footpeg
9 Return spring
10 Rider's footpeg rubber pad
11 Rider's left footpeg bracket
*12 Passenger footpeg rubber pad**
*13 Passenger right footpeg**
*14 Passenger left footpeg**
*15 Washer**
*16 Detent plate***
*17 Right passenger footpeg***
*18 Left passenger footpeg***
19 Rider's footpeg bracket bolt
20 Rider's footpeg pad bolts
21 Rider's footpeg bracket ground bolt
22 Washer
23 Cotter pin (split pin)
*24 Pivot pin**
*25 Pivot pin***
*26 Ball bearing***
**Fitted to models with rubber passenger footpegs*
***Fitted to models with alloy passenger footpegs*

10 Undo the two retaining bolts and remove the bracket assembly from the frame.

Passenger footpegs

11 On models with rubber passenger footpegs, remove the cotter pin (split pin) and washer then slide out the pivot pin and remove the footpeg from the bracket along with its washer. If necessary, separate the rubber pad from the footpeg.

12 On models with alloy passenger footpegs, remove the cotter pin (split pin) and washer then slide out the pivot pin and remove the footpeg from the bracket. As the footpeg is removed, recover the footpeg detent plate, spring and ball bearing, noting the correct fitted positions of each component.

Left passenger footpeg bracket

13 Remove the left side cover (see Chapter 8, if necessary).

14 Undo the retaining bolts and remove the footpeg bracket from the motorcycle.

Right passenger footpeg bracket

15 Remove the right side cover (see Chapter 8, if necessary).

16 Slacken and remove the mounting bolt securing the exhaust system muffler (silencer) to the footpeg bracket. Tie the muffler (silencer) to the frame to prevent strain on the exhaust system.

17 Undo the retaining bolts and remove the footpeg bracket from the motorcycle.

Installation

Rider's footpegs

18 Installation is the reverse of removal. Use a new cotter pin (split pin).

Left rider's footpeg bracket

19 Install the bracket and securely tighten its mounting bolts.

20 Apply a smear of grease to the bearing surface of the gearshift lever pivot bolt. Position the washer behind the gearshift lever, then fit the pivot bolt, tightening it securely.

Right rider's footpeg bracket

21 Install the bracket and securely tighten its mounting bolts.

22 Apply a few drops of locking compound to the threads of the master cylinder reservoir bolt, then fit the bolt and tighten it to the specified torque setting (see Chapter 7).

23 Connect the banjo fitting to the top of the master cylinder, using a new sealing washer on each side of the fitting. Tighten the banjo fitting bolt to the specified torque setting (see Chapter 7).

24 Reconnect the brake light switch wiring, ensuring it is correctly routed.

25 Fill the fluid reservoir with the specified fluid (see Chapter 1) and bleed the system following the procedure in Section 11 of Chapter 7. Install the fuel tank as described in Chapter 4.

Passenger footpegs

26 Installation is the reverse of removal. Use a new cotter pin (split pin).

Passenger footpeg brackets

27 Installation is the reverse of removal.

4 Side and centerstand - maintenance

1 The centerstand is attached to the frame by a pivot shaft. Periodically, remove the cotter pin (split pin) then undo the retaining screw and slide out the pivot shaft. Inspect the shaft for signs of wear and replace if necessary. Apply a smear of grease to the shaft and fit it to the motorcycle. Securely tighten the retaining screw and fit a new cotter pin (split pin).

2 Make sure the return spring is in good condition. A broken or weak spring is an obvious safety hazard.

3 The sidestand is attached to a bracket on the frame. An extension spring anchored to the bracket ensures that the stand is held in the retracted position.

4 Make sure the pivot bolt is tight and the extension spring is in good condition and not over-stretched. An accident is almost certain to occur if the stand extends while the machine is in motion.

5 Handlebars - removal and installation

Removal

Right handlebar

1 Set the bike on its centerstand.

2 Disconnect the wiring connector from the front brake light switch.

3 Remove the two clamp bolts and remove the mounting clamp from the master cylinder. Position the master cylinder clear of the handlebar, ensuring no strain is placed on the hydraulic hose. Keep the master cylinder upright to prevent possible fluid leakage.

4 Unscrew the two handlebar switch screws and free the switch from the handlebar.

5 Disconnect the throttle cables from the carburetors, then free the cables from the throttle grip (see Chapter 4).

6 Pry off the snap ring from the top of the fork tube.

7 Slacken the clamp bolt and slide the handlebar off the fork.

5.13 Slacken the clamp bolt (arrow) and remove the handlebar

5.11a Free the switch from the left handlebar . . .

8 If necessary, undo the retaining screw, then remove the weight from the end of the handlebar and slide off the throttle twistgrip.

Left handlebar

9 Set the bike on its centerstand.

10 Remove the two clamp bolts and remove the mounting clamp from the clutch lever. Position the lever clear of the handlebar.

11 Unscrew the two handlebar switch screws and free the switch from the handlebar, disconnecting the choke cable from its lever **(see illustrations)**.

12 Pry off the snap ring from the top of the fork tube.

13 Slacken the clamp bolt and slide the handlebar off of the fork **(see illustration)**.

14 If necessary, undo the retaining screw, then remove the weight from the end of the handlebar and pull off the handlebar grip and the choke lever **(see illustration)**.

Installation

Right handlebar

15 Where removed, apply a smear of grease to the throttle twistgrip and slide the grip on the handlebar. Apply non-permanent thread locking compound to the retaining screw, install the weight and securely tighten the screw.

16 Align the handlebar locating lug with the slot in the triple clamp. Fit the snap ring ensuring it is correctly located in its groove.

17 Tighten the handlebar clamp bolt to the specified torque while pushing the handlebar fully forward.

18 Reconnect the throttle cables to the twistgrip.

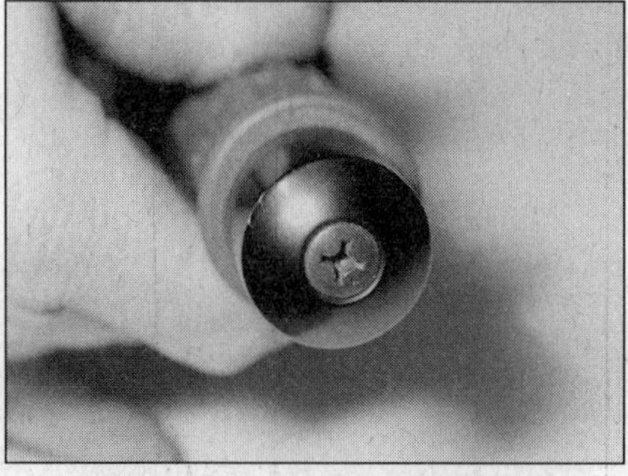

5.14 Handlebar end weight retaining screw

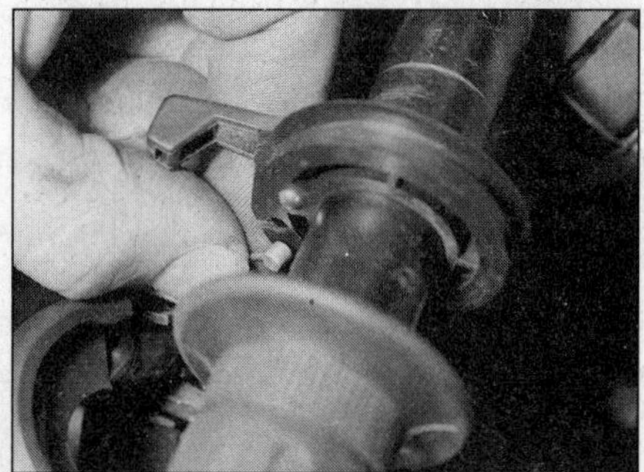

5.11b . . . and disconnect the choke cable from the lever

19 Fit the switch lower half to the handlebar, locating its peg in the handlebar hole. Fit the top half of the switch and securely tighten the screws.

20 Adjust the throttle cables as described in Chapter 1.

21 Install the master cylinder, making sure the 'UP' mark on the clamp is upwards, and tighten its clamp bolts to the specified torque setting (see Chapter 7).

22 Reconnect the front brake light switch wiring.

Left handlebar

23 Where removed, slide on the choke lever. Apply a suitable adhesive to the inside of the throttle grip and slide it on the handlebar. Apply non-permanent thread locking compound to the retaining screw then install the weight and securely tighten the screw.

24 Align the handlebar locating lug with the slot in the triple clamp. Fit the snap ring ensuring it is correctly located in its groove.

25 Tighten the handlebar clamp bolt to the specified torque while pushing the handlebar fully forward.

26 Reconnect the choke cable to the lever.

27 Fit the switch lower half to the handlebar, locating its peg in the handlebar hole. Fit the top half of the switch and securely tighten the screws.

28 Check the choke cable operation and, if necessary, adjust as described in Chapter 1.

29 Install the clutch lever, making sure the 'UP' mark on the clamp is upwards, and securely tighten the clamp bolts **(see illustration)**.

30 Reconnect the clutch switch wiring.

5.29 Install the clutch lever mounting clamp ensuring the 'UP' mark is the correct way up

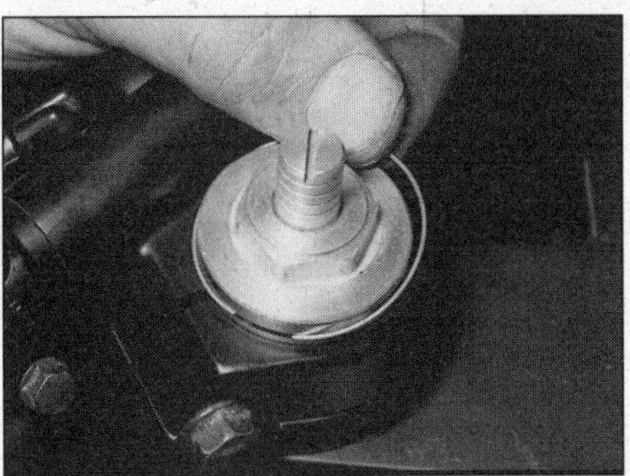
6.3 Remove the snap-ring from the top of the fork tube

6.5 Slide off the left handlebar assembly and position it clear of the fork tube

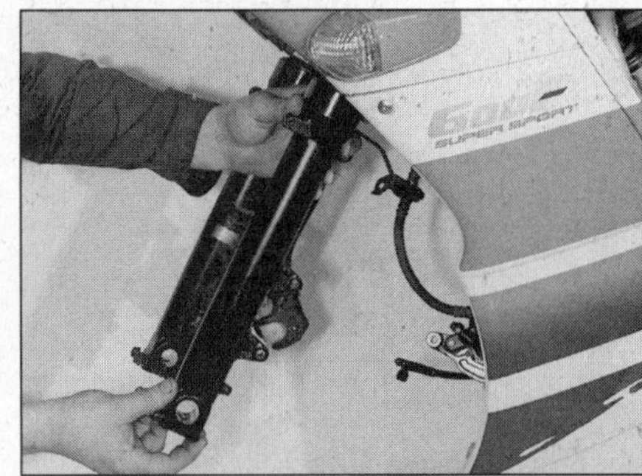
6.8 Slide the fork tube out of the triple clamps using a twisting motion

6.10a Position the fork tube so the lower groove (arrow) aligns with the top triple clamp surface . . .

6.10b . . . then tighten the upper . . .

6 Forks - removal and installation

Removal

1 Remove the front wheel as described in Chapter 7.

2 Remove the front fender/mudguard as described in Chapter 8.

3 Carefully pry off the snap-ring from the top of each fork tube **(see illustration)**.

4 Slacken the right handlebar clamp bolt. Slide the handlebar off the fork tube and support it to prevent straining the hydraulic hose or leakage of brake fluid from the master cylinder.

5 Slacken the left handlebar clamp bolt. Slide the handlebar off the fork tube and position it clear of the triple clamp **(see illustration)**.

6 Undo the two bolts and free the right brake caliper from the fork slider.

7 Tie the caliper to the bike to prevent any strain being placed on the hydraulic hose or pipe.

Note: *If the fork legs are to be dismantled it is preferable to slacken the top bolts while they are still held in the triple clamps.*

8 Slacken the top and bottom triple clamp bolts and remove the forks by twisting them and pulling them downwards **(see illustration)**.

If the fork legs are seized in the triple clamps, spray the area with penetrating oil and allow time for it to soak in before trying again.

Installation

9 Remove all traces of corrosion from the triple clamps and slide the fork legs back into place.

10 Position each leg so that the lower groove on the fork tube aligns with the top surface of the top triple clamp, then tighten the top and bottom triple clamp pinch bolts to the specified torque setting **(see illustrations)**.

11 Install the handlebars to the top of the fork tubes, ensuring that the lug on the bottom of each casting is correctly located with the cutout on the top triple clamp.

12 Fit the snap-ring to each fork tube making sure they are correctly located in their grooves.

13 If the fork legs have been dismantled, the fork tube top bolts should now be tightened to the specified torque setting **(see illustration)**.

6.10c . . . and lower triple clamp pinch bolts to the specified torque setting

6.13 With the tube held in the triple clamps tighten the top bolt to the specified torque setting

6.14 Tighten the handlebar clamp bolts to the specified torque setting while pushing the handlebar forward

14 Tighten the handlebar clamp bolts to the specified torque setting while pushing each handlebar fully forward **(see illustration)**.

15 Install the front fender/mudguard as described in Chapter 8.

16 Fit the right brake caliper to the fork slider and tighten its mounting bolts to the specified torque (see Chapter 7).

17 Install the front wheel as described in Chapter 7.

18 Adjust the fork settings as described in Section 12. Check the operation of the front forks and brake before taking the machine out on the road.

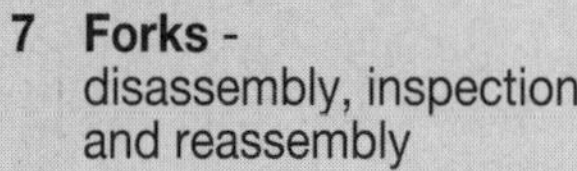

7 Forks - disassembly, inspection and reassembly

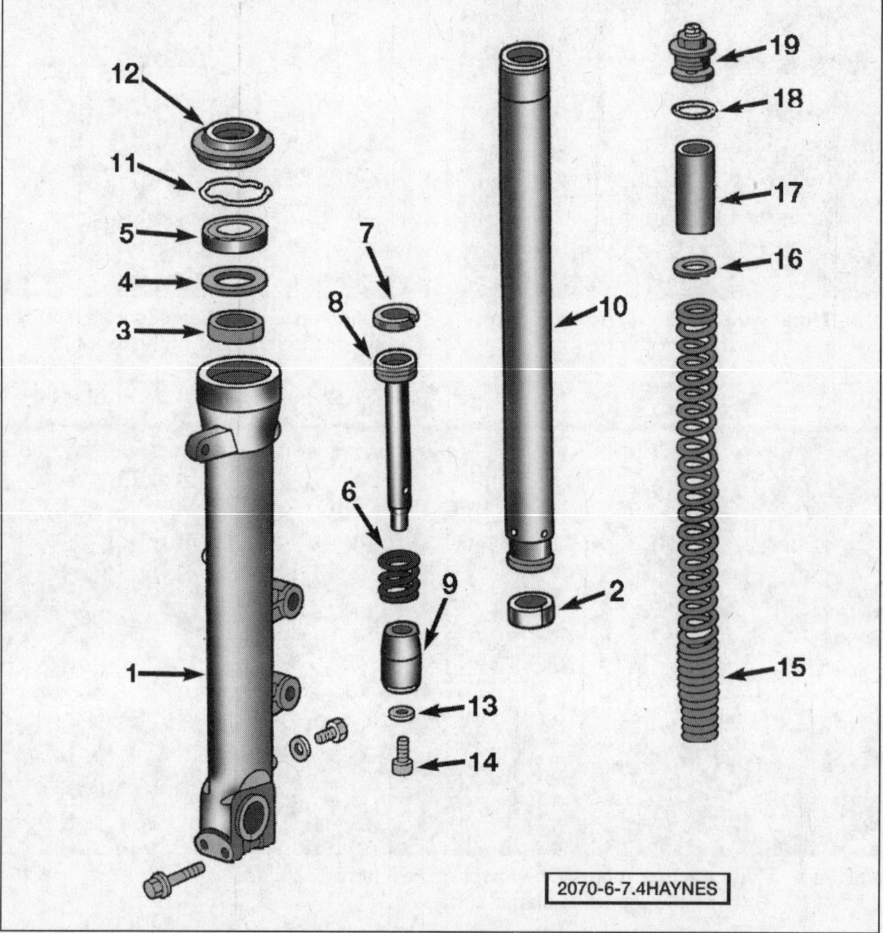

7.4 Exploded view of a front fork - M and N (1991 and 1992) models

1 Fork slider
2 Lower bushing
3 Upper bushing
4 Washer
5 Oil seal
6 Damper rod spring
7 Damper rod piston ring
8 Damper rod
9 Damper rod seat
10 Fork tube
11 Snap ring
12 Dust seal
13 Sealing washer
14 Damper rod Allen bolt
15 Fork spring
16 Spring seat
17 Spacer
18 O-ring
19 Top bolt

Disassembly

1 Always dismantle the fork legs separately to avoid interchanging parts and thus causing an accelerated rate of wear. Store all components in separate, clearly marked containers.

2 Clamp the fork slider securely in a vise equipped with soft jaws, being careful not to overtighten it. Slacken the damper rod assembly Allen bolt which passes up through the bottom of the slider. **Note:** *The bolt is slackened at this point because the tension applied by the fork spring will keep the damper rod from spinning in the fork tube as the bolt is turned. Don't remove the bolt completely, but make sure it's loose enough to turn easily.*

3 Release the slider from the vise and then carefully clamp the fork tube in the vise, taking care not to overtighten or score its surface, in an upright position. On S, T, V and W (1995 to 1998) models, remove the fork protector from the top of each slider by inserting two screwdrivers between the bottom of the protector and the slider and levering up to release the retaining tabs from the groove, taking care not to scratch the slider or damage the dust seal. Follow the procedure given under the relevant sub-heading for the remainder of the disassembly procedure.

M and N (1991 and 1992) models

4 To minimize spring pressure on the top bolt, fully unscrew the preload adjuster **(see illustration)**.

7.8 Use a flat-bladed screwdriver to free the dust seal . . .

5 Unscrew the top bolt from the top of the tube, making sure it is not expelled forcibly by spring pressure as the last threads of the bolt are unscrewed.

6 Withdraw the spacer, spring seat and fork spring, noting which way up the spring is fitted.

7 Invert the fork leg over a suitable container and pump the tube vigorously to expel as much fork oil as possible.

8 Pry out the dust seal from the top of the slider to gain access to the oil seal retaining snap-ring **(see illustration)**.

9 Carefully remove the snap-ring while taking care not to scratch the surface of the tube **(see illustration)**.

10 Remove the damper rod retaining Allen bolt and washer from the bottom of the slider.

11 To separate the tube from the slider it will be necessary to displace the top bushing and oil seal. The lower bushing should not pass

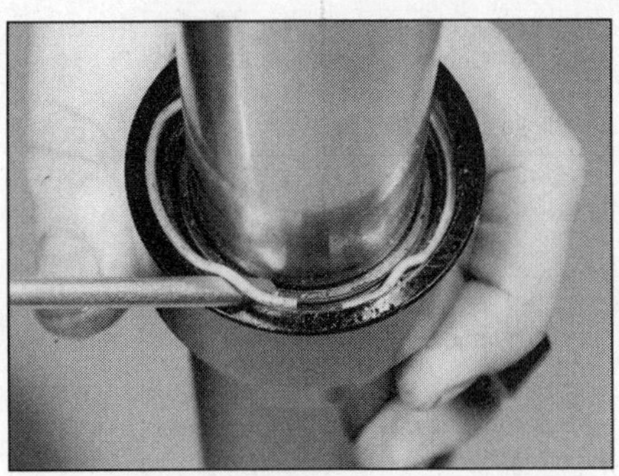

7.9 . . . then pry the snap-ring out of the slider

through the top bushing, and this can be used to good effect. Push the tube gently inwards until it stops against the damper rod seat. Take care not to do this forcibly or the seat may be damaged. Then pull the tube sharply outwards until the lower bushing strikes the top bushing. Repeat this operation until the top bushing and seal are tapped out of the slider.

12 With the tube removed, slide off the oil seal and washer, noting which way up it is fitted. The top bushing can then also be slid off its upper end.

Caution: Do not remove the lower bushing from the tube unless it is to be replaced.

13 Tip up the fork tube and remove the damper rod and spring.

Caution: Do not remove the piston ring from the damper rod unless it is to be replaced.

14 Tip the damper rod seat out of the slider.

P, R, S, T, V and W (1993 to 1998) models

15 To minimize spring pressure fully unscrew the preload adjuster **(see illustration)**.

16 Unscrew the top bolt until it is free from the top of the fork tube.

17 Carefully clamp the fork slider in the vise and, with the aid of an assistant, push the spring downwards, to compress it. Unscrew

7.15 Exploded view of a front fork - P, R, S, T, V and W (1993 to 1998) models

DUST SEAL
SNAP RING
TOP BOLT
OIL SEAL
WASHER
UPPER BUSHING
SLOTTED COLLAR
SPRING SEAT
DAMPER ROD/PISTON ASSEMBLY
SPACER (S,T,V,W MODELS)
SPRING SEAT (S,T,V,W MODELS)
FORK SLIDER
FORK SPRING
FORK TUBE
LOWER BUSHING
DAMPER ROD/PISTON ASSEMBLY SEAT
SEALING WASHER
DAMPER ROD/PISTON ASSEMBLY ALLEN BOLT
2070-6-7.15 HAYNES

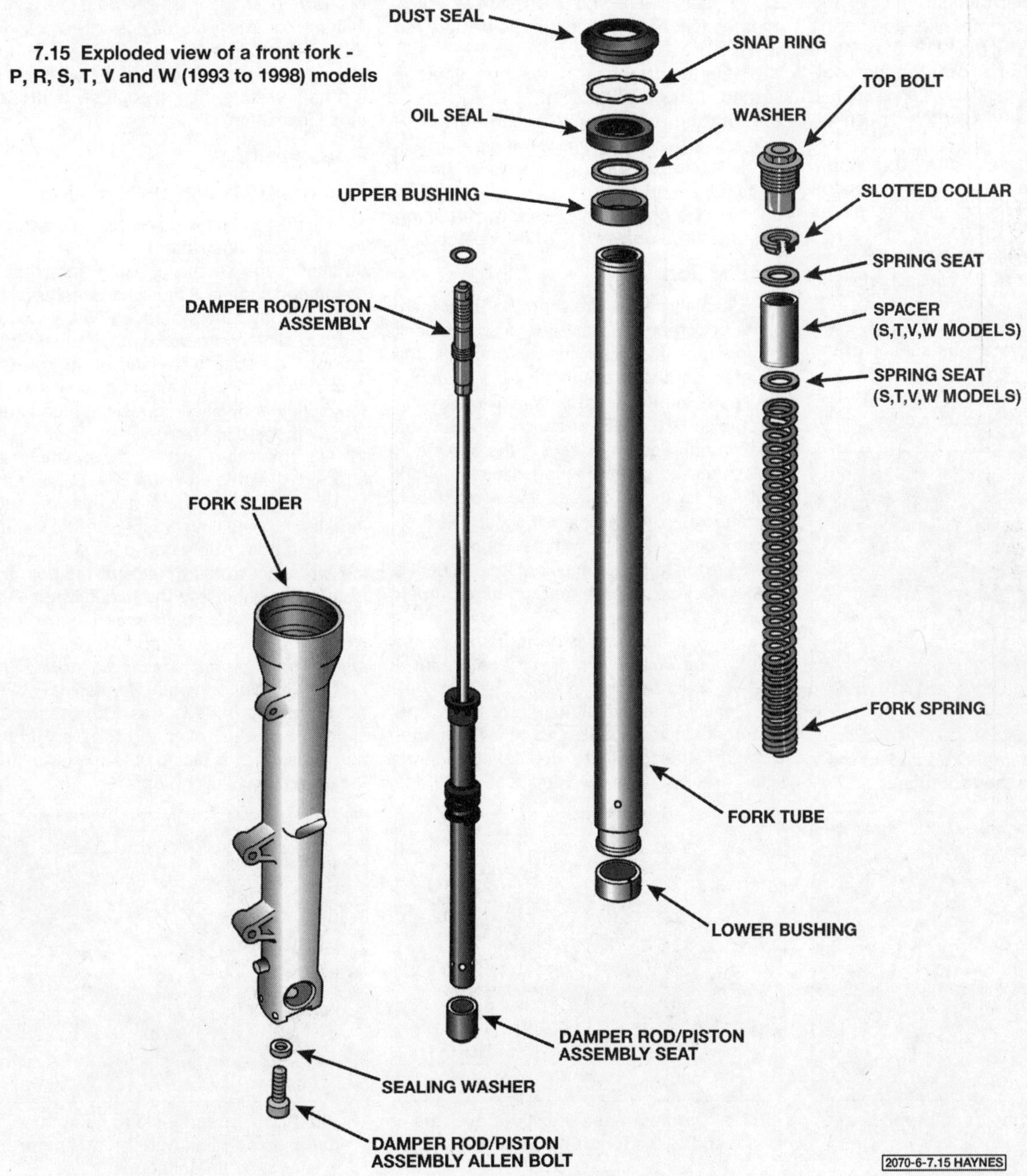

7.25 Inspect the damper rod piston ring for signs of damage and replace if worn

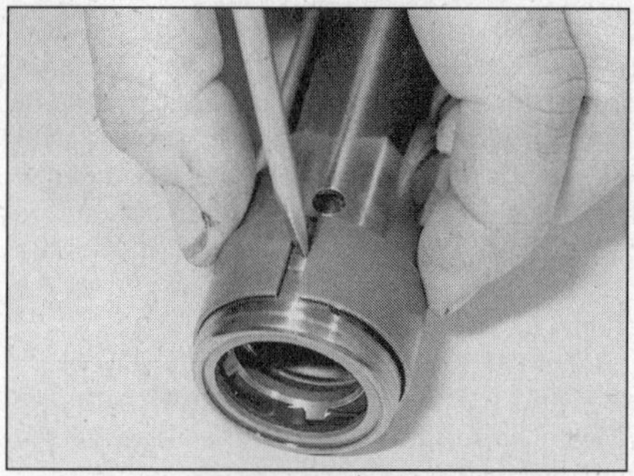

7.28 Pry the ends of the lower bushing apart with a screwdriver and remove it from the fork tube

7.29 Lubricate the top bushing and washer and slide them onto the tube

the top bolt from the preload adjuster and remove the slotted spring collar and spring seat, and on S, T, V and W (1995 to 1998) models, the spacer and lower spring seat. Slowly release the spring until all pressure has been relieved, then withdraw the fork spring from the tube.

18 Invert the fork leg over a suitable container and pump the damper rod piston vigorously to expel as much fork oil as possible.

19 Pry out the dust seal from the top of the slider to gain access to the oil seal retaining snap-ring.

20 Carefully remove the snap-ring while taking care not to scratch the surface of the tube.

21 Remove the damper rod retaining Allen bolt and washer from the bottom of the slider.

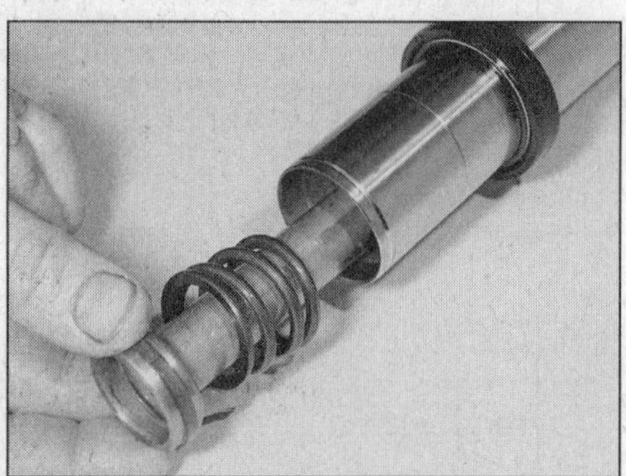

7.31a Insert the damper rod and spring down through the fork tube . . .

22 Withdraw the damper rod/piston assembly from the fork tube and tip out the damper rod seat

23 Separate the fork tube and slider as described above in Step 11.

24 With the tube removed slide off the oil seal and washer, noting which way up it is fitted. The top bushing can then also be slid off its upper end.

Caution: Do not remove the lower bushing from the tube unless it is to be replaced.

Inspection

25 Clean all parts in solvent and blow them dry with compressed air, if available. Check the fork tube and slider, the bushings and the damper rod/piston assembly (as applicable) for score marks, scratches, flaking of the chrome and excessive or abnormal wear **(see illustration)**. Look for dents in the tubes and replace them if any are found. Check the fork seal seat for nicks, gouges and scratches. If damage is evident, leaks will occur. Replace worn or defective parts with new ones.

26 Have the fork tube checked for runout at a dealer service department or other repair shop.

Warning: If it is bent, it should not be straightened; replace it with a new one.

27 Measure the overall length of the spring and check it for cracks and other damage. Compare the length to the service length listed in this Chapter's Specifications. If it's defective or sagged, replace both fork springs with new ones. Never replace only one spring.

28 If it's necessary to replace the fork tube lower bushing, pry it apart at the slit and slide it off. Make sure the new one seats properly **(see illustration)**.

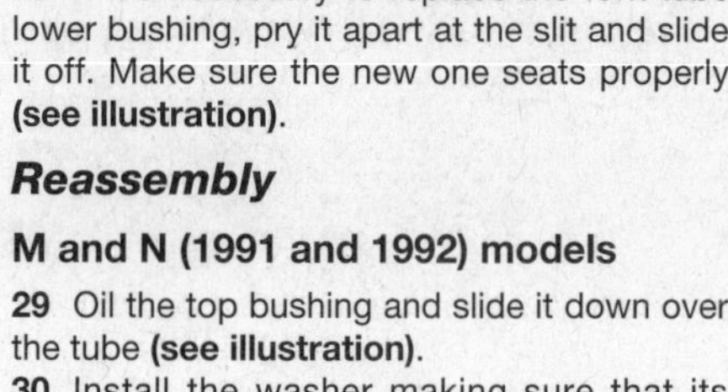

Reassembly

M and N (1991 and 1992) models

29 Oil the top bushing and slide it down over the tube **(see illustration)**.

30 Install the washer making sure that its chamfered surface is facing the top bushing.

31 Install the rebound spring on the damper rod and slide it into place in the tube. Fit the damper rod seat to the end of the rod **(see illustrations)**. Pass a length of dowel, or the fork spring and spacer, down the tube to hold the damper rod in place.

32 Oil the tube and lower bushing and support it vertically with the damper rod uppermost. Lower the slider over the tube. Install a new sealing washer on the damper rod Allen bolt. Apply non-permanent thread locking agent to the threads of the bolt, then install and tighten it to the torque listed in this Chapter's Specifications **(see illustrations)**. **Note:** *If necessary, temporarily fit the fork spring, spring seat, spacer and top bolt to prevent the damper rod from rotating.*

33 Smear the oil seal lips with grease and slide the oil seal over the tube so that its marked surface is facing upwards (away from the slider) **(see illustration)**.

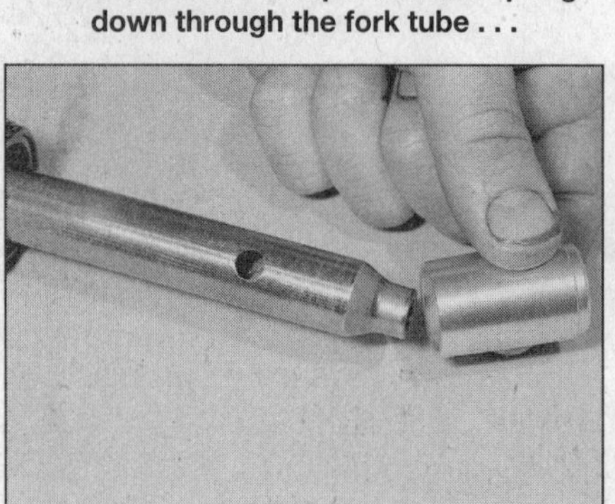

7.31b . . . and fit the damper rod seat

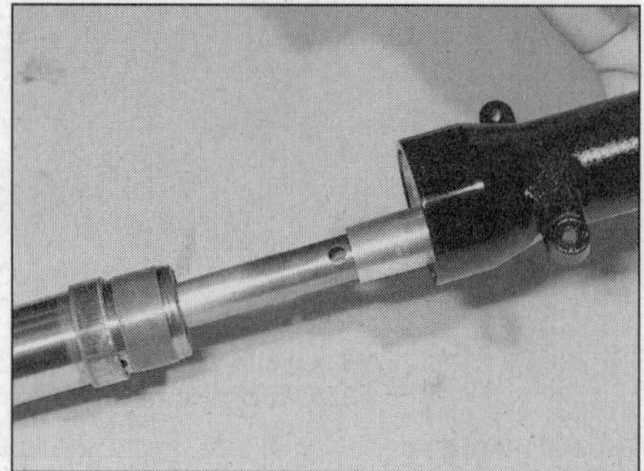

7.32a Carefully ease the slider over the end of the fork tube assembly

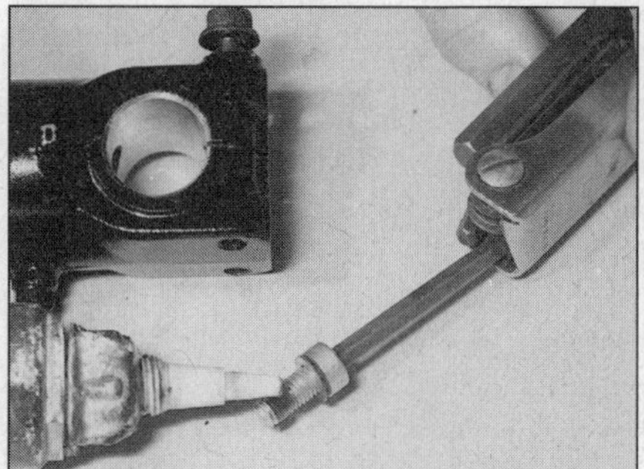

7.32b Apply thread locking compound to damper rod Allen bolt threads before installation

7.33 Slide the seal onto the tube making sure its marked surface is facing upwards

7.34 Using a piece of metal tubing as a form of slide-hammer to tap the fork seal into place

7.35 Secure the seal in place with the snap-ring . . .

7.36 . . . then slide the dust seal into position

7.37a Fill the fork leg with the specified type and amount of fork oil . . .

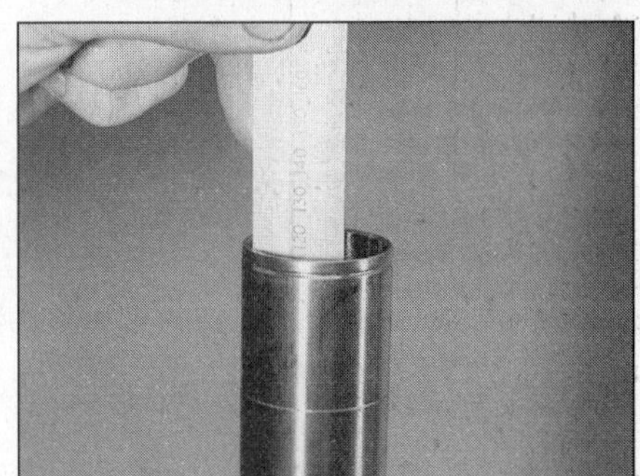
7.37b . . . then check the oil level as described in text

34 To fit the bushing and seal into their recesses it will be necessary to use the Honda service tool or devise an alternative tubular drift. The best method is to use a length of tubing slightly larger in diameter than the tube. Place a large plain washer against the oil seal and then tap it home using the tube as a form of slide hammer **(see illustration)**. Take care not to scratch the tube during this operation; it is best to make sure that the fork tube is pushed fully into the slider so that any accidental scoring is confined to the area above the seal.

7.39 Install the fork spring making sure its tighter pitched coils (or tapered end) are at the bottom

35 Once the oil seal is correctly seated, fit the snap-ring, ensuring that it is correctly located in its groove **(see illustration)**.

36 Lubricate the lips of the dust seal, then slide it down the fork tube and press it into position **(see illustration)**.

37 Fill the fork leg with the specified amount and type of fork oil and pump the fork leg slowly to distribute the oil. Compress the assembly fully and check the oil level **(see illustrations)**. Add or subtract oil, as necessary, until it is at the level given in this Chapter's Specifications.

38 Clamp the tube securely in a vise equipped with soft jaws, taking care not to overtighten it or score the tube's surface.

39 Insert the fork spring, ensuring that its tighter pitched coils or tapered end (as appropriate) is at the bottom **(see illustration)**.

40 Insert the spring seat and spacer and fit a new O-ring to the top bolt. Install the top bolt to the tube **(see illustrations)**. **Note:** *The top bolt can be tightened to the specified torque setting at this stage if it can be held firmly enough, but do not risk overtightening the tube. A better method is to tighten the top bolt when the fork leg is securely clamped in the triple clamps.*

41 Install the forks as described in Section 6.

7.40a Fit the spring seat . . .

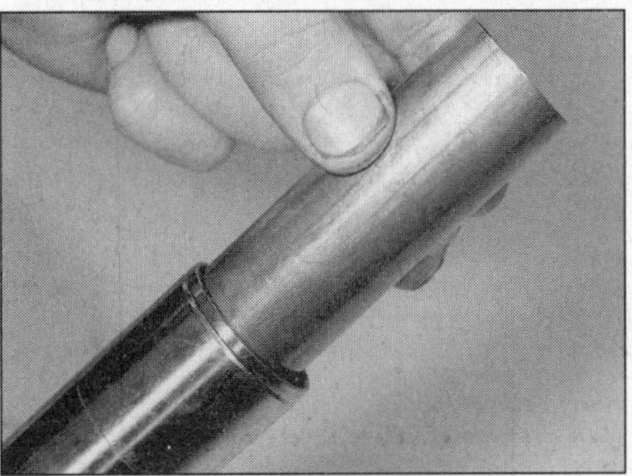
7.40b . . . followed by the spacer

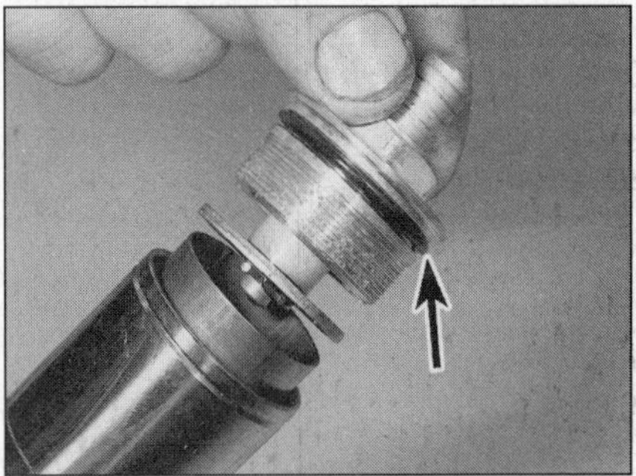
7.40c Fit a new O-ring (arrow) to the top bolt and screw the top bolt into the fork tube

P, R, S, T, V AND W (1993 to 1998) models

42 Oil the fork tube and lower bushing and insert it into position in the fork slider.

43 Install the top bushing, washer, oil seal, snap-ring and dust seal as described above in Steps 29 to 36.

44 Fit the damper rod seat to the base of the damper rod/piston assembly. Insert the damper rod/piston assembly into the fork tube.

45 Apply non-permanent thread locking compound to the threads of the damper rod Allen bolt. Install the bolt using a new sealing washer and tighten it to the specified torque setting. **Note:** *If necessary, temporarily fit the fork spring, spring seat, washer and top bolt to prevent the damper rod/piston assembly from rotating.*

46 Slowly pour in the specified amount and grade of fork oil while pushing the damper rod piston up and down. Once the oil has been added, slowly pump the fork tube in and out at least five times, and pump the damper rod piston at least another 10 times. This will ensure that the fork oil is evenly distributed. Fully insert both the tube and damper rod, then check the fork oil level. Add or subtract fork oil until the oil is at the specified level listed in this Chapter's Specifications.

47 Clamp the slider securely in a vise and fully extend the damper rod. Tie a piece of wire around the rod; the wire can then be used to hold the rod in the extended position while the slotted spring collar is installed.

48 Insert the fork spring, ensuring that its tapered end is at the bottom, and on S, T, V and W (1995 to 1998) models, the lower spring seat and spacer, followed by the spring seat. Fit a new O-ring to the preload adjuster and lubricate it with a smear of fork oil.

49 With the aid of an assistant push down on the spring seat, compressing the fork spring, and slide the slotted spring collar into position. Screw the top bolt fully onto the preload adjuster then slowly release the fork spring, making sure the slotted collar is correctly seated against the base of the preload adjuster.

50 Carefully screw the top bolt into the fork tube making sure it is not cross-threaded. **Note:** *The top bolt can be tightened to the specified torque setting at this stage if it can be held firmly enough but do not risk overtightening the tube. A better method is to tighten the top bolt when the fork leg has been installed and is securely held in the triple clamps.*

TOOL TIP ***Use a ratchet-type tool when installing the fork top bolt. This makes it unnecessary to remove the tool from the bolt while threading it in, making it easier to maintain a downward pressure on the spring.***

51 On S, T, V and W (1995 to 1998) models, fit the fork protector onto the top of each slider, making sure the tabs locate properly in the groove.

52 Install the forks as described in Section 6.

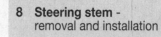

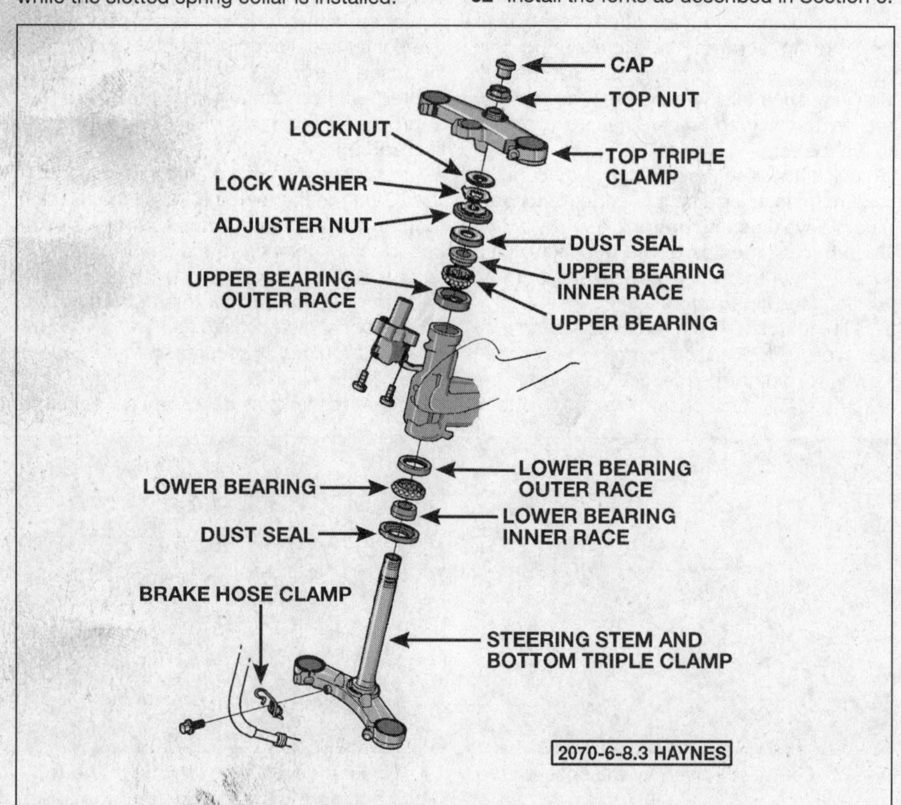

8.3 Exploded view of steering stem and bearings

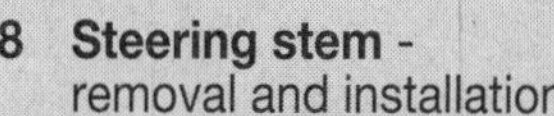

8 Steering stem - removal and installation

Caution: Although not strictly necessary, before removing the steering stem it is recommended that the fuel tank be removed. This will prevent accidental damage to the paintwork.

Removal

1 Remove the forks as described in Section 6 of this Chapter.

2 Remove the ignition switch as described in Chapter 9.

3 Pry off the cap from the steering stem top nut. Slacken and remove the nut and lift off the top triple clamp **(see illustration)**.

4 Undo the bolt securing the brake hose clamp to the bottom triple clamp.

5 Straighten the tabs of the steering stem adjuster nut lock washer.

6 Using a suitable C-wrench, slacken and remove the adjuster nut locknut.

7 Remove the lock washer and discard it; a new one must be fitted on reassembly.

8 Support the bottom triple clamp and slacken the adjuster nut.

9 Lift off the nut, dust seal, inner race and upper bearing from the top of the steering head.

10 Gently lower the bottom triple clamp and steering stem out of the frame. Remove the lower bearing from the steering stem.

11 Remove all traces of old grease from the bearings and races and check them for wear or damage as described in Section 9. **Note:** *Do not attempt to remove the outer races from the frame or the lower inner race and dust seal from the steering stem unless they are to be replaced.*

Installation

12 Smear a liberal quantity of grease on both inner and outer races and the steering stem. Work the grease well into both the upper and lower bearing races.

13 Fit the lower bearing onto the steering stem.

14 Carefully lift the steering stem into position and fit the upper bearing and inner race.

15 Apply grease to the underside of the dust seal and fit it to the steering stem.

16 Apply clean engine oil to the threads of the adjuster nut and tighten it using hand pressure only.

17 To preload the bearings to the torque specified by the manufacturer (see Specifications) it will be necessary to use the service tool, part no. 07916-3710100, which is a socket that fits the adjuster nut. Using the service tool, tighten the adjuster nut to the specified torque setting, then turn the steering stem from lock to lock approximately 5 times to settle the bearings and races in position. After preloading the bearings, slacken the adjuster nut one full turn then tighten it again to the specified torque setting. **Note:** *It is important to check the feel of the steering afterwards as described below; if it is too tight readjust the bearings as described below.*

18 If the service tool is not available, tighten the adjuster nut hard using a conventional C-wrench to preload the bearings, then adjust as follows.

19 Slacken the adjuster nut slightly until pressure is just released, then turn it slowly clockwise until resistance is just evident. The object is to set the adjuster nut so that the bearings are under a very light loading, just enough to remove any freeplay.

Caution: Take great care not to apply excessive pressure because this will cause premature failure of the bearings.

20 With the bearings correctly adjusted, fit a new lock washer to the adjuster nut. Bend down two opposite lock washer tabs into the grooves of the adjuster nut.

21 Install the locknut and tighten it finger-tight only.

22 Hold the adjuster nut, to prevent it from moving, and tighten the locknut approximately 90° more until its slots align with the remaining lock washer tabs. Secure the locknut in position by bending up the tabs into its slots.

23 Fit the top triple clamp to the steering stem and install the stem top nut.

24 Temporarily fit the fork legs, to align the triple clamps, tighten the steering stem top nut to the specified torque setting. Fit the cap.

25 Install the ignition switch as described in Chapter 9.

26 Fit the brake hose clamp, tightening its retaining bolt securely.

27 Install the fork legs as described in Section 6 of this Chapter.

28 Check that the steering head bearings are correctly adjusted as soon as the forks and front wheel are installed (see Chapter 1).

9 Steering head bearings - inspection and replacement

Inspection

1 Remove the steering stem as described in Section 8.

2 Remove all traces of old grease from the bearings and races and check them for wear or damage.

3 The ball bearing tracks of the races should be polished and free from indentations. Inspect the ball bearings for signs of wear, damage or discoloration, and examine the bearing retainer cage for signs of cracks or splits. If there are signs of wear on any of the above components both upper and lower bearing assemblies must be replaced as a set.

Replacement

4 The outer races are an interference fit in the steering head and can be tapped from position with a suitable drift. Tap firmly and evenly around each race to ensure that it is driven out squarely. It may prove advantageous to curve the end of the drift slightly to improve access.

5 Alternatively, the races can be removed using a slide-hammer type bearing extractor; these can often be rented from tool shops.

6 The new races can be pressed into the head using the drawbolt arrangement **(see illustration)**, or by using a large diameter tubular drift which bears only on the outer edge of the race. Ensure that the drawbolt washer or drift (as applicable) bears only on the outer edge of the race and does not contact the race bearing surface.

Installation of new head bearing races is made much easier if the races are left overnight in the freezer. This causes them to contract slightly, making them a looser fit.

7 To remove the inner race from the steering stem, use two screwdrivers placed on opposite sides of the race to work it free.

8 With the inner race removed, lift off the dust seal. Inspect the seal for wear or damage and replace it if necessary.

9 Install the dust seal and slide on the new inner race. A length of tubing with an internal diameter slightly larger than the steering stem will be needed to tap the new race into position. Ensure that the drift bears only on the inner edge of the race and does not contact the bearing surface.

10 Install the steering stem (see Section 8).

10 Rear shock absorber - removal and installation

Removal

1 Set the bike on its centerstand.

2 Remove the seat (see Chapter 8, if necessary). On S, T, V and W (1995 to 1998) models, remove the fuel tank (see Chapter 4).

3 Remove the swingarm-mounted rear fender/mudguard as described in Chapter 8. Proceed as described under the relevant sub-heading.

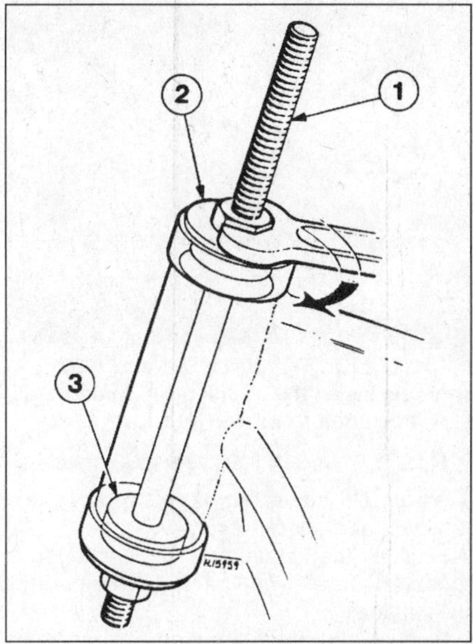

9.6 Drawbolt arrangement for fitting steering head bearing outer races

1 *Long bolt or threaded bar*
2 *Thick washer*
3 *Guide for lower outer race*

M and N (1991 and 1992) models

4 Slacken and remove the shock absorber upper mounting nut and bolt.

5 Slacken and remove the shock absorber lower mounting nut and bolt and maneuver the shock absorber out from the frame **(see illustration)**.

6 Withdraw the inner sleeve from the shock absorber lower mounting **(see illustration)**. Inspect the sleeve, bearing and dust seals for signs of wear and replace worn components as necessary. The bearing is a press-fit and can be removed and installed using a drawbolt arrangement similar to that used in Section 9.

7 All shock absorber components are available separately. However, disassembly requires the use of a suitable spring compressor. It is therefore recommended that the unit be taken to a Honda dealer who will have the necessary service tools to dismantle the unit.

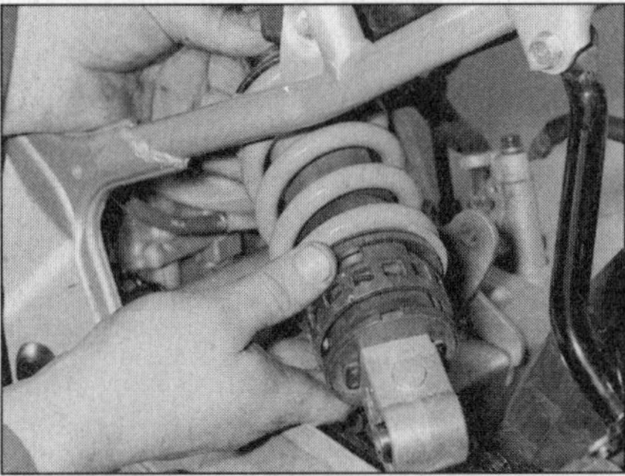

10.5 Removing the rear shock absorber - M and N (1991 and 1992) models

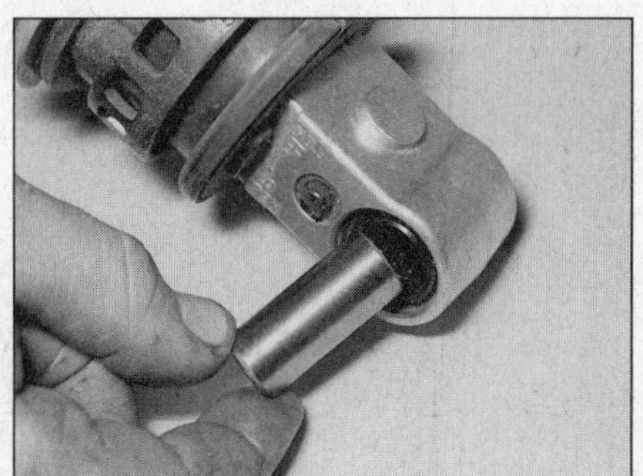

10.6 Examine shock absorber lower mounting sleeve and bearings for wear

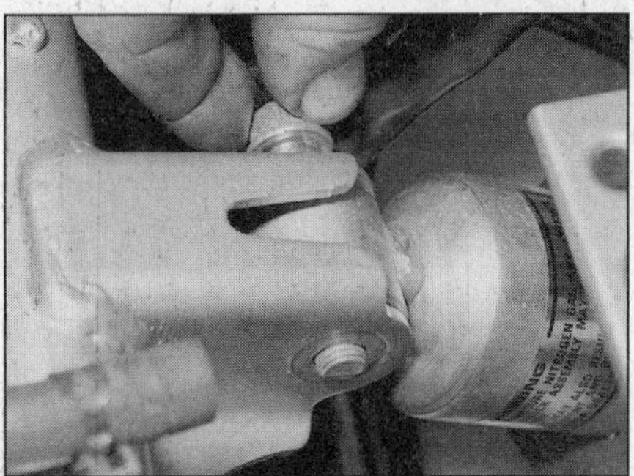

10.17a On M and N (1991 and 1992) models insert the shock upper mounting bolt from the right . . .

10.17b . . . and the lower mounting bolt from the left

10.18 Tighten both shock absorber mounting bolts to the specified torque setting

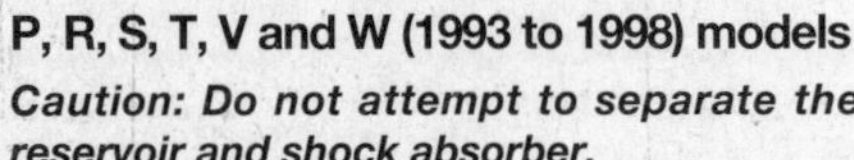

P, R, S, T, V and W (1993 to 1998) models

Caution: Do not attempt to separate the reservoir and shock absorber.

8 Slacken the retaining clip securing the shock absorber reservoir to the frame and slide off the clip.

9 Release the clips securing the reservoir hose to the frame.

10 Unscrew the rear brake master cylinder reservoir retaining bolt and position the reservoir clear of the shock absorber. Keep the reservoir upright to prevent fluid loss.

11 Slacken and remove the shock absorber upper mounting nut and bolt.

12 Slacken and remove the shock absorber lower mounting nut and bolt and maneuver the shock absorber and reservoir assembly out from the frame.

13 Inspect the shock absorber lower mounting components as described above in Step 6.

14 Apart from the lower mounting bearing, dust seals and inner sleeve, no shock absorber components are available separately. Damage to any other component will require the replacement of the complete shock absorber assembly.

Installation

M and N (1991 and 1992) models

15 Check that the mounting bolts are unworn, replacing them if necessary, and apply molybdenum disulfide grease to their shanks.

16 Install the shock absorber so that the rebound damping adjuster is on the right side of the bike.

17 Insert the upper mounting bolt from the right side and insert the lower mounting bolt from the left side **(see illustrations)**.

18 Fit both the upper and lower mounting bolt nuts and tighten them to the specified torque setting **(see illustration)**. Install the seat and fender/mudguard as described in Chapter 8.

19 Check the operation of the rear suspension and adjust the suspension settings as described in Section 12.

P, R, S, T, V and W (1993 to 1998) models

20 Check that the mounting bolts are unworn, replacing them if necessary, and apply molybdenum disulfide grease to their shanks.

21 Install the shock absorber so that the rebound damping adjuster is on the right side of the bike.

22 Make sure the reservoir hose is correctly routed and insert both the shock absorber mounting bolts from the left side.

23 Fit the mounting bolt nuts and tighten them to the specified torque setting.

24 Slide the reservoir into position, engaging it with the frame cutout, and securely tighten its retaining clip. Fit the hose retaining clips.

25 Apply a few drops of locking compound to the threads of the master cylinder reservoir bolt, then fit the bolt and tighten it to the specified torque setting (see Chapter 7). On S, T, V and W (1995 to 1998) models, install the fuel tank (see Chapter 4). Install the seat and fender/mudguard as described in Chapter 8.

26 Check the operation of the rear suspension and adjust the suspension settings as described in Section 12.

11 Rear suspension linkage - removal, inspection and installation

Removal

1 Set the bike on its centerstand.

2 Remove the swingarm-mounted rear fender/mudguard as described in Chapter 8.

3 Slacken and remove the shock absorber lower mounting nut and bolt.

4 Slacken and remove the nut and pivot bolt securing the linkage to the frame **(see illustration)**.

5 Slacken and remove the nut and pivot bolt securing the linkage to the swingarm and remove the linkage from the frame **(see illustration)**.

11.4 Withdrawing the suspension linkage-to-frame pivot bolt

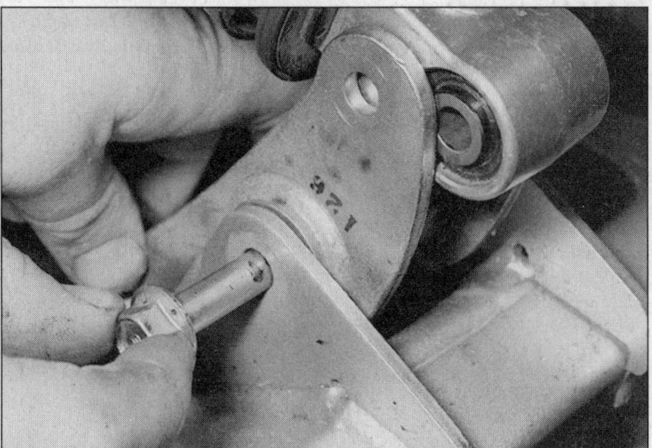

11.5 Withdrawing the suspension linkage-to-swingarm pivot bolt

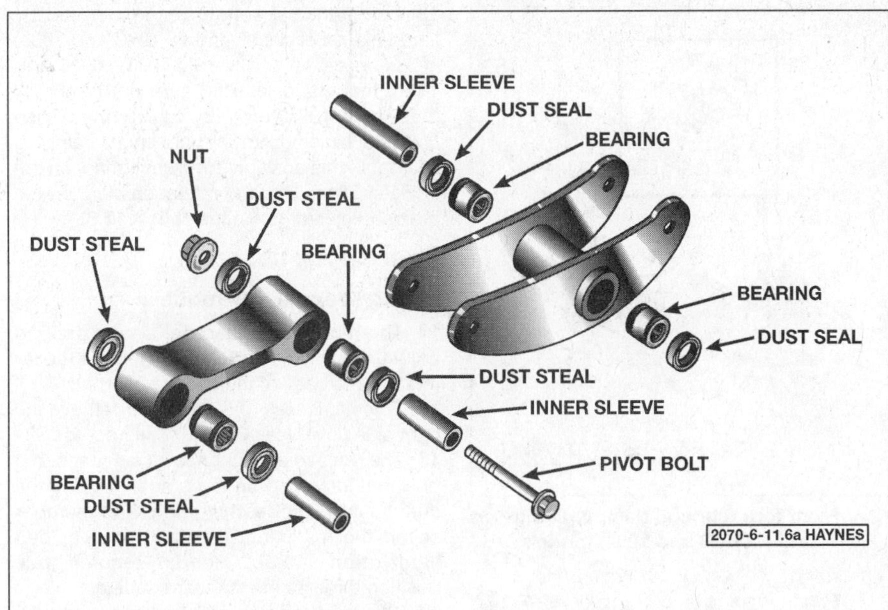

11.6a Exploded view of rear suspension linkage components

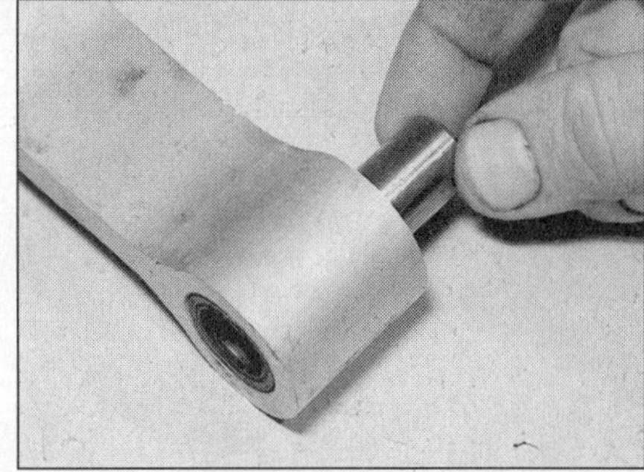

11.6b Inspect the suspension linkage inner sleeves and bearings for wear

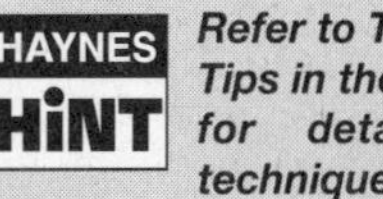

Refer to Tools and Workshop Tips in the Reference section for details of drawbolt techniques.

Inspection

6 Undo the nut and remove the pivot bolt and separate the two linkage components. Withdraw the inner sleeves from both links **(see illustrations)**.

7 Thoroughly clean all components, removing all traces of dirt, corrosion and grease.

8 Inspect all components closely, looking for obvious signs of wear such as heavy scoring, or for damage such as cracks or distortion.

9 Carefully lever out the dust seals, using a flat-bladed screwdriver, and check them for signs of wear or damage; replace them if necessary.

10 Worn bearings can be driven out of their bores, but note that removal will destroy them; new bearings should be obtained before work commences. The new bearings should be pressed or drawn into their bores rather than driven into position. In the absence of a press, a suitable drawbolt arrangement can be made up as described below.

11 It will be necessary to obtain a long bolt or a length of threaded rod from a local hardware store, engineering works or some other supplier. The bolt or rod should be about one inch longer than the combined length of either link, and one bearing. Also required are suitable nuts and two large and strong washers having a larger outside diameter than the bearing housing. In the case of the threaded rod, fit one nut to one end of the rod and stake it in place for convenience.

12 Fit one of the washers over the bolt or rod so that it rests against the head, then pass the assembly through the relevant bore. Over the projecting end place the bearing, which should be greased to ease installation, followed by the remaining washer and nut.

13 Holding the bearing to ensure that it is kept square, slowly tighten the nut so that the bushing or bearing is drawn into its bore.

14 Once it is fully home, remove the drawbolt arrangement and, if necessary, repeat the procedure to fit the opposite bearing. The dust seals can then be pressed into place.

15 Lubricate all the seals, needle roller bearings, inner sleeves and the pivot bolts with molybdenum disulfide grease. Insert the sleeves into the links.

16 Couple the two suspension links, making sure the 'F MV9' or 'FR MAL' mark on the rear link is positioned on the left side with the arrow pointing forward **(see illustration)**. Insert the pivot bolt and tighten its nut to the torque listed in this Chapter's Specifications.

Installation

17 If not already done, lubricate the seals, needle roller bearings, inner sleeves and the pivot bolts with molybdenum disulfide grease.

18 Maneuver the linkage assembly into position making sure that the 'F MV9' or 'FR MAL' mark on the rear link is on the left side **(see illustration)**.

19 Insert both pivot bolts and the shock absorber bolt from the left side of the bike and tighten the retaining nuts to the specified torque setting **(see illustration)**.

20 Install the rear fender/mudguard (see Chapter 8).

21 Check the operation of the rear suspension before taking the machine on the road.

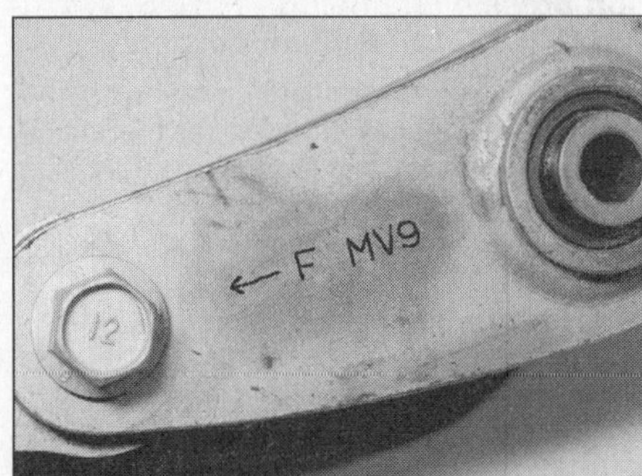

11.16 Couple the suspension links making sure the 'F MV9' mark is on the left with the arrow pointing forward

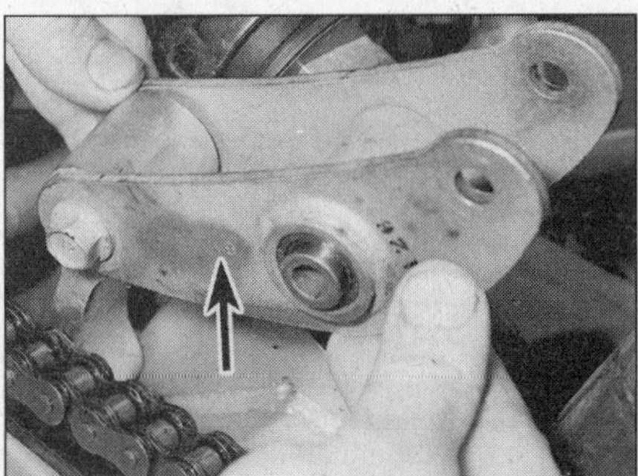

11.18 Install the suspension linkage ensuring that the marking (arrow) is on the left

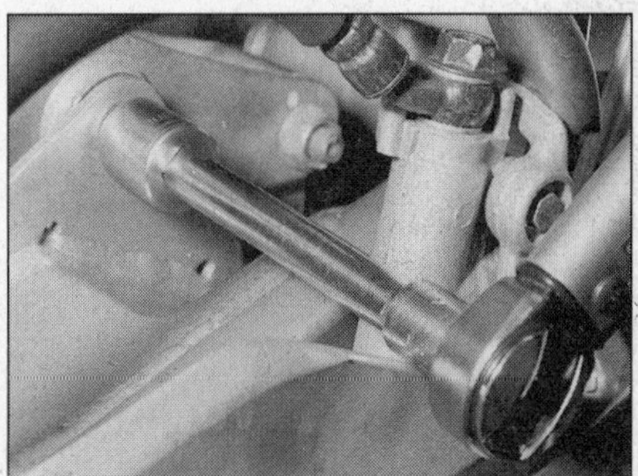

11.19 Tighten all suspension linkage pivot bolts to the specified torque setting

12.1 Adjusting the front fork spring preload

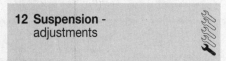

12 Suspension - adjustments

Front forks

Caution: Always ensure that both front fork settings are the same. Uneven settings will upset the handling of the machine and could cause it to become unstable.

Spring preload - all models

1 The front fork spring preload adjuster is located in the center of each fork top bolt **(see illustration)**.

2 To reduce the preload (ie soften the ride), rotate the adjuster counterclockwise (anti-clockwise) using a suitable wrench/screw-driver (as applicable).

3 To increase the preload (ie stiffen the ride), rotate the adjuster clockwise using a suitable wrench/screwdriver (as applicable).

4 Always ensure both adjusters are set to the same position.

5 Adjuster position is indicated by the number of grooves which are visible above the top of the fork top bolt. Ensure the same number of grooves are visible on both the left and right adjusters. On all except M and N (1991 and 1992) models, the standard setting recommended is with the 3rd groove visible.

Rebound damping - P, R, S, T, V and W (1993 to 1998) models only

6 The rebound damping adjuster is situated in the center of the preload adjuster **(see illustration)**.

12.19 Adjusting the rear shock absorber rebound damping

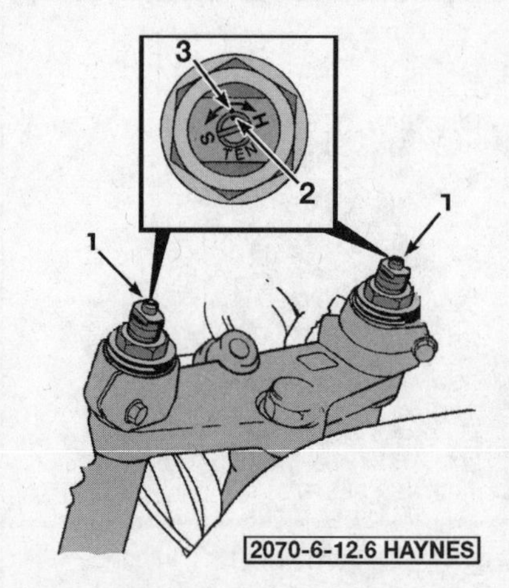

12.6 Front fork rebound damping adjuster - P and R (1993 and 1994) models

1 Adjuster
2 Punch mark
3 Reference mark

7 To reduce the rebound damping, turn the adjuster counterclockwise (anti-clockwise) using a suitable screwdriver.

8 To increase the rebound damping, turn the adjuster clockwise using a suitable screwdriver.

9 Always ensure both adjusters are set to the same position.

10 Adjuster position is indicated by counting the number of clicks emitted by the adjuster or the number of turns out from the maximum position.

11 Turn one of the adjusters fully clockwise, while counting the number of clicks emitted or the number of turns, until it seats, then rotate it back to its original position. Repeat the procedure on the other adjuster to ensure both are set in the same position.

12 Both adjusters can then be repositioned by the required number of clicks or turns.

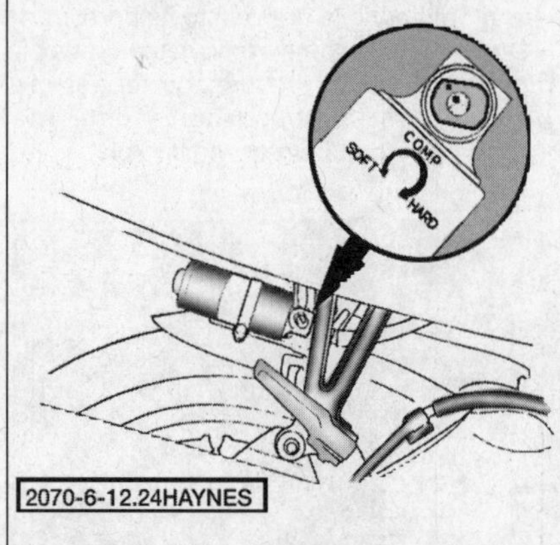

12.24 Rear suspension compression damping adjuster - P and R (1993 and 1994) models

1 Adjuster
2 Punch mark
3 Reference mark

13 The standard setting recommended by Honda is six clicks (P and R (1993 and 1994) models), seven clicks (S and T (1995 and 1996) models) or one full turn out (V and W (1997 and 1998) models) counterclockwise (anti-clockwise) from the maximum damping setting. In this position, the punch mark on the adjuster aligns with the reference mark on the preload adjuster **(see illustration 12.6)**.

Rear shock absorber

Spring preload - all models

14 The rear shock absorber spring preload adjuster is in the form of a stepped collar fitted to the base of the shock absorber.

15 To gain access to the adjuster remove the right side cover (see Chapter 8, if necessary).

16 The preload adjuster has seven numbered positions stamped on it, number 1 being the minimum (ie softest) setting and number seven the maximum (hardest) setting **(see illustration 10.5)**. Honda recommends position three as the standard setting.

17 The rebound adjuster is rotated using a suitable C-wrench. One is supplied in the bike's tool kit.

18 When the preload is correctly set, install the side cover.

Rebound damping - all models

19 The rear suspension rebound damping adjuster is situated at the base of the shock absorber and is accessible through the hole in the swingarm-mounted fender/mudguard **(see illustration)**.

20 To reduce the damping, turn the adjuster counterclockwise (anti-clockwise) using a suitable screwdriver.

21 To increase the damping, turn the adjuster clockwise using a suitable screwdriver.

22 To establish the current setting, turn the adjuster fully clockwise while counting the number of turns until it seats, then rotate it back to its original position. Reposition the adjuster by the required amount.

23 The standard setting recommended by Honda is one turn counterclockwise (anti-clockwise) from the maximum damping setting. In this position, the punch mark on the adjuster aligns with the reference mark on the shock absorber.

Compression damping - P, R, S, T, V and W (1993 to 1998) models only

24 The rear suspension compression damping adjuster is situated on the shock absorber reservoir, mounted on the right side of the bike **(see illustration)**.

25 To reduce the damping, turn the adjuster counterclockwise (anti-clockwise) using a suitable screwdriver.

26 To increase the damping, turn the adjuster clockwise using a suitable screwdriver.

27 To establish the current setting, turn the adjuster fully clockwise while counting the number of turns until it seats, then rotate it back to its original position. Reposition the adjuster by the required amount.

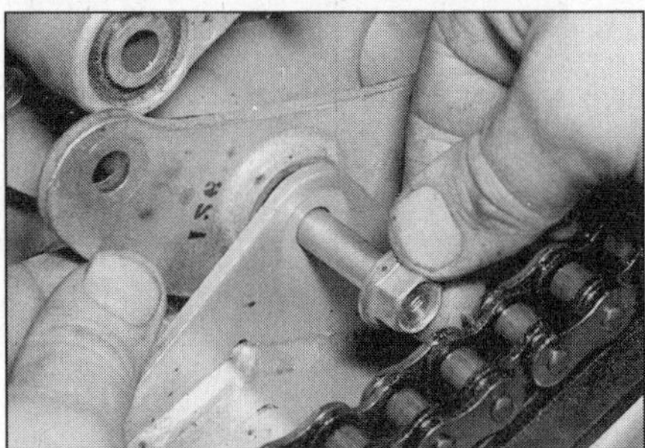
14.5 Withdraw the swingarm-to-suspension linkage pivot bolt to free the linkage from the swingarm

14.6 Remove the cap from the frame . . .

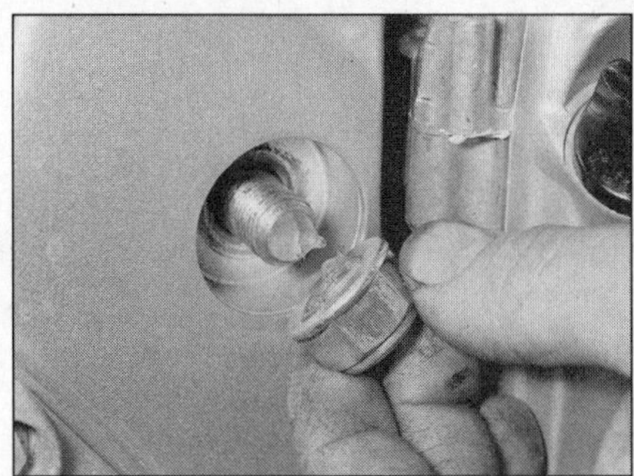
14.7a . . . then unscrew the nut . . .

28 The standard setting recommended by Honda is one turn counterclockwise (anti-clockwise) from the maximum damping setting. In this position, the punch mark on the adjuster aligns with the reference mark on the reservoir.

13 Swingarm bearings - check

1 Refer to Chapter 7 and remove the rear wheel, then refer to Section 10 of this Chapter and remove the rear shock absorber.

2 Grasp the rear of the swingarm with one hand and place your other hand at the junction of the swingarm and the frame. Try to move the rear of the swingarm from side-to-side. Any wear (play) in the bearings should be felt as movement between the swingarm and the frame at the front. The swingarm will actually be felt to move forward and backward at the front (not from side-to-side). If any play is noted, the bearings should be replaced (see Section 15).

3 Next, move the swingarm up and down through its full travel. It should move freely, without any binding or rough spots. If it does not move freely, refer to Section 14 for servicing procedures.

14 Swingarm - removal and installation

Removal

1 Set the bike on its centerstand.

2 Remove the rear wheel as described in Chapter 7.

3 Remove the swingarm-mounted rear fender/mudguard as described in Chapter 8.

4 Unscrew the nut and withdraw the shock absorber lower mounting bolt.

5 Slacken and remove the nut and pivot bolt securing the linkage to the swingarm **(see illustration)**.

6 Carefully pry out the cap from each side of the frame to gain access to the swingarm pivot bolt and nut **(see illustration)**. On 1995 to 1998 California models, disconnect the No. 1 and 4 hose from the EVAP canister under the swingarm.

7 Undo the nut and withdraw the swingarm pivot bolt while supporting the arm **(see illustrations)**. If the shaft is stuck firmly in place with corrosion apply a penetrating fluid, and allow time for this to work before trying again. Rotate the pivot shaft head in an attempt to free it, or in stubborn cases use a long drift to drive the shaft out.

8 Remove the swingarm.

9 Remove the spacers from the right and left sides of the swingarm and withdraw the inner sleeve from the left side of the swingarm. Inspect all components for wear or damage as described in the following Section.

Installation

10 Lubricate the dust seals, bearings, spacers and inner sleeve, and the pivot shaft with grease.

11 Insert the inner sleeve from the left side and fit the spacer to each side of the swingarm **(see illustrations)**.

12 Install the swingarm, passing it through the drive chain, and insert the pivot shaft from the left side **(see illustration)**.

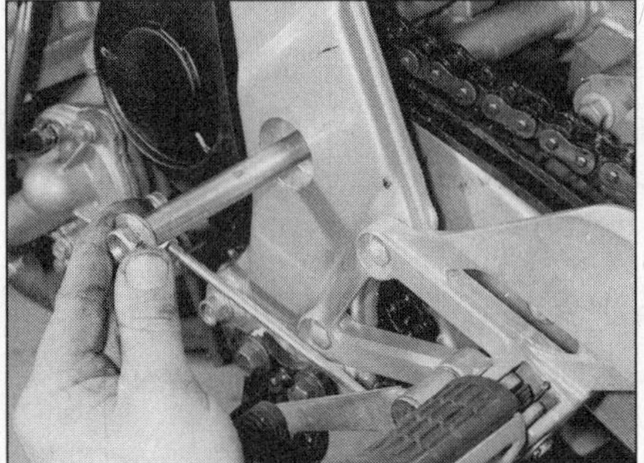
14.7b . . . and withdraw the swingarm pivot bolt

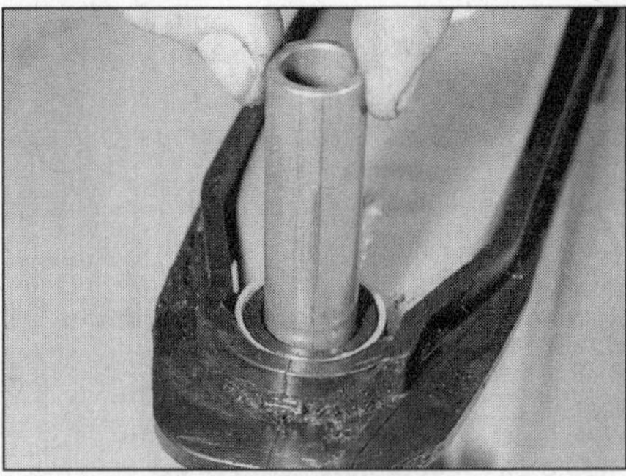
14.11a Insert the inner sleeve in the left side of the swingarm

14.11b Fit the longer spacer to the left side of the swingarm . . .

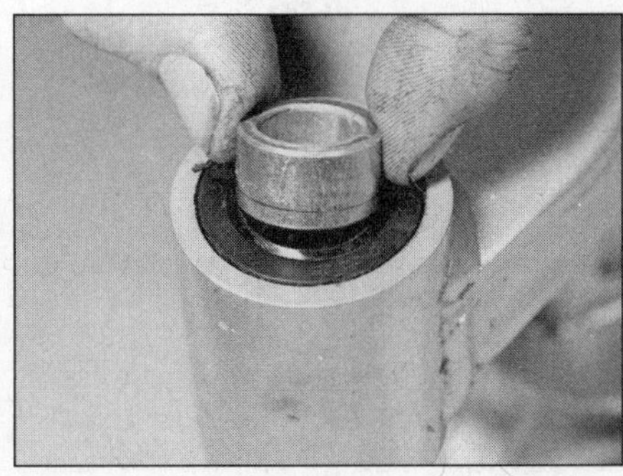
14.11c . . . and the shorter spacer to the right side

14.12 Install the swingarm ensuring it is correctly engaged with the drive chain and suspension linkage (arrows)

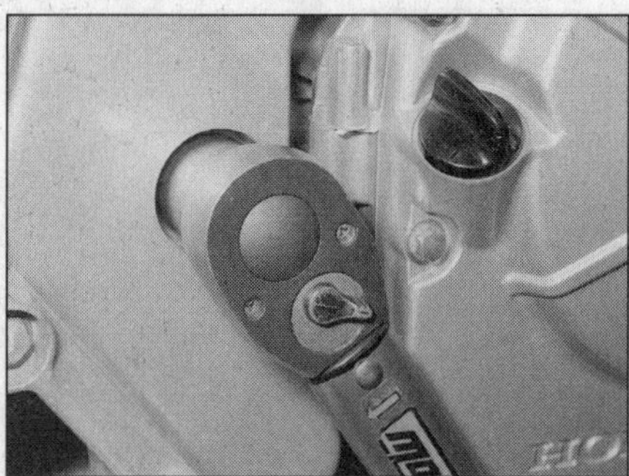

14.13 Tighten the swingarm pivot bolt nut to the specified torque setting

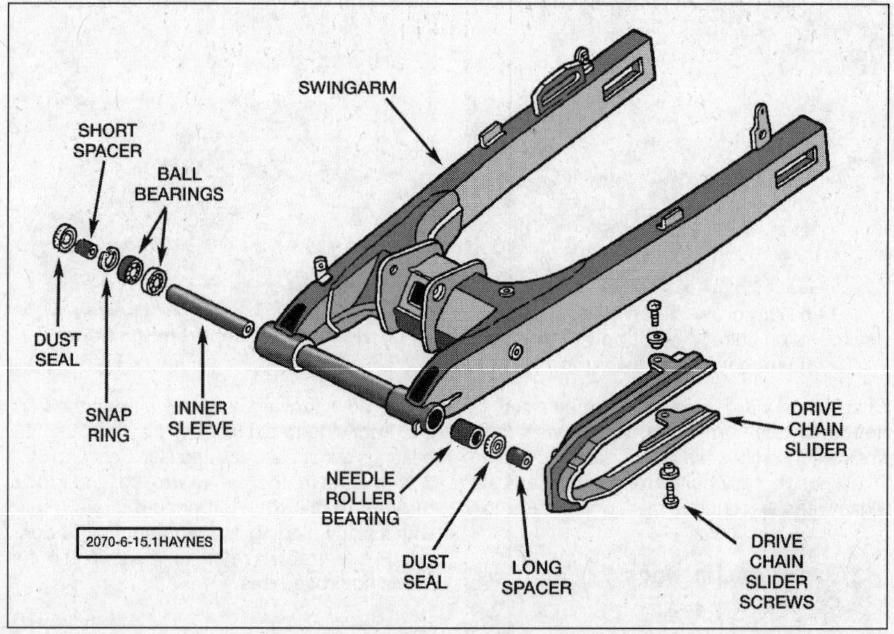

15.1 Exploded view of swingarm components

13 Fit the pivot shaft nut and tighten it to the torque setting listed in this Chapter's Specifications **(see illustration)**. Fit the cap to each side of the frame.

14 Install the shock absorber lower mounting bolt and the suspension linkage to swingarm pivot bolt from the left side. Fit both nuts and tighten them to the torque setting listed in this Chapter's Specifications.

15 Install the rear fender/mudguard as described in Chapter 8.

16 Install the rear wheel as described in Chapter 7.

17 Check the operation of the rear suspension before taking the machine on the road.

15 Swingarm - inspection and bearing replacement

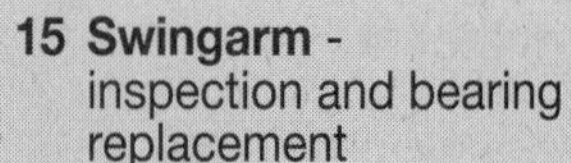

Inspection

1 Thoroughly clean all components, removing all traces of dirt, corrosion and grease **(see illustration)**.

2 Inspect all components closely, looking for obvious signs of wear such as heavy scoring, and cracks or distortion due to accident damage. Any damaged or worn component must be replaced.

3 If the painted finish of the swingarm has deteriorated it is worth taking the opportunity to repaint the affected area, ensuring that the surface is correctly prepared beforehand.

Bearing replacement

4 Lever out the dust seals, using a flat-bladed screwdriver, and inspect them for signs of wear or damage; replace them if necessary.

5 Using snap-ring pliers, remove the snap-ring from the right side of the swingarm **(see illustration)**.

6 The two right side bearings can be driven out of position simultaneously, using a hammer and suitable drift inserted from the left side of the swingarm. Move the drift around the face of the bearing while driving it out of position, so that the bearings leave the swingarm squarely.

7 Wash the bearings thoroughly in a high flash-point solvent to remove all traces of the old grease.

8 Check the bearing tracks and balls for wear, pitting or damage to hardened surfaces. A small amount of side movement in the bearing is normal but no radial movement should be detectable.

9 Check the bearings for play and roughness when they are spun by hand. All bearings will emit a small amount of noise when spun but they should not chatter or sound rough. If there is any doubt about the condition of the bearings they should be replaced.

10 Pack the bearings with grease and drift them separately into position using a suitable tubular drift which bears only on the outer race of the bearing.

11 Secure the bearings in position with the snap-ring, ensuring that it is correctly seated in its groove.

12 The needle roller bearing fitted to the left side of the swingarm can, if necessary, be replaced as described in Section 11 of this Chapter.

13 Press the dust seals into position using a suitable tubular spacer which bears only on the hard outer edge of the seal **(see illustration)**.

14 Inspect the chain slider fitted to the left side of the swingarm. If this shows any sign of wear it should be replaced.

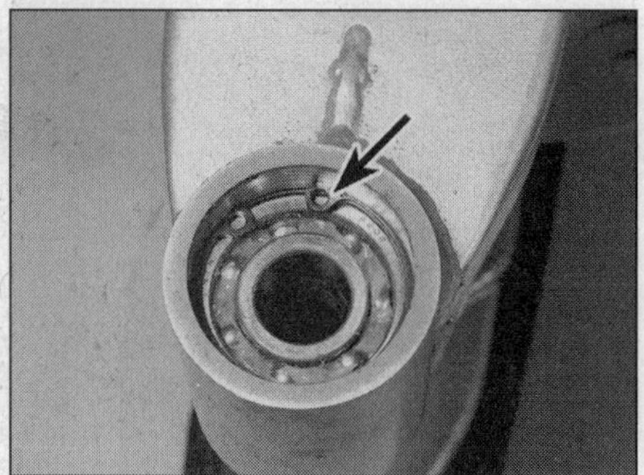

15.5 Swingarm right side bearings are retained by a snap-ring (arrow)

15.13 Press the dust seals into position with a suitable tubular spacer

16 Drive chain - removal, cleaning and installation

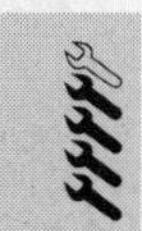

Removal - endless type chain

Note: *An endless chain has no riveted (soft) link - all links and pins are the same.*

1 Unscrew the two screws securing the front sprocket cover to the engine unit, noting the position of the wiring clamp **(see illustration 17.2)**.

2 Remove the cover and drive chain guide plate **(see illustrations 17.3a and 17.3b)**.

3 Remove the rear wheel as described in Chapter 7.

4 Remove the swingarm (see Section 14).
5 Slip the chain off the front sprocket and remove it from the bike.

Removal - riveted link chain

Note: *The riveted (soft) link can be identified by its identification markings on the side plate and usually slightly different color. Also the staked ends of the link's two pins look as if they have been deeply center-punched, instead of peened over as with all other pins.*
6 Locate the joining link in a suitable position to work on by rotating the back wheel; midway between the sprockets is ideal.
7 Slacken the drive chain as described in Chapter 1.
8 Split the chain at the joining link using an approved chain breaker tool. Honda produce a service tool (pt. no. 07HMH-MR1010B for US models or 07HMH-MR10102 for UK models) or you could use one of the commercially available types - see *Tools and Workshop Tips* in the Reference section. Remove the chain from the bike, noting its routing through the swingarm.

Cleaning

9 Soak the chain in kerosene (paraffin) for approximately five or six minutes.
Caution: Don't use gasoline (petrol), solvent or other cleaning fluids which might damage its internal sealing properties. Don't use high-pressure water. Remove the chain, wipe it off, then blow dry it with compressed air immediately. The entire process shouldn't take longer than ten minutes - if it does, the O-rings in the chain rollers could be damaged.

Installation - endless chain

10 Installation is the reverse of the removal procedure. On completion adjust and lubricate the chain following the procedures described in Chapter 1.
Caution: Use only the recommended lubricant - see Chapter 1.

Installation - riveted link chain

Warning: NEVER install a drive chain which uses a clip-type master (split) link. If you do not have access to a chain riveting tool, have the chain fitted by a dealer service department.

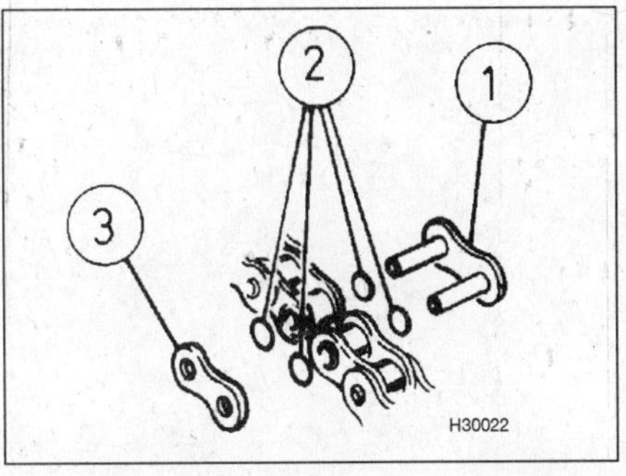

16.14 Drive chain joining link components

1 Joining link
2 O-rings
3 Side plate

11 Unscrew the two screws securing the front sprocket cover to the engine unit, noting the position of the wiring clamp **(see illustration 17.2)**.
12 Remove the cover and drive chain guide plate **(see illustrations 17.3a and 17.3b)**.
13 Install the drive chain through the swingarm sections and around the front sprocket, leaving the two ends in a convenient position to work on.
14 Install the **new** soft link from the inside run of the chain, with the four O-rings correctly located between the link plates **(see illustration)**. Never reuse the old soft link. Install the new side plate with its identification marks facing out and use the chain tool to press the side plate into position. Note that Honda specify a figure for the amount of link pin extension from the side plate for the RK and DID chains fitted as standard to S, T, V and W (1995 to 1998) models (see Specifications). Stake the new link pins using the chain riveting tool, following carefully the instructions of both the chain manufacturer and the tool manufacturer.
15 After riveting, check the soft link pin ends for any signs of cracking. If there is any evidence of cracking, the soft link, O-rings and side plate must be removed and the procedure repeated with a new soft link **(see illustration)**. Note that Honda specify a figure for the diameter of the riveted pin ends for the RK and DID chains fitted as standard to S, T, V and W (1995 to 1998) models (see Specifications).

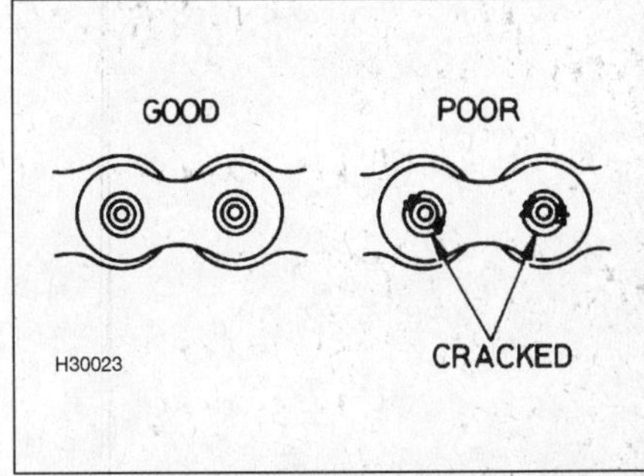

16.15 Check the joining link to make sure it is properly staked

16 Install the drive chain guide plate and front sprocket cover.
17 On completion, adjust and lubricate the chain following the procedures described in Chapter 1.
Caution: Use only the recommended lubricant.

17 Sprockets - check and replacement

Check

1 Set the bike on its centerstand.
2 Unscrew the two screws securing the front sprocket cover to the engine unit, noting the position of the wiring clamp **(see illustration)**.
3 Remove the sprocket cover and the drive chain guide plate **(see illustrations)**.
4 Check the wear pattern on both sprockets (see Chapter 1). If the sprocket teeth are worn excessively, replace the chain and both sprockets as a set. Whenever the drive chain is inspected, the sprockets should be inspected also. If you are replacing the chain, replace the sprockets as well.

Replacement

5 To remove the rear sprocket, remove the rear wheel as described in Chapter 7. Unscrew the nuts holding the sprocket to the wheel coupling and lift it off. Check the condition of the rubber damper under the rear wheel coupling (see Section 18).

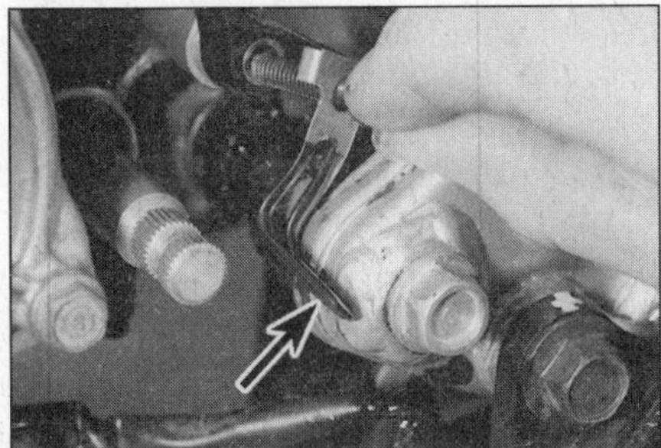

17.2 Remove the sprocket cover screws noting the wiring clip (arrow) fitted to the lower screw

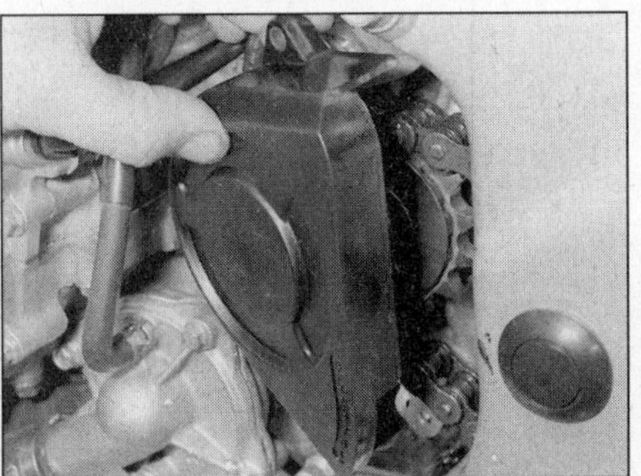

17.3a Remove the front sprocket cover from the engine . . .

17.3b . . . and remove the drive chain plate

17.6 Tighten the rear sprocket retaining bolts to the specified torque setting

17.8 Remove the front sprocket retaining bolt and washer . . .

17.9 . . . then slide the sprocket off the shaft and disengage it from the drive chain

6 Fit the new sprocket. Apply a smear of clean oil to the threads of the retaining nuts prior to fitting and tighten them to the torque setting listed in this Chapter's Specifications **(see illustration)**.
7 To replace the front sprocket, begin by installing the chain and rear wheel.
8 With the chain now in place, have an assistant apply the rear brake, then slacken and remove the sprocket retaining bolt and washer **(see illustration)**.
9 Pull the engine sprocket and chain off the shaft, then separate the sprocket from the chain **(see illustration)**.
10 Engage the new sprocket with the chain and slide it onto the shaft. Install the washer and retaining bolt and tighten it to the specified torque setting.
11 Fit the drive chain guide and sprocket cover. Fit the retaining screws, not forgetting the wiring clamp fitted to the lower screw, and tighten them securely.
12 Adjust and lubricate the chain following the procedures described in Chapter 1.

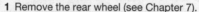

18 Rear wheel coupling/ rubber damper - check and replacement

1 Remove the rear wheel (see Chapter 7).
2 Remove the spacer from the center of the sprocket coupling.
3 Lift the sprocket coupling away from the wheel leaving the rubber dampers in position in the wheel. Take care not to lose the spacer from the inside of the coupling bearing.
4 Lift the rubber damper segments from the wheel and check them for cracks, hardening and general deterioration **(see illustration)**. Replace the rubber dampers as a set if necessary.
5 Checking and replacement procedures for the sprocket coupling bearing are described in Section 16 of Chapter 7.
6 Installation is the reverse of the removal procedure ensuring the sprocket coupling spacers are correctly positioned.
7 Install the rear wheel as described in Chapter 7.

18.4 Remove the rubber dampers from the rear wheel and inspect them for wear and damage

Chapter 7
Brakes, wheels and tires

Contents

Degrees of difficulty

Easy, suitable for novice with little experience

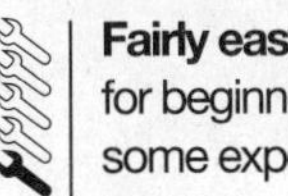

Fairly easy, suitable for beginner with some experience

Fairly difficult, suitable for competent DIY mechanic

Difficult, suitable for experienced DIY mechanic

Very difficult, suitable for expert DIY or professional

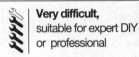

Specifications

Brakes

Brake fluid type	See Chapter 1
Front disc thickness	
M, N, P and R (1991 to 1994) models	
New	4.8 to 5.2 mm (0.19 to 0.20 in)
Service limit	4.0 mm (0.20 in)
S and T (1995 and 1996) models	
New	3.8 to 4.2 mm (0.15 to 0.17 in)
Service limit	3.5 mm (0.14 in)
V and W (1997 and 1998) models	
New	4.4 to 4.6 mm (0.19 to 0.20 in)
Service limit	3.5 mm (0.14 in)
Rear disc thickness	
New	4.8 to 5.2 mm (0.19 to 0.20 in)
Service limit	4.0 mm (0.20 in)
Disc maximum runout (front and rear)	0.3 mm (0.012 in)
Caliper bore ID	
Front	
New	25.400 to 25.450 mm (1.000 to 1.002 in)
Service limit	25.460 mm (1.0021 in)
Rear	
New	38.180 to 38.230 mm (1.503 to 1.505 in)
Service limit	38.240 mm (1.506 in)
Caliper piston OD	
Front	
New	25.335 to 25.368 mm (0.997 to 0.999 in)
Service limit	25.330 mm (0.997 in)
Rear	
New	38.098 to 38.148 mm (1.499 to 1.501 in)
Service limit	38.090 mm (1.500 in)

Brakes (continued)

Front master cylinder bore ID	
New	12.700 to 12.743 mm (0.500 to 0.501 in)
Service limit	12.760 mm (0.502 in)
Front master cylinder piston OD	
New	12.657 to 12.684 mm (0.498 to 0.499 in)
Service limit	12.650 mm (0.498 in)
Rear master cylinder bore ID	
M, N, P and R (1991 to 1994) models	
New	12.700 to 12.743 mm (0.500 to 0.501 in)
Service limit	12.760 mm (0.502 in)
S, T, V and W (1995 to 1998) models	
New	14.000 to 14.043 mm (0.551 to 0.553 in)
Service limit	14.055 mm (0.553 in)
Rear master cylinder piston OD	
M, N, P and R (1991 to 1994) models	
New	12.657 to 12.684 mm (0.498 to 0.499 in)
Service limit	12.650 mm (0.498 in)
S, T, V and W (1995 to 1998) models	
New	13.957 to 13.984 mm (0.549 to 0.550 in)
Service limit	13.945 mm (0.549 in)

Wheels

Maximum wheel runout (front and rear)	
Axial (side-to-side)	2.0 mm (0.08 in)
Radial (out-of-round)	2.0 mm (0.08 in)
Maximum axle runout (front and rear)	0.2 mm (0.01 in)

Tires

Tire pressures	See Chapter 1
Tire sizes	
Front	120/60 ZR 17
Rear	160/60 ZR 17

Torque settings

	Nm	ft-lbs
Front brake caliper		
Mounting bolts		
M, N, P and R (1991 to 1994) models	27	20
S, T, V and W (1995 to 1998) models	31	22
Pad retaining pins	18	13
Upper slider pin	23	17
Lower slider pin	13	9
Front brake disc retaining bolts		
M, N, P and R (1991 to 1994) models	43	31
S, T, V and W (1995 to 1998) models	20	14
Front brake master cylinder clamp bolts	12	9
Front brake lever pivot bolt locknut	6	4
Rear brake caliper		
Mounting bolt	23	17
Pad retaining pin	18	13
Slider pin	28	20
Rear brake disc retaining bolts	43	31
Rear brake master cylinder		
Mounting bolts		
M, N, P and R (1991 to 1994) models	12	9
S and T (1995 and 1996) models	9	7
V and W (1997 and 1998) models	12	9
Fluid reservoir mounting bolt		
M, N, P and R (1991 to 1994) models	9	7
S and T (1995 and 1996) models	12	9
V and W (1997 and 1998) models	9	7
Brake hose banjo fitting bolt	35	25
Brake pipe flare nuts	17	12
Brake caliper bleeder valves	6	4
Front axle bolt	60	43
Front axle clamp bolts	22	16
Rear axle nut	95	69
Drive chain adjuster locknuts	22	16

1 General information

The models covered in this manual are fitted with cast aluminum wheels designed to accept tubeless tires. Both front and rear brakes are hydraulically operated disc brakes, the front using a twin disc set up and the rear a single disc. The front brake calipers are of the dual piston sliding type, while the rear is of the single piston sliding type.

Caution: Disc brake components rarely require disassembly. Do not disassemble components unless absolutely necessary. If any hydraulic brake line is loosened, the entire system must be disassembled, drained, cleaned and then properly filled and bled upon reassembly. Do not use solvents on internal brake components. Solvents will cause the seals to swell and distort. Use only clean brake fluid or alcohol for cleaning. Use care when working with brake fluid as it can injure your eyes and it will damage painted surfaces and plastic parts.

2 Front brake pads - replacement

Warning: When replacing the front brake pads always replace the pads in BOTH calipers - never just on one side. The dust created by the brake system may contain asbestos, which is harmful to your health. Never blow it out with compressed air and don't inhale any of it. An approved filtering mask should be worn when working on the brakes.

2.3a Unscrew the caliper mounting bracket bolts (arrows) . . .

2.4a Unscrew and remove the pad pins . . .

2.2a Unscrew the plugs from the caliper body . . .

M, N, P and R (1991 to 1994) models

1 Set the bike on its centerstand.

2 Unscrew both plugs from the caliper body to reveal the pad pin retaining bolt heads then loosen both pad pins **(see illustrations)**.

3 Slacken and remove the two caliper mounting bracket retaining bolts and slide the caliper assembly off the disc, taking care not to place any undue strain on the hydraulic hose **(see illustrations)**.

4 Unscrew and remove both pad pins from the caliper and withdraw the brake pads **(see illustrations)**.

2.3b . . . and slide the caliper assembly off the disc

2.4b . . . and withdraw the pads from the caliper

2.2b . . . and loosen both pad pins

5 Remove the anti-rattle springs from the caliper body and the mounting bracket, noting their correct fitted positions.

6 Inspect the surface of each pad for contamination and check that the friction material has not worn beyond its service limit groove, or down to expose the cutout in the pad's rear edge. If either pad is worn to or beyond the service limit groove (ie the grooves are no longer visible), fouled with oil or grease, or heavily scored or damaged by dirt and debris, both pads must be replaced as a set **(see illustration)**. Note that it is not possible to degrease the friction material; if the pads are contaminated in any way they must be replaced.

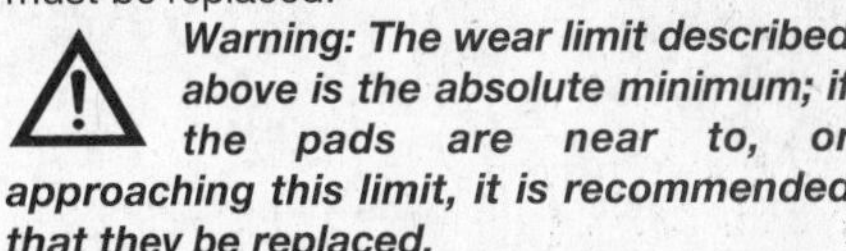

Warning: The wear limit described above is the absolute minimum; if the pads are near to, or approaching this limit, it is recommended that they be replaced.

7 If the pads are in good condition clean them carefully, using a fine wire brush which is completely free of oil and grease, to remove all traces of road dirt and corrosion. Using a pointed instrument, clean out the grooves in the friction material and dig out any embedded particles of foreign matter. Any areas of glazing may be removed using emery cloth.

8 Check the condition of the brake disc (see Section 4).

9 Remove all traces of corrosion from the pad pins. Inspect the pins and anti-rattle springs for signs of damage and replace if necessary.

10 Push the pistons as far back into the caliper as possible using hand pressure only.

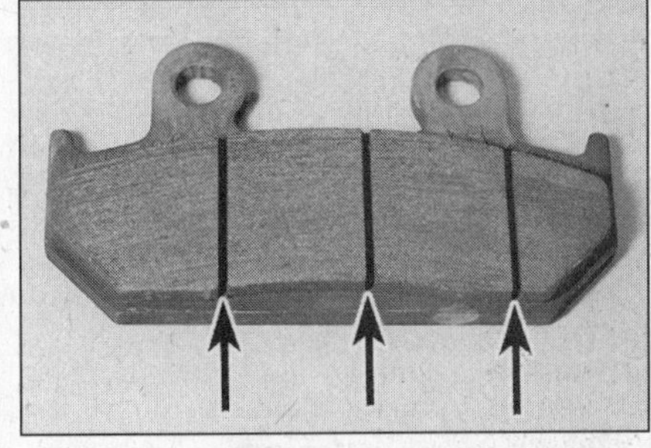

2.6 Brake pads must be replaced when the wear grooves (arrows) are no longer visible

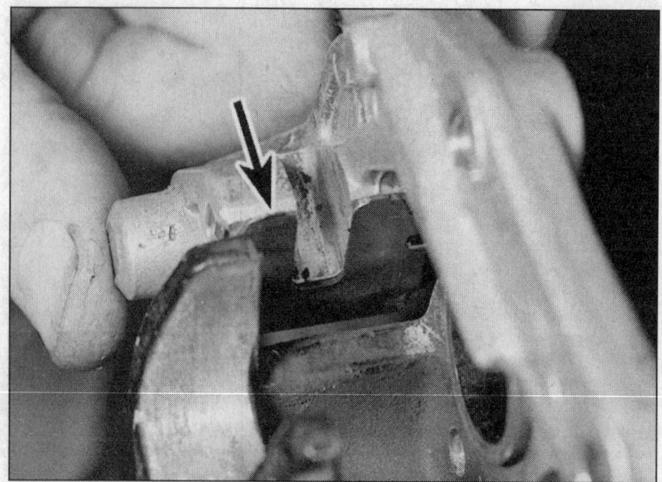
2.11a Ensure both the small pad spring (arrow) . . .

2.11b . . . and large pad spring are correctly installed in the caliper body

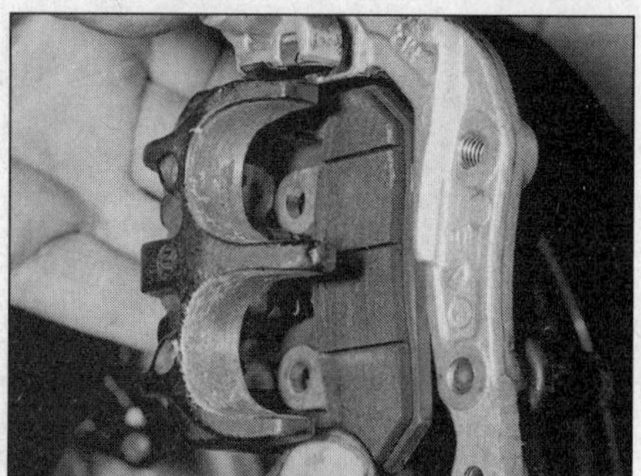
2.12 Position the pads in the caliper so that their friction material is facing the brake disc

2.13 Slide the caliper assembly into position and tighten its retaining bolts to the specified torque

Due to the increased friction material thickness of new pads, it may be necessary to remove the master cylinder reservoir cap, plate and diaphragm and siphon out some fluid.

11 Install the anti-rattle springs in the caliper body ensuring each one is correctly positioned **(see illustrations)**.

12 Insert the pads into the caliper, ensuring both anti-rattle springs remain correctly positioned, so that the friction material of each pad is facing the disc **(see illustration)**. Insert the pad retaining pins making sure that they pass through the holes in both pads correctly.

13 Slide the caliper assembly onto the disc and fit the caliper bracket mounting bolts, tightening them to the specified torque setting **(see illustration)**.

14 Tighten the pad retaining pins to the specified torque setting then fit the pad pin plugs, tightening them securely.

15 Top up the master cylinder reservoir (see *'Daily (pre-ride) checks'*) and fit the diaphragm, plate and seal.

16 Operate the brake lever several times to bring the pads into contact with the disc. Check the master cylinder fluid level (see *'Daily (pre-ride) checks'*) and the operation of the brake before riding the motorcycle.

S, T, V and W (1995 to 1998) models

17 Set the bike on its centerstand. Before removing the pads, push the caliper body against the disc to press the pistons fully back into their bores in the caliper - this provides clearance for the new pads to be installed. It may be necessary to remove the master cylinder reservoir cap, plate and diaphragm and siphon out some fluid.

18 Unscrew the plug from the caliper body to reveal the pad pin retaining bolt head then loosen the pad pin **(see illustration)**.

19 Unscrew and remove the pad pin from the caliper and withdraw the brake pads **(see illustrations)**.

20 Inspect the surface of each pad for contamination and check that the friction material has not worn down to expose the cutout in the pad's edge **(see illustration)**. If either pad is worn, fouled with oil or grease, or heavily scored or damaged by dirt and debris, both pads must be replaced as a set. Note that it is not possible to degrease the friction material; if the pads are contaminated in any way they must be replaced.

Warning: The wear limit described above is the absolute minimum; if the pads are near to, or approaching this limit, it is recommended that they be replaced.

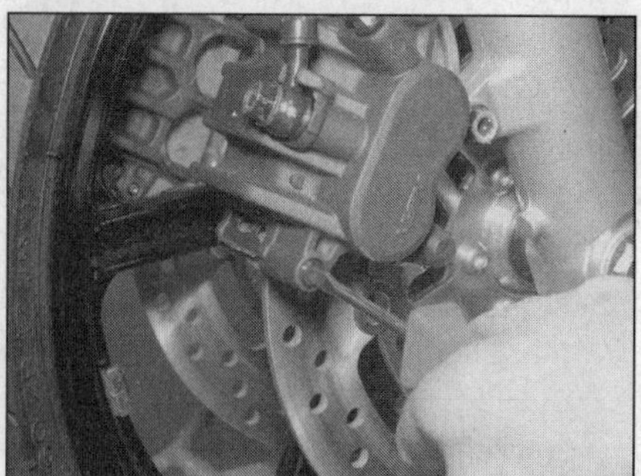
2.18 Unscrew the pad pin plug . . .

2.19a . . . then remove the pad pin . . .

2.19b . . . and withdraw the pads

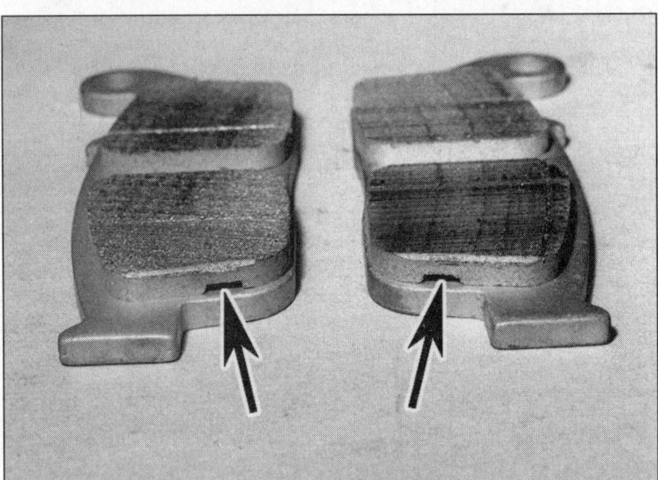
2.20 Brake pad wear limit cutouts (arrow)

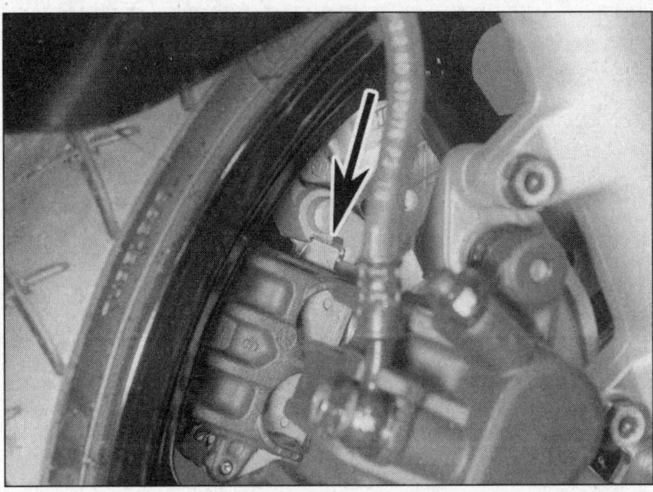
2.25a Make sure the pads locate correctly against the inner pad spring (arrow) . . .

21 If the pads are in good condition clean them carefully, using a fine wire brush which is completely free of oil and grease, to remove all traces of road dirt and corrosion. Using a pointed instrument, clean out the grooves in the friction material and dig out any embedded particles of foreign matter. Any areas of glazing may be removed using emery cloth.

22 Check the condition of the brake disc (see Section 4).

23 Remove all traces of corrosion from the pad pins. Inspect the pins and anti-rattle springs for signs of damage and replace if necessary.

24 Check that each pad spring is correctly positioned.

25 Insert the pads into the caliper, ensuring both anti-rattle springs remain correctly positioned, so that the friction material of each pad is facing the disc **(see illustrations)**. Press each pad up against the spring to align the holes and insert the pad retaining pin, making sure that it passes through the hole in each pad.

26 Tighten the pad retaining pin to the specified torque setting then fit the pad pin plug and, tighten it securely **(see illustration)**.

27 Top up the master cylinder reservoir (see *'Daily (pre-ride) checks'*) and fit the diaphragm, plate and seal.

28 Operate the brake lever several times to bring the pads into contact with the disc. Check the master cylinder fluid level (see *'Daily (pre-ride) checks'*) and the operation of the brake before riding the motorcycle.

3 Front brake caliper - removal, overhaul and installation

Warning: If a caliper indicates the need for an overhaul (usually due to leaking fluid or sticky operation), all old brake fluid should be flushed from the system. Also, the dust created by the brake system may contain asbestos, which is harmful to your health. Never blow it out with compressed air and don't inhale any of it. An approved filtering mask should be worn when working on the brakes. Do not, under any circumstances, use petroleum-based solvents to clean brake parts. Use clean brake fluid, brake cleaner or denatured alcohol only.

Removal

1 Place the bike on its centerstand.

2 Remove the brake hose banjo fitting bolt and separate the hose from the caliper. Plug the hose end or wrap a plastic bag tightly around it to minimize fluid loss and prevent dirt entering the system. Discard the sealing washers; new ones must be used on installation. **Note:** *If you're planning to overhaul the caliper and don't have a source of compressed air to blow out the pistons, just loosen the banjo bolt at this stage and retighten it lightly. The bike's hydraulic system can then be used to force the pistons out of the body once the pads have been removed. Disconnect the hose once the pistons have been sufficiently displaced.*

2.25b . . . and the outer pad spring

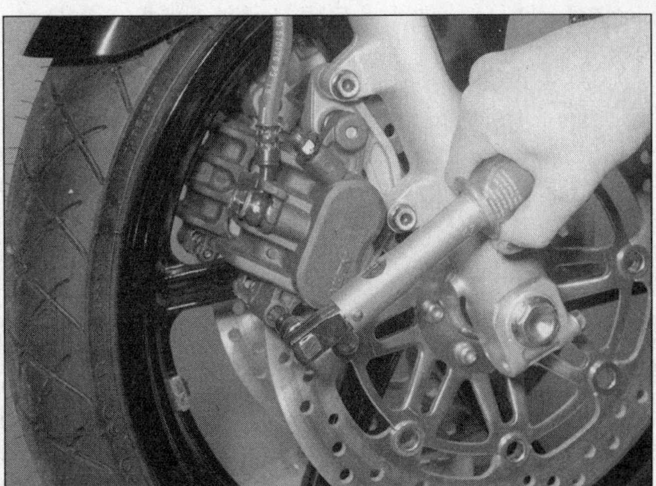
2.26 Tighten the pad pin to the specified torque

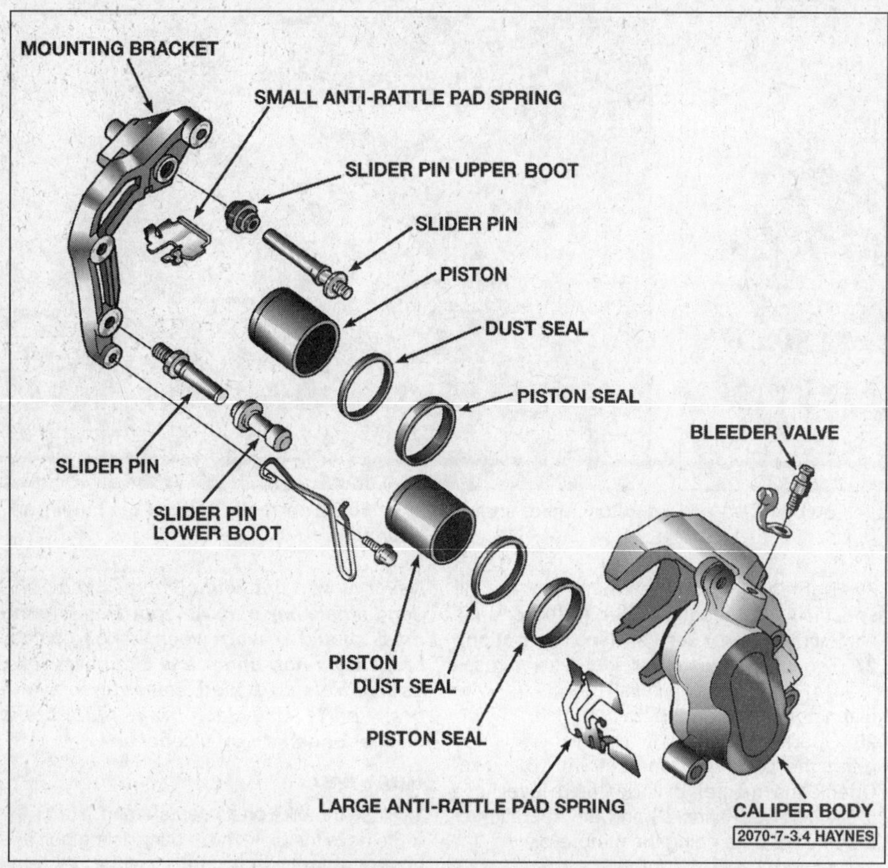

3.4 Exploded view of a front brake caliper (M, N, P and R (1991 to 1994) model type shown)

3 Remove the brake pads and anti-rattle springs as described in Section 2. On S, T, V and W (1995 to 1998) models, unscrew the caliper mounting bolts and remove the caliper. Note that on S, T, V and W (1995 to 1998) models, Honda specify that the mounting bolts should be discarded and new ones used for installation.

Overhaul

4 Clean the exterior of the caliper with denatured alcohol or brake system cleaner **(see illustration)**.

5 Slide the caliper off the mounting bracket and recover the rubber boots from the slider pins **(see illustration)**.

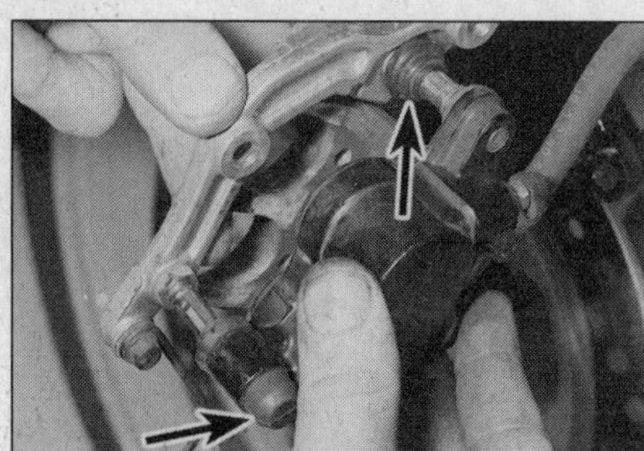

3.5 Slide the caliper off the mounting bracket and remove the rubber boots (arrows)

6 If the pistons weren't forced out using the bike's hydraulic system, place a wad of rag between the piston and caliper frame to act as a cushion, then use compressed air directed into the fluid inlet to force the pistons out of the body. Use only low pressure to ease the pistons out and make sure both pistons are displaced at the same time. If the air pressure is too high and the pistons are forced out, the caliper and/or pistons may be damaged.

Warning: Never place your fingers in front of the pistons in an attempt to catch or protect them when applying compressed air, as serious injury could result.

7 Using a wooden or plastic tool, remove the dust seals from the caliper bores. If a metal tool is being used, take great care not to damage the caliper bores.

3.12 Examine the slider pins for wear and replace if necessary

8 Remove both the piston seals in the same way.

9 Clean the pistons and bores with denatured alcohol, clean brake fluid or brake system cleaner.

Caution: Do not, under any circumstances, use a petroleum-based solvent to clean brake parts. If compressed air is available, use it to dry the parts thoroughly (make sure it's filtered and unlubricated).

10 Inspect the caliper bores and pistons for signs of corrosion, nicks and burrs and loss of plating. If surface defects are present, the caliper assembly must be replaced. If the caliper is in bad shape the master cylinder should also be checked.

11 If the necessary measuring equipment is available, compare the dimensions of the caliper bores and pistons to those given in this Chapter's Specifications, replacing any component that is worn beyond the service limit.

12 Temporarily install the caliper bracket. Make sure that it slides smoothly in-and-out of the caliper and check that the pins are a snug fit in their bores. If not check the slider pins and their bores for burrs or excessive wear, replacing worn components as necessary **(see illustration)**. The slider pin boots should be replaced as a matter of course.

13 Lubricate the new piston seals with clean brake fluid and install them in their grooves in the caliper bores.

14 Lubricate the new dust seals with clean brake fluid and install them in their grooves in the caliper bores.

15 Lubricate the pistons with clean brake fluid and install them in the caliper bores. Using your thumbs, push the pistons all the way in, making sure they enter the bore squarely.

16 If the slider pins have been removed, apply a few drops of thread locking compound to the pin threads then fit the pin to the caliper body or mounting bracket (as applicable) and tighten it to the specified torque setting.

17 Install the new slider pin boots.

18 Apply a thin coat of PBC (poly butyl cuprysil) grease, or silicone grease designed for high-temperature brake applications, to each of the slider pins. Install the mounting bracket on the caliper and seat the boots over the lips on the bracket.

Installation

19 Install the anti-rattle springs and brake pads as described in Section 2.

20 On S, T, V and W (1995 to 1998) models, slide the caliper assembly onto the disc and fit the caliper bracket mounting bolts (Honda specify that new ones should be used), tightening them to the specified torque setting.

21 Connect the brake hose to the caliper, using new sealing washers on each side of the fitting. Tighten the banjo fitting bolt to the specified torque setting.
22 Fill the master cylinder with the recommended brake fluid (see Chapter 1) and bleed the hydraulic system as described in Section 11.
23 Check for leaks and thoroughly test the operation of the brake before riding the motorcycle.

4 Front brake discs - inspection, removal and installation

Inspection

1 Set the bike on its centerstand.
2 Visually inspect the surface of the discs for score marks and other damage. Light scratches are normal after use and won't affect brake operation, but deep grooves and heavy score marks will reduce braking efficiency and accelerate pad wear. If the discs are badly grooved they must be machined or replaced.
3 To check disc runout, mount a dial indicator to a fork leg, with the plunger on the indicator touching the surface of the disc about 10 mm (1/2 inch) from the outer edge **(see illustration)**. Have an assistant sit on the seat to raise the front wheel off the ground, then rotate the wheel and watch the indicator needle, comparing your reading with the limit listed in this Chapter's Specifications. If the runout is greater than allowed, check the hub bearings for play. If the bearings are worn, replace them and repeat this check. If the disc runout is still excessive, it will have to be replaced, although machining by a competent engineering shop may be a solution.
4 The disc must not be machined or allowed to wear down to a thickness less than the service limit, listed in this Chapter's Specifications (check also for wear limits stamped on the disc itself). The thickness of the disc can be checked with a micrometer **(see illustration)**. If the thickness of the disc is less than the minimum allowable, it must be replaced.

Removal

5 Remove the wheel (see Section 14).
Caution: Don't lay the wheel down and allow it to rest on one of the discs - the disc could become warped. Set the wheel on wood blocks so the disc doesn't support the weight of the wheel.
6 Mark the relationship of the disc to the wheel, so it can be installed in the same position. Remove the bolts that retain the disc to the wheel. Loosen the bolts a little at a time, in a criss-cross pattern, to avoid distorting the disc.
7 Remove the disc, and on M, N, P and R (1991 to 1994) models recover the six shims which are positioned between the disc and wheel. If both discs are to be removed mark them Left and Right to ensure they are correctly positioned on installation.

Installation

8 On M, N, P and R (1991 to 1994) models, position a shim on each of the disc's threaded holes in the wheel.
9 Install the disc on the wheel, aligning the previously applied matchmarks (if you're reinstalling the original disc). Make sure the arrow (stamped on the disc) marking the normal direction of rotation is pointing in the direction of wheel rotation and is on the outer face of the disc **(see illustration)**.
10 Install the bolts, ensuring the shims remain in position, and tighten them evenly and progressively to the specified torque setting. Clean off all grease from the brake disc(s) using acetone or brake system cleaner. If new brake discs have been installed, remove any protective coating from their working surfaces.
11 Install the wheel (see Section 14).

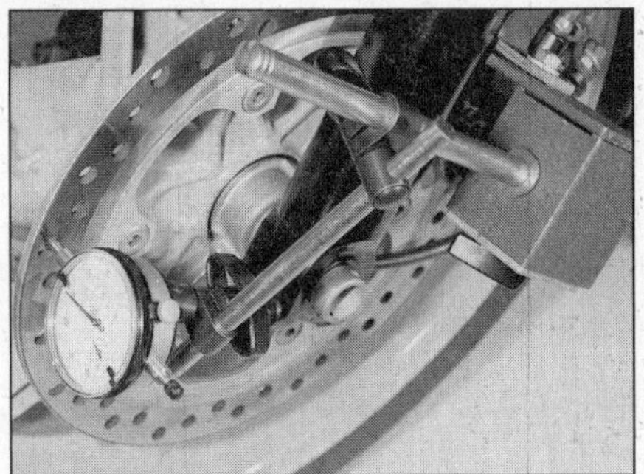

4.3 Using a dial indicator to measure disc runout

12 Operate the brake lever several times to bring the pads into contact with the disc. Check the operation of the brakes carefully before riding the motorcycle.

5 Front brake master cylinder - removal, overhaul and installation

1 If the master cylinder is leaking fluid, or if the lever does not produce a firm feel when the brake is applied, and bleeding the brakes does not help, master cylinder overhaul is recommended. Before disassembling the master cylinder, read through the entire procedure and make sure that you have the correct rebuild kit.
2 Also, you will need some new, clean brake fluid of the recommended type, some clean shop towels and internal snap-ring pliers. **Note:** *To prevent damage to the paint from spilled brake fluid, always cover the fuel tank when working on the master cylinder.*
Caution: Disassembly, overhaul and reassembly of the brake master cylinder must be done in a spotlessly clean work area to avoid contamination and possible failure of the brake hydraulic system components.

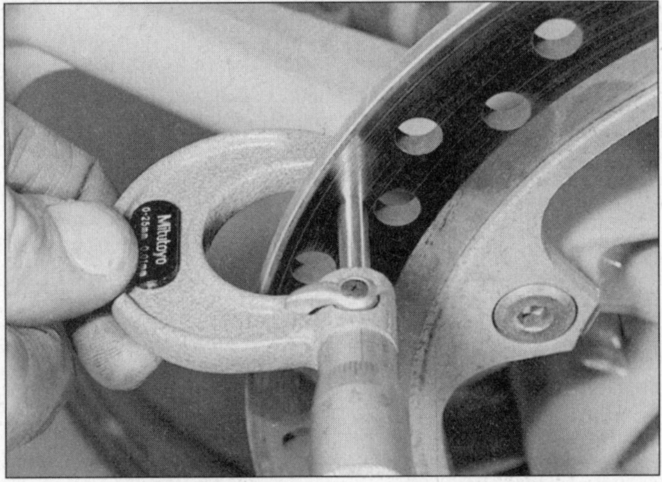

4.4 Using a micrometer to measure disc thickness

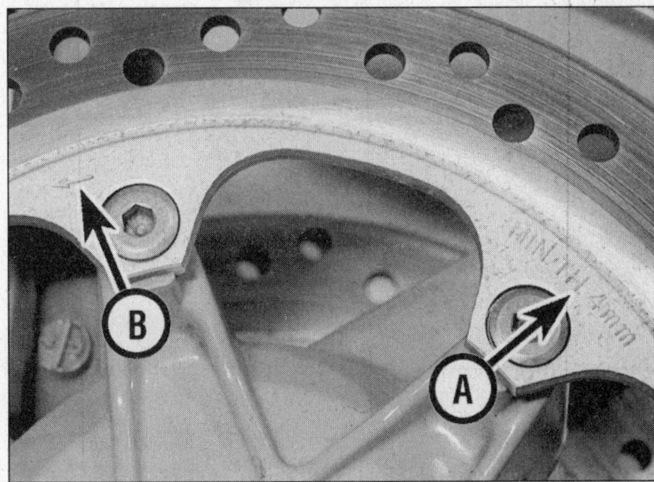

4.9 Disc minimum thickness (A) stamped on disc. Ensure the arrow (B) is pointing in the normal direction of wheel rotation

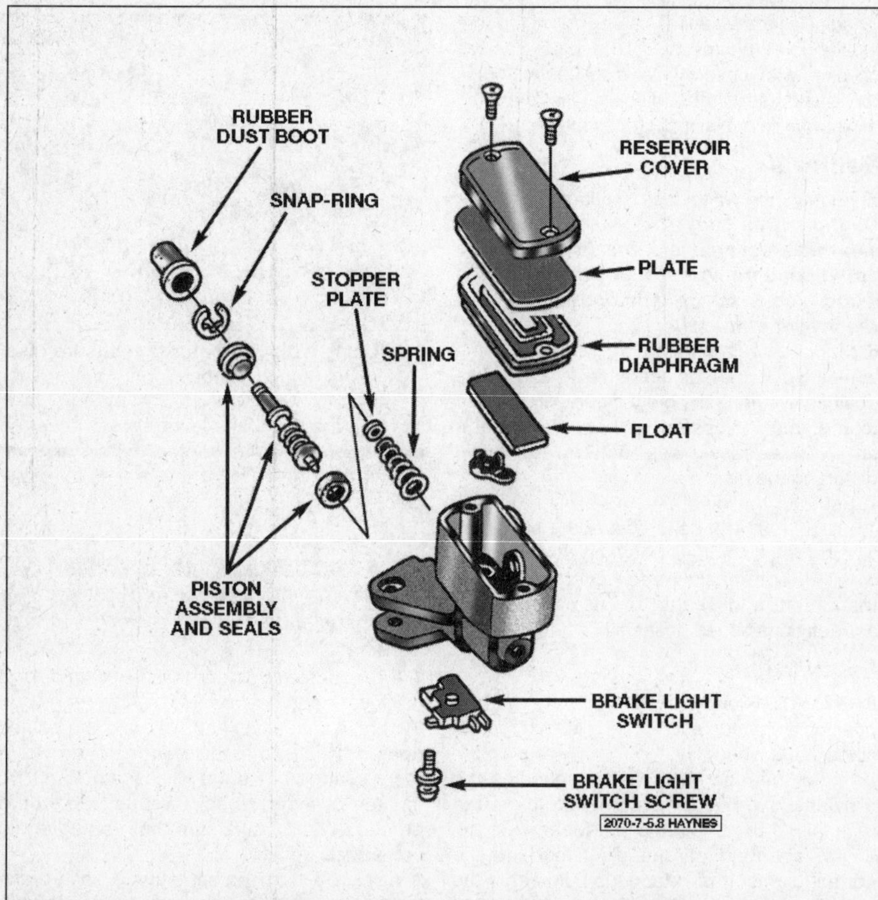

5.8 Exploded view of the front brake master cylinder

Removal

3 Loosen, but do not remove, the screws holding the reservoir cover in place.
4 Disconnect the electrical connectors from the brake light switch.
5 Pull back the rubber boot, loosen the banjo fitting bolt and separate the brake hose from the master cylinder. Wrap the end of the hose in a clean rag and suspend the hose in an upright position or bend it down carefully and place the open end in a clean container. The objective is to prevent excessive loss of brake fluid, fluid spills and system contamination.
6 Remove the locknut from the underside of the brake lever pivot bolt, then unscrew the bolt and remove the brake lever.
7 Remove the master cylinder mounting bolts then remove the clamp and lift the master cylinder away from the handlebar.
Caution: Do not tip the master cylinder upside down or brake fluid will run out.

Overhaul

8 Detach the reservoir cover and remove the plate, rubber diaphragm and float then drain the brake fluid into a suitable container **(see illustration)**. Wipe any remaining fluid out of the reservoir with a clean rag.
9 Undo the screw and remove the brake light switch.
10 Carefully remove the rubber dust boot from the end of the piston.
11 Using snap-ring pliers, remove the snap-ring and slide out the piston assembly and the spring. Lay the parts out in the proper order to prevent confusion during reassembly.
12 Clean all of the parts with brake system cleaner (available at auto parts stores), isopropyl alcohol or clean brake fluid.
Caution: Do not, under any circumstances, use a petroleum-based solvent to clean brake parts. If compressed air is available, use it to dry the parts thoroughly (make sure it's filtered and unlubricated).
13 Check the master cylinder bore for corrosion, scratches, nicks and score marks. If damage is evident, the master cylinder must be replaced with a new one. If the master cylinder is in poor condition, then the calipers should be checked as well.
14 If the necessary measuring equipment is available, compare the dimensions of the master cylinder bore and piston to those given in this Chapter's Specifications, replacing any component that it is worn beyond the service limit.
15 The dust boot, piston assembly and spring are included in the rebuild kit. Use all of the new parts, regardless of the apparent condition of the old ones.
16 Before reassembling the master cylinder, soak the piston and the rubber cup seals in clean brake fluid for ten or fifteen minutes. Lubricate the master cylinder bore with clean brake fluid, then carefully insert the piston and related parts in the reverse order of disassembly. Make sure the lips on the cup seals do not turn inside out when they are slipped into the bore and ensure the spring is fitted the correct way around.
17 Depress the piston, then install the snap-ring (make sure the snap-ring is properly seated in the groove). Install the rubber dust boot (make sure the lip is seated properly in the piston groove).
18 Install the brake light switch and securely tighten its retaining screw.

Installation

19 Attach the master cylinder to the handlebar then fit the clamp making sure the 'UP' mark is facing upwards. Tighten the clamp bolts to the torque setting listed in this Chapter's Specifications.
20 Connect the brake hose to the master cylinder, using new sealing washers. Tighten the banjo fitting bolt to the specified torque setting.
21 Install the lever and pivot bolt. Install the pivot bolt locknut and tighten it to the torque setting listed in this Chapter's Specifications. Connect the brake light switch wiring.
22 Refer to Section 11 and bleed the air from the system.

6 Rear brake pads - replacement

Warning: The dust created by the brake system may contain asbestos, which is harmful to your health. Never blow it out with compressed air and don't inhale any of it. An approved filtering mask should be worn when working on the brakes.

1 Set the bike on its centerstand. Before removing the pads, push the caliper body against the disc to press the pistons fully back into their bores in the caliper - this provides clearance for the new pads to be installed. It may be necessary to remove the master cylinder reservoir cap, plate and diaphragm and siphon out some fluid.
2 Unscrew the plug from the caliper body to reveal the pad retaining pin head then slacken and remove the pad pin **(see illustrations)**.
3 Unscrew the caliper mounting bolt then release the brake hose from its retaining clips and pivot the caliper upwards **(see illustration)**. Do not place any excess strain on the hydraulic hose.
4 Slide out the pads along with the insulating pad and shim which are fitted to the rear of each pad **(see illustrations)**.
5 If required, remove the anti-rattle springs from the caliper bracket and body, noting their correct fitted positions **(see illustration)**.

6.2a Unscrew the plug from the rear brake caliper body . . .

6.2b . . . then slacken the pad pin with an Allen wrench . . .

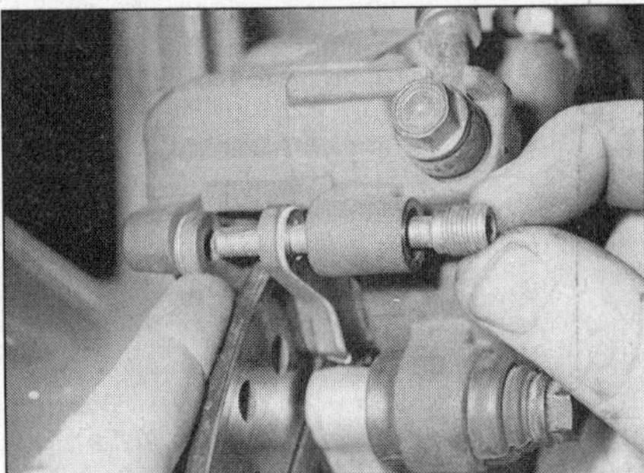

6.2c . . . and withdraw the pin from the caliper

6.3 Unscrew the caliper mounting bolt . . .

6.4a . . . then pivot the caliper away from the disc and recover the inner . . .

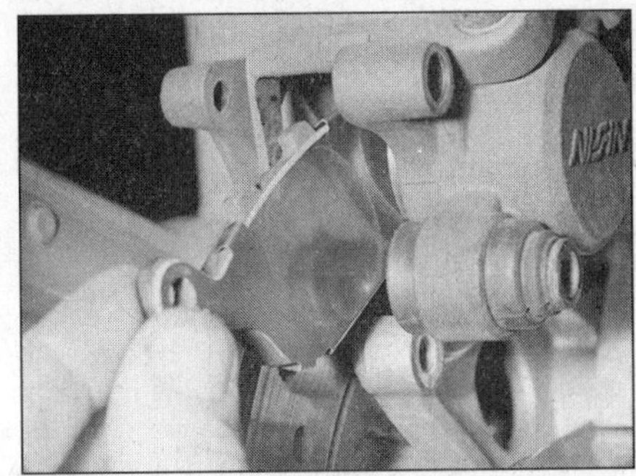

6.4b . . . and outer pads noting the correct fitted locations of the insulating pads and shims

6 Inspect the brake pads and associated components as described in Steps 6 to 10 of Section 2.

7 If removed, fit the small anti-rattle spring to the caliper bracket and clip the large spring into the caliper body. Make sure both springs are correctly fitted and clipped securely in position.

8 Install the insulating pad and shim to the rear of each pad backing plate **(see illustrations)**.

9 Install the pads with the friction material of each pad facing the disc, and locate the leading edge of each pad against the pad spring in the caliper bracket. Lower the caliper onto the pads, making sure the spring in the caliper remains correctly positioned. Press the pads up against the spring and insert the pad retaining pin, making sure that it passes through the hole in both pads as well as the insulating pads and shims.

10 Fit the caliper mounting bolt, and tighten it to the specified torque setting.

11 Locate the brake hose in the retaining clips on the rear fender/mudguard. Ensure the hose is securely retained by each clip.

12 Tighten the pad retaining pin to the specified torque setting then install the pad pin plug, tightening it securely.

13 Refill the master cylinder reservoir up to the level line with DOT 4 brake fluid and fit the diaphragm and cap.

14 Operate the brake pedal several times to bring the pads into contact with the disc. Check the master cylinder fluid level (see *'Daily (pre-ride) checks'*) and the operation of the brake before riding the motorcycle.

7 Rear brake caliper - removal, overhaul and installation

Warning: If the caliper indicates the need for an overhaul (usually due to leaking fluid or sticky operation), all old brake fluid should be flushed from the system. Also, the dust created by the brake system may contain asbestos, which is harmful to your health. Never blow it out with compressed air and don't inhale any of it. An approved filtering mask should be worn when working on the brakes. Do not, under any circumstances, use petroleum-based solvents to clean brake parts. Use clean brake fluid, brake cleaner or denatured alcohol only.

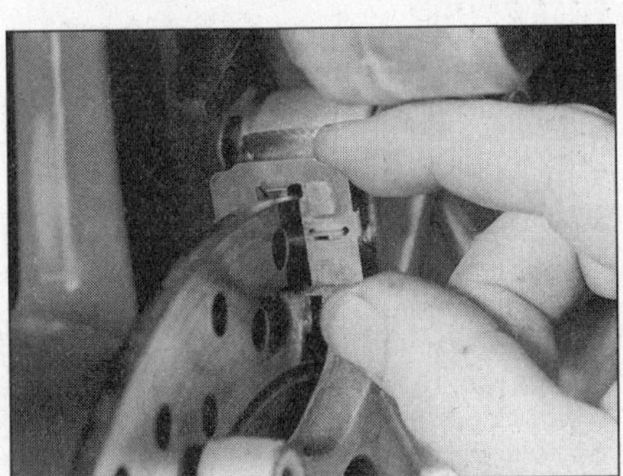

6.5 Remove anti-rattle spring from the caliper bracket for safe-keeping

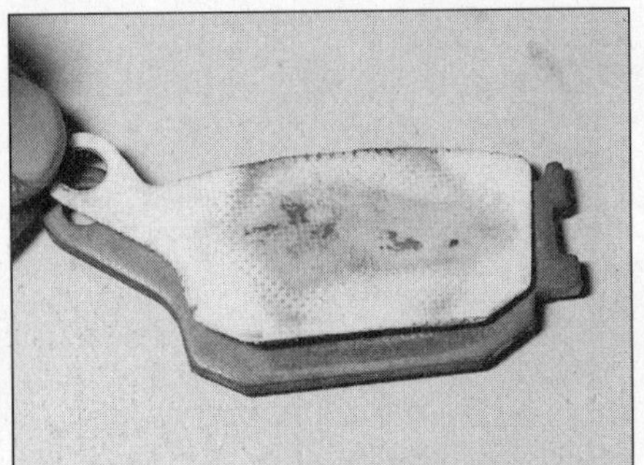

6.8a Prior to installing, fit the insulating pad . . .

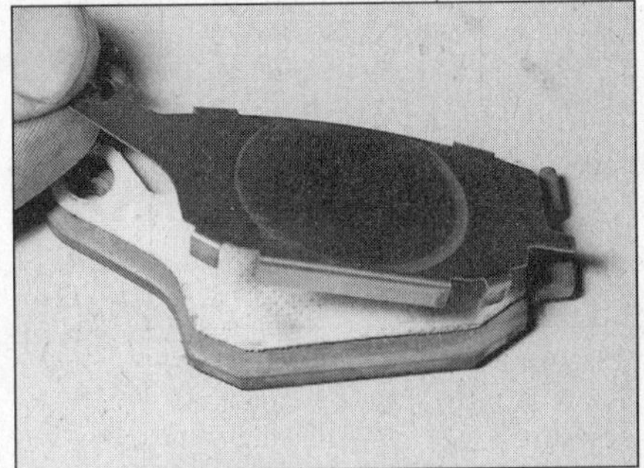

6.8b . . . and shim to the rear of each rear brake pad

Removal

1 Place the bike on its centerstand.

2 Remove the brake hose banjo fitting bolt and separate the hose from the caliper. Plug the hose end or wrap a plastic bag tightly around it to minimize fluid loss and prevent dirt entering the system. Discard the sealing washers; new ones must be used on installation. **Note:** *If you're planning to overhaul the caliper and don't have a source of compressed air to blow out the pistons, just loosen the banjo bolt at this stage and retighten it lightly. The bike's hydraulic system can then be used to force the piston out of the body once the pads have been removed. Disconnect the hose once the pistons have been sufficiently displaced.*

3 Remove the brake pads and anti-rattle springs as described in Section 6.

4 Slide the caliper away from its mounting bracket and recover the slider pin rubber boot.

Overhaul

5 Clean the exterior of the caliper with denatured alcohol or brake system cleaner **(see illustration)**.

6 If the piston wasn't forced out using the bike's hydraulic system, place a wad of rag between the piston and caliper frame to act as a cushion, then use compressed air directed into the fluid inlet to force the piston out of the body. Use only low pressure to ease the piston out. If the air pressure is too high and the piston is forced out, the caliper and/or piston may be damaged.

Warning: Never place your fingers in front of the piston in an attempt to catch or protect it when applying compressed air, as serious injury could result.

7 Using a wooden or plastic tool, remove the dust seal from the caliper bore. If a metal tool is being used, take great care not to damage the caliper bore.

8 Remove the piston seal in the same way.

9 Clean the piston and bore with denatured alcohol, clean brake fluid or brake system cleaner.

Caution: Do not, under any circumstances, use a petroleum-based solvent to clean brake parts. If compressed air is available, use it to dry the parts thoroughly (make sure it's filtered and unlubricated).

10 Inspect the caliper bore and piston for signs of corrosion, nicks and burrs and loss of plating. If surface defects are present, the caliper assembly must be replaced. If the caliper is in bad shape the master cylinder should also be checked.

11 If the necessary measuring equipment is available, compare the dimensions of the caliper bore and piston to those given in this Chapter's Specifications, replacing any component that is worn beyond the service limit.

12 Temporarily install the caliper to its mounting bracket. Make sure that it slides smoothly in-and-out and check that the slider pin and the slider bushing are a snug fit in their bores. If not check the slider pin/bushing and their bores for burrs or excessive wear, replacing worn components as necessary. The slider pin/bushing boots should be replaced as a matter of course.

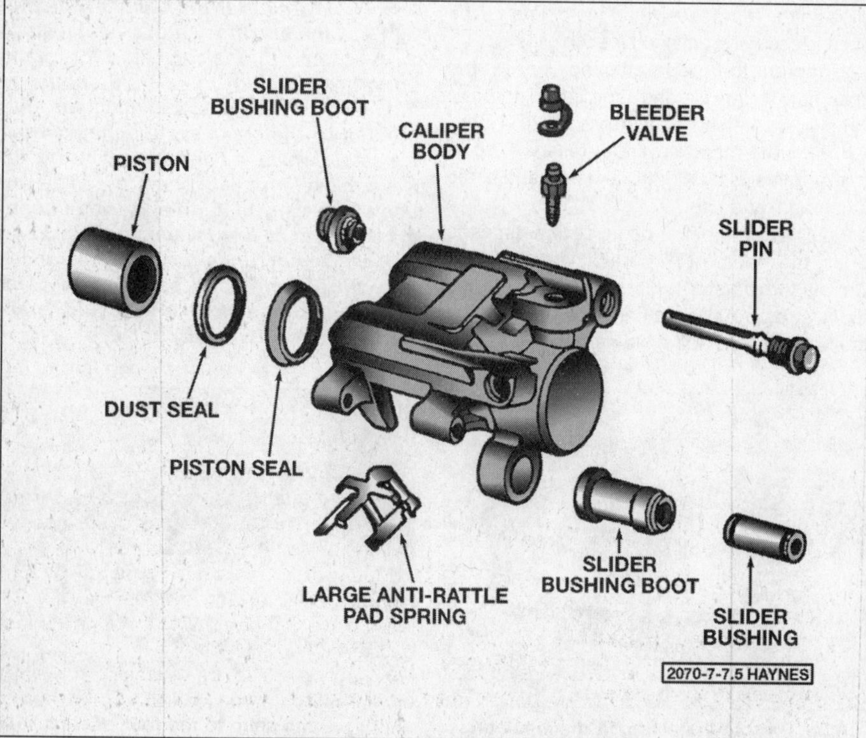

7.5 Exploded view of the rear brake caliper

13 Lubricate the new piston seal with clean brake fluid and install it in the groove in the caliper bore.

14 Lubricate the new dust seal with clean brake fluid and install it in the groove in the caliper bore.

15 Lubricate the piston with clean brake fluid and install it in the caliper bore. Using your thumbs, push the piston all the way in, making sure it enters the bore squarely.

16 If the slider pin has been removed, apply a few drops of thread locking compound to its threads then fit the pin to the caliper body and tighten it to the specified torque setting.

17 Install the new slider pin/bush boots.

18 Apply a thin coat of PBC (poly butyl cuprysil) grease, or silicone grease designed for high-temperature brake applications, to the slider pin and bushing. Slide the slider bushing into position in the caliper body ensuring the boot is correctly seated in the groove on each end of the bushing.

Installation

19 Slide the caliper into position on the mounting bracket. Make sure the slider pin boot is correctly located in its grooves on the body and bracket.

20 Install the anti-rattle springs and brake pads as described in Section 6.

21 Connect the brake hose to the caliper, using new sealing washers on each side of the fitting. Tighten the banjo fitting bolt to the torque setting listed in this Chapter's Specifications.

22 Fill the fluid reservoir up to the level line with DOT 4 brake fluid and bleed the hydraulic system as described in Section 11.

23 Check for leaks and thoroughly test the operation of the brake before riding the motorcycle on the road. Check the rear brake fluid level (see *'Daily (pre-ride) checks'*).

8 Rear brake disc - inspection, removal and installation

Inspection

1 Refer to Section 4 of this Chapter, noting that the dial indicator should be attached to the swingarm.

Removal

2 Remove the wheel (see Section 15).

Caution: Don't lay the wheel down and allow it to rest on the disc - the disc could become warped. Set the wheel on wood blocks so the disc doesn't support the weight of the wheel.

3 Mark the relationship of the disc to the wheel, so it can be installed in the same position. Remove the bolts that retain the disc to the wheel. Loosen the bolts a little at a time, in a criss-cross pattern, to avoid distorting the disc then remove the disc **(see illustration)**.

Installation

4 Position the disc on the wheel, aligning the previously applied matchmarks (if you're reinstalling the original disc). Make sure the arrow (stamped on the disc) marking the direction of rotation is pointing in the proper direction and is on the outer face of the disc **(see illustration 4.9)**.

5 Clean the threads of the disc bolts and apply a suitable thread locking compound to the threads of each bolt.

6 Install the bolts and tighten them evenly and progressively to the torque setting listed in this Chapter's Specifications. Clean off all grease from the brake disc using acetone or brake system cleaner. If a new brake disc has been installed, remove any protective coating from its working surfaces.

7 Install the wheel as described in Section 15.

8 Operate the brake pedal several times to bring the pads into contact with the disc. Check the operation of the brake carefully before riding the motorcycle.

9 Rear brake master cylinder - removal, overhaul and installation

1 If the master cylinder is leaking fluid, or if the pedal does not produce a firm feel when the brake is applied, and bleeding the brakes does not help, master cylinder overhaul is recommended. Before disassembling the master cylinder, read through the entire procedure and make sure that you have the correct rebuild kit.

2 Also, you will need some new, clean brake fluid of the recommended type, some clean shop towels and internal snap-ring pliers.

Caution: Disassembly, overhaul and reassembly of the brake master cylinder must be done in a spotlessly clean work area to avoid contamination and possible failure of the brake hydraulic system components.

Removal

3 Set the bike on its centerstand. Remove the right side cover (see Chapter 8 if necessary).

4 Unscrew the banjo union bolt from the top of the master cylinder. Discard the sealing washers on each side of the fitting. Wrap the end of the hose in a clean shop towel and suspend the hose in an upright position or bend it down carefully and place the open end in a clean container. The objective is to prevent excessive loss of brake fluid, fluid spills and system contamination.

5 Loosen the master cylinder mounting bolts then remove the right footpeg bracket retaining bolts (see Chapter 6).

6 Move the footpeg bracket slightly away from the motorcycle then unhook and remove the brake light switch spring and the brake pedal return spring. Free the brake light switch from its mounting bracket.

8.3 Rear brake disc is retained by four bolts (arrows)

7 Remove the cotter pin (split pin) and slide out the clevis pin securing the master cylinder to the brake pedal.

8 Using snap-ring pliers, remove the snap-ring then remove the washer and slide of the brake pedal. Recover the dust seals from each side of the pedal.

9 Remove the bolt securing the master cylinder reservoir to the frame. Unscrew the reservoir cap and pour the contents into a container.

10 Remove the snap-ring then disengage the reservoir hose from the master cylinder and remove the reservoir assembly. Discard the O-ring.

11 Remove the master cylinder mounting bolts and separate it from the footpeg bracket.

Overhaul

12 Tap out the lock pin **(see illustration)**.

13 Hold the clevis with a pair of pliers and loosen the locknut. Mark the position of the clevis on the pushrod as an aid for installation, then unscrew the clevis and locknut from the pushrod. Carefully remove the rubber dust boot from the pushrod.

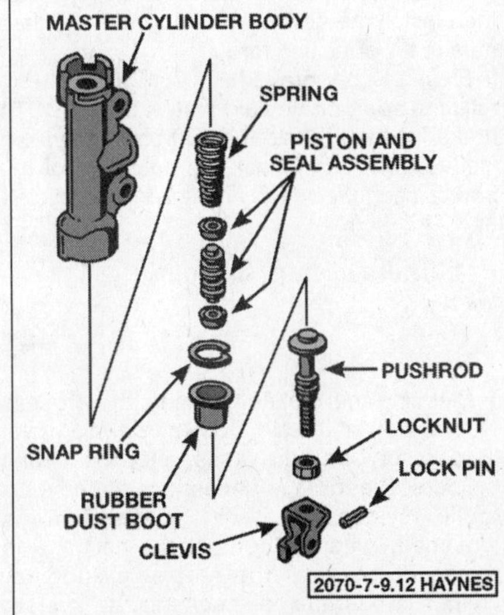

9.12 Exploded view of the rear brake master cylinder

14 Depress the pushrod and, using snap-ring pliers, remove the snap-ring. Slide out the piston assembly and spring. Lay the parts out in the proper order to prevent confusion during reassembly.

15 Clean all of the parts with brake system cleaner (available at auto parts stores), isopropyl alcohol or clean brake fluid.

Caution: Do not, under any circumstances, use a petroleum-based solvent to clean brake parts. If compressed air is available, use it to dry the parts thoroughly (make sure it's filtered and unlubricated).

16 Check the master cylinder bore for corrosion, scratches, nicks and score marks. If damage is evident, the master cylinder must be replaced with a new one. If the master cylinder is in poor condition, then the caliper should be checked as well.

17 If the necessary measuring equipment is available, compare the dimensions of the master cylinder bore and piston to those given in this Chapter's Specifications, replacing any component that it worn beyond the service limit.

18 A new piston and spring are included in the rebuild kit. Use them regardless of the condition of the old ones.

19 Before reassembling the master cylinder, soak the piston and the rubber cup seals in clean brake fluid for ten or fifteen minutes. Lubricate the master cylinder bore with clean brake fluid, then carefully insert the parts in the reverse order of disassembly, ensuring the tapered end of the spring is facing the piston. Make sure the lips on the cup seals do not turn inside out when they are slipped into the bore.

20 Depress the pushrod, then install the snap-ring (make sure the snap-ring is properly seated in the groove). Note that the snap-ring must be fitted with its chamfered edge towards the master cylinder piston.

21 Install the rubber dust boot (make sure the lip is seated properly in the groove).

22 Install the locknut and clevis to the end of the pushrod, setting the clevis at the position previously marked, or on S, T, V and W (1995 to 1998) models setting the distance between the lower mounting bolt hole and the clevis pin hole at 66 mm (2.6 in), then tighten the locknut. Install the lock pin.

Installation

23 Fit the master cylinder to the footpeg bracket and lightly tighten its retaining bolts.

24 Fit a new O-ring to the reservoir hose union and fit the union. Secure it in position with the snap-ring making sure it is correctly located in the master cylinder groove. Also ensure the chamfered edge of the snap-ring is facing the master cylinder.

25 Apply a few drops of locking compound to the threads of the master cylinder reservoir bolt then fit the bolt and tighten it to the specified torque setting.

26 Fit the dust seals to the brake pedal and apply a smear of grease to the pedal pivot.

27 Slide the pedal onto the bracket. Install the washer and fit the snap-ring, making sure it is correctly located in the bracket groove. Also ensure the chamfered edge of the snap-ring is facing the pedal.

28 Align the pedal with the master cylinder clevis and slide in the clevis pin. Secure the clevis pin in position with a new cotter pin (split pin).

29 Fit the brake light switch to its retaining bracket and hook the switch spring and pedal return spring onto the bracket.

30 Install the bracket assembly on the frame and securely tighten its retaining bolts.

31 Tighten the master cylinder mounting bolts to the specified torque.

32 Connect the banjo fitting to the top of the master cylinder, using a new sealing washer on each side of the fitting. Tighten the banjo fitting bolt to the specified torque setting.

33 Fill the fluid reservoir up to the level line with DOT 4 brake fluid and bleed the system following the procedure in Section 11. Install the right side cover (see Chapter 8, if necessary).

34 Check the position of the brake pedal and adjust the brake light switch (see Chapter 1). Check the operation of the brake carefully before riding the motorcycle. Check the rear brake fluid level (see *'Daily (pre-ride) checks'*).

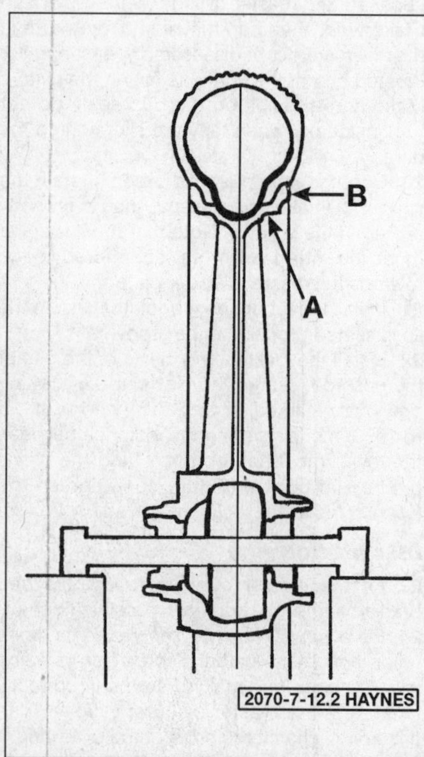

12.2 Use a dial indicator to measure wheel runout

A Radial runout
B Axial runout

10 Brake pipe and hoses - inspection and replacement

Inspection

1 Once a week, or if the motorcycle is used less frequently, before every ride, check the condition of the brake hoses.

2 Twist and flex the rubber hoses while looking for cracks, bulges and seeping fluid. Check extra carefully around the areas where the hoses connect with the banjo fittings, as these are common areas for hose failure.

3 Inspect the metal banjo union fittings connected to brake hoses. If the fittings are rusted, scratched or cracked, replace them.

4 Inspect the metal pipe linking the two front brake caliper hoses. If the plating on the metal pipe is chipped or scratched, the lines may rust. If the fittings are rusted, scratched or cracked, replace the pipe assembly.

Replacement

5 The brake hoses have banjo union fittings on each end of the hose. Cover the surrounding area with plenty of shop towels and unscrew the banjo bolt on each end of the hose. Detach the hose from any clips that may be present and remove the hose. Discard the sealing washers.

6 Position the new hose, making sure it isn't twisted or otherwise strained, between the two components. Make sure the metal tube portion of the banjo fitting is located between the protrusions on the component it's connected to, if equipped. Install the banjo bolts, using new sealing washers on both sides of the fittings, and tighten them to the specified torque setting.

7 The metal pipe has a flare nut at each end, and can be removed once both nuts have been slackened. Apply a few drops of locking compound to each of the flare nut threads then install the new pipe and tighten the flare nuts to the specified torque.

8 Flush the old brake fluid from the system, refill the appropriate fluid reservoir with DOT4 brake fluid and bleed the air from the system (see Section 11). Check the operation of the brakes carefully before riding the motorcycle.

11 Brake system bleeding

1 Bleeding the brakes is simply the process of removing all the air bubbles from the brake fluid reservoirs, the lines and the brake calipers. Bleeding is necessary whenever a brake system hydraulic connection is loosened, when a component or hose is replaced, or when the master cylinder or caliper is overhauled. Leaks in the system may also allow air to enter, but leaking brake fluid will reveal their presence and warn you of the need for repair.

2 To bleed the brakes, you will need some new, clean DOT 4 brake fluid, a length of clear vinyl or plastic tubing, a small container partially filled with clean brake fluid, some shop towels and a wrench to fit the brake caliper bleeder valves.

3 Cover the fuel tank and other painted components to prevent damage in the event that brake fluid is spilled.

4 Remove the reservoir cap or cover and slowly pump the brake lever or pedal a few times, until no air bubbles can be seen floating up from the holes at the bottom of the reservoir. Doing this bleeds the air from the master cylinder end of the line. Reinstall the reservoir cap or cover.

5 Attach one end of the clear vinyl or plastic tubing to the bleeder valve and submerge the other end in the brake fluid in the container.

6 Remove the reservoir cap or cover and check the fluid level. Do not allow the fluid level to drop below the lower mark during the bleeding process.

7 Carefully pump the brake lever or pedal three or four times and hold it in (front) or down (rear) while opening the caliper bleeder valve. When the valve is opened, brake fluid will flow out of the caliper into the clear tubing and the lever will move toward the handlebar or the pedal will move down.

8 Retighten the bleeder valve, then release the brake lever or pedal gradually. Repeat the process until no air bubbles are visible in the brake fluid leaving the caliper and the lever or pedal is firm when applied.

9 Replace the reservoir cap or cover, wipe up any spilled brake fluid and check the entire system for leaks.

If bleeding is difficult, it may be necessary to let the brake fluid in the system stabilize for a few hours (it may be aerated). Repeat the bleeding procedure when the tiny bubbles in the system have settled out.

12 Wheels - inspection and repair

1 Place the motorcycle on the centerstand, then clean the wheels thoroughly to remove mud and dirt that may interfere with the inspection procedure or mask defects. Make a general check of the wheels and tires as described in *'Daily (pre-ride) checks'*.

2 With the motorcycle on the centerstand and the wheel in the air, attach a dial indicator to the fork slider or the swingarm and position its stem against the side of the rim **(see illustration)**. Spin the wheel slowly and check the side-to-side (axial) runout of the rim, then compare your readings with the value listed in this Chapter's Specifications. In order to accurately check radial runout with the dial indicator, the wheel would have to be

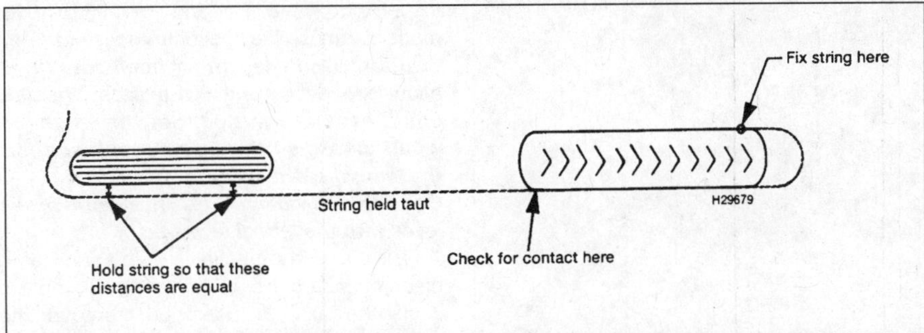

13.5 Checking wheel alignment with string

removed from the machine. With the axle clamped in a vise, the wheel can be rotated to check the runout.

3 An easier, though slightly less accurate, method is to attach a stiff wire pointer to the fork slider or the swingarm and position the end a fraction of an inch from the wheel (where the wheel and tire join). If the wheel is true, the distance from the pointer to the rim will be constant as the wheel is rotated. **Note:** *If wheel runout is excessive, check the wheel bearings very carefully before replacing the wheel.*

4 The wheels should also be visually inspected for cracks, flat spots on the rim and other damage. Since tubeless tires are fitted, look very closely for dents in the area where the tire bead contacts the rim. Dents in this area may prevent complete sealing of the tire against the rim, which leads to deflation of the tire over a period of time.

5 If damage is evident, or if runout in either direction is excessive, the wheel will have to be replaced with a new one. Never attempt to repair a damaged cast aluminum wheel.

13 Wheels - alignment check

1 Misalignment of the wheels, which may be due to a cocked rear wheel or a bent frame or triple clamps, can cause strange and possibly serious handling problems. If the frame or triple clamps are at fault, repair by a frame specialist or replacement with new parts are the only alternatives.

2 To check the alignment you will need an assistant, a length of string or a perfectly straight piece of wood and a ruler graduated in 1/64 inch increments. A plumb bob or other suitable weight will also be required.

3 Place the motorcycle on the centerstand, then measure the width of both tires at their widest points. Subtract the smaller measurement from the larger measurement, then divide the difference by two. The result is the amount of offset that should exist between the front and rear tires on both sides.

4 If a string is used, have your assistant hold one end of it about half way between the floor and the rear axle, touching the rear sidewall of the tire.

5 Run the other end of the string forward and pull it tight so that it is roughly parallel to the floor. Slowly bring the string into contact with the front sidewall of the rear tire, then turn the front wheel until it is parallel with the string. Measure the distance from the front tire sidewall to the string **(see illustration)**.

6 Repeat the procedure on the other side of the motorcycle. The distance from the front tire sidewall to the string should be equal on both sides.

7 As was previously pointed out, a perfectly straight length of wood may be substituted for the string. The procedure is the same **(see illustration)**.

8 If the distance between the string and tire is greater on one side, or if the rear wheel appears to be cocked, refer to Chapter 6, Swingarm bearings - check, and make sure the swingarm is tight.

9 If the front-to-back alignment is correct, the wheels still may be out of alignment vertically.

10 Using the plumb bob, or other suitable weight, and a length of string, check the rear wheel to make sure it is vertical. To do this, hold the string against the tire upper sidewall and allow the weight to settle just off the floor. When the string touches both the upper and lower tire sidewalls and is perfectly straight, the wheel is vertical. If it is not, place thin spacers under one leg of the centerstand.

11 Once the rear wheel is vertical, check the front wheel in the same manner. If both wheels are not perfectly vertical, the frame and/or major suspension components are bent.

14 Front wheel - removal and installation

Removal

1 Place the motorcycle on the centerstand, then raise the front wheel off the ground by tying down the rear of the machine. If this is not possible, remove the lower fairing panels (see Chapter 8) and place a floor jack, with a wood block on the jack head, under the engine; raise the jack to lift the wheel off the ground.

2 Unscrew the two bracket retaining bolts then slide the left brake caliper off the disc

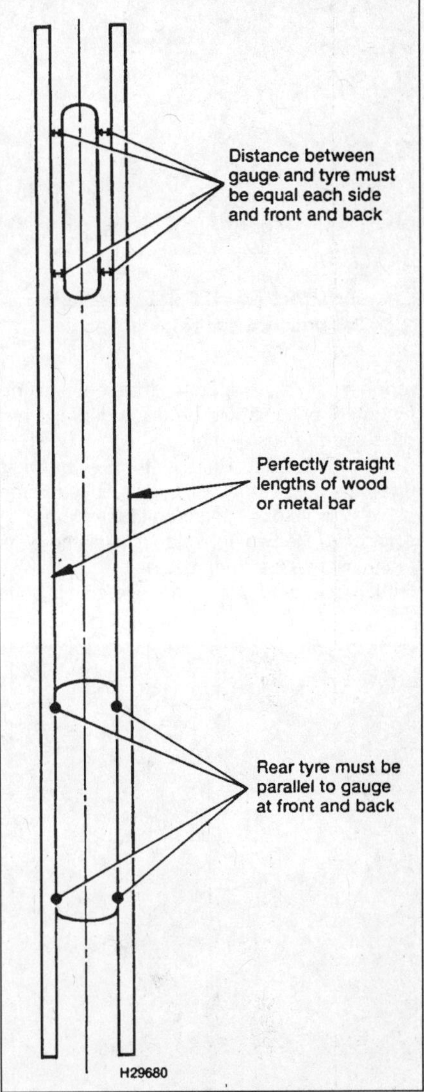

13.7 Checking wheel alignment with a straight-edge

and support the caliper with a piece of wire, taking care not to place any undue strain on the hydraulic hose **(see illustration)**. Don't disconnect the brake hose from the caliper. Note that on S, T, V and W (1995 to 1998)

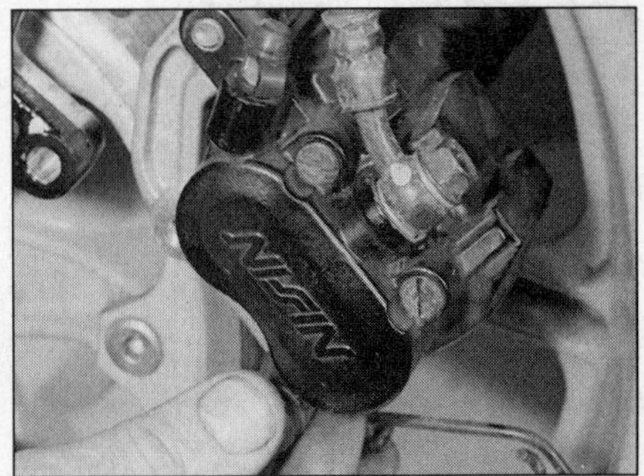

14.2 To ease front wheel removal, undo the two mounting bolts and release the left caliper bracket from the fork

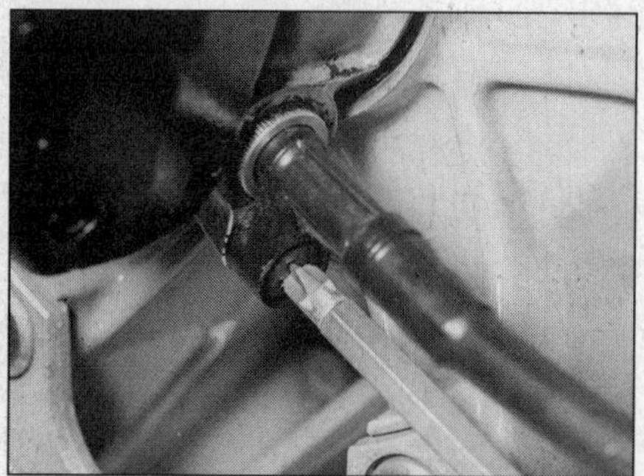
14.3a Unscrew the retaining screw . . .

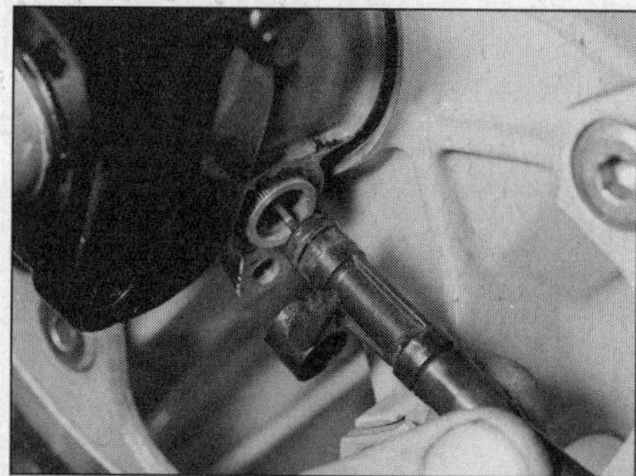

14.3b . . . and detach the speedometer cable from its drive unit

models, Honda specify that the caliper mounting bolts should be discarded and new ones used for installation.

3 On M, N, P and R (1991 to 1994) models, undo the screw and detach the speedometer cable from its drive unit **(see illustrations)**.

4 Slacken the two right side axle clamp bolts, then unscrew the front axle bolt.

5 Slacken the two left side axle clamp bolts. Support the wheel then pull out the axle and carefully lower the wheel. Disengage the right brake caliper from the disc and slide the caliper outwards to gain the necessary clearance to withdraw the wheel from the forks **(see illustrations)**.

6 Remove the spacer from the right side of the wheel. On M, N, P and R (1991 to 1994) models remove the speedometer drive from the left side. On S, T, V and W (1995 to 1998) models, remove the spacer from the left side.

Caution: Don't lay the wheel down and allow it to rest on one of the discs - the disc could become warped. Set the wheel on wood blocks so the disc doesn't support the weight of the wheel.

Caution: Do not operate the front brake lever with the wheel removed.

7 Roll the axle on a flat surface such as a piece of plate glass. If it's bent at all, replace it. If the axle is corroded, remove the corrosion with fine emery cloth.

8 Check the condition of the wheel bearings (see Section 16).

Installation

9 On M, N, P and R (1991 to 1994) models fit the speedometer drive to the left side wheel aligning its drive gear slots with the driveplate tabs. On S, T, V and W (1995 to 1998) models, install the spacer in the left side. On all models install the spacer in the right side of the wheel **(see illustrations)**.

14.5a Withdraw the axle from the left side of the bike . . .

14.5b . . . and roll the front wheel out from between the forks

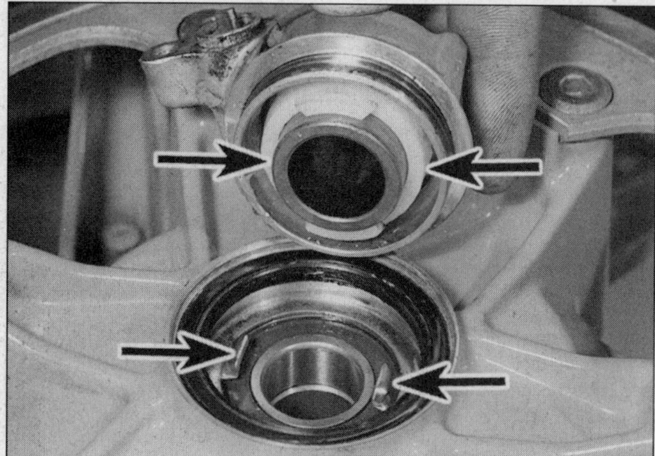
14.9a Align the speedometer drive gear slots with the driveplate tabs (arrows) on installation

14.9b Do not omit the spacer from the right side of the front wheel

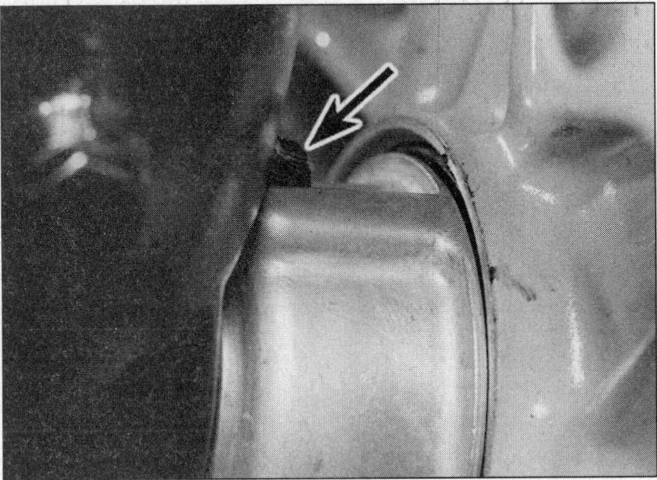

14.12a Rotate the speedometer drive until its lug abuts the rear of the fork slider lug (arrow) . . .

14.12b . . . then tighten the left clamp bolts to the specified torque

14.13a Install the axle bolt . . .

14.13b . . . and tighten it to the specified torque setting

10 Maneuver the wheel into position. Apply a thin coat of grease to the axle.

11 Engage the right brake disc with the caliper and lift the wheel into position making sure the spacer remains in place.

12 On M, N, P and R (1991 to 1994) models, position the speedometer drive lug against the rear of the lug on the fork slider. Slide the axle into position, then tighten the left axle clamp bolts to the torque setting listed in this Chapter's Specifications **(see illustrations)**.

13 Install the axle bolt and tighten it to the specified torque setting **(see illustrations)**.

14 Install the left brake caliper and tighten its mounting bolts to the specified torque setting. On S, T, V and W (1995 to 1998) models, Honda specify that new caliper bolts should be used.

15 On M, N, P and R (1991 to 1994) models, connect the speedometer cable to the drive, aligning the inner cable slot with the drive dog, and securely tighten its retaining screw.

16 Remove the support from under the engine and rest the front wheel on the ground. Pump the front forks a few times to settle all components in position and tighten the right axle clamp bolts to the specified torque setting.

17 Using feeler gauges, check the clearance between each brake disc and its relevant

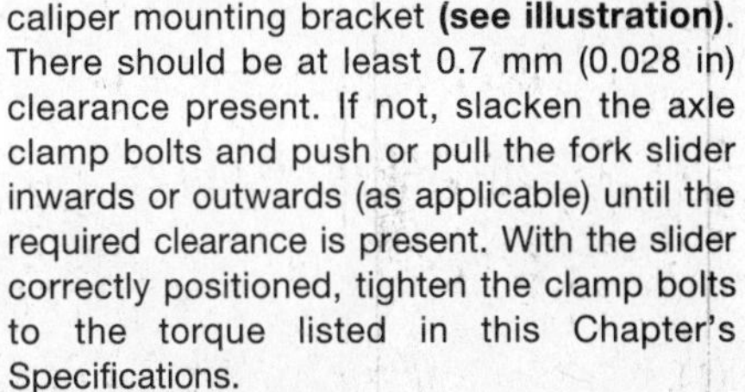

caliper mounting bracket **(see illustration)**. There should be at least 0.7 mm (0.028 in) clearance present. If not, slacken the axle clamp bolts and push or pull the fork slider inwards or outwards (as applicable) until the required clearance is present. With the slider correctly positioned, tighten the clamp bolts to the torque listed in this Chapter's Specifications.

18 Apply the front brake, pump the forks up and down several times and check for proper brake operation.

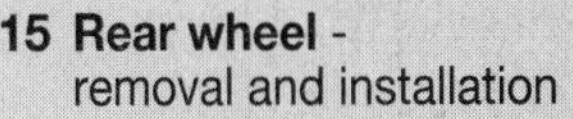

15 Rear wheel - removal and installation

Removal

1 Set the bike on its centerstand.

2 Undo the brake caliper lower mounting bolt. Release the brake hose from its retaining clips then pivot the caliper away from the disc and slide it off its pin. Tie the caliper to the frame to prevent any strain being placed on the hydraulic hose. Recover the rubber boot from the slider pin. Remove the pad spring from the caliper bracket for safe-keeping **(see illustrations)**.

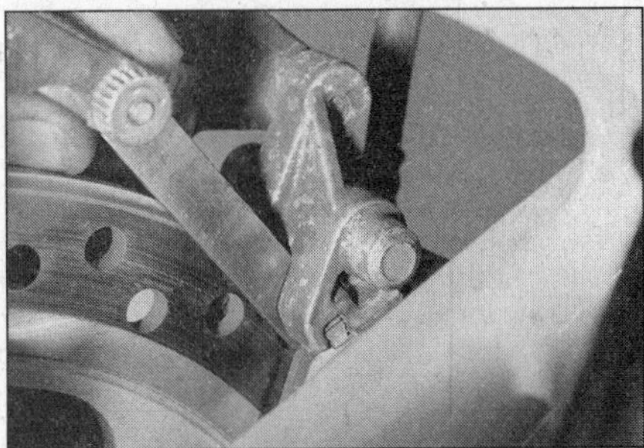

14.17 Use a feeler blade to check the caliper bracket-to-disc clearance - see text

15.2a Unscrew the rear brake caliper mounting bolt . . .

15.2b . . . then pivot the caliper clear of the disc, slide it off its pin and recover the pad spring (arrow)

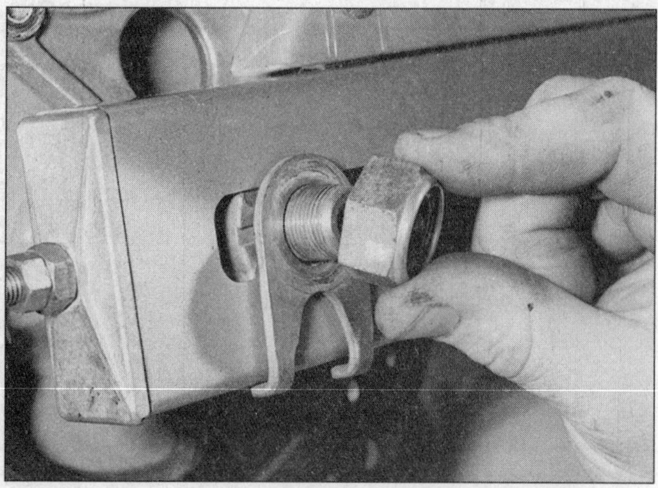
15.4 Unscrew the rear axle nut and remove the washer

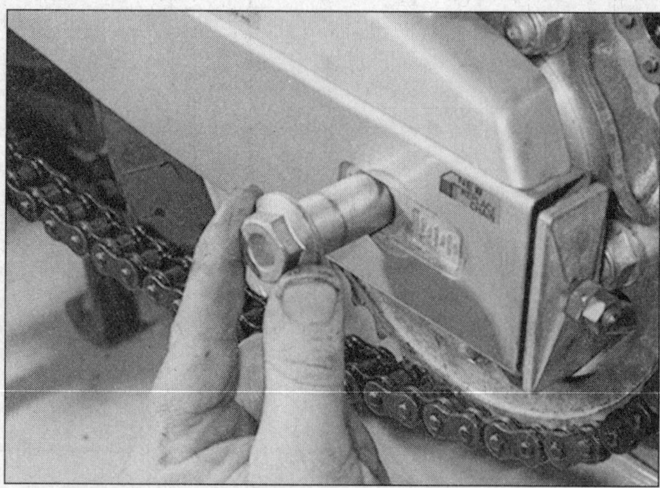
15.5 Withdraw the axle from the left side of the bike and lower the rear wheel to the ground

15.6a Disengage the drive chain from the sprocket and remove the wheel from the swingarm

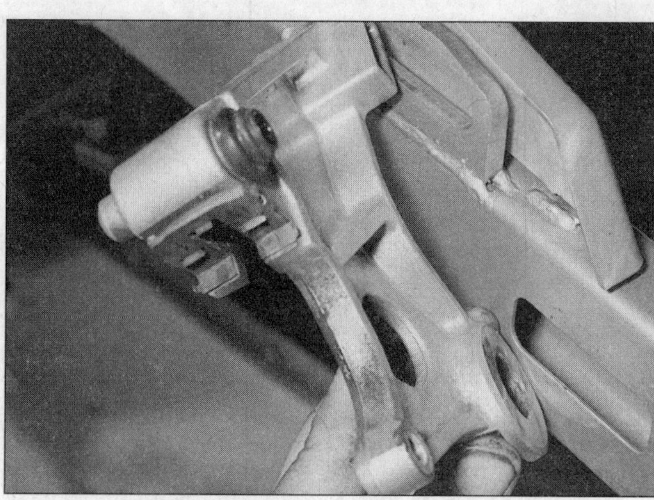
15.6b With the wheel removed, remove the caliper mounting bracket from the swingarm

3 Slacken the locknuts and fully slacken the drive chain adjuster nuts.

4 Unscrew the rear axle nut and remove it along with its washer **(see illustration)**.

5 Support the wheel then slide out the axle and lower the wheel to the ground **(see illustration)**.

6 Disengage the chain from the sprocket and remove the wheel from the swingarm, being careful not to lose the spacers on each side of the hub **(see illustration)**.

Caution: Don't lay the wheel down and allow it to rest on the disc or the sprocket - they could become warped. Set the wheel on wood blocks so the disc or the sprocket doesn't support the weight of the wheel. Do not operate the brake pedal with the wheel removed.

Remove the brake caliper mounting bracket from the swingarm **(see illustration)**.

7 Check the axle for straightness by rolling it on a flat surface such as a piece of plate glass (if the axle is corroded, first remove the corrosion with fine emery cloth). If the axle is bent at all, replace it.

8 Check the condition of the wheel bearings (see Section 16).

15.9a Apply grease to the seal lips and install the left . . .

15.9b . . . and right spacers in the rear wheel

Installation

9 Apply a thin coat of grease to the seal lips, then slide the spacers into their proper positions on both sides of the hub **(see illustrations)**. On S, T, V and W (1995 to 1998) models, the left-side spacer is shouldered.

10 Ensure both chain adjusters are correctly installed with their marked faces outwards and locate the brake caliper mounting bracket in its swingarm slot **(see illustration)**.

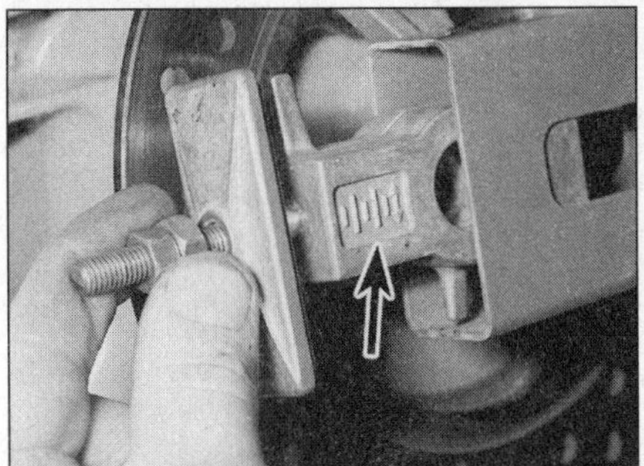

15.10 Ensure that each drive chain adjuster is installed in the swingarm with its markings (arrow) facing outwards

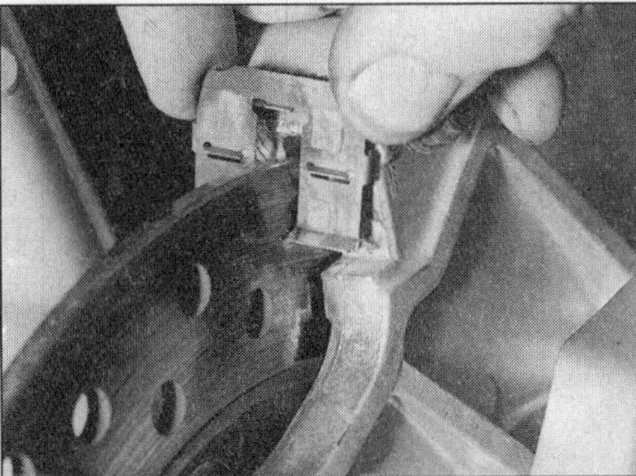

15.14 Locate the anti-rattle spring on the caliper bracket making sure it is the correct way around

15.15 With the rear caliper correctly installed, tighten its mounting bolt to the specified torque

11 Apply a thin coat of grease to the axle and slide the axle into position in the left chain adjuster.

12 Engage the drive chain with the sprocket and lift the wheel into position ensuring both spacers remain in position and the brake caliper mounting bracket is correctly positioned.

13 Slide the axle into position and fit the washer and axle nut, but do not tighten yet.

14 Fit the pad anti-rattle spring to the caliper bracket and slide the caliper onto its pin, making sure the rubber boot is correctly located in its grooves **(see illustration)**.

15 Pivot the caliper back down into position, making sure the disc is correctly positioned between the pads. Fit the caliper mounting bolt and tighten it to the torque setting listed in this Chapter's Specifications **(see illustration)**. Ensure the brake hose is securely retained by all its relevant retaining clips.

16 Adjust the chain slack (see Chapter 1) and tighten the adjuster locknuts to the specified torque.

17 Tighten the axle nut to the specified torque setting.

18 Operate the brake pedal several times to bring the pads into contact with the disc. Check the operation of the brakes carefully before riding the motorcycle.

16 Wheel bearings - removal, inspection and installation

Front wheel bearings

Note: *Always replace the wheel bearings in pairs. Never replace the bearings individually.*

1 Remove the wheel (see Section 14).

2 Set the wheel on blocks so as not to allow the weight of the wheel to rest on the brake discs.

3 If not already done, remove the spacer from the right side of the wheel. On M, N, P and R (1991 to 1994) models remove the speedometer drive from the left side. On S, T, V and W (1995 to 1998) models, remove the spacer from the left side **(see illustrations)**.

4 Using a flat-bladed screwdriver, pry out the grease seal from the left side of the wheel, then on UK M, N, P and R (US 1991 to 1994) models withdraw the speedometer driveplate **(see illustration)**.

5 Pry out the grease seal from the right side of the wheel.

6 Using a metal rod (preferably a brass drift punch) inserted through the center of the hub bearing, tap evenly around the inner race of

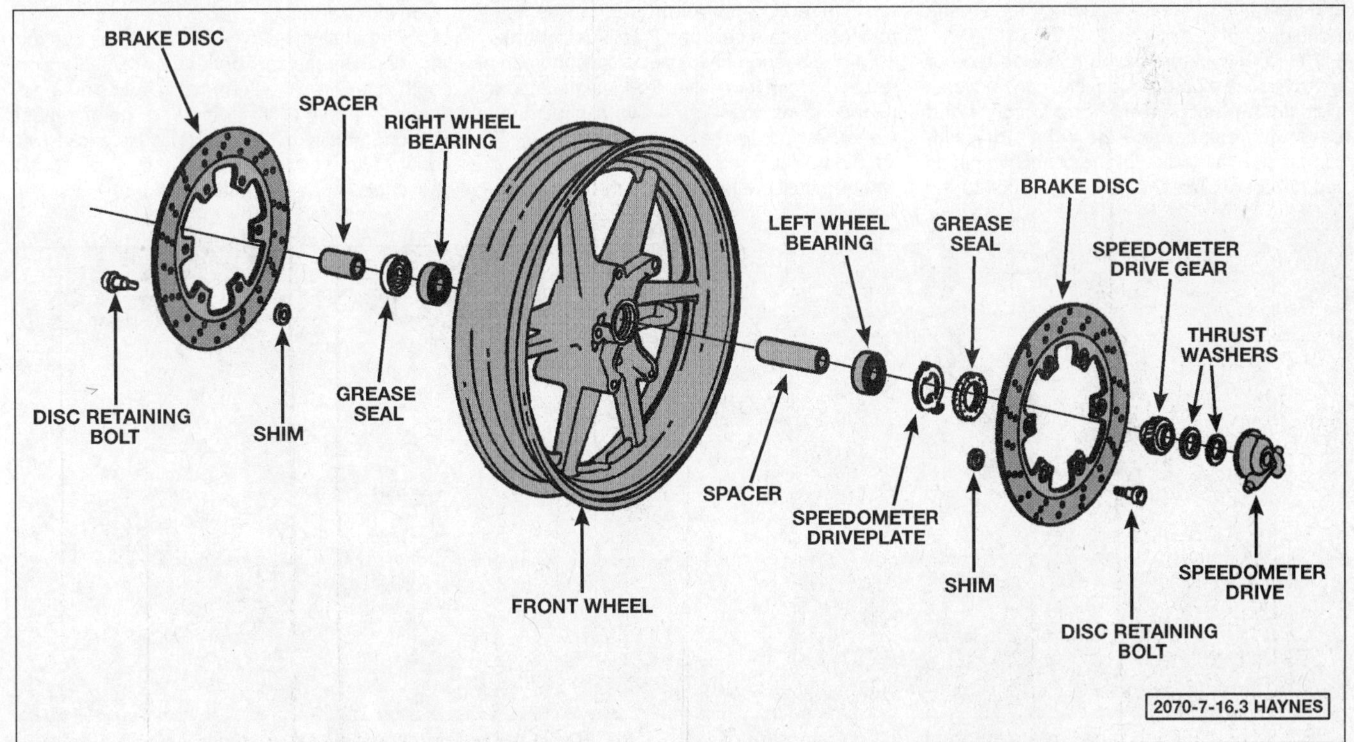

16.3a Front wheel and associated components - M, N, P and R (1991 to 1994) models

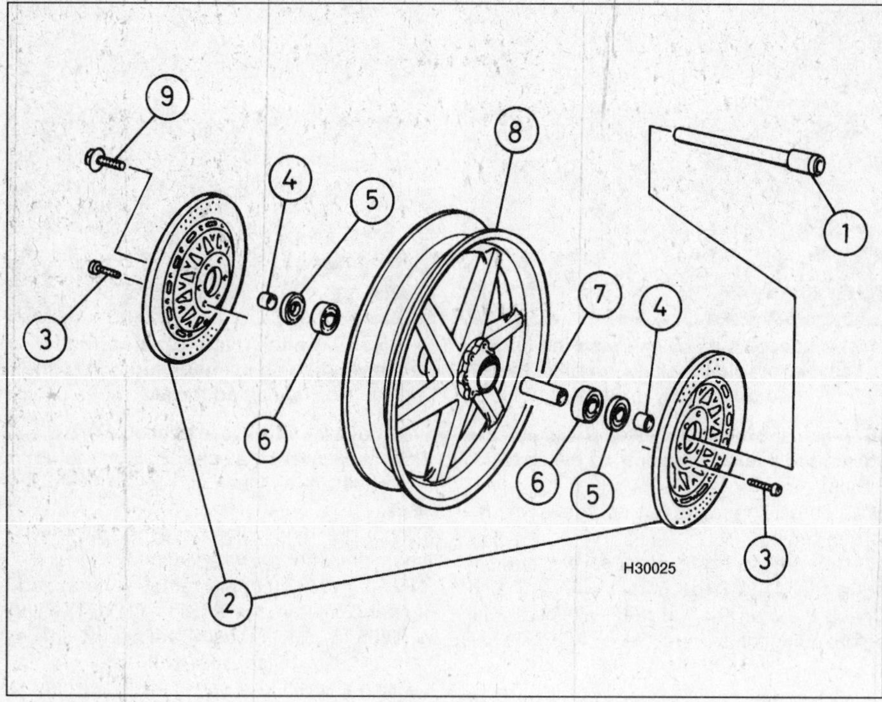

16.3b Front wheel and associated components - S, T, V and W (1995 to 1998) models

1 Axle
2 Brake discs
3 Brake disc bolts
4 Spacers
5 Grease seals
6 Bearings
7 Bearing spacer
8 Wheel
9 Axle bolt

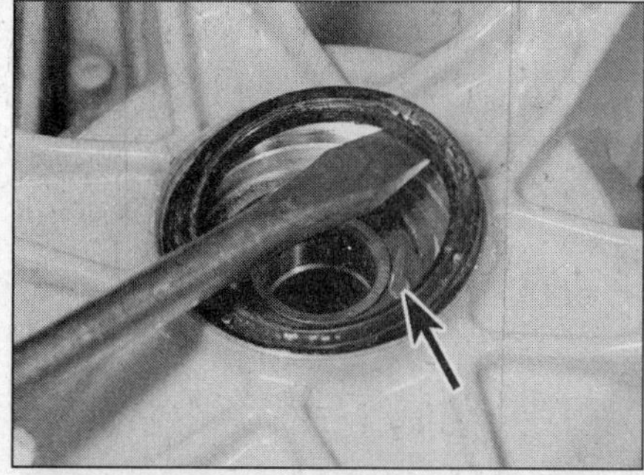

16.4 Pry out the grease seal and where fitted remove the speedometer driveplate (arrow)

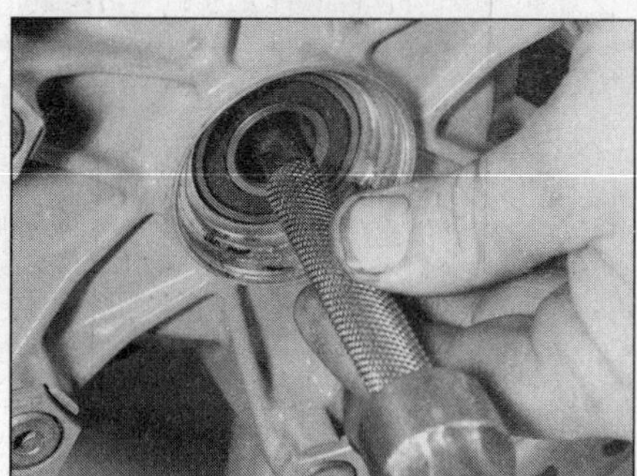

16.6 Drift the first wheel bearing out using a metal rod passed through from the opposite side of the wheel

the opposite bearing to drive it from the hub **(see illustration)**. The bearing spacer will also come out.

7 Lay the wheel on its other side and remove the remaining bearing using the same technique.

8 If the bearings are of the unsealed type or are only sealed on one side, clean them with a high flash-point solvent (one which won't leave any residue) and blow them dry with compressed air (don't let the bearings spin as you dry them). Apply a few drops of oil to the bearing. **Note:** *If the bearing is sealed on both sides don't attempt to clean it.*

9 Hold the outer race of the bearing and rotate the inner race - if the bearing doesn't turn smoothly, has rough spots or is noisy, replace it with a new one **(see illustration)**.

10 If the bearing checks out okay and can be re-used, wash it in solvent once again and dry it, then pack the bearing with high-quality wheel bearing grease.

11 Thoroughly clean the hub area of the wheel. Install the bearing into the recess in the hub, with the marked or sealed side facing out. Using a bearing driver or a socket large enough to contact the outer race of the bearing, drive it in until it's completely seated **(see illustration)**.

12 Turn the wheel over and install the bearing spacer. Unless the bearings are sealed on both sides, pack the remaining space no more than 2/3 full of high-melting point wheel bearing grease. Once the grease is packed in, driving the second bearing into place as described above **(see illustrations)**.

16.9 Check bearing races rotate smoothly without any sign of roughness

16.11 Drive the bearing squarely into the hub, using a tubular spacer which bears on the bearing's outer race . . .

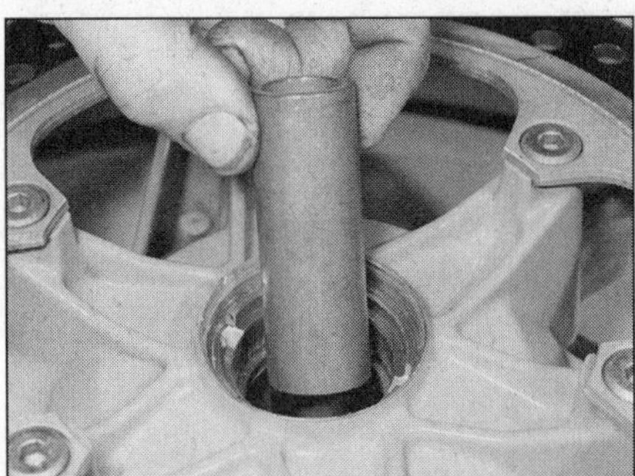

16.12a . . . then turn the wheel over, insert the spacer . . .

16.14 Press in a new grease seal

16.12b . . . and install the second bearing

13 On M, N, P and R (1991 to 1994) models, fit the speedometer driveplate to the left side of the wheel ensuring its locating tangs are correctly located in the hub slots **(see illustration)**.

14 Install new grease seals, using a seal driver, large socket or a flat piece of wood to drive them into place **(see illustration)**.

15 On M, N, P and R (1991 to 1994) models fit the speedometer drive to the left side wheel aligning its drive gear slots with the driveplate tabs. On S, T, V and W (1995 to 1998) models, install the spacer in the left side. On all models install the spacer in the right side of the wheel.

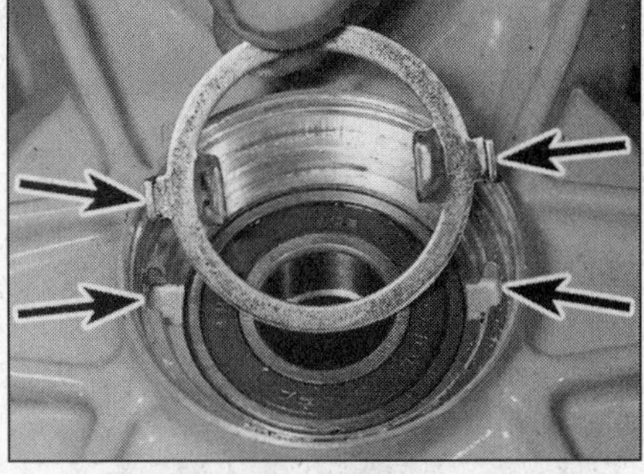

16.13 On M, N, P and R (1991 to 1994) models, fit the speedometer driveplate to the left side of the wheel, making sure its tangs are correctly seated in the hub slots (arrows)

Clean off all grease from the brake discs using acetone or brake system cleaner then install the wheel as described in Section 14.

Sprocket coupling bearing

16 Remove the rear wheel as described in Section 15 and remove the spacer from the center of the sprocket coupling (see Chapter 6) **(see illustration)**.

17 Lift the sprocket coupling away from the wheel leaving the rubber dampers in position in the wheel **(see illustration)**.

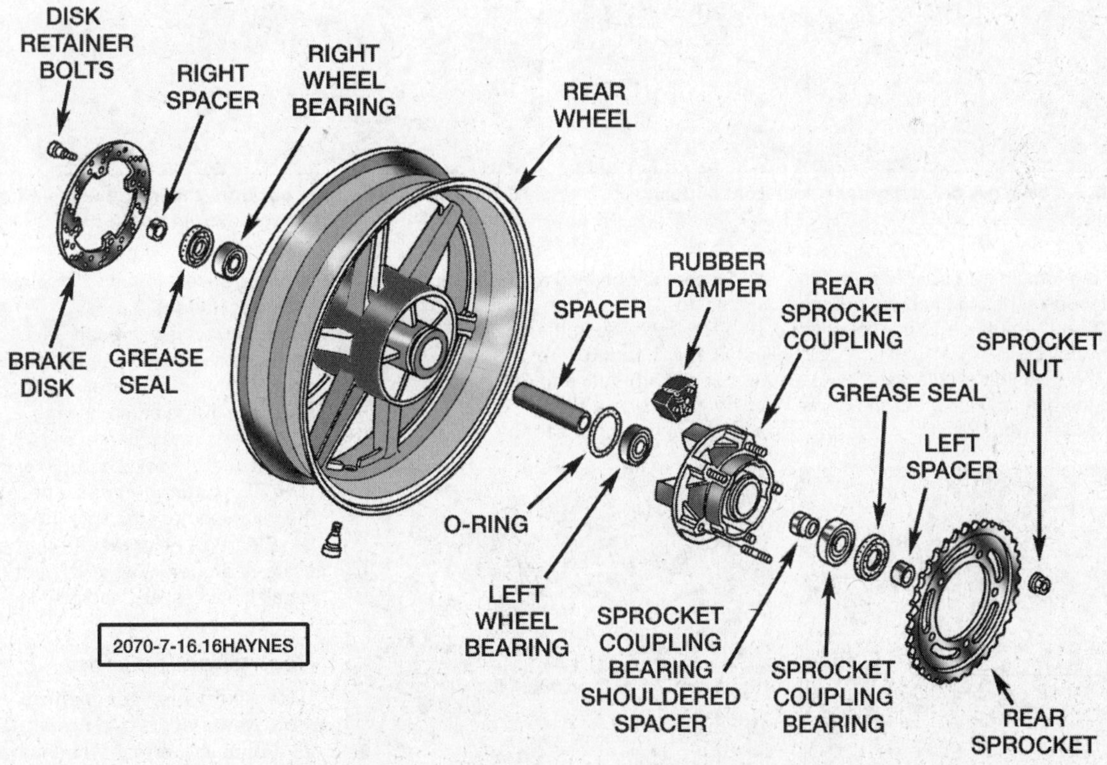

DISK RETAINER BOLTS
RIGHT SPACER
RIGHT WHEEL BEARING
REAR WHEEL
BRAKE DISK
GREASE SEAL
RUBBER DAMPER
SPACER
REAR SPROCKET COUPLING
SPROCKET NUT
GREASE SEAL
LEFT SPACER
O-RING
LEFT WHEEL BEARING
SPROCKET COUPLING BEARING SHOULDERED SPACER
SPROCKET COUPLING BEARING
REAR SPROCKET
2070-7-16.16HAYNES

16.16 Rear wheel and associated components

Note that on S, T, V and W (1995 to 1998) models the left spacer is shouldered

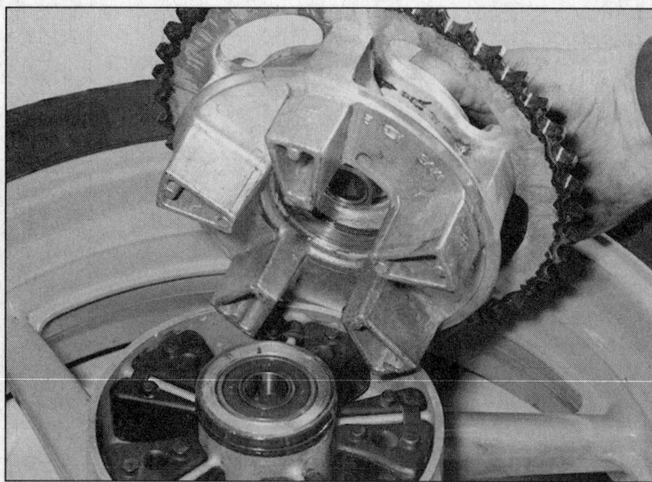
16.17 Remove the sprocket coupling ensuring the rubber dampers remain in position in the wheel

16.18a Remove the spacer from inside the coupling bearing . . .

16.18b . . . then pry out the grease seal from coupling

16.19 Drive the bearing out from the inside using a hammer and bearing driver or socket

18 Remove the shouldered spacer from the inside of the coupling bearing and pry out the grease seal from the outside of the coupling **(see illustrations)**.

19 Support the coupling on blocks of wood and drive out the bearing with a bearing driver or socket **(see illustration)**.

16.21 Drive the new coupling bearing into position using a large tubular drift which bears only on the bearing's outer race

20 Inspect the bearing as described above in Steps 8 to 10.

21 Thoroughly clean the bearing recess then install the bearing into the recess in the coupling, with the marked or sealed side facing out. Using a bearing driver or a socket large enough to contact the outer race of the bearing, drive it in until it's completely seated **(see illustration)**.

16.23 Ensure the hub O-ring is in position on the wheel and apply a smear of oil to it to aid installation

22 Install a new grease seal, using a seal driver, large socket or a flat piece of wood to drive them into place. Fit the shouldered spacer to inside of the bearing.

23 Apply a smear of grease to the hub O-ring and fit the sprocket coupling to the wheel **(see illustration)**. Grease the lip of the seal then fit the outer spacer to the coupling.

24 Clean off all grease from the brake disc using acetone or brake system cleaner then install the wheel as described in Section 15.

Rear wheel bearings

Note: *Always replace the wheel bearings in pairs. Never replace the bearings individually.*

25 Remove the rear wheel as described in Section 15.

26 Lift the sprocket coupling away from the wheel leaving the rubber dampers in position in the wheel. Take care not to lose the spacers from inside and outside of the sprocket coupling.

27 Remove the spacer from the right side of the wheel and pry out the grease seal.

28 Set the wheel on blocks so as not to allow the weight of the wheel to rest on the brake disc.

29 Remove, inspect and install the bearings as described above in Steps 6 to 12.

30 Install a new grease seal to the right side of the wheel, using a seal driver, large socket or a flat piece of wood to drive them into place. Fit the spacer into the seal.

31 Apply a smear of grease to the hub O-ring and fit the sprocket coupling to the wheel, ensuring both the spacers are in position.

32 Clean off all grease from the brake disc using acetone or brake system cleaner then install the wheel as described in Section 15.

17 Tires - general information and fitting

General information

1 The cast wheels fitted to all models are designed to take tubeless tires only.

2 Refer to *'Daily (pre-ride) checks'* at the beginning of this manual and to the scheduled checks in Chapter 1 for tire and wheel maintenance.

Fitting new tires

3 When selecting new tires, refer to the tire information label and the tire options listed in the owner's handbook. Ensure that front and rear tire types are compatible, the correct size and correct speed rating; if necessary seek advice from a Honda dealer or tire fitting specialist **(see illustration)**.

4 It is recommended that tires are fitted by a motorcycle tire specialist rather than attempted in the home workshop. This is particularly relevant in the case of tubeless tires because the force required to break the seal between the wheel rim and tire bead is substantial, and is usually beyond the capabilities of an individual working with normal tire levers. Additionally, the specialist will be able to balance the wheels after tire fitting.

5 In the case of tubeless tires, note that punctured tires can in some cases be repaired. Honda recommend that a repaired tire should not be used at speeds above 50 mph (80 kmh) for the first 24 hours after the repair, and thereafter not above 80 mph (130 kmh).

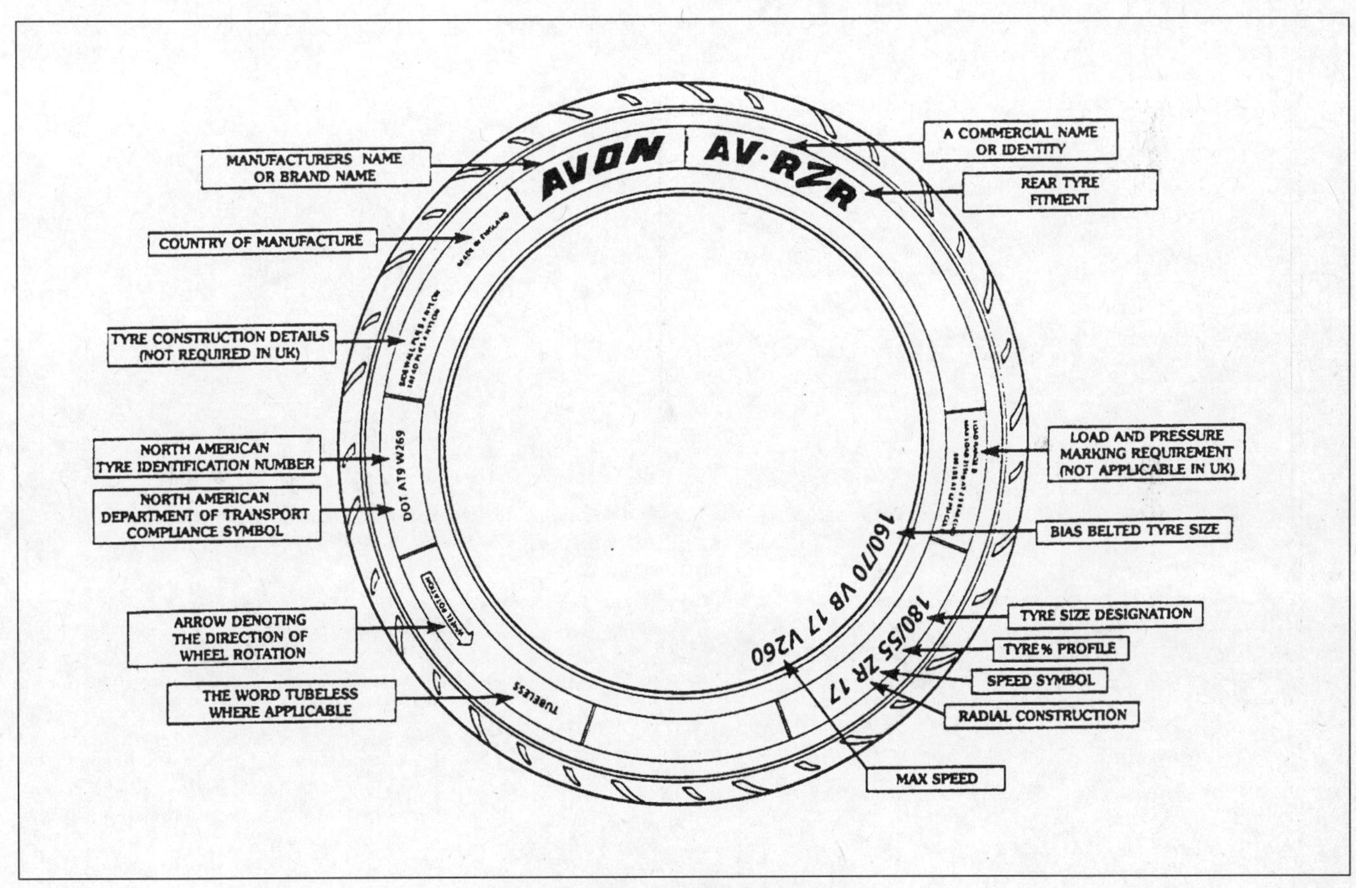

17.3 Common tire sidewall markings

Chapter 8
Fairing and bodywork

Contents

Degrees of difficulty

Easy, suitable for novice with little experience 

Fairly easy, suitable for beginner with some experience 

Fairly difficult, suitable for competent DIY mechanic 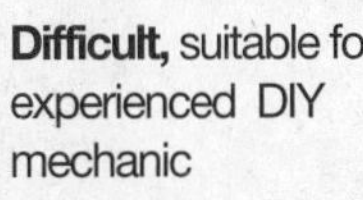

Difficult, suitable for experienced DIY mechanic 

Very difficult, suitable for expert DIY or professional

1 General information

This Chapter covers the procedures necessary to remove and install the fairing and other body parts. Since many service and repair operations on these motorcycles require the removal of the fairing and/or other body parts, the procedures are grouped here and referred to from other Chapters.

In the case of damage to the fairing or other body parts, it is usually necessary to remove the broken component and replace it with a new (or used) one. The material that the fairing and other body parts are composed of doesn't lend itself to conventional repair techniques. There are however some shops that specialize in 'plastic welding', so it may be worthwhile seeking the advice of one of these specialists before consigning an expensive component to the bin.

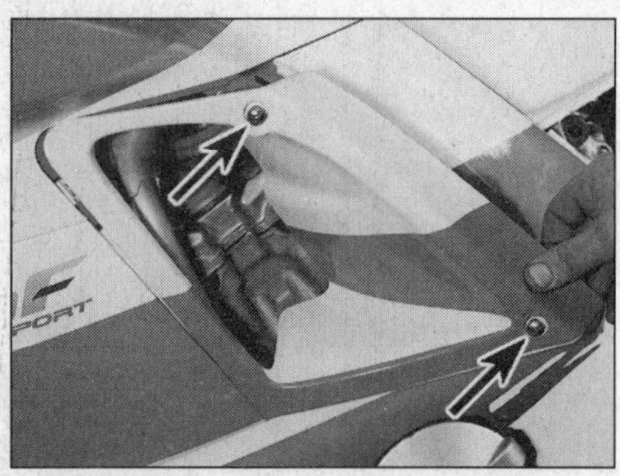

2.3a Undo the two screws (arrows) and remove the access cover

2 Fairing panels - removal and installation

Removal

1 Set the bike on its centerstand.

Lower fairing panels - M, N, P and R (1991 to 1994) models

2 Remove the side covers as described in Section 6.

3 Remove the access cover from both the left and right sides of the fairing. Each panel is retained by two screws **(see illustrations)**.

4 Undo the two screws and remove the headlight access cover from the base of the upper fairing. Take great care not to break the cover tabs when releasing the cover from the fairing mounting stay **(see illustration)**.

5 Release the two fasteners, situated at the bottom of the fairing front panels, securing the left and right lower fairing panels together, and the fastener securing each lower fairing panel to the underside of the upper fairing. Each fastener is released by pulling out the center pin **(see illustrations)**.

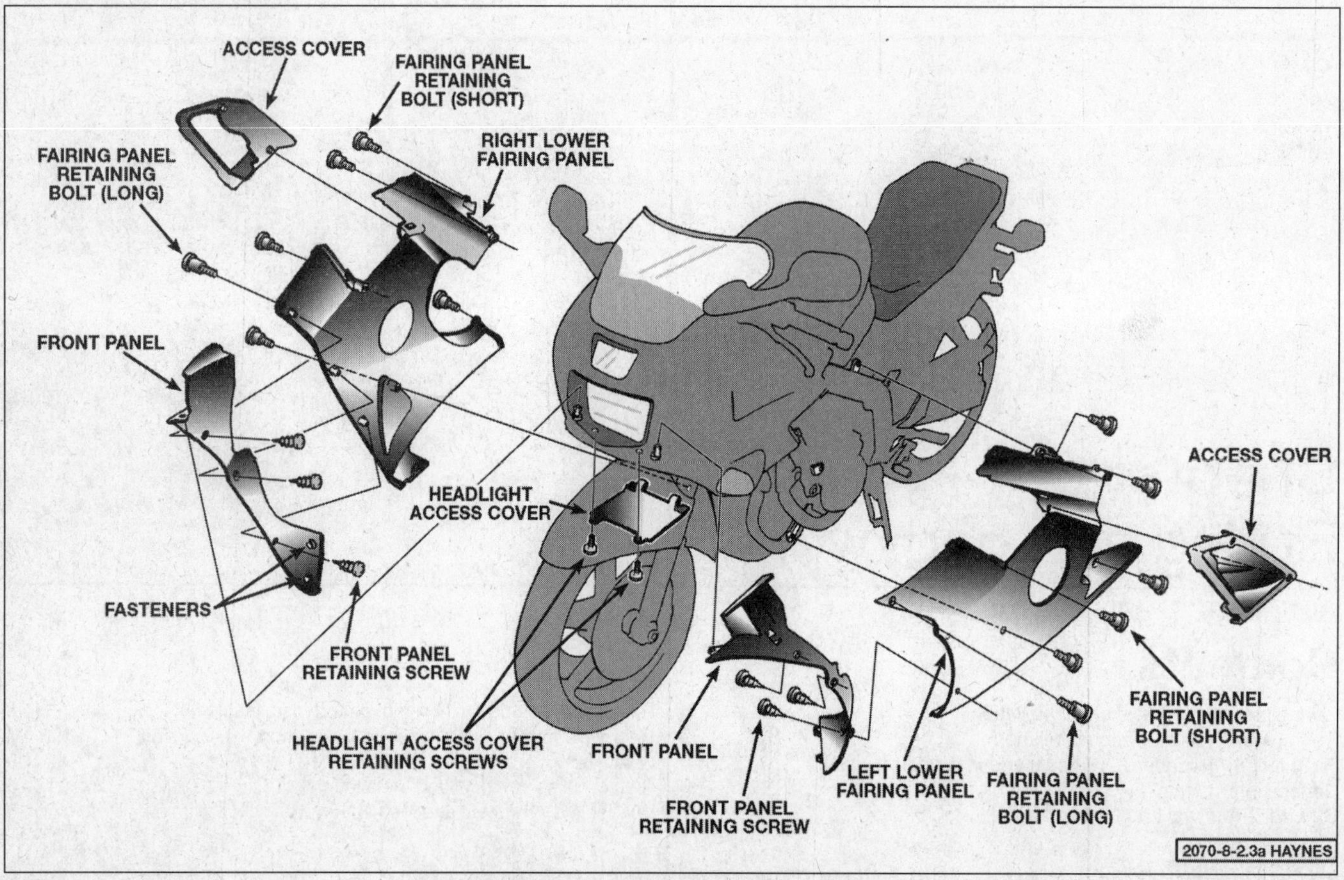

2.3b Lower fairing panel components and fasteners

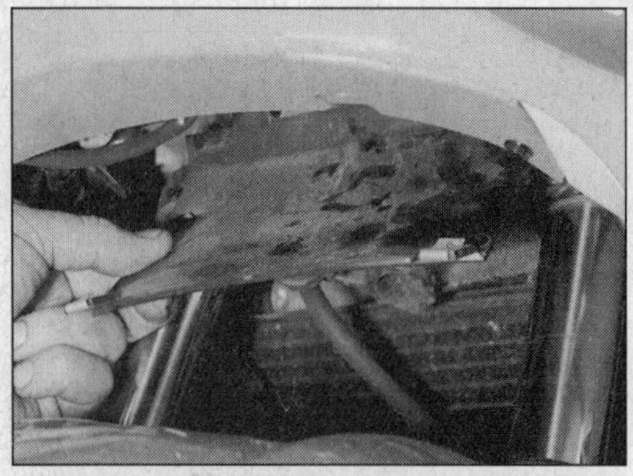

2.4 Removing the headlight access cover from the base of the upper fairing

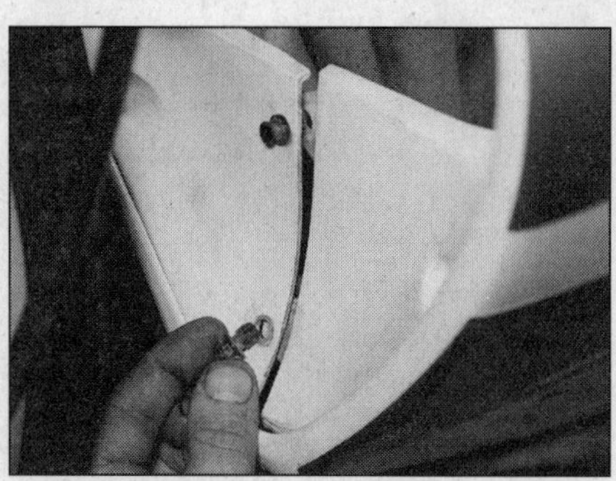

2.5a Release the two fasteners securing the left and right lower fairing panels together . . .

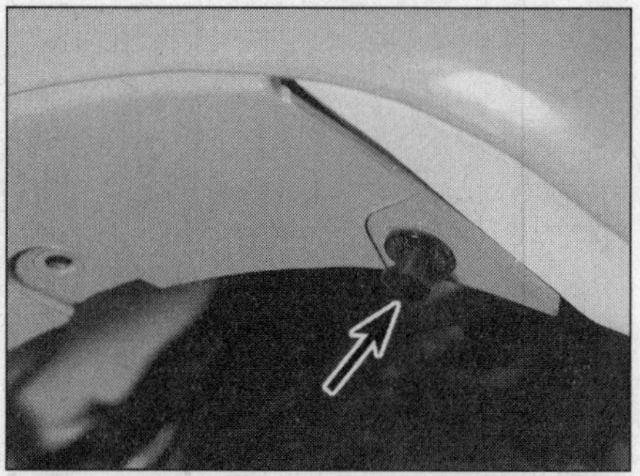

2.5b . . . and the fastener securing each lower fairing panel to the upper fairing by pulling out the center pin (arrow)

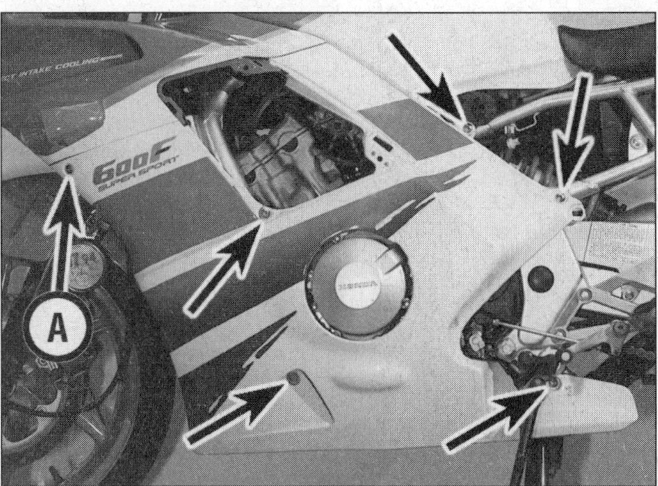

2.6 Left lower fairing panel retaining screw (arrows), the longer screw should be fitted in position 'A'

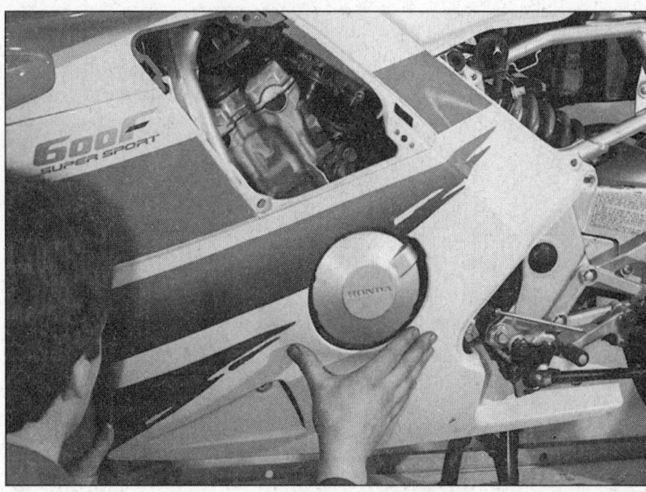

2.8 Move the left lower fairing panel forward to disengage it and remove it from the bike

6 Undo the six left lower fairing panel retaining screws, noting the correct location of the longer screw **(see illustration)**.

7 Free the speedometer cable from its retaining clips on the inside of the left fairing panel.

8 Move the left panel forward, to disengage it from the hooks on the bottom of the right panel, and remove it from the motorcycle **(see illustration)**.

9 Undo the six retaining screws, again noting the correct location of the longer screw, and remove the right lower fairing panel.

10 If necessary, the front panels can then be removed from each lower fairing panel. The front panels are each retained by three screws.

Lower fairing panels - S, T, V and W (1995 to 1998) models

11 Remove the side covers as described in Section 6.

12 Remove the access cover from both the left and right sides of the fairing. Each panel is retained by two screws **(see illustrations)**.

13 If only removing the right panel, remove the quick fastener from the bottom of the inner cover by turning it 90° anti-clockwise (counter-clockwise), and remove the top right screw from the inner cover **(see illustration)**. If only removing the left panel, remove the screw from the underside of the fairing panels, and remove the top left screw from the inner cover **(see illustration)**. If removing both lower fairing panels, remove all the above fasteners.

14 Undo the lower fairing panel six retaining screws, noting the correct location of the longer screw **(see illustration)**. When removing the left panel, lower the sidestand to improve access to the rear screw.

15 Move the panel to disengage its tabs from the upper fairing, and remove it from the motorcycle.

Upper fairing assembly - M, N, P and R (1991 to 1994) models

16 Remove both the lower fairing panels as described above.

17 Remove the rear view mirrors as described in Section 4 **(see illustration)**.

18 Remove the windshield as described in Section 3.

19 Undo the two upper fairing assembly retaining screws (one on either side) and move the upper fairing assembly forward until access can be gained to the wiring connectors located in front of the instrument cluster **(see illustrations)**.

20 Support the fairing then trace the wiring back from each turn signal assembly and the sidelight (UK models only) and disconnect the three wiring connectors **(see illustration)**.

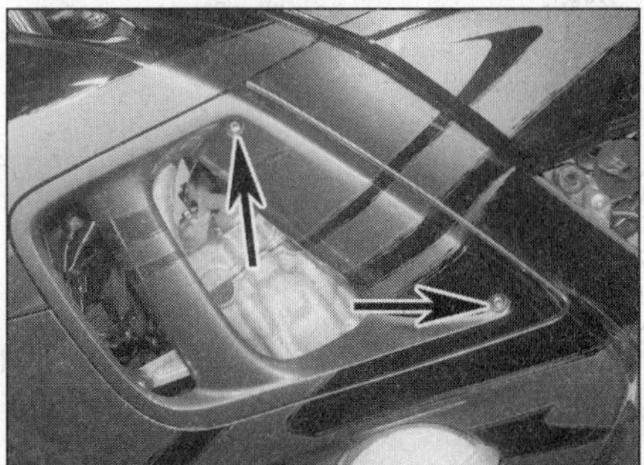

2.12a Unscrew the fasteners (arrows) . . .

2.12b . . . and remove the cover

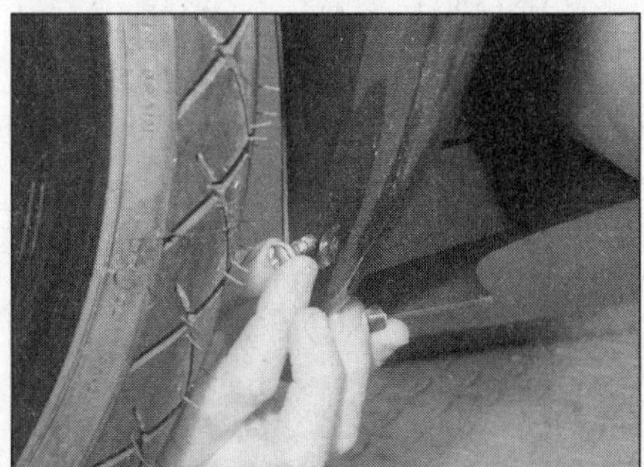

2.13a Remove the front screw to release the right panel . . .

2.13b . . . and the bottom screw (arrow) to release the left panel

2.14 Remove the six screws (arrows), noting the position of the longer screw (A)

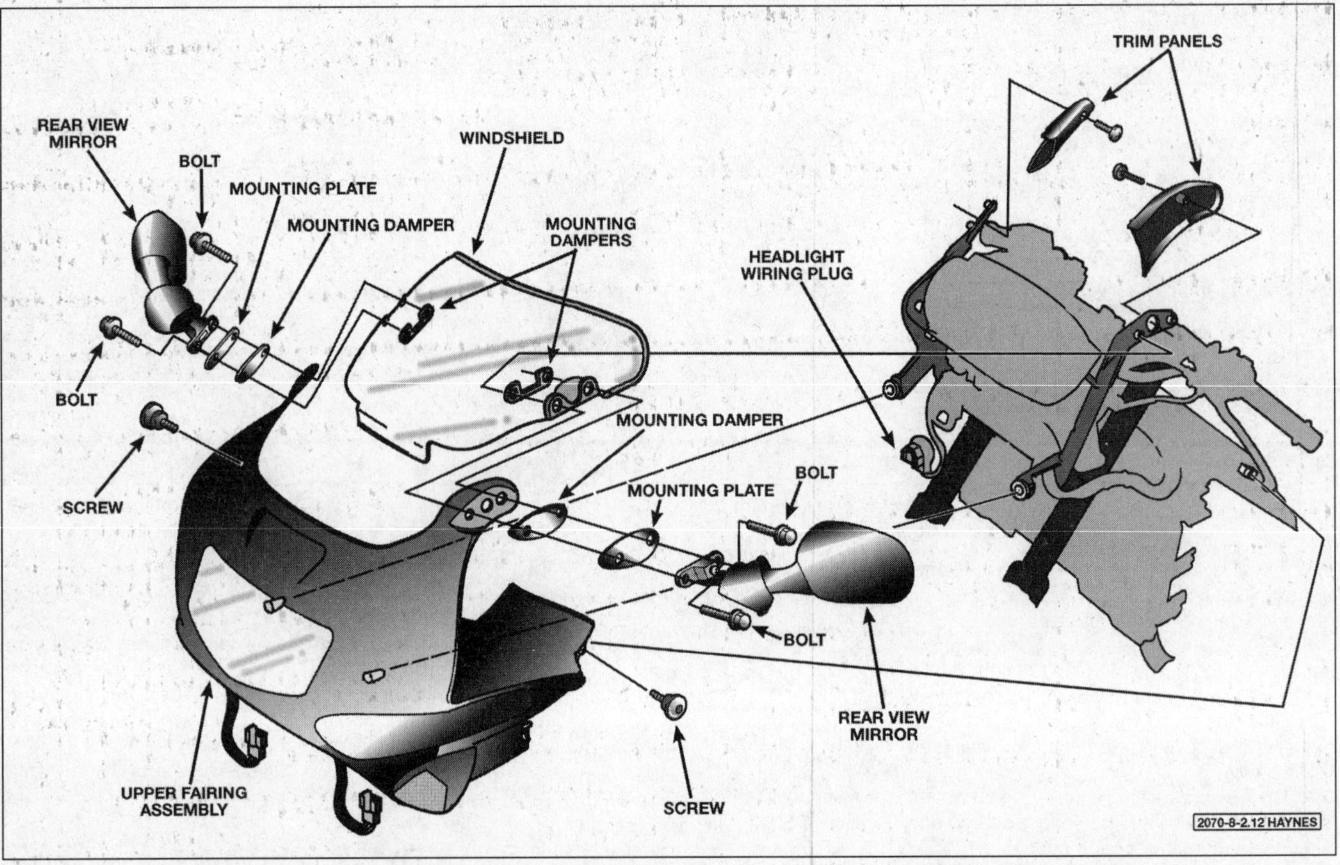

2.17 Upper fairing assembly and associated components - M, N, P and R (1991 to 1994) models

2.19a Undo the upper fairing retaining screws . . .

21 Disconnect the wiring plug from the rear of the headlight unit and remove the upper fairing from the motorcycle **(see illustration)**. Examine the fairing mounting dampers for signs of damage and replace if necessary.

Upper fairing assembly - S, T, V and W (1995 to 1998) models

22 Remove both the lower fairing panels as described above.

23 Remove the rear view mirrors as described in Section 4.

24 Remove the access cover from the underside of the front of the fairing by pulling out the two trim tabs, then drawing the cover back to release the tabs **(see illustration)**. Remove the screw securing each DAI (Direct Air Induction) system air nozzle and position the hoses clear **(see illustration)**.

25 Remove the screw securing the fusebox cover in the right side of the fairing and remove the cover. On UK models, remove the sidelight bulbholder from the base of the headlight.

26 Undo the two upper fairing assembly retaining screws (one on either side) and move the upper fairing assembly forward until access can be gained to the turn signal and headlight wiring connectors **(see illustration)**.

27 Support the fairing then trace the wiring

2.19b . . . and move the fairing forward and away from the bike

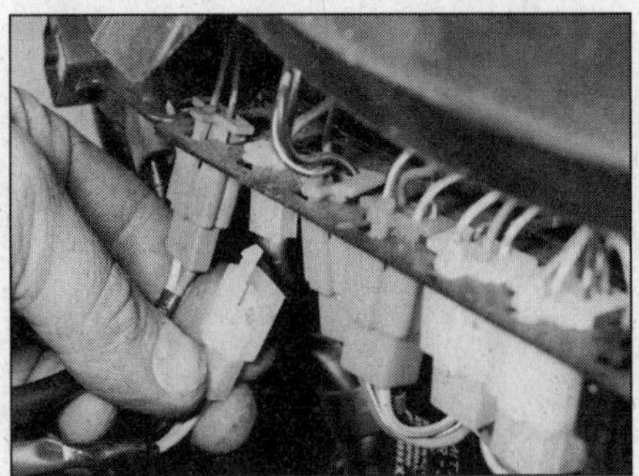

2.20 Disconnect the turn signal and sidelight (UK models only) wiring at the wiring connectors . . .

2.21 . . . then disconnect the wiring plug from the headlight bulb and remove the upper fairing

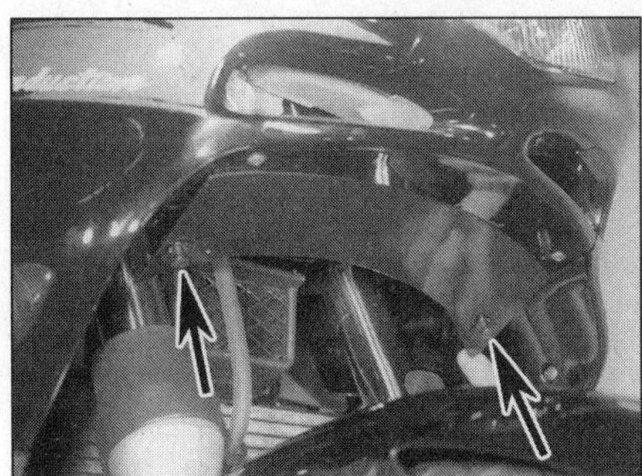
2.24a Pull out the trim clips (arrows) and remove the panel

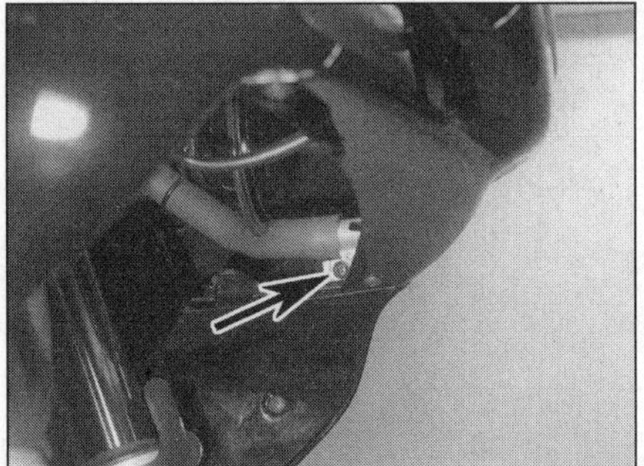
2.24b Remove the screw (arrow) securing each air nozzle

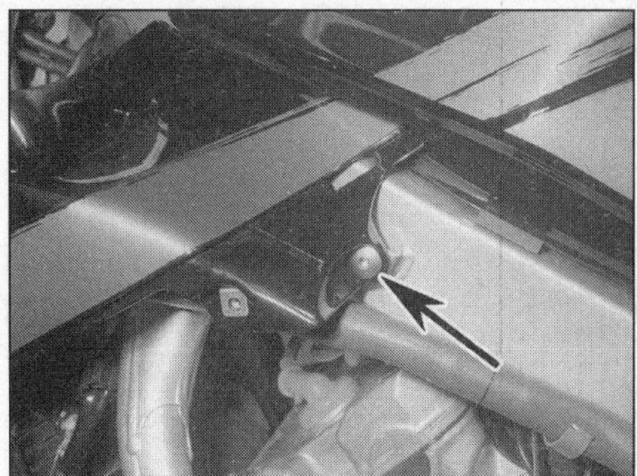
2.26 The fairing is secured by a screw on each side (arrow)

back from each turn signal assembly and disconnect the wiring connectors.

28 Disconnect the wiring plug from the rear of the headlight unit and remove the upper fairing from the motorcycle **(see illustration 2.21)**. Remove the windshield **(see illustration 3.3)**.

Installation

Lower fairing panels

29 Installation is the reverse of removal ensuring the lower fairing panels are correctly hooked together and secured in position by all the relevant screws and fasteners. Note that the longer screw for each panel is for the front top mounting.

Upper fairing assembly

30 Installation is the reverse of removal, making sure the pegs on the headlight are correctly aligned with dampers on the fairing stay. Do not forget to connect the headlight and turn signal wiring connectors, and on UK models to fit the sidelight into the base of the headlight. On completion check the headlight aim as described in Chapter 9.

3 Windshield - removal and installation

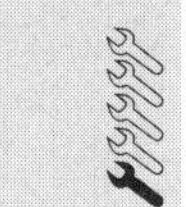

Removal

M, N, P and R (1991 to 1994) models

1 Remove both rear view mirrors as described in Section 4.

2 Carefully lift the windshield away from the upper fairing assembly and recover the mounting damper from each side of the fairing mounting stay **(see illustration)**.

S, T, V and W (1995 to 1998) models

3 Remove the upper fairing as described in Section 2, then remove the windshield **(see illustration)**.

Installation

4 Installation is the reverse of removal.

4 Rear view mirrors - removal and installation

Removal

1 Undo the screw and remove the rear view mirror trim panel from inside the upper fairing **(see illustrations)**.

2 Peel back the rubber cover then undo the two retaining bolts and remove the rear view mirror along with its mounting plate and damper **(see illustrations)**.

Installation

3 Fit the mounting plate onto the mirror. On M, N, P and R (1991 to 1994) models, the left mirror the plate must be fitted with its marked side facing the mirror and the arrows stamped on the plate pointing upwards and forward. On the right mirror the plate must be fitted with its marked side facing the fairing and the arrows stamped on the plate pointing upwards and forward **(see illustration)**. On S, T, V and W (1995 to 1998) models, the left mirror the plate must be fitted with its marked side facing the fairing and the arrows stamped on the plate pointing downwards and forward.

3.2 Recover the mounting damper (arrow) from each side of the fairing stay

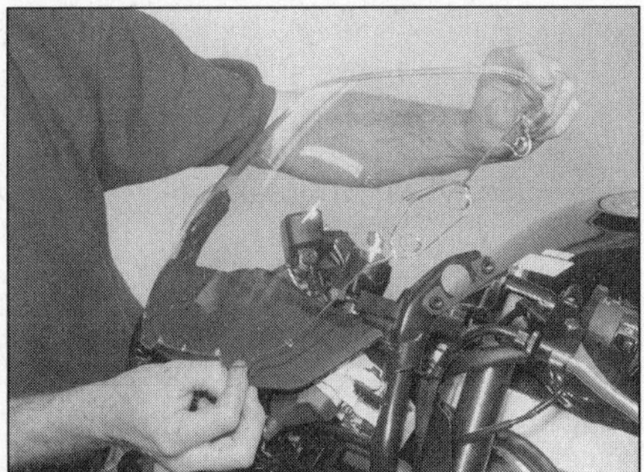
3.3 The windshield can be lifted away after removing the upper fairing

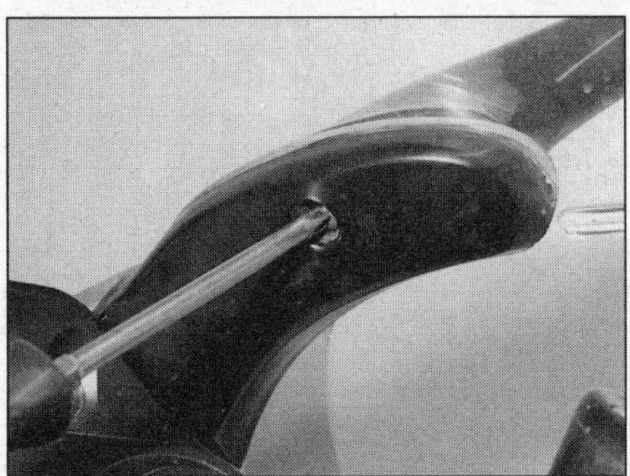
4.1a Undo the retaining screw . . .

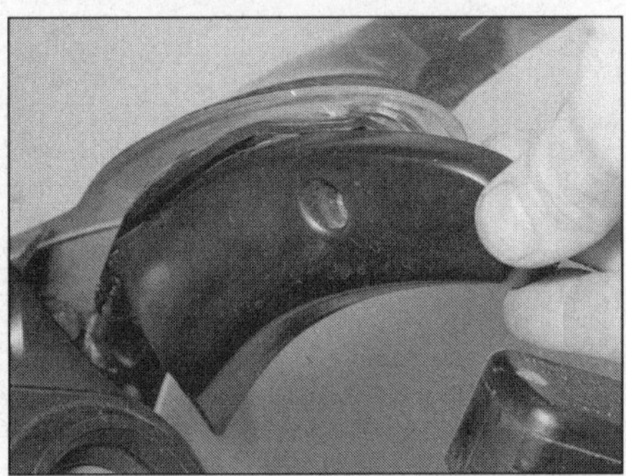
4.1b . . . and remove the rear view mirror trim panel from the upper fairing

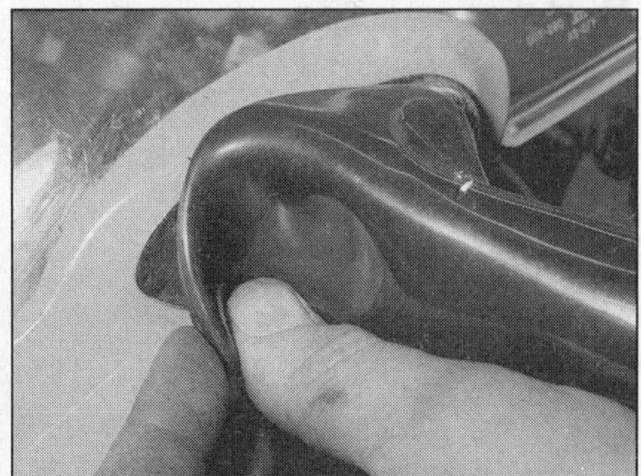
4.2a Peel back the rubber cover . . .

4.2b ... then undo the two retaining bolts ...

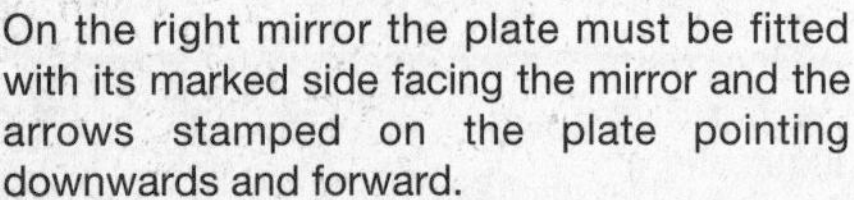

On the right mirror the plate must be fitted with its marked side facing the mirror and the arrows stamped on the plate pointing downwards and forward.

4 Fit the mounting damper onto the mirror. On M, N, P and R (1991 to 1994) models, the left mirror the damper should be fitted so that the 'MT4-L' marking is facing the fairing. On the right mirror the damper must be fitted so that the 'MT4-R' marking is facing the fairing **(see illustration)**. On S, T, V and W (1995 to 1998) models, the left mirror the damper should be fitted so that the 'MT4-L' marking is facing the mirror and upside down. On the right mirror the damper must be fitted so that the 'MT4-R' marking is facing the mirror and upside down.

5.3 Make a note of the correct routing of all wiring before disconnecting it and removing the fairing stay

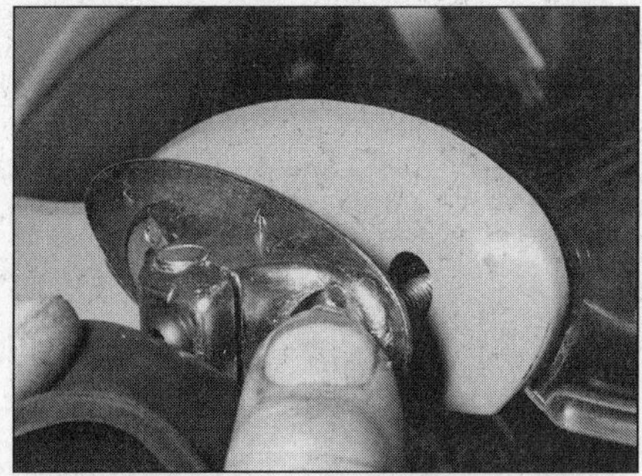

4.2c ... and remove the mirror complete with mounting plate and damper

5 Install the mirror on the fairing and securely tighten its retaining bolts. Slide the rubber cover back into position over the mounting plate.

6 Fit the trim panel to the inside of the fairing.

5 Fairing stay - removal and installation

Removal

1 Remove the upper fairing assembly as described in Section 2.

2 Remove the instrument cluster as described in Chapter 9.

3 Carefully note the correct routing of the wiring harness around the stay. Disconnect the wiring relevant connectors, then release the retaining clips and detach the harness from the stay **(see illustration)**.

4 Undo the stay mounting nuts and bolts and take the fairing stay off the bike.

Installation

5 Installation is the reverse of removal.

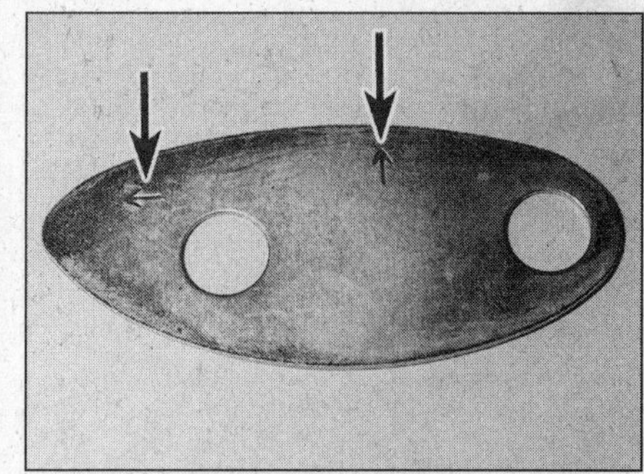

4.3 Make sure the mounting plate arrows (arrows) are positioned as described in text

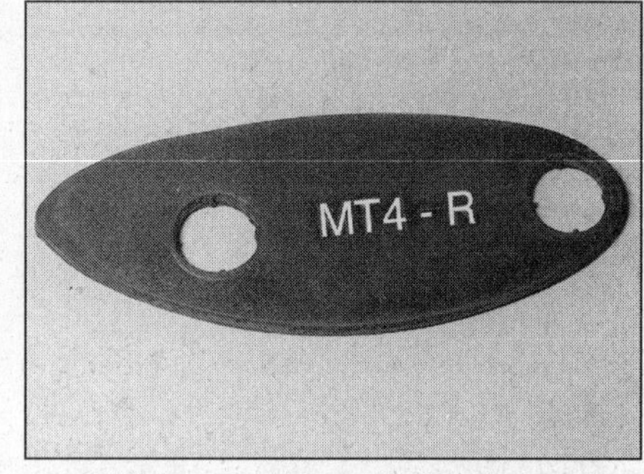

4.4 Make sure the mounting damper is installed with its identification mark (highlighted) correctly positioned

6 Side covers - removal and installation

Removal

1 Release the side cover fastener by rotating it through 90° so that its longer slot is aligned with the dot on the cover **(see illustration)**.

2 Release the tab and the hole on the side cover from the slot and the pin in the tail cowl and carefully pull it squarely away from the machine to release its retaining pegs from their grommets **(see illustrations)**.

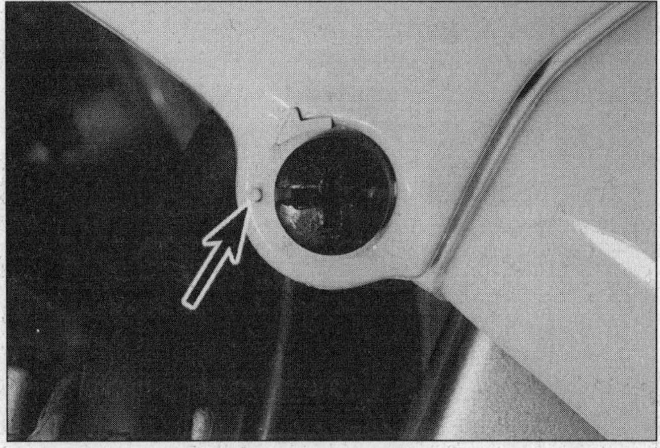

6.1 Release the cover fastener by rotating it 90° so that its longer slot is aligned with the cover dot (arrow) ...

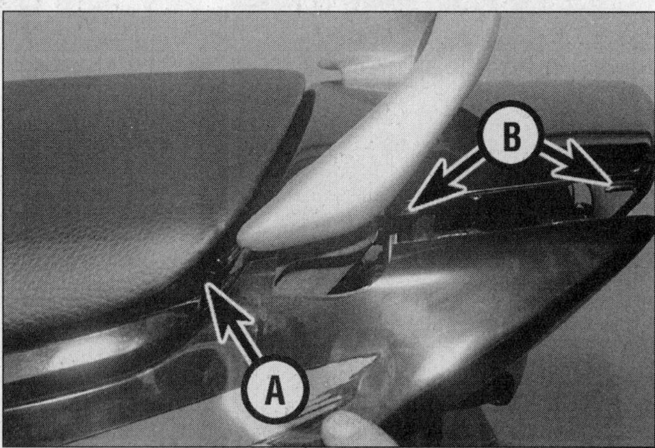

6.2a ... carefully release the pin (A) and tabs (B) ...

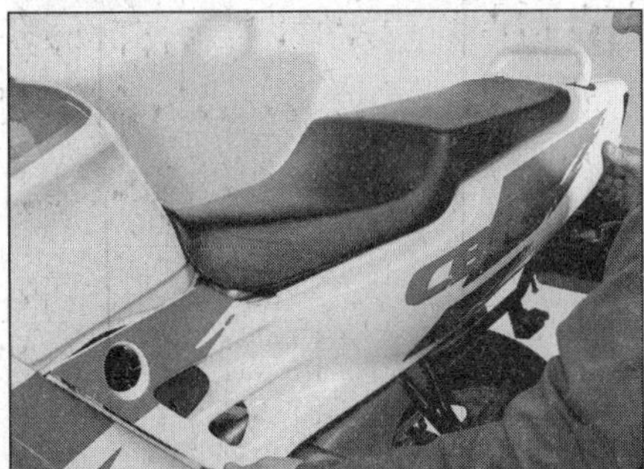

6.2b ... then pull the side cover away from the bike to release its retaining pegs

Installation

3 Offer up the side cover and engage it with the slot and the pin in the tail cowl and the grab rail rubber grommet (where fitted).

4 Align the cover retaining pegs with their grommets and clip the cover into position.

5 Secure the cover in position by rotating its fastener through 90° so that the triangular mark on the fastener is aligned with the dot on the cover **(see illustration)**.

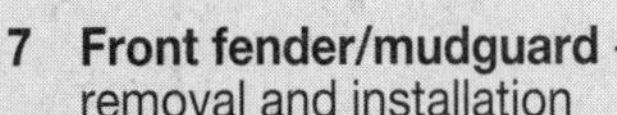

7 Front fender/mudguard - removal and installation

Removal

1 Set the bike on its centerstand.

2 Undo the four mounting bolts and remove the fender/mudguard, taking care not to damage its painted finish **(see illustrations)**.

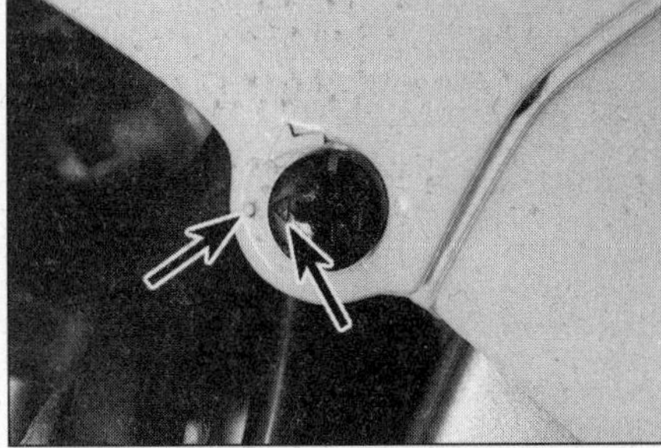

6.5 Secure the cover in position by rotating the fastener through 90° so that its arrow is aligned with the cover dot (arrows)

Installation

3 Installation is the reverse of removal not forgetting to position the brake pipe retainers behind the rear mounting bolts.

8 Rear fender/mudguard - removal and installation

Removal

Frame-mounted fender/mudguard

1 Where fitted, remove the grab rail as described in Section 10.

2 Undo the two bolts, and on V and W (1997 and 1998) models the two screws, then pull the tail cowl upwards to release its retaining peg (except V and W (1997 and 1998) models) and remove it from the bike.

3 Disconnect the wiring connectors from the rear turn signal assemblies.

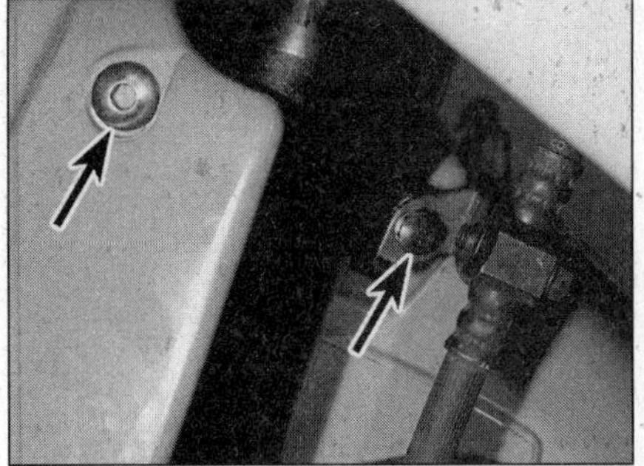

7.2a Undo the mounting bolts on each side (arrows) ...

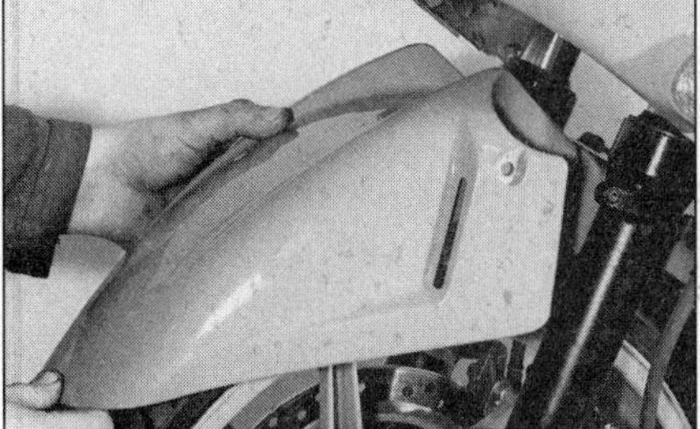

7.2b ... and remove the front fender/mudguard

4 On M, N, P and R (1991 to 1994) models, undo the two retaining bolts and remove the left pillion footpeg bracket.

5 Undo the bolt from the front of the fender/mudguard and remove the assembly from the left side of the bike. Examine the fender/mudguard rubber mounts for signs of damage and replace if necessary.

Swingarm-mounted fender/mudguard

6 Undo the screws and remove the drive chain guard **(see illustrations)**.

7 Undo the two retaining bolts and remove the left pillion footpeg bracket. Release the brake hose from its clips on the fender/mudguard **(see illustration)**.

8 Undo the retaining screws and remove the fender/mudguard from the swingarm taking care not to damage its painted finish **(see illustrations)**.

8.6a Undo the two screws ...

8.6b ... and remove the drive chain guard from the swingarm

8.7 Release the rear brake hose from its clips (arrows) ...

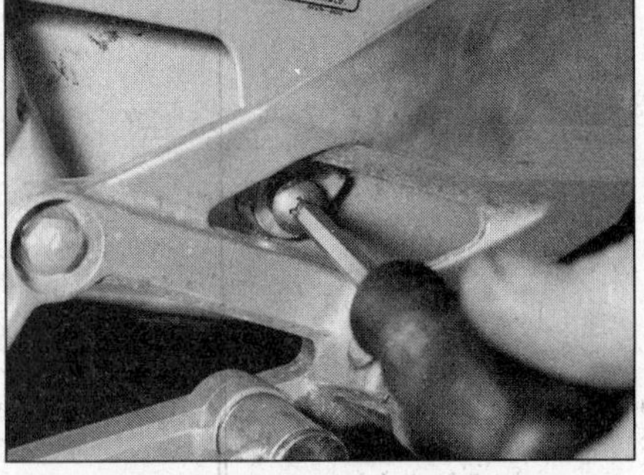

8.8a ... then undo the retaining screws ...

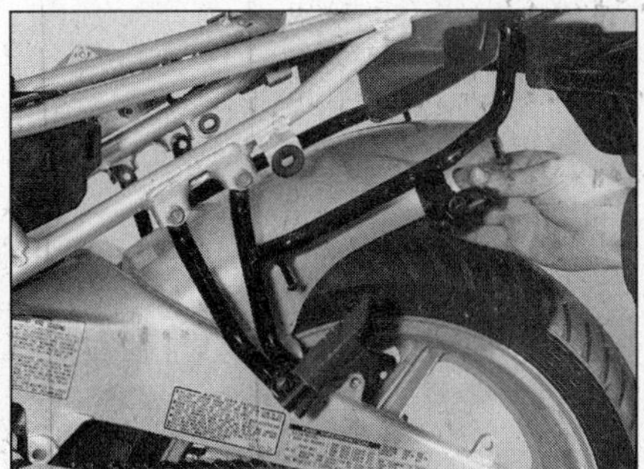

8.8b ... and remove the fender/mudguard from the bike

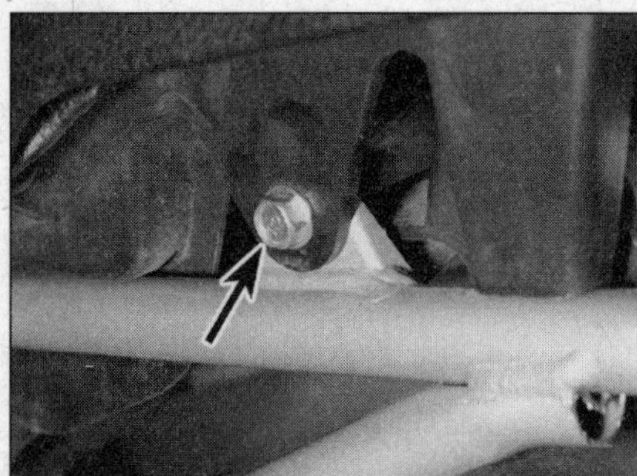

9.2a Undo the seat retaining bolt (arrow) from each side . . .

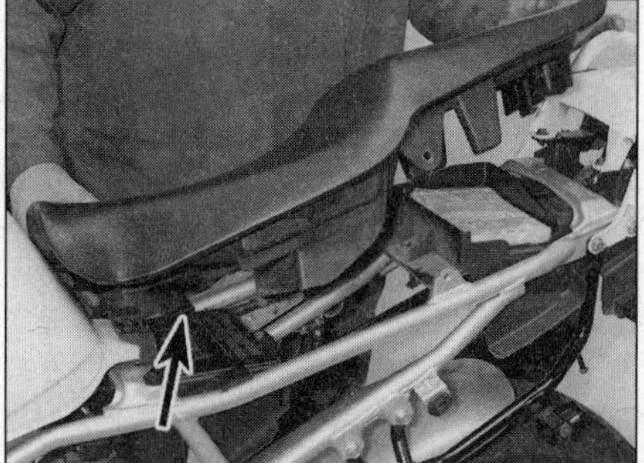

9.2b . . . then slide the seat to the rear to release its locating hook (arrow) from the fuel tank

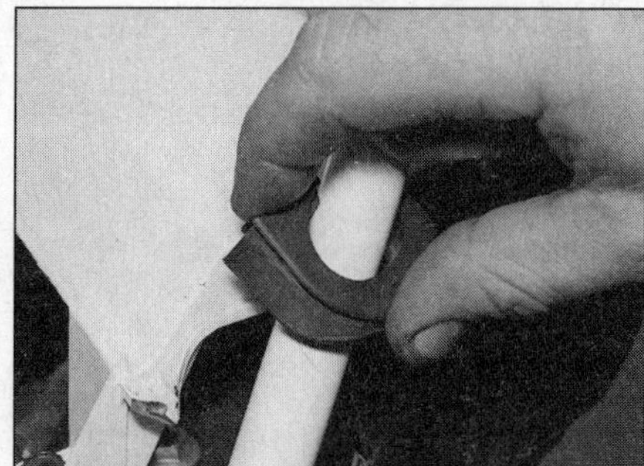

10.2 Remove both rubber mounts from the grab rail

Installation

Frame-mounted fender/mudguard

9 Installation is the reverse of removal. On completion check the operation of the turn signals before taking the machine on the road.

Swingarm-mounted fender/mudguard

10 Installation is the reverse of removal ensuring the brake hose is securely clipped in position.

9 Seat - removal and installation

Removal

1 Remove the side covers as described in Section 6. On V and W (1997 and 1998) models, remove the access flap from the left side of the toolbox.

2 Undo the two retaining bolts (one each side) then slide the seat to the rear to disengage its tabs from the fuel tank at the front and the toolbox at the back, and remove it from the bike **(see illustrations)**.

Installation

3 Installation is the reverse of removal. Make sure the tabs engage correctly with the tank and toolbox.

10 Grab rail - removal and installation

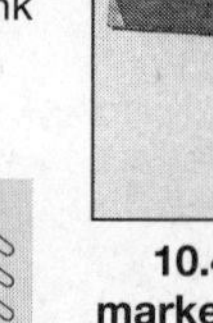

Removal

1 Remove the seat as described in Section 9.

2 Remove the rubber mount from each side of the grab rail **(see illustration)**.

3 Undo the four bolts and remove the grab rail from the bike.

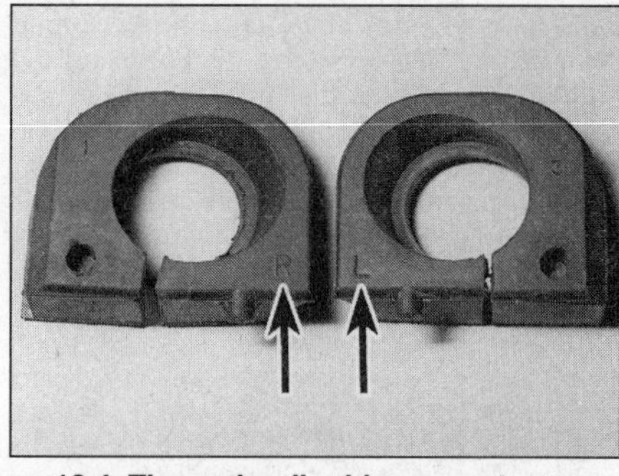

10.4 The grab rail rubber mounts are marked for identification purposes and are not interchangeable

Installation

4 Installation is the reverse of removal. Ensure the grab rail rubber mounts are correctly installed so that their locating pegs engage with the tail cowl. The mounts are different; the right mount is marked 'R' and the left mount 'L' **(see illustration)**.

Chapter 9
Electrical system

Contents

Degrees of difficulty

Easy, suitable for novice with little experience

Fairly easy, suitable for beginner with some experience

Fairly difficult, suitable for competent DIY mechanic

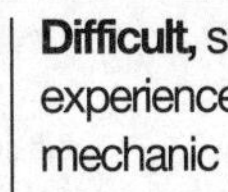

Difficult, suitable for experienced DIY mechanic

Very difficult, suitable for expert DIY or professional

Specifications

Battery

Capacity	12V, 8Ah

Alternator

Type	Three-phase AC
Output	350 watts at 5000 rpm
Charging voltage	13.0 to 15.5 volts at 5000 rpm
Stator coil resistance	0.1 to 1.0 ohms at 20°C (68°F)

Starter motor

Brush length	
New	12 to 13 mm (0.47 to 0.51 in)
Service limit	4.5 mm (0.18 in)

Fuses

Main fuse (on starter relay)	30A
All other fuses (in fusebox)	3 x 10A and 1 x 15A*

**See fusebox lid for circuits protected*

Bulbs	US models	UK models
Headlight	12V 60/55W	12V 60/55W
Sidelight	-	12V 5W
Stop/taillight	12V 32/3cp	12V 21/5W
Turn signal lights	12V 23/8W (front) 23W (rear)	12V 21W
License plate light	12V 4cp	-
Instrument illuminating lights	12V 1.7W	12V 1.7W
Warning lamps		
Sidestand warning light	12V 1.7W	12V 1.7W
Neutral indicator light		
M, N, P and R (1991 to 1994) models	12V 3.4W	12V 3.4W
S, T, V and W (1995 to 1998) models	12V 1.7W	12V 1.7W
Oil pressure warning light		
M, N, P and R (1991 to 1994) models	12V 3.4W	12V 3.4W
S, T, V and W (1995 to 1998) models	12V 1.7W	12V 1.7W
High beam indicator light		
M, N, P and R (1991 to 1994) models	12V 3.4W	12V 3.4W
S, T, V and W (1995 to 1998) models	12V 1.7W	12V 1.7W
Turn signal indicator lights		
M, N, P and R (1991 to 1994) models	12V 3.4W	12V 3.4W
S, T, V and W (1995 to 1998) models	12V 3.0W	12V 3.0W

Torque settings	Nm	ft-lbs
Ignition (main) switch bolts	25	18
Neutral switch	12	9
Oil pressure switch	12	9
Sidestand switch bolt	10	7
Alternator stator coil bolts	12	9

1 General information

The machines covered by this manual are equipped with a 12-volt electrical system. The components include a three-phase alternator and a regulator/rectifier unit.

The regulator/rectifier unit maintains the charging system output within the specified range to prevent overcharging and converts the AC (alternating current) output of the alternator to DC (direct current) to power the lights and other components and to charge the battery.

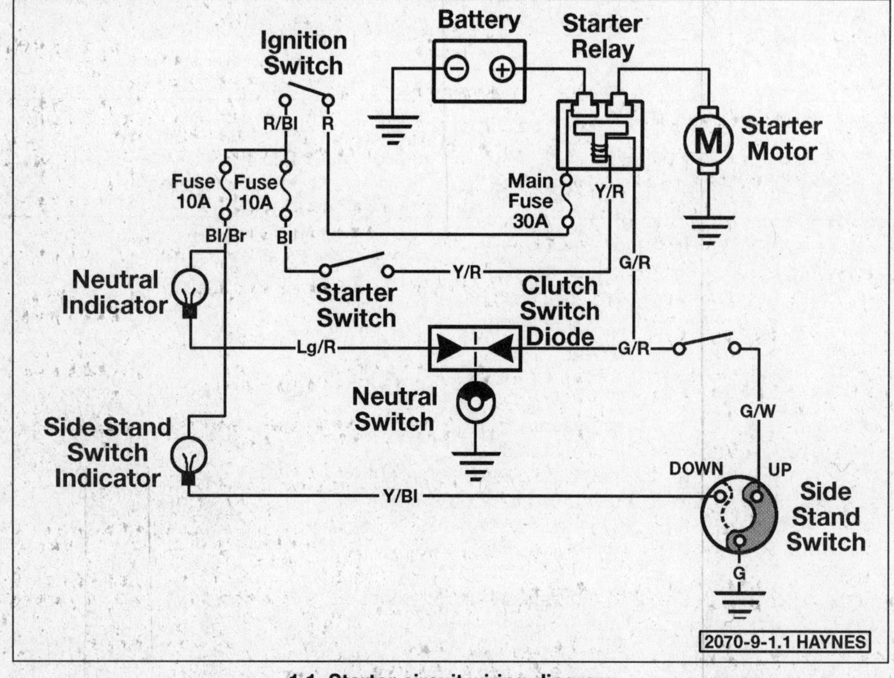

1.1 Starter circuit wiring diagram

Bl Black *G Green* *W White* *Lg Light green*
Y Yellow *R Red* *Br Brown*

An electric starter mounted to the engine case behind the cylinders is standard equipment. The starting system includes the motor, the battery, the relay and the various wires and switches. If the engine stop switch and the main key switch are both in the Run or On position, the circuit relay allows the starter motor to operate only if the transmission is in Neutral (Neutral switch on) or the clutch lever is pulled to the handlebar (clutch switch on) and the sidestand is up (sidestand switch on) **(see illustration)**.

Note: *Keep in mind that electrical parts, once purchased, can't be returned. To avoid unnecessary expense, make very sure the faulty component has been positively identified before buying a replacement part.*

2 Electrical fault finding

Warning: To prevent the risk of short circuits, the ignition (main) switch must always be OFF and the battery negative (-ve) terminal should be disconnected before any of the bike's other electrical components are disturbed. Don't forget to reconnect the terminal securely once work is finished or if battery power is needed for circuit testing.

A typical electrical circuit consists of an electrical component, the switches, relays, etc. related to that component and the wiring and connectors that hook the component to both the battery and the frame. To aid in locating a problem in any electrical circuit, refer to the wiring diagrams at the end of this Chapter.

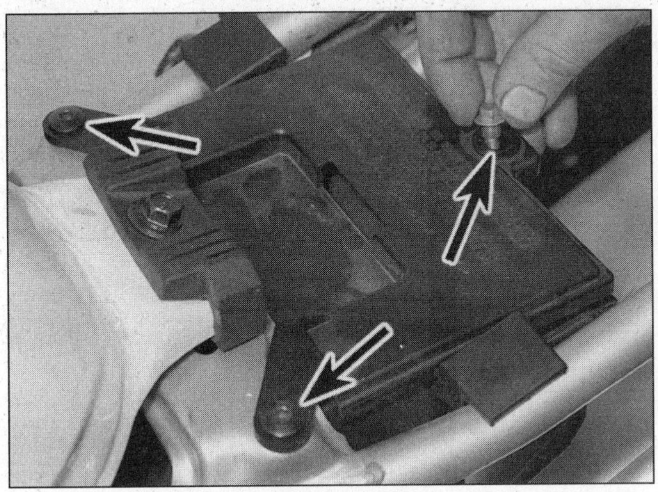
3.2a Unscrew the three bolts (arrows) . . .

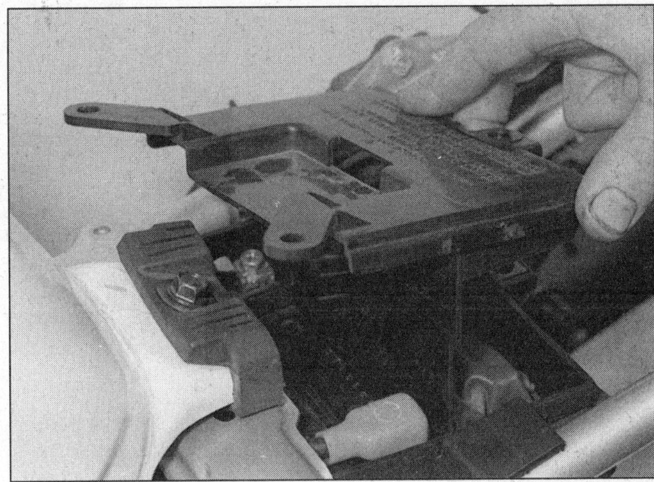
3.2b . . . and remove the cover to gain access to the battery

Before tackling any troublesome electrical circuit, first study the appropriate diagrams thoroughly to get a complete picture of what makes up that individual circuit. Trouble spots, for instance, can often be narrowed down by noting if other components related to that circuit are operating properly or not. If several components or circuits fail at one time, chances are the fault lies in the fuse or ground (earth) connection, as several circuits often are routed through the same fuse and ground (earth) connections.

Electrical problems often stem from simple causes, such as loose or corroded connections or a blown fuse. Prior to any electrical fault finding, always visually check the condition of the fuse, wires and connections in the problem circuit. Intermittent failures can be especially frustrating, since you can't always duplicate the failure when it's convenient to test. In such situations, a good practice is to clean all connections in the affected circuit, whether or not they appear to be good. All of the connections and wires should also be wiggled to check for looseness which can cause intermittent failure.

If testing instruments are going to be utilized, use the diagrams to plan where you will make the necessary connections in order to accurately pinpoint the trouble spot.

The basic tools needed for electrical fault finding include a battery and bulb test circuit, a continuity tester, a test light, and a jumper wire. A multimeter capable of reading volts, ohms and amps is also very useful as an alternative to the above, and is necessary for performing more extensive tests and checks.

Refer to Fault Finding Equipment in the Reference section for details of how to use electrical test equipment.

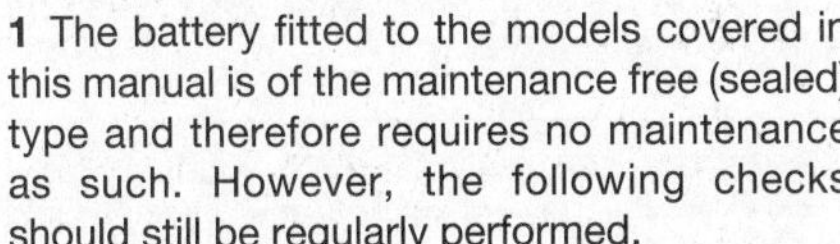

3 Battery - inspection and maintenance

1 The battery fitted to the models covered in this manual is of the maintenance free (sealed) type and therefore requires no maintenance as such. However, the following checks should still be regularly performed.

2 Remove the seat (see Chapter 8) then unscrew the three bolts and lift off the battery cover **(see illustrations)**.

3 Check the battery terminals and leads for tightness and corrosion. If corrosion is evident, disconnect the leads from the battery, disconnecting the negative (-ve) terminal first. Clean the terminals and lead ends with a wire brush or knife and emery paper **(see illustration)**. Reconnect the leads, connecting the negative (-ve) terminal last.

Warning: Always disconnect the negative lead first and connect it last. If the positive lead is disconnected or reconnected while the negative lead is attached to the battery, the resulting sparks could ignite hydrogen gas given off by the battery, causing the battery to explode and spray acid.

Haynes Hint Apply a thin coat of petroleum jelly to the connections to slow further corrosion.

4 The battery case should be kept clean to prevent current leakage, which can discharge the battery over a period of time (especially when it sits unused). Wash the outside of the case with a solution of baking soda and water. Rinse the battery thoroughly, then dry it.

5 Look for cracks in the case and replace the battery if these are found.

6 If the motorcycle sits unused for long periods of time, disconnect the cables from the battery terminals. Refer to Section 4 and charge the battery approximately once every month.

7 The condition of the battery can be assessed by measuring the voltage present at the battery terminals; voltmeter positive probe to the battery positive terminal and negative probe to battery negative terminal. When fully charged there should be approximately 13 volts present. If the voltage falls below 12.3 volts the battery must be removed, disconnecting the negative (-ve) terminal first, and recharged as described below in Section 4.

4 Battery - charging

1 To charge the battery it is first necessary to remove it from the motorcycle. To do this remove the seat (see Chapter 8) then unscrew the three bolts and lift off the battery cover. Disconnect the leads from the battery, disconnecting the negative (-ve) terminal first, and lift the battery out of its box.

2 Honda recommends that the battery is charged at rate of 0.9 amps for between 5 and 10 hours. Exceeding this figure can cause the battery to overheat, buckling the plates and rendering it useless. Few owners will have access to an expensive current controlled

3.3 Always disconnect the battery negative lead first, and reconnect it last

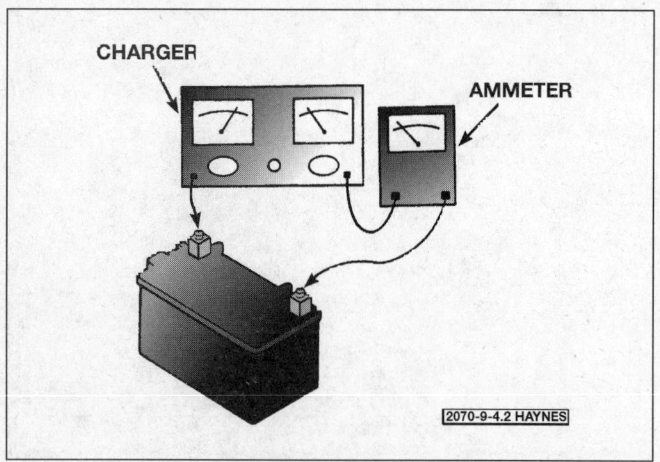

4.2 If the charger doesn't have an ammeter built in, connect one in series as shown; DO NOT connect the ammeter between the battery terminals or it will be ruined

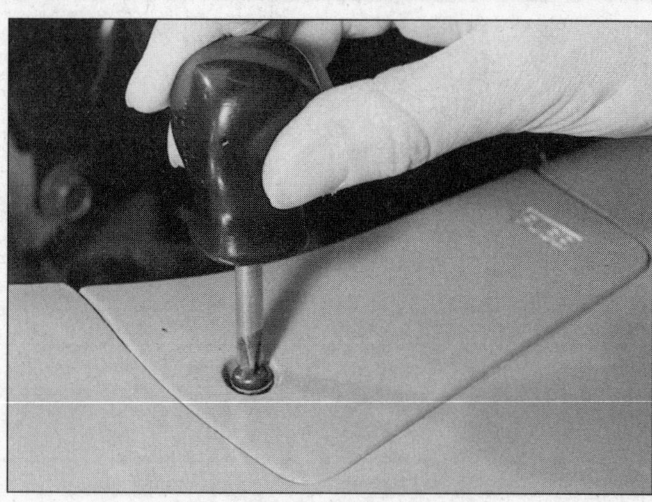

5.2a Undo the retaining screw . . .

charger, so if a normal domestic charger is used check that after a possible initial peak, the charge rate falls to a safe level **(see illustration)**. If the battery becomes hot during charging **stop**. Further charging will cause damage. **Note:** *In emergencies Honda states that the battery can be charged at a rate of 4 amps for a period of 1 hour. However, this is not recommended and the low amp charge is by far the safer method of charging the battery.*

3 If the recharged battery discharges rapidly when left disconnected it is likely that an internal short caused by physical damage or sulphation has occurred. A new battery will be required. A good battery will tend to lose its charge at about 1% per day.

4 On installation, clean the battery terminals and lead ends with a wire brush or knife and emery paper. Reconnect the leads, connecting the negative (-ve) terminal last. Fit the battery cover and install the seat as described in Chapter 8.

Apply a thin coat of petroleum jelly to the connections to slow further corrosion.

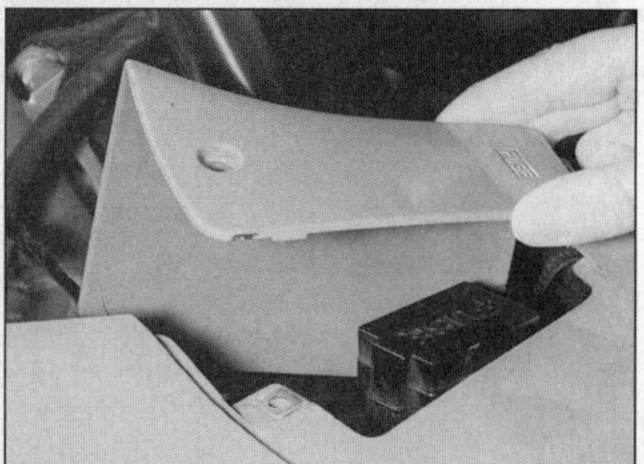

5.2b . . . and lift off the access cover from the upper fairing to reveal the fusebox

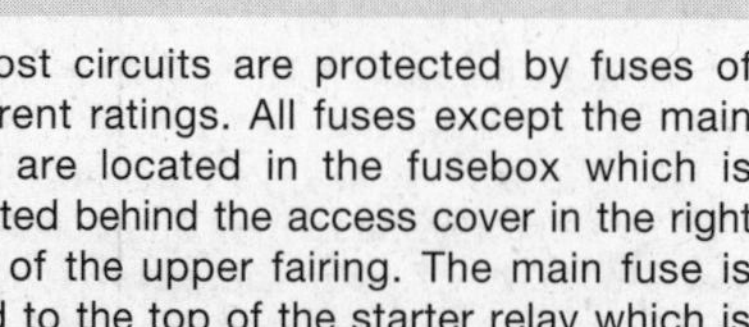

5 Fuses - check and replacement

1 Most circuits are protected by fuses of different ratings. All fuses except the main fuse are located in the fusebox which is situated behind the access cover in the right side of the upper fairing. The main fuse is fitted to the top of the starter relay which is behind the left side cover **(see illustration 26.1)**. All fusebox fuses are labeled for easy identification.

2 To gain access to the fusebox, undo the retaining screw and remove the fusebox access cover from the right side of the upper fairing then unclip and remove the fusebox lid. To gain access to the main fuse remove the left side cover (see Chapter 8) **(see illustrations)**.

3 The fuses can be removed and checked visually. If you can't pull the fuse out with your fingertips, use a pair of needle-nose pliers. A blown fuse is easily identified by a break in the element **(see illustration)**. Each is clearly marked with its rating and must only be replaced by a fuse of the correct rating.

Caution: Never put in a fuse of a higher rating or bridge the terminals with any other substitute, however temporary it may be. Serious damage may be done to the circuit, or a fire may start. Spare fuses of each rating are located in the fusebox, and a spare main fuse is clipped to the base of the starter relay. If the spare fuses are used, always replace them so that a spare fuse of each rating is carried on the machine at all times.

4 If a fuse blows, be sure to check the wiring circuit very carefully for evidence of a short-circuit. Look for bare wires and chafed, melted or burned insulation. If a fuse is replaced before the cause is located, the new fuse will blow immediately.

5.2c Unclip the fusebox lid . . .

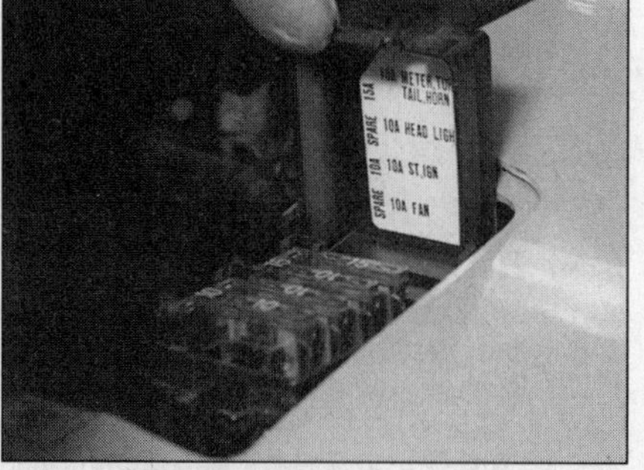

5.2d . . . to access the fuses, fuse locations are marked on the inside of the lid

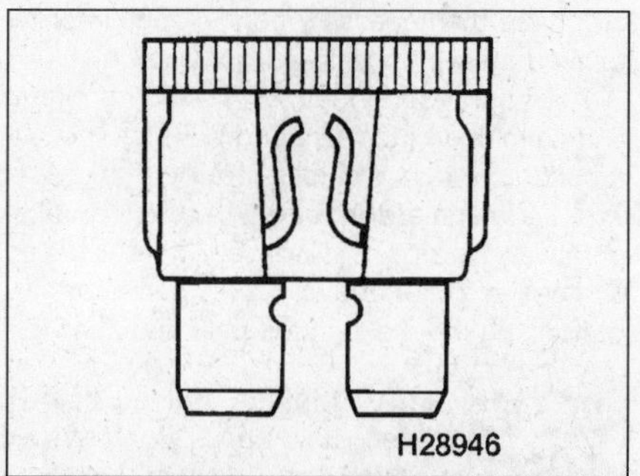

5.3 A blown fuse can be easily identified by a break in its element

7.2 Remove the rubber cover from the rear of the headlight . . .

7.3a . . . then unhook the retaining clip . . .

5 Occasionally a fuse will blow or cause an open-circuit for no obvious reason. Corrosion of the fuse ends and fusebox terminals may occur and cause poor fuse contact. If this happens, remove the corrosion with a wire brush or emery paper, then spray the fuse ends and terminals with electrical contact cleaner.

6 Lighting system - check

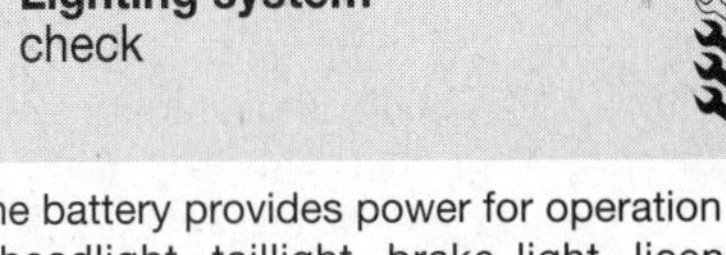

1 The battery provides power for operation of the headlight, taillight, brake light, license plate light and instrument cluster lights. If none of the lights operate, always check battery voltage before proceeding. Low battery voltage indicates either a faulty battery or a defective charging system. Refer to Section 3 for battery checks and Sections 29 and 30 for charging system tests. Also, check the condition of the fuses and replace any blown fuses with new ones.

Headlight

2 If the headlight is out when the engine is running (US models) or it won't switch on (UK models), check the fuse first with the key On (see Section 5), then unplug the electrical connector for the headlight and use jumper wires to connect the bulb directly to the battery terminals. If the light comes on, the problem lies in the wiring or one of the switches in the circuit. Refer to Section 19 for the switch testing procedures, and also the wiring diagrams at the end of this Chapter.

Taillight/license plate light

3 If the taillight fails to work, check the bulbs and the bulb terminals first, then check for battery voltage at the taillight electrical connector. If voltage is present, check the ground (earth) circuit for an open or poor connection.

4 If no voltage is indicated, check the wiring between the taillight and the ignition switch, then check the switch. On UK models, check the lighting switch as well.

Brake light

5 See Section 13 for the brake light switch checking procedure.

Neutral indicator light

6 If the neutral light fails to operate when the transmission is in Neutral, check the fuses and the bulb (see Sections 5 and 16). If the bulb and fuses are in good condition, check for battery voltage at the connector attached to the neutral switch on the left side of the engine. If battery voltage is present, refer to Section 21 for the neutral switch check and replacement procedures.

7 If no voltage is indicated, check the wiring between the switch and the bulb for open-circuits and poor connections.

Oil pressure warning light

8 See Section 17 for the oil pressure switch check.

Sidestand switch warning light

9 If the sidestand light fails to operate when the stand is extended down, check the fuses and the bulb (see Sections 5 and 16). If the bulb and fuses are in good condition, refer to Section 22 for the sidestand switch check and replacement procedures.

10 If the switch is functioning correctly check for voltage at the switch wiring connector. If no voltage is indicated, check the wiring between the switch and the bulb for open-circuits and poor connections.

7 Headlight bulb and sidelight (UK models only) - bulb replacement

Note: *The headlamp bulb is of the quartz-halogen type. Do not touch the bulb glass as skin acids will shorten the bulb's service life. If the bulb is accidentally touched, it should be wiped carefully when cold with a rag soaked in solvent and dried before fitting.*

Warning: Allow the bulb time to cool before removing it if the headlight has been used.

Headlight

1 Undo the two screws or pull out the two trim clips and remove the headlight access cover from the base of the upper fairing assembly. Take care not to break the cover tabs.

2 Unplug the wiring connector from the headlight bulb and remove the rubber dust cover **(see illustration)**.

3 Release the retaining clip and swing it away, then remove the bulb **(see illustrations)**.

4 Fit the new bulb, bearing in mind the information in the note and warning at the start of this Section and secure it in position with the retaining clip.

5 Install the dust cover, making sure it's correctly seated, and connect the wiring plug.

6 Check the operation of the headlight, then install the access cover and securely tighten its retaining screws.

Sidelight (UK models only)

7 Remove the access cover as described in Step 1.

8 Pull the bulbholder out from the base of the headlight. Pull the bulb out of its holder **(see illustrations)**. If the socket contacts are dirty

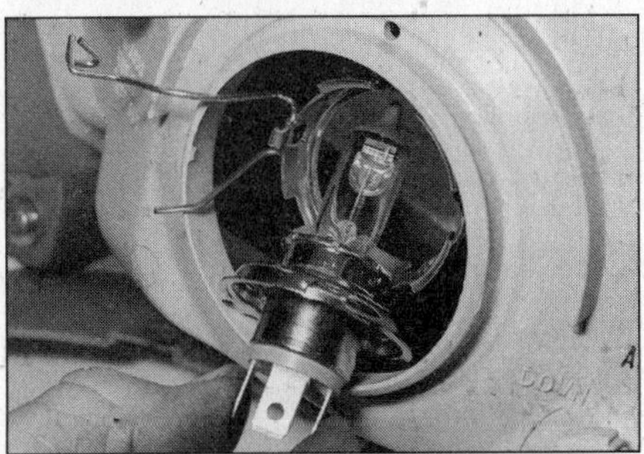

7.3b . . . and withdraw the bulb; DO NOT touch the bulb glass (fairing removed for clarity)

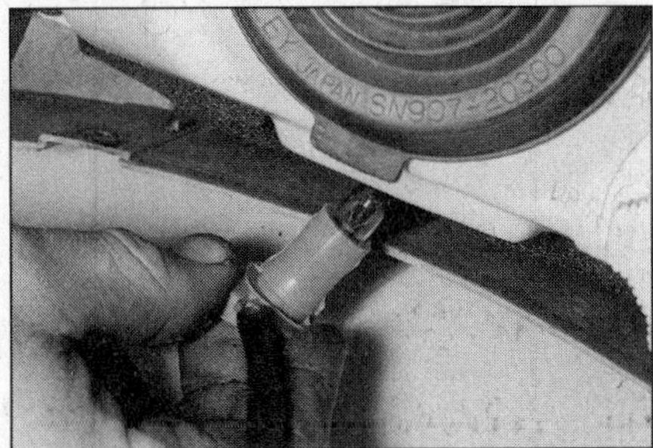

7.8a On UK models, pull the sidelight bulbholder out the base of the headlight unit . . .

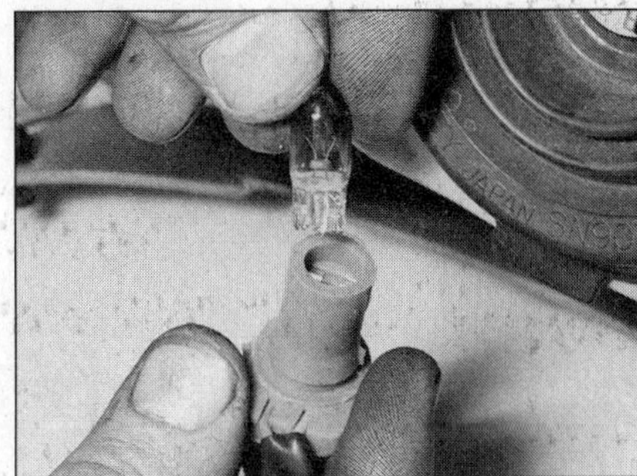

7.8b . . . and pull the bulb from the holder (fairing removed for clarity)

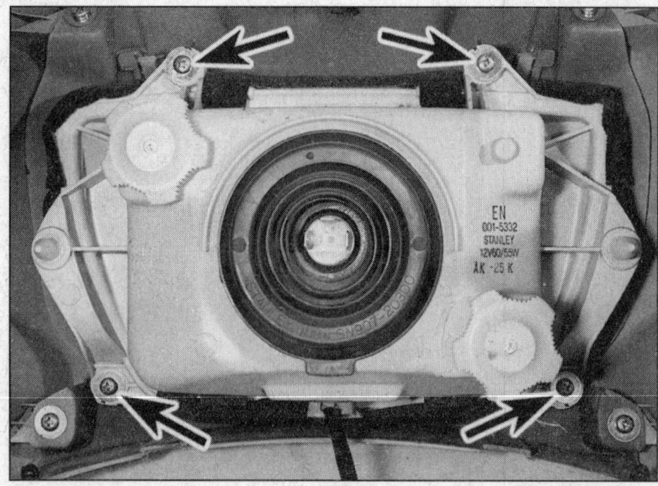

8.2 Headlight unit retained by four screws (arrows

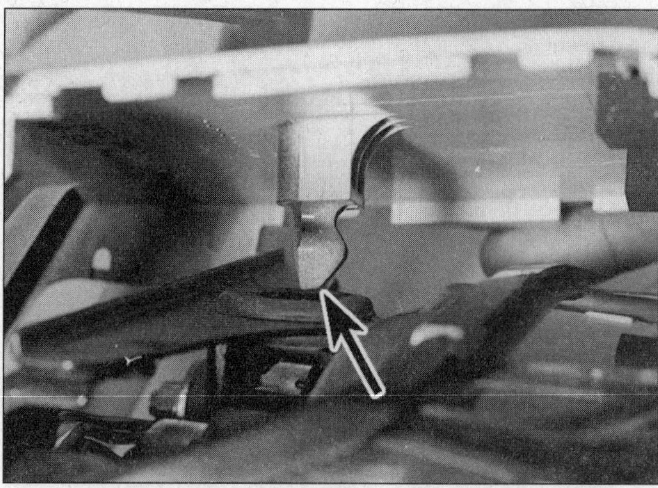

9.3 On all except V and W (1997 and 1998) models, pull the tail cowl section upwards to release its retaining peg (arrow)

or corroded, they should be scraped clean and sprayed with electrical contact cleaner before the new bulb is installed.

9 Carefully push the new bulb into position, then push the bulbholder back into the headlight unit.

10 Check the operation of the sidelight, then install the access cover and securely tighten its retaining screws.

8 Headlight assembly - removal and installation

Removal

1 Remove the upper fairing assembly as described in Chapter 8.

2 Slacken and remove the four screws and washers and remove the headlight assembly from the fairing **(see illustration)**.

Installation

3 Ensure the headlight assembly is correctly seated and fit the four retaining screws and washers, tightening them securely.

4 Install the upper fairing as described in Chapter 8.

9.4 Twist the bulbholder counterclockwise (anti-clockwise) to release it from the taillight unit

9 Taillight bulbs - replacement

1 Remove the seat as described in Chapter 8.

2 Remove the rubber mount from each side of the grab rail.

3 Undo the two bolts, and on V and W (1997 and 1998) models the two screws, then pull the tail cowl upwards to release its retaining peg (except V and W (1997 and 1998) models) and remove it from the bike **(see illustration)**.

4 Twist the relevant bulbholder counter-clockwise (anti-clockwise) to release it from the light unit **(see illustration)**.

5 Push the bulb into the holder and twist it counter-clockwise (anti-clockwise) to remove it. Check the socket terminals for corrosion and clean them if necessary. Line up the pins of the new bulb with the slots in the socket, push in and turn the bulb clockwise until it locks into place **(see illustration)**. **Note:** *The pins on the bulb are offset so it can only be installed one way.*

HAYNES HiNT ***It is a good idea to use a paper towel or dry cloth when handling the new bulb to prevent injury if the bulb should break and to increase bulb life.***

9.5 Note that the pins of the taillight bulb are offset (arrows)

6 Fit the tail cowl and securely tighten its bolts/screws.

7 Fit the rubber mounts to the grab rail. Ensure each mount is correctly fitted so that its locating peg is correctly engaged with the tail cowl. The mounts are different; the right mount is marked 'R' and the left mount 'L'.

8 Install the seat as described in Chapter 8.

10 Turn signal bulbs - replacement

Front

1 On M, N, P, R, S and T (1991 to 1996) models, remove the retaining screw from the base of the turn signal and withdraw the turn signal lens assembly. On V and W (1997 and 1998) models, remove the screw securing the lens and remove the lens.

2 On M, N, P, R, S and T (1991 to 1996) models, twist the bulbholder counterclockwise (anti-clockwise) to release it from the lens.

3 Push the bulb into the holder and twist it counterclockwise (anti-clockwise) to remove it. Check the socket terminals for corrosion and clean them if necessary. Line up the pins of the new bulb with the slots in the socket, push in and turn the bulb clockwise until it locks into place.

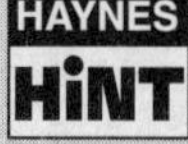

It is a good idea to use a paper towel or dry cloth when handling the new bulb to prevent injury if the bulb should break and to increase bulb life.

4 On M, N, P, R, S and T (1991 to 1996) models, fit the bulbholder into the lens and twist the bulbholder clockwise until it is locked into place.

5 Fit the turn signal lens assembly and securely tighten its retaining screw.

Rear

6 Remove the screw from the turn signal assembly and remove the lens.

7 Replace the bulb as described above in Step 3. Check the lens seal and replace if damaged.

8 Fit the lens and install the screw. Be careful not to overtighten the screw as the lens is easily cracked.

11 Turn signal assemblies - removal and installation

Removal

Front

1 On M, N, P and R (1991 to 1994) models, unscrew the retaining screw from the base of the turn signal and withdraw the turn signal from the upper fairing. Twist the bulbholder counterclockwise (anti-clockwise) to release it from the lens and remove the lens assembly. If necessary, the bulbholder and wiring can be removed once the upper fairing assembly has been removed as described in Chapter 8.

2 On S, T, V and W (1995 to 1998) models, trace the wiring back from the turn signal and disconnect its wiring connectors. Undo the nut securing the assembly to the inside of the fairing and remove the assembly along with its mounting base.

Rear

3 Remove the seat as described in Chapter 8.

4 Trace the wiring back from the turn signal and disconnect its wiring connectors.

5 Undo the two screws securing the assembly to the inside of the rear fender/mudguard, and remove them along with the collar and rubber mount which is fitted to each screw.

6 Remove the turn signal from the fender/mudguard along with its mounting base and collars.

Installation

7 Installation is the reverse of the removal procedure. On rear turn signal assemblies do not omit the collars from the rear of the assembly or the collar and mount from the mounting screw.

12 Turn signal circuit - check

1 The battery provides power for operation of the signal lights, so if they do not operate, always check the battery voltage first. Low battery voltage indicates either a faulty battery or a defective charging system. Refer to Section 3 for battery checks and Sections 29 and 30 for charging system tests. Also, check the fuses (see Section 5) and the switch (see Section 19).

2 Most turn signal problems are the result of a burned out bulb or corroded socket. This is especially true when the turn signals function properly in one direction, but fail to flash in the other direction. Check the bulbs and the sockets (see Section 10).

3 If the bulbs and sockets check out okay, check for power at the turn signal relay with the ignition ON. The relay is mounted onto the fairing mounting stay **(see illustration)**; for access remove the upper fairing assembly as described in Chapter 8. Refer to *wiring diagrams* at the end of the book to identify the power source terminal.

4 If power is present, check the wiring between the relay and the turn signal lights (see the *wiring diagrams* at the end of the book).

5 If the wiring checks out okay, replace the turn signal relay.

13 Brake light switches - check and replacement

Circuit check

1 Before checking any electrical circuit, check the bulb (see Section 10) and fuses (see Section 5).

2 Using a test light connected to a good ground (earth), check for voltage at the brake light switch wiring connector (see Steps 8 and 9 for the rear brake pedal switch). If there's no voltage present, check the wire between the switch and the fusebox (see the *wiring diagrams* at the end of this Chapter).

3 If voltage is available, touch the probe of the test light to the other terminal of the switch, and pull the brake lever or depress the brake pedal. **Note:** *The wiring connector halves must be joined for this test and the probes inserted in the back of the connector.* If the test light doesn't light up, replace the switch.

4 If the test light does light, check the wiring between the switch and the brake lights (see the *wiring diagrams* at the end of the book).

Switch replacement

Front brake lever switch

5 Remove the mounting screw and unplug the electrical connector from the switch **(see illustration)**.

6 Detach the switch from the bottom of the front brake master cylinder.

7 Installation is the reverse of the removal procedure. The brake lever switch isn't adjustable.

Rear brake pedal switch

8 Remove the fuel tank as described in Chapter 4.

12.3 The turn relay unit is mounted on the fairing stay

13.5 The front brake light switch (arrow) is mounted on the underside of the master cylinder

14.2a Unscrew the three instrument cluster mounting bolts (arrows) . . .

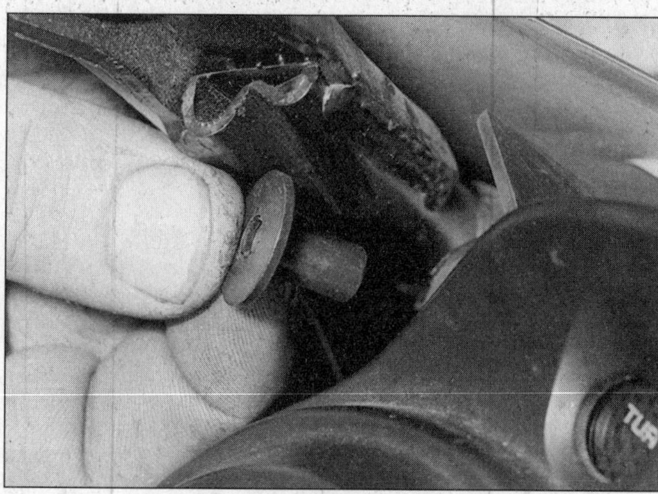

14.2b . . . and recover the collar from each mounting damper

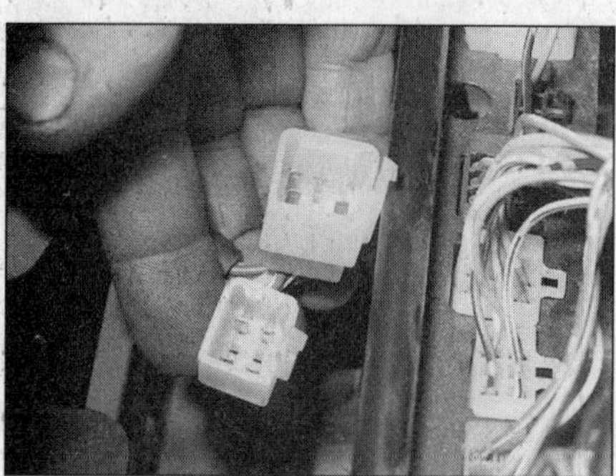

14.4 Disconnect both the cluster wiring connectors . . .

9 Trace the wiring back from the switch and disconnect it at its wiring connector in the junction box. Work back along the wiring releasing it from any relevant retaining clips and ties.

10 Unhook the spring from the switch and brake pedal and remove it from the bike.

11 Free the switch from the right footpeg bracket and remove it from the bike.

12 Install the switch by reversing the removal procedure, then adjust the switch by following the procedure described in Chapter 1.

14 Instrument cluster and speedometer cable or speed sensor - removal and installation

Removal

Instrument cluster - M, N, P and R (1991 to 1994) models

1 Remove the windshield (see Chapter 8).

2 Unscrew the three instrument cluster mounting bolts and withdraw the collars from the cluster mounting dampers **(see illustrations)**. Turn the handlebars if required to improve access to the lower bolt. Note the fitted position of the long collar.

3 Undo the screw securing the lower end of the speedometer cable to the drive gearbox and detach the cable.

4 Carefully maneuver the instrument cluster assembly out of position and disconnect the two cluster wiring connectors as they become accessible **(see illustration)**.

5 Unscrew the retaining ring and detach the speedometer cable from the rear of the instruments and remove the instrument cluster from the bike **(see illustrations)**.

6 Inspect the cluster mounting dampers for signs of damage and replace if necessary.

Instrument cluster - S, T, V and W (1995 to 1998) models

7 Remove the upper fairing (see Chapter 8).

8 Remove the rubber blanking cap from the lower mounting bolt **(see illustration)**. Unscrew the three instrument cluster mounting bolts and withdraw the collars from the cluster mounting dampers **(see illustrations 14.2a and b)**. Turn the handlebars if required to improve access to the lower bolt.

14.5a . . . then unscrew the retaining ring and detach the speedometer cable . . .

14.5b . . . and lift the instrument cluster assembly away from the bike

14.8 Remove the blanking plug from the lower mounting

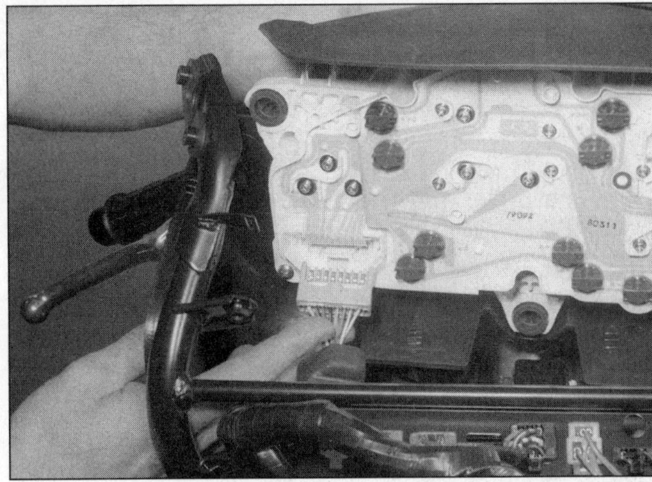
14.9 Disconnect the cluster wiring connectors as they become accessible

9 Carefully maneuver the instrument cluster assembly out of position and disconnect the two wiring connectors as they become accessible **(see illustration)**.

10 Inspect the cluster mounting dampers for signs of damage and replace if necessary.

Speedometer cable - M, N, P and R (1991 to 1994) models

11 Remove the instrument cluster as described above in Steps 1 to 5.

12 Free the cable from its retaining clip on the left lower fairing panel and remove it from the bike, noting its correct routing.

Speed sensor - S, T, V and W (1995 to 1998) models

13 Remove the right lower fairing panel (see Chapter 8) and the fuel tank (see Chapter 4).

14 Trace the wiring from the speed sensor, which is mounted on the crankcase behind the cylinders, and disconnect it at the connector **(see illustration)**.

15 Unscrew the sensor mounting bolts and remove the sensor **(see illustration)**. Remove and discard its O-ring as a new one must be used. Plug the sensor orifice with clean rag to prevent anything falling into the engine.

Installation

Instrument cluster - M, N, P and R (1991 to 1994) models

16 Maneuver the instrument cluster into position. Attach the speedometer cable to the cluster and securely tighten its retaining ring.

17 Connect the cluster wiring connectors and seat the cluster on the fairing stay, ensuring the rubber cover is tucked down behind the fairing.

18 Fit the collars to the cluster, making sure the longer collar is fitted to the center damper **(see illustration)**. Install the mounting bolts and tighten them securely.

19 Make sure the O-ring is fitted to the lower end of the speedometer cable. Align the inner cable slot with the drive gear dog and connect the cable to the speedometer drive. Secure the cable in position with the retaining screw.

20 Install the windshield (see Chapter 8).

Instrument cluster - S, T, V and W (1995 to 1998) models

21 Maneuver the instrument cluster into position and connect the wiring connectors **(see illustration 14.9)**.

22 Fit the collars then install the mounting bolts and tighten them securely **(see illustrations 14.2b and a)**. Fit the rubber blanking plug onto the lower bolt **(see illustration 14.8)**.

23 Install the fairing (see Chapter 8).

Speedometer cable - M, N, P and R (1991 to 1994) models

24 Ensure the cable is correctly routed and clip it into position on the left lower fairing panel.

25 Install the instrument cluster as described above.

26 On completion check that the cable doesn't cause the steering to bind or interfere with any other components.

Speed sensor - S, T, V and W (1995 to 1998) models

27 Installation is the reverse of removal, using a new O-ring.

15 Meters and gauges - check and replacement

Check

Temperature gauge

1 The temperature gauge check is described in Chapter 3.

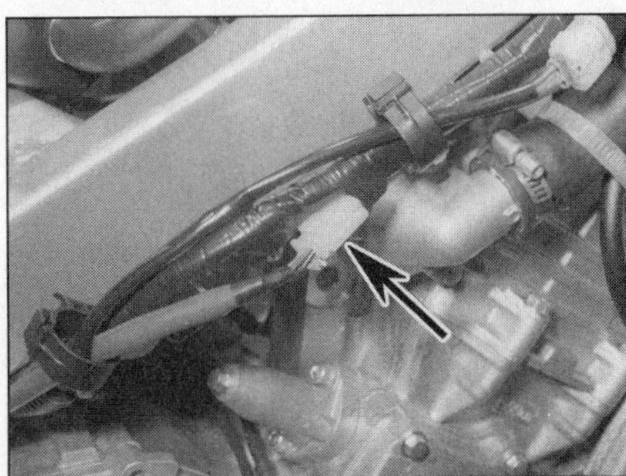
14.14 Disconnect the speed sensor wiring connector . . .

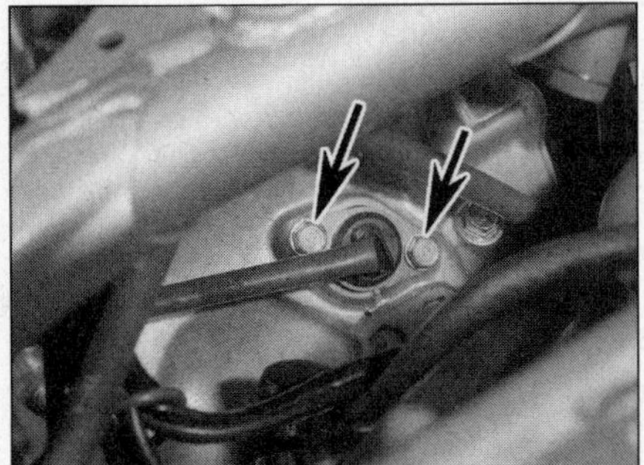
14.15 . . . then unscrew the two bolts (arrows) and remove the sensor

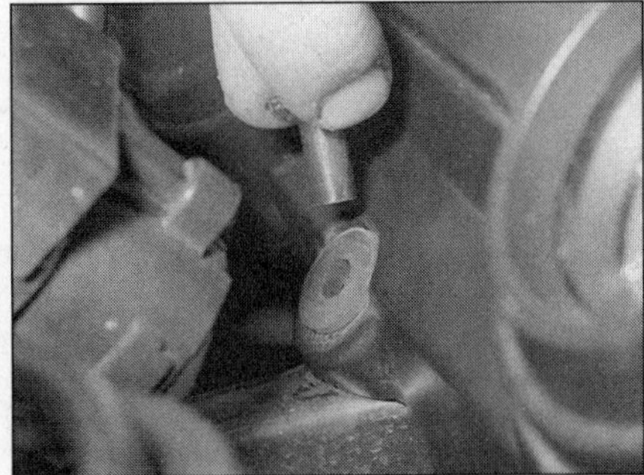
14.18 Make sure the longer collar is fitted to the cluster's center mounting damper

15.5a Check the instrument cluster wiring connectors

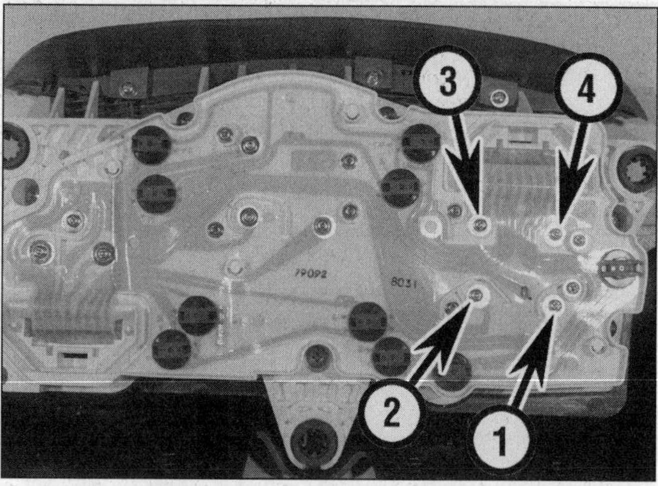

15.5b Instrument cluster wiring terminal identification

1 Black/brown
2 Green/black
3 Pink/green
4 Pink

Tachometer and speedometer - M, N, P and R (1991 to 1994) models

2 Special instruments are required to properly check the operation of these meters. Take the machine to a Honda dealer service department or other qualified repair shop for diagnosis.

Tachometer - S, T, V and W (1995 to 1998) models

3 Remove the right side cover and the upper fairing (see Chapter 8). Disconnect the ignition spark unit wiring connector and the instrument cluster wiring connector with the yellow/green wire **(see illustration 14.9)**. Check for continuity from one end of the yellow/green wire to the other. If there is no continuity there is a break in the wire or faulty connector. Refer to the wiring diagrams and trace and rectify the fault. If continuity exists, either the tachometer or the ignition spark unit is faulty. Special instruments are required to properly check their operation. Take the machine to a Honda dealer service department or other qualified repair shop for diagnosis.

Speedometer - S, T, V and W (1995 to 1998) models

4 First check the fuse (see Section 5), and that the battery is fully charged.

5 Remove the right side cover (see Chapter 8). Disconnect the speed sensor wiring connector and check for loose or broken connections **(see illustration 14.14)**. With the ignition switch ON, check for battery voltage between the black/brown and green/black terminals on the wiring loom side of the connector, then turn the ignition OFF and remake the connector. If there is no voltage, refer to the wiring diagrams and check the circuit. If there is voltage, remove the upper fairing (see Chapter 8), then disconnect the instrument cluster wiring connectors and check for loose or broken connections **(see illustration)**. With the ignition ON, check for battery voltage between the black/brown and green/black terminals on the rear of the instrument cluster **(see illustration)**. If there is no voltage, refer to the wiring diagrams and check the circuit. If there is voltage, with the ignition switch OFF check for continuity between the pink/green wire on the loom side of the speed sensor wiring connector and the

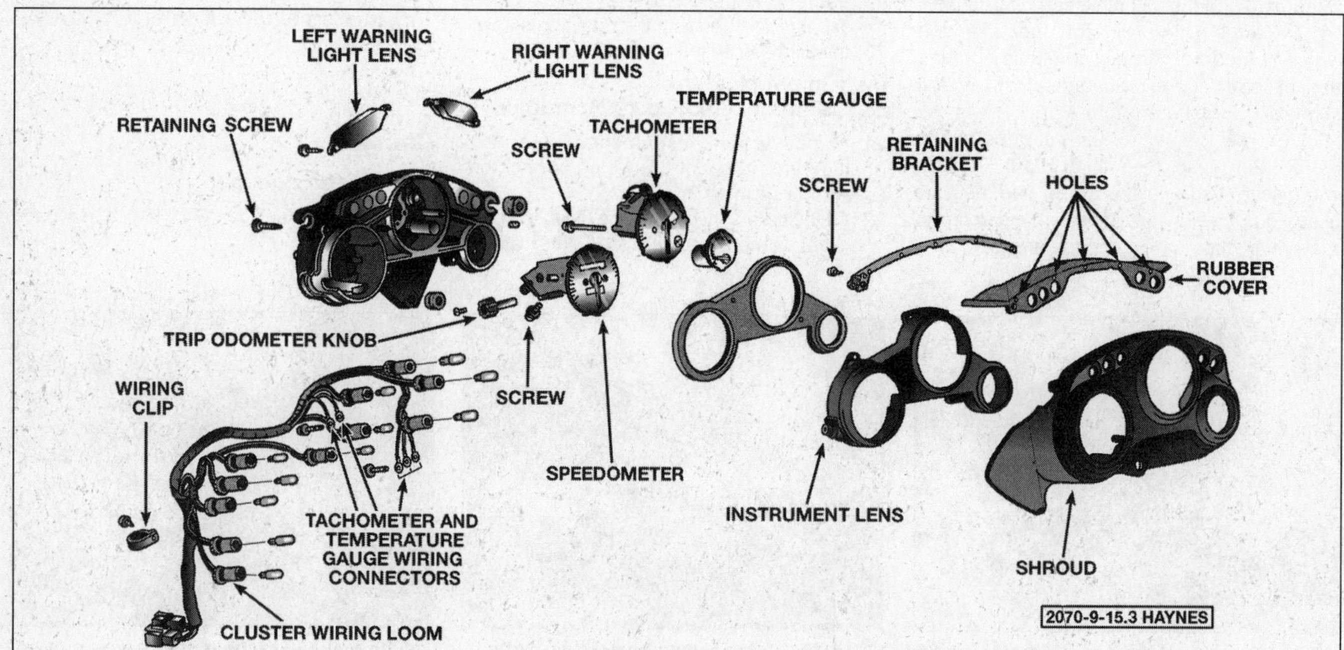

15.6 Exploded view of the instrument cluster - M, N, P and R (1991 to 1994) models

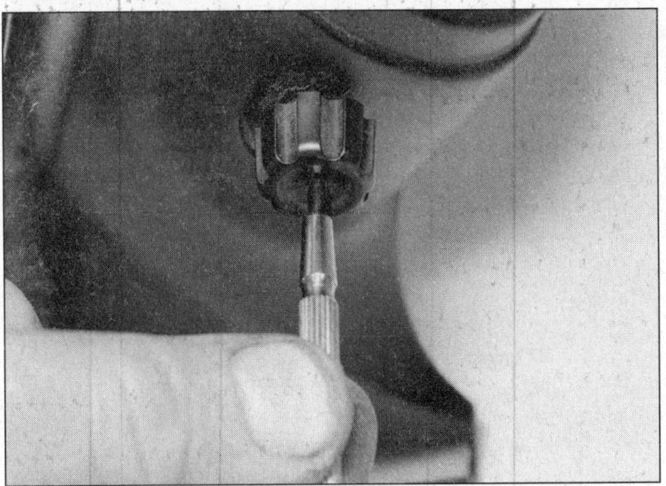

15.7 Trip odometer knob retained by a small screw in the center of the knob

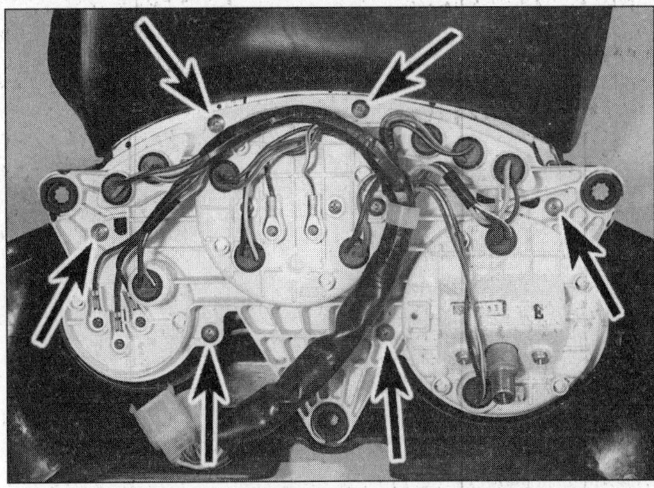

15.8a Undo the retaining screws (arrows) . . .

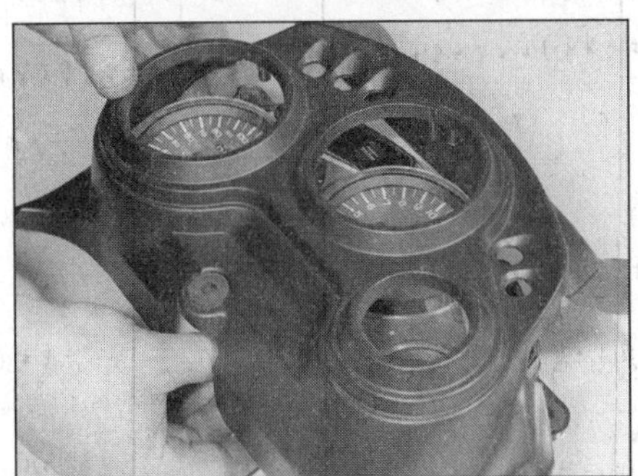

15.8b . . . and remove the shroud from the front of the instrument cluster

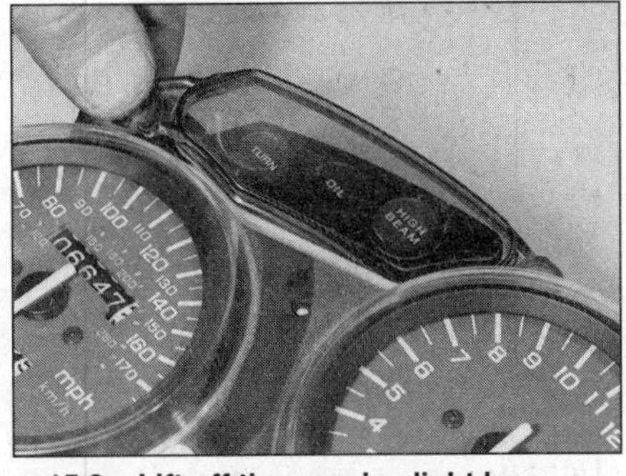

15.9a Lift off the warning light lens . . .

15.9b . . . and instrument lens

pink/green terminal on the rear of the instrument cluster. If there is no continuity, check the circuit for loose or broken connections. If there is continuity, connect a voltmeter between the pink/green and green/black terminals on the rear of the instrument cluster. With the machine on its centerstand and the ignition switch ON, turn the rear wheel by hand and check that a fluctuating voltage reading between 0 - 5 volts is obtained. If a reading is obtained, the speedometer is probably faulty. Special instruments are required to properly check the operation of the speedometer. Take the machine to a Honda dealer service department or other qualified repair shop for diagnosis. If no reading is obtained, and the wiring is good, then the sensor is faulty.

Replacement - M, N, P and R (1991 to 1994) models

6 Remove the cluster from the motorcycle as described in Section 14 and proceed as described under the relevant sub-heading below **(see illustration)**.

Speedometer

7 Unscrew the retaining screw from the center of the trip odometer knob and remove the knob **(see illustration)**.

8 Unscrew the six retaining screws and lift the shroud away from the front of the cluster assembly **(see illustrations)**.

9 Remove the warning light and instrument lenses **(see illustrations)**.

10 Undo the two retaining screws and lift the speedometer out of the casing **(see illustration)**.

11 Install the speedometer by reversing the removal sequence. Take care not to overtighten the retaining screws as the components are very fragile and can be easily damaged.

Tachometer

12 Carry out the operations described above in Steps 7 to 9.

13 Note the correct fitted positions of the tachometer wires then undo the retaining screws and detach the wiring **(see illustration)**.

14 Unscrew the two screws and lift the tachometer out of the casing.

15 Install the tachometer by reversing the removal sequence. Take care not to overtighten the retaining screws as the components are very fragile and can be easily damaged.

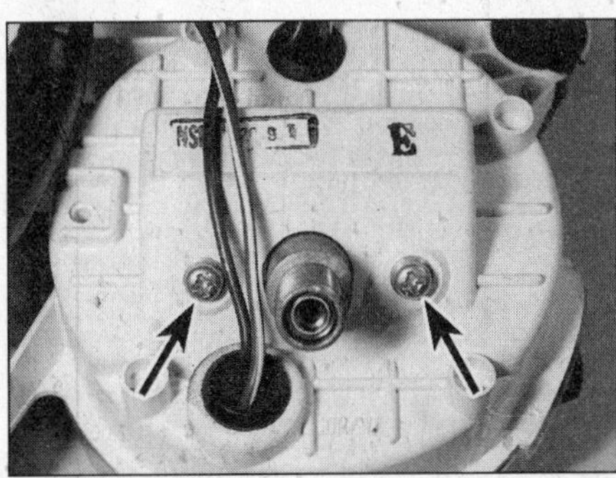

15.10 Speedometer is retained by two screws (arrows)

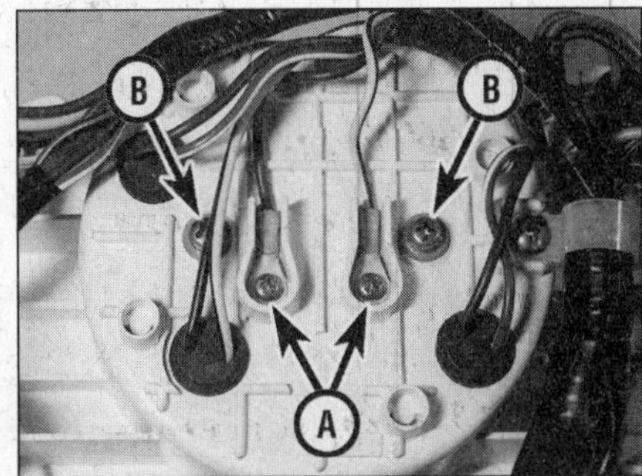

15.13 Undo the wiring screws (A) followed by the retaining screws (B) and lift out the tachometer

15.17 Temperature gauge is retained by the three wiring screws, wire colors are marked on the casing

Temperature gauge

16 Carry out the operations described above in Steps 7 to 9.

17 Note the correct fitted positions of the temperature gauge wires, then undo the retaining screws and detach the wiring; the wiring color locations should be marked on the casing **(see illustration)**. The temperature gauge can then be lifted out of the casing.

18 Install the temperature gauge by reversing the removal sequence. Take care not to overtighten the retaining screws as the components are very fragile and can be easily damaged.

Replacement - S, T, V and W (1995 to 1998) models

19 Remove the cluster from the motorcycle as described in Section 14 **(see illustration)**.

20 Remove the retaining screws and lift the cover away from the front of the cluster assembly **(see illustration)**.

21 Remove the screws and lift the relevant instrument out of the casing.

22 Install the instrument by reversing the removal sequence. Take care not to overtighten the retaining screws as the components are very fragile and can be easily damaged.

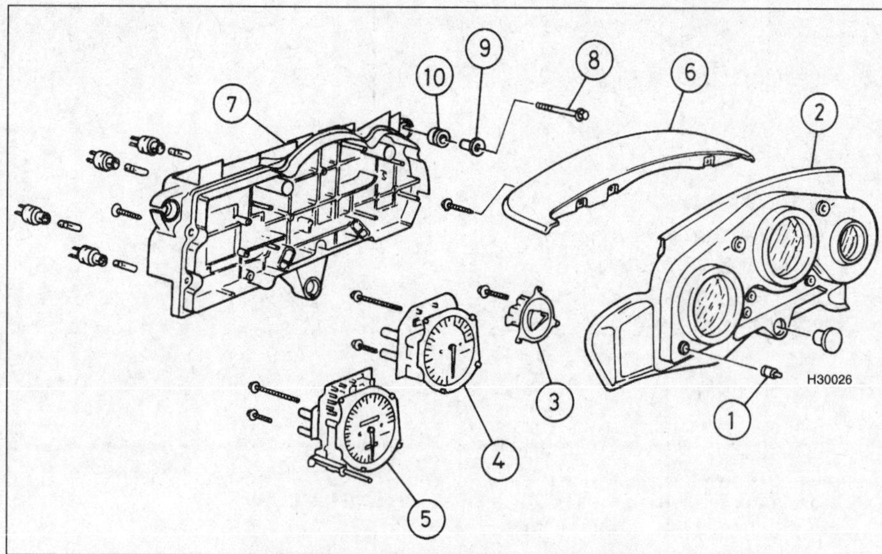

15.19 Exploded view of the instrument cluster - S, T, V and W (1995 to 1998) models

1 Reset knob
2 Cover
3 Temperature gauge
4 Tachometer
5 Speedometer
6 Shield
7 Instrument housing
8 Mounting bolt
9 Collar
10 Grommet

16 Instrument and warning light bulbs - replacement

M, N, P and R (1991 to 1994) models

1 Unscrew the three instrument cluster mounting bolts. Withdraw the collars from the cluster mounting dampers noting the fitted position of the long collar **(see illustrations 14.2a and 14.2b)**.

2 Undo the screw securing the lower end of the speedometer cable to the drive gearbox and detach the cable.

3 Taking great care not to damage the windshield, carefully maneuver the instrument cluster assembly slightly out of position and fold back the rubber cover to gain access to the bulbholders.

4 Pull the relevant bulbholder out of the back of the cluster then pull the bulb out of its holder **(see illustrations)**. If the socket contacts are dirty or corroded, they should be scraped clean and sprayed with electrical contact cleaner before a new bulb is installed.

5 Carefully push the new bulb into position, then push the bulbholder back into the rear of the cluster.

6 Seat the cluster on the fairing stay ensuring

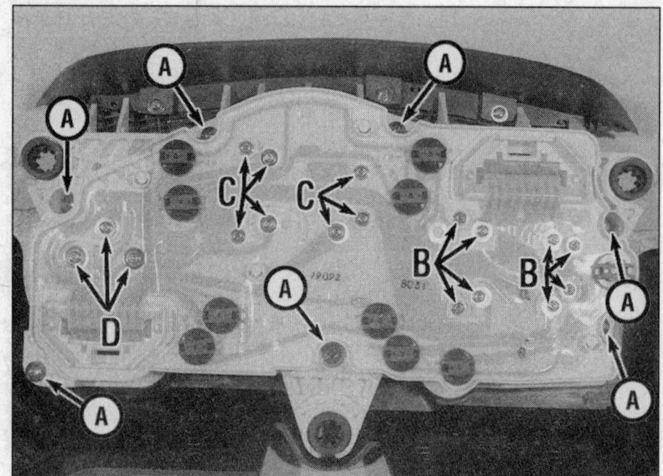

15.20 Cover screws (A), speedometer screws (B), tachometer screws (C), temperature gauge screws (D)

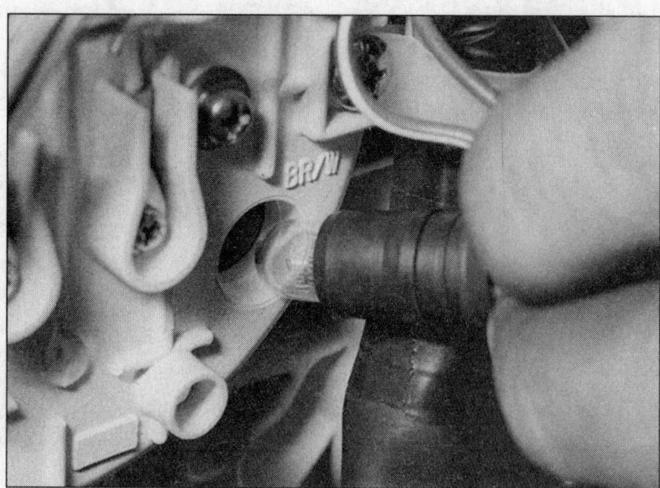

16.4a Pull the relevant bulbholder out from the cluster . . .

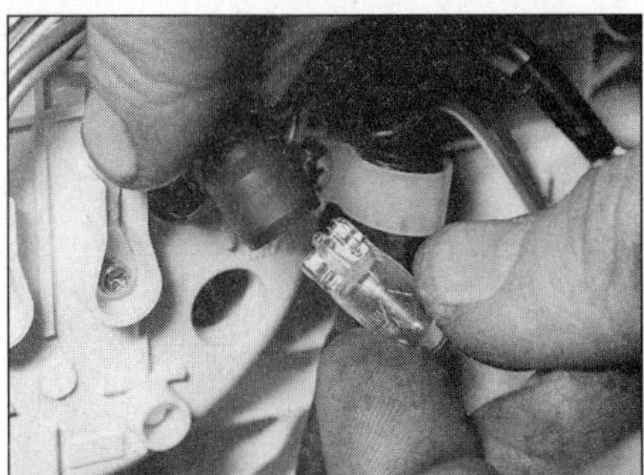

16.4b . . . and pull the bulb out of its holder

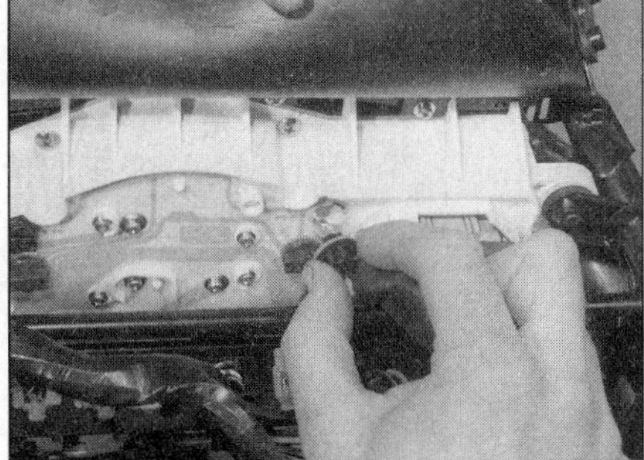

16.10a Release the bulbholder from the cluster . . .

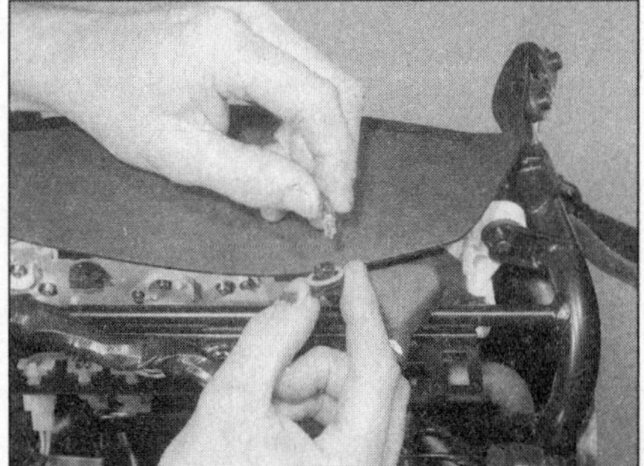

16.10b . . . and pull the bulb out of its holder

the rubber cover is tucked down behind the fairing.

7 Fit the collars to the cluster, making sure the longer collar is fitted to the center rubber **(see illustration 14.18)**. Install the mounting bolts and tighten them securely.

8 Make sure the O-ring is fitted to the lower end of the speedometer cable. Align the inner cable slot with the drive gear dog and connect the cable to the speedometer drive. Secure the cable in position with the retaining screw.

S, T, V and W (1995 to 1998) models

9 Remove the upper fairing (see Chapter 8).

10 Turn the relevant bulbholder anti-clockwise (counter clockwise) and draw it out of the back of the cluster, then pull the bulb out of its holder **(see illustrations)**. If the socket contacts are dirty or corroded, they should be scraped clean and sprayed with electrical contact cleaner before a new bulb is installed.

11 Carefully push the new bulb into position, then fit the bulbholder back into the rear of the cluster and turn it clockwise to lock it.

12 Install the upper fairing (see Chapter 8).

17 Oil pressure switch - check and replacement

Check

1 Before checking the electrical circuit, check the bulb (see Section 16) and fuses (see Section 5).

2 Remove the right lower fairing panel as described in Chapter 8 to gain access to the oil pressure switch. On M, N, P and R (1991 to 1994) models it is screwed into the top of the crankcase - if necessary, also remove the fuel tank (see Chapter 4) to improve access to the switch. On S, T, V and W (1995 to 1998) models, it is screwed into the right side of the crankcase, below the crankshaft end cover.

3 Peel back the rubber cover, then undo the retaining screw and detach the wiring connector from the switch **(see illustrations)**.

4 With the wire detached and the ignition switched on, the light should be out. If it's illuminated, the wire between the switch and instrument cluster must be grounded (earthed) at some point.

5 Ground (earth) the wire on the crankcase and check that the warning light comes on. If the light does come on, either the switch is defective or the engine oil pressure is low. Perform an oil pressure check as described in Chapter 2. If the oil pressure checks out okay the switch is defective and must be replaced.

6 If the light does not come on when the wire is grounded (earthed), check for voltage at the wire terminal using a test light. If there's no voltage present, check the wire between the switch, the instrument cluster and fusebox for continuity (see the *wiring diagrams* at the end of the book).

Replacement

7 Detach the wire from the switch as described above in Steps 2 and 3.

8 Unscrew the switch from the crankcase.

9 Ensure the switch threads are clean and dry and apply a thin coat of suitable sealant to the 3 to 4 mm (approximately ⅛ inch) of its threads that are closest to the hex on the switch.

10 Screw the switch into the top of the crankcase and tighten it to the torque setting specified at the beginning of the Chapter.

11 Attach the wire, tightening its retaining screw securely, then seat the rubber cover correctly over the switch.

12 Check the operation of the oil pressure warning light, then install the fairing panel as described in Chapter 8.

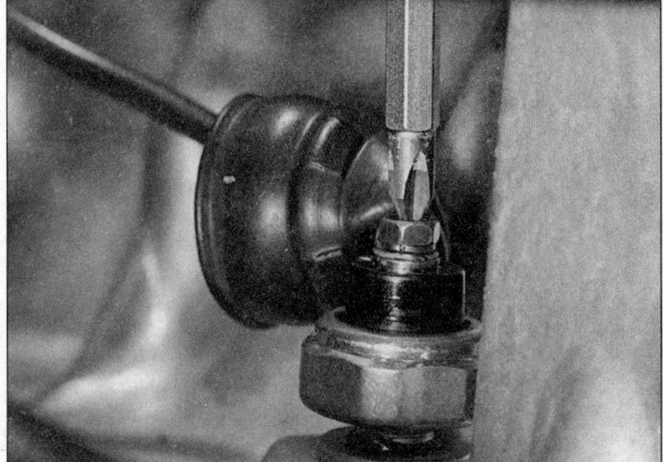

17.3a On M, N, P and R (1991 to 1994) models the oil pressure switch is screwed into the crankcase directly behind the cylinders

17.3b On S, T, V and W (1995 to 1998) models the oil pressure switch is screwed into the crankcase directly below the right end cover

18 Ignition (main) switch - check, removal and installation

Check

1 Disconnect the switch wiring connector as described in Steps 4 and 5.

2 Using an ohmmeter, check the continuity of the terminal pairs (see the *wiring diagrams* at the end of the book). Continuity should exist between the terminals connected by a solid line when the switch is in the indicated position.

3 If the switch fails any of the tests, replace it.

Removal

4 On M, N, P and R (1991 to 1994) models, remove the instrument cluster (see Section 14). On S, T, V and W (1995 to 1998) models, remove the upper fairing (see Chapter 8).

5 Trace the wiring back from the base of the switch, releasing it from any necessary retaining clips, and disconnect it at the wiring connector which is clipped to the front of the fairing stay.

6 Undo the two Torx bolts securing the switch to the underside of the top triple clamp and remove the switch from the bike.

Installation

7 Maneuver the switch assembly into position making sure the wiring is correctly routed.

8 Thoroughly clean the switch bolts and apply a few drops of suitable locking compound to them. Install the bolts and tighten them to the specified torque setting.

9 Secure the switch wiring in position with any relevant clips or ties. Pass the connector through the fairing stay and reconnect it.

10 Install the instrument cluster (Section 14).

19 Handlebar switches - check

1 Generally speaking, the switches are reliable and trouble-free. Most troubles, when they do occur, are caused by dirty or corroded contacts, but wear and breakage of internal parts is a possibility that should not be overlooked. If breakage does occur, the entire switch and related wiring harness will have to be replaced with a new one, since individual parts are not usually available.

2 The switches can be checked for continuity with a multimeter set to the resistance function (ohmmeter) or a continuity test light. Always disconnect the battery negative cable, which will prevent the possibility of a short circuit, before making the checks.

3 On M, N, P and R (1991 to 1994) models, remove the instrument cluster (see Section 14). On S, T, V and W (1995 to 1998) models, remove the upper fairing (see Chapter 8). Trace the wiring harness of the switch in question back to its connector(s) which are clipped to the front of the fairing stay. Unplug the relevant electrical connector(s).

4 Using the multimeter or test light, check for continuity between the terminals of the switch harness with the switch in the various positions (see the *wiring diagrams* at the end of this Chapter).

5 If the continuity check indicates a problem exists, refer to Section 20, remove the switch and spray the switch contacts with electrical contact cleaner. If they are accessible, the contacts can be scraped clean with a knife or polished with crocus cloth. If switch components are damaged or broken, it will be obvious when the switch is disassembled.

20.4 Each handlebar switch is retained by two screws

20 Handlebar switches - removal and installation

Removal

1 On M, N, P and R (1991 to 1994) models, remove the instrument cluster (see Section 14). On S, T, V and W (1995 to 1998) models, remove the upper fairing (see Chapter 8). Proceed as described under the relevant sub-heading.

Left handlebar switch

2 Trace the wiring harness back from the switch to the wiring connectors which are clipped to the front of the fairing stay. Unplug the relevant electrical connector.

3 Work back along the harness, freeing it from all the relevant clips and ties, while noting its correct routing.

4 Unscrew the two handlebar switch screws and free the switch from the handlebar, disconnecting the choke cable from its lever **(see illustration)**.

5 Unscrew the choke cable from the lower half of the switch and remove the switch from the bike.

Right handlebar switch

6 Disconnect the switch wiring connectors as described above in Steps 2 and 3.

7 Disconnect the throttle cables from the carburetors, then free the cables from the switch as described in Section 10 of Chapter 4.

8 Remove the switch from the bike.

Installation

Left handlebar switch

9 Installation is a reversal of the removal procedure, making sure that the locating peg on the lower half of the switch is correctly located in the handlebar hole. On completion check the choke cable operation and, if necessary, adjust as described in Chapter 1.

Right handlebar switch

10 Installation is a reversal of the removal procedure, making sure that the locating peg on the lower half of the switch is correctly located in the handlebar hole. Adjust the throttle cables as described in Chapter 1.

21 Neutral switch - check and replacement

Check

1 Before checking the electrical circuit, check the bulb (see Section 16) and fuses (see Section 5).

2 Remove the left lower fairing panel as described in Chapter 8 to gain access to the neutral switch. The switch is screwed into the left side of the crankcase, where it is situated directly in front of the engine sprocket cover.

3 Disconnect the wiring connector from the switch and shift the transmission into neutral.

4 With the wire detached and the ignition switched on, the neutral light should be out. If not, the wire between the switch and instrument cluster must be grounded (earthed) at some point.

5 Ground (earth) the wire on the crankcase and check that the neutral light comes on. If the light does come on, the switch is defective.

6 If the light does not come on when the wire is grounded, check for voltage at the wire terminal using a test light. If there's no voltage present, check the wire between the switch, the instrument cluster and fusebox (see the *wiring diagrams* at the end of the book).

Replacement

7 Remove the left lower fairing panel as described in Chapter 8.

8 Disconnect the wiring connector from the switch which is situated directly in front of the engine sprocket cover.

9 Unscrew the switch and remove it from the crankcase. Recover the sealing washer and plug the switch opening to minimize oil loss while the switch is removed.

10 Clean the threads of the switch and fit a new sealing washer to it.

11 Remove the plug from the crankcase and install the switch. Tighten the switch to the specified torque, then reconnect the wiring connector.

12 Check the operation of the neutral light.

13 Check the oil level as described in *'Daily (pre-ride) checks'* and top up if necessary.

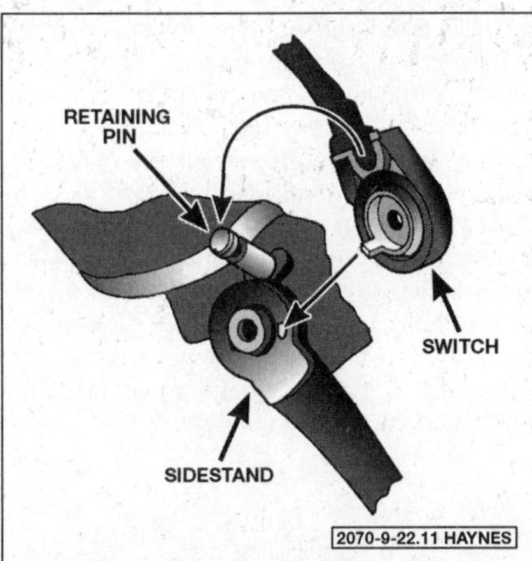

22.11 Ensure the sidestand switch lug engages the stand hole and the switch recess engages the retaining pin

22 Sidestand switch - check and replacement

Check

1 Before checking any electrical circuit, check the bulb (see Section 16) and fuses (see Section 5).

2 To gain access to the switch wiring connector remove the fuel tank as described in Chapter 4. The sidestand switch connector is the green 3-pin wiring connector situated in the junction box.

3 Disconnect the wiring connector and check the operation of the switch using an ohmmeter or continuity test light.

4 Set the meter to the ohms x 1 scale and connect the meter to the Yellow/black and Green wires on the switch side of the wiring connector. With the sidestand down (extended) there should be continuity between the terminals, and with the stand up there should be no continuity (infinite resistance).

5 Connect the meter to the Green/white and Green wires on the switch side of the connector. With the sidestand up there should be continuity between the terminals, and with the stand down there should be no continuity (infinite resistance).

6 If the switch does not perform as expected, it is defective and must be replaced.

7 If the switch checks out okay, check the wiring between the wiring connector, instrument cluster and fusebox (see the *wiring diagrams* at the end of this book).

Replacement

8 Disconnect the switch wiring connector as described above in Step 2.

9 Work back along the switch wiring, freeing it from any relevant retaining clips and ties, noting its correct routing. Access to the wiring can be improved by removing the left lower fairing panel as described in Chapter 8.

10 Unscrew the bolt securing the switch to the sidestand mounting bracket and remove the switch from the bike.

11 Fit the new switch to the rear of the sidestand bracket making sure the switch lug engages the hole in the sidestand, and the switch recess engages with the retaining pin **(see illustration)**. Install the switch retaining bolt and tighten it to the specified torque setting.

12 Ensure the wiring is correctly routed up to the junction box and retained by all the necessary clips and ties.

13 Securely reconnected the wiring connector and check the operation of the warning light.

14 Install the fuel tank as described in Chapter 4 and, if necessary, the fairing panel as described in Chapter 8.

23 Clutch diode - check and replacement

1 The clutch diode is plugged into the main wiring harness clipped onto the right side of the frame. The diode is part of the starter safety circuit **(see illustration 1.1)** which prevents the starter motor operating while the transmission is in gear unless the clutch lever is pulled in. If the starter circuit is faulty, first check the fuses (see Section 5).

2 To gain access to the diode remove the right side lower fairing panel as described in Chapter 8.

3 Remove the insulating tape and unplug the diode from the wiring harness. Using a multimeter set to the resistance scale (ohmmeter) or a continuity test light, check for continuity between any two of the terminals on the diode. Now transpose the meter probes and check for continuity between the same terminals but in the opposite direction. Repeat the checks between each pair of terminals in turn, taking six readings in all. If the diode is serviceable there should be continuity in one direction (indicated by the arrow on the diode) and no continuity (infinite resistance) in the other. If not, the diode must be replaced.

4 If the diode checks out okay, check the other components in the starter circuit (clutch switch, neutral switch and starter relay) as described in the relevant sections of this Chapter. If all components check out fine, check the wiring between the various components (see the *wiring diagrams* at the end of this book).

5 Plug the diode back into position and install the lower fairing panel as described in Chapter 8.

24.2 Clutch switch (arrow) is mounted in the clutch lever bracket

24 Clutch switch - check and replacement

Check

1 The clutch switch is situated in the lever mounting bracket. The switch is part of the starter safety circuit (see Section 1) which prevents the starter motor operating while the transmission is in gear unless the clutch lever is pulled in. If the starter circuit is faulty, first check the fuses (see Section 5).

2 To check the switch, disconnect the wiring connectors **(see illustration)**. Using a multimeter set to the resistance scale (ohmmeter) or a continuity test light, check for continuity between the terminals of the switch with the lever pulled into the handlebar and no continuity (infinite resistance) with the lever released. If this is not the case, the switch is faulty and must be replaced.

3 If the switch checks out okay, check the other components in the starter circuit (clutch diode, neutral switch and starter relay) as described in the relevant sections of this Chapter. If all components check out fine, check the wiring between the various components (see the *wiring diagrams* at the end of this book).

Replacement

4 Disconnect the wiring connectors from the clutch lever switch.

5 Slacken the upper adjuster to obtain maximum freeplay in the clutch cable then slacken and remove the clutch lever nut and pivot bolt.

6 Free the lever from the mounting bracket and remove the switch.

7 Install the new switch and fit the lever. Securely tighten the pivot bolt and nut then connect the switch wiring connectors.

8 Adjust the clutch cable as described in Chapter 1.

25 Horn - check and replacement

Check

1 On M, N, P and R (1991 to 1994) models, remove the left lower fairing panel (see Chapter 8). On S, T, V and W (1995 to 1998) models, remove the upper fairing (see Chapter 8).

26.1 Starter relay is located behind the left side cover

2 Unplug the wiring connectors from the horn. Using two jumper wires, apply battery voltage directly to the terminals on the horn. If the horn sounds, check the switch (see Section 19) and the wiring between the switch and the horn (see the *wiring diagrams* at the end of this Chapter).
3 If the horn doesn't sound, replace it.

Replacement

4 On M, N, P and R (1991 to 1994) models, remove the left lower fairing panel (see Chapter 8). On S, T, V and W (1995 to 1998) models, remove the upper fairing (see Chapter 8).
5 Unplug the wiring connectors from the horn then unscrew the bolt securing the horn to its mounting bracket and remove it from the machine.
6 Connect the wiring connectors to the new horn and securely tighten its retaining bolt.

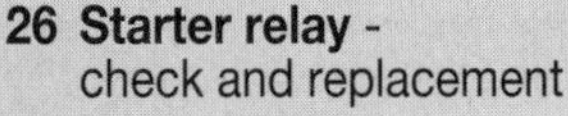

26 Starter relay - check and replacement

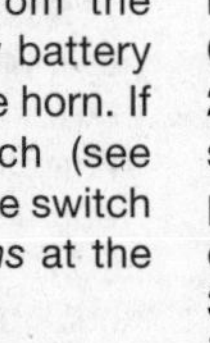

Check

1 If the starter circuit is faulty, first check the fuses (see Section 5). The starter relay is located behind the left side cover (see Chapter 8, if necessary) **(see illustration)**.
2 With the ignition switch ON, the engine kill switch in RUN and the transmission in neutral, press the starter switch. The relay should click.
3 If the relay doesn't click, switch off the ignition and remove the relay as described below and test as follows.
4 Set a multimeter to the ohms x 1 scale and connect it across the relay's starter motor and battery lead terminals. Using a fully-charged 12 volt battery and two insulated jumper wires, connect the positive terminal of the battery to the Yellow/red terminal of the relay, and the negative terminal to the Green/red terminal of the relay. At this point the relay should click and the multimeter read 0 ohms (continuity). If this is the case the relay is serviceable and the fault lies in the starter switch circuit (check the clutch diode, clutch switch and neutral switch as described elsewhere in this Chapter). If the relay does not click when battery voltage is applied and indicates no continuity across its terminals, it is faulty and must be replaced.

Replacement

5 Remove the seat as described in Chapter 8.
6 Undo the three screws and remove the cover from the battery box. Disconnect the battery terminals, remembering to disconnect the negative (-ve) terminal first.
7 Peel back the rubber cover, then undo the two retaining screws and disconnect the starter motor and battery leads from the relay.
8 Disconnect the relay wiring connector and remove the relay from the bike.
9 Installation is the reverse of removal ensuring the terminal screws are securely tightened. Connect the negative lead last when reconnecting the battery.

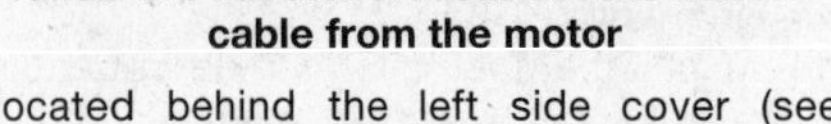

27.3 Peel back the rubber cover, then undo the nut and disconnect the starter cable from the motor

27 Starter motor - removal and installation

Removal

1 Remove the fuel tank as described in Chapter 4 and the left lower fairing panel as described in Chapter 8.
2 Undo the three retaining screws, then remove the battery box cover and disconnect the battery negative (-ve) lead.
3 Peel back the rubber cover and unscrew the nut securing the starter cable to the motor **(see illustration)**.
4 Unscrew the starter motor retaining bolts, noting the correct fitted positions of the ground (earth) lead and wiring clamp **(see illustration)**.
5 Slide the starter motor out from the crankcase and remove it from the left side of the machine **(see illustration)**.
6 Inspect the O-ring on the end of the starter motor and replace if necessary.

Installation

7 Make sure the O-ring is correctly seated in its groove and apply a smear of engine oil to it to aid installation.

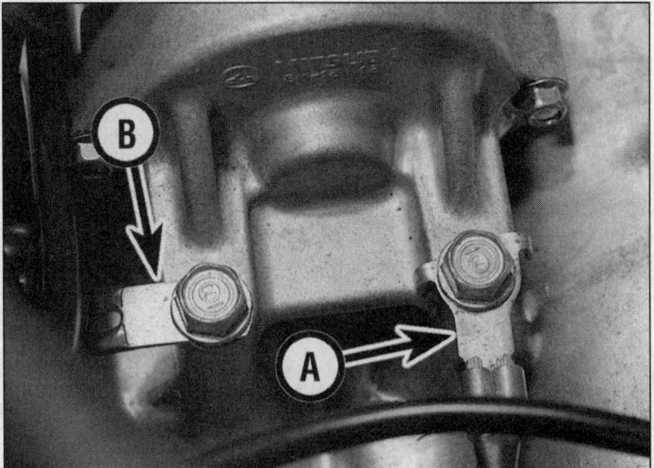

27.4 Undo the starter motor retaining bolts, noting the fitted position of the earth lead (A) and wiring clamp (B) . . .

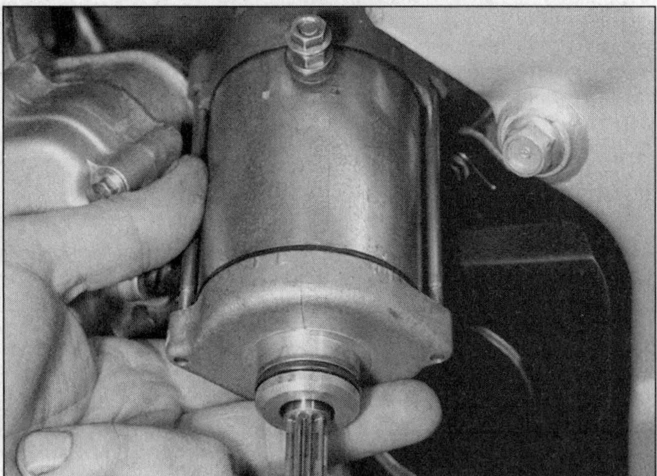

27.5 . . . and maneuver the motor out from the left side of the frame

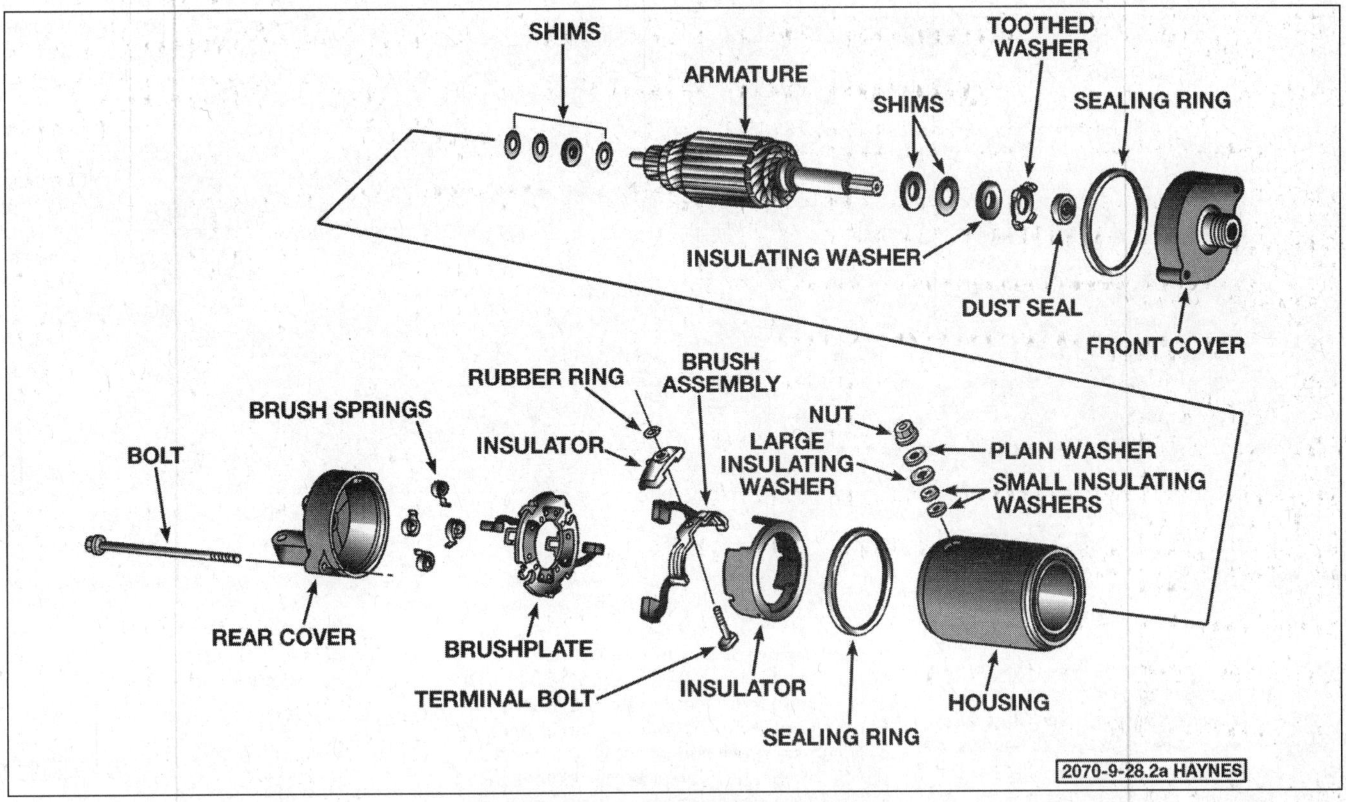

SHIMS
ARMATURE
SHIMS
TOOTHED WASHER
SEALING RING
INSULATING WASHER
DUST SEAL
FRONT COVER
RUBBER RING
BRUSH ASSEMBLY
BRUSH SPRINGS
NUT
INSULATOR
LARGE INSULATING WASHER
PLAIN WASHER
SMALL INSULATING WASHERS
BOLT
REAR COVER
BRUSHPLATE
TERMINAL BOLT
INSULATOR
SEALING RING
HOUSING
2070-9-28.2a HAYNES

28.2a Exploded view of the starter motor

Note that on V and W (1997 and 1998) models the bolts fit through the front cover and thread into the rear cover

8 Maneuver the motor into position and slide it into the crankcase.

9 Fit the retaining bolts, ensuring the wiring clip is correctly fitted underneath the rear bolt and the ground lead underneath the front bolt, and tighten them securely.

10 Connect the cable and securely tighten the nut. Make sure the rubber cover is correctly seated over the terminal.

11 Connect the battery and install the battery box cover.

12 Install the fuel tank as described in Chapter 4 and fairing panel as described in Chapter 8.

28 Starter motor - disassembly, inspection and reassembly

Disassembly

1 Remove the starter motor (see Section 27).

2 Make alignment marks between the housing and end covers **(see illustrations)**.

3 Unscrew the two long bolts, then remove the rear cover from the motor along with its sealing ring. Remove the shim(s) from the rear end of the armature noting their correct fitted locations.

4 Remove the front cover from the motor along with its sealing ring. Recover the toothed washer from the cover and slide off the insulating washer and shim(s) from the front end of the armature, noting their correct fitted locations.

5 Withdraw the armature from the housing.

6 Noting the correct fitted location of each washer, unscrew the nut from the terminal bolt and remove the plain washer, the various insulating washers and the rubber ring **(see illustration)**. Withdraw the terminal bolt and brushplate assembly from the housing and recover the insulator.

7 Lift the brush springs and slide the brushes out from their holders **(see illustration)**.

28.2b Make alignment marks between the housing and end covers before disassembly

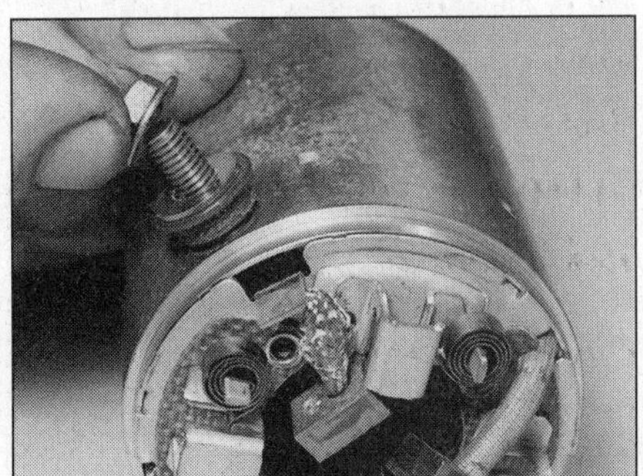

28.6 Unscrew the nut and remove the washers from the terminal bolt noting their correct fitted order

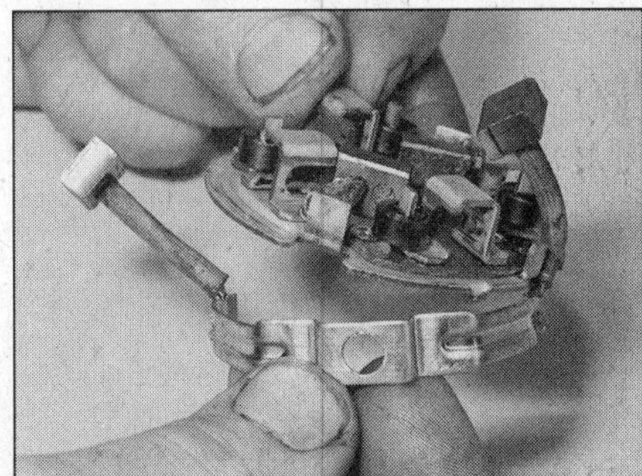

28.7 Lift the brush springs and slide the brushes out from their holders

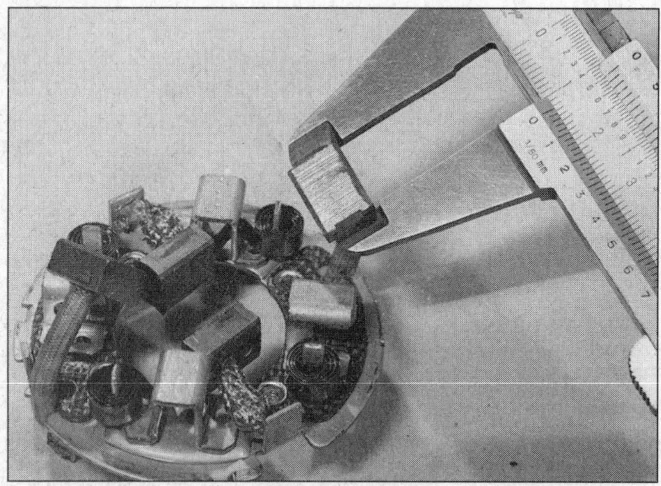

28.8 Measuring brush length - replace brushes if they are worn beyond service limit

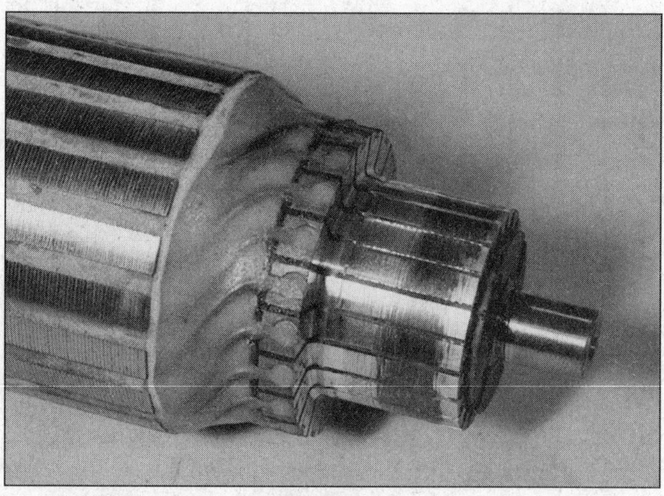

28.9 Inspect commutator segments for wear and test as described in text

Inspection

8 The parts of the starter motor that are most likely to require attention are the brushes. Measure the length of the brushes and compare the results to the brush length listed in this Chapter's Specifications **(see illustration)**. If any of the brushes are worn beyond the service limit, replace the brushplate assembly with a new one. If the brushes are not worn excessively, nor cracked, chipped, or otherwise damaged, they may be re-used.

9 Inspect the commutator for scoring, scratches and discoloration **(see illustration)**. The commutator can be cleaned and polished with crocus cloth, but do not use sandpaper or emery paper. After cleaning, wipe away any residue with a cloth soaked in electrical system cleaner or denatured alcohol.

10 Using an ohmmeter or a continuity test light, check for continuity between the commutator bars. Continuity should exist between each bar and all of the others. Also, check for continuity between the commutator bars and the armature shaft. There should be no continuity between the commutator and the shaft. If the checks indicate otherwise, the armature is defective.

11 Check the starter pinion gear for worn, cracked, chipped and broken teeth. If the gear is damaged or worn, replace the starter motor.

12 Inspect the insulating washers and front cover dust seal for signs of damage and replace if necessary.

Reassembly

13 Lift the brush springs and slide all the brushes back into position in their holders.

Lifting the end of the brush spring so that it is against the top of the brush holder and not pressing the brush inwards makes it much easier to install the armature.

14 Fit the insulator to the housing and install the brushplate. Insert the terminal bolt through the brushplate and housing **(see illustrations)**.

15 Slide the rubber ring and small insulating washer(s) onto the bolt, followed by the large insulating washer(s) and the plain washer. Fit the nut to the terminal bolt and tighten it securely **(see illustrations)**.

16 Locate the brushplate assembly in the housing making sure its tab is correctly located in the housing slot **(see illustration)**.

28.14a Locate the insulator in the housing . . .

28.14b . . . and install the brushplate assembly and terminal bolt

28.15a Slide the rubber ring onto the terminal bolt . . .

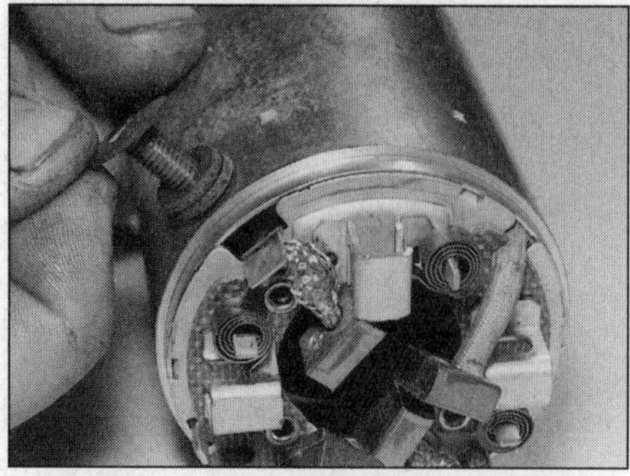

28.15b . . . followed by the insulating washers . . .

28.15c . . . and plain washer, fit the nut and tighten it securely

28.16 Make sure the brushplate tab (arrow) is correctly located in the housing slot

28.17a Insert the armature from the front of the housing . . .

28.17b . . . and locate the brushes on the commutator

28.18 Fit the toothed washer to the front cover so that its teeth engage with the cover ribs

28.19a Install the shims and washers on the front of the armature making sure they are correctly fitted

28.19b Fit the sealing ring (arrow) and install the front cover

17 Insert the armature in the front of the housing and locate the brushes on the commutator bars. Check that each brush is securely pressed against the commutator by its spring and is free to move easily in its holder **(see illustrations)**.

18 Fit the toothed washer to the front cover so that its teeth are correctly located with the cover ribs **(see illustration)**. Apply a smear of grease to the cover dust seal lip.

19 Slide the shim(s) onto the front end of the armature shaft then fit the insulating washer. Fit the sealing ring to the housing and carefully slide the front cover into position, aligning the marks made on removal **(see illustrations)**.

20 Fit the shims to the rear of the armature shaft **(see illustration)**.

21 Ensure the brushplate inner tab is correctly located in the housing slot and fit the sealing ring to the housing **(see illustration)**.

22 Align the rear cover groove with the brushplate outer tab and install the cover **(see illustration)**.

28.20 Fit the rear shims to the armature in the order noted on removal

28.21 Make sure the brushplate tab is correctly located in the housing (arrow) . . .

28.22 . . . and install the rear cover, aligning its groove with the brushplate outer tab (arrows)

28.23 Align the marks made on removal and install the starter motor bolts

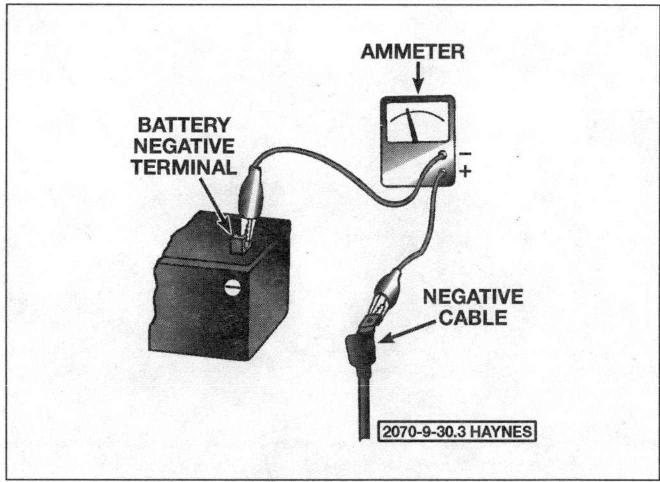

30.3 Checking the charging system leakage rate, connect meter as shown

23 Check the marks made on removal are correctly aligned, then fit the long bolts and tighten them securely **(see illustration)**.

24 Install the starter motor (see Section 27).

29 Charging system testing - general information and precautions

1 If the performance of the charging system is suspect, the system as a whole should be checked first, followed by testing of the individual components (the alternator stator coils and the voltage regulator/rectifier). **Note:** *Before beginning the checks, make sure the battery is fully charged and that all system connections are clean and tight.*

2 Checking the output of the charging system and the performance of the various components within the charging system requires the use of a multimeter (with voltage, current and resistance checking facilities).

3 When making the checks, follow the procedures carefully to prevent incorrect connections or short circuits, as irreparable damage to electrical system components may result if short circuits occur.

4 If a multimeter is not available, the job of checking the charging system should be left to a dealer service department or a reputable motorcycle repair shop.

30 Charging system - leakage and output test

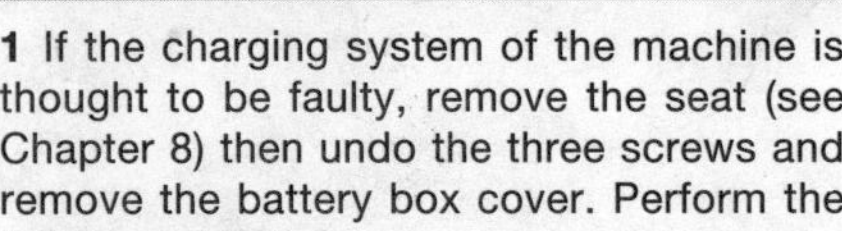

1 If the charging system of the machine is thought to be faulty, remove the seat (see Chapter 8) then undo the three screws and remove the battery box cover. Perform the following checks.

Leakage test

2 Turn the ignition switch OFF and disconnect the lead from the battery negative (-ve) terminal.

3 Set the multimeter to the mA (milli Amps) function and connect its negative probe to the battery negative terminal, and positive probe to the disconnected negative lead **(see illustration)**. With the meter connected like this the reading should not exceed 1.2 mA.

4 If the reading exceeds the specified amount it is likely that there is a short circuit in the wiring. Thoroughly check the wiring between the various components (see the *wiring diagrams* at the end of this book).

5 If the reading is below the specified amount, the leakage rate is satisfactory. Disconnect the meter and connect the negative (-ve) lead to the battery, tightening it securely. Check the alternator output as described below.

Output test

6 Start the engine and warm it up to normal operating temperature. Stop the engine.

7 Connect a multimeter set to the 0-20 volts scale (voltmeter) across the terminals of the battery (positive lead to battery positive terminal, negative lead to battery negative terminal). Start the engine and allow it to idle, then slowly increase the engine speed to 5000 rpm and note the voltmeter reading obtained. At this speed the voltage should be 13.0 to 15.5 volts. If the voltage is below this it will be necessary to check the alternator and regulator as described in the following Sections. **Note:** *Occasionally the condition may arise where the charging voltage is excessive. This condition is almost certainly due to a faulty regulator/rectifier which should be tested as described in Section 32.*

Clues to a faulty regulator are constantly blowing bulbs, with brightness varying considerably with engine speed and battery overheating.

31 Alternator stator coils - check and replacement

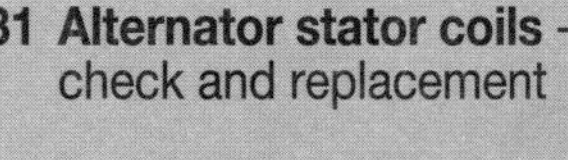

Check

1 Remove the fuel tank as described in Chapter 4 to gain access to the junction box wiring connectors located in the front of the battery box.

2 Disconnect the 3-pin block connector containing the yellow wires. Using a multimeter set to the ohms x 1 (ohmmeter) scale measure the resistance between each of the yellow wires on the alternator side of the connector, taking a total of three readings, then check for continuity between each terminal and ground (earth). If the stator coil windings are in good condition there should be no continuity (infinite resistance) between any of the terminals and ground (earth) and the three readings should be within the range shown in the Specifications at the start of this Chapter. If not, the alternator stator coil assembly is at fault and should be replaced. **Note:** *Check the fault is not due to damaged wiring between the connector and coils.*

Replacement

3 Remove the left crankcase end cover as described in Section 22 of Chapter 2.

4 Unscrew the bolt and remove the wiring retaining clip from inside the cover **(see illustration)**.

5 Undo the four bolts and separate the stator coil assembly from the cover.

6 Remove all trace of sealant from the wiring grommet and apply a smear of fresh sealant to the grommet.

7 Clean the crankcase and bolt threads and apply a few drops of suitable locking compound to the stator retaining bolts. Fit the stator coil assembly to the cover and tighten the retaining bolts to the torque listed in this Chapter's Specifications.

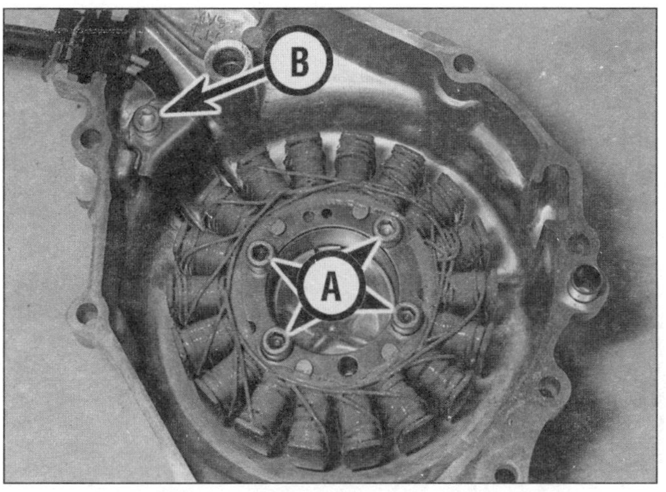

31.4 Alternator stator coil retaining bolts (A) and wiring clip bolt (B)

32.1 The regulator/rectifier unit is mounted behind the right side cover

8 Ensure the grommet is correctly seated in the casing, then install the retaining clip and securely tighten its retaining screw.

9 Fit the cover to the engine as described in Section 22 of Chapter 2.

32 Regulator/rectifier unit - check and replacement

Check

1 Remove the right side cover (see Chapter 8, if necessary) and disconnect the wiring connector from the regulator/rectifier unit **(see illustration)**.

2 Connect the negative (-) probe of the multimeter to a suitable ground (earth) point then switch the ignition switch On and carry out the following checks.

3 Set the multimeter to the 0 - 20 dc volts setting then connect the meter positive (+ve) probe to the Red/white terminal of the wiring connector and check for voltage. Full battery voltage should be present. Switch the ignition switch Off.

4 Switch the multimeter to the resistance (ohms) scale. Check for continuity between the Green terminal of the wiring connector and ground (earth), then check the resistance between the two Yellow terminals of the wiring connector. There should be continuity between the Green terminal and ground (earth) and a resistance reading of 0.1 to 1.0 ohms should be obtained between the two Yellow terminals of the wiring connector. Also check for continuity between each yellow terminal and ground (earth) - there should be no continuity.

5 If the above checks do not provide the expected results check the wiring between the battery, regulator/rectifier and alternator (see the *wiring diagrams* starting overleaf).

6 If the wiring checks out, the regulator/ rectifier unit is probably faulty. To check the unit, using a multimeter set to the appropriate resistance scale check the resistance between the various terminals of the regulator/rectifier **(see illustration)**. If the readings do not compare closely with those shown in the accompanying table the regulator/rectifier unit can be considered faulty. **Note:** *The use of certain multimeters could lead to false readings being obtained. Therefore, if the above check shows the regulator/rectifier unit to be faulty take the unit to a Honda dealer for confirmation of its condition before replacing it.*

Replacement

7 Remove the right side cover (see Chapter 8, if necessary).

8 Disconnect the wiring connector from the rectifier/regulator unit, then unscrew the two bolts and remove the unit.

9 On installation, tighten the retaining bolts securely and connect the wiring connector. Install the side cover (see Chapter 8, if necessary).

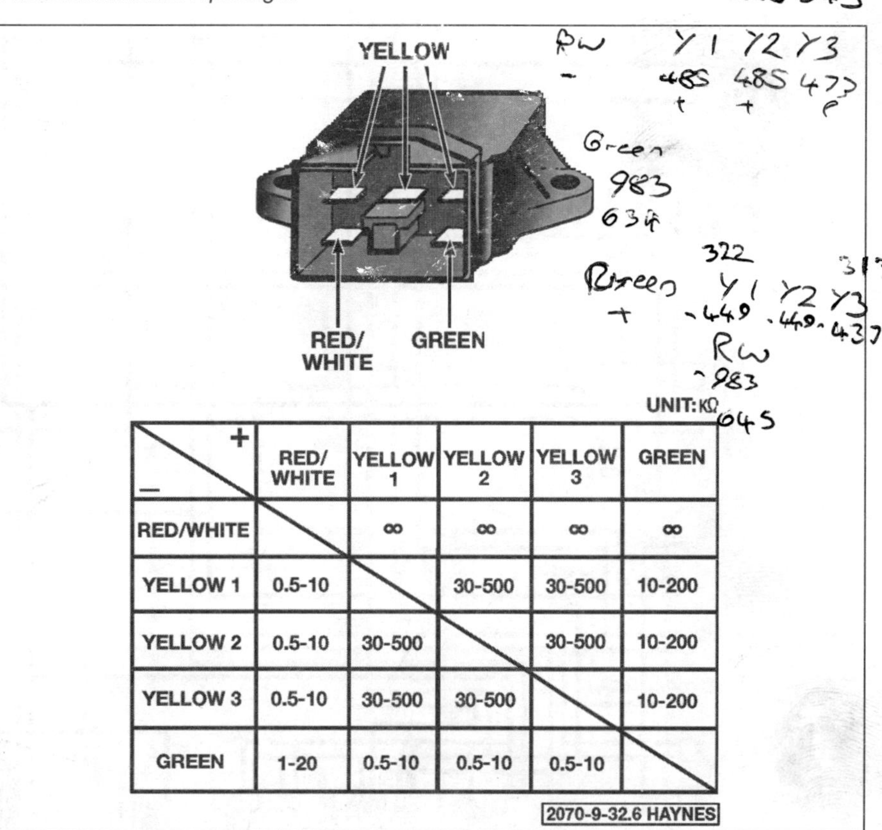

− \ +	RED/ WHITE	YELLOW 1	YELLOW 2	YELLOW 3	GREEN
RED/WHITE		∞	∞	∞	∞
YELLOW 1	0.5-10		30-500	30-500	10-200
YELLOW 2	0.5-10	30-500		30-500	10-200
YELLOW 3	0.5-10	30-500	30-500		10-200
GREEN	1-20	0.5-10	0.5-10	0.5-10	

32.6 Regulator/rectifier unit terminal identification and resistance readings

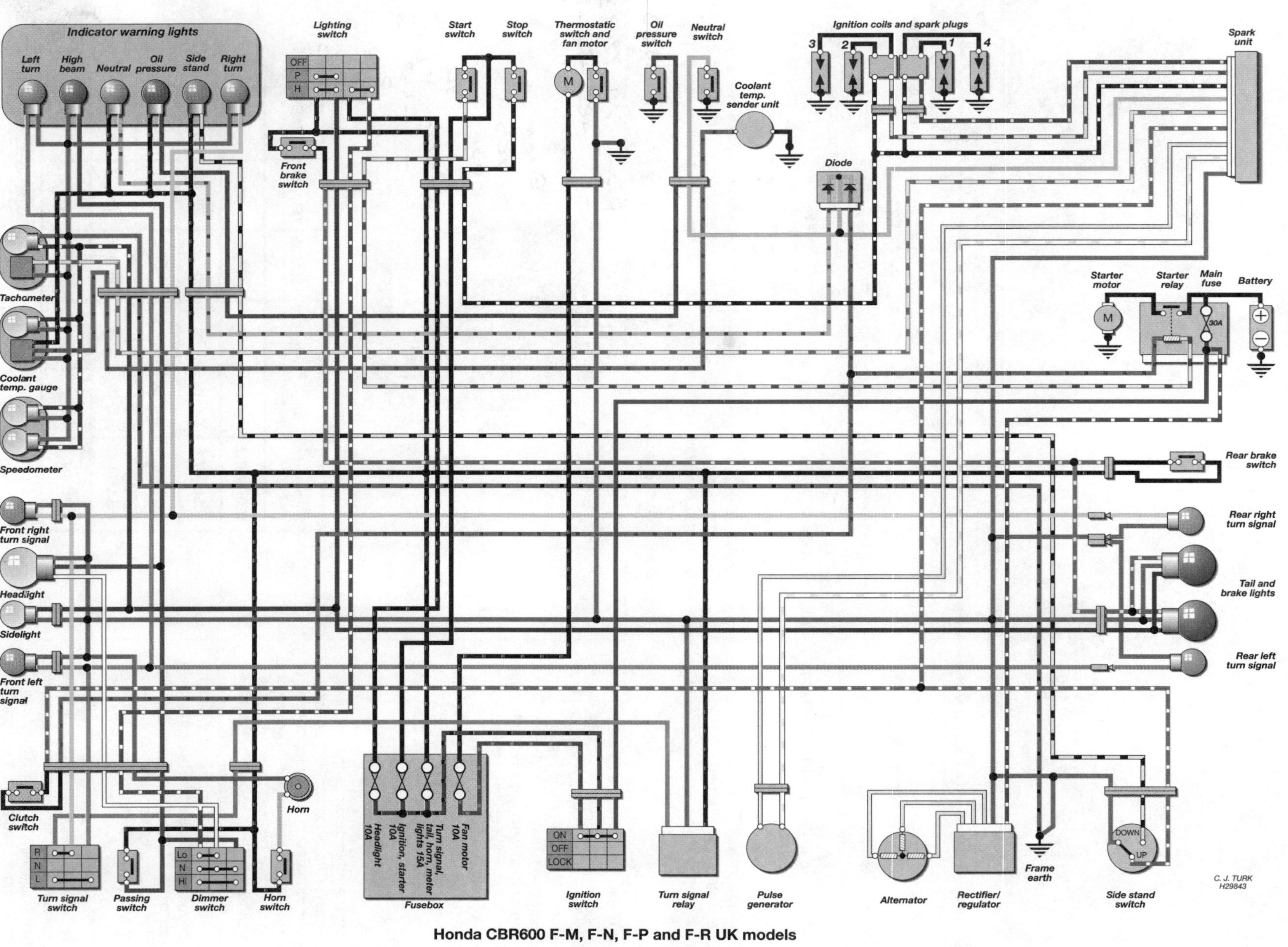
Indicator warning lights
Left turn
High beam
Neutral
Oil pressure
Side stand
Right turn
Lighting switch
OFF
P
H
Front brake switch
Start switch
Stop switch
Thermostatic switch and fan motor
M
Oil pressure switch
Neutral switch
Coolant temp. sender unit
Ignition coils and spark plugs
3
2
1
4
Diode
Spark unit
Tachometer
Coolant temp. gauge
Speedometer
Starter motor
Starter relay
Main fuse
30A
Battery
Rear brake switch
Front right turn signal
Rear right turn signal
Headlight
Tail and brake lights
Sidelight
Front left turn signal
Rear left turn signal
Clutch switch
Horn
R
N
L
Turn signal switch
Passing switch
Lo
N
Hi
Dimmer switch
Horn switch
Fan motor 10A
Turn signal, tail, horn, meter lights 15A
Ignition, starter 10A
Headlight 10A
Fusebox
ON
OFF
LOCK
Ignition switch
Turn signal relay
Pulse generator
Alternator
Rectifier/ regulator
Frame earth
DOWN
UP
Side stand switch
C. J. TURK
H29843
Honda CBR600 F-M, F-N, F-P and F-R UK models

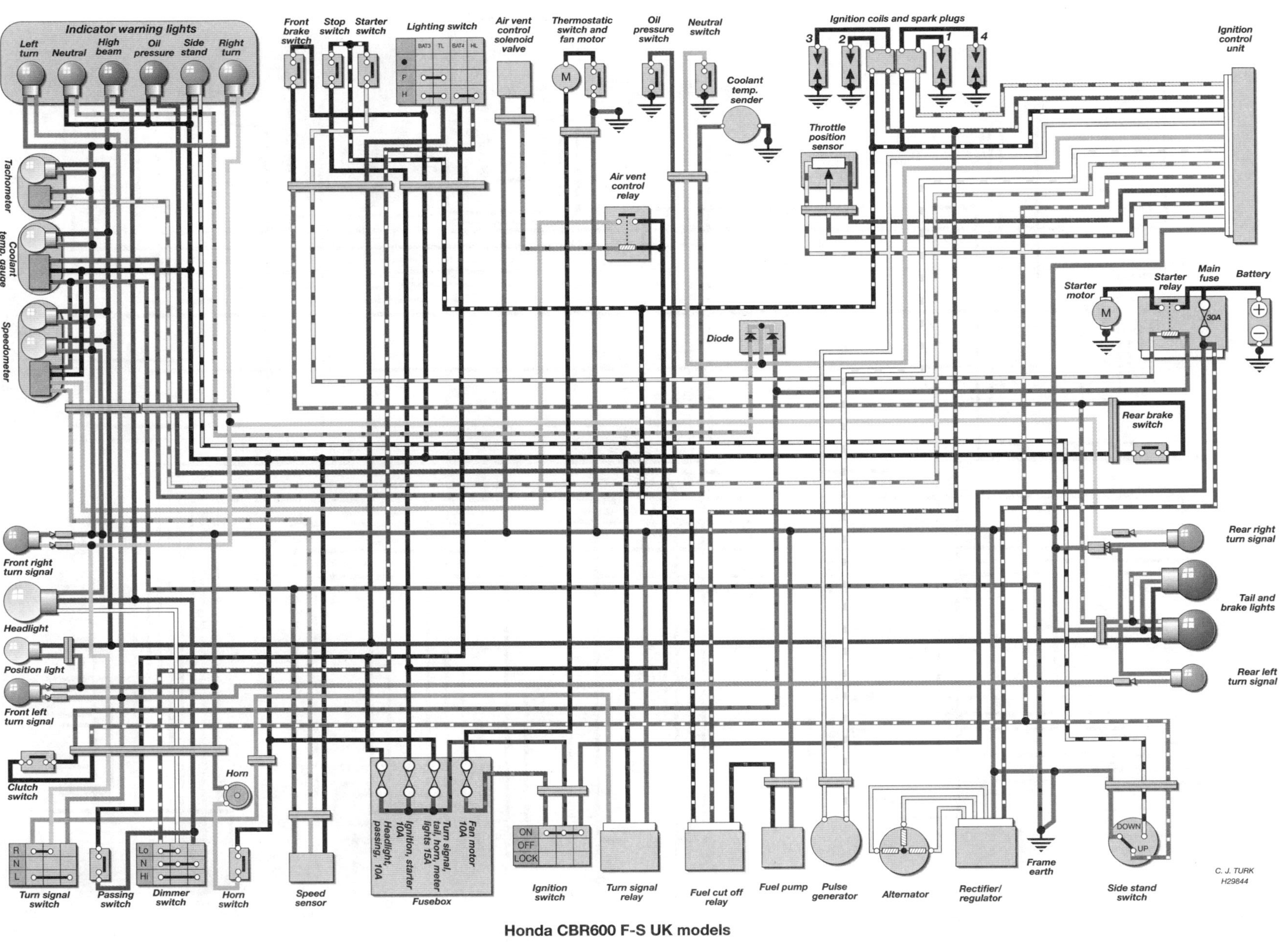

Honda CBR600 F-S UK models

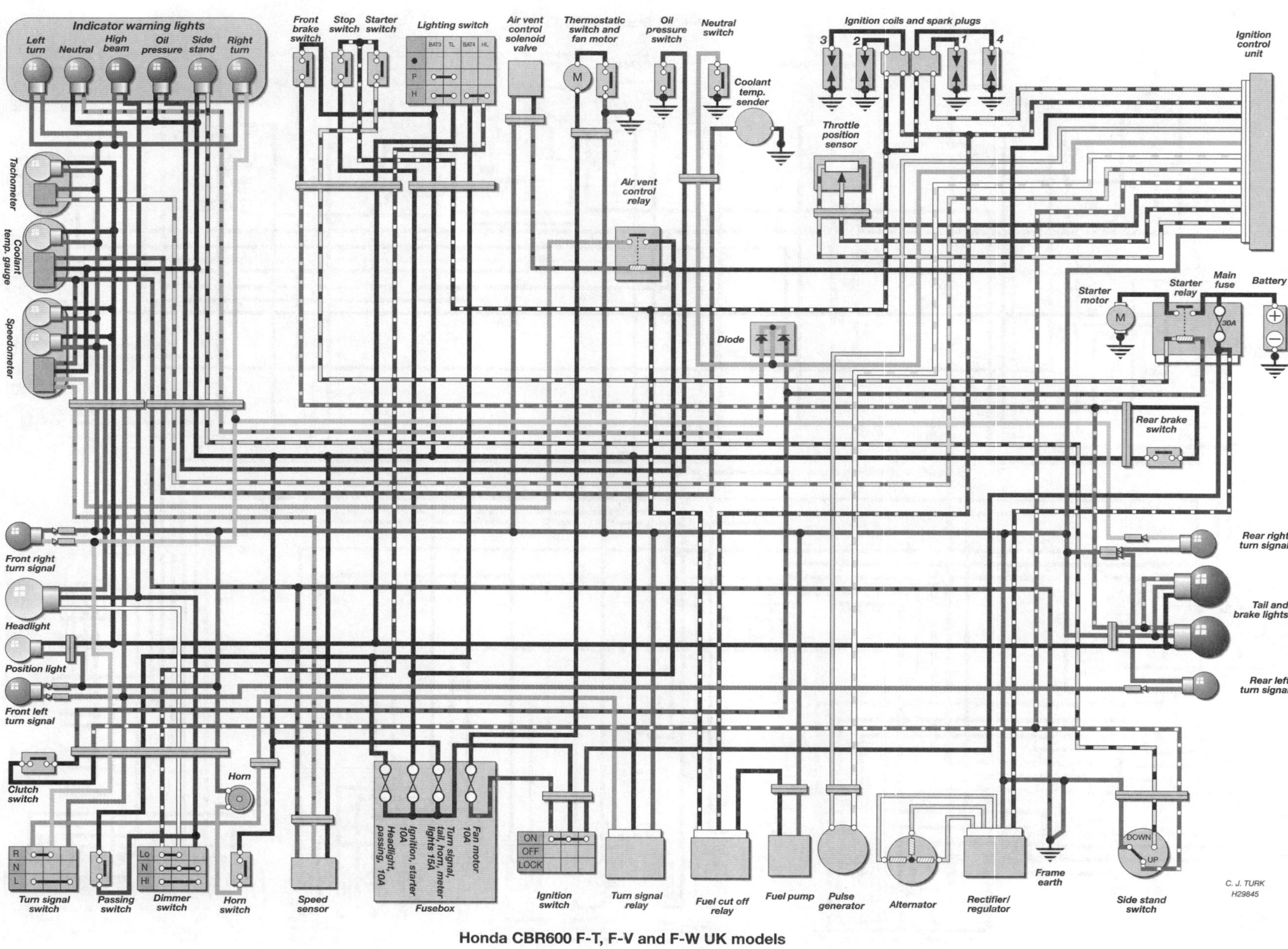

Honda CBR600 F-T, F-V and F-W UK models

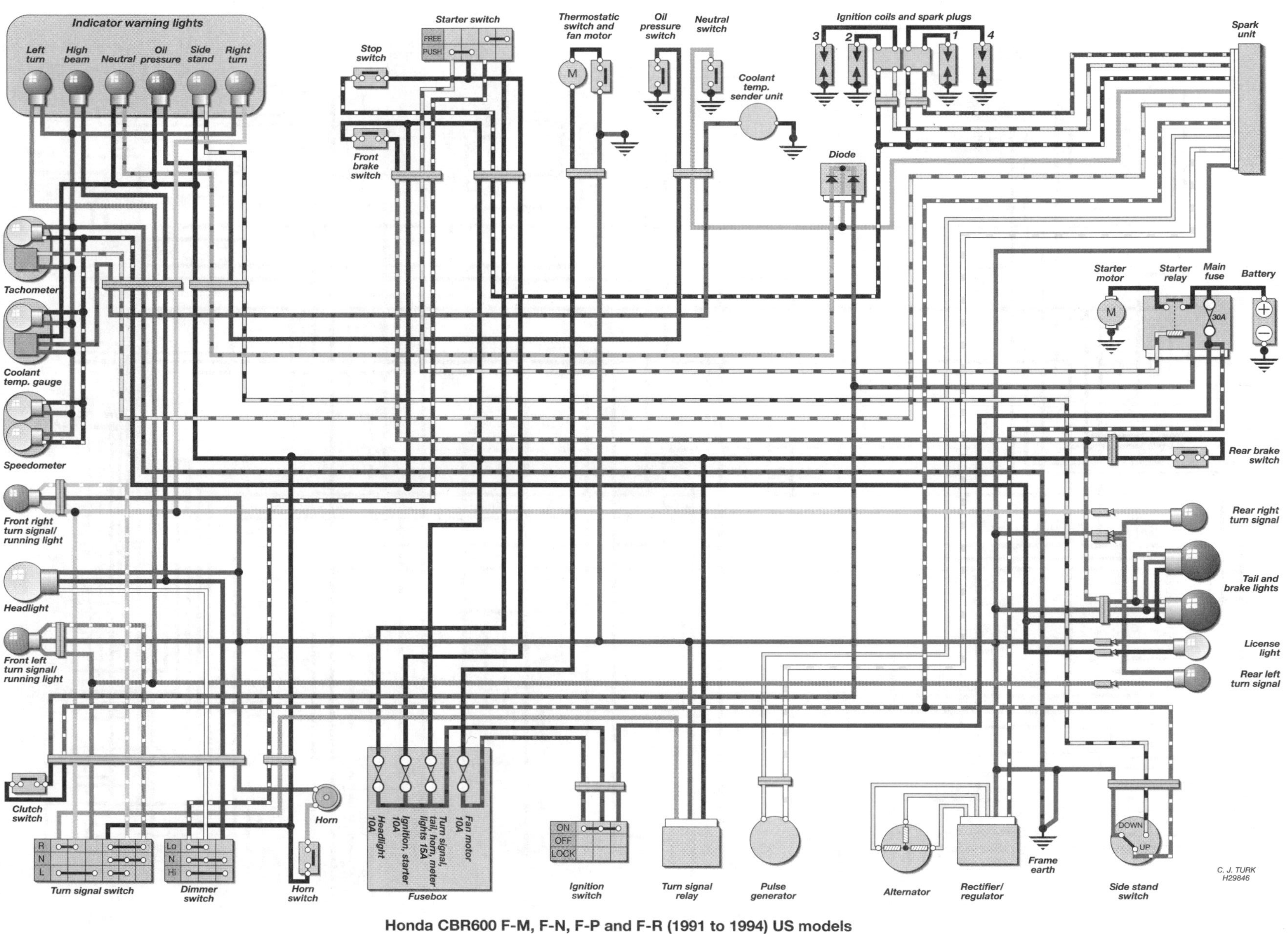

Honda CBR600 F-M, F-N, F-P and F-R (1991 to 1994) US models

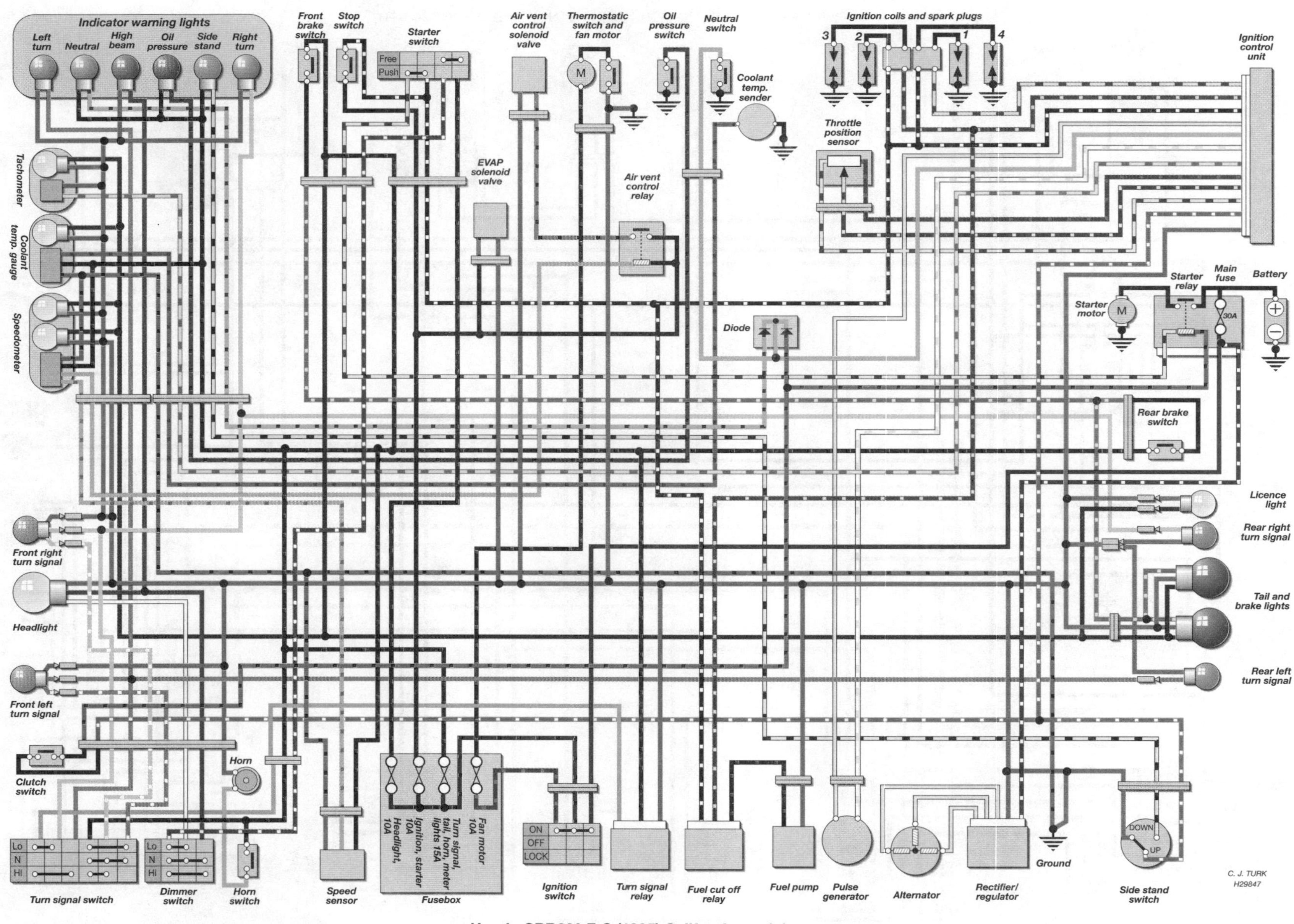

Honda CBR600 F-S (1995) California model

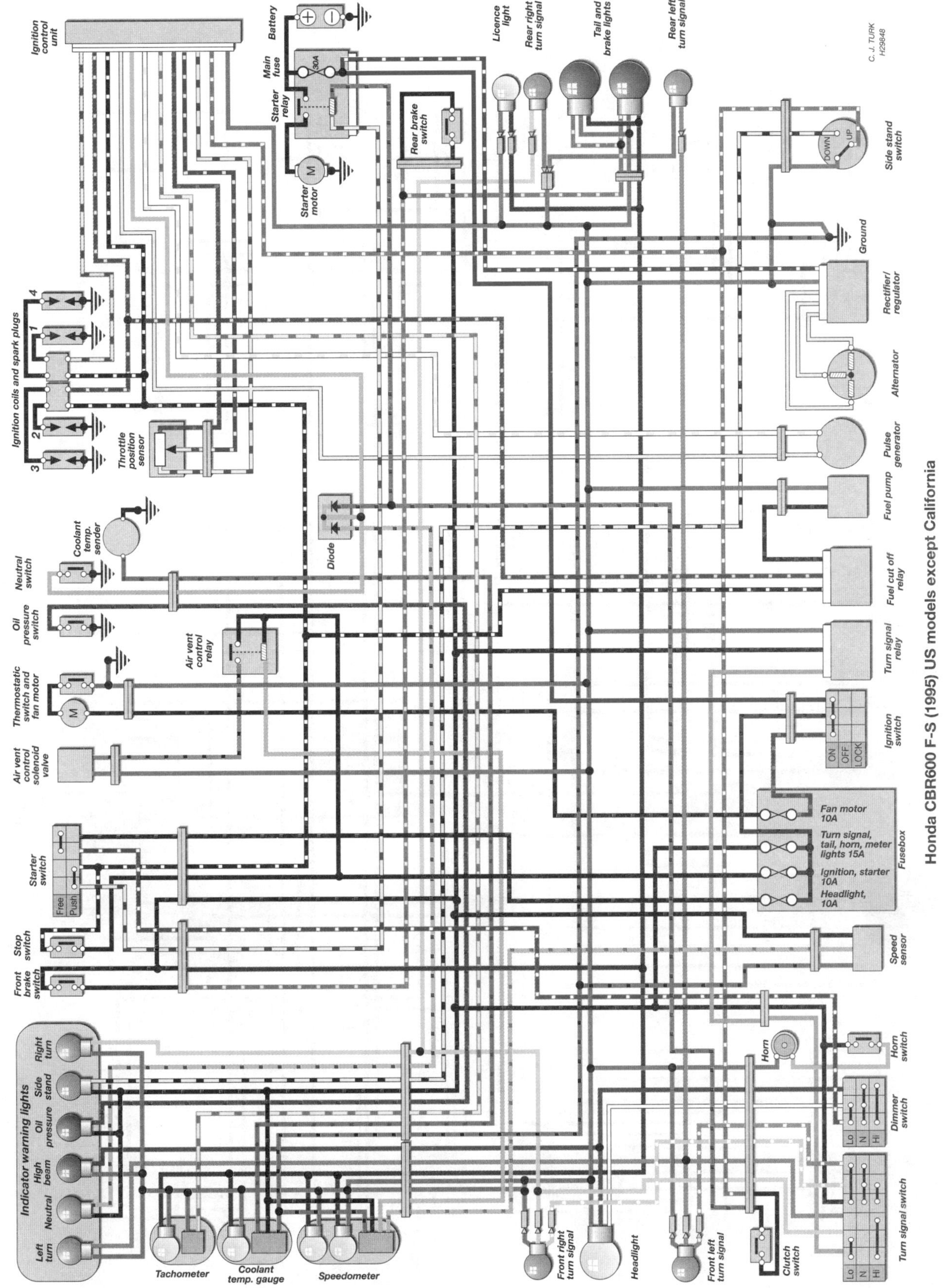
Honda CBR600 F-S (1995) US models except California
Ignition control unit
Battery
Main fuse
30A
Starter relay
Starter motor
M
Rear brake switch
Licence light
Rear right turn signal
Tail and brake lights
Rear left turn signal
C. J. TURK
H29848
Side stand switch
DOWN
UP
Ground
Rectifier/regulator
Alternator
Pulse generator
Fuel pump
Fuel cut off relay
Turn signal relay
Ignition switch
ON
OFF
LOCK
Fusebox
Fan motor 10A
Turn signal, tail, horn, meter lights 15A
Ignition, starter 10A
Headlight, 10A
Speed sensor
Horn
Horn switch
Dimmer switch
Lo
N
Hi
Turn signal switch
Clutch switch
Front left turn signal
Headlight
Front right turn signal
Speedometer
Coolant temp. gauge
Tachometer
Indicator warning lights
Left turn
Neutral
High beam
Oil pressure
Side stand
Right turn
Front brake switch
Stop switch
Starter switch
Free
Push
Air vent control solenoid valve
Thermostatic switch and fan motor
Oil pressure switch
Neutral switch
Coolant temp. sender
Air vent control relay
Diode
Throttle position sensor
Ignition coils and spark plugs
1
2
3
4

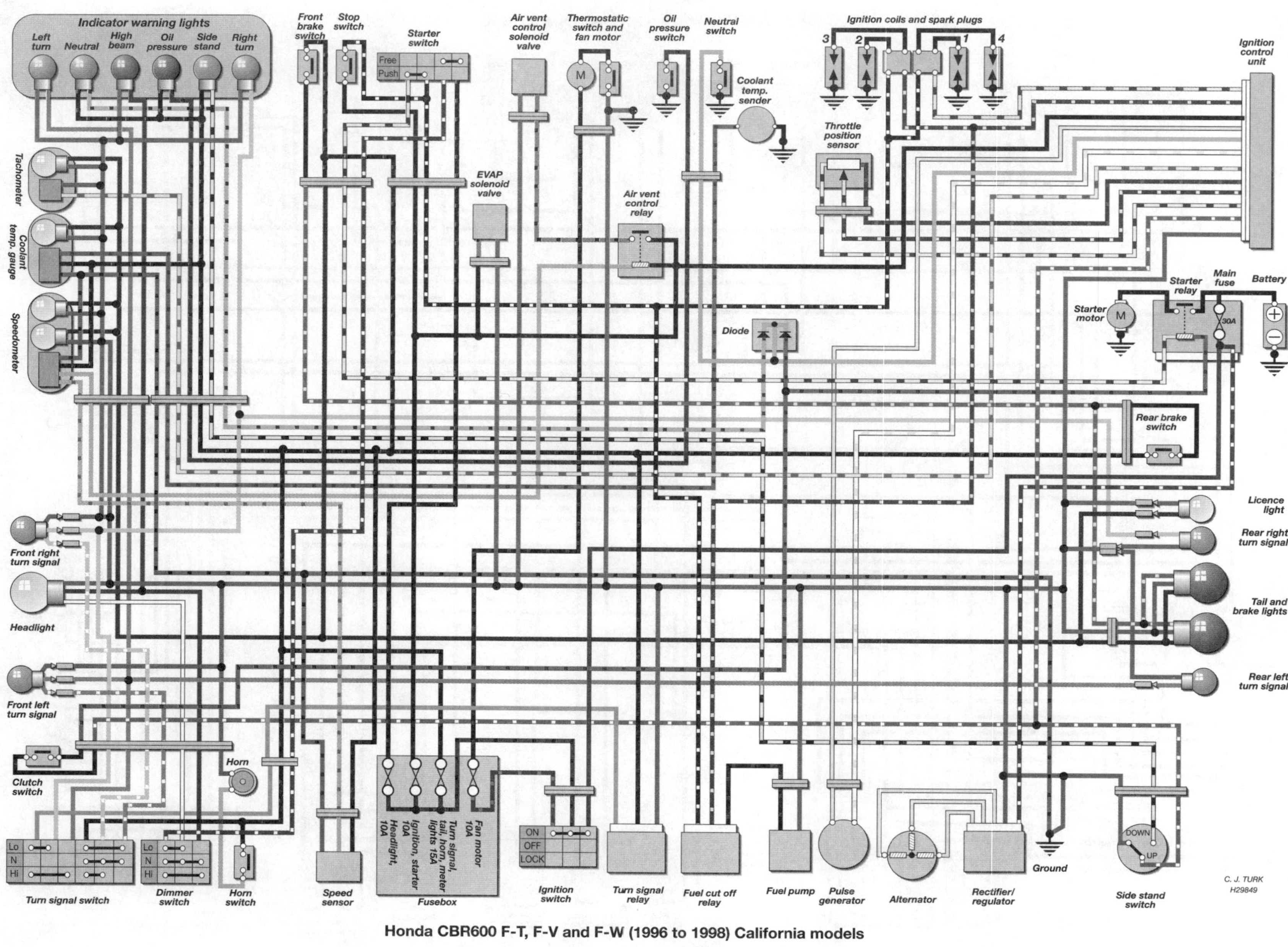

Honda CBR600 F-T, F-V and F-W (1996 to 1998) California models

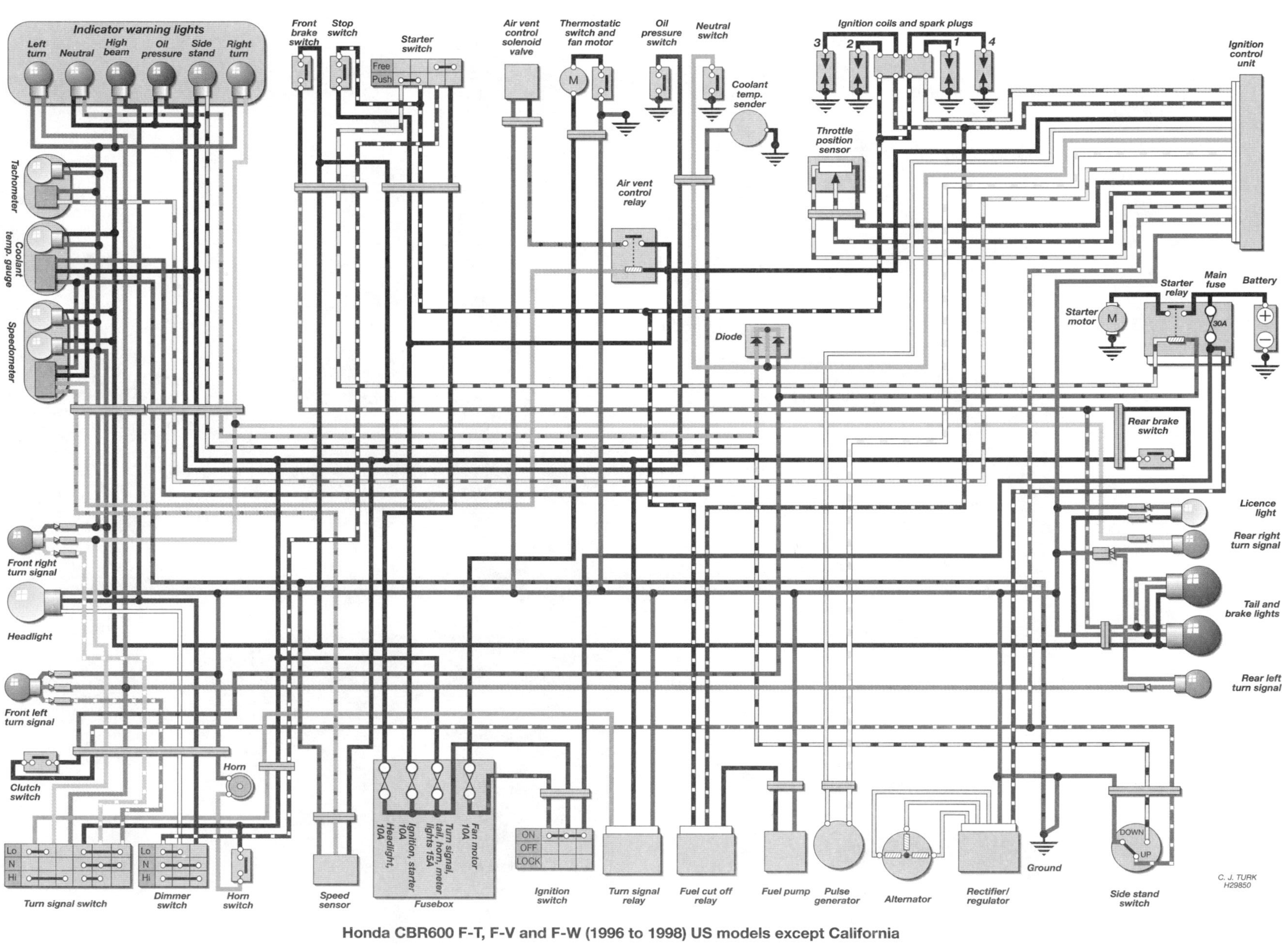

Honda CBR600 F-T, F-V and F-W (1996 to 1998) US models except California

Dimensions and weights

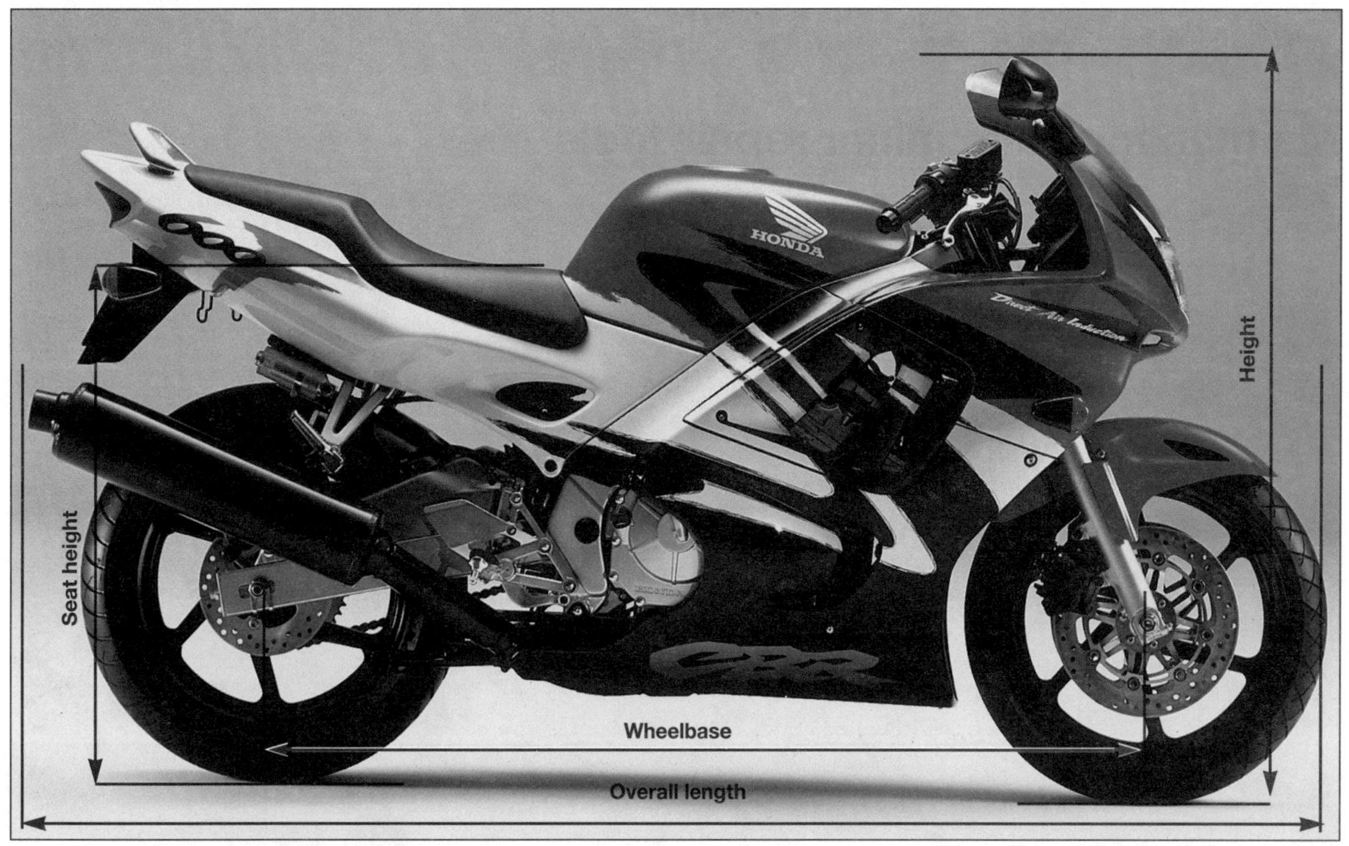

Wheelbase
All models. . . . . .1405 mm (55.3 in)

Overall length
US 1991 to 1994 models . . . . .2040 mm (80.3 in)
US 1995 to 1998 models . . . . .2055 mm (80.9 in)
UK M, N, P and R models .2010 mm (79.1 in)
UK S, T, V and W models .2055 mm (80.9 in)

Overall width
M, N, P and R (1991 to 1994) models . . . . .695 mm (27.4 in)
S, T, V and W (1995 to 1998) models . . . . .685 mm (27.0 in)

Overall height
M, N, P and R (1991 to 1994) models . . . . .1130 mm (44.5 in)
S, T, V and W (1995 to 1998) models . . . . .1135 mm (44.7 in)

Seat height
All models . . . . .810 mm (31.9 in)

Ground clearance
M, N, P and R (1991 to 1994) models . . . . .145 mm (5.7 in)
S, T, V and W (1995 to 1998) models . . . . .130 mm (5.1 in)

Weight (with oil and full fuel tank)
California 1991 to 1994 models . . . . .206 kg (454 lb)
California 1995 to 1996 models . . . . .208 kg (459 lb)
California 1997 to 1998 models . . . . .209 kg (461 lb)
US 1991 to 1994 models (except California) . . . . .204 kg (450 lb)
US 1995 to 1996 models (except California) . . . . .206 kg (454 lb)
US 1997 to 1998models (except California) . . . . .207 kg (456 lb)
UK M, N, P and R models . . . . .205 kg (452 lb)
UK S, T, V and W models . . . . .207 kg (456 lb)

Buying tools

A toolkit is a fundamental requirement for servicing and repairing a motorcycle. Although there will be an initial expense in building up enough tools for servicing, this will soon be offset by the savings made by doing the job yourself. As experience and confidence grow, additional tools can be added to enable the repair and overhaul of the motorcycle. Many of the specialist tools are expensive and not often used so it may be preferable to hire them, or for a group of friends or motorcycle club to join in the purchase.

As a rule, it is better to buy more expensive, good quality tools. Cheaper tools are likely to wear out faster and need to be renewed more often, nullifying the original saving.

> ***Warning: To avoid the risk of a poor quality tool breaking in use, causing injury or damage to the component being worked on, always aim to purchase tools which meet the relevant national safety standards.***

The following lists of tools do not represent the manufacturer's service tools, but serve as a guide to help the owner decide which tools are needed for this level of work. In addition, items such as an electric drill, hacksaw, files, soldering iron and a workbench equipped with a vice, may be needed. Although not classed as tools, a selection of bolts, screws, nuts, washers and pieces of tubing always come in useful.

For more information about tools, refer to the Haynes *Motorcycle Workshop Practice TechBook* (Bk. No. 3470).

Manufacturer's service tools

Inevitably certain tasks require the use of a service tool. Where possible an alternative tool or method of approach is recommended, but sometimes there is no option if personal injury or damage to the component is to be avoided. Where required, service tools are referred to in the relevant procedure.

Service tools can usually only be purchased from a motorcycle dealer and are identified by a part number. Some of the commonly-used tools, such as rotor pullers, are available in aftermarket form from mail-order motorcycle tool and accessory suppliers.

Maintenance and minor repair tools

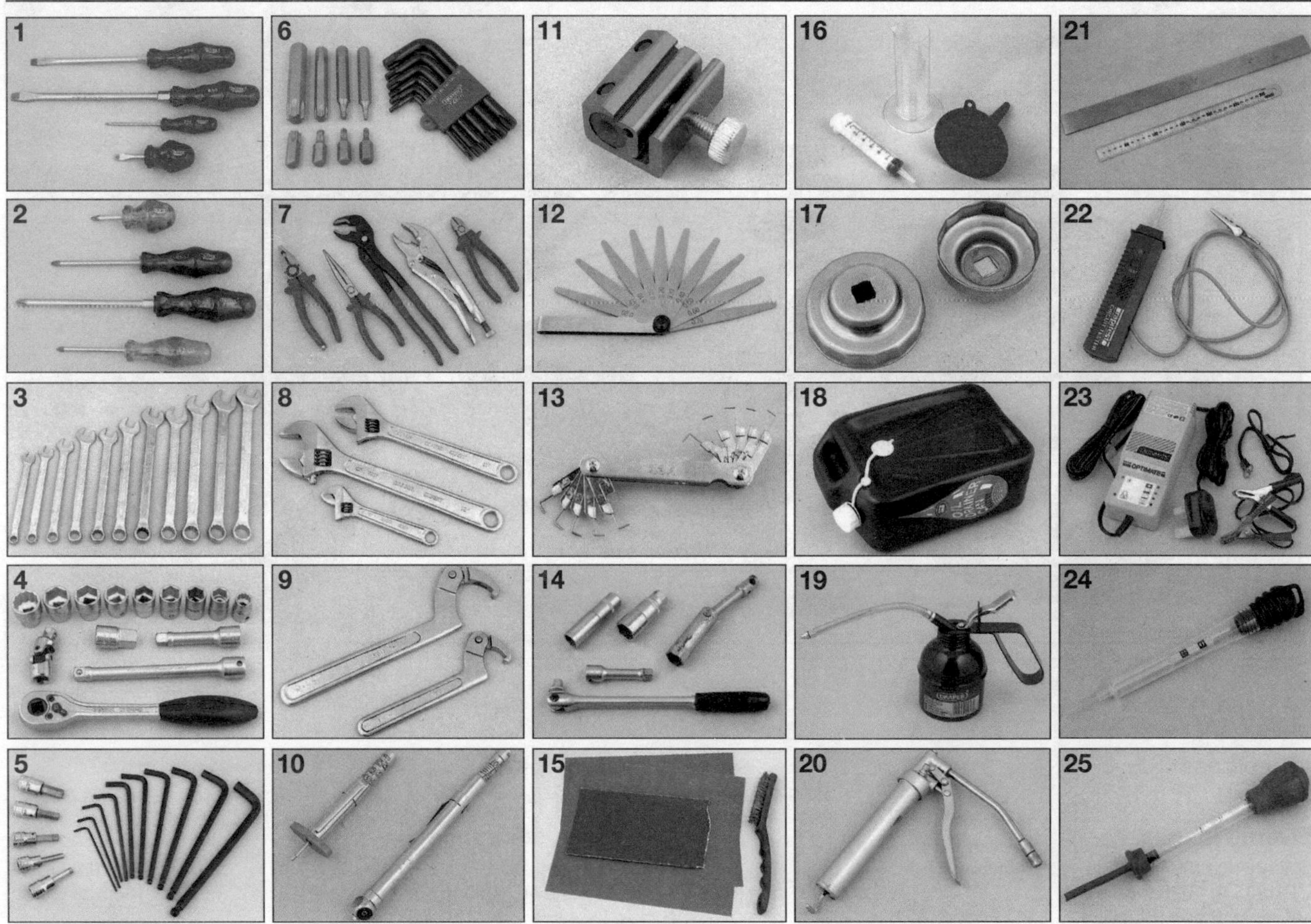

1 Set of flat-bladed screwdrivers
2 Set of Phillips head screwdrivers
3 Combination open-end and ring spanners
4 Socket set (3/8 inch or 1/2 inch drive)
5 Set of Allen keys or bits
6 Set of Torx keys or bits
7 Pliers, cutters and self-locking grips (Mole grips)
8 Adjustable spanners
9 C-spanners
10 Tread depth gauge and tyre pressure gauge
11 Cable oiler clamp
12 Feeler gauges
13 Spark plug gap measuring tool
14 Spark plug spanner or deep plug sockets
15 Wire brush and emery paper
16 Calibrated syringe, measuring vessel and funnel
17 Oil filter adapters
18 Oil drainer can or tray
19 Pump type oil can
20 Grease gun
21 Straight-edge and steel rule
22 Continuity tester
23 Battery charger
24 Hydrometer (for battery specific gravity check)
25 Anti-freeze tester (for liquid-cooled engines)

Repair and overhaul tools

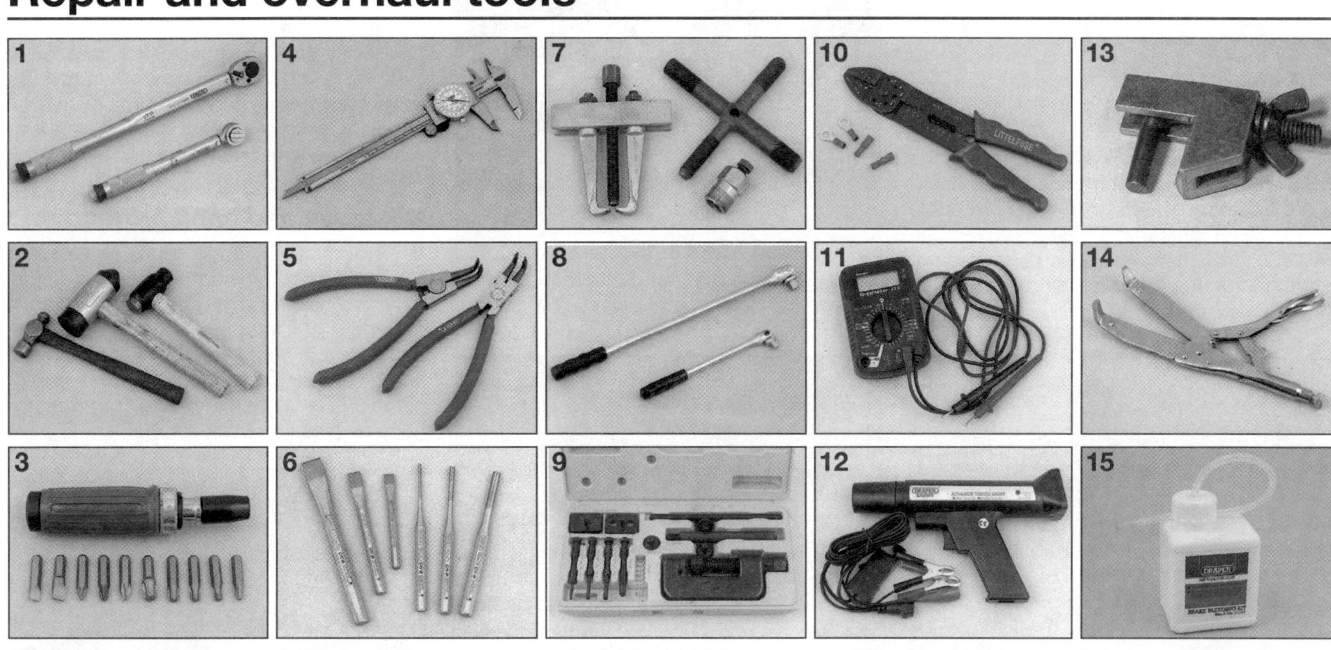

1 *Torque wrench (small and mid-ranges)*
2 *Conventional, plastic or soft-faced hammers*
3 *Impact driver set*
4 *Vernier gauge*
5 *Circlip pliers (internal and external, or combination)*
6 *Set of cold chisels and punches*
7 *Selection of pullers*
8 *Breaker bars*
9 *Chain breaking/ riveting tool set*
10 *Wire stripper and crimper tool*
11 *Multimeter (measures amps, volts and ohms)*
12 *Stroboscope (for dynamic timing checks)*
13 *Hose clamp (wingnut type shown)*
14 *Clutch holding tool*
15 *One-man brake/clutch bleeder kit*

Specialist tools

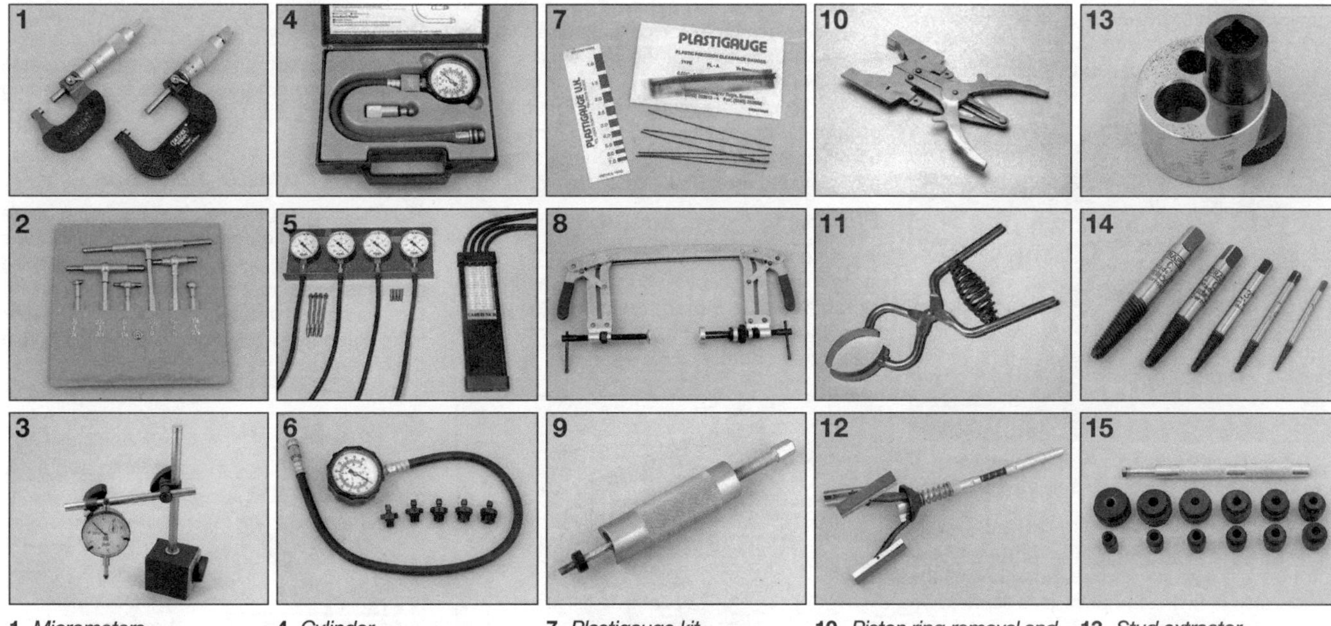

1 *Micrometers (external type)*
2 *Telescoping gauges*
3 *Dial gauge*
4 *Cylinder compression gauge*
5 *Vacuum gauges (left) or manometer (right)*
6 *Oil pressure gauge*
7 *Plastigauge kit*
8 *Valve spring compressor (4-stroke engines)*
9 *Piston pin drawbolt tool*
10 *Piston ring removal and installation tool*
11 *Piston ring clamp*
12 *Cylinder bore hone (stone type shown)*
13 *Stud extractor*
14 *Screw extractor set*
15 *Bearing driver set*

1 Workshop equipment and facilities

The workbench

● Work is made much easier by raising the bike up on a ramp - components are much more accessible if raised to waist level. The hydraulic or pneumatic types seen in the dealer's workshop are a sound investment if you undertake a lot of repairs or overhauls **(see illustration 1.1)**.

1.1 Hydraulic motorcycle ramp

● If raised off ground level, the bike must be supported on the ramp to avoid it falling. Most ramps incorporate a front wheel locating clamp which can be adjusted to suit different diameter wheels. When tightening the clamp, take care not to mark the wheel rim or damage the tyre - use wood blocks on each side to prevent this.

● Secure the bike to the ramp using tie-downs **(see illustration 1.2)**. If the bike has only a sidestand, and hence leans at a dangerous angle when raised, support the bike on an auxiliary stand.

1.2 Tie-downs are used around the passenger footrests to secure the bike

● Auxiliary (paddock) stands are widely available from mail order companies or motorcycle dealers and attach either to the wheel axle or swingarm pivot **(see illustration 1.3)**. If the motorcycle has a centrestand, you can support it under the crankcase to prevent it toppling whilst either wheel is removed **(see illustration 1.4)**.

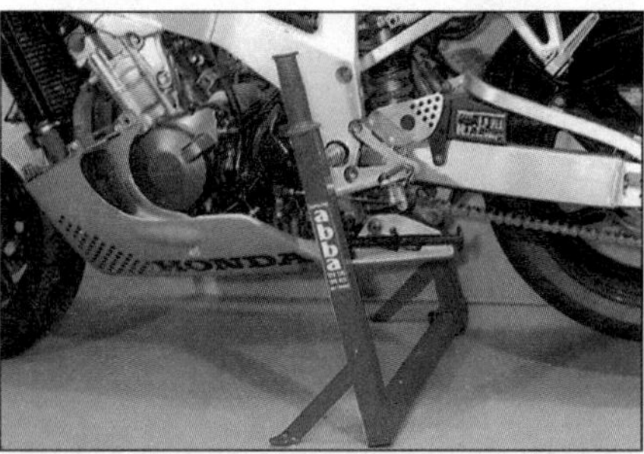

1.3 This auxiliary stand attaches to the swingarm pivot

1.4 Always use a block of wood between the engine and jack head when supporting the engine in this way

Fumes and fire

● Refer to the Safety first! page at the beginning of the manual for full details. Make sure your workshop is equipped with a fire extinguisher suitable for fuel-related fires (Class B fire - flammable liquids) - it is not sufficient to have a water-filled extinguisher.

● Always ensure adequate ventilation is available. Unless an exhaust gas extraction system is available for use, ensure that the engine is run outside of the workshop.

● If working on the fuel system, make sure the workshop is ventilated to avoid a build-up of fumes. This applies equally to fume build-up when charging a battery. Do not smoke or allow anyone else to smoke in the workshop.

Fluids

● If you need to drain fuel from the tank, store it in an approved container marked as suitable for the storage of petrol (gasoline) **(see illustration 1.5)**. Do not store fuel in glass jars or bottles.

1.5 Use an approved can only for storing petrol (gasoline)

● Use proprietary engine degreasers or solvents which have a high flash-point, such as paraffin (kerosene), for cleaning off oil, grease and dirt - never use petrol (gasoline) for cleaning. Wear rubber gloves when handling solvent and engine degreaser. The fumes from certain solvents can be dangerous - always work in a well-ventilated area.

Dust, eye and hand protection

● Protect your lungs from inhalation of dust particles by wearing a filtering mask over the nose and mouth. Many frictional materials still contain asbestos which is dangerous to your health. Protect your eyes from spouts of liquid and sprung components by wearing a pair of protective goggles **(see illustration 1.6)**.

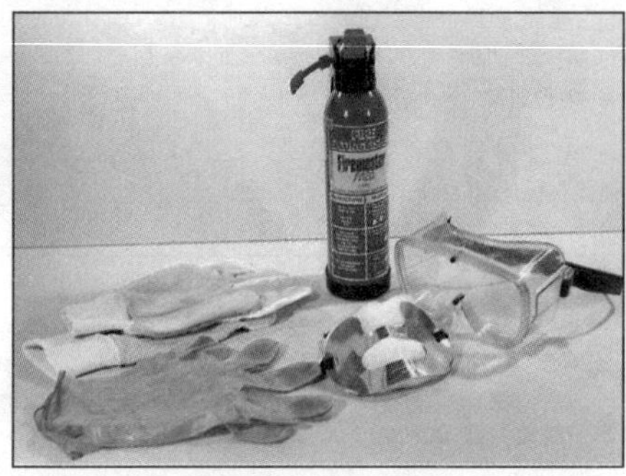

1.6 A fire extinguisher, goggles, mask and protective gloves should be at hand in the workshop

● Protect your hands from contact with solvents, fuel and oils by wearing rubber gloves. Alternatively apply a barrier cream to your hands before starting work. If handling hot components or fluids, wear suitable gloves to protect your hands from scalding and burns.

What to do with old fluids

● Old cleaning solvent, fuel, coolant and oils should not be poured down domestic drains or onto the ground. Package the fluid up in old oil containers, label it accordingly, and take it to a garage or disposal facility. Contact your local authority for location of such sites or ring the oil care hotline.

OIL CARE
FOLLOW THE CODE
OIL BANK LINE
0800 66 33 66

Note: It is antisocial and illegal to dump oil down the drain. To find the location of your local oil recycling bank, call this number free.

In the USA, note that any oil supplier must accept used oil for recycling.

2 Fasteners - screws, bolts and nuts

Fastener types and applications

Bolts and screws

● Fastener head types are either of hexagonal, Torx or splined design, with internal and external versions of each type **(see illustrations 2.1 and 2.2);** splined head fasteners are not in common use on motorcycles. The conventional slotted or Phillips head design is used for certain screws. Bolt or screw length is always measured from the underside of the head to the end of the item **(see illustration 2.11)**.

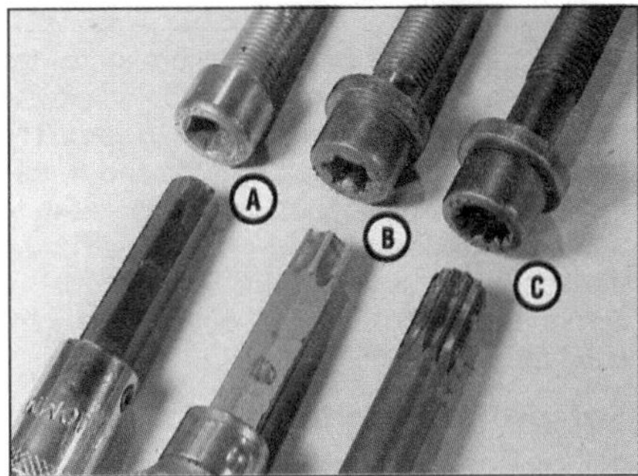

2.1 Internal hexagon/Allen (A), Torx (B) and splined (C) fasteners, with corresponding bits

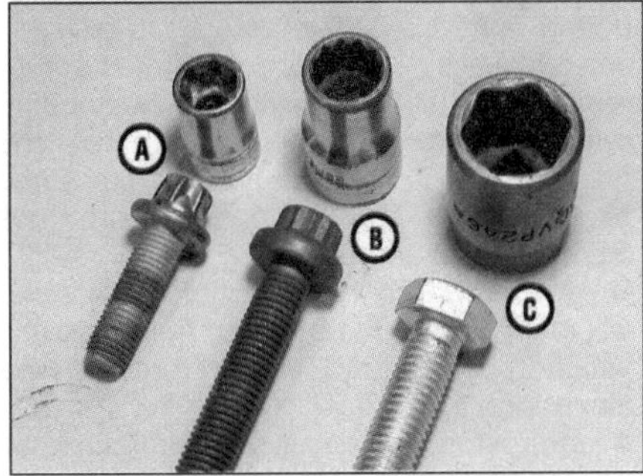

2.2 External Torx (A), splined (B) and hexagon (C) fasteners, with corresponding sockets

● Certain fasteners on the motorcycle have a tensile marking on their heads, the higher the marking the stronger the fastener. High tensile fasteners generally carry a 10 or higher marking. Never replace a high tensile fastener with one of a lower tensile strength.

Washers (see illustration 2.3)

● Plain washers are used between a fastener head and a component to prevent damage to the component or to spread the load when torque is applied. Plain washers can also be used as spacers or shims in certain assemblies. Copper or aluminium plain washers are often used as sealing washers on drain plugs.

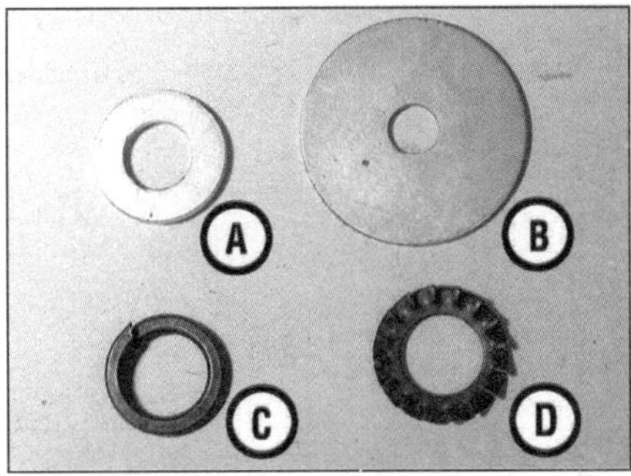

2.3 Plain washer (A), penny washer (B), spring washer (C) and serrated washer (D)

● The split-ring spring washer works by applying axial tension between the fastener head and component. If flattened, it is fatigued and must be renewed. If a plain (flat) washer is used on the fastener, position the spring washer between the fastener and the plain washer.

● Serrated star type washers dig into the fastener and component faces, preventing loosening. They are often used on electrical earth (ground) connections to the frame.

● Cone type washers (sometimes called Belleville) are conical and when tightened apply axial tension between the fastener head and component. They must be installed with the dished side against the component and often carry an OUTSIDE marking on their outer face. If flattened, they are fatigued and must be renewed.

● Tab washers are used to lock plain nuts or bolts on a shaft. A portion of the tab washer is bent up hard against one flat of the nut or bolt to prevent it loosening. Due to the tab washer being deformed in use, a new tab washer should be used every time it is disturbed.

● Wave washers are used to take up endfloat on a shaft. They provide light springing and prevent excessive side-to-side play of a component. Can be found on rocker arm shafts.

Nuts and split pins

● Conventional plain nuts are usually six-sided **(see illustration 2.4)**. They are sized by thread diameter and pitch. High tensile nuts carry a number on one end to denote their tensile strength.

2.4 Plain nut (A), shouldered locknut (B), nylon insert nut (C) and castellated nut (D)

● Self-locking nuts either have a nylon insert, or two spring metal tabs, or a shoulder which is staked into a groove in the shaft - their advantage over conventional plain nuts is a resistance to loosening due to vibration. The nylon insert type can be used a number of times, but must be renewed when the friction of the nylon insert is reduced, ie when the nut spins freely on the shaft. The spring tab type can be reused unless the tabs are damaged. The shouldered type must be renewed every time it is disturbed.

● Split pins (cotter pins) are used to lock a castellated nut to a shaft or to prevent slackening of a plain nut. Common applications are wheel axles and brake torque arms. Because the split pin arms are deformed to lock around the nut a new split pin must always be used on installation - always fit the correct size split pin which will fit snugly in the shaft hole. Make sure the split pin arms are correctly located around the nut **(see illustrations 2.5 and 2.6)**.

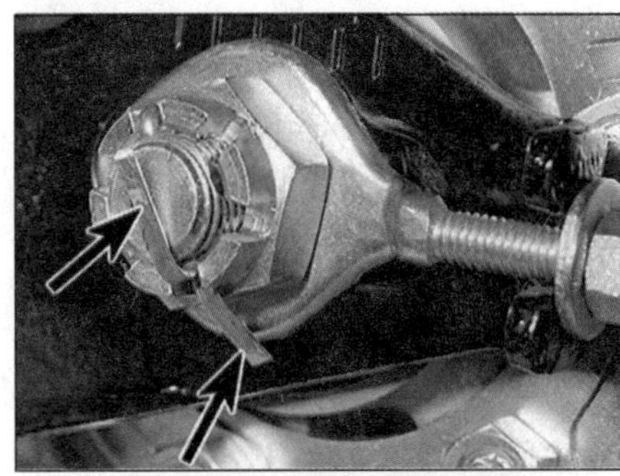
2.5 Bend split pin (cotter pin) arms as shown (arrows) to secure a castellated nut

2.6 Bend split pin (cotter pin) arms as shown to secure a plain nut

Caution: If the castellated nut slots do not align with the shaft hole after tightening to the torque setting, tighten the nut until the next slot aligns with the hole - never slacken the nut to align its slot.

● R-pins (shaped like the letter R), or slip pins as they are sometimes called, are sprung and can be reused if they are otherwise in good condition. Always install R-pins with their closed end facing forwards **(see illustration 2.7)**.

2.7 Correct fitting of R-pin. Arrow indicates forward direction

Circlips (see illustration 2.8)

● Circlips (sometimes called snap-rings) are used to retain components on a shaft or in a housing and have corresponding external or internal ears to permit removal. Parallel-sided (machined) circlips can be installed either way round in their groove, whereas stamped circlips (which have a chamfered edge on one face) must be installed with the chamfer facing away from the direction of thrust load **(see illustration 2.9)**.

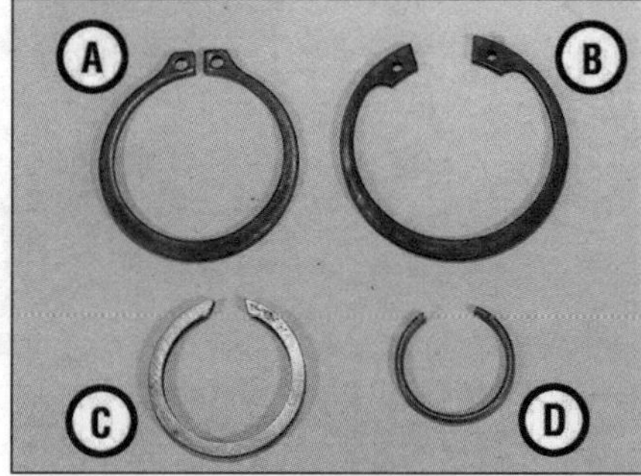

2.8 External stamped circlip (A), internal stamped circlip (B), machined circlip (C) and wire circlip (D)

● Always use circlip pliers to remove and install circlips; expand or compress them just enough to remove them. After installation, rotate the circlip in its groove to ensure it is securely seated. If installing a circlip on a splined shaft, always align its opening with a shaft channel to ensure the circlip ends are well supported and unlikely to catch **(see illustration 2.10)**.

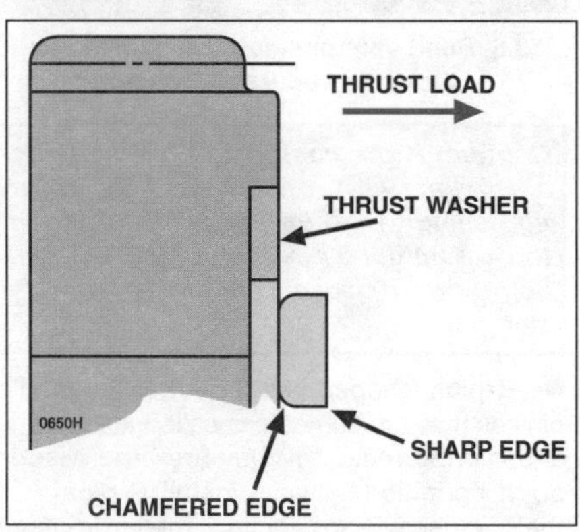

2.9 Correct fitting of a stamped circlip

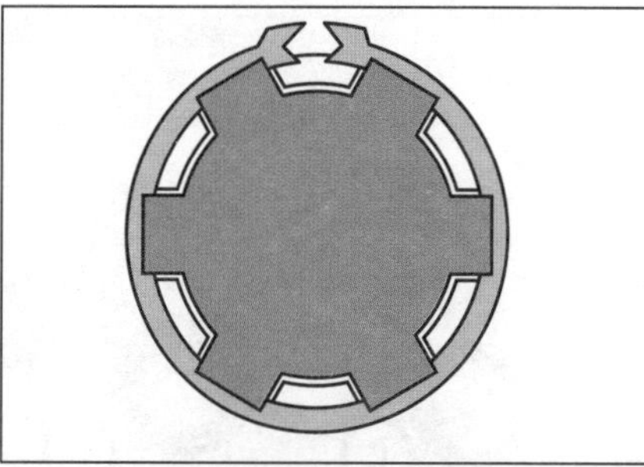

2.10 Align circlip opening with shaft channel

● Circlips can wear due to the thrust of components and become loose in their grooves, with the subsequent danger of becoming dislodged in operation. For this reason, renewal is advised every time a circlip is disturbed.

● Wire circlips are commonly used as piston pin retaining clips. If a removal tang is provided, long-nosed pliers can be used to dislodge them, otherwise careful use of a small flat-bladed screwdriver is necessary. Wire circlips should be renewed every time they are disturbed.

Thread diameter and pitch

● Diameter of a male thread (screw, bolt or stud) is the outside diameter of the threaded portion **(see illustration 2.11)**. Most motorcycle manufacturers use the ISO (International Standards Organisation) metric system expressed in millimetres, eg M6 refers to a 6 mm diameter thread. Sizing is the same for nuts, except that the thread diameter is measured across the valleys of the nut.

● Pitch is the distance between the peaks of the thread **(see illustration 2.11)**. It is expressed in millimetres, thus a common bolt size may be expressed as 6.0 x 1.0 mm (6 mm thread diameter and 1 mm pitch). Generally pitch increases in proportion to thread diameter, although there are always exceptions.

● Thread diameter and pitch are related for conventional fastener applications and the accompanying table can be used as a guide. Additionally, the AF (Across Flats), spanner or socket size dimension of the bolt or nut **(see illustration 2.11)** is linked to thread and pitch specification. Thread pitch can be measured with a thread gauge **(see illustration 2.12)**.

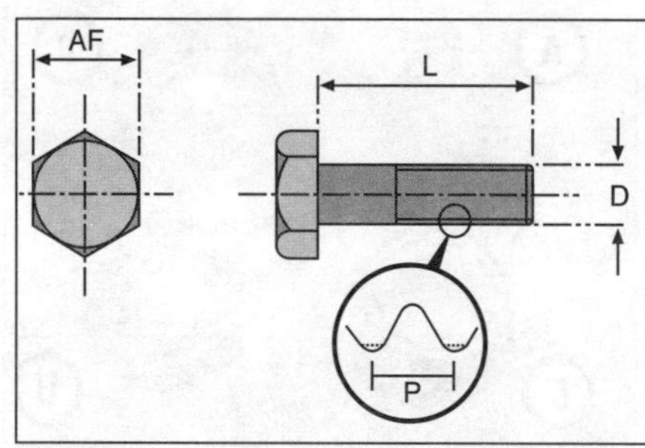

2.11 Fastener length (L), thread diameter (D), thread pitch (P) and head size (AF)

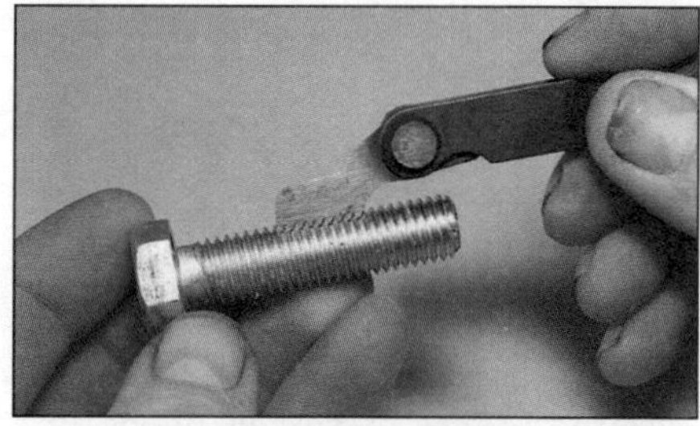

2.12 Using a thread gauge to measure pitch

AF size	Thread diameter x pitch (mm)
8 mm	M5 x 0.8
8 mm	M6 x 1.0
10 mm	M6 x 1.0
12 mm	M8 x 1.25
14 mm	M10 x 1.25
17 mm	M12 x 1.25

● The threads of most fasteners are of the right-hand type, ie they are turned clockwise to tighten and anti-clockwise to loosen. The reverse situation applies to left-hand thread fasteners, which are turned anti-clockwise to tighten and clockwise to loosen. Left-hand threads are used where rotation of a component might loosen a conventional right-hand thread fastener.

Seized fasteners

● Corrosion of external fasteners due to water or reaction between two dissimilar metals can occur over a period of time. It will build up sooner in wet conditions or in countries where salt is used on the roads during the winter. If a fastener is severely corroded it is likely that normal methods of removal will fail and result in its head being ruined. When you attempt removal, the fastener thread should be heard to crack free and unscrew easily - if it doesn't, stop there before damaging something.

● A smart tap on the head of the fastener will often succeed in breaking free corrosion which has occurred in the threads **(see illustration 2.13)**.

● An aerosol penetrating fluid (such as WD-40) applied the night beforehand may work its way down into the thread and ease removal. Depending on the location, you may be able to make up a Plasticine well around the fastener head and fill it with penetrating fluid.

2.13 A sharp tap on the head of a fastener will often break free a corroded thread

● If you are working on an engine internal component, corrosion will most likely not be a problem due to the well lubricated environment. However, components can be very tight and an impact driver is a useful tool in freeing them **(see illustration 2.14)**.

2.14 Using an impact driver to free a fastener

● Where corrosion has occurred between dissimilar metals (eg steel and aluminium alloy), the application of heat to the fastener head will create a disproportionate expansion rate between the two metals and break the seizure caused by the corrosion. Whether heat can be applied depends on the location of the fastener - any surrounding components likely to be damaged must first be removed **(see illustration 2.15)**. Heat can be applied using a paint stripper heat gun or clothes iron, or by immersing the component in boiling water - wear protective gloves to prevent scalding or burns to the hands.

2.15 Using heat to free a seized fastener

● As a last resort, it is possible to use a hammer and cold chisel to work the fastener head unscrewed **(see illustration 2.16)**. This will damage the fastener, but more importantly extreme care must be taken not to damage the surrounding component.

Caution: Remember that the component being secured is generally of more value than the bolt, nut or screw - when the fastener is freed, do not unscrew it with force, instead work the fastener back and forth when resistance is felt to prevent thread damage.

2.16 Using a hammer and chisel to free a seized fastener

Broken fasteners and damaged heads

● If the shank of a broken bolt or screw is accessible you can grip it with self-locking grips. The knurled wheel type stud extractor tool or self-gripping stud puller tool is particularly useful for removing the long studs which screw into the cylinder mouth surface of the crankcase or bolts and screws from which the head has broken off **(see illustration 2.17)**. Studs can also be removed by locking two nuts together on the threaded end of the stud and using a spanner on the lower nut **(see illustration 2.18)**.

2.17 Using a stud extractor tool to remove a broken crankcase stud

2.18 Two nuts can be locked together to unscrew a stud from a component

● A bolt or screw which has broken off below or level with the casing must be extracted using a screw extractor set. Centre punch the fastener to centralise the drill bit, then drill a hole in the fastener **(see illustration 2.19)**. Select a drill bit which is approximately half to three-quarters the

2.19 When using a screw extractor, first drill a hole in the fastener . . .

diameter of the fastener and drill to a depth which will accommodate the extractor. Use the largest size extractor possible, but avoid leaving too small a wall thickness otherwise the extractor will merely force the fastener walls outwards wedging it in the casing thread.

● If a spiral type extractor is used, thread it anti-clockwise into the fastener. As it is screwed in, it will grip the fastener and unscrew it from the casing **(see illustration 2.20)**.

2.20 . . . then thread the extractor anti-clockwise into the fastener

● If a taper type extractor is used, tap it into the fastener so that it is firmly wedged in place. Unscrew the extractor (anti-clockwise) to draw the fastener out.

Warning: Stud extractors are very hard and may break off in the fastener if care is not taken - ask an engineer about spark erosion if this happens.

● Alternatively, the broken bolt/screw can be drilled out and the hole retapped for an oversize bolt/screw or a diamond-section thread insert. It is essential that the drilling is carried out squarely and to the correct depth, otherwise the casing may be ruined - if in doubt, entrust the work to an engineer.

● Bolts and nuts with rounded corners cause the correct size spanner or socket to slip when force is applied. Of the types of spanner/socket available always use a six-point type rather than an eight or twelve-point type - better grip

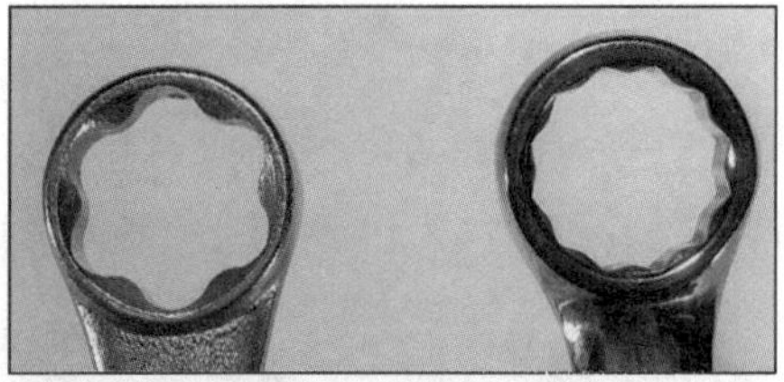

2.21 Comparison of surface drive ring spanner (left) with 12-point type (right)

is obtained. Surface drive spanners grip the middle of the hex flats, rather than the corners, and are thus good in cases of damaged heads **(see illustration 2.21)**.

● Slotted-head or Phillips-head screws are often damaged by the use of the wrong size screwdriver. Allen-head and Torx-head screws are much less likely to sustain damage. If enough of the screw head is exposed you can use a hacksaw to cut a slot in its head and then use a conventional flat-bladed screwdriver to remove it. Alternatively use a hammer and cold chisel to tap the head of the fastener around to slacken it. Always replace damaged fasteners with new ones, preferably Torx or Allen-head type.

A dab of valve grinding compound between the screw head and screwdriver tip will often give a good grip.

Thread repair

● Threads (particularly those in aluminium alloy components) can be damaged by overtightening, being assembled with dirt in the threads, or from a component working loose and vibrating. Eventually the thread will fail completely, and it will be impossible to tighten the fastener.

● If a thread is damaged or clogged with old locking compound it can be renovated with a thread repair tool (thread chaser) **(see illustrations 2.22 and 2.23)**; special thread

2.22 A thread repair tool being used to correct an internal thread

2.23 A thread repair tool being used to correct an external thread

chasers are available for spark plug hole threads. The tool will not cut a new thread, but clean and true the original thread. Make sure that you use the correct diameter and pitch tool. Similarly, external threads can be cleaned up with a die or a thread restorer file **(see illustration 2.24)**.

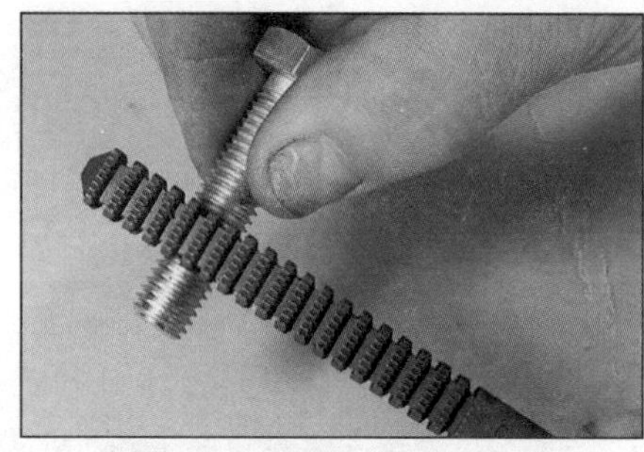

2.24 Using a thread restorer file

● It is possible to drill out the old thread and retap the component to the next thread size. This will work where there is enough surrounding material and a new bolt or screw can be obtained. Sometimes, however, this is not possible - such as where the bolt/screw passes through another component which must also be suitably modified, also in cases where a spark plug or oil drain plug cannot be obtained in a larger diameter thread size.

● The diamond-section thread insert (often known by its popular trade name of Heli-Coil) is a simple and effective method of renewing the thread and retaining the original size. A kit can be purchased which contains the tap, insert and installing tool **(see illustration 2.25)**. Drill out the damaged thread with the size drill specified **(see illustration 2.26)**. Carefully retap the thread **(see illustration 2.27)**. Install the

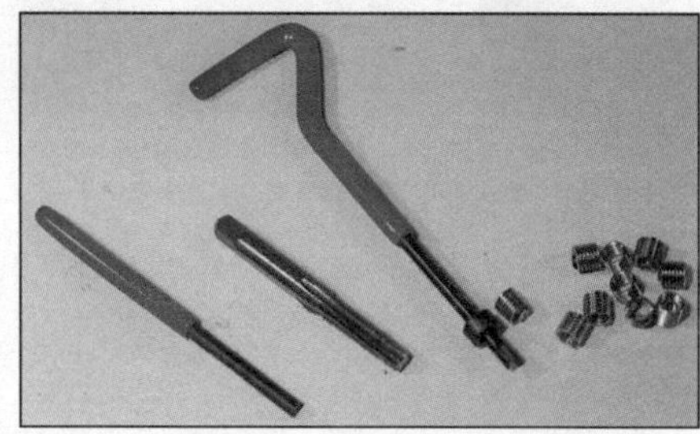

2.25 Obtain a thread insert kit to suit the thread diameter and pitch required

2.26 To install a thread insert, first drill out the original thread . . .

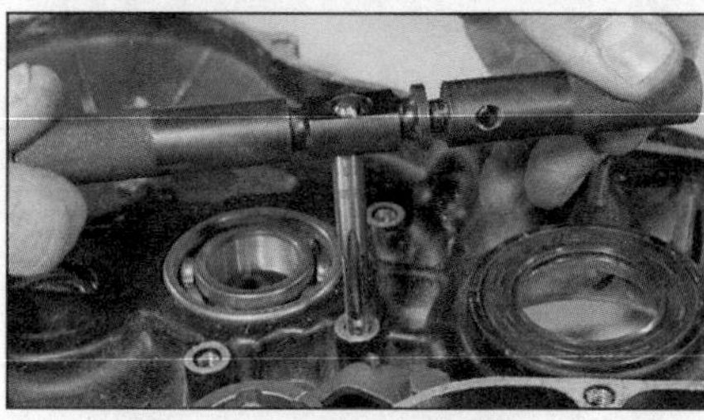

2.27 . . . tap a new thread . . .

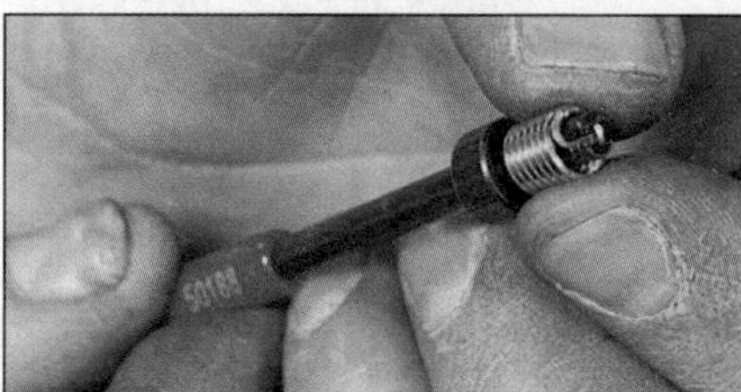

2.28 . . . fit insert on the installing tool . . .

2.29 . . . and thread into the component . . .

2.30 . . . break off the tang when complete

insert on the installing tool and thread it slowly into place using a light downward pressure **(see illustrations 2.28 and 2.29)**. When positioned between a 1/4 and 1/2 turn below the surface withdraw the installing tool and use the break-off tool to press down on the tang, breaking it off **(see illustration 2.30)**.

● There are epoxy thread repair kits on the market which can rebuild stripped internal threads, although this repair should not be used on high load-bearing components.

Thread locking and sealing compounds

- Locking compounds are used in locations where the fastener is prone to loosening due to vibration or on important safety-related items which might cause loss of control of the motorcycle if they fail. It is also used where important fasteners cannot be secured by other means such as lockwashers or split pins.
- Before applying locking compound, make sure that the threads (internal and external) are clean and dry with all old compound removed. Select a compound to suit the component being secured - a non-permanent general locking and sealing type is suitable for most applications, but a high strength type is needed for permanent fixing of studs in castings. Apply a drop or two of the compound to the first few threads of the fastener, then thread it into place and tighten to the specified torque. Do not apply excessive thread locking compound otherwise the thread may be damaged on subsequent removal.
- Certain fasteners are impregnated with a dry film type coating of locking compound on their threads. Always renew this type of fastener if disturbed.
- Anti-seize compounds, such as copper-based greases, can be applied to protect threads from seizure due to extreme heat and corrosion. A common instance is spark plug threads and exhaust system fasteners.

3 Measuring tools and gauges

Feeler gauges

- Feeler gauges (or blades) are used for measuring small gaps and clearances **(see illustration 3.1)**. They can also be used to measure endfloat (sideplay) of a component on a shaft where access is not possible with a dial gauge.
- Feeler gauge sets should be treated with care and not bent or damaged. They are etched with their size on one face. Keep them clean and very lightly oiled to prevent corrosion build-up.

3.1 Feeler gauges are used for measuring small gaps and clearances - thickness is marked on one face of gauge

- When measuring a clearance, select a gauge which is a light sliding fit between the two components. You may need to use two gauges together to measure the clearance accurately.

Micrometers

- A micrometer is a precision tool capable of measuring to 0.01 or 0.001 of a millimetre. It should always be stored in its case and not in the general toolbox. It must be kept clean and never dropped, otherwise its frame or measuring anvils could be distorted resulting in inaccurate readings.
- External micrometers are used for measuring outside diameters of components and have many more applications than internal micrometers. Micrometers are available in different size ranges, eg 0 to 25 mm, 25 to 50 mm, and upwards in 25 mm steps; some large micrometers have interchangeable anvils to allow a range of measurements to be taken. Generally the largest precision measurement you are likely to take on a motorcycle is the piston diameter.
- Internal micrometers (or bore micrometers) are used for measuring inside diameters, such as valve guides and cylinder bores. Telescoping gauges and small hole gauges are used in conjunction with an external micrometer, whereas the more expensive internal micrometers have their own measuring device.

External micrometer

Note: *The conventional analogue type instrument is described. Although much easier to read, digital micrometers are considerably more expensive.*

- Always check the calibration of the micrometer before use. With the anvils closed (0 to 25 mm type) or set over a test gauge (for the larger types) the scale should read zero **(see illustration 3.2)**; make sure that the anvils (and test piece) are clean first. Any discrepancy can be adjusted by referring to the instructions supplied with the tool. Remember that the micrometer is a precision measuring tool - don't force the anvils closed, use the ratchet (4) on the end of the micrometer to close it. In this way, a measured force is always applied.

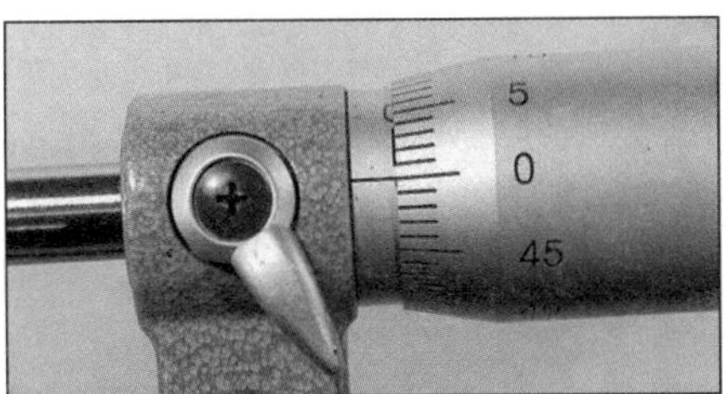

3.2 Check micrometer calibration before use

- To use, first make sure that the item being measured is clean. Place the anvil of the micrometer (1) against the item and use the thimble (2) to bring the spindle (3) lightly into contact with the other side of the item **(see illustration 3.3)**. Don't tighten the thimble down because this will damage the micrometer - instead use the ratchet (4) on the end of the micrometer. The ratchet mechanism applies a measured force preventing damage to the instrument.
- The micrometer is read by referring to the linear scale on the sleeve and the annular scale on the thimble. Read off the sleeve first to obtain the base measurement, then add the fine measurement from the thimble to obtain the overall reading. The linear scale on the sleeve represents the measuring range of the micrometer (eg 0 to 25 mm). The annular scale

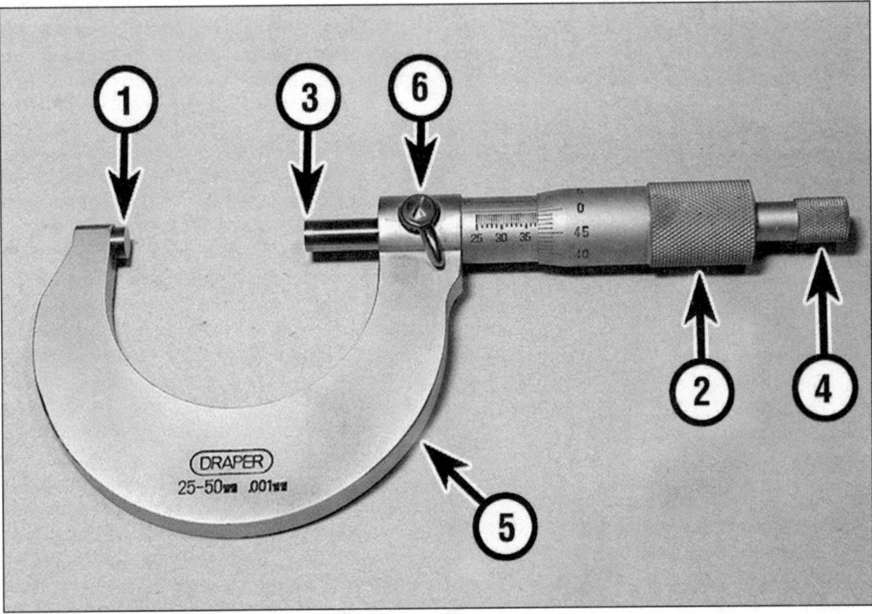

3.3 Micrometer component parts

1 Anvil
2 Thimble
3 Spindle
4 Ratchet
5 Frame
6 Locking lever

on the thimble will be in graduations of 0.01 mm (or as marked on the frame) - one full revolution of the thimble will move 0.5 mm on the linear scale. Take the reading where the datum line on the sleeve intersects the thimble's scale. Always position the eye directly above the scale otherwise an inaccurate reading will result.

In the example shown the item measures 2.95 mm **(see illustration 3.4)**:

Linear scale	2.00 mm
Linear scale	0.50 mm
Annular scale	0.45 mm
Total figure	**2.95 mm**

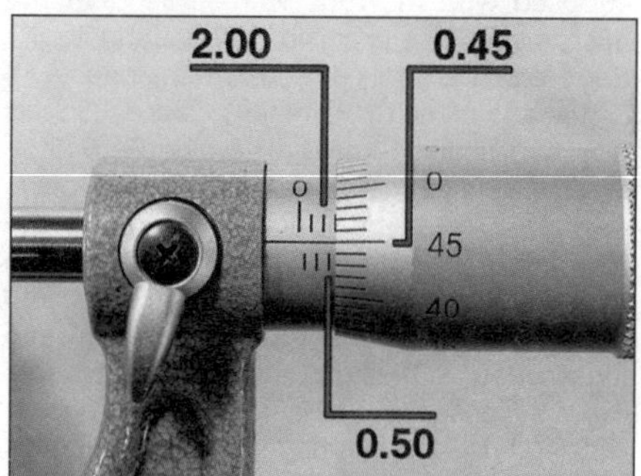

3.4 Micrometer reading of 2.95 mm

Most micrometers have a locking lever (6) on the frame to hold the setting in place, allowing the item to be removed from the micrometer.

- Some micrometers have a vernier scale on their sleeve, providing an even finer measurement to be taken, in 0.001 increments of a millimetre. Take the sleeve and thimble measurement as described above, then check which graduation on the vernier scale aligns with that of the annular scale on the thimble **Note:** *The eye must be perpendicular to the scale when taking the vernier reading - if necessary rotate the body of the micrometer to ensure this.* Multiply the vernier scale figure by 0.001 and add it to the base and fine measurement figures.

In the example shown the item measures 46.994 mm **(see illustrations 3.5 and 3.6)**:

Linear scale (base)	46.000 mm
Linear scale (base)	00.500 mm
Annular scale (fine)	00.490 mm
Vernier scale	00.004 mm
Total figure	**46.994 mm**

Internal micrometer

- Internal micrometers are available for measuring bore diameters, but are expensive and unlikely to be available for home use. It is suggested that a set of telescoping gauges and small hole gauges, both of which must be used with an external micrometer, will suffice for taking internal measurements on a motorcycle.
- Telescoping gauges can be used to measure internal diameters of components. Select a gauge with the correct size range, make sure its ends are clean and insert it into the bore. Expand the gauge, then lock its position and withdraw it from the bore **(see illustration 3.7)**. Measure across the gauge ends with a micrometer **(see illustration 3.8)**.
- Very small diameter bores (such as valve guides) are measured with a small hole gauge. Once adjusted to a slip-fit inside the component, its position is locked and the gauge withdrawn for measurement with a micrometer **(see illustrations 3.9 and 3.10)**.

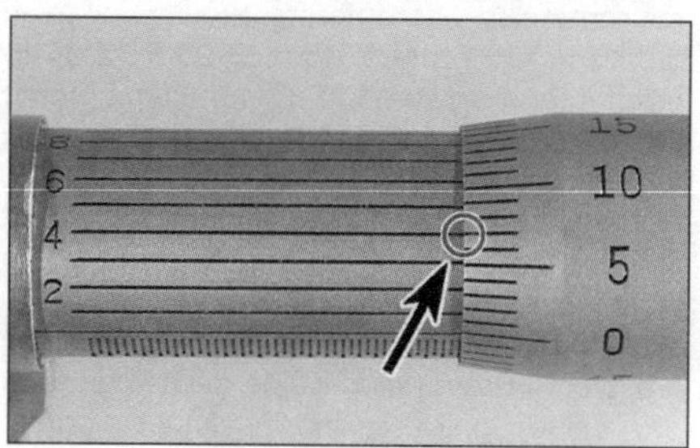

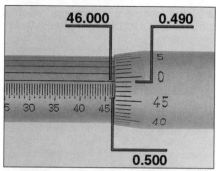

3.5 Micrometer reading of 46.99 mm on linear and annular scales . . .

3.6 . . . and 0.004 mm on vernier scale

Vernier caliper

Note: *The conventional linear and dial gauge type instruments are described. Digital types are easier to read, but are far more expensive.*

- The vernier caliper does not provide the precision of a micrometer, but is versatile in being able to measure internal and external diameters. Some types also incorporate a depth gauge. It is ideal for measuring clutch plate friction material and spring free lengths.
- To use the conventional linear scale vernier, slacken off the vernier clamp screws (1) and set its jaws over (2), or inside (3), the item to be measured **(see illustration 3.11)**. Slide the jaw into contact, using the thumb-wheel (4) for fine movement of the sliding scale (5) then tighten the clamp screws (1). Read off the main scale (6) where the zero on the sliding scale (5) intersects it, taking the whole number to the left of the zero; this provides the base measurement. View along the sliding scale and select the division which lines up exactly with any of the divisions on the main scale, noting that the divisions usually represents 0.02 of a millimetre. Add this fine measurement to the base measurement to obtain the total reading.

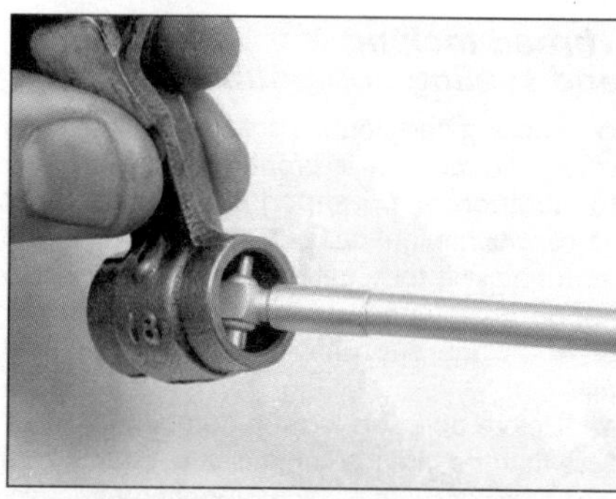

3.7 Expand the telescoping gauge in the bore, lock its position . . .

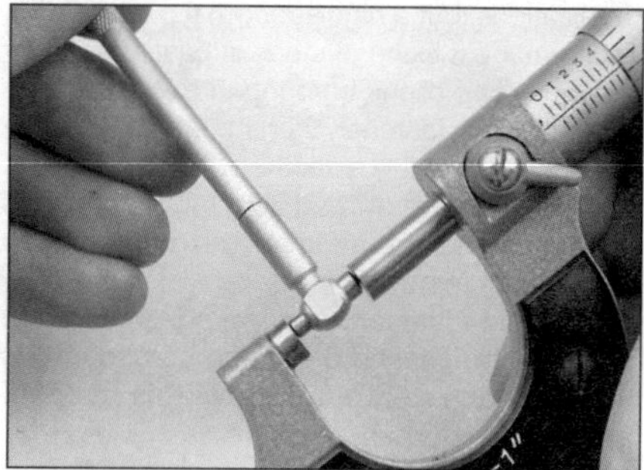

3.8 . . . then measure the gauge with a micrometer

3.9 Expand the small hole gauge in the bore, lock its position . . .

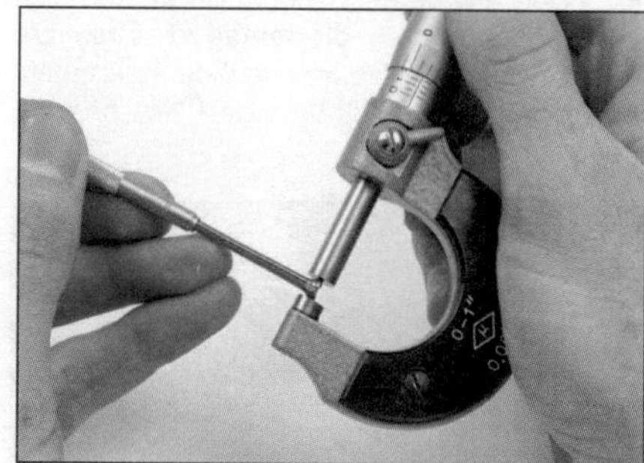

3.10 . . . then measure the gauge with a micrometer

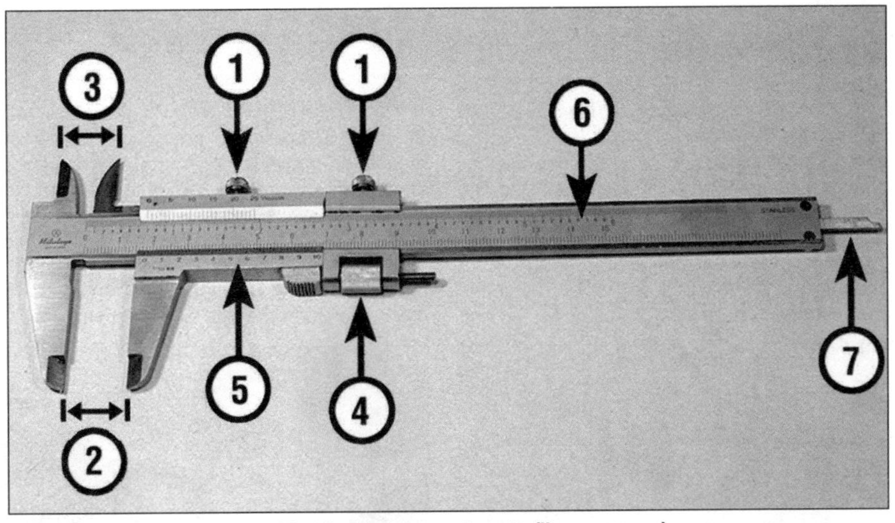

3.11 Vernier component parts (linear gauge)

1 *Clamp screws*
2 *External jaws*
3 *Internal jaws*
4 *Thumbwheel*
5 *Sliding scale*
6 *Main scale*
7 *Depth gauge*

In the example shown the item measures 55.92 mm **(see illustration 3.12)**:

Base measurement	55.00 mm
Fine measurement	00.92 mm
Total figure	**55.92 mm**

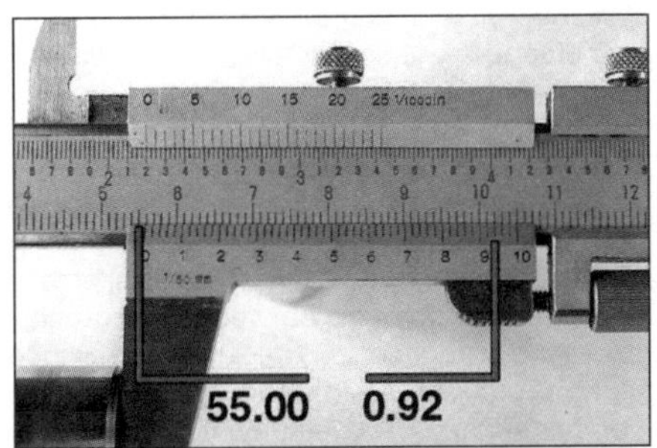

3.12 Vernier gauge reading of 55.92 mm

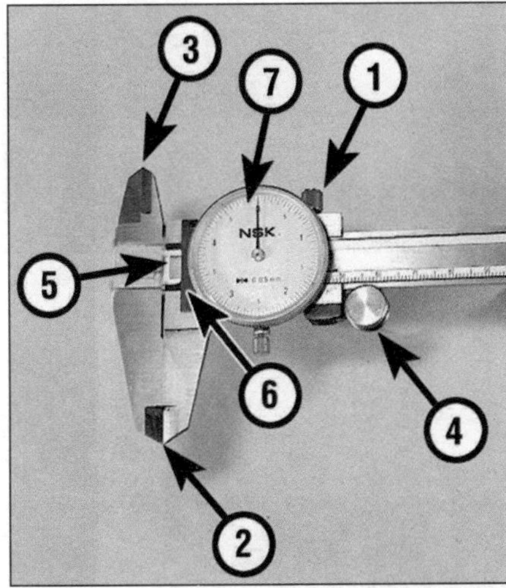

3.13 Vernier component parts (dial gauge)

1 *Clamp screw*
2 *External jaws*
3 *Internal jaws*
4 *Thumbwheel*
5 *Main scale*
6 *Sliding scale*
7 *Dial gauge*

● Some vernier calipers are equipped with a dial gauge for fine measurement. Before use, check that the jaws are clean, then close them fully and check that the dial gauge reads zero. If necessary adjust the gauge ring accordingly. Slacken the vernier clamp screw (1) and set its jaws over (2), or inside (3), the item to be measured **(see illustration 3.13)**. Slide the jaws into contact, using the thumbwheel (4) for fine movement. Read off the main scale (5) where the edge of the sliding scale (6) intersects it, taking the whole number to the left of the zero; this provides the base measurement. Read off the needle position on the dial gauge (7) scale to provide the fine measurement; each division represents 0.05 of a millimetre. Add this fine measurement to the base measurement to obtain the total reading.

In the example shown the item measures 55.95 mm **(see illustration 3.14)**:

Base measurement	55.00 mm
Fine measurement	00.95 mm
Total figure	**55.95 mm**

3.14 Vernier gauge reading of 55.95 mm

Plastigauge

● Plastigauge is a plastic material which can be compressed between two surfaces to measure the oil clearance between them. The width of the compressed Plastigauge is measured against a calibrated scale to determine the clearance.

● Common uses of Plastigauge are for measuring the clearance between crankshaft journal and main bearing inserts, between crankshaft journal and big-end bearing inserts, and between camshaft and bearing surfaces. The following example describes big-end oil clearance measurement.

● Handle the Plastigauge material carefully to prevent distortion. Using a sharp knife, cut a length which corresponds with the width of the bearing being measured and place it carefully across the journal so that it is parallel with the shaft **(see illustration 3.15)**. Carefully install both bearing shells and the connecting rod. Without rotating the rod on the journal tighten its bolts or nuts (as applicable) to the specified torque. The connecting rod and bearings are then disassembled and the crushed Plastigauge examined.

3.15 Plastigauge placed across shaft journal

● Using the scale provided in the Plastigauge kit, measure the width of the material to determine the oil clearance **(see illustration 3.16)**. Always remove all traces of Plastigauge after use using your fingernails.

Caution: Arriving at the correct clearance demands that the assembly is torqued correctly, according to the settings and sequence (where applicable) provided by the motorcycle manufacturer.

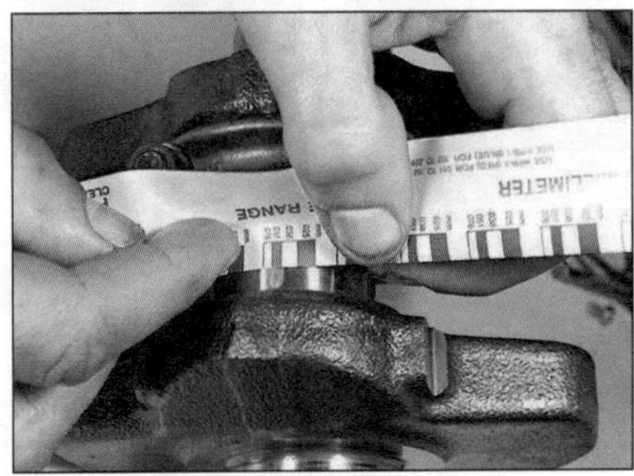
3.16 Measuring the width of the crushed Plastigauge

Dial gauge or DTI (Dial Test Indicator)

● A dial gauge can be used to accurately measure small amounts of movement. Typical uses are measuring shaft runout or shaft endfloat (sideplay) and setting piston position for ignition timing on two-strokes. A dial gauge set usually comes with a range of different probes and adapters and mounting equipment.
● The gauge needle must point to zero when at rest. Rotate the ring around its periphery to zero the gauge.
● Check that the gauge is capable of reading the extent of movement in the work. Most gauges have a small dial set in the face which records whole millimetres of movement as well as the fine scale around the face periphery which is calibrated in 0.01 mm divisions. Read off the small dial first to obtain the base measurement, then add the measurement from the fine scale to obtain the total reading.

In the example shown the gauge reads 1.48 mm **(see illustration 3.17)**:

Base measurement	1.00 mm
Fine measurement	0.48 mm
Total figure	**1.48 mm**

3.17 Dial gauge reading of 1.48 mm

● If measuring shaft runout, the shaft must be supported in vee-blocks and the gauge mounted on a stand perpendicular to the shaft. Rest the tip of the gauge against the centre of the shaft and rotate the shaft slowly whilst watching the gauge reading **(see illustration 3.18)**. Take several measurements along the length of the shaft and record the maximum gauge reading as the amount of runout in the shaft. **Note:** *The reading obtained will be total runout at that point - some manufacturers specify that the runout figure is halved to compare with their specified runout limit.*

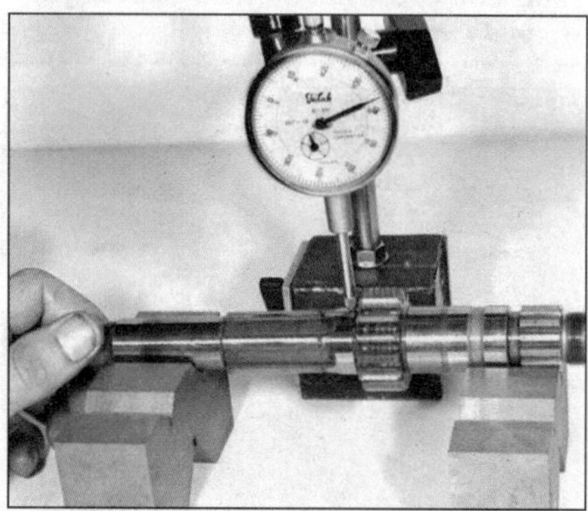

3.18 Using a dial gauge to measure shaft runout

● Endfloat (sideplay) measurement requires that the gauge is mounted securely to the surrounding component with its probe touching the end of the shaft. Using hand pressure, push and pull on the shaft noting the maximum endfloat recorded on the gauge **(see illustration 3.19)**.

3.19 Using a dial gauge to measure shaft endfloat

● A dial gauge with suitable adapters can be used to determine piston position BTDC on two-stroke engines for the purposes of ignition timing. The gauge, adapter and suitable length probe are installed in the place of the spark plug and the gauge zeroed at TDC. If the piston position is specified as 1.14 mm BTDC, rotate the engine back to 2.00 mm BTDC, then slowly forwards to 1.14 mm BTDC.

Cylinder compression gauges

● A compression gauge is used for measuring cylinder compression. Either the rubber-cone type or the threaded adapter type can be used. The latter is preferred to ensure a perfect seal against the cylinder head. A 0 to 300 psi (0 to 20 Bar) type gauge (for petrol/gasoline engines) will be suitable for motorcycles.
● The spark plug is removed and the gauge either held hard against the cylinder head (cone type) or the gauge adapter screwed into the cylinder head (threaded type) **(see illustration 3.20)**. Cylinder compression is measured with the engine turning over, but not running - carry out the compression test as described in *Fault Finding Equipment*. The gauge will hold the reading until manually released.

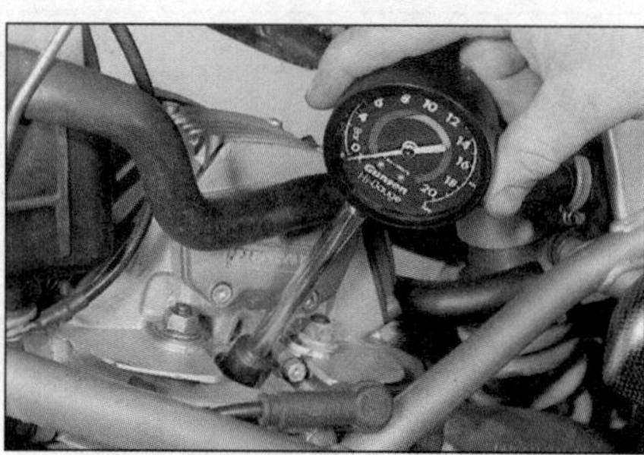

3.20 Using a rubber-cone type cylinder compression gauge

Oil pressure gauge

● An oil pressure gauge is used for measuring engine oil pressure. Most gauges come with a set of adapters to fit the thread of the take-off point **(see illustration 3.21)**. If the take-off point specified by the motorcycle manufacturer is an external oil pipe union, make sure that the specified replacement union is used to prevent oil starvation.

3.21 Oil pressure gauge and take-off point adapter (arrow)

● Oil pressure is measured with the engine running (at a specific rpm) and often the manufacturer will specify pressure limits for a cold and hot engine.

Straight-edge and surface plate

● If checking the gasket face of a component for warpage, place a steel rule or precision straight-edge across the gasket face and measure any gap between the straight-edge and component with feeler gauges **(see illustration 3.22)**. Check diagonally across the component and between mounting holes **(see illustration 3.23)**.

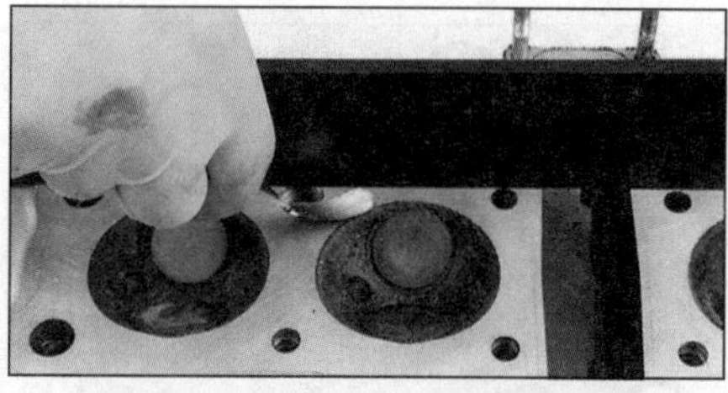

3.22 Use a straight-edge and feeler gauges to check for warpage

3.23 Check for warpage in these directions

● Checking individual components for warpage, such as clutch plain (metal) plates, requires a perfectly flat plate or piece or plate glass and feeler gauges.

4 Torque and leverage

What is torque?

● Torque describes the twisting force about a shaft. The amount of torque applied is determined by the distance from the centre of the shaft to the end of the lever and the amount of force being applied to the end of the lever; distance multiplied by force equals torque.

● The manufacturer applies a measured torque to a bolt or nut to ensure that it will not slacken in use and to hold two components securely together without movement in the joint. The actual torque setting depends on the thread size, bolt or nut material and the composition of the components being held.

● Too little torque may cause the fastener to loosen due to vibration, whereas too much torque will distort the joint faces of the component or cause the fastener to shear off. Always stick to the specified torque setting.

Using a torque wrench

● Check the calibration of the torque wrench and make sure it has a suitable range for the job. Torque wrenches are available in Nm (Newton-metres), kgf m (kilograms-force metre), lbf ft (pounds-feet), lbf in (inch-pounds). Do not confuse lbf ft with lbf in.

● Adjust the tool to the desired torque on the scale **(see illustration 4.1)**. If your torque wrench is not calibrated in the units specified, carefully convert the figure (see *Conversion Factors*). A manufacturer sometimes gives a torque setting as a range (8 to 10 Nm) rather than a single figure - in this case set the tool midway between the two settings. The same torque may be expressed as 9 Nm ± 1 Nm. Some torque wrenches have a method of locking the setting so that it isn't inadvertently altered during use.

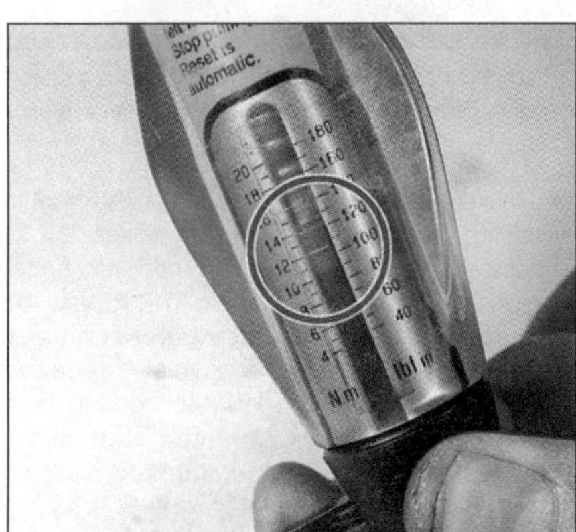

4.1 Set the torque wrench index mark to the setting required, in this case 12 Nm

● Install the bolts/nuts in their correct location and secure them lightly. Their threads must be clean and free of any old locking compound. Unless specified the threads and flange should be dry - oiled threads are necessary in certain circumstances and the manufacturer will take this into account in the specified torque figure. Similarly, the manufacturer may also specify the application of thread-locking compound.

● Tighten the fasteners in the specified sequence until the torque wrench clicks, indicating that the torque setting has been reached. Apply the torque again to double-check the setting. Where different thread diameter fasteners secure the component, as a rule tighten the larger diameter ones first.

● When the torque wrench has been finished with, release the lock (where applicable) and fully back off its setting to zero - do not leave the torque wrench tensioned. Also, do not use a torque wrench for slackening a fastener.

Angle-tightening

● Manufacturers often specify a figure in degrees for final tightening of a fastener. This usually follows tightening to a specific torque setting.

● A degree disc can be set and attached to the socket **(see illustration 4.2)** or a protractor can be used to mark the angle of movement on the bolt/nut head and the surrounding casting **(see illustration 4.3)**.

4.2 Angle tightening can be accomplished with a torque-angle gauge . . .

4.3 . . . or by marking the angle on the surrounding component

Loosening sequences

● Where more than one bolt/nut secures a component, loosen each fastener evenly a little at a time. In this way, not all the stress of the joint is held by one fastener and the components are not likely to distort.

● If a tightening sequence is provided, work in the REVERSE of this, but if not, work from the outside in, in a criss-cross sequence **(see illustration 4.4)**.

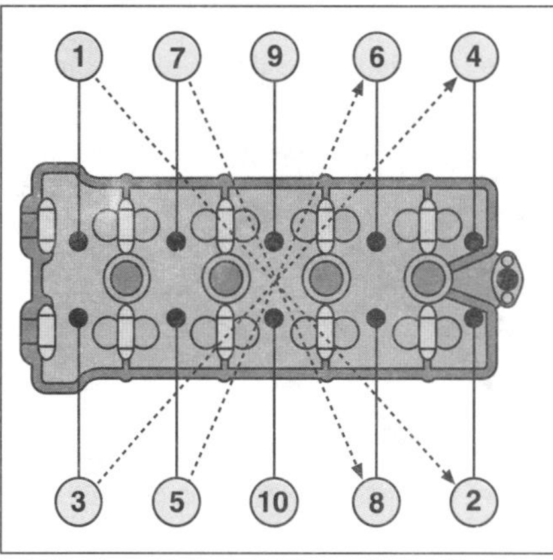

4.4 When slackening, work from the outside inwards

Tightening sequences

● If a component is held by more than one fastener it is important that the retaining bolts/nuts are tightened evenly to prevent uneven stress build-up and distortion of sealing faces. This is especially important on high-compression joints such as the cylinder head.

● A sequence is usually provided by the manufacturer, either in a diagram or actually marked in the casting. If not, always start in the centre and work outwards in a criss-cross pattern **(see illustration 4.5)**. Start off by securing all bolts/nuts finger-tight, then set the torque wrench and tighten each fastener by a small amount in sequence until the final torque is reached. By following this practice,

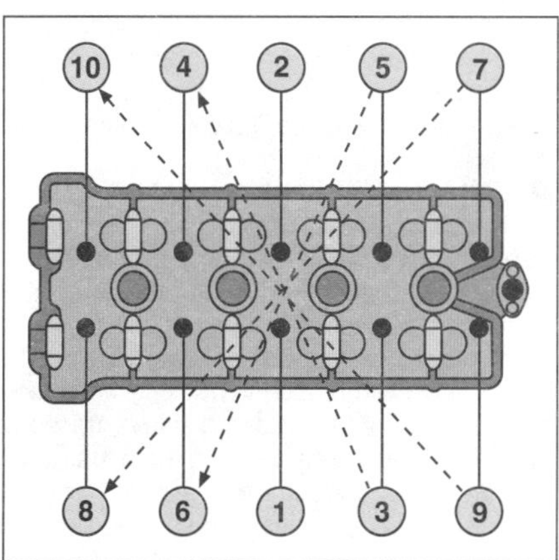

4.5 When tightening, work from the inside outwards

the joint will be held evenly and will not be distorted. Important joints, such as the cylinder head and big-end fasteners often have two- or three-stage torque settings.

Applying leverage

● Use tools at the correct angle. Position a socket wrench or spanner on the bolt/nut so that you pull it towards you when loosening. If this can't be done, push the spanner without curling your fingers around it **(see illustration 4.6)** - the spanner may slip or the fastener loosen suddenly, resulting in your fingers being crushed against a component.

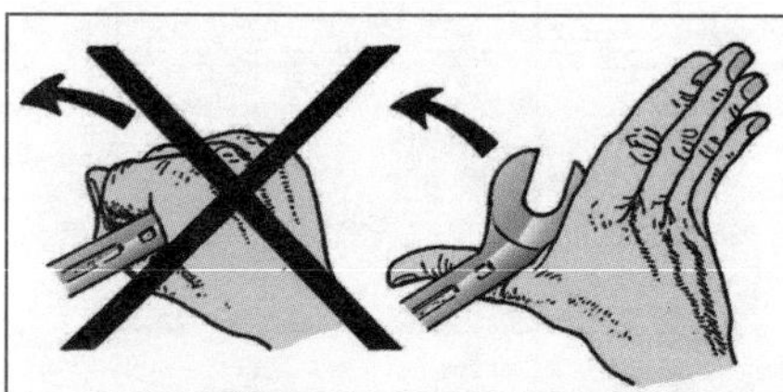

4.6 If you can't pull on the spanner to loosen a fastener, push with your hand open

● Additional leverage is gained by extending the length of the lever. The best way to do this is to use a breaker bar instead of the regular length tool, or to slip a length of tubing over the end of the spanner or socket wrench.

● If additional leverage will not work, the fastener head is either damaged or firmly corroded in place (see *Fasteners*).

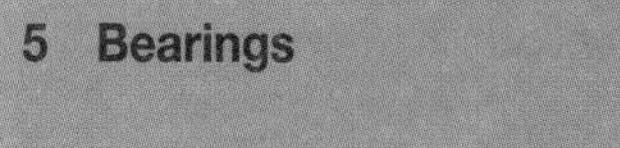

5 Bearings

Bearing removal and installation

Drivers and sockets

● Before removing a bearing, always inspect the casing to see which way it must be driven out - some casings will have retaining plates or a cast step. Also check for any identifying markings on the bearing and if installed to a certain depth, measure this at this stage. Some roller bearings are sealed on one side - take note of the original fitted position.

● Bearings can be driven out of a casing using a bearing driver tool (with the correct size head) or a socket of the correct diameter. Select the driver head or socket so that it contacts the outer race of the bearing, not the balls/rollers or inner race. Always support the casing around the bearing housing with wood blocks, otherwise there is a risk of fracture. The bearing is driven out with a few blows on the driver or socket from a heavy mallet. Unless access is severely restricted (as with wheel bearings), a pin-punch is not recommended unless it is moved around the bearing to keep it square in its housing.

● The same equipment can be used to install bearings. Make sure the bearing housing is supported on wood blocks and line up the bearing in its housing. Fit the bearing as noted on removal - generally they are installed with their marked side facing outwards. Tap the bearing squarely into its housing using a driver or socket which bears only on the bearing's outer race - contact with the bearing balls/rollers or inner race will destroy it **(see illustrations 5.1 and 5.2)**.

● Check that the bearing inner race and balls/rollers rotate freely.

5.1 Using a bearing driver against the bearing's outer race

5.2 Using a large socket against the bearing's outer race

Pullers and slide-hammers

● Where a bearing is pressed on a shaft a puller will be required to extract it **(see illustration 5.3)**. Make sure that the puller clamp or legs fit securely behind the bearing and are unlikely to slip out. If pulling a bearing

5.3 This bearing puller clamps behind the bearing and pressure is applied to the shaft end to draw the bearing off

off a gear shaft for example, you may have to locate the puller behind a gear pinion if there is no access to the race and draw the gear pinion off the shaft as well **(see illustration 5.4)**.

Caution: Ensure that the puller's centre bolt locates securely against the end of the shaft and will not slip when pressure is applied. Also ensure that puller does not damage the shaft end.

5.4 Where no access is available to the rear of the bearing, it is sometimes possible to draw off the adjacent component

● Operate the puller so that its centre bolt exerts pressure on the shaft end and draws the bearing off the shaft.

● When installing the bearing on the shaft, tap only on the bearing's inner race - contact with the balls/rollers or outer race with destroy the bearing. Use a socket or length of tubing as a drift which fits over the shaft end **(see illustration 5.5)**.

5.5 When installing a bearing on a shaft use a piece of tubing which bears only on the bearing's inner race

● Where a bearing locates in a blind hole in a casing, it cannot be driven or pulled out as described above. A slide-hammer with knife-edged bearing puller attachment will be required. The puller attachment passes through the bearing and when tightened expands to fit firmly behind the bearing **(see illustration 5.6)**. By operating the slide-hammer part of the tool the bearing is jarred out of its housing **(see illustration 5.7)**.

● It is possible, if the bearing is of reasonable weight, for it to drop out of its housing if the casing is heated as described opposite. If this

5.6 Expand the bearing puller so that it locks behind the bearing . . .

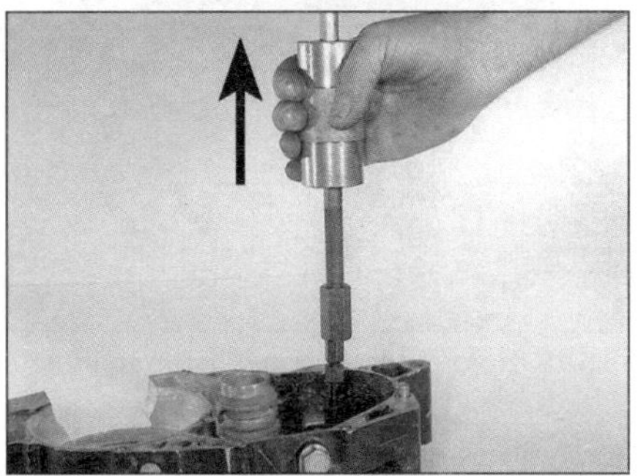
5.7 . . . attach the slide hammer to the bearing puller

method is attempted, first prepare a work surface which will enable the casing to be tapped face down to help dislodge the bearing - a wood surface is ideal since it will not damage the casing's gasket surface. Wearing protective gloves, tap the heated casing several times against the work surface to dislodge the bearing under its own weight **(see illustration 5.8)**.

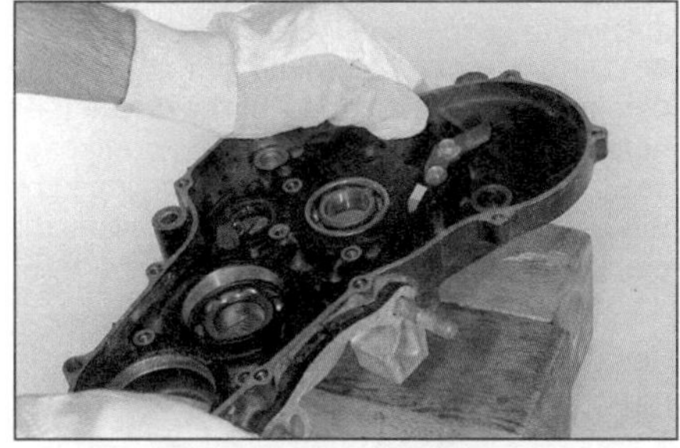
5.8 Tapping a casing face down on wood blocks can often dislodge a bearing

● Bearings can be installed in blind holes using the driver or socket method described above.

Drawbolts

● Where a bearing or bush is set in the eye of a component, such as a suspension linkage arm or connecting rod small-end, removal by drift may damage the component. Furthermore, a rubber bushing in a shock absorber eye cannot successfully be driven out of position. If access is available to a engineering press, the task is straightforward. If not, a drawbolt can be fabricated to extract the bearing or bush.

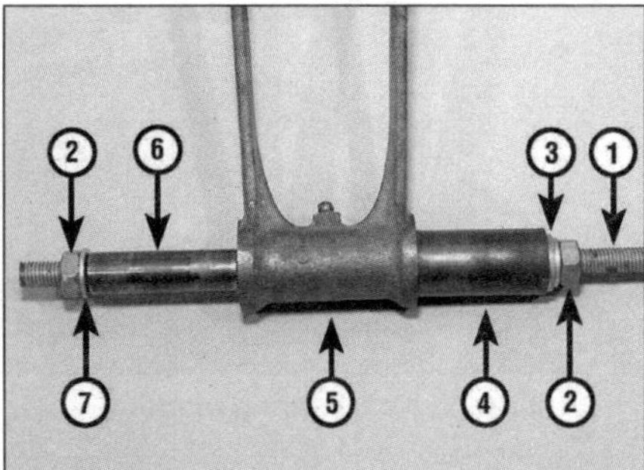

5.9 Drawbolt component parts assembled on a suspension arm

1 Bolt or length of threaded bar
2 Nuts
3 Washer (external diameter greater than tubing internal diameter)
4 Tubing (internal diameter sufficient to accommodate bearing)
5 Suspension arm with bearing
6 Tubing (external diameter slightly smaller than bearing)
7 Washer (external diameter slightly smaller than bearing)

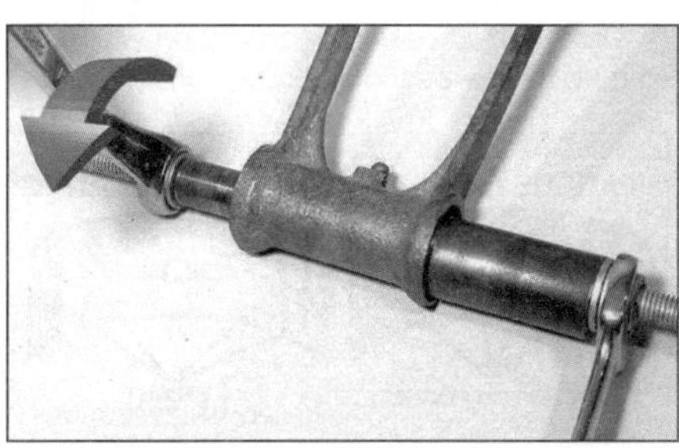
5.10 Drawing the bearing out of the suspension arm

● To extract the bearing/bush you will need a long bolt with nut (or piece of threaded bar with two nuts), a piece of tubing which has an internal diameter larger than the bearing/bush, another piece of tubing which has an external diameter slightly smaller than the bearing/ bush, and a selection of washers **(see illustrations 5.9 and 5.10)**. Note that the pieces of tubing must be of the same length, or longer, than the bearing/bush.

● The same kit (without the pieces of tubing) can be used to draw the new bearing/bush back into place **(see illustration 5.11)**.

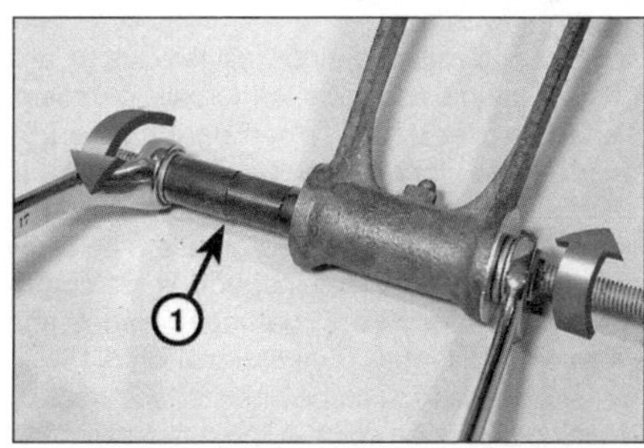

5.11 Installing a new bearing (1) in the suspension arm

Temperature change

● If the bearing's outer race is a tight fit in the casing, the aluminium casing can be heated to release its grip on the bearing. Aluminium will expand at a greater rate than the steel bearing outer race. There are several ways to do this, but avoid any localised extreme heat (such as a blow torch) - aluminium alloy has a low melting point.

● Approved methods of heating a casing are using a domestic oven (heated to 100°C) or immersing the casing in boiling water **(see illustration 5.12)**. Low temperature range localised heat sources such as a paint stripper heat gun or clothes iron can also be used **(see illustration 5.13)**. Alternatively, soak a rag in boiling water, wring it out and wrap it around the bearing housing.

Warning: All of these methods require care in use to prevent scalding and burns to the hands. Wear protective gloves when handling hot components.

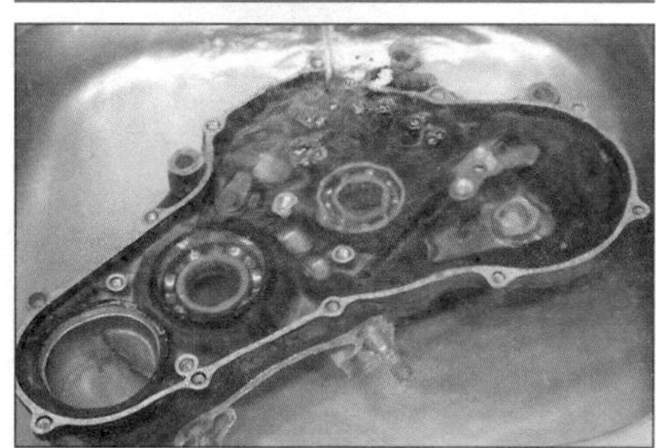
5.12 A casing can be immersed in a sink of boiling water to aid bearing removal

5.13 Using a localised heat source to aid bearing removal

● If heating the whole casing note that plastic components, such as the neutral switch, may suffer - remove them beforehand.

● After heating, remove the bearing as described above. You may find that the expansion is sufficient for the bearing to fall out of the casing under its own weight or with a light tap on the driver or socket.

● If necessary, the casing can be heated to aid bearing installation, and this is sometimes the recommended procedure if the motorcycle manufacturer has designed the housing and bearing fit with this intention.

● Installation of bearings can be eased by placing them in a freezer the night before installation. The steel bearing will contract slightly, allowing easy insertion in its housing. This is often useful when installing steering head outer races in the frame.

Bearing types and markings

● Plain shell bearings, ball bearings, needle roller bearings and tapered roller bearings will all be found on motorcycles **(see illustrations 5.14 and 5.15)**. The ball and roller types are usually caged between an inner and outer race, but uncaged variations may be found.

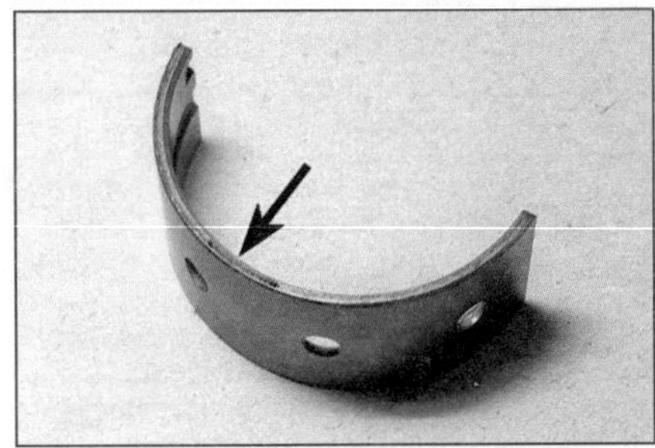

5.14 Shell bearings are either plain or grooved. They are usually identified by colour code (arrow)

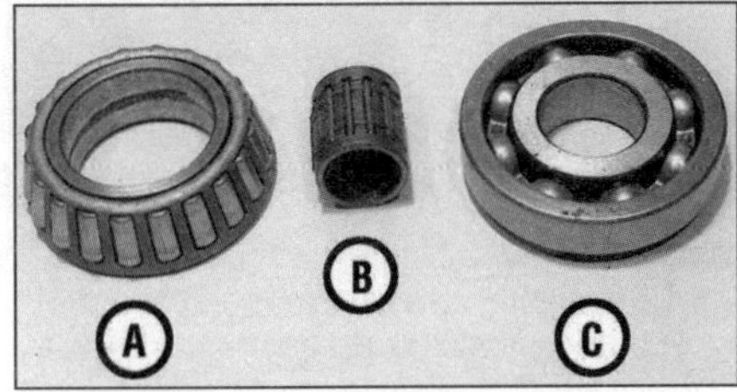

5.15 Tapered roller bearing (A), needle roller bearing (B) and ball journal bearing (C)

● Shell bearings (often called inserts) are usually found at the crankshaft main and connecting rod big-end where they are good at coping with high loads. They are made of a phosphor-bronze material and are impregnated with self-lubricating properties.

● Ball bearings and needle roller bearings consist of a steel inner and outer race with the balls or rollers between the races. They require constant lubrication by oil or grease and are good at coping with axial loads. Taper roller bearings consist of rollers set in a tapered cage set on the inner race; the outer race is separate. They are good at coping with axial loads and prevent movement along the shaft - a typical application is in the steering head.

● Bearing manufacturers produce bearings to ISO size standards and stamp one face of the bearing to indicate its internal and external diameter, load capacity and type **(see illustration 5.16)**.

● Metal bushes are usually of phosphor-bronze material. Rubber bushes are used in suspension mounting eyes. Fibre bushes have also been used in suspension pivots.

5.16 Typical bearing marking

Bearing fault finding

● If a bearing outer race has spun in its housing, the housing material will be damaged. You can use a bearing locking compound to bond the outer race in place if damage is not too severe.

● Shell bearings will fail due to damage of their working surface, as a result of lack of lubrication, corrosion or abrasive particles in the oil **(see illustration 5.17)**. Small particles of dirt in the oil may embed in the bearing material whereas larger particles will score the bearing and shaft journal. If a number of short journeys are made, insufficient heat will be generated to drive off condensation which has built up on the bearings.

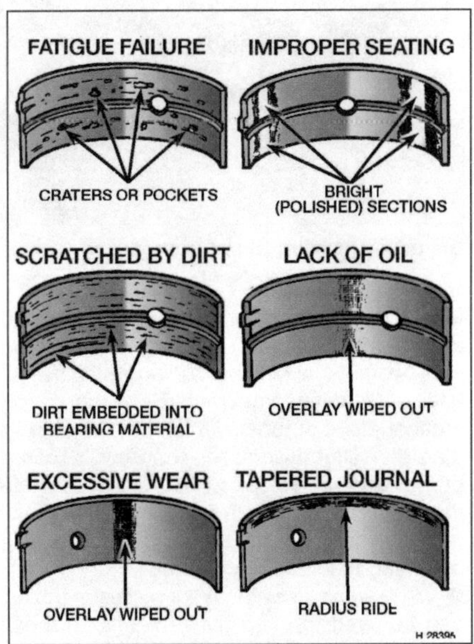

5.17 Typical bearing failures

● Ball and roller bearings will fail due to lack of lubrication or damage to the balls or rollers. Tapered-roller bearings can be damaged by overloading them. Unless the bearing is sealed on both sides, wash it in paraffin (kerosene) to remove all old grease then allow it to dry. Make a visual inspection looking to dented balls or rollers, damaged cages and worn or pitted races **(see illustration 5.18)**.

● A ball bearing can be checked for wear by listening to it when spun. Apply a film of light oil to the bearing and hold it close to the ear - hold the outer race with one hand and spin the inner race with the other hand **(see illustration 5.19)**. The bearing should be almost silent when spun; if it grates or rattles it is worn.

5.18 Example of ball journal bearing with damaged balls and cages

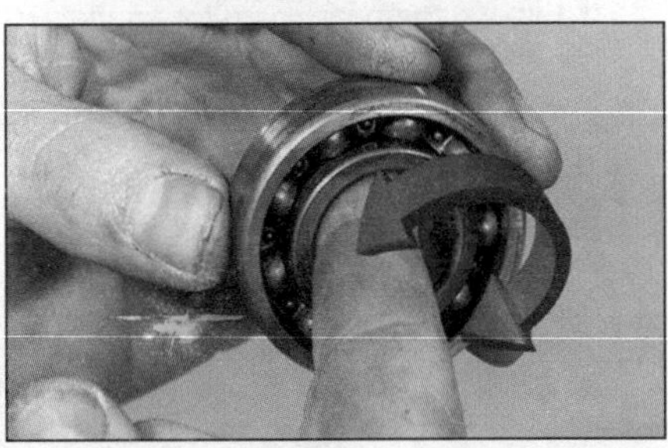

5.19 Hold outer race and listen to inner race when spun

6 Oil seals

Oil seal removal and installation

● Oil seals should be renewed every time a component is dismantled. This is because the seal lips will become set to the sealing surface and will not necessarily reseal.

● Oil seals can be prised out of position using a large flat-bladed screwdriver **(see illustration 6.1)**. In the case of crankcase seals, check first that the seal is not lipped on the inside, preventing its removal with the crankcases joined.

6.1 Prise out oil seals with a large flat-bladed screwdriver

● New seals are usually installed with their marked face (containing the seal reference code) outwards and the spring side towards the fluid being retained. In certain cases, such as a two-stroke engine crankshaft seal, a double lipped seal may be used due to there being fluid or gas on each side of the joint.

● Use a bearing driver or socket which bears only on the outer hard edge of the seal to install it in the casing - tapping on the inner edge will damage the sealing lip.

Oil seal types and markings

● Oil seals are usually of the single-lipped type. Double-lipped seals are found where a liquid or gas is on both sides of the joint.
● Oil seals can harden and lose their sealing ability if the motorcycle has been in storage for a long period - renewal is the only solution.
● Oil seal manufacturers also conform to the ISO markings for seal size - these are moulded into the outer face of the seal **(see illustration 6.2)**.

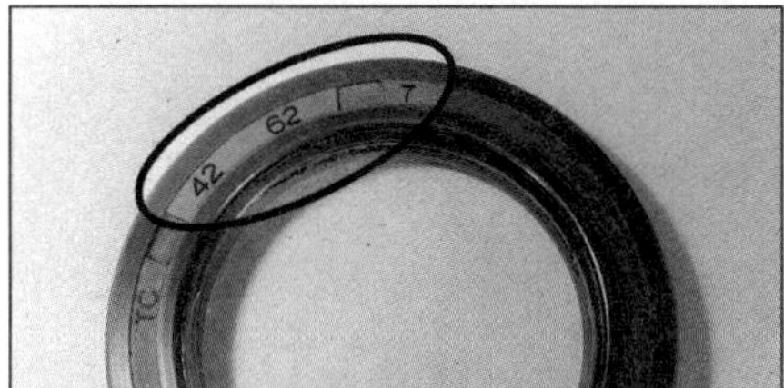

6.2 These oil seal markings indicate inside diameter, outside diameter and seal thickness

7 Gaskets and sealants

Types of gasket and sealant

● Gaskets are used to seal the mating surfaces between components and keep lubricants, fluids, vacuum or pressure contained within the assembly. Aluminium gaskets are sometimes found at the cylinder joints, but most gaskets are paper-based. If the mating surfaces of the components being joined are undamaged the gasket can be installed dry, although a dab of sealant or grease will be useful to hold it in place during assembly.
● RTV (Room Temperature Vulcanising) silicone rubber sealants cure when exposed to moisture in the atmosphere. These sealants are good at filling pits or irregular gasket faces, but will tend to be forced out of the joint under very high torque. They can be used to replace a paper gasket, but first make sure that the width of the paper gasket is not essential to the shimming of internal components. RTV sealants should not be used on components containing petrol (gasoline).
● Non-hardening, semi-hardening and hard setting liquid gasket compounds can be used with a gasket or between a metal-to-metal joint. Select the sealant to suit the application: universal non-hardening sealant can be used on virtually all joints; semi-hardening on joint faces which are rough or damaged; hard setting sealant on joints which require a permanent bond and are subjected to high temperature and pressure. **Note:** *Check first if the paper gasket has a bead of sealant impregnated in its surface before applying additional sealant.*
● When choosing a sealant, make sure it is suitable for the application, particularly if being applied in a high-temperature area or in the vicinity of fuel. Certain manufacturers produce sealants in either clear, silver or black colours to match the finish of the engine. This has a particular application on motorcycles where much of the engine is exposed.
● Do not over-apply sealant. That which is squeezed out on the outside of the joint can be wiped off, whereas an excess of sealant on the inside can break off and clog oilways.

Breaking a sealed joint

● Age, heat, pressure and the use of hard setting sealant can cause two components to stick together so tightly that they are difficult to separate using finger pressure alone. Do not resort to using levers unless there is a pry point provided for this purpose **(see illustration 7.1)** or else the gasket surfaces will be damaged.
● Use a soft-faced hammer **(see illustration 7.2)** or a wood block and conventional hammer to strike the component near the mating surface. Avoid hammering against cast extremities since they may break off. If this method fails, try using a wood wedge between the two components.

Caution: If the joint will not separate, double-check that you have removed all the fasteners.

7.1 If a pry point is provided, apply gently pressure with a flat-bladed screwdriver

7.2 Tap around the joint with a soft-faced mallet if necessary - don't strike cooling fins

Removal of old gasket and sealant

● Paper gaskets will most likely come away complete, leaving only a few traces stuck on the sealing faces of the components. It is imperative that all traces are removed to ensure correct sealing of the new gasket.
● Very carefully scrape all traces of gasket away making sure that the sealing surfaces are not gouged or scored by the scraper **(see illustrations 7.3, 7.4 and 7.5)**. Stubborn deposits can be removed by spraying with an aerosol gasket remover. Final preparation of

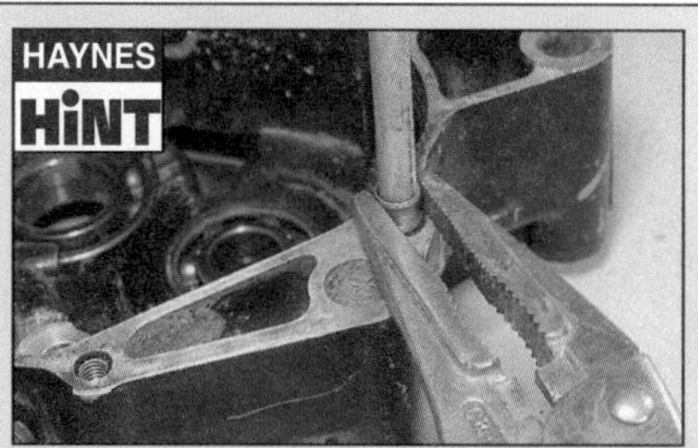

Most components have one or two hollow locating dowels between the two gasket faces. If a dowel cannot be removed, do not resort to gripping it with pliers - it will almost certainly be distorted. Install a close-fitting socket or Phillips screwdriver into the dowel and then grip the outer edge of the dowel to free it.

7.3 Paper gaskets can be scraped off with a gasket scraper tool . . .

7.4 . . . a knife blade . . .

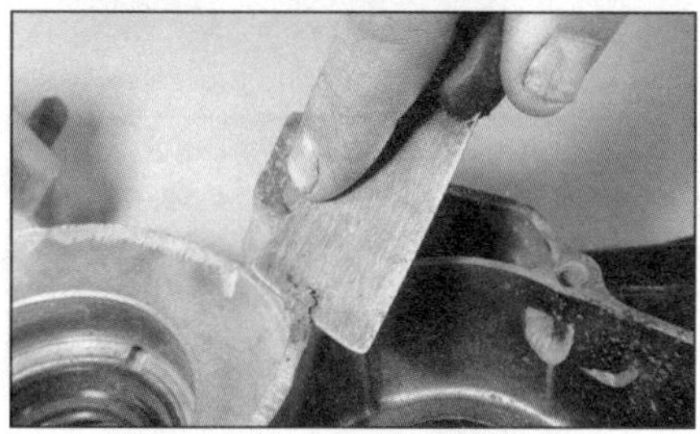

7.5 . . . or a household scraper

7.6 Fine abrasive paper is wrapped around a flat file to clean up the gasket face

7.7 A kitchen scourer can be used on stubborn deposits

the gasket surface can be made with very fine abrasive paper or a plastic kitchen scourer **(see illustrations 7.6 and 7.7)**.

● Old sealant can be scraped or peeled off components, depending on the type originally used. Note that gasket removal compounds are available to avoid scraping the components clean; make sure the gasket remover suits the type of sealant used.

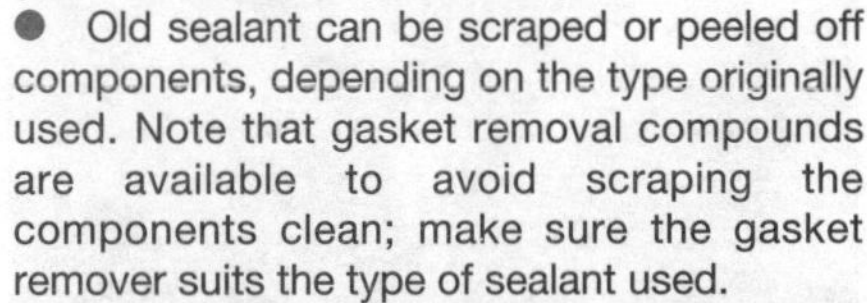

8 Chains

Breaking and joining final drive chains

● Drive chains for all but small bikes are continuous and do not have a clip-type connecting link. The chain must be broken using a chain breaker tool and the new chain securely riveted together using a new soft rivet-type link. Never use a clip-type connecting link instead of a rivet-type link, except in an emergency. Various chain breaking and riveting tools are available, either as separate tools or combined as illustrated in the accompanying photographs - read the instructions supplied with the tool carefully.

> ***Warning: The need to rivet the new link pins correctly cannot be overstressed - loss of control of the motorcycle is very likely to result if the chain breaks in use.***

● Rotate the chain and look for the soft link. The soft link pins look like they have been

8.1 Tighten the chain breaker to push the pin out of the link . . .

8.2 . . . withdraw the pin, remove the tool . . .

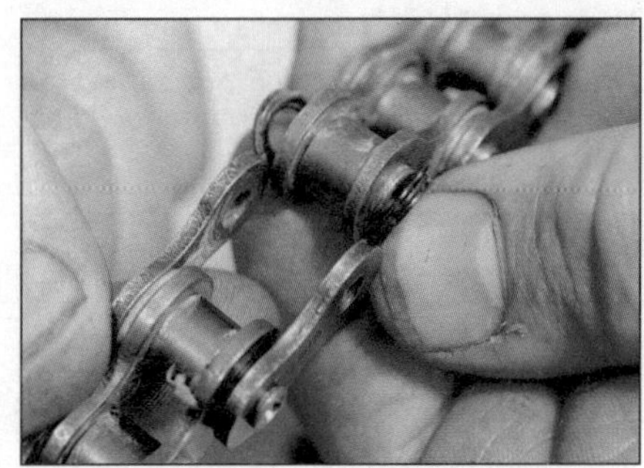

8.3 . . . and separate the chain link

deeply centre-punched instead of peened over like all the other pins **(see illustration 8.9)** and its sideplate may be a different colour. Position the soft link midway between the sprockets and assemble the chain breaker tool over one of the soft link pins **(see illustration 8.1)**. Operate the tool to push the pin out through the chain **(see illustration 8.2)**. On an O-ring chain, remove the O-rings **(see illustration 8.3)**. Carry out the same procedure on the other soft link pin.

> ***Caution: Certain soft link pins (particularly on the larger chains) may require their ends to be filed or ground off before they can be pressed out using the tool.***

● Check that you have the correct size and strength (standard or heavy duty) new soft link - do not reuse the old link. Look for the size marking on the chain sideplates **(see illustration 8.10)**.

● Position the chain ends so that they are engaged over the rear sprocket. On an O-ring

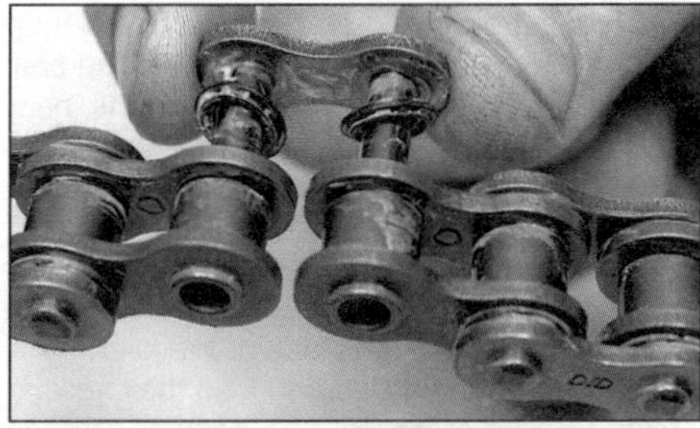

8.4 Insert the new soft link, with O-rings, through the chain ends . . .

8.5 . . . install the O-rings over the pin ends . . .

8.6 . . . followed by the sideplate

chain, install a new O-ring over each pin of the link and insert the link through the two chain ends **(see illustration 8.4)**. Install a new O-ring over the end of each pin, followed by the sideplate (with the chain manufacturer's marking facing outwards) **(see illustrations 8.5 and 8.6)**. On an unsealed chain, insert the link through the two chain ends, then install the sideplate with the chain manufacturer's marking facing outwards.

● Note that it may not be possible to install the sideplate using finger pressure alone. If using a joining tool, assemble it so that the plates of the tool clamp the link and press the sideplate over the pins **(see illustration 8.7)**. Otherwise, use two small sockets placed over

8.7 Push the sideplate into position using a clamp

8.8 Assemble the chain riveting tool over one pin at a time and tighten it fully

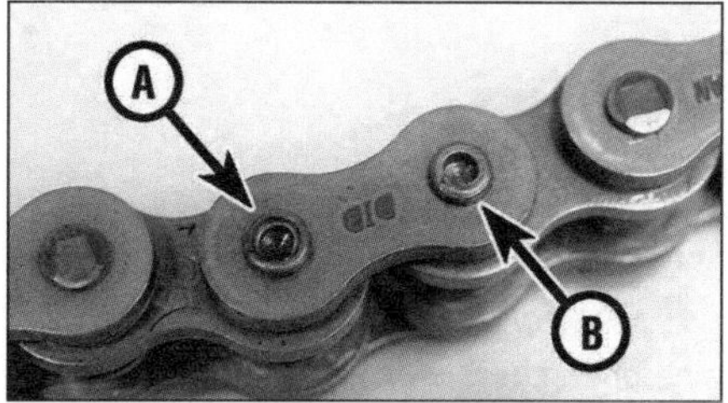

8.9 Pin end correctly riveted (A), pin end unriveted (B)

the rivet ends and two pieces of the wood between a G-clamp. Operate the clamp to press the sideplate over the pins.

● Assemble the joining tool over one pin (following the maker's instructions) and tighten the tool down to spread the pin end securely **(see illustrations 8.8 and 8.9)**. Do the same on the other pin.

> ***Warning: Check that the pin ends are secure and that there is no danger of the sideplate coming loose. If the pin ends are cracked the soft link must be renewed.***

Final drive chain sizing

● Chains are sized using a three digit number, followed by a suffix to denote the chain type **(see illustration 8.10)**. Chain type is either standard or heavy duty (thicker sideplates), and also unsealed or O-ring/X-ring type.

● The first digit of the number relates to the pitch of the chain, ie the distance from the centre of one pin to the centre of the next pin **(see illustration 8.11)**. Pitch is expressed in eighths of an inch, as follows:

8.10 Typical chain size and type marking

8.11 Chain dimensions

Sizes commencing with a 4 (eg 428) have a pitch of 1/2 inch (12.7 mm)

Sizes commencing with a 5 (eg 520) have a pitch of 5/8 inch (15.9 mm)

Sizes commencing with a 6 (eg 630) have a pitch of 3/4 inch (19.1 mm)

● The second and third digits of the chain size relate to the width of the rollers, again in imperial units, eg the 525 shown has 5/16 inch (7.94 mm) rollers **(see illustration 8.11)**.

9 Hoses

Clamping to prevent flow

● Small-bore flexible hoses can be clamped to prevent fluid flow whilst a component is worked on. Whichever method is used, ensure that the hose material is not permanently distorted or damaged by the clamp.

*a) A brake hose clamp available from auto accessory shops **(see illustration 9.1)**.*
*b) A wingnut type hose clamp **(see illustration 9.2)**.*

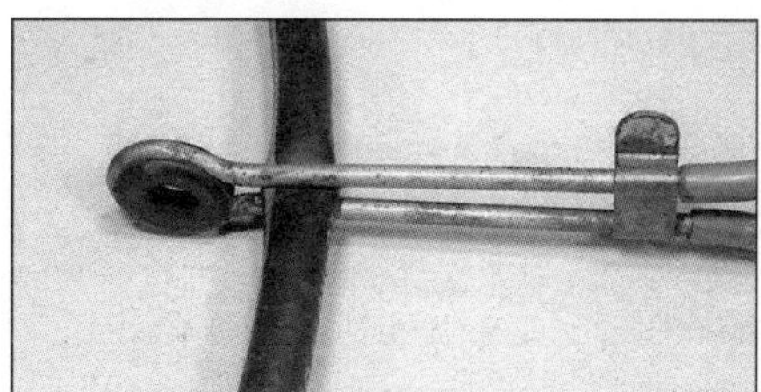

9.1 Hoses can be clamped with an automotive brake hose clamp . . .

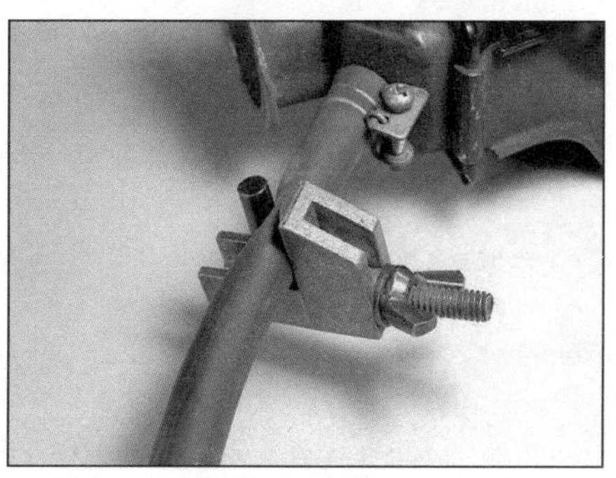

9.2 . . . a wingnut type hose clamp . . .

*c) Two sockets placed each side of the hose and held with straight-jawed self-locking grips **(see illustration 9.3)**.*
*d) Thick card each side of the hose held between straight-jawed self-locking grips **(see illustration 9.4)**.*

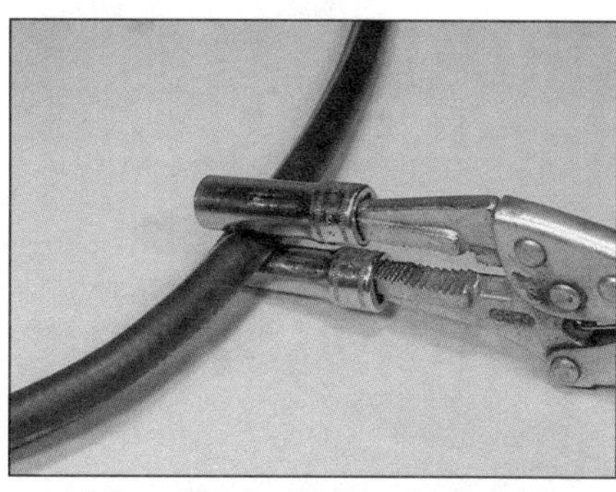

9.3 . . . two sockets and a pair of self-locking grips . . .

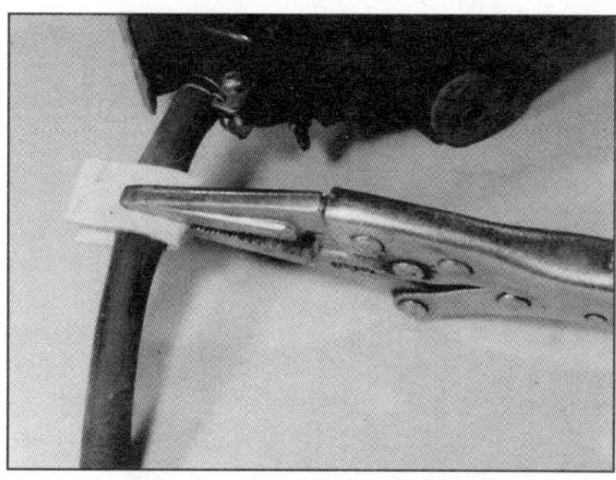

9.4 . . . or thick card and self-locking grips

Freeing and fitting hoses

● Always make sure the hose clamp is moved well clear of the hose end. Grip the hose with your hand and rotate it whilst pulling it off the union. If the hose has hardened due to age and will not move, slit it with a sharp knife and peel its ends off the union **(see illustration 9.5)**.

● Resist the temptation to use grease or soap on the unions to aid installation; although it helps the hose slip over the union it will equally aid the escape of fluid from the joint. It is preferable to soften the hose ends in hot water and wet the inside surface of the hose with water or a fluid which will evaporate.

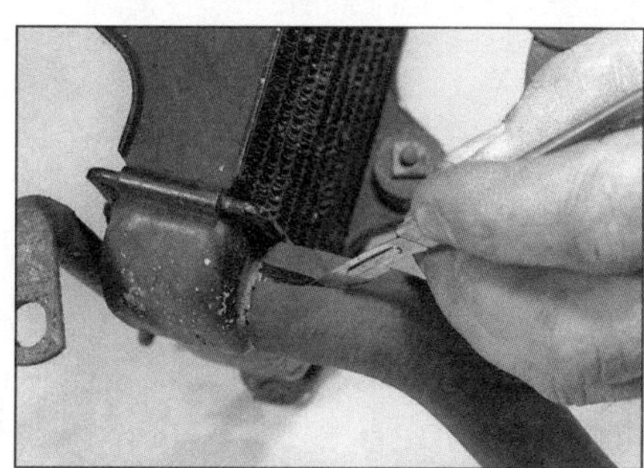

9.5 Cutting a coolant hose free with a sharp knife

Conversion Factors

Length (distance)

Inches (in)	x 25.4	= Millimetres (mm)	x 0.0394	= Inches (in)
Feet (ft)	x 0.305	= Metres (m)	x 3.281	= Feet (ft)
Miles	x 1.609	= Kilometres (km)	x 0.621	= Miles

Volume (capacity)

Cubic inches (cu in; in^3)	x 16.387	= Cubic centimetres (cc; cm^3)	x 0.061	= Cubic inches (cu in; in^3)
Imperial pints (Imp pt)	x 0.568	= Litres (l)	x 1.76	= Imperial pints (Imp pt)
Imperial quarts (Imp qt)	x 1.137	= Litres (l)	x 0.88	= Imperial quarts (Imp qt)
Imperial quarts (Imp qt)	x 1.201	= US quarts (US qt)	x 0.833	= Imperial quarts (Imp qt)
US quarts (US qt)	x 0.946	= Litres (l)	x 1.057	= US quarts (US qt)
Imperial gallons (Imp gal)	x 4.546	= Litres (l)	x 0.22	= Imperial gallons (Imp gal)
Imperial gallons (Imp gal)	x 1.201	= US gallons (US gal)	x 0.833	= Imperial gallons (Imp gal)
US gallons (US gal)	x 3.785	= Litres (l)	x 0.264	= US gallons (US gal)

Mass (weight)

Ounces (oz)	x 28.35	= Grams (g)	x 0.035	= Ounces (oz)
Pounds (lb)	x 0.454	= Kilograms (kg)	x 2.205	= Pounds (lb)

Force

Ounces-force (ozf; oz)	x 0.278	= Newtons (N)	x 3.6	= Ounces-force (ozf; oz)
Pounds-force (lbf; lb)	x 4.448	= Newtons (N)	x 0.225	= Pounds-force (lbf; lb)
Newtons (N)	x 0.1	= Kilograms-force (kgf; kg)	x 9.81	= Newtons (N)

Pressure

Pounds-force per square inch (psi; lbf/in^2; lb/in^2)	x 0.070	= Kilograms-force per square centimetre (kgf/cm^2; kg/cm^2)	x 14.223	= Pounds-force per square inch (psi; lbf/in^2; lb/in^2)
Pounds-force per square inch (psi; lbf/in^2; lb/in^2)	x 0.068	= Atmospheres (atm)	x 14.696	= Pounds-force per square inch (psi; lbf/in^2; lb/in^2)
Pounds-force per square inch (psi; lbf/in^2; lb/in^2)	x 0.069	= Bars	x 14.5	= Pounds-force per square inch (psi; lbf/in^2; lb/in^2)
Pounds-force per square inch (psi; lbf/in^2; lb/in^2)	x 6.895	= Kilopascals (kPa)	x 0.145	= Pounds-force per square inch (psi; lbf/in^2; lb/in^2)
Kilopascals (kPa)	x 0.01	= Kilograms-force per square centimetre (kgf/cm^2; kg/cm^2)	x 98.1	= Kilopascals (kPa)
Millibar (mbar)	x 100	= Pascals (Pa)	x 0.01	= Millibar (mbar)
Millibar (mbar)	x 0.0145	= Pounds-force per square inch (psi; lbf/in^2; lb/in^2)	x 68.947	= Millibar (mbar)
Millibar (mbar)	x 0.75	= Millimetres of mercury (mmHg)	x 1.333	= Millibar (mbar)
Millibar (mbar)	x 0.401	= Inches of water (inH_2O)	x 2.491	= Millibar (mbar)
Millimetres of mercury (mmHg)	x 0.535	= Inches of water (inH_2O)	x 1.868	= Millimetres of mercury (mmHg)
Inches of water (inH_2O)	x 0.036	= Pounds-force per square inch (psi; lbf/in^2; lb/in^2)	x 27.68	= Inches of water (inH_2O)

Torque (moment of force)

Pounds-force inches (lbf in; lb in)	x 1.152	= Kilograms-force centimetre (kgf cm; kg cm)	x 0.868	= Pounds-force inches (lbf in; lb in)
Pounds-force inches (lbf in; lb in)	x 0.113	= Newton metres (Nm)	x 8.85	= Pounds-force inches (lbf in; lb in)
Pounds-force inches (lbf in; lb in)	x 0.083	= Pounds-force feet (lbf ft; lb ft)	x 12	= Pounds-force inches (lbf in; lb in)
Pounds-force feet (lbf ft; lb ft)	x 0.138	= Kilograms-force metres (kgf m; kg m)	x 7.233	= Pounds-force feet (lbf ft; lb ft)
Pounds-force feet (lbf ft; lb ft)	x 1.356	= Newton metres (Nm)	x 0.738	= Pounds-force feet (lbf ft; lb ft)
Newton metres (Nm)	x 0.102	= Kilograms-force metres (kgf m; kg m)	x 9.804	= Newton metres (Nm)

Power

Horsepower (hp)	x 745.7	= Watts (W)	x 0.0013	= Horsepower (hp)

Velocity (speed)

Miles per hour (miles/hr; mph)	x 1.609	= Kilometres per hour (km/hr; kph)	x 0.621	= Miles per hour (miles/hr; mph)

Fuel consumption*

Miles per gallon (mpg)	x 0.354	= Kilometres per litre (km/l)	x 2.825	= Miles per gallon (mpg)

Temperature

Degrees Fahrenheit = (°C x 1.8) + 32

Degrees Celsius (Degrees Centigrade; °C) = (°F - 32) x 0.56

** It is common practice to convert from miles per gallon (mpg) to litres/100 kilometres (l/100km), where mpg x l/100 km = 282*

A number of chemicals and lubricants are available for use in motorcycle maintenance and repair. They include a wide variety of products ranging from cleaning solvents and degreasers to lubricants and protective sprays for rubber, plastic and vinyl.

- **Contact point/spark plug cleaner** is a solvent used to clean oily film and dirt from points, grime from electrical connectors and oil deposits from spark plugs. It is oil free and leaves no residue. It can also be used to remove gum and varnish from carburettor jets and other orifices.

- **Carburettor cleaner** is similar to contact point/spark plug cleaner but it usually has a stronger solvent and may leave a slight oily reside. It is not recommended for cleaning electrical components or connections.

- **Brake system cleaner** is used to remove grease or brake fluid from brake system components (where clean surfaces are absolutely necessary and petroleum-based solvents cannot be used); it also leaves no residue.

- **Silicone-based lubricants** are used to protect rubber parts such as hoses and grommets, and are used as lubricants for hinges and locks.

- **Multi-purpose grease** is an all purpose lubricant used wherever grease is more practical than a liquid lubricant such as oil. Some multi-purpose grease is coloured white and specially formulated to be more resistant to water than ordinary grease.

- **Gear oil** (sometimes called gear lube) is a specially designed oil used in transmissions and final drive units, as well as other areas where high friction, high temperature lubrication is required. It is available in a number of viscosities (weights) for various applications.

- **Motor oil**, of course, is the lubricant specially formulated for use in the engine. It normally contains a wide variety of additives to prevent corrosion and reduce foaming and wear. Motor oil comes in various weights (viscosity ratings) of from 5 to 80. The recommended weight of the oil depends on the seasonal temperature and the demands on the engine. Light oil is used in cold climates and under light load conditions; heavy oil is used in hot climates and where high loads are encountered. Multi-viscosity oils are designed to have characteristics of both light and heavy oils and are available in a number of weights from 5W-20 to 20W-50.

- **Petrol additives** perform several functions, depending on their chemical makeup. They usually contain solvents that help dissolve gum and varnish that build up on carburettor and inlet parts. They also serve to break down carbon deposits that form on the inside surfaces of the combustion chambers. Some additives contain upper cylinder lubricants for valves and piston rings.

- **Brake and clutch fluid** is a specially formulated hydraulic fluid that can withstand the heat and pressure encountered in brake/clutch systems. Care must be taken that this fluid does not come in contact with painted surfaces or plastics. An opened container should always be resealed to prevent contamination by water or dirt.

- **Chain lubricants** are formulated especially for use on motorcycle final drive chains. A good chain lube should adhere well and have good penetrating qualities to be effective as a lubricant inside the chain and on the side plates, pins and rollers. Most chain lubes are either the foaming type or quick drying type and are usually marketed as sprays. Take care to use a lubricant marked as being suitable for O-ring chains.

- **Degreasers** are heavy duty solvents used to remove grease and grime that may accumulate on engine and frame components. They can be sprayed or brushed on and, depending on the type, are rinsed with either water or solvent.

- **Solvents** are used alone or in combination with degreasers to clean parts and assemblies during repair and overhaul. The home mechanic should use only solvents that are non-flammable and that do not produce irritating fumes.

- **Gasket sealing compounds** may be used in conjunction with gaskets, to improve their sealing capabilities, or alone, to seal metal-to-metal joints. Many gasket sealers can withstand extreme heat, some are impervious to petrol and lubricants, while others are capable of filling and sealing large cavities. Depending on the intended use, gasket sealers either dry hard or stay relatively soft and pliable. They are usually applied by hand, with a brush, or are sprayed on the gasket sealing surfaces.

- **Thread locking compound** is an adhesive locking compound that prevents threaded fasteners from loosening because of vibration. It is available in a variety of types for different applications.

- **Moisture dispersants** are usually sprays that can be used to dry out electrical components such as the fuse block and wiring connectors. Some types can also be used as treatment for rubber and as a lubricant for hinges, cables and locks.

- **Waxes and polishes** are used to help protect painted and plated surfaces from the weather. Different types of paint may require the use of different types of wax polish. Some polishes utilise a chemical or abrasive cleaner to help remove the top layer of oxidised (dull) paint on older vehicles. In recent years, many non-wax polishes (that contain a wide variety of chemicals such as polymers and silicones) have been introduced. These non-wax polishes are usually easier to apply and last longer than conventional waxes and polishes.

About the MOT Test

In the UK, all vehicles more than three years old are subject to an annual test to ensure that they meet minimum safety requirements. A current test certificate must be issued before a machine can be used on public roads, and is required before a road fund licence can be issued. Riding without a current test certificate will also invalidate your insurance.

For most owners, the MOT test is an annual cause for anxiety, and this is largely due to owners not being sure what needs to be checked prior to submitting the motorcycle for testing. The simple answer is that a fully roadworthy motorcycle will have no difficulty in passing the test.

This is a guide to getting your motorcycle through the MOT test. Obviously it will not be possible to examine the motorcycle to the same standard as the professional MOT tester, particularly in view of the equipment required for some of the checks. However, working through the following procedures will enable you to identify any problem areas before submitting the motorcycle for the test.

It has only been possible to summarise the test requirements here, based on the regulations in force at the time of printing. Test standards are becoming increasingly stringent, although there are some exemptions for older vehicles. More information about the MOT test can be obtained from the TSO publications, *How Safe is your Motorcycle* and *The MOT Inspection Manual for Motorcycle Testing*.

Many of the checks require that one of the wheels is raised off the ground. If the motorcycle doesn't have a centre stand, note that an auxiliary stand will be required. Additionally, the help of an assistant may prove useful.

Certain exceptions apply to machines under 50 cc, machines without a lighting system, and Classic bikes - if in doubt about any of the requirements listed below seek confirmation from an MOT tester prior to submitting the motorcycle for the test.

Check that the frame number is clearly visible.

HAYNES HiNT ***If a component is in borderline condition, the tester has discretion in deciding whether to pass or fail it. If the motorcycle presented is clean and evidently well cared for, the tester may be more inclined to pass a borderline component than if the motorcycle is scruffy and apparently neglected.***

Electrical System

Lights, turn signals, horn and reflector

✔ With the ignition on, check the operation of the following electrical components. **Note:** *The electrical components on certain small-capacity machines are powered by the generator, requiring that the engine is run for this check.*

a) Headlight and tail light. Check that both illuminate in the low and high beam switch positions.

b) Position lights. Check that the front position (or sidelight) and tail light illuminate in this switch position.

c) Turn signals. Check that all flash at the correct rate, and that the warning light(s) function correctly. Check that the turn signal switch works correctly.

d) Hazard warning system (where fitted). Check that all four turn signals flash in this switch position.

e) Brake stop light. Check that the light comes on when the front and rear brakes are independently applied. Models first used on or after 1st April 1986 must have a brake light switch on each brake.

f) Horn. Check that the sound is continuous and of reasonable volume.

✔ Check that there is a red reflector on the rear of the machine, either mounted separately or as part of the tail light lens.

✔ Check the condition of the headlight, tail light and turn signal lenses.

Headlight beam height

✔ The MOT tester will perform a headlight beam height check using specialised beam setting equipment **(see illustration 1)**. This equipment will not be available to the home mechanic, but if you suspect that the headlight is incorrectly set or may have been maladjusted in the past, you can perform a rough test as follows.

✔ Position the bike in a straight line facing a brick wall. The bike must be off its stand, upright and with a rider seated. Measure the height from the ground to the centre of the headlight and mark a horizontal line on the wall at this height. Position the motorcycle 3.8 metres from the wall and draw a vertical line up the wall central to the centreline of the motorcycle. Switch to dipped beam and check that the beam pattern falls slightly lower than the horizontal line and to the left of the vertical line **(see illustration 2)**.

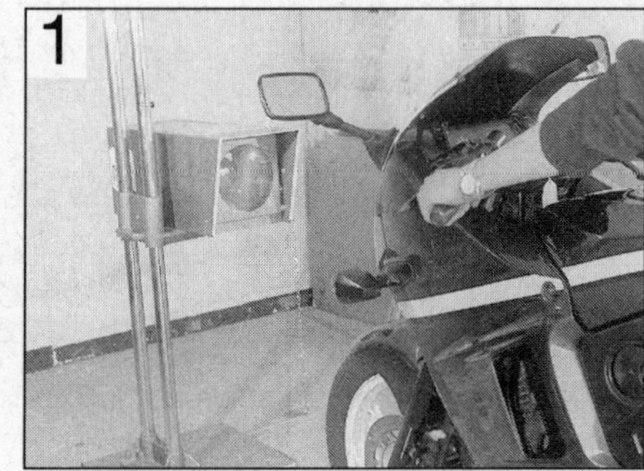

Headlight beam height checking equipment

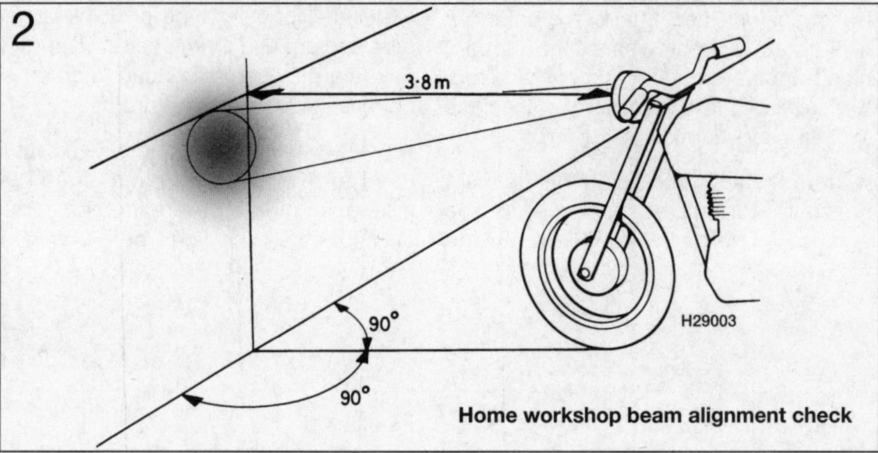

Home workshop beam alignment check

Exhaust System and Final Drive

Exhaust

✔ Check that the exhaust mountings are secure and that the system does not foul any of the rear suspension components.

✔ Start the motorcycle. When the revs are increased, check that the exhaust is neither holed nor leaking from any of its joints. On a linked system, check that the collector box is not leaking due to corrosion.

✔ Note that the exhaust decibel level ("loudness" of the exhaust) is assessed at the discretion of the tester. If the motorcycle was first used on or after 1st January 1985 the silencer must carry the BSAU 193 stamp, or a marking relating to its make and model, or be of OE (original equipment) manufacture. If the silencer is marked NOT FOR ROAD USE, RACING USE ONLY or similar, it will fail the MOT.

Final drive

✔ On chain or belt drive machines, check that the chain/belt is in good condition and does not have excessive slack. Also check that the sprocket is securely mounted on the rear wheel hub. Check that the chain/belt guard is in place.

✔ On shaft drive bikes, check for oil leaking from the drive unit and fouling the rear tyre.

Steering and Suspension

Steering

✔ With the front wheel raised off the ground, rotate the steering from lock to lock. The handlebar or switches must not contact the fuel tank or be close enough to trap the rider's hand. Problems can be caused by damaged lock stops on the lower yoke and frame, or by the fitting of non-standard handlebars.

✔ When performing the lock to lock check, also ensure that the steering moves freely without drag or notchiness. Steering movement can be impaired by poorly routed cables, or by overtight head bearings or worn bearings. The tester will perform a check of the steering head bearing lower race by mounting the front wheel on a surface plate, then performing a lock to lock check with the weight of the machine on the lower bearing **(see illustration 3)**.

✔ Grasp the fork sliders (lower legs) and attempt to push and pull on the forks **(see illustration 4)**. Any play in the steering head bearings will be felt. Note that in extreme cases, wear of the front fork bushes can be misinterpreted for head bearing play.

Front wheel mounted on a surface plate for steering head bearing lower race check

✔ Check that the handlebars are securely mounted.

✔ Check that the handlebar grip rubbers are secure. They should by bonded to the bar left end and to the throttle cable pulley on the right end.

Front suspension

✔ With the motorcycle off the stand, hold the front brake on and pump the front forks up and down **(see illustration 5)**. Check that they are adequately damped.

Checking the steering head bearings for freeplay

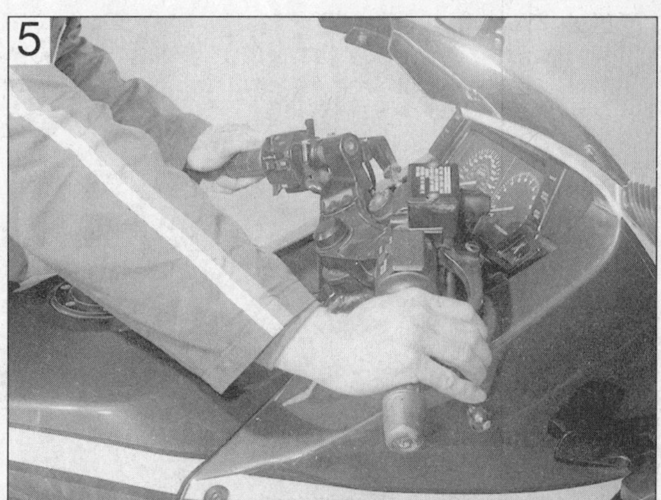

Hold the front brake on and pump the front forks up and down to check operation

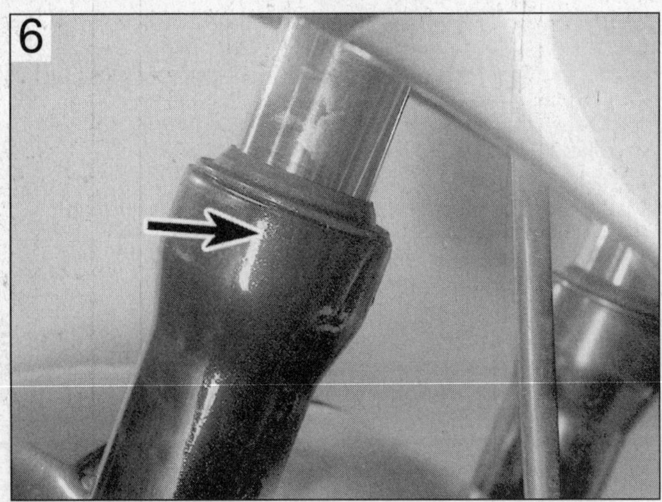

Inspect the area around the fork dust seal for oil leakage (arrow)

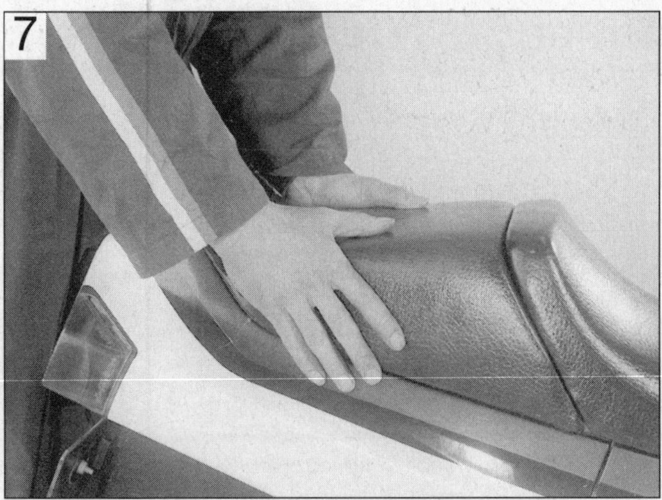

Bounce the rear of the motorcycle to check rear suspension operation

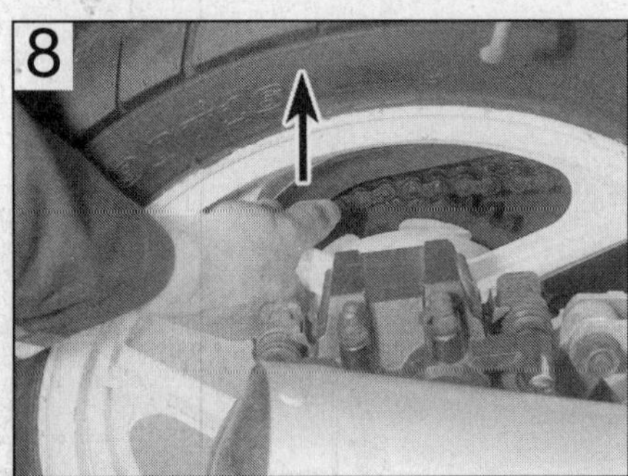

Checking for rear suspension linkage play

✔ Inspect the area above and around the front fork oil seals **(see illustration 6)**. There should be no sign of oil on the fork tube (stanchion) nor leaking down the slider (lower leg). On models so equipped, check that there is no oil leaking from the anti-dive units.

✔ On models with swingarm front suspension, check that there is no freeplay in the linkage when moved from side to side.

Rear suspension

✔ With the motorcycle off the stand and an assistant supporting the motorcycle by its handlebars, bounce the rear suspension **(see illustration 7)**. Check that the suspension components do not foul on any of the cycle parts and check that the shock absorber(s) provide adequate damping.

✔ Visually inspect the shock absorber(s) and check that there is no sign of oil leakage from its damper. This is somewhat restricted on certain single shock models due to the location of the shock absorber.

✔ With the rear wheel raised off the ground, grasp the wheel at the highest point and attempt to pull it up **(see illustration 8)**. Any play in the swingarm pivot or suspension linkage bearings will be felt as movement. **Note:** *Do not confuse play with actual suspension movement.* Failure to lubricate suspension linkage bearings can lead to bearing failure **(see illustration 9)**.

✔ With the rear wheel raised off the ground, grasp the swingarm ends and attempt to move the swingarm from side to side and forwards and backwards - any play indicates wear of the swingarm pivot bearings **(see illustration 10)**.

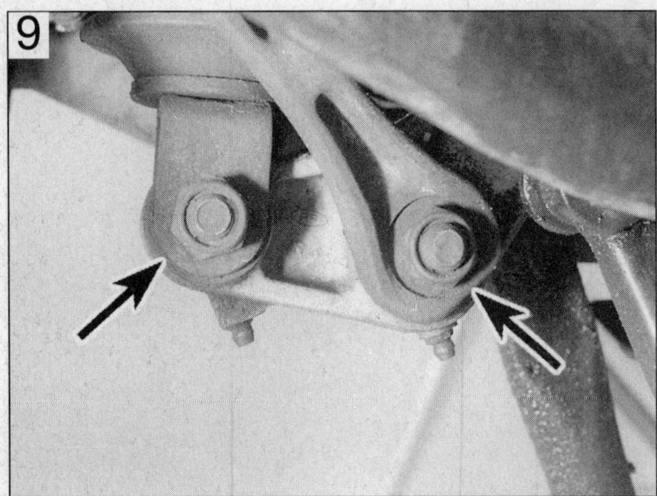

Worn suspension linkage pivots (arrows) are usually the cause of play in the rear suspension

Grasp the swingarm at the ends to check for play in its pivot bearings

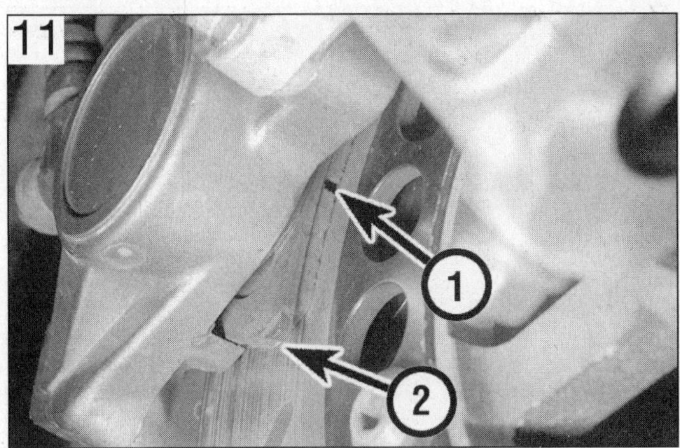

Brake pad wear can usually be viewed without removing the caliper. Most pads have wear indicator grooves (1) and some also have indicator tangs (2)

On drum brakes, check the angle of the operating lever with the brake fully applied. Most drum brakes have a wear indicator pointer and scale.

Brakes, Wheels and Tyres

Brakes

✔ With the wheel raised off the ground, apply the brake then free it off, and check that the wheel is about to revolve freely without brake drag.

✔ On disc brakes, examine the disc itself. Check that it is securely mounted and not cracked.

✔ On disc brakes, view the pad material through the caliper mouth and check that the pads are not worn down beyond the limit **(see illustration 11)**.

✔ On drum brakes, check that when the brake is applied the angle between the operating lever and cable or rod is not too great **(see illustration 12)**. Check also that the operating lever doesn't foul any other components.

✔ On disc brakes, examine the flexible hoses from top to bottom. Have an assistant hold the brake on so that the fluid in the hose is under pressure, and check that there is no sign of fluid leakage, bulges or cracking. If there are any metal brake pipes or unions, check that these are free from corrosion and damage. Where a brake-linked anti-dive system is fitted, check the hoses to the anti-dive in a similar manner.

✔ Check that the rear brake torque arm is secure and that its fasteners are secured by self-locking nuts or castellated nuts with split-pins or R-pins **(see illustration 13)**.

✔ On models with ABS, check that the self-check warning light in the instrument panel works.

✔ The MOT tester will perform a test of the motorcycle's braking efficiency based on a calculation of rider and motorcycle weight. Although this cannot be carried out at home, you can at least ensure that the braking systems are properly maintained. For hydraulic disc brakes, check the fluid level, lever/pedal feel (bleed of air if its spongy) and pad material. For drum brakes, check adjustment, cable or rod operation and shoe lining thickness.

Wheels and tyres

✔ Check the wheel condition. Cast wheels should be free from cracks and if of the built-up design, all fasteners should be secure. Spoked wheels should be checked for broken, corroded, loose or bent spokes.

✔ With the wheel raised off the ground, spin the wheel and visually check that the tyre and wheel run true. Check that the tyre does not foul the suspension or mudguards.

✔ With the wheel raised off the ground, grasp the wheel and attempt to move it about the axle (spindle) **(see illustration 14)**. Any play felt here indicates wheel bearing failure.

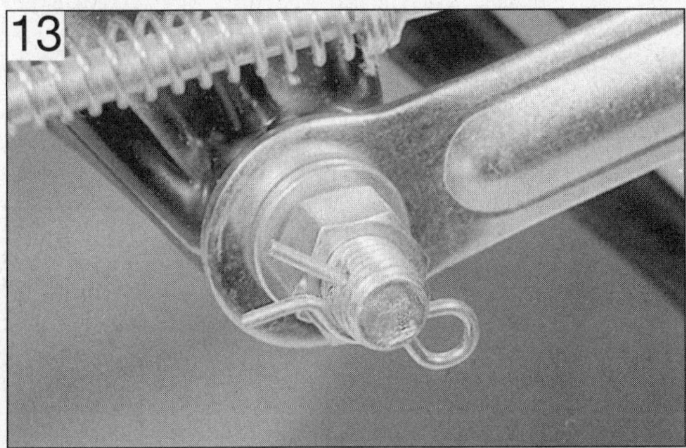

Brake torque arm must be properly secured at both ends

Check for wheel bearing play by trying to move the wheel about the axle (spindle)

15
Checking the tyre tread depth

16
Tyre direction of rotation arrow can be found on tyre sidewall

17
Castellated type wheel axle (spindle) nut must be secured by a split pin or R-pin

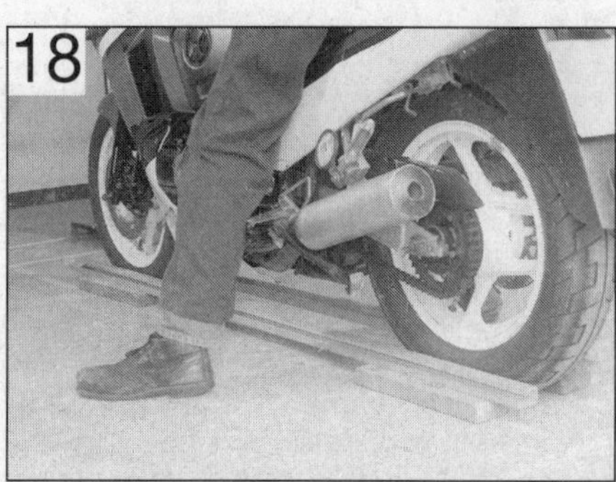
18
Two straightedges are used to check wheel alignment

✔ Check the tyre tread depth, tread condition and sidewall condition **(see illustration 15)**.

✔ Check the tyre type. Front and rear tyre types must be compatible and be suitable for road use. Tyres marked NOT FOR ROAD USE, COMPETITION USE ONLY or similar, will fail the MOT.

✔ If the tyre sidewall carries a direction of rotation arrow, this must be pointing in the direction of normal wheel rotation **(see illustration 16)**.

✔ Check that the wheel axle (spindle) nuts (where applicable) are properly secured. A self-locking nut or castellated nut with a split-pin or R-pin can be used **(see illustration 17)**.

✔ Wheel alignment is checked with the motorcycle off the stand and a rider seated. With the front wheel pointing straight ahead, two perfectly straight lengths of metal or wood and placed against the sidewalls of both tyres **(see illustration 18)**. The gap each side of the front tyre must be equidistant on both sides. Incorrect wheel alignment may be due to a cocked rear wheel (often as the result of poor chain adjustment) or in extreme cases, a bent frame.

General checks and condition

✔ Check the security of all major fasteners, bodypanels, seat, fairings (where fitted) and mudguards.

✔ Check that the rider and pillion footrests, handlebar levers and brake pedal are securely mounted.

✔ Check for corrosion on the frame or any load-bearing components. If severe, this may affect the structure, particularly under stress.

Sidecars

A motorcycle fitted with a sidecar requires additional checks relating to the stability of the machine and security of attachment and swivel joints, plus specific wheel alignment (toe-in) requirements. Additionally, tyre and lighting requirements differ from conventional motorcycle use. Owners are advised to check MOT test requirements with an official test centre.

Preparing for storage

Before you start

If repairs or an overhaul is needed, see that this is carried out now rather than left until you want to ride the bike again.

Give the bike a good wash and scrub all dirt from its underside. Make sure the bike dries completely before preparing for storage.

Engine

● Remove the spark plug(s) and lubricate the cylinder bores with approximately a teaspoon of motor oil using a spout-type oil can **(see illustration 1)**. Reinstall the spark plug(s). Crank the engine over a couple of times to coat the piston rings and bores with oil. If the bike has a kickstart, use this to turn the engine over. If not, flick the kill switch to the OFF position and crank the engine over on the starter **(see illustration 2)**. If the nature on the ignition system prevents the starter operating with the kill switch in the OFF position, remove the spark plugs and fit them back in their caps; ensure that the plugs are earthed (grounded) against the cylinder head when the starter is operated **(see illustration 3)**.

Warning: It is important that the plugs are earthed (grounded) away from the spark plug holes otherwise there is a risk of atomised fuel from the cylinders igniting.

HAYNES HiNT ***On a single cylinder four-stroke engine, you can seal the combustion chamber completely by positioning the piston at TDC on the compression stroke.***

● Drain the carburettor(s) otherwise there is a risk of jets becoming blocked by gum deposits from the fuel **(see illustration 4)**.

● If the bike is going into long-term storage, consider adding a fuel stabiliser to the fuel in the tank. If the tank is drained completely, corrosion of its internal surfaces may occur if left unprotected for a long period. The tank can be treated with a rust preventative especially for this purpose. Alternatively, remove the tank and pour half a litre of motor oil into it, install the filler cap and shake the tank to coat its internals with oil before draining off the excess. The same effect can also be achieved by spraying WD40 or a similar water-dispersant around the inside of the tank via its flexible nozzle.

● Make sure the cooling system contains the correct mix of antifreeze. Antifreeze also contains important corrosion inhibitors.

● The air intakes and exhaust can be sealed off by covering or plugging the openings. Ensure that you do not seal in any condensation; run the engine until it is hot,

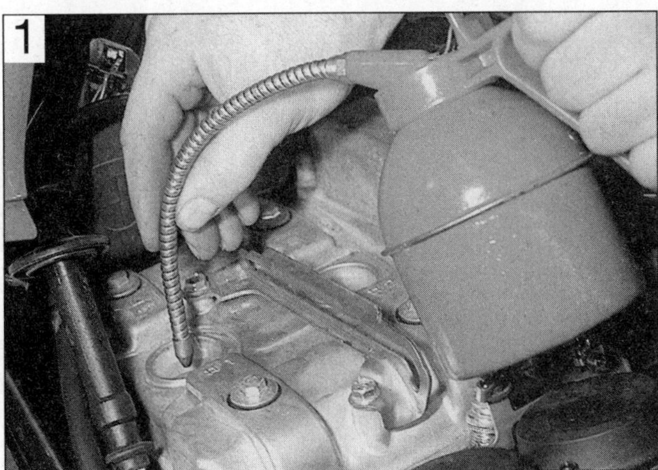

1 **Squirt a drop of motor oil into each cylinder**

2 **Flick the kill switch to OFF . . .**

3 **. . . and ensure that the metal bodies of the plugs (arrows) are earthed against the cylinder head**

4 **Connect a hose to the carburettor float chamber drain stub (arrow) and unscrew the drain screw**

Exhausts can be sealed off with a plastic bag

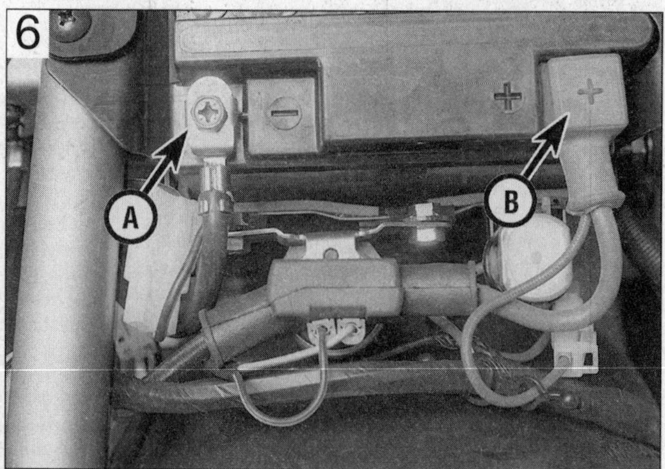

Disconnect the negative lead (A) first, followed by the positive lead (B)

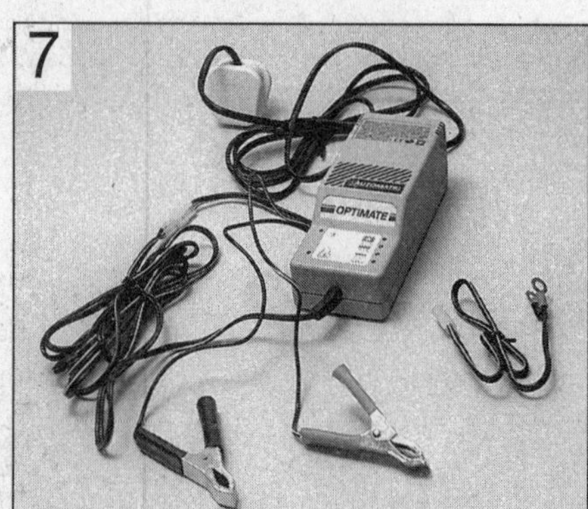
Use a suitable battery charger - this kit also assess battery condition

then switch off and allow to cool. Tape a piece of thick plastic over the silencer end(s) **(see illustration 5)**. Note that some advocate pouring a tablespoon of motor oil into the silencer(s) before sealing them off.

Battery

- Remove it from the bike - in extreme cases of cold the battery may freeze and crack its case **(see illustration 6)**.
- Check the electrolyte level and top up if necessary (conventional refillable batteries). Clean the terminals.
- Store the battery off the motorcycle and away from any sources of fire. Position a wooden block under the battery if it is to sit on the ground.
- Give the battery a trickle charge for a few hours every month **(see illustration 7)**.

Tyres

- Place the bike on its centrestand or an auxiliary stand which will support the motorcycle in an upright position. Position wood blocks under the tyres to keep them off the ground and to provide insulation from damp. If the bike is being put into long-term storage, ideally both tyres should be off the ground; not only will this protect the tyres, but will also ensure that no load is placed on the steering head or wheel bearings.
- Deflate each tyre by 5 to 10 psi, no more or the beads may unseat from the rim, making subsequent inflation difficult on tubeless tyres.

Pivots and controls

- Lubricate all lever, pedal, stand and footrest pivot points. If grease nipples are fitted to the rear suspension components, apply lubricant to the pivots.
- Lubricate all control cables.

Cycle components

- Apply a wax protectant to all painted and plastic components. Wipe off any excess, but don't polish to a shine. Where fitted, clean the screen with soap and water.
- Coat metal parts with Vaseline (petroleum jelly). When applying this to the fork tubes, do not compress the forks otherwise the seals will rot from contact with the Vaseline.
- Apply a vinyl cleaner to the seat.

Storage conditions

- Aim to store the bike in a shed or garage which does not leak and is free from damp.
- Drape an old blanket or bedspread over the bike to protect it from dust and direct contact with sunlight (which will fade paint). This also hides the bike from prying eyes. Beware of tight-fitting plastic covers which may allow condensation to form and settle on the bike.

Getting back on the road

Engine and transmission

- Change the oil and replace the oil filter. If this was done prior to storage, check that the oil hasn't emulsified - a thick whitish substance which occurs through condensation.
- Remove the spark plugs. Using a spout-type oil can, squirt a few drops of oil into the cylinder(s). This will provide initial lubrication as the piston rings and bores comes back into contact. Service the spark plugs, or fit new ones, and install them in the engine.
- Check that the clutch isn't stuck on. The plates can stick together if left standing for some time, preventing clutch operation. Engage a gear and try rocking the bike back and forth with the clutch lever held against the handlebar. If this doesn't work on cable-operated clutches, hold the clutch lever back against the handlebar with a strong elastic band or cable tie for a couple of hours **(see illustration 8)**.
- If the air intakes or silencer end(s) were blocked off, remove the bung or cover used.
- If the fuel tank was coated with a rust

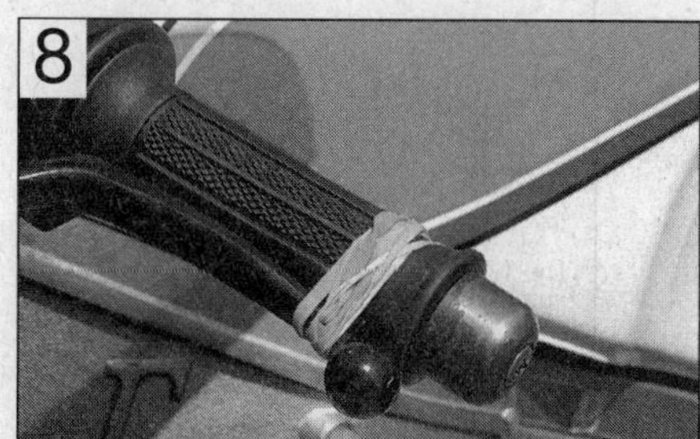
Hold clutch lever back against the handlebar with elastic bands or a cable tie

preventative, oil or a stabiliser added to the fuel, drain and flush the tank and dispose of the fuel sensibly. If no action was taken with the fuel tank prior to storage, it is advised that the old fuel is disposed of since it will go off over a period of time. Refill the fuel tank with fresh fuel.

Frame and running gear

- Oil all pivot points and cables.
- Check the tyre pressures. They will definitely need inflating if pressures were reduced for storage.
- Lubricate the final drive chain (where applicable).
- Remove any protective coating applied to the fork tubes (stanchions) since this may well destroy the fork seals. If the fork tubes weren't protected and have picked up rust spots, remove them with very fine abrasive paper and refinish with metal polish.
- Check that both brakes operate correctly. Apply each brake hard and check that it's not possible to move the motorcycle forwards, then check that the brake frees off again once released. Brake caliper pistons can stick due to corrosion around the piston head, or on the sliding caliper types, due to corrosion of the slider pins. If the brake doesn't free after repeated operation, take the caliper off for examination. Similarly drum brakes can stick due to a seized operating cam, cable or rod linkage.
- If the motorcycle has been in long-term storage, renew the brake fluid and clutch fluid (where applicable).
- Depending on where the bike has been stored, the wiring, cables and hoses may have been nibbled by rodents. Make a visual check and investigate disturbed wiring loom tape.

Battery

- If the battery has been previously removal and given top up charges it can simply be reconnected. Remember to connect the positive cable first and the negative cable last.
- On conventional refillable batteries, if the battery has not received any attention, remove it from the motorcycle and check its electrolyte level. Top up if necessary then charge the battery. If the battery fails to hold a charge and a visual checks show heavy white sulphation of the plates, the battery is probably defective and must be renewed. This is particularly likely if the battery is old. Confirm battery condition with a specific gravity check.
- On sealed (MF) batteries, if the battery has not received any attention, remove it from the motorcycle and charge it according to the information on the battery case - if the battery fails to hold a charge it must be renewed.

Starting procedure

- If a kickstart is fitted, turn the engine over a couple of times with the ignition OFF to distribute oil around the engine. If no kickstart is fitted, flick the engine kill switch OFF and the ignition ON and crank the engine over a couple of times to work oil around the upper cylinder components. If the nature of the ignition system is such that the starter won't work with the kill switch OFF, remove the spark plugs, fit them back into their caps and earth (ground) their bodies on the cylinder head. Reinstall the spark plugs afterwards.
- Switch the kill switch to RUN, operate the choke and start the engine. If the engine won't start don't continue cranking the engine - not only will this flatten the battery, but the starter motor will overheat. Switch the ignition off and try again later. If the engine refuses to start, go through the fault finding procedures in this manual. **Note:** *If the bike has been in storage for a long time, old fuel or a carburettor blockage may be the problem. Gum deposits in carburettors can block jets - if a carburettor cleaner doesn't prove successful the carburettors must be dismantled for cleaning.*
- Once the engine has started, check that the lights, turn signals and horn work properly.
- Treat the bike gently for the first ride and check all fluid levels on completion. Settle the bike back into the maintenance schedule.

This Section provides an easy reference-guide to the more common faults that are likely to afflict your machine. Obviously, the opportunities are almost limitless for faults to occur as a result of obscure failures, and to try and cover all eventualities would require a book. Indeed, a number have been written on the subject.

Successful troubleshooting is not a mysterious 'black art' but the application of a bit of knowledge combined with a systematic and logical approach to the problem. Approach any troubleshooting by first accurately identifying the symptom and then checking through the list of possible causes, starting with the simplest or most obvious and progressing in stages to the most complex.

Take nothing for granted, but above all apply liberal quantities of common sense.

The main symptom of a fault is given in the text as a major heading below which are listed the various systems or areas which may contain the fault. Details of each possible cause for a fault and the remedial action to be taken are given, in brief, in the paragraphs below each heading. Further information should be sought in the relevant Chapter.

1 Engine doesn't start or is difficult to start

- ☐ Starter motor doesn't rotate
- ☐ Starter motor rotates but engine does not turn over
- ☐ Starter works but engine won't turn over (seized)
- ☐ No fuel flow
- ☐ Engine flooded
- ☐ No spark or weak spark
- ☐ Compression low
- ☐ Stalls after starting
- ☐ Rough idle

2 Poor running at low speed

- ☐ Spark weak
- ☐ Fuel/air mixture incorrect
- ☐ Compression low
- ☐ Poor acceleration

3 Poor running or no power at high speed

- ☐ Firing incorrect
- ☐ Fuel/air mixture incorrect
- ☐ Compression low
- ☐ Knocking or pinging
- ☐ Miscellaneous causes

4 Overheating

- ☐ Engine overheats
- ☐ Firing incorrect
- ☐ Fuel/air mixture incorrect
- ☐ Compression too high
- ☐ Engine load excessive
- ☐ Lubrication inadequate
- ☐ Miscellaneous causes

5 Clutch problems

- ☐ Clutch slipping
- ☐ Clutch not disengaging completely

6 Gearshifting problems

- ☐ Doesn't go into gear, or lever doesn't return
- ☐ Jumps out of gear
- ☐ Overshifts

7 Abnormal engine noise

- ☐ Knocking or pinging
- ☐ Piston slap or rattling
- ☐ Valve noise
- ☐ Other noise

8 Abnormal driveline noise

- ☐ Clutch noise
- ☐ Transmission noise
- ☐ Final drive noise

9 Abnormal frame and suspension noise

- ☐ Front end noise
- ☐ Shock absorber noise
- ☐ Brake noise

10 Oil pressure indicator light comes on

- ☐ Engine lubrication system
- ☐ Electrical system

11 Excessive exhaust smoke

- ☐ White smoke
- ☐ Black smoke
- ☐ Brown smoke

12 Poor handling or stability

- ☐ Handlebar hard to turn
- ☐ Handlebar shakes or vibrates excessively
- ☐ Handlebar pulls to one side
- ☐ Poor shock absorbing qualities

13 Braking problems

- ☐ Brakes are spongy or don't hold
- ☐ Brake lever or pedal pulsates
- ☐ Brakes drag

14 Electrical problems

- ☐ Battery dead or weak
- ☐ Battery overcharged

1 Engine doesn't start or is difficult to start

Starter motor doesn't rotate

- ☐ Engine kill switch Off.
- ☐ Fuse blown. Check fuse block (Chapter 9).
- ☐ Battery voltage low. Check and recharge battery (Chapter 9).
- ☐ Starter motor defective. Make sure the wiring to the starter is secure. Make sure the starter relay clicks when the start button is pushed. If the relay clicks, then the fault is probably in the wiring or motor.
- ☐ Starter relay faulty. Check it according to the procedure in Chapter 9.
- ☐ Starter button not contacting. The contacts could be wet, corroded or dirty. Disassemble and clean the switch (Chapter 9).
- ☐ Wiring open or shorted. Check all wiring connections and harnesses to make sure that they are dry, tight and not corroded. Also check for broken or frayed wires that can cause a short to ground (earth) (see wiring diagram, Chapter 9).
- ☐ Ignition switch defective. Check the switch according to the procedure in Chapter 9. Replace the switch with a new one if it is defective.
- ☐ Engine kill switch defective. Check for wet, dirty or corroded contacts. Clean or replace the switch as necessary (Chapter 9).
- ☐ Faulty neutral/sidestand/clutch switch(es). Check the wiring to each switch and the switch itself according to the procedures in Chapter 9.

Starter motor rotates but engine does not turn over

- ☐ Starter motor clutch defective. Inspect and repair or replace (Chapter 2).
- ☐ Damaged idler or starter gears. Inspect and replace the damaged parts (Chapter 2).

Starter works but engine won't turn over (seized)

- ☐ Seized engine caused by one or more internally damaged components. Failure due to wear, abuse or lack of lubrication. Damage can include seized valves, followers, camshaft, pistons, crankshaft, connecting rod bearings, or transmission gears or bearings. Refer to Chapter 2 for engine disassembly.

No fuel flow

- ☐ No fuel in tank.
- ☐ Fuel tap vacuum hose broken or disconnected (M, N, P and R (1991 to 1994) models.
- ☐ Tank cap air vent obstructed (not California models). Usually caused by dirt or water. Remove it and clean the cap vent hole.
- ☐ Fuel tap filter clogged. Remove the tap and clean it and the filter (Chapter 1).
- ☐ Fuel line clogged. Pull the fuel line loose and carefully blow through it.
- ☐ Inlet needle valve clogged. For all of the valves to be clogged, either a very bad batch of fuel with an unusual additive has been used, or some other foreign material has entered the tank. Many times after a machine has been stored for many months without running, the fuel turns to a varnish-like liquid and forms deposits on the inlet needle valves and jets. The carburetors should be removed and overhauled if draining the float bowls doesn't solve the problem.
- ☐ Fuel pump faulty or in-line filter blocked (S, T, V and W (1995 to 1998) models. Check the pump and filter (Chapters 4 and 1).

Engine flooded

- ☐ Float height too high. Check as described in Chapter 4.
- ☐ Inlet needle valve worn or stuck open. A piece of dirt, rust or other debris can cause the inlet needle to seat improperly, causing excess fuel to be admitted to the float bowl. In this case, the float chamber should be cleaned and the needle and seat inspected. If the needle and seat are worn, then the leaking will persist and the parts should be replaced with new ones (Chapter 4).
- ☐ Starting technique incorrect. Under normal circumstances (e.g., if all the carburetor functions are sound) the machine should start with little or no throttle. When the engine is cold, the choke should be operated and the engine started without opening the throttle. When the engine is at operating temperature, only a very slight amount of throttle should be necessary. If the engine is flooded, turn the fuel tap off and hold the throttle open while cranking the engine. This will allow additional air to reach the cylinders. Remember to turn the fuel tap back on after the engine starts.

No spark or weak spark

- ☐ Ignition switch Off.
- ☐ Engine kill switch turned to the Off position.
- ☐ Battery voltage low. Check and recharge battery as necessary (Chapter 9).
- ☐ Spark plug dirty, defective or worn out. Locate reason for fouled plug(s) using spark plug condition chart and follow the plug maintenance procedures in Chapter 1.
- ☐ Spark plug cap or secondary (HT) wiring faulty. Check condition. Replace either or both components if cracks or deterioration are evident (Chapter 5).
- ☐ Spark plug cap not making good contact. Make sure that the plug cap fits snugly over the plug end.
- ☐ Spark unit defective. Check the unit, referring to Chapter 5 for details.
- ☐ Pulse generator defective. Check the unit, referring to Chapter 5 for details.
- ☐ Ignition coil(s) defective. Check the coils, referring to Chapter 5.
- ☐ Ignition or kill switch shorted. This is usually caused by water, corrosion, damage or excessive wear. The switches can be disassembled and cleaned with electrical contact cleaner. If cleaning does not help, replace the switches (Chapter 9).
- ☐ Wiring shorted or broken between:
  - *a) Ignition switch and engine kill switch (or blown fuse)*
  - *b) Spark unit and engine kill switch*
  - *c) Spark unit and ignition coil*
  - *d) Ignition coil and plug*
  - *e) Spark unit and pulse generator*
- ☐ Make sure that all wiring connections are clean, dry and tight. Look for chafed and broken wires (Chapters 5 and 9).

Compression low

- ☐ Spark plug loose. Remove the plug and inspect the threads. Reinstall and tighten to the specified torque (Chapter 1).
- ☐ Cylinder head not sufficiently tightened down. If the cylinder head is suspected of being loose, then there's a chance that the gasket or head is damaged if the problem has persisted for any length of time. The head bolts should be tightened to the proper torque in the correct sequence (Chapter 2).
- ☐ Improper valve clearance. This means that the valve is not closing completely and compression pressure is leaking past the valve. Check and adjust the valve clearances (Chapter 1).
- ☐ Cylinder and/or piston worn. Excessive wear will cause compression pressure to leak past the rings. This is usually accompanied by worn rings as well. A top end overhaul is necessary (Chapter 2).
- ☐ Piston rings worn, weak, broken, or sticking. Broken or sticking piston rings usually indicate a lubrication or carburetion problem that causes excess carbon deposits or seizures to form on the pistons and rings. Top end overhaul is necessary (Chapter 2).
- ☐ Piston ring-to-groove clearance excessive. This is caused by excessive wear of the piston ring lands. Piston replacement is necessary (Chapter 2).
- ☐ Cylinder head gasket damaged. If the head is allowed to become loose, or if excessive carbon build-up on the piston crown and combustion chamber causes extremely high compression, the head gasket may leak. Retorquing the head is not always sufficient to restore the seal, so gasket replacement is necessary (Chapter 2).

1 Engine doesn't start or is difficult to start (continued)

- ☐ Cylinder head warped. This is caused by overheating or improperly tightened head bolts. Machine shop resurfacing or head replacement is necessary (Chapter 2).
- ☐ Valve spring broken or weak. Caused by component failure or wear; the spring(s) must be replaced (Chapter 2).
- ☐ Valve not seating properly. This is caused by a bent valve (from over-revving or improper valve adjustment), burned valve or seat (improper carburation) or an accumulation of carbon deposits on the seat (from carburation or lubrication problems). The valves must be cleaned and/or replaced and the seats serviced if possible (Chapter 2).

Stalls after starting

- ☐ Improper choke action. Make sure the choke rod is getting a full stroke and staying in the out position.
- ☐ Ignition malfunction. See Chapter 5.
- ☐ Carburetor malfunction. See Chapter 4.
- ☐ Fuel contaminated. The fuel can be contaminated with either dirt or water, or can change chemically if the machine is allowed to sit for several months or more. Drain the tank and float bowls and check the filters (Chapters 4 and 1).
- ☐ Intake air leak. Check for loose carburetor-to-intake manifold connections, loose or missing vacuum gauge access port cap or hose, or loose carburetor top (Chapter 4).
- ☐ Engine idle speed incorrect. Turn throttle stop screw until the engine idles at the specified rpm (Chapters 1 and 4).
- ☐ Direct Air Intake system vent tube or filter blocked (UK S, T, V and W (US 1995 to 1998) models). Check and clean the system (Chapter 4).
- ☐ Fuel pump faulty (S, T, V and W (1995 to 1998) models. Check the pump (Chapter 4).

Rough idle

- ☐ Ignition malfunction. See Chapter 5.
- ☐ Idle speed incorrect. See Chapter 1.
- ☐ Carburetors not synchronized. Adjust carburetors with vacuum gauge or manometer set as described in Chapter 1.
- ☐ Carburetor malfunction. See Chapter 4.
- ☐ Fuel contaminated. The fuel can be contaminated with either dirt or water, or can change chemically if the machine is allowed to sit for several months or more. Drain the tank and float bowls and check the filters (Chapters 4 and 1).
- ☐ Intake air leak. Check for loose carburetor-to-intake manifold connections, loose or missing vacuum gauge access port cap or hose, or loose carburetor top (Chapter 4).
- ☐ Air cleaner clogged. Service or replace air filter element (Chapter 1).
- ☐ Direct Air Intake system vent tube or filter blocked, vent tubes incorrectly fitted or solenoid valve faulty (S, T, V and W (1995 to 1998) models). Check and clean the system (Chapter 4).

2 Poor running at low speed

Spark weak

- ☐ Battery voltage low. Check and recharge battery (Chapter 9).
- ☐ Spark plug fouled, defective or worn out. Refer to Chapter 1 for spark plug maintenance.
- ☐ Spark plug cap or high tension wiring defective. Refer to Chapters 1 and 5 for details on the ignition system.
- ☐ Spark plug cap not making contact.
- ☐ Incorrect spark plug. Wrong type, heat range or cap configuration. Check and install correct plugs listed in Chapter 1. A cold plug or one with a recessed firing electrode will not operate at low speeds without fouling.
- ☐ Spark unit defective. See Chapter 5.
- ☐ Pulse generator defective. See Chapter 5.
- ☐ Ignition coil(s) defective. See Chapter 5.

Fuel/air mixture incorrect

- ☐ Pilot screw(s) out of adjustment (Chapter 4).
- ☐ Pilot jet or air passage clogged. Remove and overhaul the carburetors (Chapter 4).
- ☐ Air bleed holes clogged. Remove carburetor and blow out all passages (Chapter 4).
- ☐ Air cleaner clogged, poorly sealed or missing (Chapter 1).
- ☐ Air cleaner housing poorly sealed. Look for cracks, holes or loose clamps and replace or repair defective parts.
- ☐ Fuel level too high or too low. Check the float height (Chapter 4).
- ☐ Fuel tank air vent obstructed (not California models). Make sure that the air vent passage in the filler cap is open.
- ☐ Carburetor intake manifolds loose. Check for cracks, breaks, tears or loose clamps or bolts. Repair or replace the rubber boots.
- ☐ Direct Air Intake system vent tube or filter blocked, vent tubes incorrectly fitted or solenoid valve faulty, or sub-air cleaner tube or filter blocked or tubes incorrectly fitted (S, T, V and W (1995 to 1998) models). Check and clean the system (Chapter 4).
- ☐ Fuel pump faulty - S, T, V and W (1995 to 1998) models. Check the pump (Chapter 4).

Compression low

- ☐ Spark plug loose. Remove the plug and inspect the threads. Reinstall and tighten to the specified torque (Chapter 1).
- ☐ Cylinder head not sufficiently tightened down. If the cylinder head is suspected of being loose, then there's a chance that the gasket and head are damaged if the problem has persisted for any length of time. The head bolts should be tightened to the proper torque in the correct sequence (Chapter 2).
- ☐ Improper valve clearance. This means that the valve is not closing completely and compression pressure is leaking past the valve. Check and adjust the valve clearances (Chapter 1).
- ☐ Cylinder and/or piston worn. Excessive wear will cause compression pressure to leak past the rings. This is usually accompanied by worn rings as well. A top end overhaul is necessary (Chapter 2).
- ☐ Piston rings worn, weak, broken, or sticking. Broken or sticking piston rings usually indicate a lubrication or carburation problem that causes excess carbon deposits or seizures to form on the pistons and rings. Top end overhaul is necessary (Chapter 2).
- ☐ Piston ring-to-groove clearance excessive. This is caused by excessive wear of the piston ring lands. Piston replacement is necessary (Chapter 2).
- ☐ Cylinder head gasket damaged. If the head is allowed to become loose, or if excessive carbon build-up on the piston crown and combustion chamber causes extremely high compression, the head gasket may leak. Retorquing the head is not always sufficient to restore the seal, so gasket replacement is necessary (Chapter 2).
- ☐ Cylinder head warped. This is caused by overheating or improperly tightened head bolts. Machine shop resurfacing or head replacement is necessary (Chapter 2).
- ☐ Valve spring broken or weak. Caused by component failure or wear; the spring(s) must be replaced (Chapter 2).
- ☐ Valve not seating properly. This is caused by a bent valve (from over-revving or improper valve adjustment), burned valve or seat (improper carburation) or an accumulation of carbon deposits on the seat (from carburation, lubrication problems). The valves must be cleaned and/or replaced and the seats serviced if possible (Chapter 2).

Poor acceleration

- ☐ Carburetors leaking or dirty. Overhaul the carburetors (Chapter 4).
- ☐ Timing not advancing. The pulse generator or the spark unit may be defective. If so, they must be replaced with new ones, as they can't be repaired.
- ☐ Carburetors not synchronized. Adjust them with a vacuum gauge set or manometer (Chapter 1).
- ☐ Engine oil viscosity too high. Using a heavier oil than that recommended in Chapter 1 can damage the oil pump or lubrication system and cause drag on the engine.
- ☐ Brakes dragging. Usually caused by debris which has entered the brake piston seals, or from a warped disc or bent axle. Repair as necessary (Chapter 7).
- ☐ Direct Air Intake system vent tube or filter blocked, vent tubes incorrectly fitted or solenoid valve faulty, or sub-air cleaner tube or filter blocked or tubes incorrectly fitted (S, T, V and W (1995 to 1998) models). Check and clean the system (Chapter 4).
- ☐ Fuel pump faulty (S, T, V and W (1995 to 1998) models. Check the pump (Chapter 4).

3 Poor running or no power at high speed

Firing incorrect

- ☐ Air filter restricted. Clean or replace filter (Chapter 1).
- ☐ Spark plug fouled, defective or worn out. See Chapter 1 for spark plug maintenance.
- ☐ Spark plug cap or secondary (HT) wiring defective. See Chapters 1 and 5 for details of the ignition system.
- ☐ Spark plug cap not in good contact. See Chapter 5.
- ☐ Incorrect spark plug. Wrong type, heat range or cap configuration. Check and install correct plugs listed in Chapter 1. A cold plug or one with a recessed firing electrode will not operate at low speeds without fouling.
- ☐ Spark unit defective. See Chapter 5.
- ☐ Ignition coil(s) defective. See Chapter 5.

Fuel/air mixture incorrect

- ☐ Main jet clogged. Dirt, water or other contaminants can clog the main jets. Clean the fuel tap filter, the float bowl area, and the jets and carburetor orifices (Chapter 4).
- ☐ Main jet wrong size. The standard jetting is for sea level atmospheric pressure and oxygen content.
- ☐ Throttle shaft-to-carburetor body clearance excessive. Refer to Chapter 4 for inspection and part replacement procedures.
- ☐ Air bleed holes clogged. Remove and overhaul carburetors (Chapter 4).
- ☐ Air cleaner clogged, poorly sealed, or missing (Chapter 1).
- ☐ Air cleaner housing poorly sealed. Look for cracks, holes or loose clamps, and replace or repair defective parts.
- ☐ Fuel level too high or too low. Check the float height (Chapter 4).
- ☐ Fuel tank air vent obstructed (not California models). Make sure the air vent passage in the filler cap is open.
- ☐ Carburetor intake manifolds loose. Check for cracks, breaks, tears or loose clamps or bolts. Repair or replace the rubbers (Chapter 4).
- ☐ Fuel tap filter clogged. Remove the tap and clean it and the filter (Chapter 1).
- ☐ Fuel line clogged. Pull the fuel line loose and carefully blow through it.
- ☐ Direct Air Intake system vent tube or filter blocked, vent tubes incorrectly fitted or solenoid valve faulty, or sub-air cleaner tube or filter blocked or tubes incorrectly fitted (S, T, V and W (1995 to 1998) models). Check and clean the system (Chapter 4).
- ☐ Fuel pump faulty or in-line filter blocked (S, T, V and W (1995 to 1998) models). Check the pump and filter (Chapters 4 and 1).

Compression low

- ☐ Spark plug loose. Remove the plug and inspect the threads. Reinstall and tighten to the specified torque (Chapter 1).
- ☐ Cylinder head not sufficiently tightened down. If the cylinder head is suspected of being loose, then there's a chance that the gasket and head are damaged if the problem has persisted for any length of time. The head bolts should be tightened to the proper torque in the correct sequence (Chapter 2).
- ☐ Improper valve clearance. This means that the valve is not closing completely and compression pressure is leaking past the valve. Check and adjust the valve clearances (Chapter 1).
- ☐ Cylinder and/or piston worn. Excessive wear will cause compression pressure to leak past the rings. This is usually accompanied by worn rings as well. A top end overhaul is necessary (Chapter 2).
- ☐ Piston rings worn, weak, broken, or sticking. Broken or sticking piston rings usually indicate a lubrication or carburation problem that causes excess carbon deposits or seizures to form on the pistons and rings. Top end overhaul is necessary (Chapter 2).
- ☐ Piston ring-to-groove clearance excessive. This is caused by excessive wear of the piston ring lands. Piston replacement is necessary (Chapter 2).
- ☐ Cylinder head gasket damaged. If the head is allowed to become loose, or if excessive carbon build-up on the piston crown and combustion chamber causes extremely high compression, the head gasket may leak. Retorquing the head is not always sufficient to restore the seal, so gasket replacement is necessary (Chapter 2).
- ☐ Cylinder head warped. This is caused by overheating or improperly tightened head bolts. Machine shop resurfacing or head replacement is necessary (Chapter 2).
- ☐ Valve spring broken or weak. Caused by component failure or wear; the spring(s) must be replaced (Chapter 2).
- ☐ Valve not seating properly. This is caused by a bent valve (from over-revving or improper valve adjustment), burned valve or seat (improper carburation) or an accumulation of carbon deposits on the seat (from carburation or lubrication problems). The valves must be cleaned and/or replaced and the seats serviced if possible (Chapter 2).

Knocking or pinging

- ☐ Carbon build-up in combustion chamber. Use of a fuel additive that will dissolve the adhesive bonding the carbon particles to the crown and chamber is the easiest way to remove the build-up. Otherwise, the cylinder head will have to be removed and decarbonized (Chapter 2).
- ☐ Incorrect or poor quality fuel. Old or improper grades of fuel can cause detonation. This causes the piston to rattle, thus the knocking or pinging sound. Drain old fuel and always use the recommended fuel grade.
- ☐ Spark plug heat range incorrect. Uncontrolled detonation indicates the plug heat range is too hot. The plug in effect becomes a glow plug, raising cylinder temperatures. Install the proper heat range plug (Chapter 1).
- ☐ Improper air/fuel mixture. This will cause the cylinder to run hot, which leads to detonation. Clogged jets or an air leak can cause this imbalance. See Chapter 4.

3 Poor running or no power at high speed (continued)

Miscellaneous causes

- ☐ Throttle valve doesn't open fully. Adjust the cable slack (Chapter 1).
- ☐ Clutch slipping. May be caused by loose or worn clutch components. Refer to Chapter 2 for clutch overhaul procedures.
- ☐ Timing not advancing.
- ☐ Engine oil viscosity too high. Using a heavier oil than the one recommended in Chapter 1 can damage the oil pump or lubrication system and cause drag on the engine.
- ☐ Brakes dragging. Usually caused by debris which has entered the brake piston seals, or from a warped disc or bent axle. Repair as necessary.

4 Overheating

Engine overheats

- ☐ Coolant level low. Check and add coolant (Chapter 1).
- ☐ Leak in cooling system. Check cooling system hoses and radiator for leaks and other damage. Repair or replace parts as necessary (Chapter 3).
- ☐ Thermostat sticking open or closed. Check and replace as described in Chapter 3.
- ☐ Faulty radiator cap. Remove the cap and have it checked at a service station.
- ☐ Coolant passages clogged. Have the entire system drained and flushed, then refill with fresh coolant.
- ☐ Water pump defective. Remove the pump and check the components (Chapter 3).
- ☐ Clogged radiator fins. Clean them by blowing compressed air through the fins from the backside.

Firing incorrect

- ☐ Spark plugs fouled, defective or worn out. See Chapter 1 for spark plug maintenance.
- ☐ Incorrect spark plugs.
- ☐ Faulty ignition coil(s) (Chapter 5).

Fuel/air mixture incorrect

- ☐ Main jet clogged. Dirt, water and other contaminants can clog the main jets. Clean the fuel tap filter, the float bowl area and the jets and carburetor orifices (Chapter 4).
- ☐ Main jet wrong size. The standard jetting is for sea level atmospheric pressure and oxygen content.
- ☐ Air cleaner clogged, poorly sealed or missing (Chapter 1).
- ☐ Air cleaner housing poorly sealed. Look for cracks, holes or loose clamps and replace or repair.
- ☐ Fuel level too low. Check float height(s) (Chapter 4).
- ☐ Fuel tank air vent obstructed (not California models). Make sure that the air vent passage in the filler cap is open.
- ☐ Carburetor intake manifolds loose. Check for cracks, breaks, tears or loose clamps or bolts. Repair or replace the rubbers (Chapter 4).
- ☐ Direct Air Intake system vent tube or filter blocked, vent tubes incorrectly fitted or solenoid valve faulty, or sub-air cleaner tube or filter blocked or tubes incorrectly fitted (S, T, V and W (1995 to 1998) models). Check and clean the system (Chapter 4).
- ☐ Fuel pump faulty or in-line filter blocked (S, T, V and W (1995 to 1998) models). Check the pump and filter (Chapters 4 and 1).

Compression too high

- ☐ Carbon build-up in combustion chamber. Use of a fuel additive that will dissolve the adhesive bonding the carbon particles to the piston crown and chamber is the easiest way to remove the build-up. Otherwise, the cylinder head will have to be removed and decarbonized (Chapter 2).
- ☐ Improperly machined head surface or installation of incorrect gasket during engine assembly.

Engine load excessive

- ☐ Clutch slipping. Can be caused by damaged, loose or worn clutch components. Refer to Chapter 2 for overhaul procedures.
- ☐ Engine oil level too high. The addition of too much oil will cause pressurization of the crankcase and inefficient engine operation. Check Specifications and drain to proper level (Chapter 1).
- ☐ Engine oil viscosity too high. Using a heavier oil than the one recommended in Chapter 1 can damage the oil pump or lubrication system as well as cause drag on the engine.
- ☐ Brakes dragging. Usually caused by debris which has entered the brake piston seals, or from a warped disc or bent axle. Repair as necessary.

Lubrication inadequate

- ☐ Engine oil level too low. Friction caused by intermittent lack of lubrication or from oil that is overworked can cause overheating. The oil provides a definite cooling function in the engine. Check the oil level (Chapter 1).
- ☐ Poor quality engine oil or incorrect viscosity or type. Oil is rated not only according to viscosity but also according to type. Some oils are not rated high enough for use in this engine. Check the Specifications section and change to the correct oil (Chapter 1).

Miscellaneous causes

- ☐ Modification to exhaust system. Most aftermarket exhaust systems cause the engine to run leaner, this makes it run hotter. When installing an accessory exhaust system, always rejet the carburetors.

5 Clutch problems

Clutch slipping

- ☐ Cable freeplay insufficient. Check and adjust cable (Chapter 1).
- ☐ Friction plates worn or warped. Overhaul the clutch assembly (Chapter 2).
- ☐ Steel plates worn or warped (Chapter 2).
- ☐ Clutch spring(s) broken or weak. Old or heat-damaged (from slipping clutch) springs should be replaced with new ones (Chapter 2).
- ☐ Clutch release mechanism defective. Replace any defective parts (Chapter 2).
- ☐ Clutch center or drum unevenly worn. This causes improper engagement of the plates. Replace the damaged or worn parts (Chapter 2).

Clutch not disengaging completely

- ☐ Cable freeplay excessive. Check and adjust cable (Chapter 1).
- ☐ Clutch plates warped or damaged. This will cause clutch drag, which in turn will cause the machine to creep. Overhaul the clutch assembly (Chapter 2).
- ☐ Clutch spring tension uneven. Usually caused by a sagged or broken spring. Check and replace the spring (Chapter 2).
- ☐ Engine oil deteriorated. Old, thin, worn out oil will not provide proper lubrication for the discs, causing the clutch to drag. Replace the oil and filter (Chapter 1).
- ☐ Engine oil viscosity too high. Using a heavier oil than recommended in Chapter 1 can cause the plates to stick together, putting a drag on the engine. Change to the correct weight oil (Chapter 1).
- ☐ Clutch drum seized on shaft. Lack of lubrication, severe wear or damage can cause the drum to seize on the shaft. Overhaul of the clutch, and perhaps transmission, may be necessary to repair the damage (Chapter 2).
- ☐ Clutch release mechanism defective. Worn or damaged release mechanism parts can stick and fail to apply force to the pressure plate. Overhaul the clutch cover components (Chapter 2).
- ☐ Loose clutch center nut. Causes drum and center misalignment putting a drag on the engine. Engagement adjustment continually varies. Overhaul the clutch assembly (Chapter 2).

6 Gearshifting problems

Doesn't go into gear or lever doesn't return

- ☐ Clutch not disengaging. See Section 27.
- ☐ Shift fork(s) bent or seized. Often caused by dropping the machine or from lack of lubrication. Overhaul the transmission (Chapter 2).
- ☐ Gear(s) stuck on shaft. Most often caused by a lack of lubrication or excessive wear in transmission bearings and bushings. Overhaul the transmission (Chapter 2).
- ☐ Shift drum binding. Caused by lubrication failure or excessive wear. Replace the drum and bearing (Chapter 2).
- ☐ Shift lever return spring weak or broken (Chapter 2).
- ☐ Shift lever broken. Splines stripped out of lever or shaft, caused by allowing the lever to get loose or from dropping the machine. Replace necessary parts (Chapter 2).
- ☐ Shift mechanism stopper arm broken or worn. Full engagement and rotary movement of shift drum results. Replace the arm (Chapter 2).
- ☐ Stopper arm spring broken. Allows arm to float, causing sporadic shift operation. Replace spring (Chapter 2).

Jumps out of gear

- ☐ Shift fork(s) worn. Overhaul the transmission (Chapter 2).
- ☐ Gear groove(s) worn. Overhaul the transmission (Chapter 2).
- ☐ Gear dogs or dog slots worn or damaged. The gears should be inspected and replaced. No attempt should be made to service the worn parts.

Overshifts

- ☐ Stopper arm spring weak or broken (Chapter 2).
- ☐ Gearshift shaft return spring post broken or distorted (Chapter 2).

7 Abnormal engine noise

Knocking or pinging

- ☐ Carbon build-up in combustion chamber. Use of a fuel additive that will dissolve the adhesive bonding the carbon particles to the piston crown and chamber is the easiest way to remove the build-up. Otherwise, the cylinder head will have to be removed and decarbonized (Chapter 2).
- ☐ Incorrect or poor quality fuel. Old or improper fuel can cause detonation. This causes the pistons to rattle, thus the knocking or pinging sound. Drain the old fuel and always use the recommended grade fuel (Chapter 4).
- ☐ Spark plug heat range incorrect. Uncontrolled detonation indicates that the plug heat range is too hot. The plug in effect becomes a glow plug, raising cylinder temperatures. Install the proper heat range plug (Chapter 1).
- ☐ Improper air/fuel mixture. This will cause the cylinders to run hot and lead to detonation. Clogged jets or an air leak can cause this imbalance. See Chapter 4.

Piston slap or rattling

- ☐ Cylinder-to-piston clearance excessive. Caused by improper assembly. Inspect and overhaul top end parts (Chapter 2).
- ☐ Connecting rod bent. Caused by over-revving, trying to start a badly flooded engine or from ingesting a foreign object into the combustion chamber. Replace the damaged parts (Chapter 2).
- ☐ Piston pin or piston pin bore worn or seized from wear or lack of lubrication. Replace damaged parts (Chapter 2).
- ☐ Piston ring(s) worn, broken or sticking. Overhaul the top end (Chapter 2).
- ☐ Piston seizure damage. Usually from lack of lubrication or overheating. Replace the pistons and bore the cylinders, as necessary (Chapter 2).
- ☐ Connecting rod upper or lower end clearance excessive. Caused by excessive wear or lack of lubrication. Replace worn parts.

7 Abnormal engine noise (continued)

Valve noise

- ☐ Incorrect valve clearances. Adjust the clearances by referring to Chapter 1.
- ☐ Valve spring broken or weak. Check and replace weak valve springs (Chapter 2).
- ☐ Camshaft or cylinder head worn or damaged. Lack of lubrication at high rpm is usually the cause of damage. Insufficient oil or failure to change the oil at the recommended intervals are the chief causes. Since there are no replaceable bearings in the head, the head itself will have to be replaced if there is excessive wear or damage (Chapter 2).

Other noise

- ☐ Cylinder head gasket leaking.
- ☐ Exhaust pipe leaking at cylinder head connection. Caused by improper fit of pipe(s) or loose exhaust flange. All exhaust fasteners should be tightened evenly and carefully. Failure to do this will lead to a leak.
- ☐ Crankshaft runout excessive. Caused by a bent crankshaft (from over-revving) or damage from an upper cylinder component failure. Can also be attributed to dropping the machine on either of the crankshaft ends.
- ☐ Engine mounting bolts loose. Tighten all engine mount bolts (Chapter 2).
- ☐ Crankshaft bearings worn (Chapter 2).
- ☐ Camshaft chain tensioner defective. Replace according to the procedure in Chapter 2.
- ☐ Camshaft chain, sprockets or guides worn (Chapter 2).

8 Abnormal driveline noise

Clutch noise

- ☐ Clutch drum/friction plate clearance excessive (Chapter 2).
- ☐ Loose or damaged clutch pressure plate and/or bolts (Chapter 2).

Transmission noise

- ☐ Bearings worn. Also includes the possibility that the shafts are worn. Overhaul the transmission (Chapter 2).
- ☐ Gears worn or chipped (Chapter 2).
- ☐ Metal chips jammed in gear teeth. Probably pieces from a broken clutch, gear or shift mechanism that were picked up by the gears. This will cause early bearing failure (Chapter 2).
- ☐ Engine oil level too low. Causes a howl from transmission. Also affects engine power and clutch operation (Chapter 1).

Final drive noise

- ☐ Chain not adjusted properly (Chapter 1).
- ☐ Engine sprocket or rear sprocket loose. Tighten fasteners (Chapters 2 and 6).
- ☐ Sprocket(s) worn. Replace sprocket(s) (Chapter 6).
- ☐ Rear sprocket warped. Replace (Chapter 6).
- ☐ Wheel coupling worn. Replace coupling (Chapter 6).

9 Abnormal frame and suspension noise

Front end noise

- ☐ Low fluid level or improper viscosity oil in forks. This can sound like spurting and is usually accompanied by irregular fork action (Chapter 6).
- ☐ Spring weak or broken. Makes a clicking or scraping sound. Fork oil, when drained, will have a lot of metal particles in it (Chapter 6).
- ☐ Steering head bearings loose or damaged. Clicks when braking. Check and adjust or replace as necessary (Chapters 1 and 6).
- ☐ Fork clamps loose. Make sure all fork clamp pinch bolts are tight (Chapter 6).
- ☐ Fork tube bent. Good possibility if machine has been dropped. Replace tube with a new one (Chapter 6).
- ☐ Front axle or axle clamp bolt loose. Tighten them to the specified torque (Chapter 6).

Shock absorber noise

- ☐ Fluid level incorrect. Indicates a leak caused by defective seal. Shock will be covered with oil. Replace shock (Chapter 6).
- ☐ Defective shock absorber with internal damage. This is in the body of the shock and can't be remedied. The shock must be replaced with a new one (Chapter 6).
- ☐ Bent or damaged shock body. Replace the shock with a new one (Chapter 6).

Brake noise

- ☐ Squeal caused by pad shim not installed or positioned correctly (Chapter 7).
- ☐ Squeal caused by dust on brake pads. Usually found in combination with glazed pads. Clean using brake cleaning solvent (Chapter 7).
- ☐ Contamination of brake pads. Oil, brake fluid or dirt causing brake to chatter or squeal. Clean or replace pads (Chapter 7).
- ☐ Pads glazed. Caused by excessive heat from prolonged use or from contamination. Do not use sandpaper, emery cloth, carborundum cloth or any other abrasive to roughen the pad surfaces as abrasives will stay in the pad material and damage the disc. A very fine flat file can be used, but pad replacement is suggested as a cure (Chapter 7).
- ☐ Disc warped. Can cause a chattering, clicking or intermittent squeal. Usually accompanied by a pulsating lever and uneven braking. Replace the disc (Chapter 7).
- ☐ Loose or worn wheel bearings. Check and replace as needed (Chapter 7).

10 Oil pressure indicator light comes on

Engine lubrication system

- ☐ Engine oil pump defective (Chapter 2).
- ☐ Engine oil level low. Inspect for leak or other problem causing low oil level and add recommended oil (Chapters 1 and 2).
- ☐ Engine oil viscosity too low. Very old, thin oil or an improper weight of oil used in the engine. Change to correct oil (Chapter 1).
- ☐ Camshaft or journals worn. Excessive wear causing drop in oil pressure. Replace cam and/or/cylinder head. Abnormal wear could be caused by oil starvation at high rpm from low oil level or improper weight or type of oil (Chapter 1).
- ☐ Crankshaft and/or bearings worn. Same problems as paragraph 4. Check and replace crankshaft and/or bearings (Chapter 2).

Electrical system

- ☐ Oil pressure switch defective. Check the switch according to the procedure in Chapter 9. Replace it if it is defective.
- ☐ Oil pressure indicator light circuit defective. Check for pinched, shorted, disconnected or damaged wiring (Chapter 9).

11 Excessive exhaust smoke

White smoke

- ☐ Piston oil ring worn. The ring may be broken or damaged, causing oil from the crankcase to be pulled past the piston into the combustion chamber. Replace the rings with new ones (Chapter 2).
- ☐ Cylinders worn, cracked, or scored. Caused by overheating or oil starvation. The cylinders will have to be rebored and new pistons installed.
- ☐ Valve oil seal damaged or worn. Replace oil seals with new ones (Chapter 2).
- ☐ Valve guide worn. Perform a complete valve job (Chapter 2).
- ☐ Engine oil level too high, which causes the oil to be forced past the rings. Drain oil to the proper level (Chapter 1).
- ☐ Head gasket broken between oil return and cylinder. Causes oil to be pulled into the combustion chamber. Replace the head gasket and check the head for warpage (Chapter 2).
- ☐ Abnormal crankcase pressurization, which forces oil past the rings. Clogged breather or hoses usually the cause (Chapter 3).

Black smoke

- ☐ Air cleaner clogged. Clean or replace the element (Chapter 1).
- ☐ Main jet too large or loose. Compare the jet size to the Specifications (Chapter 4).
- ☐ Choke stuck, causing fuel to be pulled through choke circuit (Chapter 4).
- ☐ Fuel level too high. Check and adjust the float height(s) as necessary (Chapter 4).
- ☐ Inlet needle held off needle seat. Clean the float bowls and fuel line and replace the needles and seats if necessary (Chapter 4).

Brown smoke

- ☐ Main jet too small or clogged. Lean condition caused by wrong size main jet or by a restricted orifice. Clean float bowl and jets and compare jet size to Specifications (Chapter 4).
- ☐ Fuel flow insufficient. Fuel inlet needle valve stuck closed due to chemical reaction with old fuel. Float height incorrect. Restricted fuel line. Clean line and float bowl and adjust floats if necessary.
- ☐ Carburetor intake manifolds loose (Chapter 4).
- ☐ Air cleaner poorly sealed or not installed (Chapter 1).

12 Poor handling or stability

Handlebar hard to turn

- ☐ Steering stem nut too tight (Chapter 6).
- ☐ Bearings damaged. Roughness can be felt as the bars are turned from side-to-side. Replace bearings and races (Chapter 6).
- ☐ Races dented or worn. Denting results from wear in only one position (e.g., straight-ahead), from a collision or hitting a pothole or from dropping the machine. Replace races and bearings (Chapter 6).
- ☐ Steering stem lubrication inadequate. Causes are grease getting hard from age or being washed out by high pressure car washes. Disassemble steering head and repack bearings (Chapter 6).
- ☐ Steering stem bent. Caused by a collision, hitting a pothole or by dropping the machine. Replace damaged part. Don't try to straighten the steering stem (Chapter 6).
- ☐ Front tire air pressure too low (Chapter 1).

Handlebar shakes or vibrates excessively

- ☐ Tires worn or out of balance (Chapter 7).
- ☐ Swingarm bearings worn. Replace worn bearings by referring to Chapter 6.
- ☐ Rim(s) warped or damaged. Inspect wheels for runout (Chapter 7).
- ☐ Wheel bearings worn. Worn front or rear wheel bearings can cause poor tracking. Worn front bearings will cause wobble (Chapter 7).
- ☐ Handlebar clamp bolts loose (Chapter 6).
- ☐ Steering stem or fork clamps loose. Tighten them to the specified torque (Chapter 6).
- ☐ Engine mounting bolts loose. Will cause excessive vibration with increased engine rpm (Chapter 2).

Handlebar pulls to one side

- ☐ Frame bent. Definitely suspect this if the machine has been dropped. May or may not be accompanied by cracking near the bend. Replace the frame (Chapter 6).
- ☐ Wheel out of alignment. Caused by improper location of axle spacers (Chapter 7) or from bent steering stem or frame (Chapter 6).
- ☐ Swingarm bent or twisted. Caused by age (metal fatigue) or impact damage. Replace the arm (Chapter 6).
- ☐ Steering stem bent. Caused by impact damage or by dropping the motorcycle. Replace the steering stem (Chapter 6).
- ☐ Fork leg bent. Disassemble the forks and replace the damaged parts (Chapter 6).
- ☐ Fork oil level uneven. Check and add or drain as necessary (Chapter 6).

Poor shock absorbing qualities

- ☐ Too hard:
  - *a) Fork oil level excessive (Chapter 6)*
  - *b) Fork oil viscosity too high. Use a lighter oil (see the Specifications in Chapter 6)*
  - *c) Fork tube bent. Causes a harsh, sticking feeling (Chapter 6)*
  - *d) Shock shaft or body bent or damaged (Chapter 6)*
  - *e) Fork internal damage (Chapter 6)*
  - *f) Shock internal damage*
  - *g) Tire pressure too high (Chapter 1)*
- ☐ Too soft:
  - *a) Fork or shock oil insufficient and/or leaking (Chapter 6)*
  - *b) Fork oil level too low (Chapter 6)*
  - *c) Fork oil viscosity too light (Chapter 6)*
  - *d) Fork springs weak or broken (Chapter 6)*
  - *e) Shock internal damage or leakage (Chapter 6)*

13 Braking problems

Brakes are spongy or don't hold

- ☐ Air in brake line. Caused by inattention to master cylinder fluid level or by leakage. Locate problem and bleed brakes (Chapter 7).
- ☐ Pad or disc worn (Chapters 1 and 7).
- ☐ Brake fluid leak. See paragraph 1.
- ☐ Contaminated pads. Caused by contamination with oil, grease, brake fluid, etc. Clean or replace pads. Clean disc thoroughly with brake cleaner (Chapter 7).
- ☐ Brake fluid deteriorated. Fluid is old or contaminated. Drain system, replenish with new fluid and bleed the system (Chapter 7).
- ☐ Master cylinder internal parts worn or damaged causing fluid to bypass (Chapter 7).
- ☐ Master cylinder bore scratched by foreign material or broken spring. Repair or replace master cylinder (Chapter 7).
- ☐ Disc warped. Replace disc (Chapter 7).

Brake lever or pedal pulsates

- ☐ Disc warped. Replace disc (Chapter 7).
- ☐ Axle bent. Replace axle (Chapter 7).
- ☐ Brake caliper bolts loose (Chapter 7).
- ☐ Brake caliper sliders damaged or sticking, causing caliper to bind. Lube the sliders or replace them if they are corroded or bent (Chapter 7).
- ☐ Wheel warped or otherwise damaged (Chapter 7).
- ☐ Wheel bearings damaged or worn (Chapter 7).

Brakes drag

- ☐ Master cylinder piston seized. Caused by wear or damage to piston or cylinder bore (Chapter 7).
- ☐ Lever balky or stuck. Check pivot and lubricate (Chapter 7).
- ☐ Brake caliper binds. Caused by inadequate lubrication or damage to caliper sliders (Chapter 7).
- ☐ Brake caliper piston seized in bore. Caused by wear or ingestion of dirt past deteriorated seal (Chapter 7).
- ☐ Brake pad damaged. Pad material separated from backing plate. Usually caused by faulty manufacturing process or from contact with chemicals. Replace pads (Chapter 7).
- ☐ Pads improperly installed (Chapter 7).
- ☐ Rear brake pedal freeplay insufficient.

14 Electrical problems

Battery dead or weak

- ☐ Battery faulty. Caused by sulfated plates which are shorted through sedimentation or low electrolyte level. Also, broken battery terminal making only occasional contact (Chapter 9).
- ☐ Battery cables making poor contact (Chapter 9).
- ☐ Load excessive. Caused by addition of high wattage lights or other electrical accessories.
- ☐ Ignition switch defective. Switch either grounds (earths) internally or fails to shut off system. Replace the switch (Chapter 9).
- ☐ Regulator/rectifier defective (Chapter 9).
- ☐ Stator coil open or shorted (Chapter 9).
- ☐ Wiring faulty. Wiring grounded (earthed) or connections loose in ignition, charging or lighting circuits (Chapter 9).

Battery overcharged

- ☐ Regulator/rectifier defective. Overcharging is noticed when battery gets excessively warm or boils over (Chapter 9).
- ☐ Battery defective. Replace battery with a new one (Chapter 9).
- ☐ Battery amperage too low, wrong type or size. Install manufacturer's specified amp-hour battery to handle charging load (Chapter 9).

Checking engine compression

● Low compression will result in exhaust smoke, heavy oil consumption, poor starting and poor performance. A compression test will provide useful information about an engine's condition and if performed regularly, can give warning of trouble before any other symptoms become apparent.

● A compression gauge will be required, along with an adapter to suit the spark plug hole thread size. Note that the screw-in type gauge/adapter set up is preferable to the rubber cone type.

● Before carrying out the test, first check the valve clearances as described in Chapter 1.

1 Run the engine until it reaches normal operating temperature, then stop it and remove the spark plug(s), taking care not to scald your hands on the hot components.

2 Install the gauge adapter and compression gauge in No. 1 cylinder spark plug hole **(see illustration 1)**.

Screw the compression gauge adapter into the spark plug hole, then screw the gauge into the adapter

3 On kickstart-equipped motorcycles, make sure the ignition switch is OFF, then open the throttle fully and kick the engine over a couple of times until the gauge reading stabilises.

4 On motorcycles with electric start only, the procedure will differ depending on the nature of the ignition system. Flick the engine kill switch (engine stop switch) to OFF and turn the ignition switch ON; open the throttle fully and crank the engine over on the starter motor for a couple of revolutions until the gauge reading stabilises. If the starter will not operate with the kill switch OFF, turn the ignition switch OFF and refer to the next paragraph.

5 Install the spark plugs back into their suppressor caps and arrange the plug electrodes so that their metal bodies are earthed (grounded) against the cylinder head; this is essential to prevent damage to the ignition system as the engine is spun over **(see illustration 2)**. Position the plugs well away from the plug holes otherwise there is a risk of atomised fuel escaping from the combustion chambers and igniting. As a safety precaution, cover the top of the valve cover with rag. Now turn the ignition switch ON and kill switch ON, open the throttle fully and crank the engine over on the starter motor for a couple of revolutions until the gauge reading stabilises.

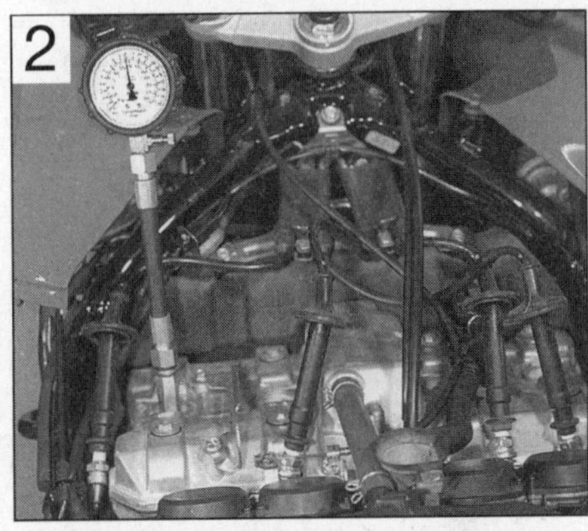

All spark plugs must be earthed (grounded) against the cylinder head

6 After one or two revolutions the pressure should build up to a maximum figure and then stabilise. Take a note of this reading and on multi-cylinder engines repeat the test on the remaining cylinders.

7 The correct pressures are given in Chapter 2 Specifications. If the results fall within the specified range and on multi-cylinder engines all are relatively equal, the engine is in good condition. If there is a marked difference between the readings, or if the readings are lower than specified, inspection of the top-end components will be required.

8 Low compression pressure may be due to worn cylinder bores, pistons or rings, failure of the cylinder head gasket, worn valve seals, or poor valve seating.

9 To distinguish between cylinder/piston wear and valve leakage, pour a small quantity of oil into the bore to temporarily seal the piston rings, then repeat the compression tests **(see illustration 3)**. If the readings show a noticeable increase in pressure this confirms that the cylinder bore, piston, or rings are worn. If, however, no change is indicated, the cylinder head gasket or valves should be examined.

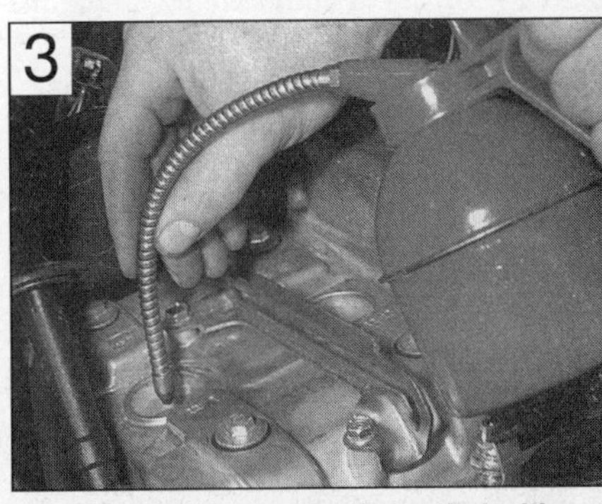

Bores can be temporarily sealed with a squirt of motor oil

10 High compression pressure indicates excessive carbon build-up in the combustion chamber and on the piston crown. If this is the case the cylinder head should be removed and the deposits removed. Note that excessive carbon build-up is less likely with the used on modern fuels.

Checking battery open-circuit voltage

Warning: The gases produced by the battery are explosive - never smoke or create any sparks in the vicinity of the battery. Never allow the electrolyte to contact your skin or clothing - if it does, wash it off and seek immediate medical attention.

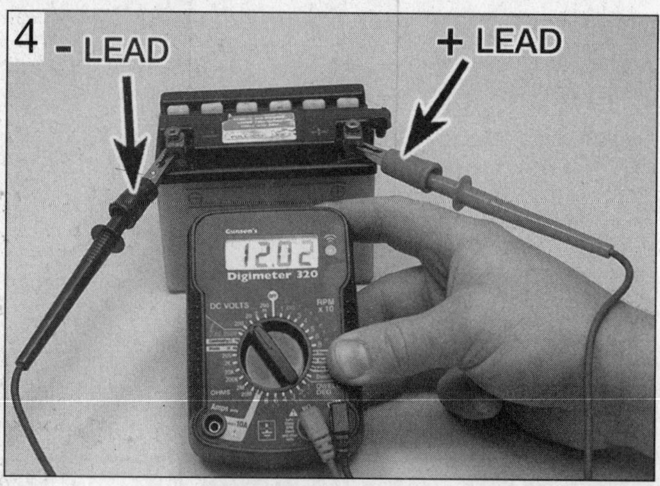

Measuring open-circuit battery voltage

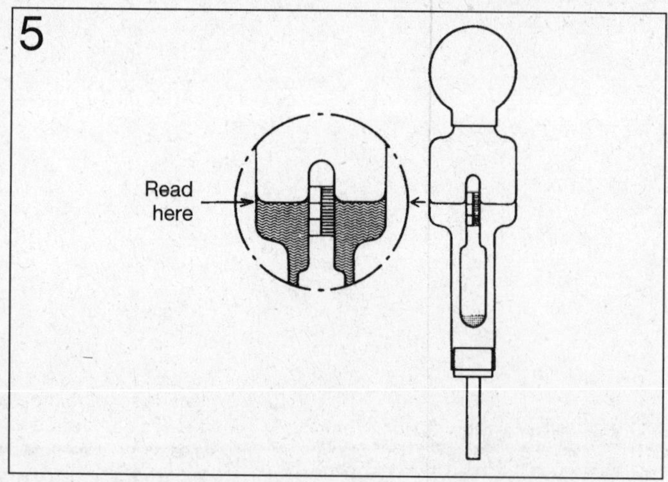

Float-type hydrometer for measuring battery specific gravity

- Before any electrical fault is investigated the battery should be checked.
- You'll need a dc voltmeter or multimeter to check battery voltage. Check that the leads are inserted in the correct terminals on the meter, red lead to positive (+ve), black lead to negative (-ve). Incorrect connections can damage the meter.
- A sound fully-charged 12 volt battery should produce between 12.3 and 12.6 volts across its terminals (12.8 volts for a maintenance-free battery). On machines with a 6 volt battery, voltage should be between 6.1 and 6.3 volts.

1 Set a multimeter to the 0 to 20 volts dc range and connect its probes across the battery terminals. Connect the meter's positive (+ve) probe, usually red, to the battery positive (+ve) terminal, followed by the meter's negative (-ve) probe, usually black, to the battery negative terminal (-ve) **(see illustration 4)**.

2 If battery voltage is low (below 10 volts on a 12 volt battery or below 4 volts on a six volt battery), charge the battery and test the voltage again. If the battery repeatedly goes flat, investigate the motorcycle's charging system.

Checking battery specific gravity (SG)

Warning: The gases produced by the battery are explosive - never smoke or create any sparks in the vicinity of the battery. Never allow the electrolyte to contact your skin or clothing - if it does, wash it off and seek immediate medical attention.

- The specific gravity check gives an indication of a battery's state of charge.
- A hydrometer is used for measuring specific gravity. Make sure you purchase one which has a small enough hose to insert in the aperture of a motorcycle battery.
- Specific gravity is simply a measure of the electrolyte's density compared with that of water. Water has an SG of 1.000 and fully-charged battery electrolyte is about 26% heavier, at 1.260.
- Specific gravity checks are not possible on maintenance-free batteries. Testing the open-circuit voltage is the only means of determining their state of charge.

1 To measure SG, remove the battery from the motorcycle and remove the first cell cap. Draw some electrolyte into the hydrometer and note the reading **(see illustration 5)**. Return the electrolyte to the cell and install the cap.

2 The reading should be in the region of 1.260 to 1.280. If SG is below 1.200 the battery needs charging. Note that SG will vary with temperature; it should be measured at 20°C (68°F). Add 0.007 to the reading for every 10°C above 20°C, and subtract 0.007 from the reading for every 10°C below 20°C. Add 0.004 to the reading for every 10°F above 68°F, and subtract 0.004 from the reading for every 10°F below 68°F.

3 When the check is complete, rinse the hydrometer thoroughly with clean water.

Digital multimeter can be used for all electrical tests

Checking for continuity

- The term continuity describes the uninterrupted flow of electricity through an electrical circuit. A continuity check will determine whether an **open-circuit** situation exists.
- Continuity can be checked with an ohmmeter, multimeter, continuity tester or battery and bulb test circuit **(see illustrations 6, 7 and 8)**.

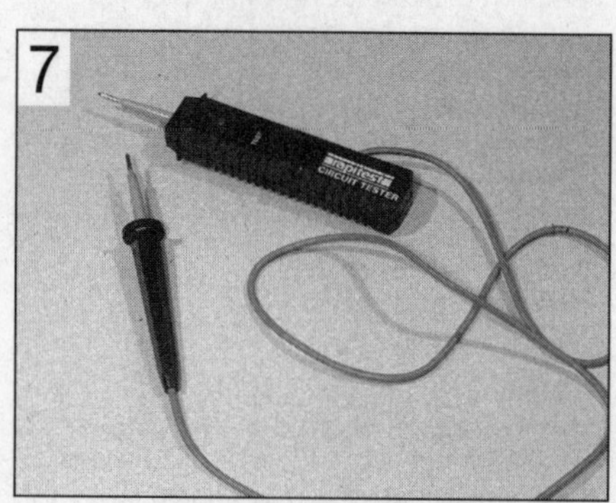

Battery-powered continuity tester

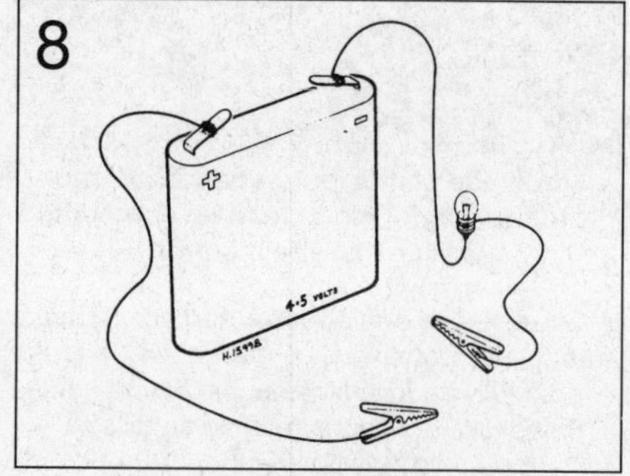

Battery and bulb test circuit

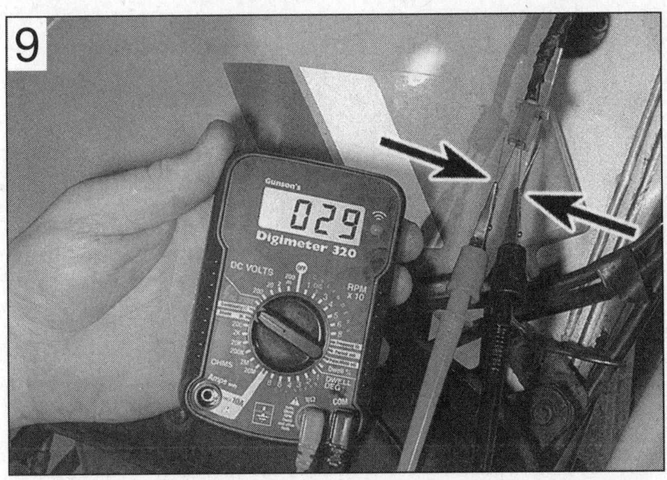

Continuity check of front brake light switch using a meter - note split pins used to access connector terminals

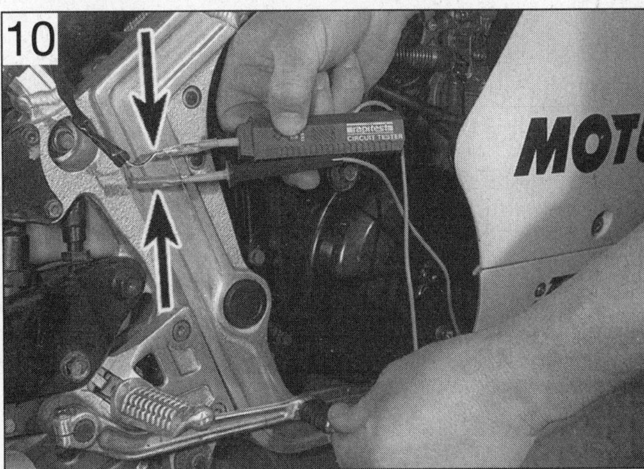

Continuity check of rear brake light switch using a continuity tester

- All of these instruments are self-powered by a battery, therefore the checks are made with the ignition OFF.
- As a safety precaution, always disconnect the battery negative (-ve) lead before making checks, particularly if ignition switch checks are being made.
- If using a meter, select the appropriate ohms scale and check that the meter reads infinity (∞). Touch the meter probes together and check that meter reads zero; where necessary adjust the meter so that it reads zero.
- After using a meter, always switch it OFF to conserve its battery.

Switch checks

1 If a switch is at fault, trace its wiring up to the wiring connectors. Separate the wire connectors and inspect them for security and condition. A build-up of dirt or corrosion here will most likely be the cause of the problem - clean up and apply a water dispersant such as WD40.

2 If using a test meter, set the meter to the ohms x 10 scale and connect its probes across the wires from the switch **(see illustration 9)**. Simple ON/OFF type switches, such as brake light switches, only have two wires whereas combination switches, like the ignition switch, have many internal links. Study the wiring diagram to ensure that you are connecting across the correct pair of wires. Continuity (low or no measurable resistance - 0 ohms) should be indicated with the switch ON and no continuity (high resistance) with it OFF.

3 Note that the polarity of the test probes doesn't matter for continuity checks, although care should be taken to follow specific test procedures if a diode or solid-state component is being checked.

4 A continuity tester or battery and bulb circuit can be used in the same way. Connect its probes as described above **(see illustration 10)**. The light should come on to indicate continuity in the ON switch position, but should extinguish in the OFF position.

Wiring checks

- Many electrical faults are caused by damaged wiring, often due to incorrect routing or chaffing on frame components.
- Loose, wet or corroded wire connectors can also be the cause of electrical problems, especially in exposed locations.

1 A continuity check can be made on a single length of wire by disconnecting it at each end and connecting a meter or continuity tester across both ends of the wire **(see illustration 11)**.

2 Continuity (low or no resistance - 0 ohms) should be indicated if the wire is good. If no continuity (high resistance) is shown, suspect a broken wire.

Checking for voltage

- A voltage check can determine whether current is reaching a component.
- Voltage can be checked with a dc voltmeter, multimeter set on the dc volts scale, test light or buzzer **(see illustrations 12 and 13)**. A meter has the advantage of being able to measure actual voltage.
- When using a meter, check that its leads are inserted in the correct terminals on the meter, red to positive (+ve), black to negative (-ve). Incorrect connections can damage the meter.
- A voltmeter (or multimeter set to the dc volts scale) should always be connected in parallel (across the load). Connecting it in series will destroy the meter.
- Voltage checks are made with the ignition ON.

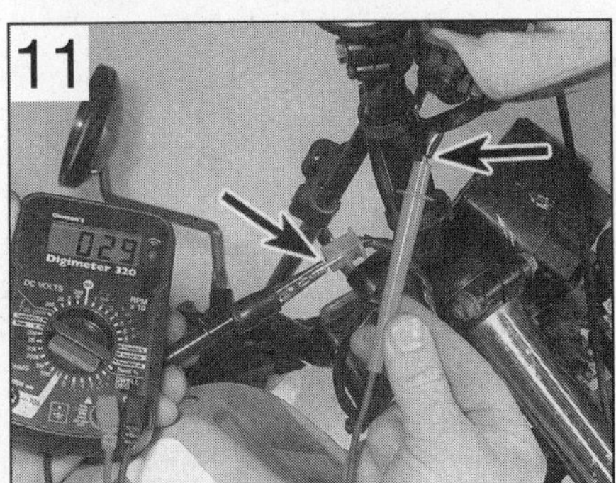

Continuity check of front brake light switch sub-harness

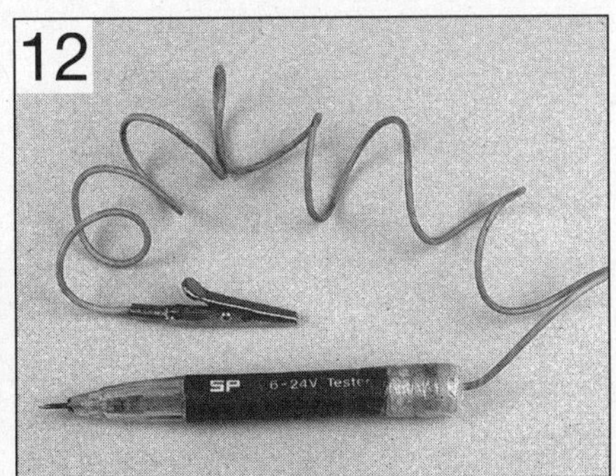

A simple test light can be used for voltage checks

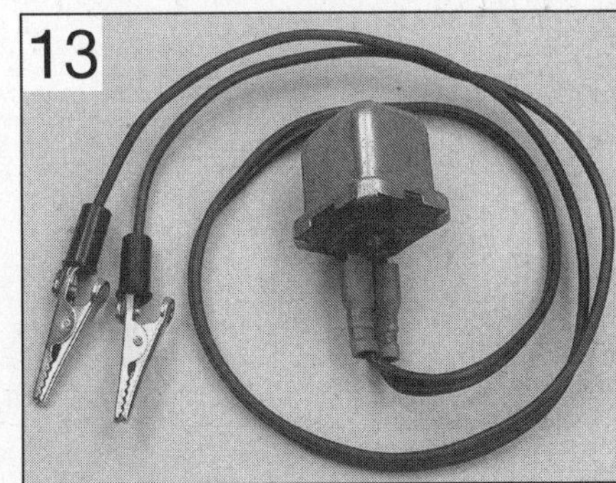

A buzzer is useful for voltage checks

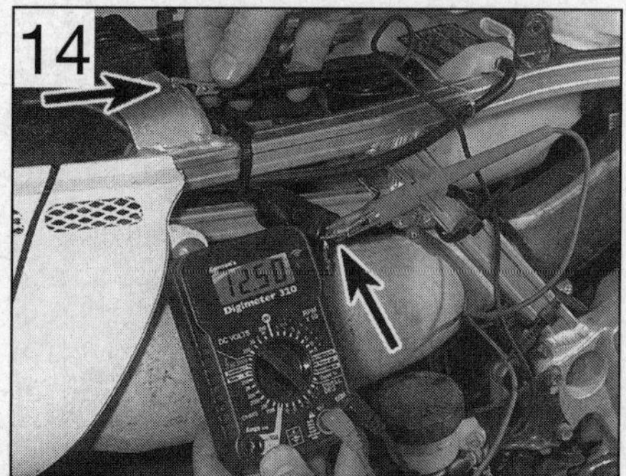

Checking for voltage at the rear brake light power supply wire using a meter . . .

1 First identify the relevant wiring circuit by referring to the wiring diagram at the end of this manual. If other electrical components share the same power supply (ie are fed from the same fuse), take note whether they are working correctly - this is useful information in deciding where to start checking the circuit.

2 If using a meter, check first that the meter leads are plugged into the correct terminals on the meter (see above). Set the meter to the dc volts function, at a range suitable for the battery voltage. Connect the meter red probe (+ve) to the power supply wire and the black probe to a good metal earth (ground) on the motorcycle's frame or directly to the battery negative (-ve) terminal **(see illustration 14)**. Battery voltage should be shown on the meter with the ignition switched ON.

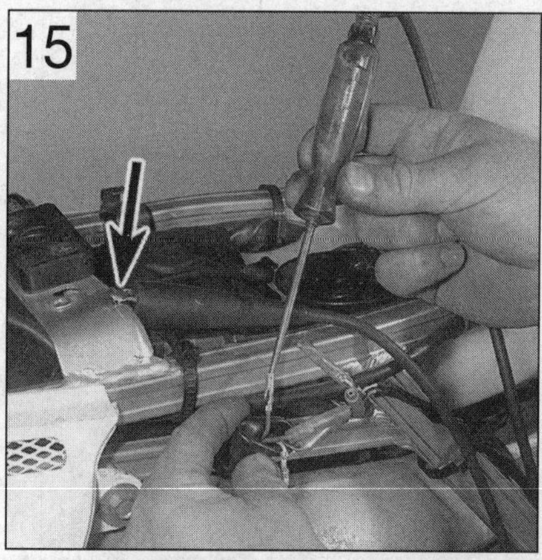

. . . or a test light - note the earth connection to the frame (arrow)

3 If using a test light or buzzer, connect its positive (+ve) probe to the power supply terminal and its negative (-ve) probe to a good earth (ground) on the motorcycle's frame or directly to the battery negative (-ve) terminal **(see illustration 15)**. With the ignition ON, the test light should illuminate or the buzzer sound.

4 If no voltage is indicated, work back towards the fuse continuing to check for voltage. When you reach a point where there is voltage, you know the problem lies between that point and your last check point.

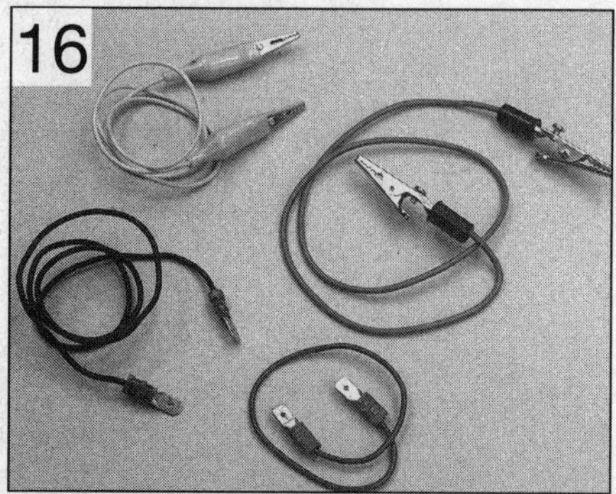

A selection of jumper wires for making earth (ground) checks

Checking the earth (ground)

- Earth connections are made either directly to the engine or frame (such as sensors, neutral switch etc. which only have a positive feed) or by a separate wire into the earth circuit of the wiring harness. Alternatively a short earth wire is sometimes run directly from the component to the motorcycle's frame.
- Corrosion is often the cause of a poor earth connection.
- If total failure is experienced, check the security of the main earth lead from the negative (-ve) terminal of the battery and also the main earth (ground) point on the wiring harness. If corroded, dismantle the connection and clean all surfaces back to bare metal.

1 To check the earth on a component, use an insulated jumper wire to temporarily bypass its earth connection **(see illustration 16)**. Connect one end of the jumper wire between the earth terminal or metal body of the component and the other end to the motorcycle's frame.

2 If the circuit works with the jumper wire installed, the original earth circuit is faulty. Check the wiring for open-circuits or poor connections. Clean up direct earth connections, removing all traces of corrosion and remake the joint. Apply petroleum jelly to the joint to prevent future corrosion.

Tracing a short-circuit

- A short-circuit occurs where current shorts to earth (ground) bypassing the circuit components. This usually results in a blown fuse.
- A short-circuit is most likely to occur where the insulation has worn through due to wiring chafing on a component, allowing a direct path to earth (ground) on the frame.

1 Remove any bodypanels necessary to access the circuit wiring.

2 Check that all electrical switches in the circuit are OFF, then remove the circuit fuse and connect a test light, buzzer or voltmeter (set to the dc scale) across the fuse terminals. No voltage should be shown.

3 Move the wiring from side to side whilst observing the test light or meter. When the test light comes on, buzzer sounds or meter shows voltage, you have found the cause of the short. It will usually shown up as damaged or burned insulation.

4 Note that the same test can be performed on each component in the circuit, even the switch.

A

ABS (Anti-lock braking system) A system, usually electronically controlled, that senses incipient wheel lockup during braking and relieves hydraulic pressure at wheel which is about to skid.

Aftermarket Components suitable for the motorcycle, but not produced by the motorcycle manufacturer.

Allen key A hexagonal wrench which fits into a recessed hexagonal hole.

Alternating current (ac) Current produced by an alternator. Requires converting to direct current by a rectifier for charging purposes.

Alternator Converts mechanical energy from the engine into electrical energy to charge the battery and power the electrical system.

Ampere (amp) A unit of measurement for the flow of electrical current. Current = Volts ÷ Ohms.

Ampere-hour (Ah) Measure of battery capacity.

Angle-tightening A torque expressed in degrees. Often follows a conventional tightening torque for cylinder head or main bearing fasteners **(see illustration)**.

Angle-tightening cylinder head bolts

Antifreeze A substance (usually ethylene glycol) mixed with water, and added to the cooling system, to prevent freezing of the coolant in winter. Antifreeze also contains chemicals to inhibit corrosion and the formation of rust and other deposits that would tend to clog the radiator and coolant passages and reduce cooling efficiency.

Anti-dive System attached to the fork lower leg (slider) to prevent fork dive when braking hard.

Anti-seize compound A coating that reduces the risk of seizing on fasteners that are subjected to high temperatures, such as exhaust clamp bolts and nuts.

API American Petroleum Institute. A quality standard for 4-stroke motor oils.

Asbestos A natural fibrous mineral with great heat resistance, commonly used in the composition of brake friction materials. Asbestos is a health hazard and the dust created by brake systems should never be inhaled or ingested.

ATF Automatic Transmission Fluid. Often used in front forks.

ATU Automatic Timing Unit. Mechanical device for advancing the ignition timing on early engines.

ATV All Terrain Vehicle. Often called a Quad.

Axial play Side-to-side movement.

Axle A shaft on which a wheel revolves. Also known as a spindle.

B

Backlash The amount of movement between meshed components when one component is held still. Usually applies to gear teeth.

Ball bearing A bearing consisting of a hardened inner and outer race with hardened steel balls between the two races.

Bearings Used between two working surfaces to prevent wear of the components and a build-up of heat. Four types of bearing are commonly used on motorcycles: plain shell bearings, ball bearings, tapered roller bearings and needle roller bearings.

Bevel gears Used to turn the drive through 90°. Typical applications are shaft final drive and camshaft drive **(see illustration)**.

Bevel gears are used to turn the drive through 90°

BHP Brake Horsepower. The British measurement for engine power output. Power output is now usually expressed in kilowatts (kW).

Bias-belted tyre Similar construction to radial tyre, but with outer belt running at an angle to the wheel rim.

Big-end bearing The bearing in the end of the connecting rod that's attached to the crankshaft.

Bleeding The process of removing air from an hydraulic system via a bleed nipple or bleed screw.

Bottom-end A description of an engine's crankcase components and all components contained there-in.

BTDC Before Top Dead Centre in terms of piston position. Ignition timing is often expressed in terms of degrees or millimetres BTDC.

Bush A cylindrical metal or rubber component used between two moving parts.

Burr Rough edge left on a component after machining or as a result of excessive wear.

C

Cam chain The chain which takes drive from the crankshaft to the camshaft(s).

Canister The main component in an evaporative emission control system (California market only); contains activated charcoal granules to trap vapours from the fuel system rather than allowing them to vent to the atmosphere.

Castellated Resembling the parapets along the top of a castle wall. For example, a castellated wheel axle or spindle nut.

Catalytic converter A device in the exhaust system of some machines which converts certain pollutants in the exhaust gases into less harmful substances.

Charging system Description of the components which charge the battery, ie the alternator, rectifer and regulator.

Circlip A ring-shaped clip used to prevent endwise movement of cylindrical parts and shafts. An internal circlip is installed in a groove in a housing; an external circlip fits into a groove on the outside of a cylindrical piece such as a shaft. Also known as a snap-ring.

Clearance The amount of space between two parts. For example, between a piston and a cylinder, between a bearing and a journal, etc.

Coil spring A spiral of elastic steel found in various sizes throughout a vehicle, for example as a springing medium in the suspension and in the valve train.

Compression Reduction in volume, and increase in pressure and temperature, of a gas, caused by squeezing it into a smaller space.

Compression damping Controls the speed the suspension compresses when hitting a bump.

Compression ratio The relationship between cylinder volume when the piston is at top dead centre and cylinder volume when the piston is at bottom dead centre.

Continuity The uninterrupted path in the flow of electricity. Little or no measurable resistance.

Continuity tester Self-powered bleeper or test light which indicates continuity.

Cp Candlepower. Bulb rating commonly found on US motorcycles.

Crossply tyre Tyre plies arranged in a criss-cross pattern. Usually four or six plies used, hence 4PR or 6PR in tyre size codes.

Cush drive Rubber damper segments fitted between the rear wheel and final drive sprocket to absorb transmission shocks **(see illustration)**.

Cush drive rubbers dampen out transmission shocks

D

Degree disc Calibrated disc for measuring piston position. Expressed in degrees.

Dial gauge Clock-type gauge with adapters for measuring runout and piston position. Expressed in mm or inches.

Diaphragm The rubber membrane in a master cylinder or carburettor which seals the upper chamber.

Diaphragm spring A single sprung plate often used in clutches.

Direct current (dc) Current produced by a dc generator.

Decarbonisation The process of removing carbon deposits - typically from the combustion chamber, valves and exhaust port/system.

Detonation Destructive and damaging explosion of fuel/air mixture in combustion chamber instead of controlled burning.

Diode An electrical valve which only allows current to flow in one direction. Commonly used in rectifiers and starter interlock systems.

Disc valve (or rotary valve) A induction system used on some two-stroke engines.

Double-overhead camshaft (DOHC) An engine that uses two overhead camshafts, one for the intake valves and one for the exhaust valves.

Drivebelt A toothed belt used to transmit drive to the rear wheel on some motorcycles. A drivebelt has also been used to drive the camshafts. Drivebelts are usually made of Kevlar.

Driveshaft Any shaft used to transmit motion. Commonly used when referring to the final driveshaft on shaft drive motorcycles.

E

Earth return The return path of an electrical circuit, utilising the motorcycle's frame.

ECU (Electronic Control Unit) A computer which controls (for instance) an ignition system, or an anti-lock braking system.

EGO Exhaust Gas Oxygen sensor. Sometimes called a Lambda sensor.

Electrolyte The fluid in a lead-acid battery.

EMS (Engine Management System) A computer controlled system which manages the fuel injection and the ignition systems in an integrated fashion.

Endfloat The amount of lengthways movement between two parts. As applied to a crankshaft, the distance that the crankshaft can move side-to-side in the crankcase.

Endless chain A chain having no joining link. Common use for cam chains and final drive chains.

EP (Extreme Pressure) Oil type used in locations where high loads are applied, such as between gear teeth.

Evaporative emission control system Describes a charcoal filled canister which stores fuel vapours from the tank rather than allowing them to vent to the atmosphere. Usually only fitted to California models and referred to as an EVAP system.

Expansion chamber Section of two-stroke engine exhaust system so designed to improve engine efficiency and boost power.

F

Feeler blade or gauge A thin strip or blade of hardened steel, ground to an exact thickness, used to check or measure clearances between parts.

Final drive Description of the drive from the transmission to the rear wheel. Usually by chain or shaft, but sometimes by belt.

Firing order The order in which the engine cylinders fire, or deliver their power strokes, beginning with the number one cylinder.

Flooding Term used to describe a high fuel level in the carburettor float chambers, leading to fuel overflow. Also refers to excess fuel in the combustion chamber due to incorrect starting technique.

Free length The no-load state of a component when measured. Clutch, valve and fork spring lengths are measured at rest, without any preload.

Freeplay The amount of travel before any action takes place. The looseness in a linkage, or an assembly of parts, between the initial application of force and actual movement. For example, the distance the rear brake pedal moves before the rear brake is actuated.

Fuel injection The fuel/air mixture is metered electronically and directed into the engine intake ports (indirect injection) or into the cylinders (direct injection). Sensors supply information on engine speed and conditions.

Fuel/air mixture The charge of fuel and air going into the engine. See **Stoichiometric ratio**.

Fuse An electrical device which protects a circuit against accidental overload. The typical fuse contains a soft piece of metal which is calibrated to melt at a predetermined current flow (expressed as amps) and break the circuit.

G

Gap The distance the spark must travel in jumping from the centre electrode to the side electrode in a spark plug. Also refers to the distance between the ignition rotor and the pickup coil in an electronic ignition system.

Gasket Any thin, soft material - usually cork, cardboard, asbestos or soft metal - installed between two metal surfaces to ensure a good seal. For instance, the cylinder head gasket seals the joint between the block and the cylinder head.

Gauge An instrument panel display used to monitor engine conditions. A gauge with a movable pointer on a dial or a fixed scale is an analogue gauge. A gauge with a numerical readout is called a digital gauge.

Gear ratios The drive ratio of a pair of gears in a gearbox, calculated on their number of teeth.

Glaze-busting see **Honing**

Grinding Process for renovating the valve face and valve seat contact area in the cylinder head.

Gudgeon pin The shaft which connects the connecting rod small-end with the piston. Often called a piston pin or wrist pin.

H

Helical gears Gear teeth are slightly curved and produce less gear noise that straight-cut gears. Often used for primary drives.

Installing a Helicoil thread insert in a cylinder head

Helicoil A thread insert repair system. Commonly used as a repair for stripped spark plug threads **(see illustration)**.

Honing A process used to break down the glaze on a cylinder bore (also called glaze-busting). Can also be carried out to roughen a rebored cylinder to aid ring bedding-in.

HT (High Tension) Description of the electrical circuit from the secondary winding of the ignition coil to the spark plug.

Hydraulic A liquid filled system used to transmit pressure from one component to another. Common uses on motorcycles are brakes and clutches.

Hydrometer An instrument for measuring the specific gravity of a lead-acid battery.

Hygroscopic Water absorbing. In motorcycle applications, braking efficiency will be reduced if DOT 3 or 4 hydraulic fluid absorbs water from the air - care must be taken to keep new brake fluid in tightly sealed containers.

I

Ibf ft Pounds-force feet. An imperial unit of torque. Sometimes written as ft-lbs.

Ibf in Pound-force inch. An imperial unit of torque, applied to components where a very low torque is required. Sometimes written as in-lbs.

IC Abbreviation for Integrated Circuit.

Ignition advance Means of increasing the timing of the spark at higher engine speeds. Done by mechanical means (ATU) on early engines or electronically by the ignition control unit on later engines.

Ignition timing The moment at which the spark plug fires, expressed in the number of crankshaft degrees before the piston reaches the top of its stroke, or in the number of millimetres before the piston reaches the top of its stroke.

Infinity (∞) Description of an open-circuit electrical state, where no continuity exists.

Inverted forks (upside down forks) The sliders or lower legs are held in the yokes and the fork tubes or stanchions are connected to the wheel axle (spindle). Less unsprung weight and stiffer construction than conventional forks.

J

JASO Quality standard for 2-stroke oils.

Joule The unit of electrical energy.

Journal The bearing surface of a shaft.

K

Kickstart Mechanical means of turning the engine over for starting purposes. Only usually fitted to mopeds, small capacity motorcycles and off-road motorcycles.

Kill switch Handebar-mounted switch for emergency ignition cut-out. Cuts the ignition circuit on all models, and additionally prevent starter motor operation on others.

km Symbol for kilometre.

kmh Abbreviation for kilometres per hour.

L

Lambda (λ) sensor A sensor fitted in the exhaust system to measure the exhaust gas oxygen content (excess air factor).

Lapping see **Grinding**.
LCD Abbreviation for Liquid Crystal Display.
LED Abbreviation for Light Emitting Diode.
Liner A steel cylinder liner inserted in a aluminium alloy cylinder block.
Locknut A nut used to lock an adjustment nut, or other threaded component, in place.
Lockstops The lugs on the lower triple clamp (yoke) which abut those on the frame, preventing handlebar-to-fuel tank contact.
Lockwasher A form of washer designed to prevent an attaching nut from working loose.
LT Low Tension Description of the electrical circuit from the power supply to the primary winding of the ignition coil.

M

Main bearings The bearings between the crankshaft and crankcase.
Maintenance-free (MF) battery A sealed battery which cannot be topped up.
Manometer Mercury-filled calibrated tubes used to measure intake tract vacuum. Used to synchronise carburettors on multi-cylinder engines.
Micrometer A precision measuring instrument that measures component outside diameters **(see illustration).**

Tappet shims are measured with a micrometer

MON (Motor Octane Number) A measure of a fuel's resistance to knock.
Monograde oil An oil with a single viscosity, eg SAE80W.
Monoshock A single suspension unit linking the swingarm or suspension linkage to the frame.
mph Abbreviation for miles per hour.
Multigrade oil Having a wide viscosity range (eg 10W40). The W stands for Winter, thus the viscosity ranges from SAE10 when cold to SAE40 when hot.
Multimeter An electrical test instrument with the capability to measure voltage, current and resistance. Some meters also incorporate a continuity tester and buzzer.

N

Needle roller bearing Inner race of caged needle rollers and hardened outer race. Examples of uncaged needle rollers can be found on some engines. Commonly used in rear suspension applications and in two-stroke engines.
Nm Newton metres.
NOx Oxides of Nitrogen. A common toxic pollutant emitted by petrol engines at higher temperatures.

O

Octane The measure of a fuel's resistance to knock.
OE (Original Equipment) Relates to components fitted to a motorcycle as standard or replacement parts supplied by the motorcycle manufacturer.
Ohm The unit of electrical resistance. Ohms = Volts ÷ Current.
Ohmmeter An instrument for measuring electrical resistance.
Oil cooler System for diverting engine oil outside of the engine to a radiator for cooling purposes.
Oil injection A system of two-stroke engine lubrication where oil is pump-fed to the engine in accordance with throttle position.
Open-circuit An electrical condition where there is a break in the flow of electricity - no continuity (high resistance).
O-ring A type of sealing ring made of a special rubber-like material; in use, the O-ring is compressed into a groove to provide the sealing action.
Oversize (OS) Term used for piston and ring size options fitted to a rebored cylinder.
Overhead cam (sohc) engine An engine with single camshaft located on top of the cylinder head.
Overhead valve (ohv) engine An engine with the valves located in the cylinder head, but with the camshaft located in the engine block or crankcase.
Oxygen sensor A device installed in the exhaust system which senses the oxygen content in the exhaust and converts this information into an electric current. Also called a Lambda sensor.

P

Plastigauge A thin strip of plastic thread, available in different sizes, used for measuring clearances. For example, a strip of Plastigauge is laid across a bearing journal. The parts are assembled and dismantled; the width of the crushed strip indicates the clearance between journal and bearing.
Polarity Either negative or positive earth (ground), determined by which battery lead is connected to the frame (earth return). Modern motorcycles are usually negative earth.
Pre-ignition A situation where the fuel/air mixture ignites before the spark plug fires. Often due to a hot spot in the combustion chamber caused by carbon build-up. Engine has a tendency to 'run-on'.
Pre-load (suspension) The amount a spring is compressed when in the unloaded state. Preload can be applied by gas, spacer or mechanical adjuster.
Premix The method of engine lubrication on older two-stroke engines. Engine oil is mixed with the petrol in the fuel tank in a specific ratio. The fuel/oil mix is sometimes referred to as "petroil".
Primary drive Description of the drive from the crankshaft to the clutch. Usually by gear or chain.
PS Pfedestärke - a German interpretation of BHP.
PSI Pounds-force per square inch. Imperial measurement of tyre pressure and cylinder pressure measurement.
PTFE Polytetrafluroethylene. A low friction substance.
Pulse secondary air injection system A process of promoting the burning of excess fuel present in the exhaust gases by routing fresh air into the exhaust ports.

Q

Quartz halogen bulb Tungsten filament surrounded by a halogen gas. Typically used for the headlight **(see illustration)**.

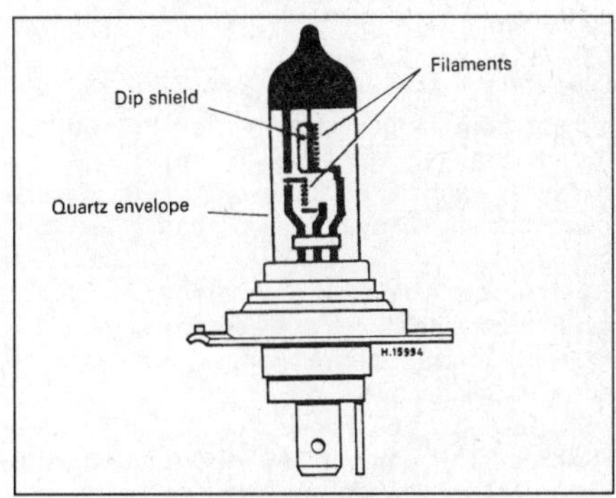

Quartz halogen headlight bulb construction

R

Rack-and-pinion A pinion gear on the end of a shaft that mates with a rack (think of a geared wheel opened up and laid flat). Sometimes used in clutch operating systems.
Radial play Up and down movement about a shaft.
Radial ply tyres Tyre plies run across the tyre (from bead to bead) and around the circumference of the tyre. Less resistant to tread distortion than other tyre types.
Radiator A liquid-to-air heat transfer device designed to reduce the temperature of the coolant in a liquid cooled engine.
Rake A feature of steering geometry - the angle of the steering head in relation to the vertical **(see illustration).**

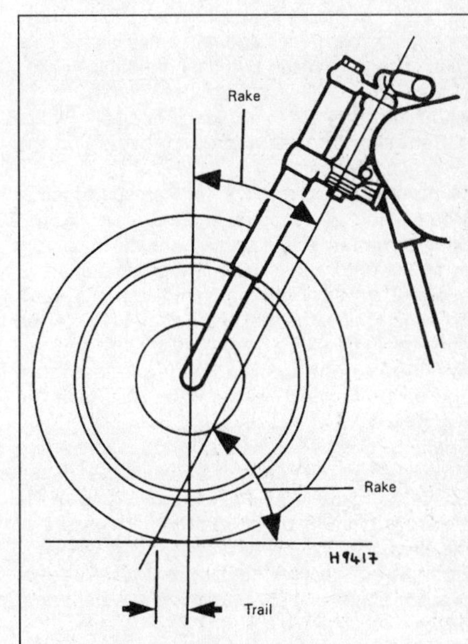

Steering geometry

Rebore Providing a new working surface to the cylinder bore by boring out the old surface. Necessitates the use of oversize piston and rings.

Rebound damping A means of controlling the oscillation of a suspension unit spring after it has been compressed. Resists the spring's natural tendency to bounce back after being compressed.

Rectifier Device for converting the ac output of an alternator into dc for battery charging.

Reed valve An induction system commonly used on two-stroke engines.

Regulator Device for maintaining the charging voltage from the generator or alternator within a specified range.

Relay A electrical device used to switch heavy current on and off by using a low current auxiliary circuit.

Resistance Measured in ohms. An electrical component's ability to pass electrical current.

RON (Research Octane Number) A measure of a fuel's resistance to knock.

rpm revolutions per minute.

Runout The amount of wobble (in-and-out movement) of a wheel or shaft as it's rotated. The amount a shaft rotates `out-of-true'. The out-of-round condition of a rotating part.

S

SAE (Society of Automotive Engineers) A standard for the viscosity of a fluid.

Sealant A liquid or paste used to prevent leakage at a joint. Sometimes used in conjunction with a gasket.

Service limit Term for the point where a component is no longer useable and must be renewed.

Shaft drive A method of transmitting drive from the transmission to the rear wheel.

Shell bearings Plain bearings consisting of two shell halves. Most often used as big-end and main bearings in a four-stroke engine. Often called bearing inserts.

Shim Thin spacer, commonly used to adjust the clearance or relative positions between two parts. For example, shims inserted into or under tappets or followers to control valve clearances. Clearance is adjusted by changing the thickness of the shim.

Short-circuit An electrical condition where current shorts to earth (ground) bypassing the circuit components.

Skimming Process to correct warpage or repair a damaged surface, eg on brake discs or drums.

Slide-hammer A special puller that screws into or hooks onto a component such as a shaft or bearing; a heavy sliding handle on the shaft bottoms against the end of the shaft to knock the component free.

Small-end bearing The bearing in the upper end of the connecting rod at its joint with the gudgeon pin.

Spalling Damage to camshaft lobes or bearing journals shown as pitting of the working surface.

Specific gravity (SG) The state of charge of the electrolyte in a lead-acid battery. A measure of the electrolyte's density compared with water.

Straight-cut gears Common type gear used on gearbox shafts and for oil pump and water pump drives.

Stanchion The inner sliding part of the front forks, held by the yokes. Often called a fork tube.

Stoichiometric ratio The optimum chemical air/fuel ratio for a petrol engine, said to be 14.7 parts of air to 1 part of fuel.

Sulphuric acid The liquid (electrolyte) used in a lead-acid battery. Poisonous and extremely corrosive.

Surface grinding (lapping) Process to correct a warped gasket face, commonly used on cylinder heads.

T

Tapered-roller bearing Tapered inner race of caged needle rollers and separate tapered outer race. Examples of taper roller bearings can be found on steering heads.

Tappet A cylindrical component which transmits motion from the cam to the valve stem, either directly or via a pushrod and rocker arm. Also called a cam follower.

TCS Traction Control System. An electronically-controlled system which senses wheel spin and reduces engine speed accordingly.

TDC Top Dead Centre denotes that the piston is at its highest point in the cylinder.

Thread-locking compound Solution applied to fastener threads to prevent slackening. Select type to suit application.

Thrust washer A washer positioned between two moving components on a shaft. For example, between gear pinions on gearshaft.

Timing chain See **Cam Chain.**

Timing light Stroboscopic lamp for carrying out ignition timing checks with the engine running.

Top-end A description of an engine's cylinder block, head and valve gear components.

Torque Turning or twisting force about a shaft.

Torque setting A prescribed tightness specified by the motorcycle manufacturer to ensure that the bolt or nut is secured correctly. Undertightening can result in the bolt or nut coming loose or a surface not being sealed. Overtightening can result in stripped threads, distortion or damage to the component being retained.

Torx key A six-point wrench.

Tracer A stripe of a second colour applied to a wire insulator to distinguish that wire from another one with the same colour insulator. For example, Br/W is often used to denote a brown insulator with a white tracer.

Trail A feature of steering geometry. Distance from the steering head axis to the tyre's central contact point.

Triple clamps The cast components which extend from the steering head and support the fork stanchions or tubes. Often called fork yokes.

Turbocharger A centrifugal device, driven by exhaust gases, that pressurises the intake air. Normally used to increase the power output from a given engine displacement.

TWI Abbreviation for Tyre Wear Indicator. Indicates the location of the tread depth indicator bars on tyres.

U

Universal joint or U-joint (UJ) A double-pivoted connection for transmitting power from a driving to a driven shaft through an angle. Typically found in shaft drive assemblies.

Unsprung weight Anything not supported by the bike's suspension (ie the wheel, tyres, brakes, final drive and bottom (moving) part of the suspension).

V

Vacuum gauges Clock-type gauges for measuring intake tract vacuum. Used for carburettor synchronisation on multi-cylinder engines.

Valve A device through which the flow of liquid, gas or vacuum may be stopped, started or regulated by a moveable part that opens, shuts or partially obstructs one or more ports or passageways. The intake and exhaust valves in the cylinder head are of the poppet type.

Valve clearance The clearance between the valve tip (the end of the valve stem) and the rocker arm or tappet/follower. The valve clearance is measured when the valve is closed. The correct clearance is important - if too small the valve won't close fully and will burn out, whereas if too large noisy operation will result.

Valve lift The amount a valve is lifted off its seat by the camshaft lobe.

Valve timing The exact setting for the opening and closing of the valves in relation to piston position.

Vernier caliper A precision measuring instrument that measures inside and outside dimensions. Not quite as accurate as a micrometer, but more convenient.

VIN Vehicle Identification Number. Term for the bike's engine and frame numbers.

Viscosity The thickness of a liquid or its resistance to flow.

Volt A unit for expressing electrical "pressure" in a circuit. Volts = current x ohms.

W

Water pump A mechanically-driven device for moving coolant around the engine.

Watt A unit for expressing electrical power. Watts = volts x current.

Wear limit see **Service limit**

Wet liner A liquid-cooled engine design where the pistons run in liners which are directly surrounded by coolant **(see illustration).**

Wet liner arrangement

Wheelbase Distance from the centre of the front wheel to the centre of the rear wheel.

Wiring harness or loom Describes the electrical wires running the length of the motorcycle and enclosed in tape or plastic sheathing. Wiring coming off the main harness is usually referred to as a sub harness.

Woodruff key A key of semi-circular or square section used to locate a gear to a shaft. Often used to locate the alternator rotor on the crankshaft.

Wrist pin Another name for gudgeon or piston pin.

Note: References throughtout this index are in the form "*Chapter number*" • "*Page number*"

D

E

F

G

H

I

L

M

N

O

P

R

S

Haynes Motorcycle Manuals – The Complete List

Title	Book No
APRILIA RS50 (99 - 06) & RS125 (93 - 06)	4298
Aprilia RSV1000 Mille (98 - 03)	◆ 4255
BMW 2-valve Twins (70 - 96)	◆ 0249
BMW K100 & 75 2-valve Models (83 - 96)	◆ 1373
BMW R850, 1100 & 1150 4-valve Twins (93 - 04)	◆ 3466
BMW R1200 (04 - 06)	◆ 4598
BSA Bantam (48 - 71)	0117
BSA Unit Singles (58 - 72)	0127
BSA Pre-unit Singles (54 - 61)	0326
BSA A7 & A10 Twins (47 - 62)	0121
BSA A50 & A65 Twins (62 - 73)	0155
DUCATI 600, 620, 750 and 900 2-valve V-Twins (91 - 05)	◆ 3290
Ducati MK III & Desmo Singles (69 - 76)	◇ 0445
Ducati 748, 916 & 996 4-valve V-Twins (94 - 01)	◆ 3756
GILERA Runner, DNA, Ice & SKP/Stalker (97 - 07)	4163
HARLEY-DAVIDSON Sportsters (70 - 03)	◆ 2534
Harley-Davidson Shovelhead and Evolution Big Twins (70 - 99)	◆ 2536
Harley-Davidson Twin Cam 88 (99 - 03)	◆ 2478
HONDA NB, ND, NP & NS50 Melody (81 - 85)	◇ 0622
Honda NE/NB50 Vision & SA50 Vision Met-in (85 - 95)	◇ 1278
Honda MB, MBX, MT & MTX50 (80 - 93)	0731
Honda C50, C70 & C90 (67 - 03)	0324
Honda XR80/100R & CRF80/100F (85 - 04)	2218
Honda XL/XR 80, 100, 125, 185 & 200 2-valve Models (78 - 87)	0566
Honda H100 & H100S Singles (80 - 92)	◇ 0734
Honda CB/CD125T & CM125C Twins (77 - 88)	◇ 0571
Honda CG125 (76 - 07)	◇ 0433
Honda NS125 (86 - 93)	◇ 3056
Honda CBR125R (04 - 07)	4620
Honda MBX/MTX125 & MTX200 (83 - 93)	◇ 1132
Honda CD/CM185 200T & CM250C 2-valve Twins (77 - 85)	0572
Honda XL/XR 250 & 500 (78 - 84)	0567
Honda XR250L, XR250R & XR400R (86 - 03)	2219
Honda CB250 & CB400N Super Dreams (78 - 84)	◇ 0540
Honda CR Motocross Bikes (86 - 01)	2222
Honda CRF250 & CRF450 (02 - 06)	2630
Honda CBR400RR Fours (88 - 99)	◇ ◆ 3552
Honda VFR400 (NC30) & RVF400 (NC35) V-Fours (89 - 98)	◇ ◆ 3496
Honda CB500 (93 - 01)	◇ 3753
Honda CB400 & CB550 Fours (73 - 77)	0262
Honda CX/GL500 & 650 V-Twins (78 - 86)	0442
Honda CBX550 Four (82 - 86)	◇ 0940
Honda XL600R & XR600R (83 - 00)	2183
Honda XL600/650V Transalp & XRV750 Africa Twin (87 to 07)	◆ 3919
Honda CBR600F1 & 1000F Fours (87 - 96)	◆ 1730
Honda CBR600F2 & F3 Fours (91 - 98)	◆ 2070
Honda CBR600F4 (99 - 06)	◆ 3911
Honda CB600F Hornet & CBF600 (98 - 06)	◇ ◆ 3915
Honda CBR600RR (03 - 06)	◆ 4590
Honda CB650 sohc Fours (78 - 84)	0665
Honda NTV600 Revere, NTV650 and NT650V Deauville (88 - 05)	◇ ◆ 3243
Honda Shadow VT600 & 750 (USA) (88 - 03)	2312
Honda CB750 sohc Four (69 - 79)	0131
Honda V45/65 Sabre & Magna (82 - 88)	0820
Honda VFR750 & 700 V-Fours (86 - 97)	◆ 2101
Honda VFR800 V-Fours (97 - 01)	◆ 3703
Honda VFR800 V-Tec V-Fours (02 - 05)	◆ 4196
Honda CB750 & CB900 dohc Fours (78 - 84)	0535
Honda VTR1000 (FireStorm, Super Hawk) & XL1000V (Varadero) (97 - 00)	◆ 3744
Honda CBR900RR FireBlade (92 - 99)	◆ 2161
Honda CBR900RR FireBlade (00 - 03)	◆ 4060
Honda CBR1000RR Fireblade (04 - 07)	◆ 4604
Honda CBR1100XX Super Blackbird (97 - 07)	◆ 3901
Honda ST1100 Pan European V-Fours (90 - 02)	◆ 3384
Honda Shadow VT1100 (USA) (85 - 98)	2313
Honda GL1000 Gold Wing (75 - 79)	0309
Honda GL1100 Gold Wing (79 - 81)	0669

Title	Book No
Honda Gold Wing 1200 (USA) (84 - 87)	2199
Honda Gold Wing 1500 (USA) (88 - 00)	2225
KAWASAKI AE/AR 50 & 80 (81 - 95)	1007
Kawasaki KC, KE & KH100 (75 - 99)	1371
Kawasaki KMX125 & 200 (86 - 02)	◇ 3046
Kawasaki 250, 350 & 400 Triples (72 - 79)	0134
Kawasaki 400 & 440 Twins (74 - 81)	0281
Kawasaki 400, 500 & 550 Fours (79 - 91)	0910
Kawasaki EN450 & 500 Twins (Ltd/Vulcan) (85 - 04)	2053
Kawasaki EX500 (GPZ500S) & ER500 (ER-5) (87 - 05)	◆ 2052
Kawasaki ZX600 (ZZ-R600 & Ninja ZX-6) (90 - 06)	◆ 2146
Kawasaki ZX-6R Ninja Fours (95 - 02)	◆ 3541
Kawasaki ZX-6R (03 - 06)	◆ 4742
Kawasaki ZX600 (GPZ600R, GPX600R, Ninja 600R & RX) & ZX750 (GPX750R, Ninja 750R)	◆ 1780
Kawasaki 650 Four (76 - 78)	0373
Kawasaki Vulcan 700/750 & 800 (85 - 04)	◆ 2457
Kawasaki 750 Air-cooled Fours (80 - 91)	0574
Kawasaki ZR550 & 750 Zephyr Fours (90 - 97)	◆ 3382
Kawasaki Z750 & Z1000 (03 - 08)	◆ 4762
Kawasaki ZX750 (Ninja ZX-7 & ZXR750) Fours (89 - 96)	◆ 2054
Kawasaki Ninja ZX-7R & ZX-9R (94 - 04)	◆ 3721
Kawasaki 900 & 1000 Fours (73 - 77)	0222
Kawasaki ZX900, 1000 & 1100 Liquid-cooled Fours (83 - 97)	◆ 1681
KTM EXC Enduro & SX Motocross (00 - 07)	◆ 4629
MOTO GUZZI 750, 850 & 1000 V-Twins (74 - 78)	0339
MZ ETZ Models (81 - 95)	◇ 1680
NORTON 500, 600, 650 & 750 Twins (57 - 70)	0187
Norton Commando (68 - 77)	0125
PEUGEOT Speedfight, Trekker & Vivacity Scooters (96 - 05)	◇ 3920
PIAGGIO (Vespa) Scooters (91 - 06)	◇ 3492
SUZUKI GT, ZR & TS50 (77 - 90)	◇ 0799
Suzuki TS50X (84 - 00)	◇ 1599
Suzuki 100, 125, 185 & 250 Air-cooled Trail bikes (79 - 89)	0797
Suzuki GP100 & 125 Singles (78 - 93)	◇ 0576
Suzuki GS, GN, GZ & DR125 Singles (82 - 05)	◇ 0888
Suzuki 250 & 350 Twins (68 - 78)	0120
Suzuki GT250X7, GT200X5 & SB200 Twins (78 - 83)	◇ 0469
Suzuki GS/GSX250, 400 & 450 Twins (79 - 85)	0736
Suzuki GS500 Twin (89 - 06)	◆ 3238
Suzuki GS550 (77 - 82) & GS750 Fours (76 - 79)	0363
Suzuki GS/GSX550 4-valve Fours (83 - 88)	1133
Suzuki SV650 & SV650S (99 - 05)	◆ 3912
Suzuki GSX-R600 & 750 (96 - 00)	◆ 3553
Suzuki GSX-R600 (01 - 03), GSX-R750 (00 - 03) & GSX-R1000 (01 - 02)	◆ 3986
Suzuki GSX-R600/750 (04 - 05) & GSX-R1000 (03 - 06)	◆ 4382
Suzuki GSF600, 650 & 1200 Bandit Fours (95 - 06)	◆ 3367
Suzuki Intruder, Marauder, Volusia & Boulevard (85 - 06)	◆ 2618
Suzuki GS850 Fours (78 - 88)	0536
Suzuki GS1000 Four (77 - 79)	0484
Suzuki GSX-R750, GSX-R1100 (85 - 92), GSX600F, GSX750F, GSX1100F (Katana) Fours	◆ 2055
Suzuki GSX600/750F & GSX750 (98 - 02)	◆ 3987
Suzuki GS/GSX1000, 1100 & 1150 4-valve Fours (79 - 88)	0737
Suzuki TL1000S/R & DL1000 V-Strom (97 - 04)	◆ 4083
Suzuki GSX1300R Hayabusa (99 - 04)	◆ 4184
Suzuki GSX1400 (02 - 07)	◆ 4758
TRIUMPH Tiger Cub & Terrier (52 - 68)	0414
Triumph 350 & 500 Unit Twins (58 - 73)	0137
Triumph Pre-Unit Twins (47 - 62)	0251
Triumph 650 & 750 2-valve Unit Twins (63 - 83)	0122
Triumph Trident & BSA Rocket 3 (69 - 75)	0136
Triumph Bonneville (01 - 07)	◆ 4364
Triumph Daytona, Speed Triple, Sprint & Tiger (97 - 05)	◆ 3755
Triumph Triples and Fours (carburettor engines) (91 - 04)	◆ 2162
VESPA P/PX125, 150 & 200 Scooters (78 - 06)	0707
Vespa Scooters (59 - 78)	0126
YAMAHA DT50 & 80 Trail Bikes (78 - 95)	◇ 0800
Yamaha T50 & 80 Townmate (83 - 95)	◇ 1247
Yamaha YB100 Singles (73 - 91)	◇ 0474

Title	Book No
Yamaha RS/RXS100 & 125 Singles (74 - 95)	0331
Yamaha RD & DT125LC (82 - 87)	◇ 0887
Yamaha TZR125 (87 - 93) & DT125R (88 - 02)	◇ 1655
Yamaha TY50, 80, 125 & 175 (74 - 84)	◇ 0464
Yamaha XT & SR125 (82 - 03)	◇ 1021
Yamaha Trail Bikes (81 - 00)	2350
Yamaha 2-stroke Motocross Bikes 1986 - 2006	2662
Yamaha YZ & WR 4-stroke Motocross Bikes (98 - 07)	2689
Yamaha 250 & 350 Twins (70 - 79)	0040
Yamaha XS250, 360 & 400 sohc Twins (75 - 84)	0378
Yamaha RD250 & 350LC Twins (80 - 82)	0803
Yamaha RD350 YPVS Twins (83 - 95)	1158
Yamaha RD400 Twin (75 - 79)	0333
Yamaha XT, TT & SR500 Singles (75 - 83)	0342
Yamaha XZ550 Vision V-Twins (82 - 85)	0821
Yamaha FJ, FZ, XJ & YX600 Radian (84 - 92)	2100
Yamaha XJ600S (Diversion, Seca II) & XJ600N Fours (92 - 03)	◆ 2145
Yamaha YZF600R Thundercat & FZS600 Fazer (96 - 03)	◆ 3702
Yamaha FZ-6 Fazer (04 - 07)	◆ 4751
Yamaha YZF-R6 (99 - 02)	◆ 3900
Yamaha YZF-R6 (03 - 05)	◆ 4601
Yamaha 650 Twins (70 - 83)	0341
Yamaha XJ650 & 750 Fours (80 - 84)	0738
Yamaha XS750 & 850 Triples (76 - 85)	0340
Yamaha TDM850, TRX850 & XTZ750 (89 - 99)	◇ ◆ 3540
Yamaha YZF750R & YZF1000R Thunderace (93 - 00)	◆ 3720
Yamaha FZR600, 750 & 1000 Fours (87 - 96)	◆ 2056
Yamaha XV (Virago) V-Twins (81 - 03)	◆ 0802
Yamaha XVS650 & 1100 Drag Star/V-Star (97 - 05)	◆ 4195
Yamaha XJ900F Fours (83 - 94)	◆ 3239
Yamaha XJ900S Diversion (94 - 01)	◆ 3739
Yamaha YZF-R1 (98 - 03)	◆ 3754
Yamaha YZF-R1 (04 - 06)	◆ 4605
Yamaha FZS1000 Fazer (01 - 05)	◆ 4287
Yamaha FJ1100 & 1200 Fours (84 - 96)	◆ 2057
Yamaha XJR1200 & 1300 (95 - 06)	◆ 3981
Yamaha V-Max (85 - 03)	◆ 4072
ATVs	
Honda ATC70, 90, 110, 185 & 200 (71 - 85)	0565
Honda Rancher, Recon & TRX250EX ATVs	2553
Honda TRX300 Shaft Drive ATVs (88 - 00)	2125
Honda TRX300EX, TRX400EX & TRX450R/ER ATVs (93 - 06)	2318
Kawasaki Bayou 220/250/300 & Prairie 300 ATVs (86 - 03)	2351
Polaris ATVs (85 - 97)	2302
Polaris ATVs (98 - 06)	2508
Yamaha YFS200 Blaster ATV (88 - 02)	2317
Yamaha YFB250 Timberwolf ATVs (92 - 00)	2217
Yamaha YFM350 & YFM400 (ER and Big Bear) ATVs (87 - 03)	2126
Yamaha Banshee and Warrior ATVs (87 - 03)	2314
Yamaha Kodiak and Grizzly ATVs (93 - 05)	2567
ATV Basics	10450
TECHBOOK SERIES	
Twist and Go (automatic transmission) Scooters Service and Repair Manual	4082
Motorcycle Basics TechBook (2nd Edition)	3515
Motorcycle Electrical TechBook (3rd Edition)	3471
Motorcycle Fuel Systems TechBook	3514
Motorcycle Maintenance TechBook	4071
Motorcycle Modifying	4272
Motorcycle Workshop Practice TechBook (2nd Edition)	3470

◇ = not available in the USA *◆ = Superbike*

The manuals on this page are available through good motorcyle dealers and accessory shops.
In case of difficulty, contact: **Haynes Publishing**
(UK) **+44 1963 442030** (USA) **+1 805 498 6703**
(SV) **+46 18 124016**
(Australia/New Zealand) **+61 3 9763 8100**